THE CAMBRIDGE COMPANION TO
HEIDEGGER'S *BEING AND TIME*

The Cambridge Companion to Heidegger's Being and Time contains seventeen chapters by leading scholars of Heidegger. It is a useful reference work for beginning students, but it also explores the central themes of *Being and Time* with a depth that will be of interest to scholars. *The Companion* begins with a section-by-section overview of *Being and Time* and a chapter reviewing the genesis of this seminal work. The final chapter situates *Being and Time* in the context of Heidegger's later work. The remaining chapters examine the core issues of *Being and Time*, including the question of being, the phenomenology of space, the nature of human being (our relation to others, the importance of moods, the nature of human understanding, language), Heidegger's views on idealism and realism and his position on skepticism and truth, Heidegger's account of authenticity (with a focus on his views on freedom, being toward death, and resoluteness), and the nature of temporality and human historicality.

Dr. Mark A. Wrathall is professor of philosophy at the University of California, Riverside. He is the author of *Heidegger and Unconcealment* (Cambridge University Press, 2010) and *How to Read Heidegger* (2006). He has edited a number of collections, including *A Companion to Heidegger* (2007), *A Companion to Phenomenology and Existentialism* (2009), *Religion after Metaphysics* (2004), and *Appropriating Heidegger* (2008). Dr. Wrathall has contributed chapters to *The Cambridge Companion to Heidegger* (2006) and *The Cambridge Companion to Merleau-Ponty* (2004), as well as numerous articles to peer-reviewed journals in philosophy. He has lectured at universities in Germany, China, Japan, Taiwan, the United Kingdom, Sweden, and Finland.

T0381865

The Cambridge Companion to

HEIDEGGER'S
BEING AND
TIME

Edited by

Mark A. Wrathall
University of California, Riverside

CAMBRIDGE
UNIVERSITY PRESS

CAMBRIDGE
UNIVERSITY PRESS

32 Avenue of the Americas, New York NY 10013-2473, USA

Cambridge University Press is part of the University of Cambridge.

It furthers the University's mission by disseminating knowledge in the pursuit of education, learning and research at the highest international levels of excellence.

www.cambridge.org
Information on this title: www.cambridge.org/9780521720564

First published 2013
Reprinted 2013

A catalogue record for this publication is available from the British Library

Library of Congress Cataloguing in Publication data
The Cambridge companion to Heidegger's Being and time / edited by Mark A.Wrathall.
    p.   cm. – (Cambridge companions to philosophy)
Includes bibliographical references (p.) and index.
ISBN 978-0-521-89595-8 (hardback) – ISBN 978-0-521-72056-4 (pbk.)
1. Heidegger, Martin, 1889–1976. Sein und Zeit.   2. Ontology.
3. Space and time.   I. Wrathall, Mark A.
B3279.H48S4433   2013
111–dc23   2012035666

ISBN 978-0-521-89595-8 Hardback
ISBN 978-0-521-72056-4 Paperback

For my parents, Donald and Anja

Contents

Contributors

WILLIAM BLATTNER is Professor of Philosophy at Georgetown University. He is the author of *Heidegger's "Being and Time": A Reader's Guide* (Continuum, 2007).

TAYLOR CARMAN is Professor of Philosophy at Barnard College, Columbia University. He is the author of *Heidegger's Analytic* (Cambridge University Press, 2003) and *Merleau-Ponty* (Routledge, 2008).

DAVID R. CERBONE is Professor of Philosophy at West Virginia University. He is the author of *Heidegger: A Guide for the Perplexed* (Continuum, 2008) and *Understanding Phenomenology* (Acumen, 2006), as well as numerous articles on Heidegger, Wittgenstein, and the phenomenological tradition. He is also the editor (with Søren Overgaard and Komarine Romdenh-Romluc) of the *Routledge Research in Phenomenology* series.

ALFRED DENKER is the former Director of the Martin-Heidegger-Archiv in Meßkirch, Germany. He is the author of *Unterwegs in Sein und Zeit: Einführung in das Leben und Denken von Martin Heidegger* (Klett-Cotta, 2011).

HUBERT L. DREYFUS is Professor in the Graduate School at the University of California, Berkeley. His recent book (with Sean Dorrence Kelly), *All Things Shining: Reading the Western Classics to Find Meaning in a Secular Age* (Free Press, 2011), was a *New York Times* best-seller.

BARBARA FULTNER is Professor of Philosophy and Director of Women's Studies at Denison University. Her publications include articles on the lifeworld, incommensurability, communicative action, and intersubjectivity. She is the editor of *Jürgen Habermas: Key Concepts* (Acumen, 2011).

PETER E. GORDON is the Amabel B. James Professor of History and Harvard College Professor at Harvard University. His most recent book was *Continental Divide: Heidegger, Cassirer, Davos* (Harvard University Press, 2010), which received the Jacques Barzun Prize from the American Philosophical Society.

BÉATRICE HAN-PILE is Professor of Philosophy at the University of Essex. She is the author of *Foucault's Critical Project: Between the Transcendental and the Historical* (Stanford University Press, 2002) and of various articles on Foucault, Nietzsche, and Heidegger.

STEPHAN KÄUFER is Professor of Philosophy at Franklin & Marshall College.

WAYNE MARTIN is Professor of Philosophy and Head of School at the University of Essex (UK); he is also Principal Investigator of the Essex Autonomy Project and Series Editor of *Modern European Philosophy* (Cambridge University Press).

DENIS MCMANUS is Professor of Philosophy at the University of Southampton. He is the author of *Heidegger and the Measure of Truth* (Oxford University Press, 2013).

MAX MURPHEY is an instructor of philosophy at the University of California, Riverside.

MATTHEW RATCLIFFE is Professor of Philosophy at Durham University, UK. He is author of *Rethinking Commonsense Psychology: A Critique of Folk Psychology, Theory of Mind and Simulation* (Palgrave, 2007) and *Feelings of Being: Phenomenology, Psychiatry and the Sense of Reality* (Oxford University Press, 2008).

JOSEPH K. SCHEAR is University Lecturer and Tutorial Fellow ("Official Student") at Christ Church, Oxford. He is completing a book entitled *Horizons of Intentionality: From Husserl to Heidegger*, and he recently edited *Mind, Reason, and Being-in-the-World: The McDowell-Dreyfus Debate* (Routledge, 2012).

THOMAS SHEEHAN is Professor of Religious Studies and, by courtesy, Philosophy at Stanford University. He is editor and translator of volume 21 of Martin Heidegger's *Gesamtausgabe: Logic: The Question of Truth* (Indiana University Press, 2010).

IAIN THOMSON is Professor of Philosophy at the University of New Mexico. His most recent book is *Heidegger, Art, and Postmodernity* (Cambridge University Press, 2011).

MARK A. WRATHALL is Professor of Philosophy at the University of California, Riverside. He is the author of *Heidegger and Unconcealment: Truth, Language and History* (Cambridge University Press, 2010) and *How to Read Heidegger* (W. W. Norton, 2006).

Acknowledgments

This volume has been many years in the making. I'd like to thank the contributors to the volume – not just for their excellent essays but also for their patience in waiting for the finished product to appear. During that time, I've had the opportunity to share the manuscript with several groups of philosophy graduate students at the University of California, Riverside. We used the book as the basis for a graduate section that I conducted while teaching *Being and Time* during the spring term of 2010. The members of the class met weekly to discuss chapters of the book and, in many cases, send comments to the authors of those chapters. I would like to thank Dan Ehrlich, Morganna Lambeth, Luis Montes, Max Murphey, Patrick Ryan, Bob Stolorow, and Justin White for their many insightful comments and pointed criticisms of the book. Max deserves special thanks for agreeing to co-author the first chapter of the book with me. During the fall term of 2011, I met in a reading group with Kevin Gin, Patrick Ryan, and Will Swanson, and they helped me to work once again through the revised chapters of the book. Kevin, Patrick, and Will also source-checked the chapters, and I owe an enormous debt of gratitude to them for their generous help in preparing the manuscript for publication. Kevin Gin deserves special recognition. He took the lead in reviewing chapters, compiling a bibliography, flagging problems, and performing other invaluable tasks as I pulled the book together into its present form. His contribution to the finished book has been invaluable. I'd like to thank Beatrice Rehl and her exceptional staff for their longanimity while awaiting the overdue manuscript, and their professionalism throughout the editing process. Finally, I'd like to thank Luane Hutchinson for her excellent work in copyediting and otherwise shepherding this book into print.

Works by Heidegger

Since this is a companion to *Being and Time*, citations of *Being and Time* are given as parenthetical references containing only page numbers. As is standard practice, we refer to the "H" numbers – the page numbers of the seventh German edition of *Sein und Zeit*, published by Verlag Max Niemeyer in 1953. These page numbers are found in the margins of both English-language translations of *Being and Time*, as well as in the margins of the *Gesamtausgabe* edition of *Sein und Zeit* (GA 2) (Klostermann, 1977). Unless otherwise noted, quotations of *Being and Time* refer to the translation by Macquarrie and Robinson.

References to other works by Heidegger will direct the reader to the *Gesamtausgabe* volume and pagination. Most newer translations of Heidegger's work include the *Gesamtausgabe* pagination in the margins, in the top header, or inserted into the text. Where this is the case, we will not generally list the page number of the translation, since the passage can be readily found by consulting the marginal numbers. Full bibliographic information for these English-language translations can be found below, included in the reference to the corresponding volume in the *Gesamtausgabe*.

When translations do not contain the marginal page numbers that refer to the *Gesamtausgabe* pagination, we will use both the *Gesamtausgabe* reference and a reference to the page number in translation. For example, *Pathmarks* – the English translation of *Wegmarken* (GA 9) – does not include a *Gesamtausgabe* reference. So a reference to *Wegmarken* (GA 9) will include the page number in GA 9, followed by a slash and the page number in *Pathmarks* – like this: (GA 9: 112/89).

Some volumes of the *Gesamtausgabe* have not yet been translated and published as a whole volume, although select essays have been translated and published in essay collections. Where this is the case, the citation will include both a citation to the *Gesamtausgabe* and a citation to the English translation, using the abbreviations listed under "Other English Translations." So a reference to Heidegger's essay "A Dialogue on Language," published in German in GA 12 and in English

in the essay collection *On the Way to Language,* will look like this: GA
12: 104/OWL 20.

VOLUMES OF HEIDEGGER'S *GESAMTAUSGABE*
(WITH INFORMATION ON ENGLISH-LANGUAGE
TRANSLATIONS, WHERE AVAILABLE)

GA 1   *Frühe Schriften.* Frankfurt am Main: Klostermann, 1978.

GA 3   *Kant und das Problem der Metaphysik.* Frankfurt am Main:
         Klostermann, 1991. Translated as: *Kant and the Problem of
         Metaphysics.* (Richard Taft, Trans.) Bloomington: Indiana University
         Press, 1997.

GA 4   *Erläuterungen zu Hölderlins Dichtung.* Frankfurt am Main:
         Klostermann, 1981. Translated as: *Elucidations of Hölderlin's
         Poetry.* (Keith Hoeller, Trans.) Amherst, New York: Humanity
         Books, 2000.

GA 5   *Holzwege.* Frankfurt am Main: Klostermann, 1977. Translated as:
         Off the Beaten Track. (Julian Young & Kenneth Haynes, Trans.)
         Cambridge: Cambridge University Press, 2002.

GA 6.1   *Nietzsche* I. Frankfurt am Main: Klostermann, 1996.

GA 6.2   *Nietzsche* II. Frankfurt am Main: Klostermann, 1997.

GA 7   *Vorträge und Aufsätze.* Frankfurt am Main: Klostermann, 2000.

GA 9   *Wegmarken.* Frankfurt am Main: Klostermann, 1996. Translated
         as: *Pathmarks.* (William McNeill, Ed.) Cambridge: Cambridge
         University Press, 1998.

GA 10   *Der Satz vom Grund.* Frankfurt am Main: Klostermann, 1997.
         Translated as: *The Principle of Reason.* (Reginald Lilly, Trans.)
         Bloomington: Indiana University Press, 1991.

GA 11   *Identität und Differenz.* Frankfurt am Main: Klostermann, 2006.

GA 12   *Unterwegs zur Sprache.* Frankfurt am Main: Klostermann, 1985.

GA 14   *Zur Sache des Denkens.* Frankfurt am Main: Klostermann, 2007.

GA 15   *Seminare.* Frankfurt am Main: Klostermann, 1986.

GA 16   *Reden und andere Zeugnisse eines Lebensweges, 1910–1976.*
         Frankfurt am Main: Klostermann, 2000.

GA 17   *Einführung in die phänomenologische Forschung.* Frankfurt
         am Main: Klostermann, 1994. Translated as: *Introduction to
         Phenomenological Research.* (Daniel O. Dahlstrom, Trans.)
         Bloomington: Indiana University Press, 2005.

GA 18   *Grundbegriffe der Aristotelischen Philosophie.* Frankfurt am
         Main: Klostermann, 2002. Translated as *The Basic Concepts of
         Aristotelian Philosophy.* (Robert D. Metcalf, Trans.) Bloomington:
         Indiana University Press, 2009.

GA 19   *Platon, Sophistes.* Frankfurt am Main: Klostermann, 1992.
         Translated as: *Plato's Sophist.* (Richard Rojcewicz & Andre
         Schuwer, Trans.) Bloomington: Indiana University Press, 1997.

GA 20   *Prolegomena zur Geschichte des Zeitbegriffs.* Frankfurt am Main: Klostermann, 1979. Translated as: *History of the Concept of Time.* (Theodore Kisiel, Trans.) Bloomington: Indiana University Press, 1985.

GA 21   *Logik: Die Frage nach der Wahrheit.* Frankfurt am Main: Klostermann, 1976. Translated as: *Logic: The Question of Truth.* (Thomas Sheehan, Trans.) Bloomington: Indiana University Press, 2010.

GA 24   *Die Grundprobleme der Phänomenologie.* Frankfurt am Main: Klostermann, 1975. Translated as: *Basic Problems of Phenomenology.* (Albert Hofstadter, Trans.) Bloomington: Indiana University Press, 1982.

GA 25   *Phänomenologische Interpretation von Kants Kritik der reinen Vernunft.* Frankfurt am Main: Klostermann, 1977. Translated as: *Phenomenological Interpretation of Kant's Critique of Pure Reason.* (Parvis Emad & Kenneth Maly, Trans.) Bloomington: Indiana University Press, 1997.

GA 26   *Metaphysische Anfangsgründe der Logik.* Frankfurt am Main: Klostermann, 1978. Translated as: *The Metaphysical Foundations of Logic.* (Michael Heim, Trans.) Bloomington: Indiana University Press, 1984.

GA 27   *Einleitung in die Philosophie.* Frankfurt am Main: Klostermann, 1996.

GA 29/30   *Die Grundbegriffe der Metaphysik: Welt, Endlichkeit, Einsamkeit.* Frankfurt am Main: Klostermann, 1983. Translated as: *The Fundamental Concepts of Metaphysics: World, Finitude, Solitude.* (William McNeill & Nicholas Walker, Trans.) Bloomington: Indiana University Press, 1995.

GA 40   *Einführung in die Metaphysik.* Frankfurt am Main: Klostermann, 1983. Translated as: *Introduction to Metaphysics.* (Gregory Fried & Richard Polt, Trans.) New Haven: Yale University Press, 2000.

GA 45   *Grundfragen der Philosophie: ausgewählte "Probleme" der "Logik."* Frankfurt am Main: Klostermann, 1984. Translated as: *Basic Questions of Philosophy. Selected "Problems" of "Logic."* (Richard Rojcewicz & Andre Schuwer, Trans.) Bloomington: Indiana University Press, 1994.

GA 49   *Die Metaphysik des deutschen Idealismus (Schelling).* Frankfurt am Main: Klostermann, 1991.

GA 56/57   *Zur Bestimmung der Philosophie.* Frankfurt am Main: Klostermann, 1987. Translated as: *Towards the Definition of Philosophy.* (Ted Sadler, Trans.) London· Continuum, 2002.

GA 58   *Grundprobleme der Phänomenologie.* Frankfurt am Main: Klostermann, 1993.

GA 59   *Phänomenologie der Anschauung und des Ausdrucks: Theorie der philosophischen Begriffsbildung.* Frankfurt am Main: Klostermann, 1993.

GA 60   *Phänomenologie des religiösen Lebens.* Frankfurt am Main: Klostermann, 1995. Translated as: *The Phenomenology of Religious Life.* (Matthias Fritsch & Jennifer Anna Gosetti-Ferencei, Trans.) Bloomington: Indiana University Press, 2004.

GA 61   *Phänomenologische Interpretationen zu Aristoteles/Einführung in die phänomenologische Forschung.* Frankfurt am Main: Klostermann, 1985. Translated as: *Phenomenological Interpretations of Aristotle.* (Richard Rojcewicz, Trans.) Bloomington: Indiana University Press, 2001.

GA 64   *Der Begriff der Zeit.* Frankfurt am Main: Klostermann, 2004. Translated as: *The Concept of Time.* (Ingo Farin, Trans.) London: Continuum, 2011.

GA 65   *Beiträge zur Philosophie (vom Ereignis).* Frankfurt am Main: Klostermann, 1989. Translated as: *Contributions to Philosophy (From Enowning).* (Parvis Emad & Kenneth Maly, Trans.) Bloomington: Indiana University Press, 1999.

GA 66   *Besinnung.* Frankfurt am Main: Klostermann, 1997. Translated as *Mindfulness.* (Parvis Emad & Thomas Kalary, Trans.) London: Athlone, 2006.

GA 81   *Gedachtes.* Frankfurt am Main: Klostermann, 2007.

GA 88   *Seminare (Übungen) 1937/38 und 1941/42.* Frankfurt am Main: Klostermann, 2008.

OTHER ENGLISH TRANSLATIONS

EGT   *Early Greek Thinking.* (David Farrell Krell & Frank A. Capuzzi, Trans.) San Francisco: Harper & Row, 1975.

EP   *The End of Philosophy.* (Joan Stambaugh, Trans.) Chicago: University of Chicago Press, 1973.

FS   *Four Seminars.* (Andrew Mitchell & François Raffoul, Trans.) Bloomington: Indiana University Press, 2003.

HS   *Heraclitus Seminar.* (Charles H. Seibert, Trans.) Evanston, IL: Northwestern University Press, 1979.

ID   *Identity and Difference.* (Joan Stambaugh, Trans.) Chicago: University of Chicago Press, 1969.

N4   *Nietzsche, vol. 4.* (David Farrell Krell, Trans.) San Francisco: Harper, 1982.

OTB   *On Time and Being.* (Joan Stambaugh, Trans.) Chicago: University of Chicago Press, 1972.

OWL   *On the Way to Language.* (Peter D. Hertz, Trans.) New York: Harper & Row, 1971.

PLT   *Poetry, Language, Thought.* (Albert Hofstadter, Trans.) New York: HarperCollins, 1971.

1   An Overview of *Being and Time*

In *Being and Time,* Heidegger aims to "work out concretely the question concerning the sense of 'being'" (1; translation modified). The published version of the book contains roughly one-third of the book Heidegger envisioned, and we have only rather sparse and sketchy indications of how the book would have looked when complete. It was to consist of two parts, with each part divided into three divisions. Part One was to offer an "explication of time as the transcendental horizon for the question of being" (38). The published portions of *Being and Time* consist of the first two divisions of Part One – the "preparatory" sections of this project. Rather than offering an account of the sense of being in general, these divisions focus on a "determinate entity": *Dasein,* the kind of entity that in each case we human beings are.[1]

Thus *Being and Time* as it exists provides a very rich preparatory analysis of human being-in-the-world (in Division I), and then argues that our way of being has its sense in temporality (in Division II). Division III, as envisaged, would have moved from the focus on Dasein toward an account of temporality as the horizon for understanding and interpreting the sense of being in general. Part Two would have used the provisional account of temporality to "destroy" the history of ontology – focusing on Kant (Division I), Descartes (Division II), and Aristotle (Division III). Part Two, Heidegger claimed, would have shown concretely how traditional ontology was consistently grounded in an experience of the temporal and historical structures of human existence. But the intention was to destroy or break down the categories of the ontological tradition that, Heidegger claimed, conceal an original experience of time (see 21–2). Neither Division III of Part One nor Part Two were ever completed (see §6 of *Being and Time* for Heidegger's overview of what he intended to accomplish in Part Two).[2]

We offer here a chapter-by-chapter overview of *Being and Time,* starting, of course, with Heidegger's Introduction.

INTRODUCTION

Inquiries into being are often dismissed as superfluous or empty because being is thought to be both so fundamental as to defy definition and yet also well understood by everybody. Heidegger agrees, in fact, that being cannot be defined in the way that concepts about entities are – that is, by deriving a definition from more basic concepts, or refining it by comparing and contrasting it to other related, well-defined concepts. And yet it is the philosopher's task, after all, to illuminate the meaning of supposedly self-evident concepts. The mere appeal to what is well understood, without any further illumination, often conceals a superficial and mistaken grasp of the matter.

But if we're not asking for a definition of "being," what is the question of being after? We make progress in understanding being, Heidegger argues, by getting clearer about the "meaning" or "sense" (Sinn) of being.[3] The way Heidegger uses the term "sense" is akin to the way we say in English that something "makes sense." Things make sense when they fit together, when there is an organized, stable, and coherent way in which they interact and bear on us and each other. We grasp the sense of something when we know our way around it, we can anticipate what kind of things can happen with respect to it, we recognize when things belong or are out of place, and so on. This is what Heidegger means when he says that "sense is that within which the intelligibility of something maintains itself... Sense is that onto which projection projects, in terms of which something becomes intelligible as something" (151, translation modified). Sense is the background way of organizing and fitting things together, which guides and shapes all our anticipations of and interactions with anything we encounter.

We explain the sense of being when we illuminate what we understand when we know our way around entities as entities, meaning that we are able to distinguish between what is and what is not, or between how something is and how it is not. The conceptual apparatus that must be brought to bear in explaining this sense, however, is anything but clear. Heidegger largely dispenses with traditional ontological categories and tries to develop his own ontological concepts by "interrogating" entities with regard to their being, viewing them in the context of their being rather than, for instance, in the context of their causal interactions with each other. Toward this end, Heidegger proposes that the inquiry should focus from the outset on a particular entity, one that is well suited for interrogation with respect to its being. Dasein has priority for the inquiry because we are defined as the kind of entity we are by our possession of an understanding of being. Moreover, we "relate to being" (see 12), meaning that we understand that there are different ways to be, and that we are capable of "deciding our existence" (12) by taking over a different way to be. Thus Dasein gets its "essential character from what is inquired about – namely, being" (7).

Dasein has priority in another way as well. It not only understands its own existence, but it "also possesses ... an understanding of the being of all entities of a character other than its own" (13). If we examine another entity with regard to its being – for instance, a physical object like a stone – we can hope only for insight into its particular mode of being. But Dasein's dealings with entities show a sensitivity to different ways of being. Thus, by analyzing Dasein's different modes of comportment, we can hope to gain insight into a number of modes of being.

Heidegger offers two rather concise arguments meant to motivate the question of being, as well as to clarify further its function and aim. The question of being, Heidegger argues, has priority over all other scientific inquiries because every science presupposes a certain ontological understanding of its subject matter. The natural sciences, for instance, operate within a pre-theoretical understanding of what it is to be a natural entity (as opposed to a cultural or historical entity). Behind the basic concepts of any positive science, Heidegger argues, lies a tacit ontology, a "productive logic" that "discloses" an area of being and guides scientific inquiry within that domain (see 10). Without an explicitly and thematically developed ontology, Heidegger argues, there is a danger that the sciences will be led astray by unfounded metaphysical assumptions (see 11).

The other motivation for asking the question of being is rooted in our essence as Dasein. The "question of existence is one of Dasein's ontical 'affairs'" (12). We care about our being, that is, about the ways in which we have decided, and will decide, our existence. We thus care about the question of being, given the reasonable assumption that having a clear-sighted understanding of being gives us guidance on how we ought to take a stand on our being.

But how is the question to be pursued? What method is to be employed? We already have a certain understanding of being. We have a sense for the difference between being and nonbeing, and we grasp pre-reflectively,[4] though imperfectly, what it is to be a human being, as opposed to a rock, as opposed to a number, and so on. Since these portions of *Being and Time* are centered on our kind of being, the initial task is to illuminate Dasein as it shows up in our pre-reflective understanding – Dasein in its everydayness. This will be done by offering a description in which "essential structures will be exhibited, which persist as determinative of being in every kind of being of factical Dasein"

(16–17, translation modified). Heidegger calls this method – description that exhibits essential structures – "phenomenology." Since it involves interpreting or laying out what we already tacitly understand, it is a "hermeneutic" phenomenology. The task of Division I is to find the right concepts to describe the structures of *everyday* Dasein, concepts that will let Dasein show itself in its being. But this will yield at best a provisional account of Dasein, since it won't show why it makes sense that those structures are determinative of the being of Dasein. Thus "this preparatory analytic of Dasein will have to be repeated on a higher and authentically ontological basis" (17) in which we uncover and articulate the sense of being. This is the task of Division II. The answer to the question of the sense of the being of Dasein is "temporality": temporality is the background against which the essential structures of Dasein are intelligible as determining the being of Dasein.[5]

DIVISION I

Heidegger begins Division I by giving a brief sketch of what Dasein is and how it differs from all other types of entities. The central claim, once again, is that Dasein is the one kind of entity that has an *understanding of being*. This does not mean that all human beings explicitly know the meaning of being, for in such a case, everyone would already be in possession of a fundamental ontology, and Heidegger's project would be superfluous. Rather, Dasein's understanding of being is for the most part implicit and vague – "pre-ontological" in the sense of lacking an explicit ontology (5–6). The philosophical development of this pre-ontological understanding will often require correcting what we think we understand about being.

Traditional ontology, Heidegger claims, has misconstrued our being as human beings by assuming that we share the same *mode of being* as other entities we encounter within the world, such as tables, rocks, dogs, atoms, or numbers. From Aristotle to Descartes and beyond, for instance, both human beings and nonhuman things were understood to be alike in that they were *substances*: discretely individuated, self-sufficient entities that possess determinate properties and stand in contingent, external relations to one another. Although different substances possess different determinative or essential properties, traditional ontology applies the same ontological categories to all of them. Heidegger argues, however, that our pre-reflective ways of distinguishing between different types of entities are grounded in an ontological difference. Much of Division I is concerned with articulating these ontological distinctions.

CHAPTER I

As an initial specification of Dasein, Heidegger observes: "we are our-selves the entities to be analysed. The being of any such entity is *in each case mine.* These entities, in their being, comport themselves towards their being ... *Being* is that which is an issue for every such entity" (41–2).

What does it mean to say that being is an *issue* for Dasein? When I say that something is an issue for me, I mean that it matters to me, that it has importance or significance for me, or that I care about it. It also implies that there is something I can do about it – that its condi-tion can be altered or affected by me. Many of Heidegger's main points are foreshadowed by this claim: that the world is to be understood as a contingent structure of significance, that entities in the world and our activities are understood on the basis of their sense, and that the being of Dasein is care.

Because Dasein can comport itself toward being, it differs fun-damentally from all other entities. Heidegger uses the term "existence" (*Existenz*) to refer to Dasein's mode of being; he calls the modes of being for entities other than Dasein "presence-at-hand" or "occurrentness" (*Vorhandenheit*), and "readiness-to-hand" or "available-ness" (*Zuhandenheit*).[6] As the name suggests, available entities are enti-ties that offer us ready, intelligible modes of use. Most of the things we encounter in everyday life are available. We are familiar with them, and they afford or solicit actions from us in response. Heidegger addresses availableness in detail in chapter 3. Occurrent entities are the enti-ties we discover when we abstract from our practical engagement with the world and take up a reflective or theoretical or scientific attitude toward it. Then we find entities that are defined not by the roles they play in our world but by their inherent physical properties. Heidegger argues that traditional ontology has focused on occurrentness and erro-neously attempted to interpret all entities as occurrent.

Because being is an issue for Dasein, it resists being explained as just one type of occurrent entity among others. In the history of philosophy, a number of different accounts have been offered regarding our essence as human beings. According to Aristotle, the essence of a human being is to be a rational animal. For Christian philosophers, the essence of a human being is to be created in the image of God. In the Cartesian para-digm, the essence of a human being is to be a conscious subject with the capacity to reflect on its mental representations. The implicit assump-tion behind each of these definitions of the essence of humanity is that human beings are ontologically homogenous with all other entities, dif-fering only in virtue of possessing different essential properties. We are different from lower animals, for instance, either because we are essentially rational or because they were created by God for us or because they are incapable of reflecting on their representations. On this traditional view, the history of different interpretations of humanity's essence can be understood as an argument over which of the properties we possess is *really* the essential one. Heidegger, however, takes this history as a sign that Dasein has an ontology fundamentally different from other entities. Namely, Dasein is *an entity that interprets its own essence*. Its essence is not found in the possession of this or that property. Its essence is found in its lack of an essential property in the traditional sense. If "existence" names our mode of being, and we are entities for whom being is an issue, then it follows, as Heidegger famously proclaims, that "the 'essence' of Dasein lies in its existence" (42).

Another way of putting this would be to say that Dasein's essence is "open." It is never fixed once and for all, and we are capable of reinterpreting ourselves. Because each of us can, at least in principle, interpret ourselves, "the being of any such entity is *in each case mine*." But, as chapter 2 argues, we are also thoroughly shaped by the people and things around us, and we inherit our possibilities from the particular shared social world we live in.

CHAPTER 2

As existing, self-interpreting entities, we stand in an essential relationship to the world. Heidegger calls our basic state "being-in-the-world," and hyphenates the term to emphasize that it is a *"unitary phenomenon"* that can only be understood when "seen as a whole" (53). Dasein and the world are fundamentally misunderstood if taken as two self-sufficient entities that can subsequently enter into an external relationship. Rather, we are entities that necessarily find ourselves in an embodied state, dealing with a world that, for its part, is prior to any particular individual. Although it is prior to any particular individual, however, the world is essentially a meaningful structure and thus only exists for entities like us who are capable of grasping meanings.

Despite focusing on each element of being-in-the-world separately – the "world" component in chapter 3, the "who" of Dasein in chapter 4, and the "being-in" relation in chapter 5 – Heidegger insists that we keep in mind that these components are abstractions from the overall unitary phenomenon.

This chapter offers a preliminary sketch of being-in-the-world, one that aims in particular to fend off our tendency to import occurrentist assumptions into ontology. For instance, if one takes Dasein as just another occurrent entity, its being-in tends to be understood on the model of spatial containment (53–4). When we say that someone is *in* the world, however, we primarily mean that he or she is at home or familiar with a certain way of *living* or *residing* in a particular organized whole of entities, activities, aims, ideals, and so on (54). This relationship of being at home in a world is poorly modeled in terms of spatial containment. Of course, we do bear a physical relationship to the objects around us – we are constrained by the particular features of the environment we find ourselves in as it bears on the particular features of us as embodied beings (our traits, dispositions, skills, and so on). Heidegger calls such features our "facticity."

Being factically "dispersed … into definite ways of being-in" (56) is different than being in determinate spatial and causal relationships to occurrent entities in our proximity. The entities within-the-world that Dasein encounters are, for the most part, the things it deals with in conducting its life: hammers, nails, pencils, paper, tables, chairs, doors, stairs, cars, clothes, food, air, the ground, the sky, and so on. We make use of these entities in various ways in our pursuit of our purposes and projects. They show up not as occurrent objects with properties but rather as the functional roles they play in these projects (87). In Heidegger's terms, the being of these entities is to be *available*: to afford or solicit particular ways of engaging with them. We can encounter them when we have *concern* (*Besorgen*) for them – we possess embodied competence for handling them, and it matters to us how they interact with each other and with us. Concern for available entities is one of our fundamental ways of being in the world (57, 66–9).

We are in the world, then, primarily by way of understanding it, by knowing our way about in it. In the preliminary sketch of being-in-the-world, Heidegger is also concerned to fend off the tendency to think of our *understanding* on the model of cognition of the occurrent world. Among the ways in which we understand entities are those specialized projects of the modern, developed world known as the *sciences*. Science, in the broadest sense, consists in the construction of theoretical representations of nature that allow us to predict and explain empirical phenomena, to manipulate natural forces, and to produce technological artifacts. All such projects share a common feature: they are ways of understanding entities in the world, as well as the world itself, in purely *occurrent* terms.

Theoretical understanding abstracts from our everyday dealings with available entities and the significance things usually have for us in order to arrive at a representation of the universe as an occurrent totality that is causally determined throughout and amenable to exhaustive mathematical representation. And yet, for all the power and utility of *knowing* the world through these theoretical representations, it is just one form of understanding among many. Moreover, it is a form of understanding that, from the standpoint of fundamental ontology, is derivative from our everyday concern (59 ff.).

CHAPTER 3

This chapter offers an account of the world and entities within-the-world as we encounter them in everyday life. We must not think of the world as simply the extended, physical universe. Instead, Heidegger uses "world" to point to the whole – the unified totality – of entities, tied together as a complex network of significant relationships. To think of the world as a mere universe, a collection of all that is, is to assume an occurrentist ontology.[7]

Heidegger's name for the available entities that we encounter "proximally and for the most part" is "equipment" (68).[8] The clothes we wear, the cars we drive, the doors we open, the ground on which we walk, the pens with which we write, the signs we read, understand, and follow – these all primarily show themselves as available. To see this, imagine what it would involve to understand these entities as occurrent substances with occurrent properties. One could attempt to give an exhaustive description of a pen, for instance, in the language of theoretical physics. This description would involve measurable quantities such as the mass and volume of the pen, an algebraic equation that describes the approximate shape of the pen, and dispositional properties such as the mechanical forces that would be exerted when the cap is removed or the button is pressed.

But in normal circumstances, when we are using the pen and it is functioning well, none of these properties show up in our experience. And we find ourselves *absorbed* (*aufgegangen*) in what we are writing. The pen itself is for the most part "transparent" or inconspicuous. However, in abnormal circumstances, some of the physical properties (shape, size, mass, forces) of the pen become *conspicuous*, or *obtrude*, in certain ways: the mass of the pen shows up when it is too heavy or too light; the shape of the pen shows up when it makes holding the pen uncomfortable; the internal forces of the pen show up when the cap is difficult to remove. But even in these cases, the pen is still not a merely occurrent substance; instead, it has a deficient mode of being that Heidegger calls "un-availableness" (73–4). The way in which one deals with a pen that is functioning poorly is not to take note of its occurrent properties but simply to toss it aside and find the closest replacement.

All the relevant parameters of the available are purpose-relative and thus not reducible to occurrent properties because they are not determinable independently of the ever-shifting contexts of use. It would be vain to seek general criteria, in Dasein-independent terms, for what counts as too heavy, uncomfortable, or difficult. Moreover, because equipment things are constituted relationally – "equipment is essentially 'something in-order-to...'" – Heidegger emphasizes that, strictly speaking, "there 'is' no such thing as *an* equipment. To the being of any equipment there always belongs a totality of equipment, in which it can be this equipment that it is" (68). Each particular item of equipment is defined *structurally* as a node in a network of relations to projects and activities, and thereby to other available entities and ultimately to Dasein. The pen, for instance, fills a place defined by its relationships to activities such as taking notes, drawing, or signing checks. It is thus brought into relationship to entities such as paper, ink, and desks, and to the roles and purposes of the human beings engaged in these activities, such as being a student, being an artist, or paying bills to support one's family (84). Unlike occurrent entities, which are essentially independent of each other, available entities are essentially *interdependent*. An individual piece of equipment only shows up as such against the background of its *involvements* (*Bewandtnis*).

A world, then, presents us with an organized totality of activities on the basis of which particular entities are able to be encountered in their involvements (ordinarily as equipment) (see 86). Dasein inhabits a world by assigning itself to a way of taking a stand on its being, in terms of which it makes sense of its particular projects and activities. So the world is that wherein Dasein can take up the tasks of interpreting and taking responsibility for its existence.

Heidegger calls the general structure of worlds "worldhood." The structure that allows for a particular world to exist is the structure of the meaningful relationships of activities and entities, the way they refer to and relate to each other, thereby affording us different possibilities for being. Heidegger calls this structure "significance" (*Bedeutung*) (87). The world and its worldhood form the background against which we understand any particular entity with its specific involvements. This background tends to withdraw from us – as long as things are working together smoothly, we don't notice it or attend to it. We typically notice how things are supposed to refer to[9] and relate to one another only in cases of breakdown, of a disruption to our ability to cope fluidly with our environment.

It is within this framework that Heidegger presents his critique of Descartes' conception of the physical world and space as *res extensa*. Just as the available entities of our everyday environment are not characterized in terms of measurable physical quantities, this environment (*Umwelt*) itself, considered as a spatial realm wherein Dasein resides, is not primarily understood as a mathematical manifold or metric space, but rather as a network of meaningful spatial relationships that are defined in terms of Dasein's activities. As we make our way around the world, we encounter available entities laid out in significant places and regions to which they *belong* (102–4). When things are placed where they belong, they are appropriately accessible to us, and our involvement with them goes smoothly; otherwise, they just "lie around" and obstruct our activities (102).

It is in terms of the varying availability of available entities that the phenomena of *distance* and *remoteness* (*Entfernung*) first show up for Dasein (104–6). In everyday life, when I say that something is "close by" or "far away," I primarily refer to the ease or difficulty involved in my accessing it (106). So, if my daily commute involves an hour-long flight between cities a few hundred miles apart, there is a distinct sense in which these cities are closer together for me than either of them is to the rural countryside in between – accessing the latter might involve making reservations at a bed-and-breakfast, renting a car, looking up directions, and bringing appropriate attire. Our everyday understanding of distances consists in comparisons of this sort, and it is only through a process of theoretical abstraction that we come to think of space as defined in terms of geometrical relations that can be measured with any degree of precision (112).[10]

The Cartesian framework, which considers these latter relations to constitute the essence of the extended world, consequently regards our everyday experience of space as insignificant and takes an abstract, albeit useful, model of space as a characterization of what space "really" is. But it is only on the basis of a familiarity with our everyday environment that the spaces of geometry or physics can have any significance for us.

CHAPTER 4

Dasein is a being-in-the-world. Chapter 3 focused on the world. In this chapter, Heidegger provides an account of everyday Dasein.

Who is Dasein? As noted at the outset of Division I, "Dasein is an entity which is in each case I myself" (114). Heidegger initially uses terms like "self," "I," and "subject" as formal indicators – that is, as ways of directing our attention in an ontologically noncommittal way to the phenomenon in question. Such terms point to the fact that Dasein has *mineness*, in other words, that I have some sort of exclusive and unique relationship to my existence. It is my affair, and I am responsible for it. They also point to the idea that there is something essential about me, something that endures across changes. But we must suspend our tendency to think about such phenomena as the *I*, the *self*, and the *subject* in an occurrentist way – in the way we might, for instance, think about the identity and constancy of an object. The "'I' ... must be interpreted existentially" (116), without assuming that there is some stable and self-identical *substance* that determines who I am.

In fact, Heidegger argues that who I am is subject to change, and Dasein can exist in quite distinct modes. But the starting point for answering the question "who is Dasein?" is the description of our everyday being in the world. How do other Dasein show up to me, and how do I show up to myself, in the course of my everyday commerce with the world?

The identity of the self is, in everyday life, constituted by those meaningful activities through which the individual partakes in norm-governed social practices. A relationship to other human beings is built into those practices. These practices are, as we have seen, defined in terms of the structure of significance: a network of available entities and their purposive relations to one another. But purposiveness presupposes a use for an agent, a role that he or she plays. For instance, a craftsperson builds things for the use of other human beings. Each individual person, before she can take responsibility for her own existence in an authentic way, already finds herself as having been interpreted in terms of her participation in social practices. As an epigram, we can say that in everyday human existence, the public is primitive and the private is derivative.

We always inhabit a shared world, and the way we exist in this world is always essentially structured by others (see 123). Conversely, the world also "frees Dasein" – that is, it opens up a space where others can be encountered as Dasein. We automatically recognize the traces of other people in the things with which they dwell in the world (117 ff.). Indeed, it is built into our experience of things that they belong to others, are well-suited to specific people, and so on. When one takes it upon oneself to trespass on another's property, for instance, it feels different; one moves and carries oneself differently than when one has been invited in. In his or her actions, the trespasser expresses an interpretation of him- or herself as disobedient to norms. Thus, even in our uncooperative or criminal activities, we never cease to interpret ourselves in terms of the very norms we have violated.

Not only do we find ourselves in a world that is meaningfully structured by the activities and purposes of others, it also seems to be a basic structure of our being that we are constantly taking measure of how we compare to or differ from others. Heidegger calls this "distantiality" (*Abständigkeit*). Everyday Dasein thus exists as "being-with" (*Mitsein*). It takes its measure from other Daseins, it has a special cognizance of them as other Daseins, and it has a primordial familiarity with them: we understand how to engage with others *as* Daseins. They show up as "Dasein-with" (*Mitdasein*). The others are "those from whom, for the most part, one does not distinguish oneself – those among whom one is too ... this 'with' is something of the character of Dasein; the 'too' means a sameness of being as circumspectively concernful being-in-the-world" (118). Thus, in addition to its ordinary concern with available entities, Dasein also exhibits *solicitude* (*Fürsorge*): a care for and about other Dasein.

One upshot of this is that in our ordinary everyday activity, there can be no "other minds" problem. We don't infer that others are Dasein (in which case, there would always be room for skeptical doubt about the accuracy of our inference). On the contrary, we couldn't even have a sense of ourselves as Dasein without already relating to other Dasein. And we immediately, unreflectively cope with others as Daseins (125).

So who is the everyday Dasein? It is not a subject who could be constituted as she is, independently of any relationship to other Daseins. It is quite the contrary, given our ordinary everyday submission to norms. Insofar as one follows the norms, one is merely *one among many*. Our distantiality disposes us to interpret ourselves in terms of these norms. But beyond that, we often fall into "inauthenticity" – that is, into "standing in subjection to others." That is, we simply accept unthinkingly the ways in which one does things. In doing so, we disburden ourselves of responsibility *for our own actions* by acting as an anonymous follower of norms. This anonymous subject or self is who we refer to when we say things like "one waits in line," "one drives on the right side," or "one just doesn't do that here." In doing so, the "who" that I am is really the others to whom I defer in deciding what to do.

Heidegger uses the impersonal pronoun "one" or "they" (*das Man*) and the related expression one-self (*Man-selbst*) to refer to the anonymous, everyday way in which Dasein generally understands itself (126 ff.). *Das Man* makes possible the social *conformity* against the background of which the individual can understand herself, her activities, and others. However, without the possibility of authenticity, in which the individual takes responsibility for her own decisions and thereby attains a unique identity for herself, there would be nothing but social *conformism*. In purely conformist scenarios, no single individual is ultimately responsible for the behavior of the group. It is not hard to see how this could (and does) lead to various forms of immoral behavior, but Heidegger does not put it in those terms. He merely says that "In Dasein's everydayness the agency through which most things come about is one of which we must say that 'it was no one'" (127).

On the one hand, we have seen that Dasein, in its everyday being-in-the-world, primarily interprets itself in terms of its world. That is, it understands its identity, as well as the identities of other Dasein, in terms of the norms that govern the use of publicly available equipment and the social interactions that are built up around cooperative projects. On the other hand, we must recognize that this everyday existence is for the most part inauthentic, meaning it is "public" (it is governed by norms available to everyone), "levelled down" (it only does what anyone could do), and "disburdened" of responsibility for its own decisions (127). Authenticity, "discovering the world in my own way" (129), is a possibility that Heidegger will take up as a theme in Division II. Authenticity is a possibility available to every Dasein simply in virtue of the basic structure of mineness. However, the achievement of authentic selfhood in any particular case only takes place against the background of the everyday, anonymous possibilities for existence that we take over from *das Man* (130).[11]

CHAPTER 5

Heidegger criticizes certain traditional approaches to ontology for their "unrestrained tendency to derive everything and anything from some simple 'primal ground'" (131). Heidegger's ontology, by contrast, is methodologically open to the possibility of "equiprimordiality." Equiprimordial phenomena cannot be derived from something more basic and cannot exist without each other. As we've seen, Heidegger argues that Dasein and world are equiprimordial. While he devotes a separate chapter to focusing on each (world in chapter 3, and Dasein in chapter 4), Heidegger emphasizes throughout that being-in-the-world is a unitary phenomenon. There cannot be a world without Dasein, and one cannot be a Dasein without a world. In chapter 5, the task is to specify the "relationship" between Dasein and world. This cannot be thought of on the model of the way two occurrent entities, each constituted independently of each other, interact on the basis of their own independently constituted properties. For instance, being-in is not the spatial containment of one object within another, and it is not a representational relationship *between* a subject (Dasein) and an object (world). It would be more accurate, Heidegger observes, to say that "Dasein is the being of this 'between'" (132). The "relation" between Dasein and world, in other words, is that a Dasein is a particular opening up of world. It is one way in which the world gets laid out and taken up as we pursue activities, identities, aims, and roles.

Dasein is *in* a world, then, insofar as it is familiar with definite ways of existing, and is engaged in taking a stand on its being. Heidegger's account of being-in in chapter 5 delineates three equiprimordial structures that are constitutive of familiarity with a world. We could characterize these structures in ordinary terms as follows: Dasein finds itself in a situation in which certain things stand out as mattering; Dasein

possesses abilities for dealing with its situation and pursuing meaningful projects; and Dasein articulates both its situation and its abilities in a way that makes particular entities and references stand out as
salient. These three structures are what Heidegger calls "disposedness"
(*Befindlichkeit*), "understanding" (*Verständnis*), and "discourse" (*Rede*)
respectively. Since these structures are equiprimordial constituents of
being-in, no one of them can be taken as more fundamental than the
others and each one must be understood in terms of the others (133).

There is a significant *passive* aspect to being-in. Dasein finds itself
already situated in a particular world that is arranged in a definite, concrete fashion and where particular things have already shown up as mattering. Heidegger refers to this as Dasein's "thrownness" (*Geworfenheit*):
we are "thrown" into the world. We also find ourselves with characteristics that shape our engagement with the world. Unlike occurrent
entities with their factual properties, our concrete characteristics are
always encountered as bearing a meaning – I'm an embodied being, with
a history, a family, and so on. These are fact-like constraints but still
meaningfully taken up and constituted. To distinguish it from "brute
facts," Heidegger calls human factuality our "facticity" (*Faktizität*) (see
135, 276). Our thrownness and facticity are disclosed to us through a
particular way of being "attuned" to the world. Heidegger calls this our
disposedness, and it involves the way we always find ourselves saddled
with dispositions, aims, desires, skills, and particular ways of making
sense of the world. Disposedness is to some extent always beyond our
control, since it provides the background against which we exercise our
abilities in order to shape our existence actively.[12]

One concrete phenomenon in which our disposedness manifests
itself is *mood* (*Stimmung*) (134). For Heidegger, a mood is not merely
an emotional state into which one falls on certain occasions based on
one's reactions to events and objects, coloring them subjectively with
a certain positive or negative valence. On the contrary, one is *always*
in a mood (134), and it is only in terms of one's mood that events and
objects show up to one as significant. Particular emotions and feelings
and passions occur against the background of this more basic mood.
The fact that we can, and must, suppress our emotions, desires, and personal interests when we engage in business or scientific research does
not mean that moods are contingent occurrences that we must avoid.
Rather, it indicates that occurrent entities are best discovered and studied when we are in a tranquil, unaffected state that facilitates placid
observation and efficient interpersonal relations (138).

Our disposedness gives us a certain familiarity with our world – a certain sense for what's important and trivial, relevant and irrelevant, to
be preferred or avoided. Our *understanding* opens up the possibility for

acting on the basis of our disposedness. In understanding, one *projects* oneself onto various possibilities. Through its disposedness, Dasein finds itself in a factical situation and in a certain mood. Through its understanding, Dasein can go beyond its current situation, freely interpret itself, and, ultimately, take responsibility for its own existence.

One might think of possibilities as events or states of affairs that could be actual but are not. We'll call such things "possible-actuals" to distinguish them from what Heidegger means by "possibility." Possibilities as Heidegger understands them are orders of meaning, whole coherent ways of organizing what is actual and possibly-actual. To use a game analogy, the rules of the game are the possibilities. They describe the different meaningful configurations into which different moves in the game and different game pieces can enter. The rules are never actual in the way that a thrown pitch in baseball is either actual or a possible-actual. The rules are, rather, in the mode of shaping the significance of all the actual things that occur.

In *understanding*, we project onto possibilities, meaning we grasp the actual in terms of the possible – that is, in terms of a space of significations that governs how the actual relates to other things, how it develops, what opportunities it affords, and so on. As one pursues those possibilities, one interprets oneself and the possibilities, developing them and working them out.[13] Heidegger calls such a commitment to a particular understanding "interpretation" (*Auslegung*). Whenever Dasein deals with available entities, it interprets them in a definite way. For example, the average individual possesses the ability to use doors. This is an open-ended ability that can be applied to an indefinite variety of particular doors, whether they have handles, knobs, or latches; whether they must be pushed or pulled; or whether they are rotating doors or car doors. In opening a door, I put this understanding to work, and refine my ability as I become precisely responsive to this particular door. Thus an interpretation need not be an explicit act of thought or assertion. To be sure, such acts also count as interpretations, but they are derivative rather than paradigmatic instances of the basic structure of interpretation that Dasein exhibits in everything that it does (149, 153 ff.). The structure of interpretation is constituted by the *affordances* that things offer to us when we understand the world. Heidegger calls the structure of affordances the "as structure" – for example, the desk shows up *as* affording writing, the knife *as* affording cutting, and so on. Every perception, cognition, or action takes things as meaningful and responds to what they afford within the world.

Assertion is a derivative form of interpretation. The basic sort of interpretation, in which we take something *as* something (i.e., experience it as affording such and such) need not pick an entity out explicitly and display it as having a determinate, propositionally communicable property. But an assertion does just this: it picks out a particular entity as subject, picks out a property of this entity as predicate, and then expresses the relationship of the entity and its property in the form of a judgment (154–5). Assertion thus involves an *abstraction* of determinate features out of a prior holistic grasp of entities in their rich network of interrelations. In assertion, available entities that already make sense to us through our circumspective understanding are reinterpreted as occurrent entities with determinate properties (157–8).

Understanding and disposedness are determined by a third equiprimordial structure of being-in: *discourse*. Discourse is the way in which Dasein *articulates* the meaningful structure of its world (161). As we have already seen, the structure of significance consists of relationships between available entities established by the shared practices and activities in which everyday Dasein takes part. While these entities are irreducibly interdependent with each other and dependent upon the activities of Dasein, they are also readily distinguishable in terms of the different functional roles they play in the structure of significance. Indeed, we are able to speak of *individual* available entities, such as hammers, pens, or doors. But if we are to understand these entities in a manner appropriate to their being, we must keep in mind that their essence consists in their holding a place in a world, thus guiding and constraining and facilitating interactions with each other and with Dasein. Dasein finds itself thrown into a situation in which certain entities show up through their significance relations; Dasein understands these entities and their relations insofar as it has the ability to make use of them in its activities. But all of this presupposes that the world has been articulated into "nodes of signification," and this is the contribution of discourse (161). On certain occasions, an individual Dasein might want or need to communicate some elements of this articulation of its world by means of *language*. Heidegger captures the relationship between language and the world in the epigram "to significations, words accrue" (161). This is just to say that significance constitutes the structure of the world, while words and sentences are the particular linguistic entities through which a person communicates an aspect of his or her understanding of significance to another person for a particular purpose.[14]

Having laid out the structure of our being in a world through the account of disposedness, understanding, and discourse, the final sections of chapter 5 describe the everyday forms of being-in. As we saw above, everyday Dasein interprets itself in terms of the public world of shared practices. If Dasein submits itself completely to the shared and public forms of intelligibility, it inauthentically rids itself of the burden of taking responsibility for its own individual existence. But even when an individual Dasein attains authenticity, it does not thereby extricate itself from *das Man* and the public world: it continues to let itself be absorbed in the activities of everyday life. In the way it is arranged, the shared public world facilitates certain kinds of activity and discourages others. There is thus a constant tendency, as we get in sync with the world around us, to become absorbed in normalized, conventional ways of doing things. This absorption in the public world is what Heidegger calls the "falling" (*Verfallen*) of Dasein (175).

Think, for instance, of the influence that one public mode of discourse in particular – our language – has on us. An individual Dasein finds itself in a public world in which the articulation of significance has already been made concrete and stabilized in an average way that is accessible to anyone who speaks a given language (168). The language affords us certain things that we can say, and well-worn manners of speech that are readily intelligible given the average ways of being in the world. When we let ourselves get drawn into and absorbed in the public, shared forms of discourse, the result is *idle talk* (*Gerede*) (167). In idle talk, Dasein does not articulate the significance of entities directly but rather does so indirectly through the mediation of what others have said, or "what one says," about these entities. Paradigmatic examples of idle talk are what we call "small talk," "hearsay," and "gossip" (168–9). If we are satisfied with the superficial understanding of the world that we can achieve through such idle forms of discourse, then we obscure the possibility of achieving a primordial relationship with the entities in our world and thereby relieve ourselves of the responsibility of attaining a first-hand articulation of them – an articulation that lends itself to one's own specific understanding and disposedness (168–70).

As long as I am skillfully pursuing something for the sake of my own highest end or purpose, I interpret my situation for myself – I see what the concrete situation requires of me given my particularities as an agent. But interpretation can succumb to the falling tendency as well – for instance, in *curiosity* (*Neugier*). When I am curious, I don't develop what is understood and make it my own. Instead, I withhold myself from committing myself to a purposive engagement in activities. I *distract* myself with a passive beholding of whatever presents itself, satisfied with whatever superficial interpretation the "one" gives to events (171–3). As we all know, one distraction often leads quickly to another. My commitment is exhausted by the desire for amusement, and the insubstantiality of such activities tends not to fulfill me, and thus puts me into a restless state of constantly craving novelty (172). The result of not interpreting the world for myself through an authentic commitment, however, is that I am completely subject to the normal, conventional way of making sense of things.

A third manifestation of falling, which Heidegger calls "ambiguity" (*Zweideutigkeit*), is a characteristic of an understanding that takes over shared, public, leveled-down ways of projecting onto possibilities. Insofar as idle talk tends to be directed toward entities that are "accessible to everyone, and about which anyone can say anything, it soon becomes impossible to decide what is disclosed in a genuine understanding, and what is not" (173). Curiosity, in its restless craving for novelty, leads to the phenomenon of a "fast-paced" social life in which everyone is trying to stay "ahead of the game" (174). In such activities, there is a pretense of concern with matters of importance and a semblance of cooperative involvement, but in reality people are focused on superficialities (174–5). The result is that it becomes impossible to tell which possibilities are genuine and which are not. We think we understand the significances that structure any particular entity or event or situation, but without a committed, concrete engagement with them, we can't be sure. The ambiguity exhibited by the publicly predominant interpretations of Dasein and of other entities perpetually hinders the individual Dasein's ability to exist authentically.

At this point, it may appear that we have diverged from the project of giving an analysis of the existential structures of Dasein and have launched into a cultural critique with a moralizing subtext. But Heidegger insists that this is not the purpose of his account of falling (167). He emphasizes that falling is not a "bad and deplorable property" (176) from which we should strive to escape, but rather an essential tendency of everyday Dasein. It is also clear, however, that the three forms of falling can be seen as enabling conditions of inauthenticity insofar as they lead an individual Dasein to interpret itself solely in terms of the anonymous self of *das Man*, and to disburden itself of responsibility for its own existence.

CHAPTER 6

Division I has been concerned with a preliminary account of the being of Dasein. Dasein, Heidegger has argued, is essentially being-in-the-world. In chapters 3 through 5, the phenomenon of being-in-the-world was analyzed into its equiprimordial moments. In chapter 6, Heidegger aims to bring the phenomenon into view as a unitary whole – that is, to direct our attention to some experience in which we can recognize the essential unity of Dasein and world, and see how their unity provides the foundation for the unity of disposedness, understanding, and discourse.

To make a somewhat long story short, the "primordially unitary phenomenon" (181) at which Heidegger arrives is *care* (*Sorge*). There is both an affective and a projective dimension to "care." The affective dimension is indicated in English expressions involving the locution "care about" – for instance, "I couldn't care less about *X*." When I say this, I indicate that *X* does not *matter* to me. Conversely, what does matter to me is something that touches me, affects me, something in which I take an interest. The projective dimension is indicated by expressions involving the locution "taking care of." If I take care of *X*, I make myself (or experience myself as already) responsible to act with respect to *X*, and I commit myself to some project that involves *X*. These ordinary meanings of care indicate the existential structures of *disposedness* and *understanding* respectively. The phenomenon of care that Heidegger is interested in involves both dimensions: the world and our place within it matters to us, it concerns us; we undertake projects with respect to it, and experience ourselves as responsible for it. It is in this sense that "Dasein's being reveals itself as care" (182).

We recognize care as the being of Dasein, Heidegger argues, in the experience of *anxiety* (*Angst*) (see 182). In anxiety, one feels an indeterminate threat from an indeterminate source – that is, in anxiety we are not worried about any particular entity or possibility being lost, and we cannot say definitely what it is that makes us feel threatened.[15] The oppressiveness of anxiety as a mood comes from the way it prevents us from getting absorbed in any activity: "environmentally available entities sink away," meaning not that they disappear but rather that they are "completely without importance" (*völlig belanglos*). Nothing, not even another Dasein, is "in a position to offer us anything" anymore (see 187). This is because no person or thing can fill the lack that we recognize in anxiety: our lack of belonging to the world – our *uncanniness* (*Unheimlichkeit*, literally, "not-at-home-ness"). When I am overcome by anxiety, it deprives me of the ability to fall into or lose myself in conventional, established activities, and thus takes away from me the ability to understand myself "in terms of the 'world' and the way things have been publicly interpreted" (187). In fact, Heidegger argues that falling (as described at the end of chapter 5) can best be understood as an effort to flee from anxiety, to "dim down" the recognition of "the 'not-at-home'" (189).

Anxiety shows us being-in-the-world as a unitary whole because, in it, I recognize (affectively) that I need to have a world and I long to be at home in or belong to world. Yet I also recognize (projectively) that I don't belong uniquely to any world, and I might find myself unable to carry on with the pretense of belonging. In anxiety, then, my mood opens up my understanding and shows me that I can't be reduced to my current involvements. I am beyond them. This makes salient, in turn, the unity that exists in the different structural elements of my being-in-the-world. In affectively showing me my uncanniness, and thus showing me that I care about being-in-the-world, anxiety at the same time makes clear that I exist "as being-possible," as free for possibilities and able to choose myself. Anxiety discloses our possibilities to us by making our uncanniness available to us as something to project upon (190–1). Anxiety thus shows up as unifying our thrownness into a world, our particular way of finding ourselves in the midst of entities in the world, with our existential freedom to pursue new possibilities.

Heidegger generalizes from the case of anxiety to offer the following formulation of the structure of care: "the being of Dasein means *ahead-of-itself-being-already-in ... as being-amidst*" (192, translation modified and emphasis supplied). In Heidegger's formulation, the "ahead-of-itself" corresponds to understanding, projection, and existence; "being-already-in" corresponds to disposedness, thrownness, and facticity; "being-alongside" corresponds to absorption and falling.

In Division II, Heidegger will develop and deepen the account of the unity by mapping this tripartite structure of care onto the three temporal "ecstases" of future, past, and present respectively (327 ff.).

The closing sections of Division I remind us of Heidegger's ultimate goal: to answer the question of the meaning of being in general. Before moving forward, he reflects on what the foregoing analytic of Dasein has taught us about the different modes of being (200). For instance, the analytic of Dasein as being-in-the-world sheds light on the being of other entities by allowing us to move beyond the traditional problem of epistemological skepticism. The latter problem, as Heidegger sees it, is based on a misinterpretation of the being of Dasein and the being of the world. The analytic of Dasein shows that the problem of the existence of the external world cannot seriously be raised: both the skeptic and the philosopher who musters a defense against the skeptic share the presuppositions that Dasein is a fundamentally occurrent subject or mind, that the external world is a occurrent manifold of "mind-independent" objects, and that the basic relationship between subject and object is that of knowledge (200–1). But once we understand that our being is care, which necessarily involves a concernful engagement with entities within-the-world, there is no room for seriously doubting the existence of the world, and hence no need to prove its existence. Indeed, doubt (including doubt of the existence of the external world) is itself, like knowledge, a derivative form of being-in, which is only intelligible on the basis of our primordial way of comporting ourselves toward the world in our everyday concern.[16]

Division I concludes with Heidegger's account of truth.[17] He wants to develop a primordial notion of truth, which he calls "unconcealment" (*Unverborgenheit*), Heidegger's translation of the Greek *alētheia*. "Uncoveredness" (*Entdecktheit*) is a species of unconcealment, and applies generally to the unveiling of any kind of entity whatsoever. We can see what entities "truly" are in practical engagements with them, Heidegger argues, and not merely through propositions, judgments, assertions, or beliefs – the focus of most philosophical accounts of truth.

"Truth, understood in the most primordial sense," Heidegger maintains, "belongs to the basic constitution of Dasein." This means both that we are always involved in uncovering entities and disclosing a world, and also that there is no disclosure without Dasein: "entities are uncovered only *when* Dasein *is;* and only as long as Dasein *is,* are they disclosed" (226). Our ability to have true beliefs or make true assertions is derivative of this primordial truth.

Untruth takes different forms in each of the different cases of uncovering. When opposed to uncovering entities in observations or assertions, untruth takes the form of false perception or erroneous belief. When opposed to uncovering available entities in absorbed activities, untruth takes the form of misuse or incompetence. This brings about a kind of uncovering of entities, but they are uncovered in the mode of being closed off, disguised, or uprooted (222). When opposed to disclosing ourselves in our self-interpretations, untruth takes the form of inauthenticity. Many of these forms of untruth are the result of Dasein's essential state of *falling,* with its idle talk, curiosity, and ambiguity. There is an inherent tendency toward a fallen engagement rather than an original, context-specific discovery of the situation. Thus it is "essential that Dasein should explicitly appropriate what has already been uncovered, defend it *against* semblance and disguise, and assure itself of its uncoveredness again and again" (222). Authenticity thus requires that we continually resist the tendency to remain in untruth by resolutely reinterpreting ourselves and the world. This is true, too, of the ontological analysis of Dasein – like any other attempt to uncover an entity in its truth, it is itself subject to the tendency toward untruth, against which it must repeatedly renew its efforts.[18]

DIVISION II

Division I of *Being and Time* offers us a preliminary account of the being of an entity (Dasein) that understands being. The aim of Division II is to articulate the sense of the being of this entity – to show on what basis we recognize these structures as the essential ontological structures of Dasein. Heidegger will argue in Division II that temporality is the sense of the being of Dasein. But before making this argument, he asks: is the preliminary account of the structures of Dasein sufficiently "originary" or "primordial" (*ursprünglich*)? A *primordial* interpretation, Heidegger explains, is one in which we have fully worked out the structures in virtue of which an entity is what it is. To do this, we must first experience and grasp in their unity all the essential structural elements of the entity. The interpretation is confirmed to the degree that it affords us a rich, detailed, and clear apprehension of the ontological constitution of the entity in question. Division II begins, then, by reflecting on the question of whether the analysis to this point has been sufficiently primordial, given that it has scarcely considered Dasein in its authentic mode (232–3). The first three chapters of Division II develop an account of authentic Dasein in order to overcome "the inadequacy of the hermeneutical situation" (235), before squarely addressing temporality and time in the final three chapters of the division.

CHAPTER I

Heidegger argues in this chapter that Dasein can only achieve wholeness through authentic being toward death. Making a case for this claim, however, will require working out what it means, in the first place, for Dasein to be a whole, as well as getting clearer about the nature of death.[19]

The problem of the wholeness of Dasein is made pressing by a paradox inherent in the nature of the care structure. Heidegger concluded in Division I that that care is "a primordial structural whole" (193, translation modified). The paradox springs from the fact that "being-ahead-of-itself" is an essential component of the care structure. To be essentially ahead-of-ourselves means that we understand ourselves, as well as everything in the world around us, in terms of open possibilities. Worldly facts and human facticity do not determine which possibilities we must use to understand the world, as we can revise them or disclose new possibilities. But this would seem to rule out completeness or wholeness: it "tells us unambiguously that in Dasein there is always something still *outstanding* ... In the essence of the basic constitution of Dasein, there accordingly lies a *constant incompleteness (Unabgeschlossenheit)*" (236, translation modified). The only way to eliminate this incompleteness is to deprive us of open, revisable possibilities, to close off our possibilities. But without open possibilities, we are "Dasein-no-longer" (*nicht-mehr-Dasein*) (236) – in other words, dead. If being a whole means having all our possibilities fixed and settled, then it seems that Dasein can't be a whole.

Obviously, we need to consider what kind of wholeness is proper to Dasein. One of the most important lessons of Division I is that it we cannot simply apply concepts drawn from one mode of being to analyze the structure of a different mode of being. The *available* is whole when all its parts are present and together in such a way that it lends itself to fluid use. Being whole in this sense is a condition for available entities to be truly available – having parts absent would render them unavailable. But possibilities aren't like components of an item of equipment, and Dasein's possibilities cannot all be present and actualized at once. To be a Dasein requires that one have possibilities *as* possibilities, and thus as open (see 243). So Dasein's wholeness must consist in a particular *way* of being open, a particular manner of comporting ourselves toward our openness, through which we achieve a unity in our being. It will require, in particular, incorporating our essential openness into our existence, and making our way of being in the world cohere with that openness. This is something we achieve, Heidegger argues, by taking up a particular relationship to death. So let's turn now to his analysis of being toward death.

Here again, it would be a mistake to draw our notions of ending or *death* from the realm of the available and the occurrent. Clearly, death is unlike the way mere objects come to an end. But defining Dasein's death is complicated, because each individual human being belongs to several overlapping types. I am a living creature; I am a social being; I am a psychological being; and I am an existing being (this is a non-exhaustive list). To each type corresponds a kind of death – an ending of a sort appropriate to that type. Heidegger reserves the term "death" for our end as existing beings (i.e., as Dasein). In order to avoid ambiguity, Heidegger refers to the ending of biological life as "perishing" (*Verenden*). All living creatures perish. But when Dasein perishes, "it does not simply perish" (247); it also effects an alteration in the constellation of psychological, biographical, legal, social, historical, and ethnological meanings. Heidegger calls such an ending a "demise" (*Ableben*). So if we take me as merely an animal, then my ending could be designated with the term "perishing." Since I am never merely an animal, however, but a social or psychological or legal or historical (etc.) being, I have a way of ending that is designated with the term "demise." Neither of these endings, however, captures what is involved in my ending as an existing being – my "death" in the specifically existential sense.

Death and demise are not entirely unrelated (see 247), but nor are they merely alternate ways of designating the same event. Indeed "death," unlike "demise," doesn't name an event at all. It names a possibility in the Heideggerian sense (for more on possibilities, see the discussion of Division I, chapter 5 above) – to be specific, "the possibility of no-longer being-able-to-be-there" (250) or "the possibility of the absolute impossibility of Dasein" (250). This isn't just any possibility. Heidegger calls it our "uttermost" possibility, because it shapes and alters the significance of every other possibility that is open to us. Our entire being in the world is fundamentally structured by a being toward death, and we are constantly coming to grips with death, Heidegger argues, even if in the mode of fleeing from it. When we "divert ourselves" into ways of life provided by the social world within which we find ourselves, we act as if death is an occasional event – something with which we all will sooner or later be involved, but not now. This treats death not as a possibility that shapes all the other possibilities of the world, but as an event that might be actual but doesn't happen to be actual now. But just like a satellite in orbit exhibits the constant pull of gravity rather than freedom from gravity, when we throw ourselves into social practices this doesn't manifest an absence of care for death. Instead, the effort to lose ourselves in life shows the constant and pervasive effects of death on the meaningful structure of our being in the world. The everyday mode of relating to death, for instance, misinterprets or tries to convert anxiety into fear – a fear focused on the event of demise and the consequences or feelings that accompany it (pain and suffering, loss of companionship, etc.). Many cultures foster fearlessness as an ideal, valorizing indifference to the fact of death. Or they encourage us to not worry about it, to put it out of mind, by throwing ourselves into the activities our world affords us. Death, they try to persuade us, is something that we all face together, in the same way (see 253). But each of these strategies for thinking about death, Heidegger argues, is actually a constant being toward death in "the mode of evasion" – an attempt to conceal from ourselves the full implications of the possibility of the impossibility of being there.

By contrast, "if Dasein stands before itself as this possibility" – that is, if I am determined as the being I am by the possibility of the impossibility of being there – "all its relations to any other Dasein are dissolved" in the sense that these relations no longer define who I am. In confronting the possibility of my impossibility, the *non-relationality* of "death lays claim to [one's own Dasein] as an individual" and "individualizes Dasein down to itself" (263). In confronting death, I see that the world could continue, and other Dasein could go on existing, even when I no longer am able to do so. Conversely (as Iain Thomson emphasizes in Chapter 12), my world could collapse, rendering it impossible for me to be there. And yet, in some sense, I could go on. In both ways, death "makes manifest that all being-amidst the things with which we concern ourselves, and all being-with others, will fail us when our ownmost ability-to-be is the issue" (263).

Because death is non-relational, it shows me that I need not treat others as normative authorities for how to be. Acknowledging this "wrenches" me away from *das Man*, and I have no choice but to take over for myself responsibility for my way of being. Of course, that doesn't mean that we can dispense with our concern for things and solicitude for other humans. Rather, authentic being toward death incorporates an understanding of death into its concern and solicitude (see 263). Having thereby lost the ability to act as if some generic or conventional way to be is the *right* way to live my life, I own up to my uncanniness (see discussion of Division I, chapter 6 above) by "assigning myself to my ownmost ability to be." This is why death, Heidegger says, is my *ownmost* possibility.

When we recognize that death is *unsurpassable* – when we see that there is no way to eliminate the possibility of the impossibility of being there – it "shatters all one's tenaciousness to whatever existence one has reached" (264). That is, it breaks down our rigid or obstinate sticking to some ideal that we think all should share. We authentically comport ourselves toward death's unsurpassability when we no longer accept as necessary "those possibilities which may accidentally thrust themselves upon one" (264). The result is that "one is liberated in such a way that for the first time one can authentically understand and choose among the factical possibilities" the world has to offer (264).

The *certainty* of the indefinite threat of death is manifest when Dasein "opens itself to a constant threat arising out of its own 'there'" – namely, the threat of being unable to maintain ourselves in our way of being. We hold open this constant threat in anxiety (see 266). The certainty of death is manifest when our being in the world shows up as fragile and transient, because we recognize that either we might lose our hold on the world, or our activities might cease to find a stable order and coherence that the world provides (or both).

According to "the full existential-ontological conception of death," then, death is "the ownmost, non-relational, certain and as such indefinite, unsurpassable possibility of Dasein" (258–9).

The possibility of death opens up or de-determines our world, whether we recognize it or not. Division I failed to fully take into account this end, because it didn't consider a way of existing that sees in the light of death and thereby owns up to and takes responsibility for its way of being in the world, without appeal to generic conventions and social norms. Authentic "dying" is a way of living – namely, experiencing the world as not determined, as offering possibilities that we must pursue without appeal to generic conventions and social norms. In dying, we see all our other possibilities to be finite. This makes us more responsive to the particularities of the concrete situation in which we find ourselves.

Unlike inauthentic fleeing from death, authentic being toward death relates to it *as* a possibility. We do this not by brooding on death, and certainly not by actualizing our demise, but rather by comporting our-selves toward our existence in such a way that we bring out and respond to the fact that our being is fragile and uncanny. Heidegger calls this "anticipation" or "running forward" into death. Anticipation casts all our other possibilities in a different light – namely, precisely as possi-bilities that we can but need not embrace. No particular possibility can show up any longer as *the* right way to make sense of ourselves and the world around us. And that, in turn, is what first allows us to understand the kind of beings that we are – existing beings and thus beings who need not exist in any particular way.

It remains to say how authentic being-toward-the-end of Dasein (death) constitutes a kind of wholeness. By forcing me to own up to my exis-tence, anticipation of death leads me to recognize myself more fully as a whole. I see most perspicuously the sense in which the "not-yet" draws on my disposedness and shapes my involvement in present situations. Authentic being-toward-the-end, Heidegger argues, would achieve a coherence between Dasein's various ontological structures, allowing us not just to recognize the whole of our being, but to be a unified whole. Thus, when we understand wholeness and ending in a way appropriate to Dasein, we see that they require and support each other. But is there any evidence that we can, in fact, be such an authentic whole? That is the topic to which Heidegger turns in the next chapter.

CHAPTER 2

As we've seen, we are thrown into a shared public world of definite pos-sibilities, inclinations, tastes, and preferences. Dasein "falls" into inau-thenticity when it lets itself be drawn into and completely absorbed in the activities that make sense for one who belongs to this world. The self of inauthentic Dasein is a "they-self" or a "one-self" (*das Man-Selbst*), meaning that it has allowed its activities, tastes, aims and goals, and so on, to be decided for it by "the one," *das Man*. It is thereby "relieved of the burden of expressly choosing these possibilities" (268). Anxiety in the face of death restores this burden to us, or rather shows us that our freedom from the burden of choice was illusory. It thus creates a space to "make up for not choosing." Being authentic involves "choosing to make this choice – deciding for an ability-to-be and making this deci-sion *from one's own self*" (268; emphasis supplied).[20]

But if I am thoroughly lost in the "they self," how could I ever make a decision from my own self? It is the call of conscience, Heidegger argues, that disrupts the complacency with which we are "lost" in "the publicness and the idle talk of the 'one'" (271; translation modified). Conscience "shows" me myself, directs me to my own factical basis for decision, and not only enables authenticity but "demands it" of me (267).

Heidegger's account of this call is an ontological and structural one. The question is not what are the causes and effects of conscience in the psychic, moral, or religious life of an agent? Rather, the question is how does conscience contribute to opening up a situation within which it is possible to be an agent? The call of conscience is a mode of discourse. It articulates the situation within which I find myself, and draws my attention to certain definite features of that situation – to be specific, my guilt. On the ordinary interpretation, in alerting me to my guilt, the conscience articulates the situation for me in moral or ethical terms. While not denying the truth of this ordinary way of hearing the call, Heidegger's focus is on a different articulation, one centered on existential rather than moral or ethical or legal guilt.[21]

On Heidegger's definition of the "formally existential idea of guilt," guilt is "being a reason for a [mode of] being determined by a nothing – that means *being the reason for a nullity*" (283; translation modified). "Reason" needs to be understood here in the broadest possible sense. The German word that it translates – *Grund* – can mean a reason in the sense of a proposition that explains or rationalizes. But it also can mean whatever is responsible for the occurrence of an event. And it can mean a background against which something can emerge. Heidegger wants to keep all of these senses in play.

Being guilty involves two kinds of nullity. First, in guilt I am the reason that something is *not* (a possibility is shut off, a state of affairs is deficient, harmony is lacking, etc.). Second, my reason is itself characterized by a nullity; it lacks adequate justification. I am guilty, for instance, when I hurt someone else (causing a nullity in their existence) and I don't have a good reason for hurting them (in Heidegger's unusual way of formulating this, I am a null reason).

An important existential source of the nullity of our reasons is our thrownness. Because of our thrownness, we "constantly lag behind our possibilities," we "never have power over our ownmost being from the ground up" (see 284), and yet we "always stand in one possibility or another" even as we are "constantly not other possibilities, and have waived these in our existentiell projection" (285). That is, we find ourselves always already saddled with dispositions, aims, desires, and particular ways of making sense of the world. These allow us to act, for they give us a foundation for understanding what our possibilities are, preferring one outcome to another, and having the skills and abilities to pursue some of those possibilities. Additionally, it is in virtue of our "reasons" that the world solicits us to respond in particular ways. As a result, Heidegger says, I don't merely *have* reasons for acting; I *am* the reason I act. This seems like the right thing to say, phenomenologically speaking. When I act, I don't generally consult reasons. Rather who I am is the reason I perform the actions that I do. At the same time, we are "released from our reasons to ourselves" (285; translation modified). Even though it is not up to me which dispositions, possibilities, habits, and standards I inherit as a result of the accidents of my birth and upbringing, I can attempt to resist, modify, alter, or reinforce them through my ongoing engagement with the world. But whenever we try to change our thrownness, we do so on the basis of our prior disposedness.

The upshot is that there is an essential nullity in my existence in a number of respects. I am thrown into being who I am, and lack a standpoint from which I could justify the reasons I am. Yet I don't have to be who I am. And in pursuing one possibility, adopting one standard, and so on, I have waived or "nullified" other possibilities and thus become answerable for who I am, even though I lacked ultimate control over my reasons for pursuing one possibility at the expense of others in the first place. "Accordingly," Heidegger concludes, "the being of Dasein means, as thrown projection: being the (null) reason of a nullity. And this means that *Dasein is as such guilty*, if the formally existential definition of 'guilt' as 'being-the-reason for a nullity' is indeed correct" (285; translation modified).

Being existentially guilty is not a "privation" – it's not a failure to live up to some ideal. It is not a condition that could be eliminated (285). Rather, being the kind of responsible beings that we *are* requires that we have nullity in our very grounds. It is a necessary condition of my being responsible that I am the reason or ground for what I do. This makes guilt both "the existential condition for the possibility of the 'morally' good and for that of the 'morally' evil" (286), since without it we cannot be morally or legally responsible for what we do.

When our conscience alerts us to our guilt, then, it articulates the fundamental nullity or lack of justification in our being. And in doing this, Heidegger argues, it "summons" the hearer out of being lost in the possibilities of the public and conventional world and "into its ownmost possibilities, as a summons to its ownmost ability-to-be-a-self" (273). But this ownmost self, for its part, has no definite, substantive features that must remain fixed (274). The call shows us, instead, that who we ordinarily think we are, defined in terms of the conventional things we do and roles we play, is not definitive of us (see 273). We cannot be indifferent to our facticity – it determines and constrains and shapes our ways of being in the world. And yet our facticity is something accidental, and our way of taking up our facticity is contingent and alterable. There is something about us that exceeds any particular worldly way of being – we are "uncanny." It is this dual relationship to our facticity – that we are it and have to be it, and yet we are not reducible to it and it offers no ultimate resolution to anything important about how to live our lives – which explains the possibility of calling to ourselves in the call of conscience. "In its 'who,' the caller is definable in a 'worldly' way by nothing at all. The caller is Dasein in its uncanniness: primordial, thrown being-in-the-world as the 'not-at-home' – the bare 'that-it-is' in the 'nothing' of the world" (276; see also 277). It calls to the factical self, who has mistaken its contingency for something essential, and summons it out of falling into the "they."

Because the appeal of the call of conscience summons us to the nullity of our ownmost self, "we cannot seek to delimit any concrete single possibility of existence" as the appropriate response to the call. It does not point us to an "ideal and universal" way to live; rather, it directs us to the ability to be that we already are (287). But it also calls Dasein "to be authentically the guilty which it is" (287) – that is, it shows us that it is a mistake to even seek sufficient justifications for our mode of life. Rather, hearing the call requires "wanting to have a conscience," that is, wanting to be responsible for who one is in the full acknowledgment that one cannot justify who one is. Thus even before Dasein acts, "it has, in being with others, on the null basis of its null projection already become guilty towards them" (288).

Heidegger's interpretation of the call of conscience seems decidedly at odds with the way the everyday understanding hears the call. This is not surprising if we recall that Heidegger's interest is in the function conscience plays in disclosing ontological structures. The everyday understanding, by contrast, is interested in the particular events that give rise to a guilty conscience, and the particular impulses or motivations that conscience produces in us. But Heidegger argues that the everyday response to conscience is not ontologically innocent. It supposes that there is a right or wrong way to "manage and reckon up" a human life, and sees the conscience solely as contributing to our ability to stay on course. It wants to guide and direct life the way one guides and directs a tool or equipment toward its designated end (see 289). "This would be as if Dasein were a 'household' whose indebtednesses simply need to be balanced off in an orderly manner so that the self may stand 'by' as a disinterested spectator while these experiences run their course" (293). Thus Heidegger contends that the everyday interpretation of conscience – as exclusively tied to particular actions – is a phenomenon of flight. It interprets the call in the way that it does precisely in order to conceal from itself our existential guilt and responsibility.

Nevertheless, Heidegger also contends that a summons to existential responsibility is presupposed in every factical instance of having a guilty conscience, even if we only hear it as directing our attention to particular acts or omissions. After all, I can only be guilty for a particular act on a particular occasion if I was already responsible for my being at the time I committed the offense. Thus "factical indebtedness" is "only the occasion for the factical calling of conscience" (290); it does not exhaust the significance of the call of conscience. It is also significant for Heidegger that the conscience does not give us maxims – it doesn't tell us what we should do. At most, it tells us that we are or will be guilty for particular things that we do (see 294). This shows that the conscience, if heard correctly, offers us an opening to decide who we will be, and thus it makes us take over our role as the agents of our actions. Authentic Dasein "wants to have a conscience," meaning that it acts without appeal to outside norms or rules to justify what it does. When I am authentic, I act *resolutely*: I act in my own name, for myself, accepting that I can neither vindicate the action nor discharge responsibility for the nullity I cause in the being of others.

"Resoluteness," then, is an existential stance in which I recognize that I am "uncanny" or "not at home" in the world – I have no inherent, natural way to be. Yet I nevertheless am disposed to act in some particular, albeit contingent, ways. In resolution, I resolve upon owning my disposedness. This will require that I accept and commit to some of my preferences, dispositions, skills, and so on, even while recognizing their ungroundedness. I can set out, of course, to alter my disposedness in resoluteness, but even this will lack ultimate justification, since the way I want to shape my disposedness is a result of my current unjustified disposedness. The mode of discourse proper to resoluteness is reticence, a way of articulating the world in which, by keeping silent, I deprive ordinary language of its power to make sense of the situation in which I find myself (see 296). The result is that the situation is articulated for me, not in terms of general and conventional significations, but in terms of the the affordances and solicitations that are salient for me, given the particular disposedness I have taken over, and the particular individual projects I have resolved to pursue (see 298). Resoluteness simultaneously discloses me in the light of my ability to be a self, and it discloses the concrete situation (*Situation*)[22] in light of the particular factical self that I am.[23]

CHAPTER 3

Division II started with an effort to assure ourselves that we had before us the phenomenon of Dasein as a whole in its unity. Anticipatorily resolute Dasein is whole because it incorporates into existence its uttermost end (death) and its grounds (guilt). Thus Heidegger argues that authentic Dasein, anxious in the face of death and resolutely wanting to have a conscience, offers us the adequate phenomenal basis for uncovering the sense of the being of Dasein. The aim of this chapter is to show that temporality is the sense of the being of Dasein because it is temporality that makes sense of anticipatory resoluteness.

The first task is to clarify the connection between anticipatory being-toward-death and resolute wanting to have a conscience. Anticipation discloses our being in the world as contingent – as transitory, ultimately individual, and uncanny (i.e., not inherently beholden to social norms). Resoluteness discloses our undischargeable and unjustifiable responsibility for our being in the world. We are only authentically resolute when we see that our way of being is not merely unjustifiable at this moment, but essentially so. Recognizing the unsurpassability of death helps us to see that our existential guilt cannot be discharged (see 306). That is, it becomes fully apparent that we can't get behind our thrownness when we confront the essential contingency of our projects. Otherwise, we might hope that our responsibility is merely a temporary condition. We might think that we've not yet hit on a justifiable way to be but that ultimately we will. Or we might imagine that the consequences of our way of being will serve, in the end, to exculpate us of guilt and responsibility for who we are. But in anticipation of the certainty and unsurpassability of death, our guilt becomes "something constant" (see 307).

At the same time, hearing the call of conscience "enables the possibility for death to attain power over the existence of Dasein and ultimately to disperse every transient self-concealment" (310; translation modified). When conscience "passes over in its appeal all 'worldly' standing and abilities" (307), it convinces us that we cannot discharge our responsibility by appealing to conventional norms and standards, and thus reaffirms the essentially non-relational nature of our being.

In anticipatory resoluteness, I am a whole in the sense that I have in view all the elements that allow me to understand my existence. I no longer deny the nullity or lack of foundations for my existence, nor do I flee anxiously from the contingency and transience of my way of being. Instead, I bring myself fully into the concrete situation, no longer dispersed into irrelevant concerns, curiosity-driven distractions, and significations that don't matter to the particular individual I am. Thus my being-ahead-of-myself, far from preventing me from being a whole, is an enabling condition of it (see 316–17). And authentic Dasein is a whole in that it alone unifies or makes coherent the three aspects of its being: the ahead-of-itself (projecting onto contingent possibilities), the already-being-in (being unjustifiably disposed for a world), and the being-amidst (being drawn into particular dealings with particular entities and people in an actual, concrete situation).

The unity of the authentic self is thus not the unity of an occurrent entity. It is the unity of a way of being that is constant, that is, consistently committed to the stand it takes on its being (see 322). The they-self, by contrast, is not authentically a *self*, even if – or rather precisely to the degree that – it achieves stability and remains self-identical, because it has not owned the stand it has taken on existence. Rather, it has surrendered to the one the decisions on how to exist. But this means that the self is precisely not something "persistently occurrent" (323). It is entirely possible that I am my own self only intermittently, if at all.

With this account of anticipatory resoluteness, then, we have before us the phenomenon of a whole Dasein in its unity (311). We also have a clear description of two modes of Dasein – the authentic and the inauthentic. Each mode instantiates the care structure, although the authentic mode manifests existence more perspicuously, because it experiences the world in the light of its guilt and being toward death, without flight or distortion. The authentic mode also lets us see more clearly the ontological distinction between Dasein and other entities. Inauthentic Dasein falls prey more readily to the illusion that life is something to be managed like equipment, or that it is a merely causally structured entity like reality. Authentic Dasein by contrast is brought face to face with its ability to be a self, and its "being-free for its ownmost possibilities" (312), and in this way grasps the distinction between the kind of beings we are and "reality." Working out this distinction in more detail will illuminate the horizon of the "idea of being in general" (314). Before we are ready to turn to that question, however, we need to have a clearer grasp of the sense of the being of Dasein.

As we saw, "sense" (or "meaning," *Sinn*) names that onto which something is projected when we understand it, the background against which we understand the possibilities that define an entity or event as the entity or event that it is (see 324). Sense is what allows us, as we say in English, "to make sense" of something. So what background understanding lets us make sense of care as a mode of being, with the possibilities that are determinative of care and that distinguish it from availableness or occurrentness? What makes it possible to be a being who cares about its being? In virtue of what do we understand the basic modalities of our being (i.e., authenticity and inauthenticity)?

Take anticipatorily resolute Dasein. The question of the sense of Dasein asks, "What makes this authentic being-a-whole of Dasein possible with regard to the unity of its articulated structural whole" (325)? Anticipatory resoluteness is a way of being in which I experience myself and my situation in terms of my "ownmost, distinctive ability to be" (*eigensten ausgezeichneten Seinkönnen*). It is only possible to experience it in this way, however, if I can belong to or "come toward" (*zukommen*) myself in my ownmost possibility – that is, if (a) I have open to me a possibility that individuates me; (b) this possibility stands before me *as* a possibility (in other words, it is not my actual state or an occurrent condition), a possibility toward which I project on the basis of the throwness that I am; and (c) I experience myself as belonging to that possibility, as being defined by it. Heidegger calls this phenomenon of being defined by a possibility that I own "the primordial phenomenon of the future." This is not the future thought in terms of an occurrent way of reckoning time. The future of existential temporality is not a "'now' which has not yet become 'actual' and which sometime will be for the first time" (325). Instead, the future is the impulse or movement of coming (*Kunft*), of self-realization, for a being that does not simply and purely coincide with itself. Anticipation is the authentically futural being of Dasein, for in anticipation we have recognized our ownmost ability to be, and we project ourselves upon it.

The lack of self-coincidence is also in part a function of my throwness – my being as I already was. Dasein's "primordial" *past* is this being as it has been, or this impulse to encounter the environing situation and to direct oneself toward goals by way of coming back to what it has been. Resoluteness is the authentic mode of coming back to what I was by way of taking over my being-guilty. I own up to and take responsibility for my throwness to the degree that I accept, own up to, and take responsibility for the dispositions, traits, desires, and so on that I find myself saddled with. In authentic Dasein, this coming back is always oriented to the primordial future. It takes responsibility for itself in order to "send itself" toward its ownmost ability to be, and in the process makes of its throwness its ownmost "as it already was" (325–6). It comes toward itself by way of coming back to itself, thereby bringing unity to its lack of self-coincidence.

Finally, Heidegger understands the *primordial present* as a "letting oneself be encountered by." We saw that anticipatory resoluteness discloses a current concrete situation. This is the authentic form of the primordial *present* – "letting itself be encountered undisguisedly by that which it seizes upon in taking action" (326).

Together, "coming to oneself" by "coming back to oneself" and, thereby, "letting oneself be encountered" by entities in the environing world constitute *primordial temporality*. It is a unified lack of self-coincidence that "releases from itself the present" as it takes up what it has been in such a way that its past belongs to its ownmost self (326). It is important not to think of this temporality in the way we ordinarily think of time – namely, as a procession of now moments.[24] This would make care into something that runs its course in time, stretched out and developing over a sequence of now moments. Instead, care is a structure that is present in every now moment, and gives to me and my activities the character that they have – me as a being concerned with my way of being, and my activities as expressions of the person that I have committed myself to being. Thus, on the ordinary conception of time, the past, for instance, is whatever "is no longer occurrent" (328). But in primordial temporality, the past is that aspect of the unified non-self-coincidence that grounds my being poised to deal with every situation I encounter and to project into possibilities.

Primordial temporality is the sense of care. We saw that care was worked out as having three moments: being ahead-of-itself (in *projecting* onto a for-the-sake-of-which), already-being-in (i.e., *thrown* into a world), and being-amidst (the innerworldly entities that encounter us). What lets each of these three moments of care be the moment that it is, and what lets them belong essentially to each other, is the underlying structure of primordial temporality. I can project onto a for-the-sake-of-which and in this way be ahead of myself only because I exist as a unified lack of self-coincidence – as an "'outside-of-itself' in and for itself" (329). If I were nothing but my current set of properties, for instance, then possibilities would in no sense define me. Thus it makes sense to treat my possibilities as determinative of me, because there is some sense in which I am unified with what I am not – with what isn't actual. The coming to oneself, coming back to oneself, and letting oneself be encountered are not independent moments of time. They are one single upsurge of non-coincidence, of "being outside itself." But we can focus nonetheless on each one as an articulated part of the unified temporality. Heidegger calls them the "ecstases" of temporality, while he refers to temporality as the "ekstatikon pure and simple" (329). An "ekstatikos" is something that is "inclined to depart from" something else, or is "able to displace or remove" something (see Liddell and Scott, *A Greek–English Lexicon*). Temporality "temporalizes" – that is, it gives a temporal dimension to entities – by setting them outside of themselves, and thus displacing or removing them from their occurrent features. Temporality has different modes because "it is determined primarily in terms of the different ecstases," but, Heidegger asserts, "primordial and authentic temporality temporalizes itself in terms of the authentic future" (329).[25]

What Heidegger has offered us to this point is hardly a satisfying and rich elaboration of existential temporality. The remainder of the extant portion of *Being and Time* develops the account he has here sketched out, as Heidegger turns his attention to showing how temporality is the sense of everyday being in the world (chapter 4), how temporality grounds historicality (chapter 5), and how the ordinary conception of time is derived from temporality (chapter 6).

CHAPTER 4

This chapter repeats the analysis of everydayness that was the focus of Division I but now on the basis of the account of temporality developed in Division II, chapter 3. Heidegger now wants to develop the account of temporality as the sense of authentic being-in-the-world, but also to show that it is the sense of inauthentic being. To do this, he describes the temporal sense of understanding, disposedness, and falling in both their everyday and authentic forms. The chapter then turns to an account of the temporal sense of circumspective concern, deliberation, and theoretical discovery, and it offers a brief overview of the temporality of spatiality.

We've described temporality in its most basic form as a unified non-self-coincidence. The temporal ecstases (which are unified in the sense that they inherently inform or constitute each other) are the future (projecting toward an ability to be, i.e., the possibilities I *understand*), the past (being brought back to my thrownness, i.e., my *disposedness*), and the present (letting myself be encountered bodily by the environing situation). Dasein is able to exist as "there" – as in a situation that is oriented toward possibilities and grounded in dispositions – only through the unified non-self-coincidence that is made possible by the belonging together of the temporal ecstases. When, in *understanding*, I project onto my ownmost ability to be, I unify my self-identification with my *disposedness* – with those of my traits, dispositions, practices, preference, desires, and skills that can support such a way of being. Indeed, my disposedness only reveals its definite character insofar as I project my dispositions, skill, and so on, forward and, in the process, bodily encounter the present situation. Projection, disposedness, and present engagement thus bear a hermeneutic relationship to one another – each one has the meaning that it does in light of the way it unfolds into the others.

Everyday, inauthentic Dasein will have a temporal unity, but not the unity of a stable self. There is a unity that deserves to be called an authentic self, only to the extent that there is a stable and constant style that governs how my preferences, desires, characteristics, and so on cohere with my intentions and other projections, and my involvements in the current situation.

Let's look more closely at the relationship between the structural elements of care (projecting-thrown-fallenness) and the temporal ecstases, with attention to the way each element can "temporalize" itself in both authentic and inauthentic modes.

Understanding is a "projecting" because it sees each thing it encounters in terms of that thing's relationships to other things, all of which are ultimately anchored in the definitive possibility that is one's for-the-sake-of-which. But this means that understanding requires the unified non-self-coincidence that is temporality, because to understand is to make sense of a current actual situation by seeing one's disposed/bodily involvement with entities in the light of one's futural possibilities. Thus understanding is grounded in temporality, and oriented primarily to the future – to the ahead-of-itself (see 336). All the same, the possibilities I can project into depend on my existing preferences, tastes, dispositions, skills, and so on.

There are different ways to unify our disposedness, our current involvements, and our projects – differences that mark the contrast between inauthentic and authentic forms of understanding. I have an authentic future when I identify myself with my ownmost ability to be (in anticipation). My future is inauthentic when I identify myself with "what is feasible, urgent, or indispensable in our everyday business" (337). Heidegger calls this latter form of projection "awaiting" or "expecting" (Gewärtigens). In awaiting, we wait for some situation which may actually obtain (getting a raise, buying a new car, getting married), and see the things we encounter in terms of that situation (i.e., as advancing us toward it or impeding us in its pursuit).

The present and past have different ways of figuring in projection, depending on whether we are anticipating or awaiting. When we await possibilities – that is, expect a particular outcome for definite objects – the situation shows up in terms of whatever allows us to achieve the outcome, and thus we give priority to the present and the past over the future in determining the stand we take on ourselves. We draw on whatever skills allow us to respond to the affordances of that present situation. Heidegger describes this experience of the present moment as a dispersal or distraction (Zerstreuung) into the nearest objects of concern (das nächst Besorgte, 338). It's a dispersal because in doing whatever it takes to bring about the desired situation, we lose a coherent sense of ourselves. This is an inauthentic temporalizing of the understanding, since we sacrifice an ownmost sense of who we are to the service of "making present" whatever will lead to the object of present concern.

When we've resolutely taken a stand on our existence in anticipation of death, by contrast, the present opens itself up in a "moment of vision" – that is, a moment in which we see through the distractions and dissipations of everyday life in order to focus on what the concrete situation offers to the person we've resolved to be. The future is given priority because our stance on the world, the way we are poised to take action, takes into consideration the wholeness of Dasein as an uncanny entity.

Disposedness is primarily related to the past – to being "what one has been." The past is manifest as the poise we carry into present situations and projects. Consider how mood, a significant component of our poise, discloses a situation. The existential character of moods is not found in the "color" or phenomenal quality they bring to our psychic condition, but rather in the way that they show us what really matters and what possibilities stand out for navigating through a situation. They show us this by bringing us back to "what we are as having been" – to the factical features (the skills, dispositions, preferences, etc.) into which we are thrown (see 340). When I fear something, for instance, I don't merely experience an unpleasant or oppressive feeling. I rather feel oppressed *because* some entity has put my projects into doubt. The snarling dog in the alleyway not only keeps me from reaching my destination, but also poses a threat to my bodily integrity and thus my ability to pursue my interests and desires. And it poses this threat because of my factical characteristics (such as a lack of skills for dealing with animals). My fear thus touches my projects and my particular involvements in the world, and brings me back from them to a concern with preservation of how I am. The specific character of a specific fear is determined by the way the object of fear threatens me in my current involvements and projects. That means, however, that moods, like fear, make sense on the basis of a temporal structure, a particular form of unified non-self-coincidence. My disposedness in general likewise only has a definite character in the way that it facilitates or obstructs some particular possibilities of being. Thus disposedness too has its sense on the basis of our being temporal creatures.

As with understanding, there are both authentic and inauthentic ways of temporalizing disposedness. Fear of demise, Heidegger argues, is an instance of an inauthentic temporalizing of the temporality of disposedness. In fear, there is no decisive self-identification. Recoiling in fear, I seize on whatever transitorily allows me to pursue the objects of my nearest concern. If my fear is prompted by the snarling dog, for instance, then I focus on whatever will allow me to stave off bodily harm. The result is that fear gives me no enduring or coherent way of unifying my traits and dispositions and practices and skills with my possibilities. No possibility is committed to, and no coherent "shape" of thrownness is repeated. Heidegger thus calls an inauthentic temporalizing of our disposedness a "self forgetting."

When moved by anxiety in the face of death, by contrast, I do not await – I'm not oriented toward any particular event or situation. Rather, I am anxious in the face of my own uncanniness, my lack of belonging to any particular way of being in the world. My uncanniness poses a threat to my current way of being in the world, because it interferes with my ability to lose myself in the activities of everyday life. It thus deprives me of anything that I could await. As anxiety brings me back to myself and my facticity, it shows me my facticity in a new light – namely, as incapable of uniquely determining how I must live in the world. Although the call of conscience presents me with the task of owning my facticity, anxiety shows me my facticity as something I must take over without any clear guidance as to how I *should* take it over. It does this by rupturing the immediate solicitations of our everyday expectations. Anxiety thus facilitates an authentic way of taking up our disposedness, which Heidegger calls a "repetition" or "retrieval" (*Wiederholung*) – a selective retrieving and owning and developing of our facticity.

When I "repeat" my past (by building a way of being in the world on the ground of inherited tastes, skills, preferences, dispositions, etc.), I unify what I've been with an anticipation directed toward my ownmost possibility. I thereby take a stand on certain aspects of who I have been and make them salient as I engage with the current situation. This is in contrast to an inauthentic temporalizing of the past in which, as we saw, I "forget" my past by not taking a stand on what I've been, not striving toward any sort of coherence in my tastes and traits, and just allowing my dispositions and skills to be activated haphazardly by the situation I find myself in or the particular urge that comes over me.

Falling is an inauthentic temporalizing of the present. Heidegger's analysis of the temporality of falling focuses on the phenomenon of curiosity. As a mode of perception, curiosity is grounded in the present – that is, in the way entities bear on our bodies (see 346). Curiosity sees, not to understand something deeply (to see through its various possibilities), but instead it "seeks to see only in order to see and to have seen" (346). This distinction between different modes of seeing, however, is a distinction amongst different ways for the bodily present to be taken up into a relationship to my thrownness and my projects. Driven by the desire for the constantly new, curiosity "seeks to extricate itself from awaiting" – that is, it is a seeing unhooked from any kind of orientation toward the accomplishment of some goal or the realization of a specific outcome. Curiosity thus tries to reduce itself to a maximally present and minimally futural orientation to the scene. It can't dispense entirely with the future, of course: curiosity wants to see what will become of something, and thus is guided by a projection onto possibilities. But it wants to be able to move on to the next interesting sight as soon as it has seen enough (347). Thus awaiting is put in the service of curiosity, rather than having sight (i.e., making bodily present) in the service of awaiting. By getting maximally entangled in the present in this way, inauthentic Dasein achieves a kind of "distraction" or "dispersion"

(*Zerstreuung*) – it loses even the minimal constancy of being guided by what it is aiming for. By the same token, it is maximally free from what it has been, and can forget immediately what has gone before because no project stabilizes its disposedness. For this maximally inauthentic engagement with the present environment, what I *have been* is simply a disorganized mass of experiences, none of which is allowed to bear on the present moment in any sort of privileged way. Curiosity is thus a temporalizing in which "making-present ... seeks to temporalize itself out of itself" (348). But it can never dispense entirely with the past and the future – it still awaits outcomes, and thus is futural. And it is ultimately motivated, Heidegger suggests, by the desire to distract itself from its guilt, and is thus constituted by its relationship to the past. By contrast, when the bodily present temporalizes itself from an authentic future, the concrete situation opens up to our perception in a "moment of vision."

Obviously, then, "temporalizing does not signify that ecstases come in a 'succession'" (350) – each ecstasis informs the others, and together they give unity to the care structure. But we are now in a better position to appreciate that authenticity is a more complete unity than inauthenticity because it is wholly connected. In authentic Dasein, each moment coheres with the others, right to its outermost temporal limits. The inauthentic temporalizing of falling doesn't see through to our ownmost possibility, and forgets and loses sight of uncanniness. With an authentic temporalizing, I am ready for events on the basis of having seen through to my end, and I encounter the concrete situation in all its richness because I've taken a coherent stand on who "I am as having been." Authentic temporalizing draws together my ownmost future possibility, who I've resolved to be, and my current situation in all its concreteness. It thus requires resoluteness *and* anticipation.

Having shown the temporal ground of Dasein's being, Heidegger turns next to showing how temporality grounds the disclosedness of the world and the discoveredness of entities (both the available and the occurrent).

To make sense of the temporality of *circumspective concern*, we can ask: how is our skillful engagement with available entities grounded in temporality? In coping with equipment, I always do so from out of an equipmental context. When I use and manipulate equipment, my coping has the meaning that it does because of the context of other equipment and other tasks within which the activity occurs (see 352). We discover the available by "letting something be involved," that is, by "projecting an involvement understandingly" (353). This projection of an involvement both orients us temporally to the things around us, but also temporally connects the things to their context. When we handle any item of equipment understandingly, we disclose the temporal structure of *awaiting* that *retains* and *makes-present*. Awaiting discovers the "toward-which" in the equipment, by showing the equipment as suitable for such and such a purpose. This awaiting is not a cognitive state in which we imagine or picture or even intend the outcome of the activity (see 353). Rather, it is a way of moving, handling, and manipulating equipment that is open to the possibilities that connect it to its toward-which. Retaining discovers the characteristics and traits and dispositions of the equipment, as it brings our own traits and skills and dispositions to bear. This is no more a cognitive state than awaiting. In retaining the equipment, I don't thematically hold on to what I know about the equipment. Instead, I let the equipment and the context to which it belongs activate the appropriate set of skills for engaging with it. Heidegger describes this as "a specific kind of *forgetting*": "in order to be able 'really' to go to work and to handle things, 'lost' in the world of equipment, the self must forget itself" (354, translation modified). Of course, the stand I've taken on myself still shapes my temporalizing (by determining which skills I "repeat" and which possibilities I "await" or "anticipate"). But it cannot be a thematic focus if I am to be drawn and solicited by the equipment and situation around me. Moreover, the awaiting and retaining are united – the skills that are activated in me depend equally on my being disposed for the equipment in its character *and* my being open to the possibilities of the equipment. In this unified awaiting and retaining, the current situation shows up as it bears bodily upon me – it is discovered in terms of those activities that it affords to *me*, given the stand I have taken on my being.

We saw in Division I that the "seeing" (apprehension) of the available is a kind of "circumspection," which means that our seeing any particular entity "is subordinate to the guidance of a more or less express survey of the equipmental totality of the current equipment-world and of the public environment which belongs to it" (359, translation modified). We've now discovered the temporal grounds for this seeing. Circumspection itself involves a unification of non-self-coincidence. It sees by taking in simultaneously the traits entities have and their possibilities for engagement, and it does so by coming back to my own disposedness for dealing with such a situation (359). But circumspection has a variety of modes, each of which are grounded in a different way of temporalizing the situation. These modes include "conspicuousness" (having a particular entity obtrude and become a focus of awareness), seeing that something is missing, being surprised by something, seeing something as an insurmountable obstacle, and seeing something as unsuitable for the task at hand. In each case, the different modes of circumspection have the meaning that they do only because of the background temporality of the situation. Something shows up as conspicuous when my progress toward an awaited outcome is "held up." Likewise, to see that something is missing, I must be awaiting something and thus engaging the current situation in the light of what I await. I can be surprised by something only because I am awaiting one thing that can stand in the possibility space of my "awaiting retaining making-present," and thus not awaiting another thing that comes over me.

But what of maximally disengaged modes of looking at objects in the world, such as the theoretical discovery of occurrent entities? This kind of seeing might seem to give the lie to the claim that making present is always grounded in some form of anticipation and retention. Heidegger's response is to show that theoretical discovery of the occurrent arises from circumspective concern by way of a particular temporal modification of the latter. Making the case for this is an important step toward accomplishing the goal of offering an account of the "temporal constitution of being-in-the-world in general" (357), and thus is preparatory to an account of the meaning of being (357).

So what is the relationship between circumspection and theoretical seeing? There are types of circumspection involved in a practical engagement that has "taken a break": inspecting as preparation for further practical engagement, reviewing how prior engagement went, and so on. These are ways of seeing that are still guided by the context of involvements, oriented by projection, dependent on thrownness, and so on. Thus it is not the case that theoretical seeing arises simply through a break in our practical engagement with a situation – through "the discontinuance of a specific manipulation in our concernful dealings" (358). Moreover, theoretical seeing in fact requires and is supported by praxis. In the scientific context, for instance, it involves a facility with the use of scientific instruments, practices for experimental design, manipulation of the objects of research, or even the recording of research findings.

So to understand the distinction, we need to identify the point at which "circumspective concern changes over into theoretical discovering" (360). Remember that circumspection involves constantly looking beyond an entity to survey the whole context (in the way that when I am using a tool like a pen, I rarely look at the tool itself, and when I do, it is always by way of aligning it with other entities in the environment). When our engagement grows less fluidly responsive to the solicitations as a whole, our sight becomes narrowed down, so that we become more focally aware of particular entities. Heidegger refers to this as "bringing the entity nearer." One way in which the entity is brought nearer is through a "deliberative making present" or "envisaging" (see 359–60).

In deliberation, we attend to the "if-then" schema to which an entity belongs, seeing the entity expressly as something that serves a particular purpose ("if we want to accomplish such and such, then we need so and so an entity, and we need to perform such and such an operation"). Obviously, our grasp of the if-then schema depends on our awareness of the context of involvements. But we're narrowing the context down from the whole context to a specific involvement, which then stands out as salient against a background of involvements.

Theoretical discovering requires a further change – a liberation of the entity from an equipmental background, and a projection of it onto a spatio-temporal background. To see it this way, we must be able to see it independently of its place, the context within which it belongs. In the change over, place "becomes a spatio-temporal position, a 'world-point,' which is in no way distinguished from any other" (362). It is against this type of temporal-spatial projection that objects can be reduced to their causal properties. This causal projection "is characterized by a distinctive kind of making-present" (363), in which we await a purely spatiotemporally specifiable event. Our ability to undergo such a changeover in our experience of entities, Heidegger suggests, has its "existentiell basis in a resoluteness by which Dasein projects itself towards its ability to be in the 'truth'" (363). The scientific-theoretical attitude, in other words, brings us back to a resolve not to be solicited to respond to the worldly signification of things. It requires scientists to break themselves out of their everyday submission to social norms, and commit themselves to the "truth" (to providing a propositionally correct account of the entities around them).

Temporality also offers the background against which something like *the world* is intelligible. Dasein or "there-being," Heidegger tells us, "is existingly its world" (364). A Dasein is not an occurrent entity, nor is it an available entity. It is rather a "there" – a particular (factical) way of being disposed, projecting onto possibilities, and uncovering a situation. When I take a stand on my being, I commit myself to a particular "location" – a particular way of activating skills and disposition in being oriented toward my possibilities, thus polarizing my situation. But I could take a stand differently; I could be a different "there" (or, more naturally, we would say "I could be there differently"). This shows that each "there" occurs within a horizon of other possible theres. The horizon of theres, of different existential "locations," is the totality of significations – that is, the world. But the world is not simply a collection of different theres, or a storehouse of different possibilities to project upon, different factical arrangements, and so on. The world itself has a unity, the source of which Heidegger locates "in the fact that temporality, as an ecstatical unity, has something like a horizon" (365). To be specific, Heidegger argues that the unity of the world is grounded in the "horizonal schema" of temporality. A schema is a form or pattern that structures the way things show up. Each ecstasis "carries us away" to a different schema in terms of which we give form to the things we encounter. The schema of the future is the "for-the-sake-of-which." The schema of the past is "that before which [Dasein] has been thrown and that to which it has been abandoned." The schema of the present is determined by the "in order to" (365). What we have been calling up until now the "unity of self-non-coincidence" is the unification that is established between the "for-the-sake-of-which," that into which I've been thrown, and the in-order-tos that solicit me. It fits or adapts each schema to the other, so that my "for-the-sake-of-which," for instance, gives direction to my disposedness and polarizes the in-order-tos so that some solicit me while others withdraw into insignificance. Temporality is a "horizonal schema" for these different ecstases in that it structures each one in such a way that it "has within itself and belonging to it a pre-delineation of the formal structure of that to which it is carried away" (GA 24: 429). Temporality assures the unity of the world, in other words, because it pre-structures the different temporal ecstases in such a way that they depend on each other. (Because *Being and Time* was never completed, we unfortunately don't have any final and detailed working out of this claim, although *The Basic Problems of Phenomenology*, quoted above, gives us some indication of how Heidegger intended to pursue this claim.)

We've been trying to show how all the elements of our being are grounded in – that is, only make sense in virtue of – the structure of temporality. We've alluded a few times, however, to the fact that our engagement with a world is also spatially structured. It thus might seem that there are two independent coordinate elements grounding our being – temporality and spatiality. Heidegger argues, however, that spatiality is "embraced" by temporality. This does not mean that spatiality can be reduced to, deduced from, or dissolved into time. Rather, the claim is that our experience of space is necessarily temporally structured. It is in falling – in being drawn into a particular situation that bears bodily upon us – that we experience ourselves as spatial. But we've already seen that this experience itself is temporally structured. This means that "Dasein is never occurrent in space" – it "does not fill up a bit of space as a real thing or item of equipment would" (368). Rather, "Dasein takes space in" – it makes space meaningful as a place for it to exist. As we saw before, space is rendered meaningful through "directionality" and "de-severance." As practically engaged, Dasein discovers regions or meaningful settings where equipment belongs, and it is on the basis of the discovery of regions that we can encounter equipment, use it, move it, and so on. But regions are structured by relationships of involvement that, as we've already seen, involve the temporal structure of awaiting retaining making-present.

CHAPTER 5

So far, we've seen how temporality provides a kind of synchronic unity – how in any given momentary engagement with things in the world, our disposedness and our projection and our absorption in a present situation are tied together. In this chapter, Heidegger turns his attention to a diachronic or "historical" unity – to a coherence and harmony that endures across a span of life, through the events that punctuate time as we ordinarily conceive of it. "In spite of the constant changing of these experiences," he observes, "the self maintains itself throughout with a certain selfsameness" (373). Heidegger argues that the historical unity of Dasein is not a mere sum of actual experiences, nor even a framework that contains various experiences. Rather, Dasein at each moment carries its past (thrownness) and future (death). Heidegger calls this "stretching along" or "persistence" *das Geschehen des Daseins* – translated as either the "historizing" or "happening" of Dasein. It is in virtue of its ability to unify an entire span of experiences, to endure as the same through a variety of experiences, that Dasein is a historical being. The historical features of existence (the individual fate and the shared destiny of a people who live within a particular world) are, for their part, shown to be "just a more concrete working out of temporality" (382). Finally, Heidegger will distinguish between authentic and inauthentic ways for individuals and for a people to relate to their historical inheritance.

The historical bears a special relationship to the past, even though the future is part of history, and historical entities can endure in the present. But what is it for things to be "past"? It is a function of the fact "that the world within which they belonged to a context of equipment and were encountered as available and used by a concernful Dasein ... is no longer" (380, translation modified). But what does it mean to say that a world "is no longer"? It means there are no longer any existing Dasein who have the sort of understanding and disposedness that such a world sustains. But that shows that the historicality of equipment is dependent on Dasein being primarily historical: "entities are historical only by reason of their belonging to the world. But the world has an historical kind of being because it makes up an ontological attribute of Dasein" (381).

The clue to understanding the relationship between Dasein and history is to ask: "from where in general can the possibilities be drawn, upon which Dasein factically projects itself?" (383, translation modified). As thrown beings, we find ourselves already in a world, and understand ourselves "in terms of those possibilities of existence which 'circulate' in the 'average' public way of interpreting Dasein today" (383). Even in breaking with the average public way of being in the world, our understanding is still tied to conventional ways of interpreting ourselves (e.g., we understand ourselves as taking a stand against public modes of being, or as realizing the true meaning of a public practice that had become obscured over time). Resolute Dasein, in taking up responsibility for its thrownness, thus "discloses current factical possibilities of authentic existence … in terms of the heritage which that resoluteness, as thrown, takes over" (383). What distinguishes a resolute, and especially an anticipatorily resolute, person is the degree to which his or her possibility is chosen and committed to, as opposed to fallen into accidentally or provisionally simply because it is one "of the endless variety of the nearest possibilities that present themselves – possibilities for pleasure, taking it easy, avoiding responsibility." Anticipatory resoluteness, by contrast, "brings Dasein into the simplicity of its fate" (384, translation modified).

By "fate," Heidegger does not mean events that necessarily occur. Fate instead refers to the way that, having committed myself to a way of being, I am subject to determinate possibilities that shape and constrain what I can do, what can befall me, what it means to succeed or fail in my endeavors, and so on. Fate is both inherited and chosen (see 384), and thus compatible with freedom – indeed, it is an expression of and realization of freedom: freedom "'is' only in having chosen to make such a choice" (384). By resolving on a fate, I am no longer abandoned to whatever I find myself drawn into, and I obtain a "clear vision" for what in the situation is essential to me versus what is accidental. Fate is "authentic historicality" (385) – it is taking up my historical situatedness and owning it.

We are not just thrown into individual possibilities, however. We also inherit, along with the coinhabitants of our world, a common set of possibilities, which Heidegger calls a "destiny" (*Geschick*). Just as an individual only becomes free by resolving upon its ownmost possibility from among all those that are available, so a generation only becomes free "in communicating and in struggling" (385) to resolve upon some possible mode of being together.

Both fate and destiny amount to an ability to gather ourselves into the possibilities that are determinative of a particular moment in time. But to seize authentically on a definite possibility, Heidegger argues, Dasein needs to "be thrown back upon its factical 'there'" (385) through the anticipation of death. The idea seems to be that only being toward death lets us confront without deception the finitude of our situation. By anticipating death, we see that we have no alternative but to seize upon some of the possibilities we've inherited.

Dasein thus always happens or "historicizes" in the form of taking up a "possibility of existence that has come down to us" (385). Authentic Dasein takes it up in a "repetition" – it "chooses its hero," or decides on its possibility of existence "expressly" by "going back into the possibilities of the Dasein that has-been-there," and choosing "the struggle of loyally following in the footsteps of that which can be repeated" (385). But "repetition" doesn't mean the precise recurrence of what went before (see 386). Rather, it takes the form of a "reciprocative rejoinder" in which the possibilities we've chosen to pursue are interpreted on the basis of what the current situation affords us, given our own particular habits, dispositions, tastes, skills, and so on.

Even when not anticipatorily resolute, Dasein happens as a taking up of historical possibilities, and it encounters the present on the basis of the possibilities and dispositions it has inherited. The priority of the past in thinking about history derives from the centrality of "the phenomena of handing down and repeating" in the happening of Dasein (386–7).

But what does our historicality teach us about the connectedness of Dasein? History is certainly not the mere sequence or causal connectedness of occurrent events. History involves a meaningful working out of possibilities. What we encounter most immediately in our everyday environment are not just equipment and objects, but "'affairs,' undertakings, incidents, mishaps" (388). Others are encountered as with us "in the swim" – we are all involved together in our activities, constantly taking measure of our progress, readjusting, reconsidering our course and relative status as each pursues some of the possibilities available in our current shared world (388). Thus the connectedness of history involves the coherent interaction of us and our equipment as we pursue our aims and goals. But is that all there is to it? There is something genuinely historical about this – Heidegger terms such historicality the "world historical." In the world historical, things and places are taken up and "incorporated into the history of the world" (388) as Dasein pursues its possibilities along with the others of its generation. When it reflects on history, it naturally thinks at first of history world historically – that is, in terms of the progress (or regress) and sequential interconnection of world historical activities (see 389). Heidegger calls such reflection "historiology": the search through world history for a connectedness of things, a narrative that can make sense of the interrelations of world historical events and sequences.

But an everyday life, immersed in world historical activities, may well lack existential interconnectedness. The ever-changing sequence of affairs will drive everyday Dasein from one pressing event to another, "so if it wants to come to itself, it must first pull itself together, from the dispersion and disconnectedness of the very things that have 'come to pass'" (390). It is constantly "awaiting the next new thing," having "already forgotten the old one" (391). The type of connectedness that the everyday understanding seeks – a coherence and order behind the sequence of experiences – precisely misses the question whether life has an inherent unity, a connectedness that makes sense of our activities in terms of their contributing to and expressing a unified stand on our existence.

Existential connectedness is the unity of "the self's resoluteness against the inconstancy of distraction," a "steadiness which has been stretched along – the steadiness with which Dasein as fate 'incorporates' into its existence birth and death and their 'between,' and holds them as thus 'incorporated,' so that in such constancy Dasein is indeed in a moment of vision for what is world-historical in its current situation" (390–1). This commitment thus anticipates or has taken in advance "every possible moment of vision that may arise from it" (391) – that is, we uncover and polarize every successive situation we encounter in terms of the stand we have taken on our existence.

As a detour to the current course of argument, but by way of preparation for the next (unwritten) division of *Being and Time*, Heidegger turns at this point to a discussion of historiology. Drawing on Dilthey and Yorck, he offers both a critique of the way historiology is ordinarily understood, and a projection of a properly existential conception of historiology. This was to have served him when it came to "destroying the history of philosophy historiologically" (392) in the unwritten Part Two of *Being and Time*. The task for historiology is that of genuinely disclosing the past – of drawing on and interpreting artifactual materials to gain insight into the world that is no longer. But we only understand world historical entities on the basis of temporality, which means by projecting them onto their possibilities. An authentic historiology thus works by recovering and thematizing the structure of possibilities that once shaped and constrained the relationships between entities in the world and the possibilities into which the past world was thrown (see 395). In helping us recognize alternative possibilities, rather than in constructing "supratemporal models" of history, authentic historiology deprives "the 'today' ... of its character as present; in other words, it becomes a way of painfully detaching oneself from the falling publicness of the 'today'" (397). It aims at "the cultivation of the hermeneutical [concrete] stituation which ... opens itself to the repetitive disclosure of what has been there" (397).

CHAPTER 6

It might strike the reader as surprising that, to this point, the analysis of temporality and historicality has largely avoided addressing the fact that Dasein and history take their course "in time." In the final chapter of *Being and Time*, Heidegger offers an account of the relationship between existential temporality and the ordinary conception of time.[26]

It's a basic feature of our human way of being that we "reckon with time" – we guide, orient, and regulate our actions by taking time into consideration. This "reckoning with time" is, of course, prior to and independent of our possessing any equipment for measuring time. It is an "elemental comportment" (404), as basic as hastening our work as the sun begins to set, or deciding not to start mowing the lawn with a storm front moving in. The account of temporality must be able to show why such reckoning is both possible and necessary. But attending to our ordinary time reckoning in dealing with entities is also an important step forward in the context of the overall project of *Being and Time*, since it helps show how entities other than Dasein are also within time.

As already noted, everyday concernful engagement with equipment in the surrounding world is temporally structured. Directed toward futural possibilities, our concern is constantly "reckoning up, planning, making provisions, and taking precautions" (406, translation modified). This need not be occasioned by an interruption in work, a breakdown, or failure of any sort. It certainly need not take the form of explicit reflection or an occurrent cognitive act. Rather, in the slightest nuances of the movement of a hand, the shifting of attention, the way our bodies brace themselves for what is to come, or the way we lay some piece of equipment aside but at the ready, we are constantly orienting ourselves to what happened before, to what will happen next, and to what now needs to be dealt with. Our concernful activities thus bear a structure of coordination of activities with one another – a coordination that involves simultaneity as well as sequentiality. Heidegger calls this coordinated relational structure "datability." Our engagement with the world expresses a particular coordination that results from a particular way of projecting ourselves onto possibilities, and a particular responsiveness to the affordances of a situation. As we saw before, Heidegger calls the commitment to a determinate possibility that develops and makes salient certain relationships "interpretation" or "laying out." Thus concernful action amounts to an "interpretation" or "laying out" of my temporality, as I commit myself to definite possibilities and, in the process, "date" or make salient certain correspondences between actions.

"Time," as we ordinarily think of it, Heidegger argues, is "the making-present which interprets itself ... This simply makes known to us that temporality ... is familiar, proximally and for the most part, only as interpreted in this concernful manner" (408). That is to say, time is the way activities show up in dated relationships to each other as a result of our commitment to a particular possibility. This time, moreover, which lifts into salience certain orders and simultaneities, is also "spanned" – we understand our activities as lasting or enduring from one event to the next. But spanned or enduring time is not a continuous sequence of nows – it might very well have "gaps" in it, moments when we become so absorbed in our activities that we're not attending to the orders and simultaneities that structure our engagement with the world (see 409). We're all familiar with this phenomenon. One "loses oneself" in an activity: it is only later, upon reflection (if ever), that one is even aware of the sequence of moments that unfolded in the course of it.

Time as we ordinarily experience it is *public*. Our activities occur within "an intelligibility which is public and average" – that is, what we do always makes some sort of sense in terms of our shared, common, and conventional framework for understanding the world. This allows us to date each other's activities with respect to our own ("I will cook the pasta then when she sets the table"). We can also correlate our activities with respect to environmental events and features that are relevant to both of our activities, such as the position of the sun. We are all thrown into a world with features that both enable and constrain our activities. For instance, "everyday circumspective *being-in-the-world* needs the *possibility of sight* (and this means that it needs brightness) if it is to deal concernfully with what is available" (412, translation modified). So we are all together "surrendered to the changes of day and night" (412, translation modified). Of course, this passage of days in astronomical time is not a brute occurrence, but it is "interpreted" or taken up into our existence in different ways depending on our tasks – it means something different for a hunter than a photographer, for instance. Nevertheless, it allows us to share, "within certain limits" a common time with others: "in the 'most intimate' being-with-one-another of several people, they can say 'now' and say it 'together,' though each of them gives a different date to the 'now' which he is saying: 'now that this or that has come to pass'" (411).

Public time is not just datable in a more or less common way. We also experience it within a shared structure of appropriateness, given our world's way of ordering activities:

Time which has been interpreted has by its very nature the character of "the time for something" or "the wrong time for something." ... [T]he time which has been made public makes manifest that structure with which we have earlier become acquainted as significance, and which constitutes the worldhood of the world. As "the time for something," the time which has been made public has essentially a world-character. Hence the time which makes itself public in the temporalizing of temporality is what we designate as "world-time." (414)

Because time is public in this way, as dated to features of the shared world, it is possible for us to have equipment the sole purpose of which is to allow us to reckon with time more regularly, predictably, and determinately – the clock. As clocks become more sophisticated, it becomes possible to measure time, and to measure it with increasing precision. That gives rise to the illusion that time is itself an entity, a stream of occurrent moments that arise and pass away sequentially. But this illusion only occurs if we ignore or abstract away from the essentially meaningful structure of temporality that grounds the use of clocks. Occurrent time, in other words, arises in a particular "interpretation" or "laying out" of temporality – one in which our concern is with measurement of time itself, and time is dated by reference to equipment for timekeeping (417). This equipment functions by maximally decontextualizing those features by which we date the passage of time – the clock uses a pointer moving across a spatial stretch between numbers on the clock face that, as much as possible, has been reduced to an occurrent, insignificant spatial entity. We need to be able to measure or count the space – a space that eventually can be dispensed with, replaced with the numbers that represent it on digital clocks. But when our ability to use a clock swings free of the richer equipmental time – the time of the "right" time to do this, or of the appropriate time to do that – then our experience of temporality gets leveled down to a mere sense of earlier and later, of succession without significance. Heidegger calls this leveled down time "now-time" (421). In this interpretation or laying out of temporality, time appears to be a pure "sequence of 'nows' which are constantly 'occurrent,' simultaneously passing away and arriving" (422, translation modified). Now-time "covers up" the significance that time has in an engaged immersion in the world. The "now" appears free of any essential relationships of datability or appropriateness. It is not tied to any particular world (see 423). It appears to be gapless, constantly present in its continuous transformations, and infinite.[27]

Heidegger by no means denies the correctness of the ordinary conception of time. It is one way of laying out or interpreting temporality. But it is neither fundamental to temporality, nor exclusive of other modes of laying it out and making it definite in a particular situation (see 426). And he argues that now-time is derivative, since we only understand its characteristics (its character as passing away, for instance) on the basis of an understanding of a more original temporality. In addition, it is only disclosed for inauthentic Dasein, which, as we've seen, can itself only be fully understood on the basis of a more whole conception of Dasein (426).

We are led astray, moreover, if we try to reduce or even to correlate strictly the moments of now-time with the ecstases of other ways of laying out time. The future of now time is a now that has not yet arrived. The future of world time, by contrast, is a datable and significant "then" – an event from which the present derives its significance (see 427).

Heidegger argues that, from Aristotle forward, philosophy has struggled to explain how subjects can inhabit time, understood as an occurrent succession of nows – Hegel being the most sustained, rigorous, and thus illuminating, failure in this regard (see §82). For Heidegger, by contrast, the starting point has been "the 'concretion' of factically thrown existence itself." Existing beings are already immersed in time and happen as historical beings. There is no need to explain how we inhabit time, since to be a Dasein at all is to be temporally extended.

CONCLUSION

Being and Time concludes by marking out the questions that surround the findings of the first two divisions. These findings include a sketch of several different modes of being – existence, availableness, occurrentness. For one of these modes – existence – an argument has been offered to show that has its sense in (i.e., only makes sense because of) original temporality.

But Heidegger warns that this is still only "the point of departure for the ontological problematic" (437). We still need to understand, for instance, why ontology, for so long, has understood being in terms of occurrentness. And while he has suggested that temporality is also the sense of other modes of being, the analysis is far from complete. Indeed, what it even means to ask about the sense of being has not yet been fully clarified. The book thus ends with an unanswered question: "Does time itself manifest itself as the horizon of being?" (437).[28]

NOTES

1   Dasein is not precisely synonymous with human being, but it's a good first approximation of its extension, if not its meaning. See Chapter 4 for a discussion of the difficulties involved in the semantics of Dasein.

2   For more on the circumstances surrounding the publication of *Being and Time*, see Chapter 2.

3   The existing English editions of *Being and Time* translate "*Sinn*" as "meaning." We prefer "sense," both because it is etymologically closer to

Heidegger's term "*Sinn*," and also because "meaning" tends to be heard as restricted to linguistic or semantic meaning, whereas Heidegger's notion of sense is much broader than that.

4 It is helpful to distinguish between (1) the *pre-reflective* understanding of being that is embodied, at least in part, by all Dasein in their everyday dealings with the world; (2) the *pre-theoretical* understanding of being, alluded to above, that a scientific theory presupposes as applying to its particular domain of entities; and (3) the *pre-ontological* understanding of being that we have prior to making being our explicit theme in ontology.

5 For more on the question of the sense of being, see Chapter 3.

6 We prefer "the occurrent" and "the available" to "the present-at-hand" and "the ready-to-hand." While students of Heidegger eventually acclimate themselves to these unwieldy locutions, we find them awkward and cumbersome.

7 Heidegger discusses four different uses of the term "world" in Division I, chapter 3 (see 64–5). While it is legitimate to use "world" to refer to the "all" of occurrent entities, a mere collection, Heidegger preserves the term as a name for the organized totality of entities within which we dwell. When he uses it in the former sense, he indicates this by suspending the term in scare quotes.

8 Our "proximal" grasp of things is, for Heidegger, always the public meaning they have – the way they function in our shared practices. "For the most part" means the way things show up "as a rule" – that is, in accordance with normal expectations. See 370.

9 Heidegger offers an analysis of signs in order to clarify by contrast with signs the sort of reference relationship that characterizes worldly entities. See §17.

10 For more on Heidegger's account of space and spatiality, see Chapter 5.

11 For more on being-with others and "the one," see Chapter 6.

12 For more on moods and disposedness, see Chapter 7.

13 See Chapter 8 for a more in-depth discussion of understanding and interpretation.

14 For more on discourse, language, and assertion, see Chapter 9.

15 Anxiety is distinguishable on these grounds from fear, which is always directed at some more or less definite threat to a more or less definite aspect of our existence.

16 For more on Heidegger's relationship to debates over the reality or ideality of the external world, see Chapter 10.

17 For more on truth and skepticism, see Chapter 11.

18 This also indicates the motivation for the unfinished Part Two of *Being and Time* – the "destruction" of the history of ontology to recover the original experience of temporality that informed the entire philosophical tradition.

19 For more on death and demise, see Chapter 12.

20 For more on freedom and authenticity, see Chapter 13.

21 Heidegger also offers an elegant analysis of the ordinary conception of guilt, and discusses its relationship to existential guilt. See 282 ff.

22 Heidegger uses "die Lage" to refer to the generic situation – the situation as it shows up when articulated by the norms and concerns of *das Man*. He uses *die Situation*, "the concrete situation," to refer to the situation as it shows up for me when I take a stand on being myself.

23 For more on authenticity and resoluteness, see Chapter 14.
24 Heidegger will argue that the ordinary conception of temporality as a succession of nows arises from inauthentic temporality, which itself is ontologically dependent on primordial temporality.
25 For more on temporality, see Chapter 15.
26 For more on this connection, see Chapter 16.
27 Heidegger speculates that the leveling of world time down to now-time is motivated by a desire, born in anxiety, for an infinity of time. See 424–5.
28 For more on the connection of *Being and Time* to Heidegger's later work, and on his lifelong effort to make sense of things, see Chapter 17.

2 Martin Heidegger's *Being and Time*
A Carefully Planned Accident?

When Martin Heidegger's most famous book, *Being and Time*, was published in 1927, it caused a sensation and brought its author world fame. Like Immanuel Kant who had published his revolutionary work *Critique of Pure Reason* after a decade of silence, Heidegger had not published anything since his qualifying dissertation on Duns Scotus in 1916. Although *Being and Time* remained a torso – only a third of the originally planned two-volume work was published – to its readers, it appeared to have sprung from Heidegger's head like the Greek goddess Athena sprung from Zeus' head. Heidegger himself did his best to leave his early beginnings in a shroud of mystery. His early writings were only republished in 1972 and in the original plan of the Collected Edition of his works, the *Gesamtausgabe*, he excluded his early Freiburg lecture courses from 1919 until 1923. According to Heidegger's self-interpretation, the story of *Being and Time* should start with his first lecture course of the winter semester 1923–4 at the University of Marburg. But as we know, an author is usually not the best interpreter of his own work.

Today the complex story of the genesis of *Being and Time* has been told in great detail, thanks to the pioneering work of Thomas Sheehan and Theodore Kisiel. They followed Heidegger's trail in archives and unearthed a wealth of new material. The biggest fruit of their labors is the publication of the early lecture courses in the *Gesamtausgabe* and Kisiel's magnum opus *The Genesis of Heidegger's* Being and Time.[1] Here Kisiel tells the story of *Being and Time*'s genesis in full, and any serious reader of *Being and Time* should work his way through this book. As early as 1922, Heidegger carefully planned a book on Aristotle's philosophy to further his academic career. When he left for Todtnauberg in February 1926 to finally put together a publishable manuscript, he accidentally came up with a work called *Being and Time*. In my paper, I will try to shine some fresh light on the origins of the carefully planned accident that *Being and Time* perhaps was.

EARLY BEGINNINGS: FROM A WELL-ORDERED WORLD TO
THE DISCOVERY OF FACTICITY

Where does the story of *Being and Time* begin? According to Heidegger, the starting point of philosophy is simply the "es gibt," "it gives, there is." The moment we open our eyes, there is a well-ordered world we experience – it is given to us. This is the basic fact of human life we cannot deny nor ignore nor get beyond. We have to accept the world as it is given to us and take it from there. "Es gibt" – the act of giving – implies three moments: someone or something (1) that gives this gift (2) to someone (3). To the young Heidegger, the someone behind the gift of the well-ordered world was God. As a philosopher, he came to the insight that there is no way we can experience anything on the other side of the gift and that we have to accept the "it gives" as the basic fact of our lives. It is from this experience that *Being and Time* ultimately sprang.

Martin Heidegger was born on September 26, 1889, in the south German town of Meßkirch. His father was cooper and sexton of Saint Martin's church, where Heidegger served as an altar boy from time to time. His mother was born and raised on a farm in nearby Göggingen, where Heidegger spent most of his holidays as a boy. His parents were neither poor nor rich; they were devout Roman Catholics. The well-ordered world of his childhood, he often described in his later "autobiographical writings," was created by God who invested all being with meaning, sense, and purpose. The laws of nature, the laws of logic, and the principles of ethics spring from God as first cause of all being. One of the consequences of this – what I would like to call "Augustinian" world view – was Heidegger's anti-modernist attitude as a student of theology. The principle of autonomy (Descartes, Kant) is the cause of the problems of the modern world. Body and Mind, the physical and the psychic world, are separate regions that cannot be reduced one to the other. God as first cause is the explanation of the connection between Body and Mind, Nature and Thought. The order of the different regions of being make the human understanding of being possible. On his long way of thought, Heidegger attempts again and again to come to grips with this primal understanding of being through phenomenological description of what is given to us and to describe the conditions of the possibility of this understanding.

At the beginning of the twentieth century, the world of Meßkirch was still well ordered. But there were clouds on the horizon. Modern life and modern science were unstoppable. And the world as Heidegger knew it slowly disappeared: it was no longer given. From a biographical point of view, Heidegger's move to Constance in 1903 marks the beginning of his intellectual education and the end of the idyll of the well-ordered Catholic world of his hometown. For boys from modest families, the financial support of Roman Catholic endowments was necessary to finish their high school education. In return, they were expected to study theology and later become priests. While visiting the gymnasium, Heidegger lived from 1903 until 1906 at the Konradihaus, the seminary where Conrad Gröber was rector. Gröber was not only Heidegger's fatherly friend who gave him a copy of Brentano's dissertation on Aristotle as a birthday present in 1907, but also later the Archbishop of Freiburg.

In Constance, Heidegger came to know a whole new world, and he also experienced the disharmony of the modern world in his everyday existence. The gymnasium was a modern humanist school, and most students were sons of the local bourgeoisie, most of the teachers were free thinkers – the seminary on the other hand resembled a monastery. Heidegger's lifelong friend, Bruno Leiner, was the son of the town's rich and famous pharmacist. The conflict between modernism and Catholic anti-modernism, between Catholic saints and theology on the one hand, the great men of Greece, Rome, and the Renaissance, modern science and literature on the other, determined Heidegger's intellectual and philosophical development.

Heidegger's later professor of theology, Carl Braig, formed the concept of modernism. He uses it to describe the point of view, popular among Protestant theologians, that after Kant's rebuttal of rational theology, religion can only be grounded in the subjective feeling of the individual subject. Therewith, the door is opened for autonomy, psychologism, and materialism. Pope Pius X used the term "modernism" to indicate a movement within Catholic theology that mistook the eternal truths of Christian dogma for the products of subjective imagination and feeling. He also singles out Kant as the villain who through his critique of natural theology cut off our intellect from God.[2] Because Kant's critical philosophy means a refutation of scholasticism, that is, a metaphysics that reaches its summit in rational theology, modernism can only be overcome by a return to this scholastic tradition. Neo-Scholasticism, based on the work of Saint Thomas Aquinas, became the necessary fundament of Catholic theology. It is based on natural theology, and implies that all sciences – philosophy included – are ancillae theologiae. This means that scientific truth cannot contradict dogmas of Catholic faith. There is ("es gibt") only one truth of which the condition of the possibility is faith. Heidegger internalized this conflict, and it took him some twenty-five years to find a solution.

From 1906 until 1909, Heidegger lived in Freiburg, where he graduated from the Berthold's gymnasium in the summer of 1909. As expected, he began his novitiate with the Jesuits of Tisis in September, but after two weeks, he was dismissed for reasons of health. He subsequently moved to the seminary in Freiburg and continued his theological studies at the university. In February 1911, a deteriorating heart condition forced Heidegger to abandon all plans to become a priest. In October 1911, he registered in the new department of mathematics and physics. He took courses in mathematics, history, physics, and philosophy. In philosophy, Professor Heinrich Rickert became his most influential teacher.[3] On July 26, 1913, Heidegger received a doctorate in philosophy with his inaugural dissertation, entitled *The Doctrine of Judgment in Psychologism*. Heidegger's future looked promising. Philosophy Professor Arthur Schneider, who held the Catholic chair, and history Professor Heinrich Finke began grooming the talented young scholar for the Freiburg University's chair of Catholic philosophy. A grant from the Catholic Church enabled Heidegger to start working on his qualifying dissertation. On the advice of his mentors, Heidegger decided to write on Duns Scotus' doctrine of categories and meaning. At this time, he still thought his lifework would be taken up with a comprehensive presentation of medieval logic and psychology in the light of modern phenomenology. It therefore came as a great shock and bitter disappointment when a year after he had successfully completed his qualifying dissertation and obtained his veni legendi on July 26, 1915, the department of philosophy accorded the chair to Josef Geyser.

When discussing Heidegger's intellectual biography in his student years, it is important to remember that there was a strong Protestant and liberal influence at Freiburg University. After his decision to give up theology and consequently the priesthood, Heidegger was no longer under the obligation to attend specific lecture courses and seminars. Students of theology were not allowed to attend any courses outside the department of theology. As a student of mathematics, history, physics, and philosophy, Heidegger got his first real taste of academic freedom. The two people who had the greatest influence on his philosophical development, Heinrich Rickert and Edmund Husserl, were a Protestant and a free Christian.[4]

We find a first clear sign that Heidegger moved beyond the strict anti-modernist world view he defended in his earliest writings in a letter he wrote to his friend and colleague Father Engelbert Krebs on July 19, 1914. "The Motu proprio[5] on philosophy is still missing. Perhaps as an 'academic' you could demand a better method, that all people, to whom having an independent thought may occur, will have their brain removed and replaced by 'Italian salad.'"[6] An obvious question is why did Heidegger get so upset by this decree of Pope Pius X? The answer is obvious: if the restriction imposed on theologians by the Motu proprio would be extended to Roman Catholic philosophers, Heidegger would no longer be able to follow his own train of thought. Financially, he was dependent on grants from Roman Catholic foundations, and they would have to take the papal guidelines into account. This would considerably diminish his chances of obtaining further endowments and put his continued existence as a philosopher at risk.

At this time, Heidegger was working on his qualifying dissertation on Duns Scotus' theory of categories and meaning. In his book, he followed a two-way strategy: on the one hand, he used modern logic (Emil Lask, Rickert, and Husserl) to make fluid the solidified tradition of medieval scholasticism; on the other, he searched for solutions to modern philosophical problems in that same tradition. Here we already find the famous structure of *Being and Time*: the systematic analytic of being-there in the first part that was to be followed by a destruction of the history of ontology. The notion of "making fluid" (a clear sign of his intense study of Dilthey) shows how far Heidegger has come and how strong the influence of life philosophy on his thought had become. In his 1911 review of Friedrich Wilhelm Förster's book *Authority and Freedom*, he still celebrated "the eternal treasure of truth" (GA 16: 7). The guarantee of this immutable and eternal treasure is the authority of the Roman Catholic Church. There can be neither development nor progress. In 1914, Heidegger had apprehended that human life in all its facets is an ongoing everyday transformation, a continued reappropriation of times past, and an ever-new projecting of the future. Even logic and mathematics are not completed and finished sciences; they too have their history. From here, it is a small but decisive step to the insight that religion in general and Christianity in particular are historical phenomena. As such phenomena, they bring the fundamental historicality (*Geschichtlichkeit*) of human life to light. Therefore, there can no longer be an eternal and immutable truth. God's Word is not only spoken to all times, it is also spoken in time. Each generation has to breathe new life into the Word of God and find its own understanding of its meaning. Here I cannot go into all the details of this slow but ongoing development of Heidegger's basic beliefs and philosophical convictions.[7] Suffice to know that this transformation was accelerated by the most decisive event in Heidegger's life.

On March 20, 1917, he married a young woman by the name of Elfride Petri, to whom he would dedicate almost 60 years later the *Gesamtausgabe*. She was a student of national economics with a strong philosophical interest. She attended Heidegger's first lecture course on the history of medieval and scholastic philosophy and his seminar on Kant's *Prolegomena* in winter semester 1915–16. As an old German saying teaches us, "where two confessions share a pillow, the devil sleeps in between"; the long and intense discussions between the fiancés would not bring Elfride into the fold of the Roman Catholic Church, and they ultimately led to Heidegger's break with "the *system* of Catholicism."[8] On December 23, 1918, Elfride visited Father Krebs, who had mediated between Heidegger and his parents concerning his marriage to a Protestant and celebrated the marriage in the University chapel in Freiburg cathedral. Elfride was pregnant with her first child. The oldest son Jörg was later born on January 21, 1919. She and her husband had decided that they would not baptize him, as they had promised at their wedding as part of their wedding vows. After her visit, Krebs jotted the essence of their conversation down.

My husband no longer has his Catholic faith and I have not found it. Already at our wedding his faith was undermined by doubts. But I insisted on the Catholic marriage and hoped to find faith with his help. We read, discussed, thought and prayed a lot together, but the result is that we both now think foremost in a Protestant way, that is to say we believe in a personal God without any fixed dogmatic ties, we pray to Him in the spirit of Christ, but without Protestant or Catholic orthodoxy.[9]

There are no grounds to doubt the truthfulness of Elfride's statement. From other sources, we also know that Heidegger studied Protestant theology (Troeltsch, von Harnack, Overbeck, and Schleiermacher, among others) from 1915 on. At the same time, he pursued his interest in mysticism. He also studied Nietzsche and Kierkegaard, as well as Simmel and Bergson. We find traces of all this in *The Phenomenology of Religious Life* (GA 60).

Heidegger's oldest student and lifelong friend, Heinrich Ochsner, gives us an important clue in a letter he wrote to an unnamed and unknown woman on August 5, 1917. "It is such a pity that you could not hear Heidegger's exposition of the problem of the religious. This whole week I am still impressed by it. But perhaps we will read the second speech of Schleiermacher's 'On religion' together. It contains the essence of Heidegger's exposition."[10] It is the first clear evidence we have that Heidegger was studying Protestant theology at the time.

During his training as a meteorologist in the summer of 1918[11] in Berlin, Heidegger had enough time on his hands to attend lectures at the university and socialize with the theologian Deißmann and the phenomenologist Stumpf. All these different and apparent loose biographical pieces will fall into place when we add the missing link. On April 1, 1916, Husserl came to Freiburg as the successor of Rickert. He and Heidegger had been corresponding since 1914. From May 1916 on, Heidegger would learn daily through his close association and joint philosophizing with Husserl.[12] Through his apprenticeship in Husserl's phenomenological "school," Heidegger obtained the necessary tools to develop a phenomenology of religious life.

After the end of World War I, Heidegger returned to Freiburg in December 1918. On January 9, 1919, he wrote his famous and enlightening letter to Father Krebs. "Epistemological insights extending to a theory of historical knowledge have made the *system* of Catholicism problematic and unacceptable to me, but not Christianity and metaphysics – these, though, in a new sense."[13] It is important not to overestimate the importance of this sentence. Heidegger is breaking with the system of Catholicism, not with Catholic faith. This is also the reason why, all of his life, he remained so attached to the Benedictine Monastery in Beuron. Here he could still experience authentic religious life. It was one of the places where people still cared for the inner life and so preserved a place where the Divine and the Holy could be present. The last sentence of his letter is also remarkable. "I believe that I have the inner calling to philosophy and, through my research and teaching, to do what stands in my power for the sake of the eternal vocation of the inner man, and *to do it for this alone,* and so justify my existence [*Dasein*] and work ultimately before God" (italics in original).[14] Heidegger did not become a philosopher because he needed to earn his keep; it was a vocation. It would perhaps not be an exaggeration to say that he felt God called him to philosophy. His need to justify his existence and work before God clearly shows the influence of Luther.

Heidegger started teaching again in the so-called war emergency semester of 1919. If we take a closer look at the lecture courses he taught between 1919 and 1923, it becomes evident that he was working out his phenomenological method through a phenomenology of religious life.[15] As we have seen above, Heidegger had lost faith in dogmatism – be it of the Roman Catholic or one of the many Protestant varieties. Dogmatism with its obsession for clear and final answers goes against the natural movement of life. It offers an unchanging interpretation of religious experience. Instead of opening up the vista of immediate experiences of the Divine and the Holy, dogmatism closes the door on any possible lived experience and throws away the key. To break through this closure, Heidegger needs to scrape off layer after layer of solidified dogmatic statement to get to the beating heart of the underlying lived and immediate experience of the Divine and the Holy. For all his shouting, the dogmatist cannot hear the gentle call of God's voice. Heidegger is searching for those pivotal moments in the history of Christianity where lived experience of the Divine erupts and is expressed immediately.[16] However tremendous these eruptions may be, they are soon absorbed and therefore deformed by dogmatism, orthodoxy, and scholasticism. Heidegger is using religious life to develop his phenomenological method. This should not blind us to the fact that his ultimate goal is a phenomenology of human life as it is lived and expresses itself. We could almost say that he is trying to come to grips with his own religious life. At the same time, his focus on religious life betrays the strong influence of Jaspers and his psychology of limit situations.

In his philosophical autobiography, Jaspers reminisces about how he met Heidegger for the first time in the spring of 1920. After a birthday party, he visited Heidegger's study and was impressed by the intensity of his Luther studies.[17] He and Heidegger share the prejudice that human existence shows itself most clearly in the extremes of the limit situations (death, love, faith, sickness). In the following years, Heidegger would free himself from this presupposition. In *Being and Time*, being-there no longer shows itself first and foremost in limit situations but in the averageness of everyday life. Human life has the tendency to fall away from itself and follow in the clear and familiar footsteps of the Anyone instead of living its own life. But however that may be, it has now become obvious why he focused on primal Christianity, Augustine, medieval mysticism, Luther, and Kierkegaard. Hard work taught Heidegger that it is not enough to move beyond crystallized dogmatism. Nor does it suffice to clarify our own hermeneutic situation. It does not even help much to read the New Testament or the works of Kierkegaard. Human life, language, and thought are historical to the bone. No writing can ever be innocent because every expression of immediate lived experience mediates and thus transforms the experience. A phenomenological description of lived experience that keeps the experience alive is the proverbial needle Heidegger tries to find in the haystack of phenomenology. What makes a phenomenology of religious lived experience so difficult is its double movement. The first step is the clarification of our hermeneutic situation. The second step is the destruction of the hermeneutic situation of the author. Heidegger's phenomenological method is specifically designed to meet these requirements, and it took him some six years to work it out. The key elements of his method are hermeneutic situation, formal indication, content sense, relation sense, actualization sense, destruction, and lived experience. Two things are very important. Heidegger is convinced that the method of phenomenology can only be learned through concrete phenomenological descriptions of phenomena. Only by doing phenomenology can we learn what it is. But at the same time, phenomenology is not a method; it is philosophy itself.[18] This means that philosophy as Heidegger understands it is only possible as phenomenology and is a way of living our life. Philosophy should do justice to the fundamental historicality of human existence and therefore follow the two-way strategy mentioned above: it should clarify its own hermeneutic situation through a destruction of a tradition and simultaneously clarify the hermeneutic situation of that tradition through a destruction of the present. In other words, in phenomenology and philosophy, we circle ever closer around the truth but we may never touch it. Thus they reflect the finitude of human existence.

FROM CHRISTIAN RELIGION TO ARISTOTLE

In January 1922, Paul Natorp wrote to Husserl to inquire after Heidegger. Natorp would be retiring shortly and Nicolai Hartmann would be taking his place, leaving the junior position in philosophy at Marburg University vacant. Heidegger had already made a name for himself as an outstanding teacher. The rumour of the "hidden king" was circulating in student circles throughout Germany.[19] To have any real chance of obtaining the post, Heidegger needed to publish something urgently or at least to come up with a publishable manuscript. He took three weeks off and labored over his manuscripts. The fruit of his labor was a typescript addressed to Natorp and Georg Misch at Göttingen University, which has become famous under the title of the "Natorp-Bericht." It is a very interesting text and a major step toward *Being and Time*. Ultimately, it would lead to Heidegger's appointment at Marburg University in 1923. In the "Natorp-Bericht," or "Phenomenological Interpretations with Respect to Aristotle. Indication of the Hermeneutic Situation," as it is called in full, Heidegger founds and develops the hermeneutic situation in which Aristotle's texts are to be interpreted. The first part is a kind of research report summarizing his work of the previous three years. Heidegger also breaks new ground and finds a solution to the problem of fusing the historical with the systematic approach in phenomenology. He outlines the double-pronged program of a fundamental ontology and a destruction of the history of ontology. The averageness of the public "Anyone" and fallenness are juxtaposed with the possibility of a more original seizure of my own death in order to define an ontological way of access to the temporality and historicality of human being-there. Heidegger designates existence as the countermovement against falling. Here existence has the meaning of life's most unique and authentic possibility. In the second part, Heidegger discusses the problem of an original retrieval of Greek philosophy rooted in *alētheia*, *logos*, and *physis*. He also gives an interpretation of *Nicomachean Ethics VI* that centers on the different ways in which the soul "trues" (*wahrnimmt*). Phronēsis is the interpretative insight into a concrete situation of action coupled with resolute decision and truth as countermovement to concealment.

The "Natorp-Bericht" is an introduction to a book on Aristotle that was scheduled for publication in volume 7, 1924–5 (*Being and Time* would be published in volume 9) of Husserl's *Jahrbuch für Philosophie und phänomenologische Forschung*. This may come as a surprise, since he had been working on a phenomenology of religious life since 1915. Why Aristotle? Where did he come from and what did Heidegger find in his philosophy?

To find an answer to these questions, we need to take a step back and approach Heidegger's philosophical development from another angle. Heidegger's work is a collection of paths of thinking. This is also the reason why his work can be interpreted in such different ways. When Heidegger returned home in the winter of 1918, an era had come to an end, and in many ways he had become homeless. He had lost his Catholic faith and not found the answers he needed in the Protestant tradition. He didn't believe in Neo-Scholasticsm nor in Neo-Kantianism. Germany was no longer an empire; it had become a republic and was a shambles. Life as he had known it had come to an end.

According to Hans-Georg Gadamer, one of Heidegger's oldest and most brilliant students, after his return from the battlefields, Heidegger came face to face with the existential question of how modern science and enlightenment could be reconciled with Christian existence.[20] But Gadamer failed to understand how radical Heidegger really was. Heidegger asked himself the most basic question of human life: who am I? This question unfolds itself into three different ones that are yet intertwined. The first question (a) is – as we read in his letter to Krebs – what is philosophy? The second question (b) is what is the essence of Modern Times? And the third question (c) is what does it mean to be a Christian? These three questions come together in a fourth (d): is it still possible to be a philosopher and Christian in this day and age?[21] One could argue that *Being and Time* is the answer to that final question.

What Is the Essence of Philosophy?

As a philosopher, Heidegger needs to define what the essence of philosophy is. The idea of philosophy is a constant theme in his early Freiburg lecture courses. In his War Emergency Course of 1919, he says:

The idea of science ... means for the immediate consciousness of life an intervention that changes it in some way; it involves a transition to a new attitude of consciousness and therewith its own form of movement of life. Undoubtedly this intervention of the idea of science in the context of the natural consciousness of life can only be found in an original, radical way in philosophy as primal science. (GA 56/57: 3–4)

Heidegger acknowledges Husserl's project of philosophy as a strict science. Until 1929, he held onto the thought that phenomenological philosophy had to be a primal science. Heidegger clearly rejects the influential thesis that every philosophy can only be a world view. In a world view, the spiritual unrest, which is so characteristic of human life, quietens down in a construction of eternal norms and values. Both the Neo-Kantians and the philosophers of life tried to develop such world views.

The idea of philosophy is that it is a primal science. Heidegger uses "idea" in the original Kantian meaning and not in the Platonic-Neo-Kantian sense. This implies that primal science as an idea of philosophy is not constitutive for philosophy; it is only regulative and a never-ending task. In his lecture course, Heidegger states phenomenology is the investigation of life in itself. In this sense, it is the opposite of a world view.

> Phenomenology is never closed off, it is always provisional in its absolute immersion in life as such. In it no theories are in dispute, but only genuine insights versus the ungenuine. The genuine ones can be obtained only by an honest and unreserved immersion in life itself in its genuineness, and this is ultimately possible only through the genuineness of a personal life.[22]

A personal life is always my life of someone. In his personal life, Heidegger is an academic teacher, and as such he has to be a "spiritual guide." Real spiritual life can only be lived, and the student should partake in this particular form of life. Only by doing philosophy under the guidance of a teacher like Heidegger can we learn what philosophy is. We cannot define nor look at it from the outside; we need to live the philosopher's life. This is the existentialist core of Heidegger's philosophy that made it so easy to mistake his work for existentialism. It also explains why students were so attracted to his teaching.

What Is the Essence of Modern Times?

In his lecture course, Heidegger also takes part in the intense debate on the status of science and world views, to which Max Weber's famous talk "Science as Calling" was one of the most important contributions. World War I had left Germany in chaos. Armed gangs ruled the streets, and the country was in a state of revolutionary upheaval. In Munich, well-meaning writers like Toller and Mühsam founded a soviet republic after several weeks of civil war. They thought that the millennium of light, beauty, and reason had finally begun. Politics had to take care of the happiness of the citizens and make it possible for them to lead meaningful lives. The world should any day become a flower bed. Weber offered in his Munich talk a sober and profound analysis of his time. At first sight, his talk seems to be about the scientific *ethos*; in

reality, he tries to answer the question how a meaningful life is possible in the rationalized civilization of his time. Weber makes it clear
that science has to be devoid of value judgments. Science can teach
us whether a means can achieve a certain goal. It can also analyze the
possible inner contradiction of our goal and examine whether or not it
conflicts with other goals we have set ourselves. However, science cannot teach us whether or not it is meaningful to aspire to certain goals.[23]
Science cannot bear the responsibility for our value judgments. This
is the liberation that the enlightenment has brought us. *Sapere aude!*
Human beings should think for themselves and live their own lives.
Unfortunately, we let slip this freedom because science has become
our fateful destiny. The technical uses of science have changed our life,
destroyed the enchantment of our world, and proven how destructive
they can be in World War I.[24] Science has lost all its old illusions. It is
no longer *"the way to true being, the way to true art, the way to true
nature, the way to the true God and the way to true happiness."*[25]
Science has become meaningless because it has no answer to the only
question that is of the utmost importance to us: *"What we should do,
how we should live?"*[26] As Friedrich Nietzsche would say, we killed
God with the rationalization of our world, although we did not know
what we were doing.

According to Weber, our civilization has become so rationalized that
we expect scientific answers to our vital questions. We do not make
use of the liberty science leaves us to answer ourselves questions of
value and meaning, but we demand the certainty of scientific answers.
We hide behind the pseudoscientific world views that the prophets of
the pulpit provide us with, and do not accept responsibility for our own
lives. These prophets react to the disenchantment of our rationalized
world by putting the last true magic left to us – our personality and
freedom – in the irons of pseudo-rationality. They create the illusion
of science and mislead their readers and listeners. Weber opposes this
deceit with a dualism. We must, on the one hand, approach the world
scientifically and, on the other hand, respect the mystery of the human
person.[27] God has disappeared from our disenchanted world. If God
still exists somewhere, then He can only exist in the soul of individual
human beings. The living faith is not of this world and demands *"the
sacrifice of the intellect."*[28] Weber emancipates personal and responsible life from the custody of science. As a scientist, he factually leaves
people to their fate. How should we live, what should we do? To these
questions, no scientific answer is possible. Heidegger accepts Weber's
critique of world views, but he does not want to leave us to our fate. He
tries to develop a new concept of science that should make scientific
answers to our most intimate and important questions possible. Two

things follow from this. First, Heidegger has to develop philosophy as a strict science in such a way that it can provide insight into the facticity of our individual lives. Second, he has to show that meaningfulness is given with the bare fact of our existence. A reinterpretation of Husserl's phenomenology will enable Heidegger to achieve both these goals in his early Freiburg lecture courses.

What Does It Mean to be a Christian?

What does it mean to be a Christian? The decisive insight that formed Heidegger's path of thinking is that Christian religion is not a world view but imitation. A Christian follows in the footsteps of Christ.

In his courses on the phenomenology of (Christian) religion, Heidegger tries to get to the origins of the religious experience. Religion puts us in touch with the fullness of our existence as human beings. As he put in a letter to Elisabeth Husserl:[29]

We must again be able to wait and have faith in the grace which is present in every genuine life, with its humility before the inviolability of one's own and the other's experience. Our life must be brought back from the dispersion of multiple concerns to its original wellspring of expansive creativity. Not the fragmentation of life into programs, no aetheticising glosses or genial posturing, but rather the mighty confidence in union with God and original pure, and effective action. Only life overcomes life and not matters and things, not even logicised "values" and "norms."

This original Christian experience was expressed through the vocabulary and conceptuality of Greek philosophy. Greek philosophy had developed its most important categories and concepts from factic life itself. But the original life experience of the Greeks was different from the Christian experience of life. From this follows a double covering up. Original Christian life experience is covered up by the Greek conceptuality used to express it. At the same time, our Christian world view blinds us to the original Greek life experience. This is why Heidegger spends so much time developing his method of destruction. We cannot distinguish between Greek and Christian life experience as long as we do not know what is original and genuine in both these life experiences. But since there is no such thing as "a view from nowhere," the only way to get to the original life experience is a scraping off of the layers of the non-original expression of this original life experience. As we can see in his courses of the phenomenology of religion and Augustine, Heidegger tries to actualize the original life experience in his own life. Originally, Heidegger believed that the all-controlling place science occupies in the modern world was a consequence of the Greek's contemplative world view. For the Greeks, the highest purpose and activity in human life is pure thought. As a kind of antidote, he used the Christian ideal of life: care (*Sorge*). A Christian should not admire and enjoy the wonders of the world but rather care about himself and the state of his eternal soul.

Heidegger studied Greek philosophy (Plato and Aristotle) as a means to uncover original and genuine Christian life experience. But in Aristotle – the all-important philosopher of the Middle Ages and scholasticism – he found a phenomenology of human life and to his surprise the moment of care and a kairological experience of time. According to Aristotle, being human means to have logos. While he has logos, his primal way of being is to behold (noein). As beholding living beings, humans collect entities in their being and discover the sense and meaning of being. This beholding unfolds itself into five different ways that each experience senses in different ways and thus opens up different regions of being: nous (pure beholding), sophia (authentic inspective understanding), phronesis (solicitous circumspection), techne (productive working procedure), and episteme (inspectional demonstrative determination).

Now we can take a step back. Greek, Christian, and modern ways of life are all possible ways of being human (Dasein). So the structure of being human that makes these three different ways of actualizing human life possible becomes the phenomenon Heidegger tries to uncover. This is the purpose of the existential analytic in *Being and Time*: to uncover the fundament of three fundamental ways of being human. As a phenomenologist, Heidegger can only describe actual phenomena. This is the reason why these three "existentiell" ideals of being human determine his existential analytic.

The interpretation of Aristotle's philosophy became an unavoidable task for Heidegger. He was a phenomenologist *avant la lettre*. Not only had he developed his concepts out of human life experience, but he had also analyzed the basic structure of human life as being-in-the-world. Human beings have the logos and behold the being of entities. His philosophy determined the conceptuality of Christian and modern life experience.

Is It Still Possible to Be a Christian in Our Day and Age?

The answer to this question is obviously yes, although the real imitation of Christ was only taking place in such unique places as Beuron. But Heidegger was a philosopher – he had given up theology and the priesthood way back in 1911 – and a Christian philosophy is a round square. His starting point is life, such as it expresses itself, and not a holy book. The philosopher digs ever deeper in the fundaments of human life experience. Although every *a priori* structure that underlies a genuine way of being human is in itself historical, Heidegger still believed that, beneath all these historical structures, a nonhistorical structure could be uncovered.

Heidegger's final course at Freiburg university as a *Privatdozent*,[30] "Ontology: Hermeneutics of Facticity," is an important step on the way to *Being and Time*. As the title indicates, Heidegger develops his ontology as a hermeneutics of facticity. Facticity is the being of our own being-there. Here Heidegger uses being-there for the first time as a formal indication of the central phenomenon of phenomenology. It indicates the particular whileness that each of us is and has. After a historical overview of the history of hermeneutics, Heidegger interprets hermeneutics not as a science of interpretation but as explicating communication. Hermeneutics is not so much a method for interpreting texts as it is a way to understand human life in its everyday form and expressions. Its goal is the self-understanding of being-there. Since interpretation is an outstanding possibility of the being of factual life itself, hermeneutics is an essential possibility of facticity. In order to keep the term being-there ontologically neutral, we must deconstruct the traditional concepts of human being such as rational animal and person. Existence is being-there's most unique and most intense possibility. It is being-there's ability to hold itself awake and be alert to itself in its ultimate possibility. After a discussion of the contemporary state of philosophy, Heidegger comes to his phenomenological analysis of being-there.

The being of being-there is determined as being in a world. In order to characterize the everyday world and to develop the formal indication of being-there as being-in-the-world, Heidegger formulates the trio of questions, which we also find in *Being and Time*: (1) What does a world mean? (2) What does in a world imply? (3) How does being in a world appear? Only the first question is worked out in any detail in the course. We encounter world in three different ways as environment, with-world, and self-world. Environment is a meaningful context that discloses the being of entities as equipment. Our everyday openness toward entities is made possible by the fundamental phenomenon of care. Because in the everydayness of our lives we are first and foremost concerned with entities, the potential authenticity of our being-there is at the same time concealed. Heidegger calls this potential authenticity discovery. In *Being and Time*, the meaning of disclosedness and discovery will be reversed.

When Heidegger assumed his post as professor of philosophy at Marburg University, he continued to follow the same paths of thought. He still labored over his book on Aristotle's philosophy. But he also found a new path of thought: the concept of time. He had already dealt with this topic in his formal "test lecture" as part of his *Habilitation* in July 1915 titled "The Concept of Time in Historical Science." Yet, when he began to walk down this path, another central element of *Being and Time* fell into place. Heidegger presented a public address, "The Concept of Time," nine years later on July 25, 1924, to the Marburg Theological Society. It contains the core structure of *Being and Time*. The central topic of the lecture is the question what is time? Heidegger analyzes first the everyday concept of time. Time is related to movement. Aristotle and Albert Einstein agree that time exists only because of the events that happen within it. In natural science, time is measured by a now that is so much later than an earlier now and so much earlier than a later now. Yet, as Augustine has shown, we can measure time only through our disposedness. Time is closely related to the being-there of human beings.

Heidegger picked this theme up in his famous summer semester 1925 lecture course on the *History of the Concept of Time. Prolegomena Toward the Phenomenology of History and Nature* (GA 20).[31] In this course, he develops a new research program that ultimately will result in the book *Being and Time*. It is a logical continuation of his earlier work on early Christianity, Aristotle, Plato, and Dilthey. The question of the meaning of being has become the fundamental problem of Heidegger's phenomenology. This question enables him to show the link between the systematic part of his research, the hermeneutics of factic life experience, and the historical part, the destruction of the philosophy of Aristotle, Augustine, and Descartes. Heidegger explains this link in the subtitle of the course. The prolegomena offers an interpretation of the history of the concept of time as an introduction to the phenomenology of history and nature. As Kisiel pointed out, Heidegger reworks the roots of his early philosophical work in this course.[32]

History and nature are the subject matter of the two main groups of science: the humanities and natural science. According to Heidegger, phenomenology should not make the mistake of the Neo-Kantians and Dilthey, looking at reality through the eyes of science, because in this way they fall prey to scientific prejudice. Phenomenology is an original discovering of history and nature in their different realities (GA 20: 2). This is only possible if we can discover history and nature within a horizon through which they can also be distinguished (GA 20: 7).[33] Such horizon can, according to Heidegger, only be disclosed by way of the history of the concept of time. "The history of the concept of time is … the history of the question of the being of beings" (GA 20: 8).[34] Because the being of beings was understood by the Greeks as presence and this view also determines the way we understand the being of beings, the history of the concept of time is really a destruction of the history of ontology and metaphysics.

During his WS 1924–5 lecture course on Plato (GA 19), Heidegger's main discovery was that the question of the stranger from Elea: "What is being?" should be the starting point of radical phenomenological research. The consequences of this ontological turning become visible in the lecture course on the history of time.[35] "The question of being as such, however, when it is put in a sufficiently formal manner, is the *most universal* and *emptiest*, but perhaps also the *most concrete* question, which a scientific inquiry can ever raise" (GA 20: 186).[36] To ask this question in a phenomenological way, we have to make a being as being visible in its being. Through this radicalization of phenomenology in its own most possibility, the questioning of Plato and Aristotle becomes alive again. Phenomenology is: "the repetition, the retaking of the beginning of our scientific philosophy" (GA 20: 184). Heidegger next shows that the question of the meaning of being has a threefold structure. We can distinguish between (1) that which we want to know, (2) that which is asked (the being of beings), and (3) that which is questioned (the being in question; GA 20: 195). Posing the question of being is a way of being of a specific being, which is characterized by an implicit understanding of being and that in its being cares about its being (GA 20: 405). Heidegger formally indicates this being as *being-there*. A phenomenology of being-there is a necessary preparation for the question of the meaning of being because being-there has an explicit relation to being.[37]

The ontological turn in his phenomenology poses four problems for Heidegger. First, what is the question of the meaning of the being of beings (GA 20: 200)? As we will see, this question is really posed by being-there itself which in its being cares about its being (GA 20: 185).[38] It is only through our own being that we have access to being. Being concerns us; we are involved in it. Second, what is being-there? The answer to this question is the hermeneutics of primal facticity that Heidegger developed from 1923 on. The being of being-there is not only historical (Dilthey, Yorck) but is thoroughly temporal. Third, what is the reason the question of being was forgotten? The forgetfulness of being is a consequence of being-there's falling in to the world and the "They" in its everydayness and ends in the crisis of modernity.[39] Finally, this implies that a solution to this crisis can only be found when being-there retrieves its authenticity – that means, it poses the question of being again (GA 20: 179–80).

In the introduction of his lecture course, Heidegger discusses the meaning and task of phenomenological research. This cannot be an ordinary introduction in which the main results of phenomenology are neatly presented, since phenomenological research must always be

repeated by us (GA 20: 32). In other words, an introduction to phenomenology falls under Husserl's famous maxim: "to the things themselves"
(GA 20: 104).

Heidegger's introduction is a repetition of Husserl's phenomenological
"breakthrough." Heidegger will try to show that his hermeneutic ontological phenomenology is a consequence of taking Husserl's maxim "to
the things themselves" seriously. In his course, he transforms Husserl's
three fundamental and revolutionary breakthroughs: intentionality,
categorical intuition, and the *a priori* into care, understanding, and time
(GA 20: 420, 355, 99).

Phenomenology's first major discovery is intentionality (GA 20: 34).
To discover what intentionality is, we need to get to the thing itself
and not be deceived by traditional philosophical opinions. We need to
uncover the structure of intentionality. The result of this process will
be that care is the fundamental structure of being-there. Factually, it is a
fact that there is being-there. The primal phenomenon for Heidegger is
the structure of being-there. His phenomenology could be described as
a structural analysis in which the structure of being-there is described
through formal indication and existential concepts. Heidegger only
describes structures and functions. He wants to discover of what being
intentionality is the structure and how it is this structure. This is
only possible if we examine intentionality in its factic historical reality. This leads us to Husserl's second discovery: categorical intuition
(GA 20: 63). Categorial intuition is "a concretion of the basic constitution of intentionality" (GA 20: 98–9). It makes the structures within
which we discover beings visible. In categorial intuition, the categorial
is first grasped as an element of a being and only later is it determined as
a category. In other words, we always already live in the categorial. Life
explains and understands itself. We live in a world that always already
is filled with meaning. Implicitly we understand the structure of life
because we are involved in it and care about it. We grasp the categorial by living our lives. "It is not so much that we see the objects and
things, but rather that we first talk about them. To put it more precisely: we do not say what we see, but rather the reverse; we see what
one says about the matter" (GA 20: 75). Only in a new approach can
we make the categorial explicit and develop a doctrine of categories.
The task of Heidegger's hermeneutical phenomenology is the explication of the structure of our lived experience. "There is no ontology
alongside a phenomenology. Rather, *scientific ontology is nothing but
phenomenology*" (GA 20: 98).

This leads us to Husserl's third discovery – the *a priori*. Categories are
earlier than any experience. "The *a priori* to something is that which
already always is the earlier" (GA 20: 99). Here Heidegger establishes

for the first time a link between the problem of time and its relation to being. Heidegger follows Dilthey and takes his distance from Kant and Husserl. The *a priori* is historical and is not beyond time. The *a priori* that is grasped through categorial intuition is a formal indication of a dynamic structure of being-there.

We live in categorial structures like being-in-the-world, being-with, and existence, within which we discover and meet beings. "We shall see that our comportments, lived experiences taken in the broadest sense, are through and through expressed experiences; even if they are not uttered in words, they are nonetheless expressed in a definite articulation by an understanding that I have of them as I simply live in them without regarding them thematically" (GA 20: 65).[40] Life articulates itself and discloses beings in their being. We are in a world because *it worlds* for us. The primal something is that there is being-there. This is as the primal form of intentionality truth as unconcealment (*aletheia*) and it has a logical structure (*logos*). The world is the *a priori* of all the beings that we discover within it. It is at the same time an always-receding horizon. In this lecture course, Heidegger uses Husserl's phenomenon of appresentation from the unpublished manuscript of Ideas II.[41]

Heidegger only uses the concept of appresentation in this course. Later it will be replaced by meaningfulness: "We always already live in an understanding of the 'is' without being able to say more precisely what it actually means" (GA 20: 194). In every aspect of our factic life experience, we have an implicit understanding of being. This implicit understanding, that is being-there, must be made explicit as the primal form of intentionality. In every experience of the being of an entity, being itself is also experienced. The world appresents things and thus lets them be present, encountered, and discovered. That which is primarily given is for Heidegger the world as intentional structure and not the things within it: the primary appresentation is the meaningfulness and not the thing or object. This brings us to the heart of Heidegger's phenomenology.

Heidegger uses the term "meaningfulness" to indicate the link between the primal phenomenon of factic life and the meaning of words (GA 20: 275). The expression meaningfulness is not the best, but Heidegger could not come up with anything better (GA 20: 275).[42] His main concern is the relation between being and language. The world is always already filled with meaning, and that is why we can discover meaning in it and talk about it. There is always and everywhere meaning. Originally, we experience the unconcealment of our being-there, that is, the primal facticity, as a logical structure. Because we are always already in the truth, Heidegger can avoid Natorp's critique of phenomenology. The structure of meaning within which we live can be expressed in words. "Live" has here the double meaning of living (*leben*), and experiencing (*erleben*). We can now take the next step. This meaningfulness can only be if the meaning of the world is understood. For this reason, Heidegger calls understanding a more primal phenomenon of "being-in-the-world" than meaningfulness (GA 20: 288). Understanding appresents the world. Understanding is fundamentally a relation that belongs to our "being-in-the-world." "Understanding is the primary being-relationship of Dasein to the world and to itself" (GA 20: 286). In everyday life, we are always already familiar with the world and ourselves. Getting around (*Umgang*) with myself is as primal as getting around with the world. I discover myself in discovering the world. I always already have myself in a self-world (GA 20: 350). In other words, I am not a pure I but far more a hermeneutical situation. This is what Heidegger formally indicates as disposition (*Befindlichkeit*). "Disposition expresses a way of finding that Dasein is in its being as being in each instance its own there, and how it is this there" (GA 20: 352). In disposition, we discover both how we are and that we are. In understanding, we realize the possibilities of being that are given to us in discoveredness and disposition. "Understanding as disposed disclosure and having disclosed the world is as such a disclosive self-finding" (GA 20: 356). Understanding always intends the world, being-with-others, and our own being-there. The self-, with-, and surrounding world are equiprimordial. Understanding is the fundamental form of all knowledge (GA 20: 281). So now we come to a second meaning of appresentation in order of knowledge that is contrary to its meaning in the order of being. Understanding appresents the world through the presentation of beings in the world (perception). Both forms of appresentation have a common base that we could call primary appresenting (GA 20: 347). In ontological appresentation, the world appresents the beings, and appresent understanding concerns the world itself. In understanding, appresenting the world and our "being-in" are appresented. At the end of the course, Heidegger will show that understanding is the *lumen naturale* of being-there (GA 20: 411). We can see ourselves and the world. We are, as it were, a between or a clearing in the massive being of nature. In understanding, we are beyond ourselves (intentionality) and already with and in being. Heidegger also uses understanding in its other meaning. We can say a carpenter understands his trade, which means that he is good at his job. Understanding here means having an ability. This ability is having the possibility to do something. Being-there is nothing other than a can-be. "I am, that means, I can" (GA 20: 412).

The world cannot only appresent things; it can also appresent the being-there of others and myself. A field appresents the farmer that ploughed it. A nightgown on a chair appresents the lover that wore it. Although others may be physically absent, they can be appresented by things. The world appresents, for instance, beings as equipment that can be used in a certain way. A hammer is for hammering, a knife is made for cutting. All equipment is appresented in structures of meaningfulness. The structure of the appresentation of other being-there is different. The others are not appresented as suitable for a certain kind of use. We meet them in the how of their going about the world. Even when we meet them in person, they are appresented "in a concern or non-concern according to their in-being" (GA 20: 331).[43] The world appresents the being-there of others in their functioning. A human being is what he does. In this way, Heidegger reduces the being of being-there to a functioning. The existential analytic of being-there is understanding the structure of the functioning of being-there. Heidegger's analytic is a form structuralism and not so much a form of ontology. He replaces the concept of substance with that of function.

Being-there is as being-in-the-world at the same time a being-with-others (GA 20: 328). I am in the world with others and others are in the world with me. We are in the world together. This being-with-others implies that we depend upon each other. "The worldhood of the world appresents not only world-things – the environing world in the narrower sense – but also, although not as a worldly being, the co-Dasein of others and my own self" (GA 20: 333).[44] From the being of being-there, we must understand our "being-in," our "being-with," and the "in each case mineness" (Jemeinigkeit) as ways of ex-istence. Here we find one of the reasons why Heidegger gave a central role to the formal indication of existence in Being and Time.

We now come to a crossing on Heidegger's path of thinking. Particular whileness (Jeweiligkeit) is a formal indication of the temporality of being-there. Being-there is the being that has to be as my being (GA 20: 206).[45] Having-to-be is a formal indication of a dynamic structure that comprises both a must and a can.[46] In Being and Time, having-to-be will disappear in the dynamics of existence. With "having-to-be," Heidegger has discovered the most fundamental structure of being-there. In being-there, there is a fundamental relation to being: the primal form of intentionality. Being-there is the being that is characterized by an implicit understanding of being and that appresents being. Heidegger can refer to a fundamental insight of Parmenides at the beginning of the history of philosophy. Being-there understands in its being the being of beings (GA 20: 200).[47] Being-there cares about its being. Being-there intends to be being and this intention of being-there is in itself care. Heidegger thus destructs Husserl's understanding of intentionality as a pure form of consciousness.

Heidegger's course on the history of the concept of time is an important step on the way to Being and Time. But there are still some important structures missing, like existence, thrownness, and mineness. During the final hour of the course, Heidegger stumbles upon a phenomenon that we can consider to be the missing link in his phenomenology. "Not 'time is' but 'Dasein qua time temporalizes its being'" (GA 20: 442). When Heidegger tries to come to grips with this phenomenon, he will make use of Kant's doctrine of schematism in the *Critique of Pure Reason* and the existential vocabulary he had avoided for so long. Being-there temporizes and actualizes in time its being. In other words, being-there exists in the three dimensions of time that correspond with the history of factic life experience: historical consciousness (Dilthey) that characterizes modern times (the past), Greek life experience of being present (the present), and the kairos experience of early Christianity and Aristotle's practical philosophy. Together they form the there as a sequence of hermeneutical situations in which being-there is always mine. In this there, being-there appresents being. Conversely, being appresents being-there in the course of history in its three different ways. Being can only be understood from the ways in which it realized itself in time. Time is the transcendental horizon of the question of the meaning of being.

On November 5, 1925, Heidegger began his lecture course on logic. This winter semester 1925–6 lecture course, the last one Hannah Arendt attended, is a milestone on the way to *Being and Time*. It moves toward the interface where language is born. Heidegger wants to develop a philosophical logic that can discover existentials and their hermeneutically indicative sentences. In the first part of the course, he rehearses his own prior steps toward such a logic. After a discussion of Edmund Husserl's critique of psychologism, he criticizes the Neo-Kantian sense of truth as the validity of judgment. To get to the essence of truth, it is necessary to return to Aristotle's prejudicative truth of "nous" or simple apprehension. This truth of intuition binds Aristotle and Husserl together in a juxtaposition of Greek and German thinking.

After this course, Heidegger gathered his manuscripts and left for Todtnauberg, where he would write the first 175 pages of *Being and Time*. In 1925, Heidegger came under increasing pressure from the philosophy department to finally publish another book. Nicolai Hartmann left Marburg to become Max Scheler's colleague at the University of Cologne. The University of Marburg wanted Heidegger to be his successor, but his lack of publications was the reason for the Ministry of Science, Art, and National Education in Berlin to remain reluctant in appointing Heidegger. Just before the Christmas break, Heidegger changed the subject matter of his course. Instead of a further destruction of Aristotle's concept of truth, Heidegger developed a phenomenological interpretation of Kant's *Critique of Pure Reason* (GA 21: 194).[48]

This brings us to two questions: (1) why did Heidegger choose logic as the subject matter of the course, and (2) why did he switch from Aristotle to Kant?

In his previous course on the history of the concept of time, Heidegger had offered his students a destruction of Husserl's phenomenology based on his concept of phenomenon. In this course, he will destruct Husserl's concept of logic. The term "phenomenology" consists of both "phenomenon" and "logic." Heidegger's Interpretation of Kant's *Critique of Pure Reason* is a first draft of the history of the concept of time that Heidegger announced in his program for research.[49] This part should have become the first chapter of the unpublished second part of *Being and Time* (40).

As a phenomenologist, Heidegger had been studying for years the structure beneath intuition and intentionality. In this lecture course, he will no longer use Husserl's terminology of appresent and appresentation. He will try to show that the structure of understanding in its profoundest sense lies beneath intuition and makes it possible. Husserl's principle of all principles is intuition, that is, the giving and having of an entity in its bodily presence. Heidegger shows that, underlying intuition, there is a more fundamental understanding of that intuition that at once understands itself. The primary form of simple apprehension is a having of something as something in the ways we can use it. We discover entities first as pieces of equipment, which are given in their in-order-to. The "as" of primary understanding is the original articulation of my getting around and dealings with the world. In this way, we acquire the habits of our habitat that constitute our most immediate having. The "as" of primary understanding makes it possible for us to explicate in assertions the structure of our being. The "as" of primary understanding can thus become the hermeneutic "as." Assertion is a demonstrative letting see or uncovering. Heidegger can now distinguish between worldly assertions that let entities see in their being and categorial assertions or existentials that indicate the being of being-there.

Identification or proof is an intentional matter. It is carried out; and thereby, without any reflection on its part, it attains to a clarification of itself. If this moment of unreflected self-understanding, which lies in the intentional performance of identification, is specially apprehended of and by itself, then it is to be taken as what we call evidence.

Evidence is the self-understanding act of identification. This self-understanding is given with the act itself, since the intentional sense of the act intends something identical *qua* identical; and thereby, in and with its intending, it *eo ipso* clarifies itself ... Evidence is not an act that accompanies proof and attaches itself to it. Evidence is the very enactment of, or a special mode of, proof. (GA 21: 107–8)[50]

In intuition, we are not only with the entity that is given in intuition; we also know that what we thought was given in intuition ("the table is white") is identical to the entity that we intuit in its bodily presence ("the white table"). "Truth as an identity is a relation between the meant and the intuited" (GA 21: 109). The judgment "the table is white" is true because the relation between table and being white can be demonstrated in the intuition of the bodily present white table. The identity of table and being white is intuited. Understanding is the condition of the possibility of intuition. Here in the heart of the problem of truth, Heidegger will come across the phenomenon of time. He will analyze the understanding that is the *a priori* of intuition with help of Aristotle's doctrine of truth. First, he will sketch the history of the concept of intuition and introduce Kant as a spokesperson for the thesis that knowledge is intuition (GA 21: 114–15).

In the second part of his lecture course on the decisive beginning of philosophical logic and the roots of traditional logic, Heidegger will destruct Aristotle's logic (GA 21: 127). On the one hand, Heidegger introduces his students to the method of phenomenological destruction. To get access to Aristotle's original thinking, all the prejudices and misunderstandings that accumulated over the centuries must be destructed. On the other hand, Heidegger destructs Aristotle's thought so it becomes clear what he thought, and we can explain how these prejudices and misunderstandings could arise (GA 21: 128). Aristotle is not only the father of philosophical logic, he is also at the origin of scholastic logic. Heidegger will deal with two important prejudices concerning Aristotle's logic: (1) Aristotle supposedly claimed that the place of truth is judgment, and (2) he supposedly taught that truth is the correspondence of thinking and the entity (GA 21: 128).

After the Christmas break, Heidegger abandons the original outline of his course. Instead of Aristotle's question of truth, he discusses Immanuel Kant's doctrine of schematism. This interpretation of Kant would ultimately result in his later book, *Kant and the Problem of Metaphysics*. Heidegger shows that the original self-affection of the mind is time. Time gives itself unthematically as the constant precursory encounter that lets entities be. It lets entities be seen and makes our intuition of entities possible. The making present of an entity as something is a comportment of being-there, for being-there is itself time.

At the end of the lecture course, Heidegger summarizes the results of his interpretation of Kant. He wants to make clear that Kant implicitly makes use of a concept of time that is not a sequence of "now-moments" and that can only be explained from the temporality of being-there. "Time is an original pure and general self-affection" (GA 21: 400). That which time affects, is a manifold of intuitions, a manifold given as a sequence of "nows." It is not grasped thematically by the "I think." The sequence of now-moments is a horizon that, through its constant intending, shows something. The now is a pointing in a direction where something can be encountered and so essentially a form of intentionality. The now is in a sense waiting for something that it can make present. Knowledge in the Kantian sense is, according to Heidegger, that now as a synthesis of the "I think" and the manifold of intuitions that are given in a sequence of "now-moments." Behind the synthesis of knowledge, we find intentionality as the making present of something. This making present of something is the now as that in which something becomes present. Because Kant made a strict and clear distinction between time and the "I think," the structure of intentionality remained invisible for him and therefore also the principal connection between time and the "I think." The making present expresses itself in the now. "Making-present is ... a factical present*ing*" (GA 21: 402). The present, understood as an existential, is a formal indication of the structure of being-there.

During the final hour of his course, Heidegger takes a terminological decision that will have far-reaching consequences: "We designate the ever-temporal [*jeweilige*], authentic ontological possibility of factical human existence (however that possibility be chosen and determined) as *Existenz*" (GA 21: 402). Heidegger replaces the formal indication of being-there's having-to-be with existence. Why he does so, he unfortunately does not explain.[51] A little later he remarks, "If *Gegenwart* [present] constitutes a mode of time and, as a mode of time, determines the meaning of the being of human existence (insofar as human existence is being at home with the world), then time itself must be understood as the basic existential of human existence" (GA 21: 403). In *Being and Time*, Heidegger will no longer call time an existential. This shows how fluid his terminology is at the time. What is the essential difference between "having-to-be" and "existence" as formal indication of being-there? "Having-to-be" implies the primacy of possibility. Being-there is essentially a possibility and so a "can-be." This formal indication has one big disadvantage. Heidegger wants to overcome Aristotle's "ousological" doctrine of being. Being is not an entity. "Having-to-be" implies, however, an entity that has to be. Being-there threatens to become an entity that has the special quality of "having-to-be" instead of the entity that has the *logos*. Heidegger, however, wants to disclose being-there not as an entity but as a structure of movement. Being-there is not an entity. It is essentially intentionality. Existence is a more appropriate formal indication because "being-out-toward" is a kind of "*ek-sistence*" or "standing-out," being beyond oneself. Heidegger can of course at the same time turn traditional ontology upside-down because existence becomes the essence of being-there. As existence, being-there has no essence in its traditional sense but always a range of possibilities it can be.

Heidegger ends his lecture course with a sketch of a phenomenological chronology. What is time (GA 21: 205)? Heidegger's interpretation of Kant is focused on this question. In the first step of his interpretation, Heidegger discloses the intentional function time has in the *Critique of Pure Reason* as a "being-toward." This function hides itself in the making present of entities in their categorial structures and is made visible in the second step of his interpretation. Third, Heidegger can then disclose time in a phenomenological analysis. "The ontological transition *from* the *pre*-theoretical relation to the world, *to* a pure [theoretical] making-present, is itself a mode of temporality – and it would be absolutely impossible if human existence were not itself time" (GA 21: 407). Being-there is time. Heidegger first raised the question "is being-there time?" in his 1924 lecture on the concept of time (GA 64: 125). The "is" does not have the function of the copula; it is a formal indication that should make being-there as phenomenon understandable (GA 21: 410). Being-there is time, which means being-there's being is determined by time and actualizes itself in the temporal structure of the three tensors (GA 21: 409). Being-there has the structure of care, that is, being-ahead-of-itself as being involved with the world. As being-involved-with the world, being-there makes entities present and temporalizes its being in presentness. As thrownness, a term Heidegger does not use yet in the lecture course, being-there actualizes the *a priori* of its facticity in historicity. As being-toward-death, being-there expects its own-most possibility and actualizes its being futurity (GA 21: 412). The three existential or temporal structures through which being-there actualizes its being form the horizon within which being-there exists. "The structures of human existence – temporality itself – are not at all like an ever-available framework for something that can be merely-present. Rather, in keeping with their most proper sense, these structures are possibilities for human existence to be, and only that" (GA 21: 414).

Being-there has always already decided which possibilities it will actualize, either authentically or inauthentically. Heidegger analyzes the structure of being-there still to a large extent with the help of Aristotle's theory of *dunamis*, *energeia*, and *entelecheia*. Time as the *a priori* enables being-there to be its own most possibility (GA 21: 414). Being-there is never at hand but always delivered over to itself, that is, always already in the world and beyond itself with other entities. Every possibility being-there actualizes always contains the possibility to give up this actualization. In its "having-to-be," being-there is responsible for itself and the way it actualizes its being. At the heart of Heidegger's philosophy, we find the foundation of ethics. We can take one more step on our way to *Being and Time* before we let Heidegger take his manuscripts to Todtnauberg where he would write the first part of his *magnum opus* in March 1926. The starting point of a phenomenological chronology is the question of the meaning of being. The condition of the possibility of the givenness of *being* is time (GA 21: 410). Being is the primal facticity. There just is being and not not-being. As the primal facticity, it is at the same time the primal intentionality and, as such, the fundamental structure of being-there. Being-there is actualized in time as meaningfulness. The temporality of being-there unfolds itself in the three tensors of historicity, presentness, and futurity. In other words, being can only be experienced within the horizon of temporality. This means being can only be understood if it can be experienced in the three dimensions of temporality at the same time. In one moment, *kairos*, being-there is disclosed in its temporality and being. This kairological moment can only be grounded in the mineness of being-there. The existential analytic of being-there in *Being and Time* will become a kairology.

It is important to keep in mind that *Being and Time* is both a book and a research program. From 1919 on, with harbingers in his dissertation and qualifying dissertation, Heidegger found his own path of thinking. The many pathways he followed came together in 1926 in the book called *Being and Time*. His research program "Being and Time" did not end there and would ultimately lead him beyond the book *Being and Time*. In this sense, we may call *Being and Time* a carefully planned accident.

NOTES

1   Theodore Kisiel, *The Genesis of Heidegger's* Being and Time (Berkeley: University of California Press, 1993).
2   Pius X, *Acta sanctae sedis* 40 (1907): 663.
3   See also Martin Heidegger and Heinrich Rickert, *Briefe 1912 bis 1933 und andere Dokumente*, ed. Alfred Denker (Frankfurt am Main: Vittorio Klostermann, 2002).
4   According to his *Vita*, Heidegger attended lecture courses of two Protestant professors, Richard August Reitzenstein (on Christianity and Hellenism) and Eduard Schwarz (on the Gospel of St. John) (GA 16: 41–5). For a complete list of the lecture courses and seminars Heidegger attended, see *Heidegger und die Anfänge seines Denkens, Heidegger-Jahrbuch*, eds. Alfred Denker, Hans-Helmuth Gander, and Holger Zaborowski (Freiburg: Verlag Karl Alber 1, 2004), vol. 1, 13–17.
5   The Motu proprio is a very anti-modernist decree of Pope Pius X in which important teaching restrictions for Catholic theologians in Italy were laid out. They should all adhere to the teachings of Thomas Aquinas.

6 Martin Heidegger, Briefe Martin Heideggers and Engelbert Krebs (1914–19), in *Heidegger-Jahrbuch*, vol. 1, 62 (my translation). See also Thomas Sheehan, "Heidegger's *Lehrjahre*," *The Collegium Phaenomenologicum: The First Ten Years, Phaenomenologica*, eds. John C. Sallis, Giuseppina Moneta, and Jacques Taminiaux (Dordrecht: Kluwer Academic Publishers, 1988), vol. 105, 113.

7 For a full-scale interpretation of Heidegger's life and work from 1909 until 1919, see my essay "Heideggers Lebens- und Denkweg 1909–1919," in *Heidegger-Jahrbuch*, vol. 1, 97–122.

8 See Heidegger's letter to Engelbert Krebs of January 9, 1919 (*Heidegger-Jahrbuch*, vol. 1, 67), and the English translation of this letter in *Supplements: From the Earliest Essays to* Being and Time *and Beyond*, ed. John Van Buren (Albany: State University of New York Press, 2002), 69–70.

9 Cited after: Hugo Ott, *Martin Heidegger: Unterwegs zu seiner Biographie* (Frankfurt and New York: Campus Verlag, 1988), 108 (my translation).

10 *Das Mass des Verborgenen: Heinrich Ochsner zum Gedächtnis*, eds. Curd Ochwadt and Erwin Tecklenborg (Hannover: Charis-Verlag, 1981), 92 (my translation).

11 In 1914, Heidegger had been declared unfit for active duty as a field soldier. He became a censor at the post monitoring authority in Freiburg. This enabled him to teach at Freiburg University from 1915 on. In spring 1918, he was declared fit for active duty, and with his background in natural sciences and mathematics, he was sent to Berlin to become a meteorologist. Meteorology was important in World War I because of the gas attacks.

12 See, for instance, his letter to Elisabeth Blochmann of May 1, 1919, in Martin Heidegger and Elisabeth Blochmann, *Briefwechsel 1918–1969*, ed. Joachim W. Storck (Marbach am Neckar: Deutschen Literaturarchiv, 1989), 16.

13 Van Buren, *Supplements*, 69. For a penetrating exposition of the system of Catholicism, see Johannes Schaber, "Martin Heideggers 'Herkunft' im Spiegel der Theologie- und Kirchengeschichte des 19. und beginnenden 20. Jahrhunderts," in *Heidegger-Jahrbuch*, vol. 1, 159–84.

14 Van Buren, *Supplements*, 70.

15 For a complete listing of Heidegger's writings, lectures, courses, and seminars, see Chris Bremmers' listing of his works in *Heidegger-Jahrbuch*, vol. 1, 419–598.

16 See, for instance, GA 58: 205, "This old Christian attainment was deformed by and buried under the penetration of ancient science in Christianity. From time to time it reasserts itself through tremendous eruptions (as *in* Augustine, *in* Luther, *in* Kierkegaard)."

17 Karl Jaspers, *Philosophische Autobiographie* (Munich: Piper, 1977), 93.

18 See, for instance, GA 59: 7 and GA 60: 22.

19 Hannah Arendt, "Martin Heidegger at Eighty," *Heidegger and Modern Philosophy*, ed. Michael Murray (New Haven: Yale University Press, 1978), 293.

20 Hans-Georg Gadamer, *Neuere Philosophie I, Gesammelte Werke*, 4 vols. (Tübingen: J. C. B. Mohr, 1987), vol. III, 398.

21 See his letter to Karl Löwith of August 19, 1921, published in *Im Gespräch der Zeit*, eds. Dietrich Papenfuss and Otto Pöggeler *Zur philosophischen*

Aktualität Heideggers (Frankfurt: Klosterman, 1990), vol. II, 27–32. Also cited by Kisiel, "I work concretely and factically out of my 'I am,' out of my intellectual and wholly factic origin, milieu, life-contexts, and whatever is available to me from these as a vital experience in which I live ... To this facticity of mine belongs what I would in brief call the fact that I am a 'Christian Theo*logian*'" (Kisiel, *Genesis*, 78; Heidegger's Letter to Lowith, 29).

22 From Oscar Becker's transcript of Heidegger's War Emergency Course, as cited by Kisiel in *Genesis*, 17. For the German, see Theodore Kisiel, "Das Kriegsnotsemester 1919: Heideggers Durchbruch in die Hermeneutische Phänomenologie," *Philosophisches Jahrbuch* 99 (1992): 105–12, esp. 106ff.

23 Max Weber, *Wissenschaft als Beruf/Politik als Beruf* (Tübingen: J. C. B. Mohr, 1994), 19.

24 Ibid., 9.

25 Ibid., 13.

26 Ibid., 13.

27 Ibid., 21.

28 Ibid., 22.

29 This letter from April 24, 1919, was published by Guy van Kerckhoven, in *Aut aut* 223–4 (1988), 6–14, here p. 8 (Kisiel's translation, *Genesis*, 112).

30 In the German University system, a student first acquires a PhD. The PhD thesis gives a student the possibility to obtain a license to teach at university level. This second thesis is called the *Habilitation*. After completion of the *Habilitation*, the student is now called a *Privatdozent*, which means he or she can teach at university but without the rights and duties of a full professor. Heidegger got his PhD in 1913, his *Habilitation* in 1915, and he became a full professor in 1923 at the University of Marburg.

31 In her afterword, the editor, Petra Jaeger, explains that she changed the title of the course because Heidegger never got to a discussion of the history of the concept of time and did not touch on the subject of a phenomenology of history and nature (GA 20: 444). Kisiel also points out that the subject matter of the course is too vast for a single lecture course (Kisiel, *Genesis*, 363). He fails to notice that Heidegger is developing a new research program based on his earlier studies and is not working on an "onto-erotic" version of a book called *Being and Time*.

32 Kisiel, *Genesis*, 362.

33 For Heidegger's overview of his research project, see GA 20: 10–11.

34 See also GA 20: 179.

35 The question Plato asks in his dialogue *Sophistes* (204a) is raised by Heidegger in this course (GA 20: 179).

36 See also Kisiel, *Genesis*, 366.

37 "ein *ausgezeichnetes Seinsverhältnis* in sich beschließt" (GA 20: 200).

38 See also Kisiel, *Genesis*, 366.

39 This interpretation of the history of European civilization can still be found in Heidegger's later philosophy. The forgetfulness of being that determines the history of metaphysics ends with planetary rule of nihilism and technology.

40 See also Kisiel, *Genesis*, 371.

41 See Edmund Husserl, *Die Konstitution der geistigen Welt* (Hamburg: Felix Meiner, 1984), 29.

42   See also Kisiel, *Genesis*, 376.

43   Ibid., 382.

44   Ibid., 383–8.

45   Ibid., *Genesis*, 396–7.

46   See GA 20: 209, 401, 422, 433–40.

47   Cf. Parmenides 8.35.

48   For the original plan of the course, see GA 21: 26. Cf. Kisiel, *Genesis*, 410.

49   This part consisted of a chapter on Bergson's theory of time (§21 of GA 21), a chapter on the concept of time of Newton and Kant, and finally a chapter on the discovery of time in Aristotle's philosophy (GA 20: 11).

50   Cf. Kisiel, *Genesis*, 400.

51   Ibid., 418–19.

3   The Question of Being

The fundamental question of Heidegger's thinking, early and late, is the question of *being*, or more precisely the question concerning the *meaning* of being. To understand this question, it is crucial to understand not only what Heidegger means by "being" (*Sein*), but also what he means by "meaning" (*Sinn*), and finally what he thinks a philosophical question is, and how and why, after completing *Being and Time*, he changed his mind about whether the question of being admits of a single definite answer.

What does Heidegger mean by "being"? The single most important point to grasp at the outset is that being is not itself something that exists: it is neither one entity among others, nor the totality of entities (*das Seiende*), nor a property of entities. The difference between being and entities is what Heidegger, soon after writing *Being and Time*, calls the "ontological difference" (GA 24: 22). Since his question concerns being, and since being is not an entity, Heidegger is not primarily interested in the central question of traditional ontology: what is there? Are there forms and universals or only particulars? Does God exist? Is there such a thing as substance or are there only properties? Is the mind physical? Do we have free will? Are we and everything else ultimately will to power? These are metaphysical questions; they are questions about entities, not about being. They are, in Heidegger's jargon, "ontic" as opposed to "ontological." Moreover, by fixing our attention exclusively on entities, Heidegger believes, such questions tend to eclipse and obscure the question of being. The difference is not just one of generality, for Heidegger also distinguishes the question of being from what he later calls "the fundamental question of metaphysics," namely, why is there something rather than nothing? (GA 40: ch. 1) The question of being is not about *what* there is or even *why* there is anything, but rather what it *is* for what there is – whatever it is, and for whatever reason there is any of it – to be.

What then *is* "being"? The closest Heidegger comes to a definition is to say that being is that *in virtue of which* entities are entities; it is what *makes* (in a noncausal sense of "makes") entities entities. This should not mislead us into supposing that being is a *property* of entities. Aristotle and the medieval scholastics knew that "being" does not name a peculiar feature of a kind of entity, or even entities as a whole, since a contrast class is by definition out of the question. What would "entities" lacking being *be*? They would not be entities at all. As Kant observed in his refutation of the ontological argument for the existence of God, being may be a "logical" (and linguistic) predicate, but it is not a "real predicate" or property.[1] On the surface, the sentence "Dogs exist" looks grammatically the same as "Dogs bark," but the surface grammar is misleading. We know what non-barking dogs are, but what *are* non-existent dogs? What would entities *be* without the putative property of existence? Nothing. And what could actually *have* such a property? Only entities. Yet the *entity*-ness of entities is just what possession of the property was supposed to explain.

Being, then, is neither an entity nor the totality of entities nor a property of entities. So, what *is* it? It is simply what we understand in our understanding of being, what we know when we know – however tacitly and obscurely – *that* entities are, and (more or less) *what* they are. In Heidegger's words, being is "that which defines entities as entities, that on the basis of which entities ... are in each case already understood" (6).[2]

More precisely, Heidegger's question of being is: what does it mean to be? What does Heidegger mean by "meaning"? Not linguistic meaning but *intelligibility* more broadly construed: "Meaning is that wherein the intelligibility [*Verständlichkeit*] of something maintains itself. That which is articulable in an understanding disclosure we call 'meaning' ... *Meaning is that ... in terms of which something as something is intelligible*" (151). Granted, *Being and Time* begins with a passage from Plato's *Sophist* in which the Stranger asks Theaetetus what he *means* when he says "being" (the participle ov in Greek), "for we, who formerly imagined we knew, are now at a loss."[3] Heidegger then asks, "Do we today have an answer to the question concerning what we really mean when we use the expression 'being' [*seiend*]? Not at all" (1). A few pages later Heidegger reiterates the question of "what we really mean by the expression 'being' [*Sein*]" (11).[4]

These formulations make it sound as if the question of being is a question about the meaning of the *word* "being," but it is important to see that this is not the case; Heidegger's question is not a question of semantics.[5] Heidegger often talks, for pedagogical and expository reasons, about what we mean when we say "to be" or "is" or "am," but the words with which we express our understanding of being are for him neither the only nor even the most important manifestation of that understanding. We understand equipment (*Zeug*) by using it competently, we understand objects by recognizing and responding to them intelligently, and we understand ourselves in all our distinctively human behaviors and practices. Using words is just one of many ways in which we exhibit our understanding of being.[6]

I have argued elsewhere for the importance of recognizing that Heidegger's project in *Being and Time* is not metaphysical but transcendental. Just as Kant distinguishes his own transcendental or critical philosophy from dogmatic metaphysics, so Heidegger distinguishes his own *"fundamental* ontology," which proceeds by way of hermeneutical phenomenology, from *traditional* ontology. Heidegger's dubbing his own account of human existence an "analytic of Dasein" is, of course, allusion to the Transcendental Analytic at the heart of the *Critique of Pure Reason*. Ontology, in Heidegger's sense, then, is not about entities per se, but rather what I call *hermeneutic conditions*, that is, conditions constitutive of the interpretability of entities *as* the entities they are.[7]

The transcendental orientation of *Being and Time* is grounded in the distinction between being and entities. Fundamental ontology, that is, has to do not with the nature of entities, but with the *meaning* – hence the structure and the conditions of our *understanding* – of being. In proposing, as he does, for example, that *"time* [is] the possible horizon of any understanding of being in general" (1), and that time must in turn be understood in the first instance as the situated ("thrown"), future-directed ("projecting") character of human existence, Heidegger is not asking about the objective nature or reality of time itself; he is instead describing the existential conditions of our making sense of time as we do – first as the thrown projection of our lives, then as concrete occasions for action, and finally as a mere abstract succession of moments.[8]

But is the ontological difference – the difference between being and entities, hence the distinction between *ontological* inquiry into our understanding of being and the *ontic* investigation of entities that one finds in the sciences – a *sharp* distinction? Or can it be understood instead as a *gradual* difference between relatively core aspects of things, as we understand them, and their relatively contingent features?

Cristina Lafont has argued that the project of *Being and Time* founders on this equivocation.[9] On the one hand, Heidegger's hermeneutical reorientation of phenomenology pushed him in the direction of contextualism and holism about meaning; on the other hand, he continued to cling to a sharp distinction between the transcendental *a priori* content of philosophy and the a posteriori content of the sciences. Again, the former has to do with *being*, the latter with *entities*. Following Ernst Tugendhat, Lafont tries to read Heidegger in the context of the "linguistic turn" in twentieth-century analytic philosophy, which she likens to an earlier German tradition going back to Hamann, Herder, and Humboldt. Accordingly, she systematically transposes what Heidegger says about *being* into claims about semantic content and concludes that Heidegger in effect remained wedded to Frege's idea that linguistic meaning (*Sinn*) precedes and determines reference. Quine, Putnam, Donnellan, Kripke, and Kaplan have all, in different ways, shown the Fregean thesis to be untenable, so we can now see in hindsight that Heidegger was wrong, too: meaning does not determine reference, our understanding of being cannot be sharply separated from our empirical knowledge of entities, nor is it immune to falsification and revision in light of evidence, reflection, and inquiry.

Lafont is right that, for Heidegger, the question of being is a question about "meaning" (*Sinn*) – in *some* sense of that word. But again, Heidegger's concept of meaning is much wider than the concept of *linguistic* meaning that figures in analytic philosophy of language since Frege. Lafont's attempt to force the ontological difference into the Procrustean bed of Fregean semantics, it seems to me, yields a wildly distorted picture of Heidegger's thought.[10] Nevertheless, her critique raises hard questions about the internal coherence of Heidegger's position itself. For instance, does the ontological difference commit him to a sharp rather than a gradual distinction between being and entities? And is the ontological difference as such, whether sharp or gradual, inconsistent with the avowed contextualism and holism of hermeneutical phenomenology?

It might seem that the distinction between being and entities must be sharp. For one thing, Heidegger concedes that Hegel's thesis, "*Pure being and pure nothing* are ... the same," is "correct" (*besteht zu Recht*).[11] It is correct because being is literally *no thing*, that is, not an entity. The opposite of nothing is not being but *something*, which is to say, entities. And surely the distinction between nothing and something is a perfectly sharp distinction.

But neither of those two points is obvious. First, admitting that a given thesis is "correct" is Heidegger's standard gesture of faint praise, from which we are to infer that the thesis in question is in a deeper sense *untrue*, that is, superficial and misleading. Hegel's proposition is untrue inasmuch as it suggests that being and nothing are conceptual categories and, as such, logically and phenomenologically empty, hence indistinguishable. Heidegger argues, on the contrary, that being and nothing are not concepts and that "the nothing" (*das Nichts*) figures uniquely in our experience of anxiety, of meaninglessness, of entities as a whole "slipping away," out of our grasp (GA 9: 8–10/88–9). What is true, then, is that being and nothing "belong together" in pointing beyond the totality of entities – apart from which there is, after all, *nothing* else – toward our affective apprehension that entities *are* and might *not* have been (and might not continue to be; GA 9: 16/94).[12]

Far from succumbing to pernicious metaphysical illusions of grammar, as his critics have often charged, Heidegger is keenly aware of the fallacy of supposing that the expression "nothing" refers to something. It does not, and calling it "*the* nothing," as he does, is merely a rhetorical device intended to remind us that we have an experience precisely of the *finitude* or boundedness of the totality of what there is, an experience that is part and parcel of our understanding of its *being*. Apprehending a kind of limit or horizon around entities as a whole, however, is not the same as positing something beyond the limit, certainly not something we could literally call "*the* nothing."

It is not easy, then, to infer a sharp distinction between being and entities from the essential "belonging together" of being and nothing, on the one hand, and the seemingly sharp distinction between nothing and something, on the other. Nor is it even obvious that that latter distinction is a sharp one. The notion of *degrees* of being flourished for centuries in Plato and in the Neoplatonic traditions of the early Middle Ages and the Renaissance. One also finds it in Descartes' argument for the existence of God in the Third Meditation, which stipulates that the objective reality of an idea cannot exceed the formal reality of its cause.[13] Kant, too, appeals to the notion in his response to Moses Mendelssohn's argument for the immortality of the soul, which after all, Kant observes, might cease to exist not by disintegrating into smaller constituent parts or by vanishing discontinuously, but by what he calls the "elanguescence" of its powers, that is, their growing faint, languishing, gradually diminishing from something to nothing.[14] Finally, Heidegger himself relies on a gradualist notion of being in his evidently sympathetic interpretation of the pre-Socratic concept of φύσις, which he says means "the unfolding that opens itself" (*das sich eröffnende Entfalten*), and "emerging-lingering holding sway" (*aufgehend-verweilende Walten*; GA 40: 21/15, translation modified). In the world of the archaic Greeks, as Heidegger sees it, things exist not by popping in and out of being, but by dawning, lingering, and fading away.

Today perhaps we find it hard to accept that there could be a gradual difference between something and nothing.[15] If so, that might tell us something interesting about our own understanding of being. In any case, although drawing a sharp line between something and nothing is neither easy nor obvious, the question remains what kind of difference the ontological difference between being and entities amounts to. For example, can being and entities in principle be said to have anything in common?

Like Hegel, many philosophers in the tradition have supposed that being, unlike entities, must be simple, univocal, and conceptually empty, hence, strictly speaking, unavailable to thought. One of the

most original and controversial ideas in *Being and Time* is Heidegger's
insistence that, on the contrary, the meaning of being is neither empty
nor univocal; that existence is not the same in the case of a stone or a
molecule as in the case of a hammer or a pair of shoes, and that neither
of those modes of being is comparable to the existence (*Existenz*) of a
human being (*Dasein*), whose being is *being-in-the-world*. For a mere
object like a stone or a molecule, to be is simply to be present at a discrete moment in time, to be "occurrent" (*vorhanden*). For a useful piece
of equipment (*Zeug*) like a hammer or a pair of shoes, to be is to be in
principle "available" (*zuhanden*) for use at particular times understood
as occasions for action (time to get to work, time to go for a walk).[16]
Finally, to be a human being is neither simply to occur nor to be defined
by a use, but to find oneself thrown into a situation, always already in
pursuit, however unthinkingly, of something like ends or purposes.

   One might object that these distinctions among kinds of entities
are just distinctions among kinds of properties, provided we construe
"property" in a sufficiently broad sense, and that the *being* of an entity,
of whatever kind, is the mere occurrence or instantiation of its properties. Kant's way of putting this point is to say that the "relative position" of a predicate to a subject (*S is p*) is distinct from the "absolute
position" of the subject term itself as denoting something that exists
(*S is*). Whereas predicates come in a variety of flavors, being qua absolute position is utterly univocal. Kant therefore writes, "The concept
of position or positing [*Position oder Setzung*] is perfectly simple: it is
identical with the concept of being in general [*Sein überhaupt*]."[17]

   Heidegger, by contrast, maintains that there are irreducibly different
ways in which something can be said to exist, quite apart from whatever specific properties it has. So although his denial that being can be
understood as a mere *property* of entities is in roughly the same spirit as
Kant's thesis that being is not a real predicate, his pluralism about *ways*
of being goes beyond Kant, and indeed beyond most of the metaphysical
tradition since Descartes. This is why, when he mentions Kant's thesis
in *Being and Time*, he dismisses it rather abruptly, remarking that it
"merely reproduces Descartes's proposition" that (in Heidegger's words)
"'being' itself does not 'affect' us, since it cannot be perceived" (94).[18]

   Now, just as we might be inclined to think that there must be a sharp
rather than a gradual difference between something and nothing, so too
we might suppose, with Kant, that in contrast to the wide variety of
properties things can have, being as such must be simple and univocal.
But in fact, as Kris McDaniel has observed, many ancient and medieval
thinkers, and even some later modern philosophers, have agreed with
Heidegger that there are different ways of being. Aristotle, Aquinas,
Descartes, Meinong, Moore, Russell, and Husserl were all ontological
pluralists of one sort or another.[19] But mustn't there also be a generic

sense of being, embracing and unifying the various restricted senses? Otherwise, what makes the diverse ways of being ways of *being*? Isn't it necessary to take for granted a single, generic concept, precisely in order to say what the diverse ways of being are ways *of*?

McDaniel, rightly I think, proposes that Heidegger conceives of the modes of being in *Being and* Time – occurrentness, availability, and *Existenz* or being-in-the-world – as unified not univocally, but, as Aquinas said, analogically. That is, words like "is" and "are" are not simply ambiguous (like "page"), but neither do they have quite the same meaning when applied to entities as radically different as occurrent objects, available equipment, and human beings. We *do* have a vague generic understanding of being as such, which embraces the kinds of being pertaining to those diverse entities, but that generic, unrestricted notion is not prior to, more basic, or more readily intelligible than the several specific, restricted senses. The generic sense of being is not presupposed by the restricted senses, but presupposes them, just as the generic sense of "healthy" is not presupposed by, but presupposes, the various different ways in which, say, an animal, urine, and medicine can each be called "healthy."[20]

As McDaniel points out, Heidegger cannot maintain that the *word* "being" is simply equivocal, upon pain of undermining the claim that there are multiple ways of *being*. The fact that the word "page" is ambiguous, after all, is what prevents us from saying (with a straight face) that there are two kinds of *page*: messengers and pieces of paper. For what does the word "page" mean in that sentence – *messenger* or *piece of paper*? Substituting either term obviously reduces the proposition to nonsense.[21] So too, the word "being" must have at least enough semantic unity to make sense of the proposition that the different ways of being are, after all, ways of *being*.

Must the generic notion of being be so general, so unrestricted, as to apply to the various ways of being themselves? After all, Heidegger seems to say that "there are" several of them. Does quantifying them in this way require him to apply the same generic notion to them as to entities? No. Being and ways of being are not entities, and Heidegger considers it profoundly misleading to say that being "is," or that "there are" ways of being. Indeed, he avoids doing so in the "Letter on 'Humanism'" by stipulating a radically different sense for the German expression *es gibt* (standardly "there is," but literally *it gives*) and reserving it for the kind of "being" being itself might be said to have:

Being and Time (212) purposely and cautiously says ... "there is" (*es gibt*) being.... the "it" that "gives" here is being itself.... "there is" is used first of all in order to avoid the locution, "being is"; for "is" is ordinarily said of something

that is. Such a thing we call an entity. But being "is" precisely not "an entity."
(GA 9: 165/254–5)[22]

One might be tempted to complain that this rather ingenious maneuver is just a desperate attempt to define the problem away rather than solve it. But that begs the question whether there really is a problem. Stipulating a radical distinction between the "is" that pertains to entities and the "there is" (es gibt) that pertains to being, as Heidegger does, is a way of denying that there is any *further* sense of "being" that pertains both to being and to entities. That is, if someone presses the point that Heidegger himself is forced to say that being has its own kind of being – call it "giving itself," if you like – the proper reply is to deny that that kind of being is related in any way, even loosely or analogically, to the being of entities.[23]

Nor should we suppose that there is any higher-order ontological difference, as it were, between being and the "self-giving" of being. Being and its self-giving cannot be distinguished in the way being and entities can. This is why Heidegger says, very shrewdly, that "the 'it' that 'gives' … is being itself." It must be, otherwise we would be faced with an infinite regress reminiscent of the Third Man objection to Plato's theory of forms.[24] The self-giving of being, then, is not a way of being in addition to the ways in which the various kinds of entities can be said to be.

The ways of being in Heidegger's ontology are thus loosely or analogically unified *as* (precisely) ways of *being*. Heidegger moreover has good reason to insist on an ontological difference at least robust enough to preempt a Third Man-style regress that might be entailed by application of one and the same sense of the word "being" to being itself (or ways of being) and entities alike. Heidegger was clearly aware of that potential conundrum, and his reliance on a deliberately literal construal of the locution "there is" (es gibt) is his way of nipping it in the bud. There is *some* sense in which "there are" ways of being, indeed *several* of them! The crucial point, however, is that their "being" – that is, their self-giving or self-manifesting – is not even loosely or analogically unified with the being of the entities, whose ways of being they *are*.

The ontological difference is thus deep and robust in one sense, yet not as crudely or starkly drawn as Kant's notion of the simplicity and univocality of absolute position or Hegel's emptiness thesis might suggest. The very fact that there are several ways of being, and moreover that they manifest themselves in an ordinary worldly experience susceptible to phenomenological description and interpretation, suggests that, although they are *not* entities and *cannot* be said to "exist," nevertheless they share some of the same concrete complexity, contextual richness, and metaphysical contingency as we find in entities themselves.

In a sense, then, Lafont's critique of *Being and Time* virtually answers itself. Did Heidegger's hermeneutical phenomenology overcome the sharp distinction drawn by Kant between *a priori* and *a posteriori*, transcendental and empirical, necessity and contingency, essence and accident? Yes. As Lafont herself observes, the *a priori* in *Being and Time* is not the Kantian notion of epistemic necessity determinable independent of experience, but rather what Heidegger calls the "*a priori* perfect" (*apriorisches Perfekt*; 85), that is, what we find "always already" (*immer schon*) established, factical, and relatively invariant.[25] As Heidegger says a decade later in "The Age of the World Picture," mathematics is *a priori* in precisely this sense, namely as a special case of what we more generally always already know or understand: "Tὰ μαθήματα means, for the Greeks, whatever man knows in advance in observing entities and in dealing with things: the corporeity of bodies, the vegetation of plants, the animality of animals, the humanness of man" (GA 5: 76/59).

It is true that the ontological difference must be firm enough to sustain the methodological distinction Heidegger insists on drawing between philosophy and the sciences, particularly the human sciences of psychology, anthropology, sociology, and history. So, for instance, his phenomenology of anxiety (*Angst*) is not primarily the description of a psychological state (§40); his criticism of Cassirer's theory of mythical thought is not a direct contribution to empirical anthropology; his account of social conformism (*das Man*) is not armchair sociology (§27, et passim); his later notion of the "history of being" is not itself a piece of cultural or intellectual history.[26] The methodological difference between philosophy and science, however, cannot mean for Heidegger, as it did for Kant and Husserl, that philosophy is itself an autonomous discipline or science, insulated from the contingently given contents of experience and history.[27] What we "always already" know about the being of entities in their respective ontological regions is not limited to what we can know *a priori* in the Kantian sense, but is embedded in the *de facto* cultural history and philosophical tradition into which we find ourselves thrown, to which we belong, and to which we thus for the most part remain unconsciously beholden.

Heidegger's admittedly aprioristic-*sounding* rhetoric about the priority and immunity of fundamental ontology to the merely ontic concerns of the sciences does not, then, commit him to a rigid or immovable distinction between pure, essential, transcendental meaning, on the one hand, and meanings tainted by historical contingency and facticity, on the other. The two are always inextricably interwoven. "Being is always the being of an entity" (9), just as entities are intelligible only thanks to the conditions or horizons that constitute their specific modes of being.

Indeed, the very fact that Heidegger conceives of transcendental conditions as "horizons" of intelligibility, as opposed to abstract forms of intuition or categories of thought, as they are in Kant, is an indication of their essential inseparability from the ontic contingencies they ground.[28] Ontological horizons of intelligibility are what they are depending on what particular ontic phenomena they embrace, just as the ontic phenomena are what they are thanks to the ontological horizons within which they manifest themselves. One way to put this is to say that Heideggerian horizons are transcendental conditions not just of possibility but of actuality, that is, of the concrete ways in which entities manifest themselves *as the entities they are*.

This is why Heidegger's ontological vocabulary is so systematically embroidered with terms describing ontic phenomena. One could defend the embroidery by pleading that natural language is necessarily constrained by our ordinary attention to the familiar, mundane aspects of things, but this would be to mistake a deep and important fact about the nature of phenomenological ontology for a merely unfortunate accident. Heidegger's intermingling of the ontic and the ontological is most explicit when he justifies his use of the phrase "primordial time" to refer to the kind of temporality that is distinct from and more fundamental than what we ordinarily call "time":

> If therefore we establish that the "time" that is accessible to Dasein's ordinary understanding (*Verständigkeit*) is *not* primordial, and moreover that it arises from authentic temporality, then, in accordance with the principle, *a potiori fit denominatio*, we are justified in calling the *temporality* we have now exposed *"primordial time."* (329)

The Latin phrase Heidegger invokes here (sometimes, *a parte potiori fit denominatio*) means something like, "a thing is named for its principal part." Calling a thing by its most important part is called *synecdoche*; so, for example, Aristotle calls us "rational animals" because, he thought, the rational part of our soul is its best or most essential part.

This principle of synecdoche underwrites not only Heidegger's calling human temporality "time," but also his reference in the same sentence to *"authentic* temporality," which, as William Blattner has shown, is not itself authentic, but is rather the ontological ("existential") condition of the possibility of authenticity and inauthenticity as ontic ("existentiel") modes of Dasein's being-in-the-world. In the same way, Heidegger uses the word "death" to refer not to the event that occurs at the very end of our lives, but to the closing down (or "dying off") of possibilities that we constantly undergo throughout our lives, and which gives "death" in the ordinary sense its existential significance. Similarly, what he calls "guilt" (*Schuld*) is not what we ordinarily mean by that word, but instead our being accountable or answerable in principle, which is what, in turn, makes blame, liability, delinquency, culpability, and debt intelligible. Likewise, he calls the being of a piece of equipment its "availability" (*Zuhandenheit*), whether or not it happens to be usable on any given occasion, since its *de facto* availability is the canonical ontic status that makes it what it is ontologically. An object is ontologically "present-at-hand" (*vorhanden*), whether or not it happens to be present before us right now, since the presence of things before us is the paradigmatic ontic manifestation of our understanding of things as intrinsically object-like.[29] Other examples abound in *Being and Time*.

The relation between the ontic and the ontological in Heidegger's thinking, then, is not the same as the relation between the *a priori* and the *a posteriori* in Kant, or between the immanence of pure consciousness and the transcendence of the external world in Husserl.[30] But neither is the fundamental ontology of *Being and Time* fully naturalized in the way much of analytic philosophy has been since Quine, or even in the manner of Nietzsche's radically anti-essentialist, detranscendentalized perspectivism. The ontological difference does indeed ground a distinction between horizons of intelligibility and what those horizons embrace; not any old property a thing happens to have will constitute the way in which it most fundamentally manifests itself as what it is.

The difference between what is ontologically essential and what is not, however, is not a metaphysical distinction between essential and accidental properties of things, but a methodological distinction between two different kinds of questions we can ask, one having to do with the particular features entities happen to have, the other concerning what it is that *makes* those entities (intelligible *as*) the entities they are. The first kind of question is ontic; the second is "ontological" in Heidegger's sense. Ontological questions are, to repeat, questions concerning *hermeneutic conditions*, conditions constitutive of the interpretability of entities as the entities they are. Ontological questions about equipment, for example, are questions about what it *is to be* equipmental(ly), to be defined by availability for use. That question is not about hammers and nails themselves, but rather the conditions internal to our understanding and our practices that allow us to make sense of anything *as* a piece of equipment, be it a loom or a lever or a computer keyboard. Ontological questions about social life, or what Heidegger calls "being-with" (*Mitsein*) and *das Man*, are questions not about late modern European society, but rather what it *is to be* entities defined, as we are, by our sociality.

The question of being itself thus appears to be fragmented and dispersed across the various modes of being and their respective paradigmatic entities. And yet Heidegger presents the fundamental ontology of *Being and Time* as clearing a path toward the question concerning "*the*" meaning of being (in general). Again, the book begins with a dramatic rhetorical question: "Do we today have an answer to the question concerning what we really mean when we use the expression 'being' (*seiend*)? Not at all" (1). Heidegger then proposes to "reawaken" and "work out" the question (1). But he never presumes to answer it; indeed, it is not even obvious that he thinks it can have a single, univocal answer. The most he says in *Being and Time* – indeed, the central thesis of the book – is that *time* is the "horizon of any understanding of being in general" (1), hence, *a fortiori*, "the transcendental horizon for the question of being" (39, 41). What Heidegger offers, then, is not an answer to the question of being, but an account of the hermeneutic conditions that render it intelligible.

It is only with the famous "turn" (*Kehre*) in (or toward) his later work that Heidegger drops all pretense of preparing the way for a systematic account of the meaning of being in general, in favor of a retrospective account of the history of metaphysics, or what he now calls the "history of being" (*Seinsgeschichte*), which is to say, a history of the dominant *understandings* of being that have grounded and guided Western thought since Greek antiquity.[31] By the mid-1930s, that is, Heidegger has stepped back from the constructive "scholarly" (*wissenschaftlich*) project of *Being and Time* to look back over the metaphysical tradition from a vantage point he now regards as lying just beyond it, Nietzsche having marked the both the culmination and the end of that tradition.

Whereas it might seem as if he just happens to leave the question of being unanswered in his early work of the 1920s, Heidegger now emphasizes that the question of being is not strictly speaking an interrogative at all, that is, a "question" in the grammatical or illocutionary sense, a question corresponding to an answer. It is instead an "experience" (*Erfahrung*), a mood, an unsettling, subrational *apprehension* (in both senses of that word) of the sheer *that* and *what* of things, a sense of astonishment, awe, perhaps a vague sense of dread. That uncanny sense of being is not merely a psychological state motivating an articulate question for systematic inquiry, a problem we might one day solve; it just *is* the "question."

In his later writings, then, rather than even pretend to set out in search of an answer to the question of being, Heidegger reads between the lines of the canonical texts of the metaphysical tradition with an eye to discerning the fundamental affects and understandings that constitute the history of being. His own philosophical contribution, he would later say, was to have articulated the question explicitly in the form of a question for the first time: "In the treatise *Being and Time* the question concerning the meaning of being is posed and developed specifically *as a question* for the first time in the history of philosophy" (GA 40: 89/88).[32]

NOTES

1 Immanuel Kant, *Critique of Pure Reason*, trans. and ed. Paul Guyer and Allen W. Wood (Cambridge: Cambridge University Press, 1998), A598 ff. /B626 ff. As Kant memorably puts it, "A hundred actual dollars do not contain the least bit more than a hundred possible ones" (A599/B627). Cf. Immanuel Kant, "The Only Possible Argument in Support of a Demonstration of the Existence of God," *Theoretical Philosophy: 1755–1770*, trans. and ed. D. Walford and R. Meerbote (Cambridge: Cambridge University Press, 1992), 2: 72–3.

2 Translations of Heidegger's *Sein und Zeit* are mine throughout.

3 Plato, *Sophist*, trans. F. M. Cornford, in *Plato: The Collected Dialogues*, eds. E. Hamilton and H. Cairns (Princeton: Princeton University Press, 1961), 244a.

4 Likewise in his 1928 lectures, Heidegger says, "*What does 'being' mean?* This is the fundamental question of philosophy *par excellence*" (GA 26: 171).

5 Ernst Tugendhat complains that although "Heidegger's philosophy is receptive to linguistic analysis from the outset," nevertheless, unlike Wittgenstein, Heidegger failed to recognize that philosophical questions can only be questions of language: "if someone says *being* and thereby thinks that he has evoked something that is not merely what we understand when we understand the word, this does not allow for elucidation as a matter of principle. For the sole possibility of an elucidation would consist in recourse to the word." Tugendhat's adherence to a purely linguistic conception of philosophy can seem arbitrary and dogmatic. To his credit, though, he concedes that his "linguistic-analytical interpretation" of *Being and Time* "does not correspond exactly to Heidegger's self-understanding, but it is the best I could make of Heidegger's question of being." Ernst Tugendhat, *Self-Consciousness and Self-Determination*, trans. P. Stern (Cambridge, MA: MIT Press, 1986), 145, 148, 150.

6 This is what Heidegger thought when he wrote *Being and Time*, anyway. In his later works, by around the mid-1930s, although he still maintains that there are nonlinguistic manifestations of our understanding of being – in the peasant's unthinking reliance on her shoes, in nondiscursive works of art like the Greek temple, in technological machinery like the hydroelectric plant on the Rhine – he also seems to hold that the *words* of great thinkers and poets are a privileged site for the manifestation and evolution of our collective understanding of being.

7 Taylor Carman, *Heidegger's Analytic: Interpretation, Discourse, and Authenticity in* "Being and Time" (Cambridge: Cambridge University Press, 2003), 23–30, et passim.

8 I therefore disagree with the central thesis of William Blattner's excellent book, *Heidegger's Temporal Idealism* (Cambridge: Cambridge University Press, 1999). See Carman, *Heidegger's Analytic*, 168–75. I think Heidegger was not trying to explain the sequential ordering of "ordinary time," as

Blattner has it, but rather trying to construe the *hermeneutic conditions* – the conditions of interpretability – of what, in the final chapter of *Being and Time*, he is careful to call "the ordinary *concept* of time" (*des vulgären Zeitbegriffes*), that is, our explicit *understanding* of time as a mere succession of moments. The question, as I see it, is how mere "clock time" manages to be *intelligible* to us, not how it manages to be sequential, or whether it exists independently of us.

9 Cristina Lafont, *Heidegger, Language, and World-Disclosure*, trans. G. Harman (Cambridge: Cambridge University Press, 2000).

10 For the details of this criticism, see Taylor Carman, "Was Heidegger a Linguistic Idealist?" *Inquiry* 45 (2002): 205–16; Mark A. Wrathall, "Heidegger, Truth, and Reference," *Inquiry* 45 (2002): 217–28; and William Blattner's Review, *Philosophy and Phenomenological Research* 66 (2003): 489–91.

11 Georg Wilhelm Friedrich Hegel, *Science of Logic*, trans. A. V. Miller (London: Allen & Unwin, 1969), 82; quoted in Heidegger, GA 9: 17/94.

12 Heidegger says that being and nothing "belong together" in part because it would make no sense to say they're "identical," since they're not entities. Of being and nothing, that is, one should say neither that there is one of them nor that there are two of them.

13 René Descartes, *Meditations, The Philosophical Writings of Descartes, Vol. II*, trans. J. Cottingham (Cambridge: Cambridge University Press, 1984), AT VII 41.

14 Kant, *Critique of Pure Reason*, B414.

15 To say that the distinction between something and nothing is not "sharp" is not to say that there is a middle state between them that is *neither* something nor nothing, any more than the gradual difference on the color spectrum between red and not red implies a third hue that is neither red nor not red. The logical distinction, that is, between red and not red differs from the material distinction between red and orange. (One could say, arbitrarily, either that vermilion is *neither* red nor orange or that it is *both*.) In this logical sense, then, the distinction between something and nothing could be said to be sharp, after all. It is important to see, though, that the logical sense sheds no light on Heidegger's notion of "*the* nothing," which is to say, the ontological difference between being and entities, or on his interpretation of the Greek concept of φ σις, for that matter. Phenomenologically, that is, *nothing* in Heidegger's sense is more like orange or vermilion than simply not red, which is why Heidegger denies that it is an artifact of *negation*, understood as either a logical or a psychological operation (GA 9: 5–6/85–6). Is *nothing* therefore "something," after all? No, no more than *being* is – about which there is more below.

16 I say "in principle" because equipment can still *be* even while *de facto* malfunctioning, being ill-suited to the task at hand, or not being there when you need it. These kinds of "unavailability" are to be understood as *ontic* modes that fall within the *ontological* category of availability, just as Dasein's occasional solitude is a mode of its existential "being-with" (*Mitsein*). Having no money is a *financial* condition.

17 Kant, "Only Possible Argument," 2: 73 (translation modified). Heidegger quotes this sentence in GA 24: 52.

18 What Descartes actually says is, "we cannot initially become aware of a sub-
    stance merely through its being an existing thing, since this alone does not
    of itself have any effect on us." René Descartes, *Principles of Philosophy*,
    The Philosophical Writings of Descartes, Vol. I, trans. J. Cottingham
    (Cambridge: Cambridge University Press, 1985), AT VIIIA 25.

19 Kris McDaniel, "Ways of Being," in *Metametaphysics*, eds. D. Chalmers,
    D. Manley, and R. Wasserman (Oxford: Oxford University Press, 2009),
    290. Aristotle famously says, "being is said in many ways." Aristotle,
    Metaphysics, trans. W. D. Ross, in *The Complete Works of Aristotle, Vol. II*,
    ed. J. Barnes (Princeton: Princeton University Press, 1984), Γ.2, 1003a, 33.
    Descartes's pluralism resides not in his mind–body dualism, which employs
    a single concept of substance, albeit of two essential kinds, but in his claim,
    following the scholastics, that the term *substantia* "does not apply univo-
    cally to God and his creatures." Descartes, *Principles of Philosophy*, AT
    VIIIA 24. Heidegger quotes this passage in his 1925 lectures and then again
    in *Being and Time* (93), where he charges Descartes with "evading" the
    question concerning the meaning of being embedded in the concept of sub-
    stance. See GA 20: 234.

20 See Aristotle, *Metaphysics*, Γ.2, 1003a 3–1003b, 4. Another example to con-
    sider, it seems to me, is the generic concept of love, which may be stitched
    together from a range of more basic, more concrete, hence more readily
    intelligible notions such as desire (ἔρως), friendship (φιλία), and charity
    (ἀγάπη).

21 McDaniel, "Ways of Being," 299–300. McDaniel credits Gareth Matthews
    with exposing this "sense–kind confusion." See Gareth Matthews, "Senses
    and Kinds," *Journal of Philosophy* 69 (1972): 149–57.

22 Similarly, in *Introduction to Metaphysics*, Heidegger writes, "The substan-
    tive *das Sein* implies that what is so named itself 'is.' 'Being' now itself
    becomes something that 'is,' whereas obviously only entities are, but not
    being, too" (GA 40: 73/73).

23 But if – to consider one more turn of the screw – I deny that "there is"
    a notion of being common to both being and entities, haven't I yet again
    (uncritically) used the expression "there is" precisely is my denial that there
    is any such sense of being? But why should I admit that what is at issue in
    that denial is anything like what is at issue in disputes about what kinds
    of entities exist, or indeed about how many ways of being "there are"? One
    cannot settle such disputes simply by pointing out our continual reliance
    on the standard verbal locutions at our disposal; what matters is what we
    mean by them.

24 Plato, *Parmenides*, trans. F. M. Cornford, in *Plato: The Collected Dialogues*,
    eds. E. Hamilton and H. Cairns (Princeton: Princeton University Press,
    1961), 132a–b.

25 Lafont, *Language World-Disclosure*, 253ff. In a marginal note to page 85,
    Heidegger says the *a priori* perfect could also be called the "ontological or
    transcendental perfect" (441–2).

26 For anxiety, see also "What is Metaphysics?" GA 9: 1–20/82–96. For myth,
    see his review of Cassirer's *Philosophy of Symbolic Forms, Volume 2:
    Mythical Thought*, Appendix II of GA 3.

27 See Taylor Carman, "Phenomenology as Rigorous Science," in *The Oxford Handbook of Continental Philosophy*, eds. B. Leiter and M. Rosen (Oxford: Oxford University Press, 2007).

28 The most basic transcendental condition in *Being and Time* is, of course, time, which Heidegger calls "the transcendental horizon for the question of being" (39, 41).

29 I usually prefer "occurrent" as a translation of *vorhanden*, in part because it avoids otherwise interminable verbal confusions in English, but also because it better captures the ontological status of objects as such. It must be said, however, that the older translation, "present-at-hand," is closer to the German word in its literally suggesting the presence of something "before" (*vor*) a subject or observer.

30 Husserl's transcendental phenomenology, unlike Heidegger's existential analytic, hinges on a robust dualism, what he calls "the prime differentiation of modes of being, the most cardinal that there is," namely "that between *consciousness* and *reality*." Edmund Husserl, *Ideen zu einer reinen Phänomenologie und phänomenologischen Philosophie, Erstes Buch*, 2nd ed. (Tübingen: Niemeyer, 1922), 77 (my translation).

31 Heidegger's earliest references to the "history of being" appear in his 1936–8 *Beiträge zur Philosophie*, GA 65, §161, et passim. Cf. "Nihilism as Determined by the History of Being," written around 1944–6. For a useful discussion of the emergence of the idea in Heidegger's thought, see Charles Guignon, "The History of Being," in *A Companion to Heidegger*, eds. Hubert L. Dreyfus and Mark A. Wrathall (Oxford: Blackwell, 2005), 392–406.

32 The translators have inadvertently omitted the words *erstmals in der Geschichte der Philosophie*.

4   The Semantics of "Dasein" and the Modality of *Being and Time*

Being and Time is a methodologically complex work, combining her-meneutic, transcendental, phenomenological, and ontological strat-egies in a provocative and not-obviously-stable concoction. In this article, I focus on one strand of the methodological puzzles raised by Heidegger's undertaking: the problem of warranting the modal claims that occur frequently in the course of Heidegger's project. In a number of crucial passages, we are told that one or another trait of Dasein is *necessary*, or that some ontic feature of Dasein would not be *possible* were it not for some deeper ontological feature. I undertake to determine the logical form of these doctrines, and to consider what kind of evidence might suffice to establish them. I draw on Heidegger's complex debt to Dilthey in proposing an inter-pretation of the notion of an *existeniale*, and I critically assess Taylor Carman's treatment of Heidegger's project as an extension of Kantian transcendental strategies. In the end, I argue, much comes to turn on one's account of the semantics of Heidegger's central term of art: "Dasein." I identify shortcomings in two possible approaches to this problem: one takes the extension of the term to be antecedently fixed; the other fixes the meaning of the term by specifying its intension. I then explore an alternative semantics for "Dasein" under which the modalized doctrines of *Being and Time* can be considered *de re* necessities.

All three of the semantic models that I consider here remain highly schematic – cartoons rather than fully elaborated portraits – and I do not mean to suggest that any of the three would suffice to capture the enormously complex semantic structure of Heidegger's undertak-ing. Nonetheless, I argue that the third semantic model enjoys cer-tain demonstrable advantages over the other two, both for mounting a defense of Heidegger's modal propositions and as a schema for mapping the text of *Being and Time*. It also allows us to frame a challenge that any fully adequate semantic interpretation of Heidegger's text would have to meet.

EXISTENTIALIA AND THE LOGICAL MODALITY OF *BEING AND TIME*

Much of Heidegger's phenomenological investigation in Division I of *Being and Time* unfolds through the enumeration of various traits of Dasein that are described as *Existenzialien* – "*existentialia*" in Macquarrie and Robinson's translation, or "existentials" in Stambaugh's. Examples include mineness, being-in-the-world, being-with, *das Man*, care, and so on. A good deal of subtle interpretative debate has been invested in recent years in determining the sense of these distinctively Heideggerian notions, but what exactly is meant in calling them *existentialia*? What distinguishes these features from other features of Dasein – if indeed there are other features of Dasein? Part of the answer certainly pertains to Heidegger's idiosyncratic use of the term "existence" (*Existenz*). Heidegger introduces the latter as his generic term for the mode of being of Dasein – that which distinguishes Dasein as the kind of entity that it is. According to Heidegger:

This being, the Dasein, like every other being, has a specific way of being. To this way of the Dasein's being we assign the term '*Existenz*.' (GA 24: 36)

The *existentialia* then fill out and articulate this general characterization of Dasein's mode of being; we might think of them as something like a set of attributes without which Dasein would not be what it is.

The lineage of Heidegger's notion of an *existentiale* can be traced to Kant's philosophical project, by way of the mediating figure of Wilhelm Dilthey. In his pioneering but incomplete *Introduction to the Human Sciences*, Dilthey laid out an agenda for extending Kant's philosophical project.[1] Kant's categories, according to Dilthey, provide the basic conceptual framework for applying the notion of an object and, as such, articulate the pure concepts required for the sciences that deal with objects – the *Naturwissenschaften* (the natural sciences). But Kant's project is incomplete, according to Dilthey, insofar as it fails to provide an analogous account of the categorial framework required for applying the notion of Life (*Leben*) or Spirit (*Geist*), and accordingly of the categories essential to the historical or human sciences (*Geisteswissenschaften*).

For this reason I have designated the basic task of all reflection about the human sciences as a critique of historical reason. The problem that needs to be solved for historical reason was not fully addressed by the Kantian critique of reason ... We must leave the pure and refined air of Kant's critique ... and do justice to the completely different nature of historical objects.[2]

Accordingly, Dilthey proposed to supplement Kant's categories with what he called "the categories of life." Most narrowly, these categories are the concepts required in order to identify something as what he calls "a psycho-physical life-unit" – effectively the categories necessary to any minimally adequate biography.[3] More broadly, they include the concepts necessary for the identification of any cultural or historical artifact, undertaking, or institution. Dilthey never seems to have settled on a final list of the categories of life, but one of his lists runs as follows: lived experience, duration, meaning, significance, value, whole and part, development.[4] Like Kant, Dilthey insisted that such categories must be *brought* to empirical science rather than derived therefrom; in this sense they are *pure*. One could never gain the concept of an object empirically if the very possibility of experience of objects presupposes the application of the categories. So analogously, one could never investigate something *as a human life* unless one already had available the conceptual framework that makes the relevant form of experience possible.

Heidegger's relation to Dilthey is complex, but in his use of the notion of an *existentiale*, he seems to be developing Dilthey's lead. In *Being and Time*, his initial introduction of the concept comes in close proximity to his discussion of Dilthey, whom he describes as "on his way towards the question of Life," albeit "limited [in] both his problematic and the set of concepts with which it had to be put into words" (46–7). His formal explanation of the term *existentialia* follows closely in the grooves Dilthey had established:

All *explicata* to which the analytic of Dasein gives rise are obtained by considering Dasein's existence-structure. Because the being-characteristics of Dasein are defined in terms of existentiality, we call them "*existentialia.*" These are to be sharply distinguished from what we call "categories" – determinations of Being for entities whose character is not that of Dasein ... *Existentialia* and categories are the two basic possibilities for characters of Being. (44–5)

Like Dilthey's categories of life, then, *existentialia* are introduced in an attempt to delineate the categorial framework that distinguishes, as Heidegger puts it, a *who* from a *what*.[5]

If this much is correct, then we can begin to see at least one sense in which Heidegger's project in Division I carries with it philosophical commitments that are *modally qualified*. I use "modal" here in the logician's sense; modally qualified propositions are propositions that carry a modal operator – that is, "necessarily," "possibly," "it is not possible that," and so forth.[6] If Heideggerian *existentialia* are understood in terms of this Kantian–Diltheyan lineage, then they would seem to involve modally qualified claims: *existentialia* would be *necessary* or *essential* features of Dasein; it would not be *possible* for Dasein to be without them. As we shall see in what follows, modal claims recur regularly in

Being and Time; indeed, we find them in almost every major section and in connection with each of the major new concepts that Heidegger introduces as Division I unfolds. We are told, for example, that being-in-the-world is "an essential structure of Dasein" (56), and that it is "a state of Dasein which is necessary *a priori*" (53); the "I" is described as "an essential characteristic [*essentielle Bestimmtheit*]" of Dasein (117); at page 120, we are told that Dasein is "essentially being-with." For my purposes here, I propose to steer clear of the problem of understanding the specific *content* of these claims; my concern in what follows lies with their logical *form*.

It is important to recognize that there is at least a prima facie difficulty to be addressed here, so I propose to begin with a crude statement of the problem and a rough sketch of one way in which the problem might be solved. To be clear: I do not mean to suggest that we attribute this solution to Heidegger. At risk of offending some old friends, I shall attribute versions of this first solution to Plato and Husserl.

Start with the problem. Phenomenology, it is very often said, is a *descriptive* undertaking. Indeed, this was from very early on one of its key selling points. Unlike dry scholastic abstraction (which phenomenology may all too often resemble!) or logic chopping rooted in nothing more sturdy than arbitrary definitions, phenomenology was always and ever to be anchored in a *description of the phenomena*. This was at least one part – and the larger part – of what Husserl meant by his famous slogan, "*auf die Sachen selbst!*"[7] Heidegger at one point goes so far as to insist that the expression "descriptive phenomenology" is "at bottom tautological" (35). It is perhaps worth mentioning that the figure of Dilthey once again lurks in the background here, this time in connection with his proposal for a *descriptive* (as opposed to explanatory) psychology.[8]

But now, we ordinarily think of *descriptions* as yielding information about how things (actually) are, rather than how they must or could be. If I describe the suspect who fled from the crime scene, or describe the floor plan of the house where I grew up, my description tells me nothing in the first instance about how the suspect *could* have appeared, or how the floor plan *had* to be. A careful descriptive undertaking simply tells me how it *is*. Depending on how we divide the logical terrain, we could say either that description warrants modally *unqualified* propositions, or that it warrants propositions in the modality of *actuality*. And here, in one stark form, lies the problem: how can a strictly descriptive phenomenology warrant modally robust conclusions? I certainly do not mean to suggest that this problem is insoluble. There are, indeed, a number of available solutions. Some are quite trivial. For example, it is generally agreed that *p* entails both "possibly *p*" and "not necessarily

not-*p*." By this route, descriptive methods immediately generate modally qualified results. Other solutions, as we shall see, are anything but
trivial. My only point so far is that we are owed *some* account of how
phenomenology warrants modally robust conclusions, particularly if its
basic method is a method of description.

As a first step, it will be useful to think about how a version of this
problem plays out in simplified version of Platonism. Think of Plato[9]
as having been impressed above all by the remarkable fact of strict
mathematical proof, that extraordinary tool yielding extraordinary
knowledge that had only recently come on the scene as Plato was writing. Mathematical knowledge was something palpably real in Plato's
world, and it required explanation. That task of explanation can itself
be resolved into two questions: what is the *world* like, and what are *we*
like, such that we are capable of knowledge with the strict generality
and exactitude characteristic of mathematics? These are questions from
which we might see much of Plato's metaphysics and epistemology –
not to mention his psychology and his politics – arising. And his official
solution involves a distinctive *descriptive* enterprise (recollection) oriented toward a distinctive sort of object (the Forms).

Switch now to the case of Husserl. Recall first that Husserl himself
was originally trained as a mathematician. Already in the 1890s, Husserl
was struck by the fact that from a suitably clear presentation of a single
example, a mathematician can extract knowledge that is both general
and necessary. If I can grasp with sufficient *evidence* a single exemplar
of an equilateral triangle, I can *know* that every equilateral triangle is
necessarily equiangular. Like Plato, Husserl constructs an account –
in this case an account of the semantic content of our experience – to
explain how this comes about. The opening sections of *Ideas I* lay the
foundations for Husserl's proposal. He there distinguishes between two
modes of being – "fact" (*Tatsache*) and "essence" (*Wesen*) – and accordingly between two broad families of sciences: *Tatsachenwissenschaften*
and *Wesenswissenschaften*. In the latter case, Husserl claims, scientific
investigation yields necessary truths.

> Every eidetic division and individuation of an eidetically general fact is called,
> just *in so far as* it is this, an *essential necessity* ... The consciousness of a
> necessity, or more specifically a consciousness of a judgement, in which we
> become aware of a certain matter as the specification of an eidetic generality, is
> called *apodeictic.*[10]

As is so often the case, Husserl's point is buried under a barrage of jargon. An apodeictic judgment is an example of what I am here calling a
"modally qualified" claim; it is a claim with the force of necessity. An
eidetically general fact is a fact about an essence – for example that the

equilateral triangle is equiangular. So Husserl's claim here, in brief, is that when we successfully describe an essence, we warrant an essential judgment, that is, a necessary truth.

To round out this position, Husserl needs an account of our access to this domain of essences, something to occupy the space held by the theory of recollection in the Platonic position. He famously has a theory about this, as well as a scientific practice shaped by that theory. Both the theory and the practice are complex; for present purposes, it will suffice to identify a marker that points to both:

This is done by bringing the essence ... to primordial givenness, and then in this object-giving consciousness completing the mental steps required for the "insight," for the primordial givenness, that is, of the essential content which the ... proposition openly expressed.[11]

According to Husserl, then, we have the capacity to bring essences to "primordial givenness," and to gain thereby a kind of direct insight into their structure. When supplemented with the appropriate "mental steps," this capacity for the so-called "intuition of essences" provides the distinctive epistemic basis for the *Wesenswissenschaften*.

If we help ourselves to these resources, then we find ourselves with the makings of a distinctive solution to the problem we set ourselves above. How can a descriptive enterprise warrant claims in the modality of necessity? The trick is to find the right sort of objects to describe. Husserlian essences are what I shall call "modal objects"; so are the *Spezies* of the *Logical Investigations* and the *noemata* of *Ideas*. For Husserl, to describe modal objects is to warrant modal truths. How does this solution apply to *phenomenological* investigation? Husserl's answer is more elaborate than anything I can articulate here, but the central idea is not hard to state. Husserl holds that there are modal objects, as it were, at work in human experience. A phenomenological description of the *content* of human experience must therefore include a description of this modal content. The output of phenomenological investigation thereby includes modally qualified propositions. For example, spatial objects necessarily present themselves aspectively; no experience can present a voluminous container that is larger on the inside than on the outside.

THE SEMANTICS OF "DASEIN"

In thinking about how Heidegger proposes to warrant his modal claims, I proceed by worrying my way through a question about the interpretation of the word "Dasein," which is of course one of Heidegger's central terms of art. The modal propositions of *Being and Time* all in one way or another pertain to Dasein, so we need to gain some clarity about just how this term bears meaning.

First, let me be clear, however, that it is *not* my intention to revisit the spirited debate over the proper *individuation* of Dasein – whether "Dasein" is a mass term or a count term, for instance, or whether it properly takes the indefinite article. I am going to assume that that debate has in all essentials been settled; whatever "Dasein" means, Heidegger means to say that there are as many of them in my kitchen right now as there are human bodies.[12] But it is important to recognize that this alone does not suffice to specify a semantics for Heidegger's term. Moreover, some of the open semantic questions come to have quite a direct bearing on the problem of understanding the status of Heidegger's modal claims in *Being and Time.*

In approaching this issue, let me start by constructing and contrasting two possible approaches to the semantics of Heidegger's term. The first of these gives priority to the *extension* of the term; I shall accordingly describe it as the *extensionalist* account. On the reading I have in mind, the meaning of the term "Dasein" is initially established by specifying its referents. This is accomplished by means of a coextensive term, such as "human being," "homo sapiens," or "man." "Dasein" does not *mean* the same thing as these terms; it is not a synonym for "man." But it has a meaningful use in virtue of its reference to the same set of individuals that are picked out by these more familiar terms. The extensionalist account is rarely spelled out explicitly among Heidegger's commentators, but it is a natural way of understanding a common strategy used by commentators in introducing Heidegger's technical term into commentary and analysis.[13] One commentator who paid explicit attention to the semantic niceties was the late Frederick Olafson:

[T]he concept of a human being and the concept of [Dasein] are extensionally equivalent in the sense that they apply to the same entities, [but] they are not intensionally equivalent because they take these entities in different ways.[14]

As we shall see, Olafson's position is not quite as univocal as this makes it seem, but we can at least see here the main outlines of the extensionalist approach: the initial meaning of a novel term is fixed by specifying a known range of entities to which it applies. We can then use the extension, together with the facts about those entitites, to establish an intension for the term.

The extensional account of the semantics of "Dasein" brings with it certain commitments about the structure of Heidegger's investigation. Notice first that on the extensionalist accounting, there can really be no question about whether there are nonhuman Daseins – for example whether dolphins or chimpanzees or Alpha Centurians or robots might be Dasein. Correlatively, there would seem to be no scope for asking whether there might be some normally functioning humans (perhaps in a culture quite unlike ours) who are not Dasein. On the extensionalist interpretation, these questions are settled from the outset – not by any facts about such entities, but simply by the semantics of the term. Moreover, if the term "Dasein" is fixed extensionally, then it is natural to read the analytic of Dasein as what I will call a *de re* ontological inquiry. Hence, for instance, when Heidegger claims that "Dasein is an entity which, in its very Being, comports itself understandingly toward being" (52–3), this would be read *de re*, as a claim about the comportment of a particular set of entities that have been antecedently specified.

All this points to an implicit assumption at work on the extensionalist approach: the assumption that all human beings are of the same ontological type. Call this the ontological homogeneity thesis. This may seem an obvious assumption, but it is far from uncontentious, and it not at all clear how it can be defended once it is called into question. To get a sense of what questions are being begged here, one need only think of the many religious discourses that talk of the birth of "a new being" upon one or another kind of religious conversion. Closer to home, Husserl's position in *Crisis* edges toward a conception of ontological difference within the human race. Once what he calls "European Man" has discovered the infinite ideals constitutive of reason and science, some human beings comes to be oriented by a totally new set of demands and ideals. They demand universally true principles admissible by proof and rules of conduct that hold everywhere, for all agents and in all circumstances. This might well be understood as a kind of ontological transformation within human history. The extensionalist approach rules out this possibility by fiat.

The purest alternative to the extensionalist approach would be a purely intensionalist account. On this reading, what is initially fixed is the intension or sense of the term "Dasein," leaving the question of extension to be settled independently. On this reading, the claim that every Dasein has an understanding of being, or that every Dasein comports itself toward its own being, can be taken as implicit definitions of a technical term. In this case, the question of whether Alpha Centurians or dolphins are Dasein *is* open; it is the question – no doubt hard to decide but nonetheless meaningful – as to whether those creatures have an understanding of being and ontological self-concern. It would also be open in principle to discover what is ruled out in advance by the extensionalist approach – namely, that some human beings are not Dasein. Notice that on this reading, the existential analytic would be a de dicto ontological inquiry. To say of Dasein that, for example, it is subject to moods would be to say (de dicto) of beings with an understanding of being that they are one-and-all subject to moods.

Despite his apparent endorsement of the extensionalist position, some of Olafson's remarks seem to betray an intensionalist semantics. He writes in his preface, for example:

> In the lectures [the concept of being] is developed much more fully and in a way that demonstrates just how closely it is linked to the concept of Dasein – that is, the kind of entity that human beings prove to be on Heidegger's analysis.[15]

Here the suggestion is that "Dasein" has a *conceptual* link to the concept of being; moreover, the thesis that human beings are Dasein is something that *emerges* in the course of an investigation. These suggestions fit poorly with the extensionalist semantics, since the claim that human beings are Dasein would not, under that interpretation, be the sort of thing to be discovered or proved; it would be a trivial consequence of the semantics of the term. Moreover, the suggestion of a *conceptual* link between "Dasein" and "being" would seem to require that these terms are fixed intensionally, most straightforwardly by defining Dasein by appeal to the idea of having an understanding of being or having ontological self-concern. In that case, one could indeed hope to *prove* that human beings are Dasein, though just what sort of proof would be required is a matter we will have to consider. For a more explicitly intensionalist approach, we can look to George Steiner. Steiner introduces Heidegger's term with a definition: "A being which questions Being, by first questioning its own [being], is a *Da-Sein.*"[16]

Although I have made reference here to the question of whether non-human animals or computers could be Dasein, I want to be clear that these are not the questions that interest me in this context. I raise these questions about the extension of Heidegger's term only with the aim of clarifying the logical form of the claims Heidegger makes *about us.* This seems to be worth getting clear about for its own sake, but it also bears quite significantly on the problem of establishing or assessing those claims. Allow me to comment briefly on this in order to show something of what is at stake.

The first and crucial point here is that modal operators function quite differently in de dicto and *de re* contexts. Recall the stock example: if I say, de dicto, that the tallest philosopher in the room is a philosopher, then I have uttered a necessary truth – a tautology. But if I say, *de re*, of that same individual that he is a philosopher then my claim is contingent. Depending on the context of utterance, I will have said of Charles Taylor or Paul Churchland or Shaquille O'Neal that *that individual* is a philosopher, and this is anything but a tautology. Accordingly, the choice between *de re* and de dicto interpretations of Heidegger's phenomenology makes a considerable difference to the logical form of its modal propositions. It should also be clear that the question of what can be claimed to hold necessarily of Dasein varies crucially with the semantics one chooses for the term. To take the most obvious point: on the extensionalist semantics, it is a necessary truth that all and only human beings are Dasein, while on the intensionalist semantics, it is a necessary truth that every Dasein has an understanding of being. But these necessities are not interchangeable. So it turns out that the choice between the extensionalist and the intensionalist semantic models has dramatic consequences for the interpretation of Heidegger's doctrines, quite apart from idle questions about the mode of being of Alpha Centurians.

The choice among semantic models for "Dasein" also has consequences for the methodology of phenomenology. Suppose that I undertake a close description of some particular example or examples of Dasein. Under what circumstances could the description of these *instances of Dasein* warrant general claims about *Dasein as such*? The answer to this question comes out rather differently, as it happens, depending on whether one chooses the extensionalist or the intensionalist semantic model. On the intensionalist model, rich description of a few particulars would seem to be a rather risky, even irresponsible, way of warranting claims about Dasein as such. For suppose that I find some individuals who clearly fall under the requisite intension: they have, let us say, an understanding of being and exhibit ontological self-concern. And suppose that I successfully identify the central features of *their* ontological structure. So far, I have no particular reason to conclude that the features of these individuals are attributable de dicto to Dasein as such, rather than simply being ontological features of the particular collection of individuals I selected to describe. So under the intensional semantic model, a descriptive method alone would not suffice to warrant *general* results – to say nothing of *necessary* ones.

Our extensionalist will be in better shape on this point, but only because of the commitment to the ontological homogeneity thesis. On this substantial assumption, one good study of an instance could, in principle, reveal the mode of being of the whole of humanity. And since, for the extensionalist, it is a necessary truth that all Dasein is human Dasein, that single successful case study would establish results for Dasein as such. In either case, however, phenomenological ontology requires a resource that goes beyond mere description. To put the point in the logician's terms, the move from a particular claim ("*a* is F") to its corresponding generalization ("All x are F") is warranted only under the special circumstance that *a* is a perfect exemplar of its kind. For the extensionalist, this circumstance is guaranteed under the assumption of ontological homogeneity; the intensionalist seems to require some additional resource to warrant the generalization. I turn now to consider one candidate for such a supplement.

There is one recurrent pattern of modal reasoning in *Being and Time* that suggests a strategy for interpreting and vindicating Heidegger's modal commitments. Consider three representative passages from Division I. In each case, I have altered the emphasis in order to focus attention on the modal inflection of Heidegger's commitments. A first example comes in connection with Heidegger's claims about Dasein's understanding of Others:

[B]ecause Dasein's Being is being-with, its understanding of Being already implies the understanding of Others. This understanding, like any understanding, is not acquaintance derived from knowledge about them, but a primordially existential kind of Being, which, more than anything else, MAKES such knowledge and acquaintance POSSIBLE. (123–4, emphasis added)

A second passage concerns moods and affects:

And ONLY BECAUSE the senses belong ontologically to an entity whose kind of Being is Being-in-the-World with a state-of-mind, CAN they be touched by anything or have a sense for something in such a way that what touches them shows itself in an affect. (137)

We find a third example in the context of Heidegger's claims about thrown projection:

ONLY BECAUSE the Being of the there receives its constitution through understanding and through the character of understanding as projection, ONLY BECAUSE it is what it becomes (or alternatively does not become) CAN IT say to itself "become what you are" and say this with understanding. (145)

Notice that, in each case, we find the claim that some trait or feature of Dasein figures as the *condition on the possibility* of some one of Dasein's capacities. The traits in question are said to be ontological features of Dasein; the capacities are ontic features. In each case, Heidegger explicitly invokes claims of possibility and so implicitly makes claims to necessity. If a certain ontological structure (e.g., being-with) is a condition on the possibility of some particular ontic feature (e.g., knowledge about others), then the ontological structure *must obtain* for any entity exhibiting the ontic feature.

This pattern of modal qualification will no doubt sound familiar. In arguing from some acknowledged fact to the conditions on its possibility, we can recognize the characteristic modal trajectory of transcendental inquiry, at least as it is orthodoxly understood. And this in turn suggests a strategy for handling Heidegger's modal propositions: we can understand their status if we can understand just how he proposes to adapt the transcendental tradition to his particular purposes. In assessing the prospects for this strategy, I want to consider the way in which these and related issues have been handled in Taylor Carman's elegant and illuminating study, *Heidegger's Analytic*. Carman's book is important for my purposes because it squarely (and lucidly) sets *Being and Time* in the transcendental tradition, and sets out to discharge the obligations that such a reading incurs.

My approach will be myopic, and accordingly I set aside a whole raft of issues on which Carman's book makes important contributions. I do this in order to hone in on two features of the book that are pertinent to the issues under discussion here. First, it is important to know – for reasons that will become clear – that Carman's book is *very unkind to Husserl*. The second chapter of *Heidegger's Analytic* is called "The Critique of Husserl," and Husserl emerges from Carman's mill a battered and bruised figure. I won't go into this here in any detail, but confine myself to a brief catalogue of Carman's complaints. Husserl's phenomenology, we are told, is "at once uncritical and incoherent"; it is "caught in a vicious circle" (HA 54). Husserl "never acknowledges the interpretative character of his own inquiry," but adopts "a pretense of scientific rigour" (HA 55). He relies on "ontologically obscure distinctions" (56), uncritically takes for granted the "primacy of the present [temporal moment]" (HA 61), and relies on "unexamined ontological categories" (HA 87). According to Carman, "Husserl's [phenomenological] findings are not findings at all, but metaphysical prejudices regarding the being of human beings" (HA 95). As the capstone to this barrage, Carman quotes from Heidegger's contemptuous letter to Löwith: "I am now convinced that Husserl was never a philosopher, not even for one second in his life" (HA 58).

I will return to consider the ramifications of this stance toward Husserl, but for now, I set it aside in order to focus on what is ultimately the more important contribution of Carman's book: its account of Heidegger's relation to Kant, and more specifically to the Kantian project of transcendental investigation. If Carman's Heidegger is mercilessly critical of Husserl, he is, by contrast, deeply indebted to Kant. Indeed, Carman argues, the very idea of an existential *analytic* of Dasein is "a self-conscious allusion to the Transcendental Analytic that makes up the central constructive core of the first Critique" (HA 10). Carman quotes Heidegger's own description of his project (in *Basic Problems*) as an inquiry "into the *conditions of the possibility* of the understanding of being as such" (HA 18, emphasis added). Thoroughgoing though the repudiation of Husserl may be, there is thus still a sense in which Heideggerian ontology, as Carman approaches it, is to be understood as transcendental phenomenology.[17]

So how are Heidegger's transcendental ambitions to be framed and defended? The key to Carman's reconstruction lies in the notion of a hermeneutic condition. Carman introduces this notion in self-conscious imitation of Henry Allison's controversial notion of an epistemic condition. For Allison, an epistemic condition is a condition necessary for knowledge of an object or an objective state of affairs.[18] Carman takes over this notion but crucially modifies it. For Heidegger, the aim is not to identify conditions necessary for *knowledge*, but rather conditions necessary for finding *meaning*, or for interpretation:

Heidegger, I shall argue, is interested ... in the conditions of the possibility of Interpretation ... Interpretation, for Heidegger, means explicit understanding, making sense of something *as* something – primitively, *entities as entities*, that is, as *being*. (HA 12)

The body of Carman's text is thus his attempt to show that, and how Heidegger's existential analytic of Dasein systematically exhibits the conditions necessary for the discovery of meaning in this sense.

At this point, I must beg forgiveness for reverting to the mode of unseemly quibbling over semantics. By adapting Allison's notion of an epistemic condition, Carman takes over and redeploys the logical modality distinctive of that transcendental approach. Allison's epistemic conditions track conditions on the *possibility* of knowledge; Carman's epistemic conditions are meant to track conditions on the *possibility* of interpretation. So naturally, I want to know under what semantic regime are these modal claims deployed and defended?

In considering this question, we can first go back to our initial semantic distinction: is Carman an extensionalist or an intensionalist about the semantics of "Dasein"? Some of his formulations suggest an extensionalist semantic model. Hence, in his introduction, Carman writes:

The argument of *Being and Time* therefore begins by referring ontology back to what Heidegger calls an "existential analytic of Dasein," that is, an account of the basic structures of human existence. (HA 9)

This might suggest that "Dasein" is coextensive with "human being"; it would certainly seem to betray a commitment to the ontological homogeneity thesis. But when he comes explicitly to introduce Heidegger's term-of-art, he does so in ways that seem to privilege an intension:

What is Dasein? What kind of entity exists in such a way that its existence involves an understanding of being, and consequently rests on the conditions of the interpretability of entities as entities? (HA 35)

Carman's answer to this question is "embodied human agents understood as concrete particulars" (HA 36), but notice that this way of framing the question privileges a particular definition of Dasein, which is then employed to identify suitable referents.

This indeterminacy in Carman's position has further consequences for his discussion. The most important of these concern the proper scope and specification of the hermeneutic conditions Carman seeks to identify. Following Allison's lead again, Carman claims that hermeneutic conditions are neither causal conditions (whether psychological or physiological) under which interpretation takes place, nor logical conditions (conditions that would follow "analytically" from the bare *concept* of interpretation or meaning). But in specifying this point, Carman again and again deploys a formulation that, from the perspective of my semantic obsessions, is crucially indeterminate. An inquiry into hermeneutic conditions, we are told, is "an inquiry into the conditions of anything making sense *to us* as anything" (HA 12); it aims to provide "an account of the conditions of *our* having an explicit understanding of being" (HA 13, emphasis added in both quotations).

What concerns me here is the proper interpretation of the personal pronouns in these formulations, which recur regularly through the body of Carman's analysis. In one way, of course, these pronouns are innocent enough: "our" here means "Dasein's"; the understanding or "making sense" is Dasein's understanding. But the scope of Carman's claims, their logical form, and ultimately the sort of the evidence required to warrant them vary dramatically depending on the way in which this "our" is specified. Is Carman's account meant to provide a *de re* account of the conditions under which *human beings* find meaning in their encounter with things? Or is it meant to provide a de dicto account of the conditions under which anything with an understanding of being and ontological self-concern finds such meaning?[19]

How do these issues play out in the details of Carman's elaboration of Heidegger's position? Consider a line of argument that Carman develops in explicating what Heidegger calls "discourse" (*Rede*). Discourse, according to Carman, is "*the* hermeneutic condition par excellence." I cannot here reconstruct the full range of Carman's subtle analysis, but it will be worth focusing on one of its crucial steps, a step that pertains to what Carman calls "the semantic gap." The semantic gap, for Carman, is (roughly) the difference between the object and content of discourse – the difference, in Heidegger's jargon, between *what is talked about* (*das Beredete*) and *what is said* (*das Geredete*). In explicit speech, the semantic gap is characteristically marked by the little word "as": I interpret x *as* y.

It should be clear that a certain kind of mastery of the semantic gap is required as a condition on the possibility of interpretation. This much simply falls out as an analytic consequence of Carman's account of what interpretation is. Recall that, for Carman, interpretation *is* explicit understanding, and that explicit understanding involves "making sense of something *as* something" (HA 12, quoted above; emphasis altered). In order to account for interpretation, then, we require some account of the possibility of the semantic gap. Carman states, "Only when we can speak of alternative or competing aspects ... does it makes sense to describe our perceptual reports with the qualifier '*as* such and such'" (HA 247).

Having set out the transcendental problem in this way, Carman then goes on to propose a solution in two stages. The first stage is to locate the roots of the semantic gap in our *competent use* of things, which exhibits what Heidegger calls "understanding."

Understanding is an intentional phenomenon, and is therefore aspectival, since it consists in our competent use or treatment of things *as* the things they are.... Understanding thus consists in *using as* or *treating as*, which is normative and aspectual but typically tacit and unthematic. (HA 247)

But competent use alone does not yet explain interpretation in Carman's sense, which requires *explicit* understanding. To explain this, Carman reasons, we need to understand how the tacit and unthematic aspectival structure of competent use is rendered explicit in the *as* that marks the semantic gap between the interpreted object and the interpretation we offer of it. It is exactly here that Carman locates the phenomenon of *discourse*. Discourse, according to Carman, is the "expressive-communicative dimension of practice, broadly conceived" (HA 205), and it is discourse, he claims, that makes understanding explicit. In Heidegger's terms, "discourse articulates intelligibility" (271). Discourse need not take the form of overt speech; indeed, Carman's preferred illustrations of discourse come in the form of nonverbal gestures – as when I wrinkle my nose or dramatically mop my brow, silently expressing the discomfort of a hot subway carriage. In doing so, I "meaningfully articulate the intelligibility" of my situation, exhibiting explicitly an aspect of the situation which had been only implicit. It is thus discourse that builds the bridge from understanding to interpretation. According to Carman:

Discourse is therefore a hermeneutic condition, indeed *the* condition of interpretation par excellence, for it is in virtue of the communicative dimension of discourse that interpretations make understandings explicit by bringing them to expression, linguistic or otherwise. (HA 249)

But it seems clear that there is a problem here. We can reduce this line of reasoning to its basic structure as follows:

(1) Interpretation requires a way of distinguishing content from object in intentional experience.
(2) We distinguish content from object by using things competently and rendering our understanding explicit in discourse.
(3) Competent use and discourse serve as conditions on the possibility of interpretation.

In assessing this argumentative schema, we must pay particular attention to the patterns of modality and generality in its premises. The first and third propositions either implicitly or explicitly include modal operators: "requires," "possibility." The second proposition does not. Furthermore, the first and third propositions are implicitly general: they both make claims about *all* interpretation. The generality of the second proposition is unclear; as we have seen, everything turns on the scope of its "we" and "our." The argument – if indeed it is an argument – is accordingly invalid. Simply put, the second premise identifies *one* way in which the semantic gap is opened in *our* experience; the conclusion follows only if this *one* way is the *only possible way*. But nothing in the argument suffices to establish the stronger thesis.

This vulnerability in Carman's argumentative schema reflects a problem of principle in the attempt to vindicate the modal propositions of *Being and Time* through a synthesis of phenomenology and transcendental philosophy. Phenomenological description tells us how things actually are in a more-or-less delimited set of cases. Moreover, we can expect the richness of a description to be inversely proportional to the generality of its application. Hence, the distinctive logical form of the second proposition answers to something intrinsic in the methodology that warrants it. But this in turn presents an obstacle for those, like Carman, who seek to deploy these phenomenological results in the service of transcendental claims, whose logical form is considerably more ambitious.

In the face of this concern, one natural recourse is to scale back the scope and modality of one's conclusions. Why can't we be satisfied if *Being and Time* teaches us something local and contingent about the ways in which entities become interpretable, about the amazing fact that things make sense to us? Wouldn't that be a significant result in its own right? Tacit and implicit understanding in competent use, discursive articulation, explicit interpretation..., that is the path that *we* (where "we" may be as local as you like) come to find things available for interpretation. Isn't it simply idle to worry about the merely abstract possibilities of some other route to the same hermeneutic end? I am sympathetic to this line of response, but we must be clear that it comes at a cost. To adopt it without qualification or supplement would effectively require us to abandon the modal propositions of Heidegger's text.

In at least one passage in his study, Carman explicitly addresses the questions about modality that are my central concern here. I quote the relevant passage in full:

> Reading the analytic of Dasein as an account of hermeneutic conditions might seem to promise a series of knock-down transcendental arguments that would demonstrate their necessity in true Kantian fashion. I do not believe that Heidegger provides such arguments, but neither do I think that his project avoids them as a matter of principle. And like the necessity of the forms of intuition and the categories in Kant, the necessity of the hermeneutic conditions Heidegger advances in the form of existential structures of Dasein, though stronger than mere causal necessity, will of course be considerably weaker than logical necessity. (HA 29)

I do not see how we can be satisfied by this. On the one hand, it seems right to try to locate phenomenological or hermeneutic necessity somewhere between (or alongside?) logical and causal necessity. But simply making these negative claims falls short of a positive specification of the relevant modality. But the more serious problem here concerns the suggestion that Heidegger's modally robust results are not supported by arguments sufficiently robust to warrant them. Here it is important to remember that, for Allison, the notion of an epistemic condition serves mainly as a heuristic device – a kind of hunting license to use in looking for conditions of a distinctive sort.[20] The real work comes in trying to establish that certain conditions *actually constrain* the possibility of knowledge. And it is just this work that transcendental arguments are traditionally called in to perform. If *Being and Time* gives us transcendental claims without transcendental arguments, this sounds suspiciously like giving us conclusions without premises, dogmas unsupported by evidence.

But here I can feel myself rising (or falling?) to match the rhetoric of "The Critique of Husserl," so let me change tack and consider whether there might be a way out.

AN ALTERNATE SEMANTICS FOR "DASEIN"

So far, I have considered two approaches to the semantics of "Dasein"; one fixes its meaning extensionally, the other intensionally. But of course, these two positions do not exhaust the range of semantic possibilities.

A third approach worth considering takes the initial significance of the term to be fixed by an exemplar, with the extension of the term fixed by similarity to that exemplar. On this approach, "Dasein" would operate in something like the way that natural kind terms work, at least under one of the standard treatments of the semantics for such terms. We can take our orientation from the standard (massively simplified) example. Suppose that the word "gold" were given meaning by ostension of a sample of the substance, and that both its intension and its extension were then left to be determined by further investigation. We could fix its intension by determining the chemical composition of the sample; we could then survey its extension by looking for other samples with the same composition.

In thinking through this semantic strategy, we might begin by rereading the very first sentence of Division I: "*We* are ourselves the entities to be analyzed" (41, emphasis added). Instead of reading this in the extensionalist way – as a reference to the same class picked out by the term "human being" – we might instead read Heidegger's "we" as in the first instance picking out Heidegger and me, or better: Heidegger and his reader. *We* would then be like the exemplars of gold: "Dasein" refers to Heidegger and his reader and to anything else that is relevantly like those exemplars. This semantic approach shares something in common with each of the other two. Like the intensionalist approach, it leaves the extension of the term unspecified. Anything that is like Heidegger and his reader in the relevant way would be a Dasein; hence, the question of whether Dasein is coextensive with "human being" would be left open. Like the extensionalist approach, however, this reading underwrites a *de re* account of the existential analytic. The constituent claims of Division I would in the first instance be *de re* claims about the exemplary instances of Dasein, themselves picked out by a literary variant of ostension rather than by description.

I will call this approach *exemplar semantics*. One question about exemplar semantics concerns its stability as a genuine alternative to the two approaches we have already discussed. The problem, of course, is to determine what "being like in the relevant sense" amounts to. On this semantic approach, the claim that, for example, Dasein is subject to anxiety would in the first instance be a claim about Heidegger and his reader. But this would not be the limit of the burden of the thesis; it would also amount to the claim that anyone else relevantly like Heidegger and his reader is also subject to anxiety. But who is that exactly? If the claim is to be truth-evaluable, then its scope must somehow be made determinate. Is the claim that all *philosophers* are subject to anxiety? Or that anyone who reads existentialist writings is subject to anxiety? Clearly not. But as soon as one tries to specify the scope of the thesis, one seems to be pressed toward one of the other two semantic options. Either one determines the claim by appeal to some antecedently known extension, or one specifies it by privileging some specific attributes shared by Heidegger and his "we" – for example that each has an understanding of being and is an issue for himself. So it is far from clear that exemplar semantics represents a stable middle ground.

The concern here is a genuine one, but it is worth considering whether Heidegger has resources for handling it. The key thing to remember is that, in the case of "gold," we start out with more than just the sample. My ring is a sample of gold, but of course it is also a round thing, something I am wearing, something I bought in New York City, and so forth. I am able to use it as a meaning-fixing exemplar only because I start out *both* with a sample *and* with a context of inquiry. "Gold" has in its extension my ring *and anything like it in the context of chemistry*, and more specifically, anything like it in atomic structure. It is this context of inquiry that serves to delimit the significance of "like in the relevant sense." In the case of "Dasein," I also start out both with an exemplar and with a context of inquiry. The exemplar, I am proposing, is Heidegger and me; the context of inquiry is ontology. On this semantic analysis, then, "Dasein" refers to Heidegger and to me and to anything else that shares our mode of being, our ontological structure.

This may seem to push us back toward intensionalist semantics. After all, my distinctive mode of being is, let us presume, that I have an understanding of being and ontological self-concern. Accordingly, as on the intensionalist account, the extension of "Dasein" will be fixed only once we know which things have that ontological character. Unless we know how far that extension reaches (and it seems clear that we do not know), we do not know the full burden of general claims about the existential traits of Dasein. Nonetheless, there is a crucial difference between the intensional semantic model and the exemplar approach, at least when it comes to making modal claims. In our chemical example, the claim "my ring is gold" comes out as a *de re* necessity. For given our story about how the term "gold" acquired its sense, it is simply not possible that *this thing* (the exemplary ring) is not gold. Moreover, the claim that gold has atomic number 79 also emerges as a necessary truth. Why is that? Because the intension of the term gold is determined by the chemical composition of my ring, which is to be of atomic number 79.[21] Under exemplar semantics, then, it is a necessary truth of Heidegger and his reader that each are Dasein-exemplars. Moreover, anything that pertains to the ontological character of Heidegger and his reader would amount to necessary features of Dasein. For if, in virtue of its meaning, "Dasein" refers to all and only those entities that share the ontological features of the exemplar, then all the ontological features of the exemplar are necessarily ascribable to every Dasein.

We must be careful not to overstate the merits of this proposal. By itself, it does not solve the problem of interpreting or assessing Heidegger's modal claims in *Being and Time*. But it does usefully shift the locus of the problem. For present purposes, it will suffice to bring out two features of this shift. Consider first the fit between the descriptive methods in phenomenology and modally qualified phenomenological doctrines. As I argued above, on either the extensionalist or the intensionalist semantic models for "Dasein," phenomenological description – no matter how rich and revealing – must be supplemented by some other form of argument or evidence. For the extensionalist, we need some reason to endorse the hypothesis of ontological homogeneity in the human race; for the intensionalist, we need some way of reassuring ourselves that the Dasein we have described is a perfect exemplar of its kind. On these points, it seems, exemplar semantics offers a promising way out. The exemplarist is not committed to the problematic thesis of ontological homogeneity, and so does not incur the awkward problem of vindicating it. But more importantly, the exemplarist has a cheap guarantee that the object of description is a perfect exemplar of its kind. Just as the chemical composition of my ring will fix the chemical composition of gold, so the ontological composition of our exemplary Daseins will fix the ontological composition of Dasein as such.

But difficulties remain. Let me here attend to two of them. Recall first that in our example about "gold," we can say that all and only those features of my ring pertaining to its atomic structure would come to figure as essential properties of gold. The fact that this piece of gold is mine, or that it is round, or that it serves as a symbol of marriage..., all these are by comparison contingent properties, and do not figure in the meaning of "gold." So analogously, in the case of Dasein, all and only those features of Heidegger and his reader that are part of their ontological character can be said to be necessary features of Dasein. Accordingly, we still stand in need of some method for distinguishing those features from others. I don't think this is a hopeless problem, though I have not here proposed a method for solving it.[22] Absent such a solution, one might think that we have effectively come back full circle. For surely it is by way of Heidegger's modal propositions that he seeks to identify ontological features.

There is truth in this complaint, but there is nonetheless a crucial difference introduced by the exemplarist proposal. For the question as to whether, say, being subject to anxiety is a necessary feature of Dasein is now no longer a question about whether *all human beings* are subject to anxiety, or even whether all ontological self-concern brings with it vulnerability to anxiety. Indeed, what is at issue is, in the first instance, neither a general nor a modally qualified claim. It is rather a particular and reflexive question about (Heidegger and) me: namely, whether *my* being subject to anxiety is a feature of *my* ontological makeup. We still need a way of answering this kind of question, but in a fundamental respect, its logical form has been tamed.

A second residual difficulty is related to the first. In our toy exemplarist myth about "gold," we have been assuming that the context of chemistry is antecedently established, such that we might deploy such notions as "atomic number" in establishing a semantics for "gold." But of course in real life, the situation is reversed. The term "gold" acquired its meaning long before the advent of anything we would now recognize as chemistry, and eons prior to the first halting formulations of the notion "atomic number." Any realistic deployment of exemplarist semantics must acknowledge this fact, and devise a strategy for deploying the basic exemplarist insight while taking account of the fact that the relevant context of inquiry is *dynamic*, and accordingly that "being like in the relevant sense" always has at best a provisional and unfolding meaning. And of course what applies in chemistry also applies – and more so – in the ontological context of *Being and Time*. I have been talking as if the context of ontology were somehow already fixed in introducing the term "Dasein," but Heidegger is rather of the view that ontology has by and large been forgotten.

These remaining difficulties certainly complicate the prospects for carrying through the exemplarist proposal, but it seems to me that they do so in exactly the right way. For what they bring out, in the first instance, is a deep and important sense in which the project of *Being and Time* is first-personal – the continuation, by other means, of the project inaugurated with the Delphic Injunction. A vindication of the modal propositions of *Being and Time* requires, in the first instance, that I *know myself*, and in particular that I learn something about my own ontological constitution. But our hope for doing so – this was the second complication – essentially depends on our learning (or recalling) something about ontological inquiry itself. As readers of Heidegger's text, we must simultaneously grope toward self-understanding and an understanding of ontological questioning.

A BRIEF ILLUSTRATION

In order to give life to the exemplarist proposal, we need to consider how it would play out in interpreting one of Heidegger's modally qualified doctrines, and in reconstructing the line of analysis that Heidegger uses to warrant that doctrine. My discussion here is, of necessity, brief, but it should at least go some way toward filling out and testing our semantic hypothesis.

Consider in particular Heidegger's treatment of *Befindlichkeit*. "*Befindlichkeit*" is a notoriously difficult term to translate; for present purposes, I shall simply leave it untranslated. What concerns me here is, at any rate, not the content of the term but the form of reasoning in which it occurs. When Heidegger introduces *Befindlichkeit* at the outset of §29, his first move is to mark it out as an *existentiale*:

> What we indicate *ontologically* by the term "*Befindlichkeit*" is *ontically* the most familiar and everyday sort of thing; our mood, our Being-attuned. Prior to all psychology of moods, a field which in any case still lies fallow, it is necessary to see this phenomenon as a fundamental *existentiale*, and to outline its structure. (134)

The first thing to notice here is the fact that Heidegger treats the same phenomenon as one that admits of either "ontic" or "ontological" analysis. Ontically, that phenomenon is the familiar psychological fact of being in a mood; ontologically it is *Befindlichkeit*. Having staked this claim, the following stretch of text sets out to establish it through phenomenological description. Accordingly, in the four paragraphs that follow, Heidegger describes the phenomenon of being in a mood. He begins with claims in the ontic mode, as for instance that Dasein is always in a mood ("Dasein always has some mood," 134).

How should we interpret such a claim on the various semantic models we have considered? On the extensionalist approach, this is a claim about all human beings; on the intensionalist approach it is a claim about all entities with an understanding of being and ontological self-concern. Either way, the scope of the claim is very broad. On the exemplarist approach, by contrast, the claim is (in the first instance at least) particular. It is a claim about our selected exemplars. This will not prove to be the limit of its applicability, but for the exemplarist, the initial burden is simply to provide a rich and revealing description of the selected sample.

The next stage, under the exemplarist regime, must be to show that the feature being described pertains to the ontological structure of the exemplar. And this is exactly what transpires in Heidegger's exposition. The claims he makes at this stage are among the most difficult and obscure in the section. I shall not propose an interpretation here; all that matters is to recognize that, in making them, Heidegger is eliciting the ontological dimensions of the phenomenon under interrogation. It is here that we are told, for instance, that "in having a mood Dasein is always disclosed moodwise as that entity that has been delivered over in its Being"; that in moods, "Dasein is brought before its Being as 'there'"; and that, in certain moods, "Being has become manifest as a burden" (134). Once again, on the exemplarist proposal, these are, in the first instance, descriptive claims about the particular exemplars under investigation; what they seek to establish is that the phenomenon of mood *implicates Being*, and hence pertains to the ontological structure *of those exemplars*.

Notice that, up to this point, Heidegger's claims have been in the mode of actuality: Dasein *is* always in a mood; a mood *does* deliver Dasein over in its Being. But if the exemplarist proposal is right, these modally modest claims suffice to warrant a modally robust proposition. If *Befindlichkeit* pertains to my ontological constitution, and if I am the exemplar of *Dasein*, then *Befindlichkeit* is a necessary feature of Dasein. To be sure, Heidegger never says exactly that, but he does claim title to designate *Befindlichkeit* as an *existentiale*. As we have seen, this is a status that would seem to carry modal import.

It is at just this point in the section that we encounter a cascade of explicitly modal propositions. For present purposes, I propose to consider only two of them. The first is formulated as follows:

[O]nly because the "there" has already been disclosed in a *Befindlichkeit* can immanent reflection come across "experiences" at all. (136)

As we have seen, it is all too easy to hear in this claim the familiar rhythms of transcendental philosophy. Read transcendentally, Heidegger would here be arguing from a known or acknowledged ontic fact – that we have experience – to the contentious ontological conclusion that "the there is disclosed in *Befindlichkeit*." By showing that the latter is a condition on the possibility of the former, Heidegger would be establishing that *Befindlichkeit* is an *existentiale*, an essential part of our ontological makeup.

But this reading, while in certain respects natural, does not fit well with the text. One sign of trouble can be found in the first sentence of the paragraph in which the seemingly transcendental line of argument appears. That paragraph begins: "From what has been said we can already see...." By this point in the section, Heidegger has *already* established the ontological credentials of *Befindlichkeit*. And he has done so, as we have seen, without the benefit of *any* modally robust claims; he simply provided a rich phenomenological description of moods so as to elicit their ontological dimension. The seemingly transcendental, modally qualified thesis of page 136 thus does not serve to *establish* the ontological result; *it follows from it*. Or better, it comes into view once we have recognized the ontological import of *Befindlichkeit*. And this is just what the exemplarist proposal would require.

We can better see how this works by considering a second example that appears in the following paragraph, this time with the whole sentence italicized in Heidegger's original:

The mood has already disclosed, in every case, being-in-the-world as a whole, and makes it possible first of all to direct oneself towards something. (137)

Once again, the transcendental reading would find here an example of a regressive transcendental argument, working back from the surface phenomenon to its underlying transcendental condition. Heidegger's claim, in effect, would be that any being that is intentionally directed must be subject to moods. As we have seen, there must be grave doubts about the adequacy of phenomenological evidence to establish such a result. But on the exemplarist proposal, Heidegger does not need it. The claim here should not be read as a claim about the general conditions on the possibility of intentional directedness; it is much rather a claim about the role played by moods *in me and in any entity of like ontological constitution.* For me, moods play a role in disclosing being-in-the-world as a whole; hence, *for me* moods are ontological. Together with what Heidegger thinks he has established about world-structure by this point in the text, that licenses the conclusion that, for me and anything like me, moods enable intentional directedness.

OBJECTIONS, REPLIES, AND FURTHER WORK

I am keenly aware that the proposal I have developed here, and the mode in which I have developed it, may prove controversial. By way of conclusion, allow me to review three lines of objection that I have encountered.

(a) *"Menschliche Dasein."* There are a handful of passages in *Being and Time*, and many more in the lecture courses, in which Heidegger uses the expression "human Dasein."[23] Depending upon how we understand this expression, it might be taken as evidence for a tighter semantic connection between "Dasein" and "man" than I have allowed here, and it might be taken to provide support specifically for the extensionalist semantics that we explored above.

I myself do not find this evidence conclusive. We should note, first of all, that the expression "human Dasein" can have a perfectly legitimate deployment under any one of the three semantic proposals we have considered. On the intensionalist semantic proposal, the meaning of "Dasein" is fixed by a definition. In speaking of "human Dasein," we would accordingly be speaking of those entities that satisfy that definition *and* are members of the human species. Under the exemplarist proposal, "Dasein" refers to the exemplar and anything that belongs to the same ontological kind. To speak of "human Dasein" would then restrict the scope to those entities that satisfy this condition *and* fall within the human race. In this respect, then, the occurrence of the phrase *"menschliche Dasein"* does not suffice to force our semantic hand in one way or another. Indeed, the phrase might well seem the most awkward under the extensionalist proposal, under which "human Dasein" would have to be seen as a kind of pleonasm.

When we look to the specific contexts in which the phrase occurs in *Being and Time*, there is indeed some weak reason to prefer either an intensionalist or exemplarist interpretation to the extensionalist alternative, for Heidegger characteristically uses the phrase in restrictive contexts, typically when he is concerned with the bearing of the analytic of Dasein *on the human sciences*. The phrase first appears in §11, in connection with Heidegger's brief remarks about the ethnological study of human cultures. It occurs again in Division II, chapter V, where Heidegger is concerned with the temporal underpinnings of human historiography. These are, in effect, restrictive passages – that is, they are passages where Heidegger's attention is restricted to the bearing of the analytic of Dasein on the specifically human sciences. The appearance of the phrase in these restrictive passages fits at least as well with a restrictive interpretation of "human Dasein" as with the pleonastic reading required under an extensionalist semantics.

(b) *Substantializing Dasein*. In tracing the semantic alternatives, I have in the foregoing spoken of Dasein as an entity with various features or properties, and I have proposed to treat *existentialia* as properties of Dasein that are necessary or essential. But this might seem to betray my failure to appreciate one of the central doctrines of *Being and Time*; that is to say that Dasein is not to be understood as a present-at-hand entity, and that the traditional framework of substance and properties is thus uniquely ill-suited to an understanding of its mode of being.

The issues raised by this objection are far-reaching, and I cannot hope to do justice to them here. But I would argue that this objection turns on an equivocation in the use of the term "substance." In one broad sense, to treat an entity as a substance is to treat it as a bearer of properties. In this sense, it is true that I have "substantialized Dasein." I have assumed that Dasein is the sort of entity that is possessed of a variety of properties or features, and that some among these are aptly characterized as *existentialia*. But there is also a narrower sense of "substance" that has had a long and established history in metaphysics. In this sense, a substance is something that can stand alone, and that bears its properties in such a way that involves no dependence on any other thing. It is this latter sense of substance that figures, for example, in Spinoza's definition in the *Ethics*:

By substance I mean that which is in itself and is conceived through itself; that is, that the conception of which does not require the conception of another thing from which it has been formed.[24]

I believe that it is this latter, more restrictive sense of "substance" that figures in Heidegger's critique of substantializing ontologies. Why is it, for instance, that a hammer is ontologically misconstrued if treated as a substance? The claim is not that a hammer has no properties or features – of course it has. The problem is that a hammer is what it is *only in relation to other equipment*. It is this inability to be what it is *in isolation* that distinguishes it from substance. If this is right, then simply ascribing properties or features to Dasein does not itself betray a substantializing ontology in the sense that concerns Heidegger.[25]

(c) *Reliance on External Semantic Resources.* In developing the foregoing proposals, the semantic and logical resources upon which I have relied are drawn from a philosophical tradition that is not Heidegger's own. As a technique of reading, there are some who will find this objectionable. After all, Heidegger himself has something to say about the meaning of modal terms, and he has a sophisticated and elaborate philosophy of language, even it if is not per se a "semantic theory" in the sense that has gained currency in philosophy in recent decades. So surely an interrogation of the modal propositions of *Being and Time* should be carried out on Heidegger's own terms – not in terms imposed on his project from without.

I am in very considerable sympathy with this third objection, and it is only a shortage of time, space, and insight that prevents me from taking up its counsel here. But let me be careful not to concede too much. I don't myself think that there is anything wrong with using external resources to interpret Heidegger's text. As it happens, philosophical developments quite independent of Heidegger's project have yielded tools for thinking about the semantic and modal alternatives, and I make no apologies for drawing on such resources here. But this should not blind us to the possibility that Heidegger himself had resources for thinking through these challenges, and that these resources might point us down quite different paths than those marked out on the usual maps. In order to investigate such possibilities, a fuller discussion of these matters would need to take into account, among other things, Heidegger's largely implicit account of the semantics of formal indication, his distinction between existential and logical modality, and so on. If I have not undertaken such an approach here, it is certainly not because I do not view it as worthwhile. If nothing else, I hope that the work undertaken here might prove useful for mapping out alternatives against which Heidegger's internal resources might be better understood.

Allow me to close by proposing a framing for such further work with reference to a challenge from Husserl. As we saw above, Husserl proposed a methodology for phenomenology whereby, under the right circumstances, careful descriptive attention to particulars could suffice to warrant modally robust "essential truths" about the ontological region to which those particulars belong. Husserl's proposal was metaphysically and epistemologically expensive; it requires that we buy into his account of modal objects and the epistemic capacities needed for meaningful access to them. And like many expensive and intricate commodities, it proved to be fragile when subjected to the stress of criticism. Heidegger and Heideggerians have, on the whole, not welcomed Husserl's proposal; indeed, as we have seen, they have scornfully dismissed it. Nonetheless, they have retained Husserl's habit of laying claim to modally robust phenomenological doctrines. If Heidegger's contemporary apologists refuse their Husserlian inheritance, then either they need to give up the practice of making modally qualified generalizations in phenomenology or they owe us an account of the basis upon which such modally qualified generalizations are to be warranted. The exemplarist proposal I have sketched here certainly does not follow Husserl in all its details; by comparison, it is metaphysically and epistemically modest. But its spirit is Husserlian in two critical respects. First, it retains the conviction that careful attentive phenomenological description of suitably selected exemplars yields a form of evidence that can be used to warrant modally inflected phenomenological results. And second, it undertakes to be clear and explicit about how such results can be justified.[26]

NOTES

1   References to Dilthey's works are given, where possible, to volume and page of Wilhelm Dilthey, *Selected Works*, eds. R. Makreel and F. Rodi (Princeton: Princeton University Press, 1985–).
2   Dilthey, *Works* III, 197–8.
3   Dilthey, *Works* I, 85.
4   See, for instance, "The Categories of Life," Dilthey, *Works*, III, 248–64.
5   "The entities which correspond to them require different kinds of primary interrogation respectively: any entity is either a '*who*' (existence) or a '*what*' (presence at hand in the broadest sense)" (45).
6   These modal terms sometimes appear explicitly, but they need not do so; the verbs "can" or "must," for example, can be used to express modal claims.
7   "To the things themselves!" See, for instance, Edmund Husserl, *Logical Investigations, vol. II,* trans. J. N. Findlay, ed. D. Moran (New York: Routledge,

2001), pt. I, Introduction and chapter II; or Edmund Husserl, *Ideas Pertaining to a Pure Phenomenology and to a Phenomenological Philosophy, Bk. I*, trans. F. Kersten (Norwell: Klewer Academic Publishers, 1998), §19. I leave Husserl's slogan untranslated to avoid any misleading association with Kant's notion of a "thing in itself" (*Ding an sich*). Husserlian phenomenology takes exactly no interest in things in themselves; its interest is with the appearing and appearances of things. Husserl insists that any account of such appearings must be oriented by a description of the facts (*Sache*) as they present themselves in experience.

8   See in particular Dilthey's 1894 essay, "Ideas Concerning a Descriptive and Analytical Psychology." At this time, this text is not yet included in the Princeton edition of Dilthey's works. A few key excerpts are translated in Wilhelm Dilthey, *Dilthey: Selected Writings*, trans. and ed. H. P. Rickman (Cambridge: Cambridge University Press, 1979), 88–97; for the full text in translation, see Wilhelm Dilthey, *Descriptive Psychology and Historical Understanding*, trans. R. Zaner (The Hague: Martinus Nijhoff, 1977), 23–120.

9   Or "Flato," if you are one of my friends who takes offence at this caricature.

10 *Husserl, Ideas* I, §6.

11 Ibid.

12 The debate over this question was inaugurated by John Haugeland, "Heidegger on Being a Person," *Nous* 25 (1982), 15–26. The objections to Haugeland's position are laid out concisely in Hubert Dreyfus, *Being-in-the-World: A Commentary on Heidegger's* Being and Time, Division I (Cambridge, MA: MIT Press, 1991), 14. For a more extensive analysis, see Carman Taylor, *Heidegger's Analytic: Interpretation, Discourse, and Authenticity in* Being and Time (Cambridge: Cambridge University Press, 2003), 35–43.

13 For example, Pierre Keller introduces the term "Dasein" by putting it in parentheses following the term "human being." Pierre Keller, *Husserl and Heidegger on Human Understanding* (Cambridge: Cambridge University Press, 1999), 100; see also Dermot Moran, *Introduction to Phenomenology* (London: Routledge, 2000), 193, 206.

14 Frederick Olafson, *Heidegger and the Philosophy of Mind* (New Haven: Yale University Press, 1987), 53.

15 Olafson, *Heidegger Philosophy of Mind*, xvi.

16 George Steiner, *Martin Heidegger* (Chicago: University of Chicago Press, 1978), 80.

17 This is not the only approach that has been taken to the transcendental tropes of *Being and Time*. One might dismiss Heidegger's transcendental formulations as an unfortunate accommodation to the predominant neo-Kantianism idiom of the day, or as an alien presence that Heidegger soon saw fit to excise, or even deliberately set out to reduce to absurdity. For a version of the latter suggestion, see Raymond Guess, *Outside Ethics* (Princeton: Princeton University Press, 2005), 57ff.

18 Henry Allison, *Kant's Transcendental Idealism: An Interpretation and Defense* (New Haven: Yale University Press, 1983), 10; Allison's initial definition actually characterizes epistemic conditions as conditions necessary

for the *representation* of an object or objective state of affairs, which brings it somewhat closer to Carman's notion of an epistemic condition.

19 It is worth remarking that analogs of these alternatives can be found in Kant's own version of the transcendental project. Kant seems to provide different answers to this question for different epistemic conditions. Space and time are said to be specifically forms of *human* intuition, whereas the categories are said to be necessary for any being that engages in judgment. In both cases, this is contrasted to the possibility of a divine intellect, which is not subject to the same conditions, but the boundaries of the class contrasted to the divine intellect are defined differently in the two cases.

20 For an illuminating clarification of the notion of an epistemic condition, and a review of the controversies surrounding it, see Henry Allison, "Transcendental Idealism: A Retrospective," in *Idealism and Freedom: Essays on Kant's Theoretical and Practical Philosophy* (Cambridge: Cambridge University Press, 1996), 3–26.

21 The *locus classicus* for this line of thinking is of course Saul Kripke, *Naming and Necessity* (Cambridge, MA: Harvard University Press, 1980).

22 For a penetrating discussion of exactly this question, see Taylor Carman's essay, "The Question of Being" in this volume.

23 For examples in *Being and Time*, see 51, 198, 382, 401. The formula occurs in many passages in *Basic Problems*; see inter alia GA 24: 7, 21.

24 Baruch Spinoza, *Ethics*, Bk. I, Def. 3, trans. S. Shirley, *Baruch Spinoza: The Ethics and Selected Letters* (Indianapolis: Hackett, 1982), 31.

25 For an important piece of supporting textual evidence, see *Being and Time*, 89: "The term for the Being of an entity that is in itself, is '*substantia*.'"

26 A much earlier version of this material was presented at a 2006 workshop of the *Transcendental Philosophy and Naturalism* research project. I am grateful to the late Mark Sacks, and to the other participants in the workshop, for their comments and objections on that occasion, and to the Arts and Humanities Research Council (UK) for its support of the TPN project. Many other friends and colleagues have provided feedback on subsequent drafts. Among them, I would like to thank members of the University of Essex Heidegger *Werkstatt*, participants in the post-Kantian European Philosophy Seminar at Oxford University, Mark Wrathall, and Ryan Hickerson.

5   Heidegger on Space and Spatiality

The sections of *Being and Time* devoted to spatiality (22–4) serve as the closing sections of chapter 3 of Division I. That lengthy chapter is central to Heidegger's project in Division I, as it lays out in considerable detail his notion of the "worldhood of the world," a key aspect, in turn, of Dasein's way of being as being-in-the-world. More narrowly, the discussion of spatiality appears immediately after Heidegger's detailed critique of Descartes' conception of worldhood and its appeal to the primacy of extended, material substance. The juxtaposition of Descartes' and Heidegger's own conception of Dasein's spatiality is striking, no doubt deliberately so. After all, Descartes was a geometer of considerable renown (witness Cartesian coordinates) and that geometrical understanding of space is crucially relevant to the broader conception of reality and our knowledge of it, which Descartes develops in his philosophical writings. Indeed, Descartes' fundamental notion of material substance is a spatial-geometrical one, constituted by the idea of *extension* and its various modifications (motion, divisibility, and so on). Descartes' material world is fundamentally a world whose spatiality is articulable in precise geometrical terms, and whatever eludes or evades those terms is to be dismissed as in some way second-rate, subjective, or illusory, vestiges of our confused, prescientific take on things.

Consider the following passage from the Third Meditation, wherein Descartes compares his "two ideas" of the sun:

For example, I find within myself two distinct ideas of the sun. One idea is drawn, as it were, from the senses. Now it is this idea which, of all those that I take to be derived from outside of me, is most in need of examination. By means

Versions of this paper were presented at the annual meetings of the International Society for Phenomenological Studies and the American Society for Existential Phenomenology. I am grateful to audiences at both meetings for helpful comments and criticisms, and for averting many more serious misunderstandings than may still be present in this paper. I would especially like to thank William Bracken for comments and criticisms.

of this idea the sun appears to me to be quite small. But there is another idea, one derived from astronomical reasoning, that is, it is elicited from certain notions that are innate in me, or else is fashioned by me in some other way. Through this idea the sun is shown to be several times larger than the earth. Both ideas surely cannot resemble the same sun existing outside of me; and reason convinces me that the idea that seems to have emanated from the sun itself from so close is the very one that least resembles the sun.[1]

In this passage, Descartes compares two ideas, one primarily perceptual in origin and content, the second "derived from astronomical reasoning," where one of them, the first, is shown to be wildly inaccurate in terms of its "resemblance" to the "sun itself." Implicit in this comparison of two ideas is a broader comparison of the forms of spatiality at work in each of the two ideas: the perceptual idea of the sun involves a perspectival, agent-centered spatial orientation. The sun appears small – is represented as being small – because of the tremendous distance between the perceiver and the celestial body, but that distance, and so the effect of distance on apparent size, are not accounted for in the idea: the idea represents what is in reality a large object as a small one, and so does not resemble how the sun really is. The second, more accurate idea, by contrast, gets the spatial relations right, as it represents the sun as a distant but massive object. Significantly, this second idea is "fashioned" in a manner entirely distinct from the workings of perceptual experience, from anything pertaining to our ordinary experience and activity: what Descartes labels here "astronomical reasoning" represents reality in ways that prescind from the reasoner's own location in, and involvement with, space and spatial relationships. The space of extension is a space that is not viewed or inhabited, but only represented via a process of reasoning whose location has been factored out completely. Accordingly, the spatial representations Descartes champions are well suited to the disembodied subjectivity he advocates in the *Meditations* (the Third Meditation still operates within the general strictures of the Method of Doubt, with Descartes' meditator knowing only that he exists as a "thinking thing," and the status of geometry as the essential form of the material world is vouchsafed in the Fifth Meditation, prior to Descartes' establishing that he even has a body). As an immaterial substance, the Cartesian mind is not located in space; it does not inhabit space, except indirectly by being conjoined with a material body that is spatially located but does not represent space at all.

   Heidegger's discussion of spatiality can be read as challenging this Cartesian picture, and Heidegger's strategy is pretty much the same strategy as the one he pursues throughout the opening chapters of Division I, the third chapter especially. That strategy is one of establishing the derivative, "founded" character of the central concepts and conceits of the traditional picture of the world and our relation to it, such that they have neither the primacy nor the autonomy that the traditional picture ascribes to them. As secondary and derivative, Heidegger argues that the traditional picture "passes over" phenomena that underwrite the intelligibility of that picture, and in ways that the picture cannot accommodate. At the outset of the spatiality sections, Heidegger makes it clear that the Cartesian picture of spatiality has been at issue all along:

In connection with our first preliminary sketch of being-in (see Section 12), we had to contrast Dasein with a way of being in space which we call "insideness." This expression means that an entity which is itself extended is closed round by the extended boundaries of something that is likewise extended. The entity inside and that which closes it round are both present-at-hand in space. (101)

Heidegger's goal in the spatiality section is in part to challenge the applicability of this notion of "insideness" to Dasein's distinctive form of spatiality. It is clear from this challenge that Heidegger's critique of Descartes is more radical than simply a reversal of the relation between the two "ideas" Descartes juxtaposes in the *Meditations*. That is, Heidegger is not out to establish the priority of a conception of space projected from "inside" the same space Descartes' disembodied subject represents from the "outside." Rather, his aim is to describe a form of spatiality – Dasein's spatiality – that does not appeal to containment *at all*: "Yet even if we deny that Dasein has any such insideness in a spatial receptacle, this does not in principle exclude it from having any spatiality at all, but merely keeps open the way for seeing the kind of spatiality which is constitutive for Dasein" (101).

Notice here Heidegger's efforts to distinguish the spatiality of Dasein as fundamentally different in kind from the spatiality of containment, such that Dasein's spatiality must *exclude* entirely other forms or kinds. These efforts are redoubled throughout the spatiality discussion, whose trajectory we will endeavor to trace. In following out this trajectory, I will raise a number of worries concerning the success of Heidegger's account that turn precisely on this kind of exclusivity. Heidegger's account of spatiality, though illuminating in places, ultimately bottoms out in a set of concepts whose meaning and import are difficult to make out. In other words, what Heidegger appeals to as the *sources* of Dasein's spatiality do not appear to be properly *spatial* notions at all, and so are ill suited as a basis for deriving or founding any (other) form of spatiality. When Heidegger writes that Dasein's spatiality "cannot signify anything like occurrence at a position in 'world-space,'" (104) his restriction is so severe as to invite the question of whether he is any longer describing a form of spatiality at all.

The worries I wish to raise about Heidegger's conception of Dasein's spatiality engage a more general set of worries concerning the place of the *body* in Heidegger's phenomenology of everydayness. A striking feature of the spatiality discussion that I think is responsible for much of the confusion and difficulty is the scattered, guarded, scare-quoted, cryptic character of Heidegger's remarks about Dasein's embodiment. This is, after all, the place in *Being and Time* where he says, frustratingly, that "[Dasein's] 'bodily nature' hides a whole problematic of its own," (108) about which he adds only that it will not be treated in *Being and Time*.[2] Other references to the body in these sections are likewise vague and allusive. Indeed, in his reading of the spatiality discussion, Dreyfus goes so far as to say that, for Heidegger, "the body is not essential," which is an odd thing for someone committed to the primacy of "skillful coping" to hold.[3] And in his 1996 paper, "Existence and Self-Understanding in *Being and Time*," William Blattner argues more generally that we must "accept that Heidegger is operating with a subterranean form of dualism" between "natural and self-interpreting characteristics" of Dasein.[4] He argues further that this dualism is integral to one of Heidegger's principal claims in *Being and Time*, namely that Dasein is (and only is) its ability-to-be. I want to suggest here that Blattner's detection of a "subterranean dualism" may be a way into diagnosing the difficulties that beset Heidegger's discussion of spatiality. Nowhere, I think, is the "subterranean dualism" Blattner describes closer to the surface in Division I than in the spatiality sections. There is no small irony in this, given the already-noted proximity of these sections to Heidegger's extended critique of Descartes' ontology of material substance. That Heidegger's own subsequent discussion betrays a continued commitment to a kind of dualism suggests that he is perhaps still gripped by the kind of thinking *Being and Time* is officially committed to overcoming.

Heidegger's discussion of spatiality begins more or less where it should, given the discussion leading up to it: Heidegger's appeal to the spatiality of *regions* – of significant *places* normatively characterized – as prior to homogeneously articulated objective space is unsurprising, as it recapitulates the already-asserted priority of readiness-to-hand over mere presence-at-hand. Just as what Dasein "proximally and for the most part" encounters are not mere things – chunks of matter objectively defined – but equipment, the "wherein" of those encounters is likewise manifest in similar terms. Indeed, Heidegger begins by noting that the very idea of something's being ready-*to-hand* (or "available," to cite another translation of *zuhanden*) implies a kind of proximity: "What is ready-to-hand in our everyday dealings has the character of *closeness*. To be exact, this closeness of equipment has already been intimated in the term 'readiness-to-hand,' which expresses the being of equipment." Heidegger notes, however, that "every entity that is 'to hand' has a different closeness, which is not to be ascertained by measuring distances. This closeness regulates itself in terms of circumspectively 'calculative' manipulating and using" (102). What Heidegger means here is that the "closeness" ascertained in circumspective dealings is "regulated" by the practical proprieties of the situation: what counts as close depends on the equipment being used, as well as the task in which it is put to use. As I sit working at my desk, some things need to be literally at hand (the keyboard upon which my hands rest, the coffee cup just to the right, and so on), while the proximity of my chair requires its being in contact with my backside. My desk light is the right distance when it is farther away, just out of reach at the back of my desk but nonetheless close. That each item of equipment is in the right place, at the right distance from me, is not a function of its measured distance from some zero point, even if some such measured distance can be determined in each case. Different items of equipment *belong* in different places, so that each item of equipment "has been essentially fitted up and installed, set up, and put to rights. Equipment has its *place*, or else it 'lies around'; this must be distinguished in principle from just occurring at random in some spatial position" (102).

Space is thus primarily manifest not in terms of a multidimensional container, which can be mapped via a coordinate system, but in terms of significant places: "Such a place and such a multiplicity of places are not to be interpreted as the 'where' of some random being-present-at-hand of things. In each case the place is the definite 'there' or 'yonder' of an item of equipment which *belongs somewhere*." (102) Things are manifest spatially in terms of what Heidegger calls the "region," as the "'wither,' which makes it possible for equipment to belong somewhere, and which we circumspectively keep in view ahead of us in our concernful dealings" (103). Heidegger's point here is that this kind of belonging, such that equipment can be in its place (or out of place), is more basic than, and so not definable in terms of, any set of purely numerical spatial relationships:

A three-dimensional multiplicity of possible positions which gets filled up with things present-at-hand is never proximally given. This dimensionality of space is still veiled in the spatiality of the ready-to-hand. The "above" is what is "on the ceiling"; the "below" is what is "on the floor"; the "behind" is what is "at the door"; all "wheres" are discovered and circumspectively interpreted as we go our ways in everyday dealings; they are not ascertained and catalogued by the observational measurement of space. (103)

What Heidegger here calls "the spatiality of the ready-to-hand" can neither be reduced to nor explained in terms of whatever is revealed by "the observational measurement of space." Observational measurement does not provide a more accurate take on what is initially revealed circumspectively – a better "idea" or representation, in Descartes' sense – but reveals a different kind of spatiality altogether. Quantitatively determined spatial relations are fundamentally different from the kind of practical spatial relations that suffuse Dasein's everyday activity: the *near* and *far*, the *above* and *below*, the *over there* and *right here*, the *up* and *down*, and so on of everydayness are not numerically precise notions, and to treat them in such terms is to distort their meaning. What is *near* or *far*, for example, depends on the situation, the entities at issue, and the people making the estimates. If I'm talking to someone in California about where I live in relation to the university where I work, I may say that Morgantown is "not far at all," but if I'm explaining to my son Henry why we cannot get some desired item that very day, I may point out that the item is "all the way in Morgantown," thereby suggesting that it is very far away indeed. While I could replace what I said in each case with a precise mileage – thirty-eight miles, say – that would not retain the practical significance of my original locutions.

The spatiality of regions and places underwrites the entirety of Dasein's circumspective dealings. What have their place are not just hammers and screwdrivers, coffee cups and desk lamps; rather, "anything constantly ready-to-hand of which circumspective being-in-the-world takes account beforehand, has its place." Heidegger continues:

> The "where" of its readiness-to-hand is put to account as a matter for concern, and oriented towards the rest of what is ready-to-hand. Thus the sun, whose light and warmth are in everyday use, has its own places – sunrise, midday, sunset, midnight; these are discovered in circumspection and treated distinctively in terms of changes in the usability of what the sun bestows. (103)

Heidegger's appeal to the sun recalls Descartes' "two ideas," though now without any urge to dismiss or discount how the sun is manifest in everydayness. The everyday sun is not something represented – taken, or judged, to be something small, when in fact it is large – but a familiar, indeed central, aspect of our everyday activity, circumspectively accounted for in terms of a series of places that lack astronomical significance. Whatever the merits of astronomical reasoning – and there are many – the correction of our everyday reckoning of the sun's position does not number among them.

Where the discussion of spatiality becomes murkier is in the sequel to this opening foray, when Heidegger adduces the constitutive characteristics of Dasein that found the regional spatiality initially described: "To encounter the ready-to-hand in its environmental space remains ontically possible only because Dasein itself is 'spatial' with regard to its being-in-the-world." (104) Described in the abstract, there is nothing particularly surprising about this maneuver on Heidegger's part. After all, the opening discussion of readiness-to-hand, which these sections parallel, leads ultimately to the appeal to Dasein's for-the-sake-of as the linchpin or fulcrum for the entirety of the referential totality. So, in parallel, the spatiality of regions is likewise underwritten by something pertaining more narrowly to Dasein. As Dreyfus sees it, the problem is that Heidegger's account becomes overly narrow and individualistic: as Heidegger continues, he fails to "stick to the priority of the presence of equipment in public, workshop space – which Dasein is always in and which has its regions, its places, and its accessibility to anyone."[5] Instead, his account seems to concern the "nearness or farness of specific equipment from a particular Dasein,"[6] and this is what incurs the risk of residual Cartesianism. As I see it, the problem arises from how Heidegger explicates the notions of nearness and farness at some points in §23, so that they no longer appear to be *spatial* notions at all.

Heidegger characterizes Dasein's spatiality – the spatiality that underwrites the spatiality of regions – in terms of two interlocking dimensions: *orientation* (Stambaugh translates Heidegger's term as "directionality") and what Macquarrie and Robinson translate as *de-severance* (Dreyfus opts for "dis-stance," while Stambaugh uses "de-distancing"):

> Dasein, however, is "in" the world in the sense that it deals with entities encountered within-the-world, and does so concernfully and with familiarity. So if spatiality belongs to it in any way, that is possible only because of this being-in. But its spatiality shows the characters of *de-severance* and *directionality*. (104–5)

Heidegger addresses these two notions in order, with the lion's share of his discussion being devoted to de-severance. As de-severance, more than directionality, raises the worries I wish to discuss, the bulk of my discussion will likewise concentrate on this first notion. Heidegger says that "Dasein is essentially de-severant: it lets any entity be encountered close by as the entity which it is" (105). What this remark indicates is de-severance's role in enabling Dasein's distinctive form of proximity to things. Crucial in this remark are the closing words – as the entity that it is – as they indicate that the kind of proximity in question here is not to be understood metrically. De-severance does not name Dasein's ability to get physically closer to or farther from objects – animals, heat-seeking missiles, even falling rocks can do that sort of thing – but rather the way in which Dasein can get close to things in terms of apprehending them, understanding them as the things they are. This twist on the notion of proximity again marks a parallel with the earlier chapters of Division I, as it accords with Heidegger's efforts early on to distinguish the notion of "in" in the formula being-in-the-word from the "in" of spatial containment. Indeed, Heidegger might be understood here as simply re-emphasizing this "non-containment" sense of Dasein's being-in: the proximity enabled by de-severance is the proximity characteristic of *involvement* and *engagement*, of circumspective concern, rather than physical nearness and distance.

In keeping with the general account of everydayness in Division I, Dasein's de-severance is manifest primarily in practical terms:

> Proximally and for the most part, de-severing is a circumspective bringing-close – bringing something close by, in the sense of procuring it, putting it in readiness, having it to hand. But certain ways in which entities are discovered in a purely cognitive manner also have the character of bringing them close. *In Dasein there lies an essential tendency towards closeness.* (105)

It is clear from this passage, with its mixture of bodily and cognitive forms of proximity, that "bringing-close" is not to be understood in metrical terms. To be close in the sense of de-severing is to be available for use; something is close when it is situated so as to be taken up into Dasein's ongoing activities, regardless of its physical distance in relation to Dasein. The proximity of items of equipment is not a function of their physical distance, and so the reckoning of such distances need not figure into Dasein's circumspective bringing-close: "De-severing does not necessarily imply any explicit estimation of the farness of something ready-to-hand in relation to Dasein. Above all, remoteness never gets taken as a distance" (105).

Though proximity and remoteness in the sense of de-severance is not a function of physical distance (indeed, physical distances may not even be involved if something is brought close in "a purely cognitive manner"), de-severance underwrites Dasein's everyday reckoning of distance:

> If farness is to be estimated, this is done relatively to deseverances in which everyday Dasein maintains itself. Though these estimates may be imprecise and variable if we try to compute them, in the everydayness of Dasein they have their *own definiteness* which is thoroughly intelligible. We say that to go over yonder is "a good walk," "a stone's throw," or "as long as it takes to smoke a pipe." (105)

That such estimates are "done relatively to deseverances" means that they are informed by the different ways in which Dasein brings things close: when planning to travel by air, a city several hundred miles away may be not far at all (especially compared to one located on another continent), whereas the convenience store two miles away may be too far if the road to get there is unsafe for walking. These kinds of reckonings are "thoroughly intelligible" without being "computed" in quantitative terms. It would make no sense to fault my saying of New York City that it is "not far" as I set off on a flight from Pittsburgh by pointing out that it is, after all, significantly farther away than the convenience store I just the other day claimed was "too far" from home really to be all that convenient. Such an attempt at criticism would come off as little more than a feeble joke that blithely ignores the context sensitivity of such locutions as "far" and "near." Indeed, to treat such an observation as anything more than a joke would betray just the kind of philosophical confusion Heidegger wishes to expose in *Being and Time*, the kind of confusion that leads Descartes to discredit our everyday reckoning of the sun as an inaccurate "idea" of its size. Heidegger insists that "the objective distances of things present-at-hand do not coincide with the remoteness and closeness of what is ready-to-hand within-the-world," and so reckonings of nearness and farness are not covert judgments of such objective distances.

All of this is not to say that everyday Dasein does not – or cannot – go in for exactitude, but doing so cannot take the place of the closeness of de-severance:

> Though we may know these distances exactly, this knowledge remains blind; it does not have the function of discovering the environment circumspectively and bringing it close; this knowledge is used only in and for a concernful being which does not measure stretches – a being towards the world that "matters" to one. (106)

The "knowledge" Heidegger speaks of here is "blind" if it is conceived of as sheared off from the kind of practical reckoning afforded by de-severance. If I know only the objective distance between two points, I cannot judge those points as "nearby" to, or "distant" from, one another just like that. There is no context-independent rule such that points x and y are close if and only if they are less than distance d from one another (and even within a context, there is no precise d either). To make such a judgment, I need to be oriented to a situation in which such a judgment might be made: am I reaching for a screwdriver that I stupidly left in the basement? Am I setting out on a walk in the field below my house (and am I going alone or with a young child who will undoubtedly ask to be carried within minutes of setting out)? Am I planning a trip by car and trying to figure out where to stop for the night? Am I worrying over whether or not a tree in the landscape photograph I'm composing is too close to be rendered in focus? And so on.

Consider Heidegger's favored example in *Being and Time*: the workshop. Here is a setting where explicit measurements play a significant role (just consider the adage, "Measure twice, cut once"). As Heidegger himself notes: "The spatiality of what we proximally encounter in circumspection can become a theme for circumspection itself, as well as a task for calculation and measurement, as in building and survey-ing" (111–12). A well-equipped workshop will usually contain myriad instruments for measuring length – rulers, tape measures, calipers, t-squares, and so on – and these instruments will figure centrally in a wide range of activities and projects. Use of such instruments allows for the determination of lengths and distances with varying degrees of precision, and just how precise one needs to be will vary with the proj-ect one has undertaken (sometimes, measuring to the nearest inch will suffice, while other tasks may have much smaller tolerances). Though things are manifest in the workshop in a way that begins to suggest the present-at-hand – explicit, objective measurements, coupled with a demand for constancy and exactitude (the right measurement is one that anyone determining it will get) – any such suggestion overlooks the way in which these measurements are grounded in Dasein's circum-spective concern.[7] Dasein is the being who institutes *standards* of mea-surement in the first place and insists on those standards in its ongoing activity; the degree of exactitude of a measurement is a function of Dasein's concern, and there is no such thing as exactitude in and of itself. Even the basic determination of measurement – the laying down of a ruler, the stretching of a tape measure, the spreading of calipers – presupposes a more basic orientation toward both the instruments and the material to be measured: each of these must be "brought close" in the practical sense in order to be measured, and how they are measured (to the nearest inch, the nearest millimeter, front to back, end to end, and so on) accords with the way in which they have been de-severed. Measurements, in other words, presuppose the *practice* of measuring, and such practices are sustained by a being – Dasein – who *cares* about measuring. "What is ready-to-hand in the environment is certainly not present-at-hand for an eternal observer exempt from Dasein: but it is encountered in Dasein's circumspectively concernful everydayness" (106). An "eternal observer," Heidegger suggests, would lack a practical, de-severant orientation toward any situation. Such an observer would not, and could not, be one that measures, and so whatever the nature of its observations, it is not clear that they would be *spatial* at all.

So where do difficulties emerge in Heidegger's account? What is it about his account of de-severance in particular that invites charges of a lingering, residual dualism? After all, even though Heidegger rejects any rendering of "near" and "far" as simply a function of the physical distance from our bodies, what he offers as primary still seems to appeal to our engaged, bodily activity:

When one is primarily and even exclusively oriented towards remotenesses as measured distances, the primordial spatiality of being-in is concealed. That which is presumably "closest" is by no means that which is at the smallest distance "from us." It lies in that which is deserved to an average extent when we reach for it, grasp it, or look at it. (106–7)

Reaching and grasping do not sound like the work of Cartesian subject, but precisely the kind of worldly agent Heidegger argues is primary. Moreover, his appeal to an "average extent" here would appear to diminish further any appearance of subjectivism, especially if construed in overly individualistic terms. Things show up as near or far in an average way, in ways that are predictably similar for pretty much anyone and everyone. As Dreyfus puts it, "The equipment directly accessible to me is what anyone would have accessible if he or she were in my place."[8] While this claim may require some qualification to allow for variations in accessibility (what is within reach in the kitchen is markedly different for me than it is for my wife and children), still Heidegger's point remains. Configurations of equipment, the layout of rooms and buildings, the slope of sidewalks and passageways, the width of aisles and entrances, the design of parks and playgrounds: all of these incorporate an average, whether explicitly or not, so as to be graspable, negotiable, inhabitable, utilizable by pretty much everyone and anyone; even where the use of equipment presupposes a highly specialized skill, there is still an "average extent" in terms of how it is brought close and utilized, and even where "special accommodation" is involved (wheelchair ramps, special bars and handles, and so on), such accommodation still reflects an average, typical, or standard way of being special.

Tensions only begin to emerge in Heidegger's account of de-severance insofar as he explicates it as coordinate with Dasein's *attentiveness* toward aspects of its surrounding. Consider his example of wearing spectacles:

When, for instance, a man wears a pair of spectacles which are so close to him distantially that they are "sitting on his nose," they are environmentally more remote from him than the picture on the opposite wall. Such equipment has so little closeness that often it is proximally quite impossible to find. (107)

I find this example to be difficult to parse. While there may be occasions where one's glasses do go missing because of their proximity,[9] this does not seem to be generally true. That is, my glasses strike me as generally more accessible than what I am looking at through them, even when, or even though, I'm not paying much attention to them. I can reach for them, make minor adjustments to them, check the lenses for dust or scratches, far more easily than I can reach for and adjust the picture on the far wall, even if the picture is what I'm paying attention to.

Indeed, paying attention would appear to be an odd criterion for remoteness and nearness for Heidegger to choose, given the emphasis

on the spatiality of circumspective concern. That is, in the opening section, Heidegger had characterized nearness and remoteness in terms
of practical engagement – "This closeness regulates itself in terms of
circumspectively 'calculative' manipulating and using" (102) – but a
hallmark of his account of "skillful coping" is the *transparency* and
withdrawal of the equipment with which I'm engaged. Given the glasses
example, that would mean that the hammer I'm transparently coping
with becomes remote by dint of the fact that I'm no longer attending
to it. That not only sounds odd, but contradicts what Heidegger had
previously suggested: when I grasp the hammer, raise and lower it so as
to drive in the nail, I have brought it as close as can be, even though it
tends to "withdraw" in the course of my activity. Heidegger, however,
reinforces this new construal of nearness and remoteness in terms of
attentiveness in a second example that closely follows the one with the
spectacles:

Equipment for seeing – and likewise for hearing, such as the telephone receiver –
has what we have designated as the inconspicuousness of the proximally ready-
to-hand. So too, for instance, does the street, as equipment for walking. One
feels the touch of it at every step as one walks; it is seemingly the closest and
realest of all that is ready-to-hand, and it slides itself, as it were, along certain
portions of one's body – the soles of one's feet. And yet it is farther remote than
the acquaintance whom one encounters "on the street" at a "remoteness" of
twenty paces when one is taking such a walk. (107)

Notice first the way this example involves a kind of variability and rela-
tivity that threatens the public character of practical space. Presumably,
the acquaintance is close to me because I'm noticing him, perhaps soliciting his attention or returning a greeting. For someone standing next to
me, just noticing the rock in his shoe and paying no regard to whoever
may happen to be twenty paces away, my acquaintance is not in any
way close.

   Dreyfus, for his part, is clearly puzzled by the variation in criteria
Heidegger adduces in his account:

It seems that for Heidegger for something to be near it must be both something
I am coping with and something absorbing my attention. It cannot be just the
street under my feet, nor can it be a friend far away in Paris no matter how
intense my concern. *What is near is that with which I am currently absorbedly
coping.*[10]

I'm not sure it's right to say that for Heidegger "a friend far away in Paris"
cannot be close, even closest to me. Recall something else Heidegger
says that I noted previously: "But certain ways in which entities are discovered in a purely cognitive manner also have the character of bringing
them close" (105). But this is no doubt puzzling: if I'm reaching for a

beloved coffee cup given to me by the absent friend, thereupon thinking of the friend as I reach, which is closer to me – the cup or my friend? Are we not in danger of mixing and matching different *kinds* of proximity and remoteness?

There are further problems. Despite Dreyfus' heroic effort to meld Heidegger's criteria through adverbial dexterity, he does not seem to recognize the extent of the difficulty. The problem is not merely one of trying to mix and match two separate criteria (which matters more, the coping or the attention; do the two vary jointly or independently, and so on) but that the criteria *pull against each other*. To be absorbedly coping is precisely not to be paying attention in the sense of explicitly noticing or taking account of. Thus, when Heidegger says:

Circumspective concern decides as to the closeness and farness of what is proximally ready-to-hand environmentally. Whatever this concern dwells alongside beforehand is what is closest, and this is what regulates our de-severances. (107)

It is not clear how to understand "dwelling alongside" and how this "regulates our de-severances," given Heidegger's lately introduced examples: are we to understand "alongside" in terms of practical-bodily proximity or in terms of being at the forefront of someone's attention, and if sometimes one, sometimes the other, how are the two interrelated? How can both serve to ground the more objective, "de-worlded" form of spatiality that Heidegger argues is secondary?

I want to make clear that my questions and worries here are not the same as those raised by Dreyfus in his commentary, even if his worries and mine lead to the same conclusion. Indeed, Dreyfus' worries about the overly individualistic character of Heidegger's account of de-severance strike me as misplaced. While Heidegger's account does reveal a kind of ineliminable indexicality in Dasein's spatiality – *near* and *far*, for example, are not absolute notions, but relative to agents' interests or orientations – that alone does not undermine the public intelligibility of everyday spatiality. As Jeff Malpas has pointed out in his discussion of Dreyfus' worries, any sense of de-severance understood as an essential, ontological dimension of Dasein has to be realized or instantiated in an ontical sense, and those realizations or instantiations will have some measure of indexicality, as they will involve being at some particular location in public space, undertaking some project rather than others:

The structure of equipmentality is thus prior to any particular individual being-there since it is indeed a public structure, but it always emerges into salience in the particular activity of individual being-there. Its being public is not a matter of its standing in some relation to some generalized form of being-there, as if equipment was always already taken up by a "public" mode of being that was constantly engaged – being-there, in its generality, is no more capable of concrete engagement than the *concept* of being-there is capable of using a hammer.[11]

My worry instead concerns Heidegger's account of what Malpas here refers to as the way the "public structure" of equipmentality "emerges into salience" for any individual agent, since Heidegger sometimes characterizes that "emergence" primarily in mental, cognitive terms (noticing, attending to, having in mind), rather than engaging in a more bodily manner (reaching for, grasping, manipulating, navigating). In what sense are these the *same* sense of proximity, and if they are not the same, which is more basic?

Heidegger's explication of proximity in terms of attention – what I am absorbed in or by in a cognitive sense – *does* threaten the public character of space in the way Dreyfus worries, as the individualistic nature of such a form of proximity goes beyond mere indexicality. It is not just that what is close to me is different from what is close to you – because each of us is cognitively attending to something different – but that these respective "distances" are not publicly accessible *as spatial*: what is close to you in this sense will not be manifest to me as being further from me (because it is close to you), as it – and your relation to it – may not be manifest to me at all. (And if you and I are both thinking of the same thing, are we equally close to that thing? Does proximity in this sense admit of degrees? If we both spot a mutual friend across the street at the same time, is that friend closer to each of us to the same degree than the pavement below our feet? (And what if you're wearing heels?)) The problem here is not just one of how to mix and match these different senses of proximity, but also one of how to found or derive the more homogeneous form of space that Heidegger argues is secondary. If the proximity of attention is not publicly accessible (or at least not in a manner that can be consistently coordinated in the way the proximity of equipment can) and does not readily admit of any metric, in what sense can "the space of nature" be derived from it?

In his provocative essay, "Being and the Living," Didier Franck writes:

Now it is essential – although this necessity was something that Heidegger never took into account – that *Dasein* have hands so that, all metaphors aside, the being of the being that it is could be named being-at-hand.[12]

That Heidegger fails to confront – let alone thematize – the necessity of Dasein's incarnation is evident in the way his account of Dasein's spatiality bottoms out with a notion of de-severance that is only ambiguously spatial in nature. That Heidegger makes fundamental a notion of proximity that is divorced (or divorceable) from any form of bodily proximity is indicative of his ambivalence concerning Dasein's embodiment.

But a more resolute reckoning with Dasein's "bodily nature" may have forced Heidegger to rethink the kinds of exclusions and hierarchies that are central to his account of Dasein's spatiality (and being-in-the-world more generally). Recall that Heidegger begins his discussion of spatiality by denying "that Dasein has any such insideness in a spatial receptacle" and by insisting later that "spatiality," when applied to Dasein, "cannot signify *anything like* occurrence at a position in 'world-space'" (last emphasis mine). If the "bodily nature" of Dasein were treated not just as a source of problems but as an essential dimension of its existence, Heidegger could not maintain these sorts of exclusions and distinctions. Heidegger says that "as Dasein goes along its ways, it does not measure off a stretch of space as a corporeal thing which is present-at-hand" (106). There is something right about this, of course, insofar as we go wrong in thinking about human existence in exclusively or even primarily thing-like terms, but the problem here is that Heidegger's fear of the category of presence-at-hand leads him to avoid corporeality altogether and so at the same time to miss or underestimate the way more container-like notions of space do figure into our practical engagement with the world. Dasein as Dasein does, contrary to what Heidegger insists, "devour the kilometers": our being located *within*, and not just oriented *toward*, space is part and parcel of how the everyday world is disclosed to us and this is part and parcel of our being disclosed to ourselves and one another as *bodily* beings. Everyday space is revealed in a practical-circumspective way, but also as something that surrounds us, includes us, even, dare I say, contains us, something we are *within* in just the way Heidegger wants to deny. Had Heidegger confronted this, his account of spatiality may have been far less fraught, but it may also have not allowed the kinds of derivation relations and priority claims he wants.[13]

NOTES

1   René Descartes, *Meditations on First Philosophy*, trans. D. Cress, 3rd edition (Indianapolis: Hackett, 1993), 27.
2   I have discussed Heidegger's allusion to such a hidden "problematic" elsewhere. See my "Heidegger and Dasein's 'Bodily Nature': What is the Hidden Problematic?," *International Journal for Philosophical Studies* 8 (2000): 209–30.
3   See Hubert Dreyfus, *Being-in-the-World: A Commentary on Heidegger's Being and Time, Division I* (Cambridge, MA: MIT Press, 1991). See especially chapter 7 ("Spatiality and Space"); the cited remark about the body is from p. 137.
4   See William Blattner, "Existence and Self-Understanding in *Being and Time*," *Philosophy and Phenomenological Research* 56 (1996): 97.
5   Dreyfus, *Being-in-the-World*, 132.

6 Ibid.

7 I am grateful to William Bracken for reminding me of this point.

8 Dreyfus, *Being-in-the-World*, 136.

9 In his *Heidegger's Temporal Idealism* (Cambridge: Cambridge University Press, 1999), William Blattner relates a funny story about his father searching frantically for glasses he was wearing all along. See p. 179, note 51 (and surrounding discussion). Bill Bracken has also pointed out to me that, funny stories aside, there is a more straightforward sense in which the picture may be more accessible than my glasses: reaching out and adjusting a crooked picture may require less in the way of effort and attention than, say, finding and removing a smudge on my glasses. While this may be so, the real problem in Heidegger's account is with the criterion of attentiveness as the "metric" for degrees of proximity or accessibility.

10 Dreyfus, *Being-in-the-World*, 134; emphasis in original.

11 Jeff Malpas, *Heidegger's Topology: Being, Place, World* (Cambridge, MA: MIT Press, 2006), 94.

12 Didier Franck, "Being and the Living," in *Who Comes After the Subject?*, eds. E. Cadava, P. Connor, and J.-L. Nancy (London: Routledge, 1991), 144.

13 For a fuller discussion of the hierarchical structure of Heidegger's categories in *Being and Time* and the problems this engenders, especially in relation to the issue of spatiality, see Malpas, *Heidegger's Topology*, especially chapter 3.

6   Being-with-Others

AVOIDING BEING MISUNDERSTOOD TO BE A CARTESIAN SUBJECT

Heidegger tells us that, thanks to Descartes:

[t]he question of the who [of human beings...] answers itself in terms of the "I" itself, the "Subject" ... Ontologically we understand it as something which is in each case already constantly present-at-hand ... as self-sufficient substance.[1] (114)

By substance we can understand nothing else than an entity which *is* in such a way that it needs no other entity in order to *be*. (92)

Being and Time is dedicated to undermining our belief that we are such self-sufficient Cartesian Subjects. In §§12–18, Heidegger argues that a human being becomes something non-Subject-like (i.e., a Dasein) when dealing skillfully with familiar things and people in familiar situations. As Heidegger puts it, "In this familiarity *Dasein can lose itself in what it encounters within-the-world ...*" (76, my italics). Indeed, Dasein *must lose itself* to cope at its best:

[Dasein] must forget itself if, lost in the world of equipment, it is to be able "actually" to go to work and manipulate something. (354)

At this most basic level of skilled involvement, there is no Subject: "Dasein ... is nothing but ... concerned absorption in the world" (GA 20: 268).[2]

   Heidegger wants to stress that the absorption in which Dasein loses itself cannot be understood in terms of independent Subjects' standing over against independent Objects. He tells us that "by hyphenating the term [being-in-the-world] ... we mean to indicate that this structure is a unitary one" (GA 24: 234). "[W]e define [being-in-the-world] as *absorption* in the world, being drawn in by it" (GA 20: 266–7).

The original way of encountering the environing world evidently cannot even be directly grasped, ... this phenomenon is instead typically passed over. This is no accident, inasmuch as Dasein as being-in-the-world in the sense of concern is absorbed in its world in which it is preoccupied, is so to speak *exhausted by that world*, so that precisely in the most natural and the most immediate being-in-the-world the world in its worldhood is *not experienced thematically* at all. (GA 20: 251, italics changed)

To complete the undermining of the Cartesian Subject, Heidegger lays out a basic parallel between the way Dasein as *absorbed being-in-the-world loses itself in the world* and how *absorbed social Daseins lose themselves in each other*, and how the loss of self in each case helps to undermine the idea of a self-sufficient Subject.

But, in describing being with others in the social world, Heidegger does not reach the primordial level of being-with that would annihilate the self-sufficient Self all together. That is, while in *Being and Time* Heidegger describes at length Dasein's everyday absorption in an equipmental whole made up of equipment such as hammers, and roles such as being a carpenter, he has much less to say about a parallel phenomenon of everyday absorbed being-with-others. Instead, Heidegger offers a brief description of everyday cooperation:

By "others" we ... mean ... those among whom one is too ... By reason of this *with-like* being-in-the-world, the world is always the one that I share with others. (118)

But it looks like this shared social world might well be a world of *self-sufficient* others, not the anti-Cartesian selves absorbed into each other that would parallel the absorption of Dasein into the everyday familiar equipmental whole (*Ganzheit*).[3]

HEIDEGGER'S UNDERSTANDING OF MOOD AS SELFLESS ABSORPTION

Heidegger therefore considers an alternative phenomenological approach to absorbed being-with. This approach is implicit in Heidegger's remarks in *Being and Time* on moods as "attunements." But moods as described in *Being and Time* manifest just the opposite way of being from that of being-with. Moods according to *Being and Time* give one a sense of how things are going in one's *personal life*. "A mood makes manifest how one is, and how one is faring," Heidegger says (134).

But this does not seem to satisfy Heidegger. In *Basic Problems of Phenomenology*, Heidegger's course given the same year *Being and Time* was published, he mentions mood only once, and there he says rather obscurely: "To be affectively self-finding is the formal structure of what we call mood" (GA 24: 398). The emphasis is again on moods as a way of finding one's independent self.

However, in *The Fundamental Concepts of Metaphysics*, Heidegger's lecture course given two years after the publication of *Being and Time*, as if to complete his destruction of the self-sufficient Subject, Heidegger introduces *shared* attunements as the way moods contribute to the phenomenon of absorbed being-with. Instead of trying like a Cartesian to explain how private inner states can be found in the minds of others by means of empathy or by observing the movements of people's public external bodies, Heidegger starts with the phenomenon of moods and observes that moods are *attunements* that are *directly shared*. He describes the shared mood at a party:

A human being who ... is in a good humor brings a lively atmosphere with them ... Or another ... puts a damper on everything ... What does this tell us? Attunements ... in advance determine our *being with one another*. (GA 29/30: 100–1, my italics)

Heidegger then appeals to such shared attunements to repudiate the Cartesian self, understood as a stream of private experiences:

It seems as though an attunement is in each case already there ... like an atmosphere in which we first immerse ourselves in each case and which then attunes us through and through. It does not merely seem so, it is so; and, faced with this fact, *we must dismiss the psychology of feelings, experiences, and consciousness.* (GA 29/30: 100–1, emphasis added)

But the closest Heidegger comes to the positive phenomenon of absorption in others in *Being and Time* is his brief discussion of the *contagion* of moods. Instead of trying to explain how a Subject's inner states can be discovered in the minds of other Subjects by means of empathy, Heidegger focuses on the phenomenon of mood itself. He sees that the traditional account of moods as sent from one person's inner sphere to another's cannot account for the phenomenon of the contagion of moods. He asks:

Do [moods] ... bring about an emotional experience which is then transmitted to others, in the manner [of] infectious germs? ... We do, indeed, say that attunement or mood is infectious. (GA 29/30: 100)

However, as a phenomenologist, Heidegger does not try to explain how mood contagion actually works. Rather, he describes the ontological phenomenon manifest in such mutual attunements: "It is a matter of *seeing* and *saying* what is happening here," he says. "It is clear that attunements are not something merely at hand. They themselves are precisely a fundamental way of being ... and this always directly includes being-with-one-another" (GA 29/30: 100–1). Mood then is a basic way of being-with that contributes to overcoming our mistaken ontology of ourselves as self-sufficient Subjects. The "contagion" of mood that Heidegger notes at parties suggests that just as Dasein copes at its best when it forgets itself and is unreflectively absorbed in dealing with equipment in our familiar world, so Dasein also copes at its best when it forgets itself in absorbed being-with-others. However, to describe more fully the phenomenon of the "contagion" of moods and how it relates to being-with-one-another, we need to turn to Maurice Merleau-Ponty.[4]

MERLEAU-PONTY ON INTERCORPOREALITY

Merleau-Ponty describes the absorbed being-with that fleshes out Heidegger's phenomenological account of absorption-in-others. He says, "It is precisely my body which perceives the body of another, and discovers in that other body a *miraculous* prolongation of my own intentions."[5] But Merleau-Ponty, while offering an original *description* of the way lived bodies can be absorbed into each other, still has no account of how this "miraculous" absorption is physiologically possible. (That's why he calls it miraculous.) To explain this absorption, Merleau-Ponty introduces an equally miraculous capacity he calls the *body schema*: "The body schema," he tells us, "ensures the immediate correspondence of what [a child] sees done and what [the child] himself does."[6] Merleau-Ponty is clear that "the whole difficulty is to conceive this act clearly without confusing it with a cognitive operation ... *It is as if the other person's intention inhabited my body and mine his.*"[7] This would surely be the end of the self-sufficient Subject! But, we need to ask, what would such a direct embodied "inhabiting" of the other person in me and me in him be like and how could it be physiologically possible?

Merleau-Ponty recognizes the challenge and replies, "As the parts of my body together comprise a system, so my body and the other's are one whole, two sides of one and the same phenomenon..."[8] But this description of the phenomenon of absorption in others still leaves it mysterious – even to Merleau-Ponty. As he admits, "How significance and intentionality could come to dwell in ... masses of cells [or even in a single neuron] is a thing which can never be made comprehensible, and here Cartesianism is right."[9] That is, we cannot expect to understand how isolated neuron clusters could possibly provide an explanation of meaningful, intentional comportment, let alone a meaningful, intentional comportment that is directly shared with others.

But, nonetheless, Merleau-Ponty helps himself to directly shared intentionality: "The gesture I witness sketches out the first sign of an intentional object."[10] He thus offers an original and plausible phenomenologial description of shared intentionality, but his account remains "magical" as to how it works.

THE MIRROR-NEURONAL ACCOUNT OF BEING-WITH AND DASEIN-WITH

Until recently, the way the other person's intentions could directly inhabit my body, and mine his, has indeed been "difficult to conceive," but recent work in neuroscience has cast new light on the subject. Researchers have discovered neurons, which they appropriately call mirror neurons, which, if not inhibited, fire when a monkey sees another monkey make a movement and directly trigger a similar movement.[11]

Vittorio Gallese, one of the co-discoverers of mirror-neurons, explains how human mirror neurons work:

When we observe actions performed by other individuals our motor system *"resonates"* along with that of the observed agent.[12]

The important point is that, for communication to occur, there is no need for an *interpretation* of another person's *movements*. One responds *directly* as with a reflex. Yet according to Gallese, what takes place is more meaningful and more holistic than an *isolated, mechanical reflex response*. Giaccamo Rizzolatti, another co-discoverer, explains:

Certain cells will fire when a monkey performs a single, highly specific action with its hand: pulling, pushing, tugging, grasping, picking up and putting a peanut in the mouth etc. different neurons fire in response to different actions. One might be temped to think that these are motor "command" neurons, making muscles do certain things; however, the astonishing truth is that any given mirror neuron will also fire when the monkey in question observes another monkey (or even the experimenter) performing the same action, e.g. tasting a peanut![13]

Mirror neurons enable one to give a physiological account of the phenomenon of mutual absorption, that is, cases where one finds oneself directly doing what one sees being done. Indeed, Merleau-Ponty's account of the work of the body schema anticipates Gallese's account of the "resonance" of mirror neurons. Moreover, Gallese's physiological account enables him to avoid Merleau-Ponty's need to speak of the "miraculous" imitation of another's actions.

Mirror-neuron research helps us understand why in extreme cases speaking of *contagion* seems appropriate. Gallese notes:

Demented patients with "echopraxia" ... show an impulsive tendency to imitate other people's movements ... Imitation concerns gestures that are commonly executed as well as those that are rare and even bizarre for the observing patient. It can be hypothesized that echopractic behavior represents a "release" of a covert action simulation present also in normal subjects, but normally inhibited...[14]

V. S. Ramachandran helps complete the picture by offering a physiological account of this inhibition. He hypothesizes that "the subject's own motor system automatically simulates the perceived action, but at the same time it automatically suppresses the spinal motor signal to prevent it from being carried out."[15]

But what would such normal contagious behavior be like? Remember Merleau-Ponty says it would be like having the other's body acting through yours and yours through theirs. Gallese notes that

"Contagious behavior" commonly experienced in our daily life, in which the observation of particular actions displayed by others leads to our repetition of them, [are] yawning and laughter.[16]

Indeed, when I see someone yawn, it feels as though his or her body is yawning through my body. The same sort of contagion happens with laughing, especially if some substance has lowered everyone's inhibitions.

Now, it might seem that mirror neurons offer an explanation of Merleau-Ponty's "miracle." Such an account, however, might well be an empiricist account – an account of what looks like direct intentionality as a mere meaningless reflex. A better account compatible with the phenomenon, but which replaces the recourse to the "miraculous," might well be that, for example, the caretaker responds to the baby's reflex-smile (or yawn or laugh) with a culturally meaningful loving smile, and the baby, in imitating the caretaker's meaningful smile, thanks to its mirror neurons, picks up the cultural meaning. So the phenomenon of shared being-with, which Merleau-Ponty perceptively describes, need no longer seem miraculous.

SUMMARY

Mirror neurons offer an account of the positive phenomenon of being-with that contributes to our overcoming of our mistaken ontology of ourselves as self-sufficient Cartesian Subjects. Being "transposed into another" is not merely operative on the level of yawns and laughter. The contagion of moods and the absorption of selves into each other is manifest in everyday shared coping. They show that, just as Dasein copes at its best when it forgets itself in absorbed dealing with the familiar world, so, as we saw earlier, Dasein deals with others at its best when it is unreflectively absorbed in being-with-them.

Mirror neurons provide the physiological basis of the "miracle" of absorbed Dasein-with. Ramachandran notes the importance of such a discovery. He tells us:

> The discovery of mirror neurons ... is the single most important "unreported" (or at least, unpublicized) story of the decade. I predict that mirror neurons will do for psychology what DNA did for biology: they will provide a unifying framework and help explain a host of mental abilities that have hitherto remained mysterious and inaccessible to experiments.[17]

DISMISSING THE PSYCHOLOGY OF FEELING, EXPERIENCES, AND CONSCIOUSNESS

But isn't Dasein always *experiencing* what is going on? I think Heidegger would say, "No." *Experiences* are what one thematizes on reflection, not what one is conscious of when one is fully absorbed.

Heidegger is interested in the Homeric Greeks because they seem to have had feelings and experiences, like ours, but they understood that these get in the way of absorbed coping and mood contagion. They didn't thematize their experience or reflect on their mental states. Odysseus, for example, sees inner experiences as in the way. Heidegger must have liked a passage from the Odyssey where Odysseus warns Telemacus not to reflect on his experiences but to stay in the flow. The experience of being a self-sufficient Subject only arises when there is a breakdown of our directly shared, ongoing, absorbed being-with.

Homer describes the situation in which Odysseus and Telemacus are fully in sync, skillfully hiding the weapons that the suitors might use to defend themselves.

> And now the two men sprang to work
> ... while in their path Pallas Athena
> held up a golden lamp of purest light.
> Telémakos at last burst out:
>   "Oh, Father,
> here is a marvel! All around I see
> the walls and roof beams ...
> lighted as though by white fire blazing near.
> One of the gods of heaven is in this place!"
> Then said Odysseus, ...,
>   "Be still: keep still about it. just remember it.
> The gods who rule Olympos make this light..."[18]

Here we can hear Odysseus warning Telemacus not to thematize, that is, not to pay attention to, not turn into figure, the background illumination that guides their coordinated skillful activity. Odysseus sees that

Telemacus must let the brilliant ambient illumination withdraw so it can do its work of bringing out the two men and their shared work. The idea is that when you are in the zone, when your actions are drawn out of you rather then being generated by you, when you are acting at your best, the worst thing you can do is get in the way of whatever is going on by trying to turn the indeterminate background into a determinate figure. As a field of forces, the background qua background must remain hidden. It cannot be described as having determinate features; it can only be indirectly responded to, and hinted at, as above, in metaphors like white fire blazing.

Odysseus' warning is still the best advice about the background and how it works. If you pay attention to it, it ceases to do its job as background. Generally, if you pay attention to your coping skills – draw them out of the background into the foreground – rather than just letting yourself be drawn to respond skillfully to the current situation, you will, at best, perform competently. At worst, you will lose your skill altogether.

Almost three thousand years after Homer, Heidegger sensed how, in successful hammering, the hammer and the hammerer have to withdraw. He saw that, in general, the world must withdraw in order to allow us to be absorbed in acting at our skillful best. As he says, "We can never look upon the phenomenon of world directly" (GA 29/30: 431–2).

THE NEGATIVE, NEUTRAL, AND POSITIVE FUNCTIONS OF THE ONE

The Negative Function of the One

Even absorbed being-with-others has a negative side. Heidegger ends his discussion of being-with by asking an ominous question:

When Dasein is absorbed in the world of its concern ... it is not itself. *Who* is it, then, who has taken over being as everyday being-with-one-another? (125)

Heidegger answers:

The "who" is not this one, not that one, not oneself [man selbst], not some people [einige], and not the sum of them all. The "who" is the neuter, *the "one"* [das Man]. (126)[19]

And he adds:

What is decisive is just that inconspicuous domination by others which has already been taken over unawares from Dasein as Being-with. One belongs to the others oneself and enhances their power. (126)

In one's concern with what one has taken hold of, whether with, for, or against, the others, there is constant care as to the way one differs from them ... whether one's own Dasein has lagged behind the others. (126)

Here Heidegger takes over (without giving credit) the Kierkegaardian critique of leveling.

Overnight, everything that is primordial gets glossed over as something that has long been well known. Everything gained by a struggle becomes just something to be manipulated ... This care of averageness reveals in turn an essential tendency of Dasein which we call the "leveling down" [*Einebnung*] of all possibilities of being. (127)

The Neutral Function of the "One"

This Kierkegaardian critique of everyday conforming has, however, become a familiar complaint. Heidegger has something deeper to say concerning conforming – what he calls the slyness of the "one."

To take an example of this neutral slyness, we can see that we are not normally aware that, when interacting with friends, colleagues, loved ones, and so forth, we stand at what we feel to be a comfortable distance from them. If we thought about at what distance to stand, we wouldn't know where to place our selves. Nonetheless, anthropologists seek to measure and codify the distance-standing practices in various cultures. There is even a field called *proximics* dedicated to doing just this. But our distance-standing skill, like any skill, is endlessly flexible. We feel comfortable standing farther away if the person we are interacting with has the flu, closer if there is a lot of noise in the background. In a reading room or a church, we speak more softly and stand closer. All these subtle discriminations and responses are further inflected by our relationship with the people involved.

The sense of appropriate distance was passed on to us by our parents and peers who were not aware that they had this skill. They just found themselves doing what others were doing. The way conforming works, one does not *choose* at what distance to stand. Like most social skills, we presumably mastered skills such as distance standing directly through our bodies, mirroring the actions of other people's bodies.

Norms such as distance standing control our activity without our awareness. As Heidegger puts it:

The more openly the "one" behaves, the harder it is to grasp, and the slier it is, but the less is it nothing at all. (128)

Unfortunately, Heidegger does not distinguish this neutral role of consciously or unconsciously *conforming* to norms, and the *conformism* that leads to leveling. In describing inauthenticity, Heidegger notes Dasein's tendency to cover up its groundlessness, by taking the accepted norms as justifying grounds for one's activities.

In order to appreciate what Heidegger is trying to say, we have so far dwelt on the neutral role of conforming to the inconspicuous conformist public norms. We must now focus on the positive role of the one.

The Positive Function of the "One"

Given Heidegger's Kierkegaardian critique of keeping up with others, we may well be surprised to read that:

The "one" is an existentiale; and as a primordial phenomenon, it belongs to Dasein's positive constitution. (129)

Indeed, Heidegger holds that:

the "one" itself articulates the referential context of significance. When entities are encountered, Dasein's world frees them for a whole of involvements with which the "one" is familiar, and within the limits which have been established with the "one's" averageness. (129, my italics)

And he adds:

None of these phenomena – this is characteristic precisely of the one – is in any way conscious or intentional. The obviousness, the matter-of-course way in which this movement of Dasein comes to pass also belongs to the manner of being of the one. (GA 20: 337)

That is, norms are passed on by unconscious "imitation." Of course, this is not normal, deliberate "imitation," since it is not done intentionally. Rather, it may well be the work of the mirror neurons. We have no words to describe this direct responsiveness. But Heidegger sees that this sort of imitation is primordial; that all shared background practices depend on the way that these "sly" norms work.

Pierre Bourdieu describes the positive way the body works by unconscious "imitation of actions," just as Heidegger describes the "sly" work of the one, and Gallese describes the "resonating" of mirror neurons. Bourdieu says:

The child imitates not "models" but other people's actions. *Body hexis speaks directly to the motor function* ... The principles em-bodied in this way are placed beyond the grasp of consciousness, and hence cannot be touched by voluntary, deliberate transformation, cannot even be made explicit.[20]

But how, then, do we pass on our background coping skills? While agreement on eating manners, for example, may be passed on by instruction and examples, the distance standing practices are invisible to those practicing them. The tendency to "imitate" manifested by our mirror neurons provides the invisible physiological basis of all forms of shared activity. Without our tendency to pick up directly the significance of what others are doing, shared intelligibility would be impossible.

CONCLUSION

If we see that the one is the shared practices that make a shared world possible, then we can conclude, with Heidegger, that "[If] we 'see' [the 'one'] ... with an unprejudiced eye it reveals itself as the 'realest Subject' of everydayness" (128). The job of the Cartesian Subject – the self-sufficient source of norms and intelligibility – has been taken over by the imitative activity of the one.

NOTES

1   I follow the Macquarrie and Robinson translation, with a couple of minor changes. For one thing, I will capitalize "Subject" when it refers to the Cartesian Subject as described here by Heidegger. Likewise for "Object." In addition, I translate *das Man* as "the One," rather than as "the They." Heidegger notes:

   If we understand man in this sense as Subject and consciousness, as modern idealism since Descartes has done as a matter of course, then the fundamental possibility of penetrating into the originary essence of man, i.e. of comprehending the Dasein in him, escapes our grasp from the start. All subsequent attempts to correct this situation have proved useless. (GA 29/30: 305)

2   I am grateful for helpful conversations concerning this subject with B. Scot Rousse and Mark Wrathall.

3   *Ganzheit* should be translated "whole," not "totality," as in the Macquarrie and Robinson translation. "Totality" suggests an aggregate of independent elements, which Heidegger points out the world evidently is not.

4   Maurice Merleau-Ponty, *Phenomenology of Perception*, trans. Colin Smith (London: Routledge & Kegan Paul, 1981).

5   Ibid., 354, my italics. "Intention" at this primordial level is not to be understood as a mentalistic phenomenon. My intention is what I am currently being drawn to do.

6   Ibid. "Body *schema*" is the correct translation of Merleau-Ponty's "schema corporel." "Body *image*" is a misleading mistranslation.

7   Ibid., 185, emphasis added.

8   Ibid., 354.

9   Ibid., 351.

10 Ibid., 185.

11 Rizzolatti et al. report:

   Neurons ... discharge during goal-directed hand movements such as grasping, holding, and tearing. We report here that many of these neurons become active also when the monkey observes *specific, meaningful hand movements* performed by the experimenters. The effective experimenters' movements include among others placing or retrieving a piece of food from a table, grasping food from another experimenter's hand, and manipulating objects. There is always a clear link between the effective observed movement and that executed by the monkey and, often, only movements of the experimenter identical to those controlled by a given neuron are able to activate it. These findings indicate that premotor neurons can retrieve movements not only on the basis of [isolated] stimulus characteristics ... but also on the basis of the [holistic] *meaning* of the observed actions. (G. di Pellegrino, L. Fadiga, L. Fogassi, V. Gallese, G. Rizzolatti, "Understanding motor events: a neurophysiological study," *Experimental Brain Research* 91 (1992), 176–80, my italics)

12   Vittorio Gallese, "The 'Shared Manifold' Hypothesis: From Mirror Neurons to Empathy," *Journal of Consciousness Studies* 8, no. 5–7 (2001): 38.
13   "MIRROR NEURONS and imitation learning as the driving force behind the great leap forward in human evolution," http://www.edge.org/3rd_culture/ramachandran/ramachandran_index.html, accessed May 24, 2012.
14   Gallese, "Shared Manifold," 44. V. S. Ramachandran spells out a physiological account:

[I]t is the dynamic interplay of signals from frontal inhibitory circuits, mirror neurons (both frontal and parietal), and null signals from receptors that allow you to enjoy reciprocity with others while simultaneously preserving your individuality. (*The Tell-Tale Brain: A Neuroscientist's Quest for What Makes Us Human*, New York: W. W. Norton & Company, 2012, 125).

15   Ramachandran, *Tell-Tale Brain*, 142.
16   Gallese, "Shared Manifold," 38–9.
17   Ramachandran, "Mirror Neurons."
18   Homer, *Odyssey*, trans. Robert Fitzgerald (New York: Macmillan, 1998), 354.
19   There is a normal (appropriate) way to use any piece of equipment. This norm is expressed by saying what "one" does with the equipment, as in "one eats one's peas with a fork." To refer to the *normal* user, Heidegger coins the term *das Man*, which our translators call "the They." This translation is misleading, however, since it suggests that *I* am distinguished from *them*, whereas Heidegger's whole point is that the equipment and roles of society are defined by norms that apply to anyone. But even translating *das Man* by "we" or by "anyone" does not capture the normative force of the expression. *We* or *Anyone* might try to cheat the Internal Revenue Service, but still *one* pays *one's* taxes. To preserve a feel for the appeal to normativity in statements about what one does and does not do, we must stay close to Heidegger's German and translate *das Man* by "the one."
20   Pierre Bourdieu, *Outline of a Theory of Practice* (Cambridge: Cambridge University Press, 1997), 87 (my italics); and 94. The passage goes on: "Nothing seems more ineffable, more incommunicable, more inimitable, and, therefore, more precious, than the values given body, *made* body by the transubstantiation achieved by the hidden persuasion of an implicit pedagogy."

7   Why Mood Matters

FINDING ONESELF IN THE WORLD

This chapter offers an interpretation and critical discussion of Heidegger's treatment of "mood" in *Being and Time*. I begin by explaining and defending the claim that moods constitute how we *find ourselves in the world*. The remainder of the chapter is dedicated to addressing aspects of Heidegger's account that are unclear or underdeveloped, the focus being upon (1) what it is that makes one mood deeper or more fundamental than another; (2) the diversity of moods; and (3) the relationship between mood and temporality. I suggest that Heidegger's conception of mood is highly plausible but that a lot more needs to be done to convey the enormous phenomenological richness of mood. Furthermore, an adequate phenomenological treatment of mood will need to do more than just clarify and further develop Heidegger's ideas. To an extent at least, it will also have to be revisionary.

According to Heidegger, "mood" (*Stimmung*) makes a substantial contribution to the sense that we have of belonging to a world.[1] Our moods may change, but we are always in some kind of mood, and what might seem like the absence of mood is actually the presence of an inconspicuousness mood. Being in some mood or other is, according to Heidegger, a fundamental *existentiale* of Dasein. In other words, it is essential to the distinctively human way of having a world (134). In the absence of mood, we would not find ourselves in a world at all and would therefore cease to be Dasein. Heidegger refers to the characteristic of *finding oneself in a world through a mood* as "*Befindlichkeit*," a notoriously difficult term to translate. Macquarrie and Robinson, in their 1962 translation of *Being and Time*, opt for "state of mind," but this is inappropriate. Heidegger stresses that moods are not experienced as states of mind possessed by psychological subjects, and that we do not experience moods as "out there" in the world either. Moods constitute a sense of being part of a world that is pre-subjective and pre-objective. All "states of mind" and all perceptions and cognitions of "external" things presuppose this background sense of belonging to a world. Other translations include "affectedness,"[2] "attunement,"[3] "disposedness,"[4] and "sofindingness."[5] In what follows, I will replace the term "state of mind" with "attunement" when quoting from Macquarrie and Robinson's translation of *Sein und Zeit.*[6] Elsewhere, I will refer more often to the *having of a mood* and to how we *find ourselves in the world* or *belong to a world* through a mood.

In maintaining that moods constitute a sense of belonging to the world, Heidegger does not mean that one has a subjective state called a mood and that this somehow contributes to perception of one's spatiotemporal location in relation to other entities. To find oneself in a world is not, first and foremost, to occupy the perspective of an impartial spectator, neutrally gazing upon things from a particular space–time location. Rather, the world that we belong to is a significant realm, where things can have a host of different practical meanings. An appreciation of these meanings is inextricable from our actual and potential activities. Finding oneself in the world is thus a matter of being practically immersed in it rather than looking out upon it. Consider how I currently experience my office. As I type these words, the computer keyboard does not appear to me as a conspicuous object of experience. Rather, it is seamlessly integrated into my activity, and my appreciation of its utility is inseparable from what I am doing. However, I do not take all my surroundings to be significant in quite the same way. Numerous other things that appear to me as practically significant do not solicit activities in the way that the keyboard does. For instance, the shoes sitting on the floor by my chair appear to me as functional but do not currently summon me to do anything. So we need to distinguish between having practical significance and being both significant and enticing. The pile of student essays on the table matters to me in a different way from the keyboard and shoes; they present themselves as an impediment to my current project. They still have a kind of practical significance though, which takes the form of "something I ought to or need to do, which is unappealing and requires effort." Other aspects of my situation might appear to me as urgent or pressing, safe or threatening, interesting or boring, easy, difficult or impossible, predictable or unpredictable, achievable without effort, beyond my control, and so on. Practical significance thus divides up into a range of subcategories. If another person enters the room, she or he may matter to me in yet further ways. None of the impersonal things in my room appear to me as offering up possibilities such as conversation, companionship, consolation, love, humiliation, pride, and shame. Hence, there are many different *kinds* of significance.

Particular features of my situation do not have the kinds of significance that they do in isolation from each other. I find myself situated in a holistic web of significance relations, where the significance of one thing always relates to the significance of something else, and where all of these relations reflect projects I am currently pursuing or might pursue. According to Heidegger, this web of significance depends, in part, upon mood. A mood does not determine how a particular thing is taken to be significant, such as "this pen is for writing," or even how lots of things appear significant, such as "all the people in this room are threatening." In order to encounter things in such ways, one must already be receptive to certain kinds of mattering, which in these cases are "practical utility" and "threat." Without an appreciation that things *can* matter in these ways, one could not encounter anything as threatening or useful. This is where mood comes in. Moods constitute the range of ways in which things are able to matter to us, and are thus essential to a sense of the kinds of significant possibility that the world can offer up for us.

It is commonplace to regard moods as generalized emotions, meaning emotional states that are directed at a wide range of objects. In conjunction with this, it is often maintained that they "color" perception.[7] Heidegger rejects both views. A mood, for Heidegger, does not add emotional color to pre-given objects of experience. We can only have objects of experience insofar as we already find ourselves in a world, and we would not find ourselves in a world at all without mood. For the same reason, a mood is not a generalized emotion. It is not a way in which any number of entities appear but a condition of entities being accessible to us at all: *"The mood has already disclosed, in every case, being-in-the-world as a whole, and makes it possible first of all to direct oneself towards something"* (137). Unlike an act of perceiving, believing, desiring, emoting, or remembering, a mood is not an *intentional state* directed at something within the world. Instead, it is a condition of possibility for such states. A "mood" such as "being in a bad mood with someone" is not a mood in Heidegger's sense; it is an emotional state that presupposes a mood. The mood is what allows things to matter in such a way that being annoyed with somebody is possible. The fact that things are able to "matter" in a given way is "grounded in one's attunement" (137).

If things were completely bereft of all mattering, we could not *relate* to them in any way and, therefore, would not have a sense of being *there*, amongst them. Hence, Heidegger maintains that having a mood is responsible for the "being-in" aspect of "being-in-the-world" (130–1). Of course, moods do not fully determine the nature of what we encounter. That I am capable of finding things threatening does not itself dictate the kind of significance that a particular thing has for me on a particular occasion. For example, it does not make it the case that there is a threatening tiger in front of me. However, one can only find an entity *threatening* in the context of a mood that accommodates the possibility of being threatened. Hence, mood is essential to our "thrownness" (*Geworfenheit*), the sense we have of being in a significant worldly situation that is not of our own making (135).

None of this should be taken to suggest that alternative accounts of mood are completely misguided. Heidegger's analysis almost certainly does not track every use of the English term "mood," and it may well be that certain "moods" are indeed generalized emotions. However, at least some moods seem to fit Heidegger's analysis. There is no neat and tidy way of expressing this aspect of experience, but it is something that people do attempt to communicate, especially when they undergo substantial shifts in mood. Consider predicaments such as feeling jetlagged, hung over, exhausted, or grief stricken.[8] In these and many other circumstances, people might report an all-enveloping sense of insignificance, estrangement, unfamiliarity, and so on. Sometimes, such talk refers to the way in which a particular situation is experienced, but it can also be used to convey a more encompassing way of finding oneself in the world.

Alterations in what Heidegger calls mood are especially pronounced in a range of psychiatric illnesses, including schizophrenia, depression, and depersonalization, as exemplified by many descriptions that are offered by sufferers.[9] For instance, almost every account of severe depression includes references to changes in mood or feelings that are inextricably bound up with profound alterations in how one finds oneself in the world. For some, the possibility of encountering things as mattering in certain kinds of way is altogether gone from experience. People often report that all sense of practical significance has vanished and, alongside it, a sense of the potential for emotional connectedness with other people. At the same time, other ways of mattering can become more pronounced, even all encompassing. For instance, everything might be encountered through a sense of threat, where threat is no longer a contingent possibility but an inescapable shape that all experience takes on.[10] Similar descriptions frequently appear in literature too. For instance, when Hamlet famously announces, "I have of late – but wherefore I know not – lost all my mirth, forgone all custom of exercises" (*Hamlet*, Act 2, Scene 2), he is not referring to a mood or emotion that he experiences within an already given world. Instead, the possibilities of gaining happiness from anything and of engaging in purposeful practical activity are gone from his world, which now appears but a "sterile promontory."

MOOD, UNDERSTANDING, AND DISCOURSE

Heidegger maintains that mood is not the sole determinant of being-in-the-world. Equally important are "understanding" (*Verstehen*) and "discourse" (*Rede*). These, together with the having of a mood (*Befindlichkeit*), comprise the structure of care (*Sorge*), "care" being Heidegger's term for that in virtue of which being-in-the-world is possible. Discourse, understanding, and mood are not separable components but inextricable aspects of care. "Understanding" refers to the way in which we are always oriented toward concrete future possibilities; we understand both ourselves and the things we encounter in terms of possibilities. This is not an explicit, cognitive accomplishment, a matter of "comporting oneself towards a plan that has been thought out," but something that is implicated even in routine and unthinking encounters with pieces of equipment (145). I encounter the keyboard I am using now in the context of a project that is directed at a particular outcome and, in using it, I understand it in terms of the salient possibilities that it offers.

In Division II of *Being and Time*, Heidegger explicitly prioritizes our orientation toward future possibilities over our "thrownness": "the primary item in care is the 'ahead-of-itself'" (236). So it might seem that future-oriented "understanding" has some kind of primacy over thrownness-constituting "mood." However, I suggest that this is not the case. Mood is not only responsible for a sense of "being there"; it is also essential to our sense of what the world can offer us. Indeed, the possibility of pursuing possibilities itself depends upon mood. Things only appear significant in specific ways against the backdrop of actual or potential projects, as the significance of an entity is inextricable from a sense of salient possibilities involving that entity. For example, a mallet would not appear enticing in the context of brain surgery. Thus, it is understanding that determines the kinds of significance that particular entities have for us in particular situations, and one could not inhabit a significant world without understanding. However, what understanding takes for granted is that these kinds of significance are themselves possible. And their possibility depends upon mood, insofar as it determines the range of ways in which things are able to matter to us. Regardless of whether what one finds practically significant is a football, a novel, a radio, or a fast car, the mood-constituted possibility of finding anything practically significant is presupposed. To take the extreme case, a world that did not matter in any way and thus offered no significant possibilities would be a world where pursuit of all projects was unintelligible.[11] Hence, although understanding determines whether or not a given entity *does* appear significant in some way, it is not what determines whether an entity *can be* significant in such a way. If anything, it is mood that has primacy over understanding, as mood is responsible for determining the shape of the possibility space within which understanding operates.

What Heidegger calls "discourse" (*Rede*) similarly depends upon mood. Discourse, for Heidegger, is not spoken language but a condition of possibility for spoken language, the coalescing of a world into structured patterns that are amenable to linguistic expression (160–1). The scope of what discourse can make intelligible is constrained by a space of mood-determined possibilities. However, Heidegger also maintains that modes of interpretation enabled by discourse can serve to determine the range of possible moods. For instance, "inauthentic" immersion in public ways of doing things – unthinkingly doing "what one does," aspiring to achieve what one ought to achieve and interpreting all of one's activities in terms of pre-prescribed public norms – restricts the kinds of moods that one can have, the ways in which things can matter:

The dominance of the public way in which things have been interpreted has already been decisive even for the possibilities of having a mood – that is, for the basic way in which Dasein lets the world "matter" to it. (169–70)

Hence, the dependence between mood and discourse seems to be symmetrical. How things matter constrains the possibilities for discourse, and discourse constrains how things matter. However, it is not clear how strong a claim Heidegger wishes to make regarding the influence of interpretation upon mood. The strong version would be that some modes of interpretation render some kinds of mood unintelligible and thus impossible. A weaker version would be that certain pervasive ways of interpreting oneself and the world *actually* dispose one against or prevent one from entering into certain kinds of mood, but that those moods remain amongst one's possibilities. This latter version is, in my view, more plausible. Hence, it is arguable that the kind of dependence that mood has upon discourse is not as strong as the dependence that discourse has upon mood.

DEPTH OF MOOD

Some of Heidegger's discussion seems to contradict my claim that our moods determine the ways in which things are able to matter to us. He dedicates a great deal of attention to the mood of "fear," which is surely a way of encountering something within the world, rather than a space of possibilities in the context of which such encounters are intelligible. In fact, fear does not seem to be a mood at all but an occurrent emotion (at least if we adopt the commonplace view that emotions are brief episodes with specific objects, whereas moods are longer-term states that either do not have objects or encompass a wide range of objects). Heidegger does not explicitly distinguish the categories "mood" and "emotion." However, he does seem to acknowledge that those emotional states we have within a pre-given world presuppose mood-constituted ways of mattering:

> nothing like an affect would come about ... if being-in-the-world, with its attunement, had not already submitted itself [sich schon angeweisen] to having entities within-the-world "matter" to it in a way which its moods have outlined in advance. (137)

How do we reconcile this with the emphasis upon fear? In fact, Heidegger's discussion of fear is consistent with a distinction between emotional states that presuppose a world and background moods that make them possible. He does begin by describing fear as a kind of experience that we have *within* a world. There are, Heidegger says, three complementary ways of viewing fear: we can focus upon (a) what it is that we are afraid of, that which is threatening; (b) the attitude of "fearing"; or (c) what it is we are afraid for, which Heidegger takes to be ourselves (140). In addition he emphasizes that fear is essentially future oriented insofar as we are afraid of what might happen rather than what is already the case (141).[12] Heidegger also distinguishes different kinds of fear. If the threatening possibility appears suddenly, there is "alarm"; when we are threatened by something unfamiliar, we experience "dread"; and when we are confronted with something that is both sudden and unfamiliar, there is "terror." He adds that there are further varieties of fear, including "timidity, shyness, misgiving, becoming startled" (142). At least some of these seem to be occurrent emotions directed at specific objects, rather than ways of belonging to a world. However, Heidegger makes an important distinction between encountering a specific threat and being in the mood of "fearfulness":

> in fearing, fear can ... look at the fearsome explicitly and "make it clear" to itself. Circumspection sees the fearsome because it has fear as its attunement. Fearing, as a slumbering possibility of being-in-the-world in an attunement (we call this possibility "fearfulness" ["Furchtsamkeit"]), has already disclosed the world, in that out of it something like the fearsome may come close. (141)

The possibility of fearing something depends upon already finding oneself in the world in a way that incorporates the possibility of being threatened. "Fearfulness" is not an occurrent emotion but a mood in which it is possible to encounter something as threatening and thus to be afraid:

All modifications of fear, as possibilities of having an attunement, point to the fact that Dasein as being-in-the-world is "fearful" ["furchtsam"]. This "fearfulness" is not to be understood in an ontical sense as some factical "individualized" disposition, but as an existential possibility of the essential attunement of Dasein in general, though of course it is not the only one. (142)

Referring to that in virtue of which fear is possible as "fearfulness" is a little confusing though. A mood that allows fear is also a mood that allows feelings of safety and security. Being a vulnerable entity that cares about its existence is a precondition for feeling safe just as much as it is for feeling afraid. An indifferent or invulnerable being could feel neither safe nor unsafe. So what Heidegger is referring to as fearfulness is not just presupposed by fear but also for by various other ways of encountering things.[13]

The distinction between focused emotions and the moods that make them possible is unclear in some cases. Consider the love one has for one's child. This might be described as a focused emotion but, at the same time, it is something that can "change one's world." Similarly, intense grief is specifically focused and, at the same time, a radical shift in how one finds oneself in a world. It could be argued that such cases involve interaction between two different aspects of experience: specifically focused experiences reshape background mood, thus enabling different kinds of experience, and so on. Perhaps this is what happens when major life events "sink in" – what starts off as a focused emotion leads to a change in how one finds oneself in the world.

However, it is likely, I suggest, that some emotional states are directed at a situation within the world *and* at the same time operate as backgrounds that shape other experiences. What is needed is not a simple contrast between background moods and focused emotions but a more complicated account of emotional "depth." We can understand comparative depth in terms of possibility. For example, a mood incorporating the possibility of threat is presupposed by fear. Conversely, a mood in which all sense of threat was absent would render fear impossible. More generally, a deeper kind of mood or emotion is presupposed by the intelligibility of a shallow kind or, alternatively, renders the shallower kind unintelligible.[14] And we need not settle for just two levels of depth. Suppose that y constitutes a space of possibilities presupposed by x and that y itself presupposes a space of possibilities constituted by z. This is not something that Heidegger considers in *Being and Time*. However, in a 1929–30 lecture course, published in English as *The Fundamental Concepts of Metaphysics* (Heidegger, 1995), he offers a detailed analysis of three different kinds of boredom (*Langeweile*), which seems to indicate that moods can be understood in such a way way.[15] The first form of boredom, being bored "by" something, is directed at a particular spatiotemporal situation. Heidegger offers the example of sitting in a "tasteless station of some lonely minor railway," where we explicitly feel "unease" and make an effort to "pass the time" with various idle distractions (GA 29/30: 139–44). Here, the boredom is directed at something – one's current situation. However, it also serves as a background that shapes how one experiences entities in the context of that situation. Events in the station take on the significance they do against the backdrop of boredom. Nevertheless, the boredom alone does not add up to how one finds oneself in the world, given that one retains a sense of the boredom as contingent and of there being other possibilities. Indeed, one is all too aware of the boredom, as things continue to matter in ways that are not encompassed by it but obstructed by it.

The second form of boredom, being bored "with" something, is deeper. Heidegger offers the example of being invited out to a social occasion that you do not really want to attend. You have a pleasant evening but are later struck by the fact that you were bored all night, despite not having been conspicuously, uncomfortably bored at the time. This lack of awareness, Heidegger says, arises because the whole evening is structured by the mood of boredom and so no possibilities offer themselves that might be contrasted with those encompassed by boredom. It is *"our entire comportment and behaviour that is our passing the time* – the whole evening of the invitation itself" (GA 29/30: 170). Here, the boredom is less conspicuous or "intense" than in the first case, but it is deeper, insofar as the entire situation is shaped by the boredom and other possibilities do not even present themselves. In this second mood of boredom, it would not be possible to be bored "by" something that occurred in the context of the evening, as the shallower form of boredom requires the presentation of alternatives, kinds of significance that can be contrasted with the possibilities that the boredom offers. The "seeking" that might confront the boredom is gone (GA 29/30: 179–80) and "the evening itself is our passing the time" (GA 29/30: 182).

Finding the evening boring is compatible with retaining a sense that what it offers does not exhaust the space of possibilities. But the third form of boredom is deeper still. Heidegger refers to this as boring "for one." Here, the boredom is not just a mood that determines the possibilities offered by a contingent situation. Everything is encompassed by it, and no sense remains of there being any possibilities for anyone that fall outside of the boredom. We find ourselves "in the whole of this indifference" (GA 29/30: 208). Boredom this deep is not something that one can be made easily aware of, given that there is nothing to contrast it with. This is why Heidegger (GA 29/30: 101–2) maintains that the most "powerful" moods are those we are oblivious to.

Drawing on the example of boredom, we can offer an account of depth of mood, according to which deeper moods either facilitate or exclude kinds of mattering and therefore possibility that shallower moods presuppose. Other kinds of mood are also amenable to this kind of analysis. For example, Garrett addresses the nature of despair and distinguishes three varieties: despair in relation to a specific project or state of affairs; personal despair that encompasses one's entire life and thus all of one's projects; and finally philosophical despair, a more encompassing predicament that involves a sense of all life being irrevocably bereft of meaning.[16] Garrett does not divide up despair in quite the same way that Heidegger does boredom. The first form of despair could be subdivided along the lines of Heidegger's first and second forms of boredom, whereas personal despair perhaps points to a fourth kind of boredom between forms two and three: being bored with oneself. Steinbock offers a different but equally complementary analysis of despair, which he distinguishes from disappointment and hopelessness. Disappointment involves the loss of a particular hope, whereas hopelessness is wider reaching, as it is also future directed and incorporates a sense of certain outcomes as either impossible (if good) or inevitable (if bad). But hopelessness does not eradicate the possibility of hope. Indeed, it is only insofar as hope remains intelligible that a given scenario can appear hopeless. Despair, in contrast, is described by Steinbock as a "loss of the ground of hope,"[17] a mood where the possibility of hope has gone. It is arguable that the same kind of depth analysis can be offered for a range of other emotions and moods. Hence, although Heidegger is not clear about this in *Being and Time*, I suggest that his conception of mood can be developed in a potentially fruitful way by means of a strata theory, where moods are understood in terms of the possibilities that they offer or close off.[18]

GROUND MOODS

Although Heidegger does not explicitly offer a detailed account of the depth of mood, he does acknowledge that only some moods have the status of being fundamental or "ground" moods (*Grundstimmungen*). However, it is not entirely clear what the criteria are for being a ground mood. Heidegger does emphasize what I have called "depth," but he also maintains that ground moods can play an important philosophical role, and this role seems to contribute to their status as ground moods. According to Heidegger, although moods determine how we find ourselves in a world, most moods do not make salient to us how we find ourselves in the world. They are inconspicuous and dispose us to overlook the relevant phenomenological accomplishment. Thus, in order to bring to light the role of mood and, more generally, the structure of being-in-the-world, a mood is required that serves to *reveal* rather than just to constitute that structure. So Heidegger searches for a "way of disclosure in which Dasein brings itself before itself." He finds this in the mood of anxiety (*Angst*), which he takes to be a ground mood (182).

Anxiety plays the role of shaking us out of pervasive self-misinterpretations by eradicating the kinds of significance that more mundane moods take for granted. The everyday mood is, Heidegger says, one of evasion or "falling" (139), by which he means that it does not facilitate explicit recognition of the achievement of being-in-the-world and that we consequently misinterpret ourselves in terms of the entities we discover within the world. However, in anxiety, all practical significance falls away and what we previously took for granted becomes salient in its absence. Everything appears as no longer "relevant" in any way; the world "has the character of completely lacking significance"; "everyday familiarity collapses" (186–9). We can no longer misinterpret ourselves as worldly entities, given that the kind of significance that such interpretations quietly presuppose has gone. Anxiety thus facilitates the possibility of an authentic (*Eigentlich*) self-understanding, involving the recognition that we are not simply entities within the world whose behaviour is dictated by the public norms into which we are enculturated.

Heidegger also suggests that anxiety is philosophically illuminating, as it makes conspicuous the ordinarily presupposed structure of being-in-the-world: *"that in the face of which one has anxiety [das Wovor der Angst] is Being-in-the-world as such"* (186). Hence, through anxiety, we can bring being-in-the-world into view and make it accessible to philosophical study. However, it is not clear why the capacity to facilitate any kind of insight should make something a ground mood. Enabling being-in-the-world is not the same as revealing being-in-the-world. Surely there could be equally fundamental moods that are characterized precisely by their tendency to obscure rather than enlighten. Hence, the kind of emotional depth that I described in the previous section can come apart from the potential to facilitate insight. Which, if either, makes something a ground mood for Heidegger?

Consider Heidegger's contrast between fear, which is not a ground mood, and anxiety, which is. Fear, Heidegger says, is in fact "anxiety, fallen into the 'world,' inauthentic, and, as such, hidden from itself" (189). This might sound odd – one could surely be confronted with a threat, regardless of whether or not one has misinterpreted oneself in terms of the kinds of entity that one discovers within the world. What Heidegger means, I think, is that when one is afraid of something, one fears *for* oneself, and that this is only possible if one already matters in a particular kind of way. Yet the kinds of mattering that enable fear do not facilitate a sufficient appreciation of ourselves *as* Dasein, as beings that are thrown into a space of significant possibilities, some of which we choose to make our own. This is made clearer in Division II, where Heidegger discusses fear of death. This, he says, does not incorporate an adequate understanding of death, given that what one fears is the end of an entity that resides within the world, with which one identifies oneself. A realization of the potential loss of one's own possibilities, of "the possibility of the impossibility of every way of comporting oneself towards anything, of every way of existing" (262), is altogether different.

Anxiety removes the kinds of worldly concern that make fear possible, and so also removes (temporarily, at least) the possibility of mis-interpreting one's death in a certain way. One cannot be afraid and anxious at the same time, as the possibility of fear requires that the possibilities made salient by anxiety remain hidden. However, Heidegger sometimes indicates that we do not *become* anxious at all but are somehow anxious all the time. In addition to claiming that fear rests upon a "turning away" from anxiety and that it thus depends upon anxiety, he later indicates that anxiety is never absent but is instead "covered up" (277), as though it were something lying dormant, with the threat of its awakening quietly permeating all our experiences. But what I think he is saying is that the possibilities that are made conspicuous to us through the mood of anxiety are tacitly there in the absence of anxiety. Also present all along is the possibility of their becoming conspicuous through anxiety. Hence, we might distinguish an inescapable disposition toward anxiety from an occurrent anxiety that may be rare. It is the former upon which the possibility of fear depends.

Drawing on this example, we could maintain that what makes something a ground mood is its being a condition of possibility for the presence or absence of other moods, which does not itself presuppose a further mood. Anxiety takes away possibilities that fear presupposes. This, rather than its capacity to illuminate philosophically or to offer up the possibility of authenticity, is relevant to its "ground mood" status. Hence, anxiety is both a ground mood *and* a mood that has additional attributes that are of interest to Heidegger. It is a "basic attunement of Dasein" *and* "one which is significant from the existential–ontological standpoint" (140). However Heidegger runs these two criteria together in places. He never claims that anxiety is the only mood suited to doing philosophy, but he does suggest that philosophy, or good philosophy at least, "*in each case happens in a fundamental attunement* [ground mood]" (GA 29/30: 10). He adds that there are several different ground moods, but does not list them all (GA 29/30: 89). Here there is clearly an emphasis on revelatory capacity as a criterion for being a ground mood, in addition to depth. Hence my proposal that we understand "ground moods" in terms of conditions of intelligibility alone is, to some extent, revisionary one. This, I suggest, is preferable to switching between two or more different criteria that often come apart.

It is not actually clear whether we can actually do philosophy *during* a mood such as anxiety. For example, in the essay "What is Metaphysics?," Heidegger states that anxiety "robs us of speech" and that the "lucid vision sustained by fresh remembrance" is something that can inform us philosophically (GA 9: 112/89). However, I propose that it is neither being in the mood nor having a memory of the mood that serves to inform. What does the work is the *contrast* between moods. It is shifts in the sense of belonging to a world that serve to illuminate; what one previously took for granted becomes salient and thus amenable to phenomenological reflection when it is lost or distorted. Heidegger does at least hint that mood changes more generally can play a role in revealing how we find ourselves in a world: "It is precisely when we see the 'world' unsteadily and fitfully in accordance with our moods, that the ready-to-hand shows itself in its specific worldhood, which is never the same from day to day" (138).[19] Of course, not all mood changes will be equally illuminating. For instance, the descent into a deep depression is unlikely to be philosophically enabling, although the process of recovering from it might well be.

Given that mood changes play an important phenomenological role, the question arises as to how they might be evoked. The dynamics of mood are no doubt very complicated indeed, with moods disclosing the world in ways that then allow those moods to be transformed by experiences, activities, and happenings. The understanding required to influence a mood need not add up to an understanding of that mood. One could misunderstand a mood completely and yet reliably influence it in any number of ways. Heidegger recognizes that we are not completely passive before our moods, that we are responsible to some extent for regulating them. At the same time, he emphasizes that some mood is always presupposed. Our thoughts might influence our moods, but we would not be able to think at all unless we were already in a mood:

Factically, Dasein can, should, and must, through knowledge and will, become master of its moods; in certain possible ways of existing, this may signify a priority of volition and cognition. Only we must not be misled by this into denying that ontologically mood is a primordial kind of Being for Dasein, in which Dasein is disclosed to itself *prior to* all cognition and volition, and *beyond* their range of disclosure. And furthermore, when we master a mood, we do so by way of a counter-mood; we are never free of moods. (136)

Heidegger also refers more specifically to the effects that written and spoken language can have upon mood. The orator, he says, "must understand the possibilities of moods in order to rouse them and guide them aright" (139). He also claims that, in poetic language, "the communication of existential possibilities of one's attunement can become an aim in itself, and this amounts to a disclosing of existence" (162). An implication of his discussion is that the role of philosophical prose is not just to convey information. The prose can serve to attune a reader or listener, to instill a mood through which the philosophy is best understood. Hence, we cannot cleanly divorce the style from the content of a philosophical work, as the style can serve to evoke a mood through which the content is intelligible and without which it can only be misunderstood.

THE VARIETIES OF MOOD

Heidegger only discusses a few kinds of mood in any detail. Consequently, he neglects to convey the wide range of ways in which we can find ourselves in the world. One might wonder why he focuses only on anxiety and, two years later, on boredom as ground moods through which to philosophize. What about wonder or awe, the simple amazement that "that there is something rather than nothing"?[20] However, the range of moods (and most likely the range of philosophically informative moods too) is much greater. Neither the everyday English term "mood" nor the German "Stimmung," regardless of their differing connotations, succeed in capturing all of the relevant phenomena. In English, ways of finding oneself in the world are more commonly referred to as "feelings." Many references to feeling communicate neither an awareness of bodily states nor a way in which some specific part of the world is experienced as being. Instead, they convey a felt sense of belonging to the world, which varies subtly from person to person and time to time, sometimes changing quite dramatically. People talk of all-enveloping feelings of significance, insignificance, detachment, estrangement, absence, isolation, alienation, belonging, unreality, disorientation, disconnection, familiarity, unfamiliarity, anxiety, objectless dread, awe, ecstasy, and many, many others. There are all sorts of more nuanced and lengthy descriptions too, as exemplified by good literature.

Most of these feelings have, to date, escaped tidy classification. But how many kinds are there – are most of the above just different ways of describing the same thing? There is every reason to suspect that we can find ourselves in the world in a diverse range of ways, as there are many different kinds of mattering that can be intensified, diminished, gained, or lost. For example, a world that is bereft of enticing possibilities might still take on the form of threat; a world bereft of effortless, comfortable,

practical belonging might be a place in which things still present themselves as *to be done*, but in every case as difficult or impossible. The
overall framework of mattening is susceptible to many subtly different
kinds of change. Because this aspect of experience is most often referred
to as a kind of feeling, I refer to it as "existential feeling," rather than
mood.[21] Another reason for using the term "feeling" is that, in addition
to constituting how one finds oneself in a world, many or all of these
predicaments seem to incorporate changed bodily awareness. This is
not to say that they are experiences *of* the body. As Merleau-Ponty's
Phenomenology of Perception and Sartre's *Being and Nothingness* both
make clear, bodily awareness can be a way in which the body *perceives*
rather than a way in which it is *perceived*. It is through the feeling body
that we experience the world, and so a bodily feeling need not be contrasted with experiencing something in the world or, for that matter,
with a background sense of belonging to a world.

Heidegger avoids explicit discussion of bodily experience in *Being
and Time*, stating only that our bodily nature (*Leiblichkeit*) "hides a
whole problematic of its own, though we shall not treat it here" (108).
This is a serious omission when it comes to understanding mood, as
some account is surely needed of what moods actually *are*, in addition
to what they do, and of how they relate to the feeling body. Heidegger
returns to the phenomenology of the body in his *Zollikon Seminars*,
which were held at the home of the psychiatrist Medard Boss between
1959 and 1969.[22] There, he quotes his reference to the body in *Being
and Time* and acknowledges that it is indeed an important and difficult
topic, and deserving of further study. However, despite offering several
lengthy remarks on the body, many of which resonate with themes in
Merleau-Ponty and Sartre, he still says nothing about the bodily nature
of mood.

A problem that arises from Heidegger's neglect of the diversity of
moods is a lack of clarity over exactly which moods he *does* address.
For instance, the psychiatrist Gerritt Glas distinguishes a number of
phenomenologically different forms of basic anxiety, including anxiety
as painful disconnectedness, anxiety before death, anxiety in the face of
freedom, and anxiety before meaningless.[23] All of these themes feature
in Heideggerian anxiety, and yet the phenomenological descriptions
offered by Glas indicate that there are significant differences between
them. Given the central methodological role that anxiety plays in *Being
and Time*, it would be problematic if Heidegger's description of it failed
to discriminate between several different forms of anxiety. Of course,
one might retort that there is a difference between clinical anxiety
and the kind of deep anxiety addressed by Heidegger. Real anxiety, as
Heidegger says, is rare (190). However, it is important not to trivialize

the kinds of anxiety that are reported in psychiatric contexts, which can indeed be deep moods that have a profound effect upon how one finds oneself in the world.

A related issue is that of whether and how Heidegger's "anxiety" can be distinguished from kinds of experience that many people report whilst suffering from depression. As Blattner recognizes, the two are very similar indeed, insofar as they both involve the "total insignificance of the world."[24] To complicate matters further, there are of course considerable variations in the experience of depression, and depression is itself intimately associated with anxiety. There are certainly similarities between many people's experiences of depression and what Heidegger calls "anxiety." Severe depression involves a radical transformation of the ordinarily taken-for-granted sense of belonging to a world, where the usual sense of things as practically significant is gone from experience. In addition, both depression and Heideggerian anxiety involve not only a loss of possibilities, but also a conspicuous awarness that something has been lost.[25] Heideggerian anxiety seems to be a brief episode, rather than an enduring state. However, its structure is very similar to that of depression. And, if it is not to be identified with (some kind of) depressed mood, the question arises as to which, if any, form of clinical anxiety it most resembles. Heidegger explicitly acknowledges that he has circumvented the issues of how many different kinds of mood there are and how they interrelate:

The different modes of attunement and the ways in which they are interconnected in their foundations cannot be Interpreted within the problematic of the current investigation. The phenomena have long been well-known ontically under the terms "affects" and "feelings" and have always been under consideration in philosophy. (138)

However, in avoiding this task, he also fails to acknowledge sufficiently the diversity of and subtle differences between these "modes of attunement." Consequently, the referent of the term "anxiety" starts to look a little unclear.

MOOD AND TIME

I will conclude by very briefly raising an issue about the relationship between mood and time. In Division II of *Being and Time*, Heidegger analyzes the structure of care in terms of "original temporality." This is not clock time or time conceived of in any kind of "present-at-hand" way but the unified structure that renders being-in-the-world possible: "Dasein's totality of being as care means: ahead-of-itself-already-being-in (a world) as being-alongside (entities encountered within-the-world) ... *The primordial unity of the structure of care lies in temporality*"

(327). Hence, having a mood, along with the other aspects of care, is to be analyzed in terms of temporality.

However, it is questionable whether the role of mood can be adequately analyzed in terms of time, even a "primordial" sense of time that is quite different from everyday understandings of time. It is clear that mood changes can significantly alter *how* time is experienced. For instance, people suffering from depression frequently complain that the experience of time has changed, sometimes describing it as a slowing down or cessation of time: "Time moves like treacle, running thick and heavy through my days."[26] In severe depression, the possibility of anything appearing as practically significant is gone from experience, as is the possibility of certain significant kinds of interpersonal connectedness. The world therefore *offers* nothing, and one's sense of the future is correspondingly altered. Without meaningful transitions from future to past, awareness of the difference between them is eroded. Hence, the overall structure of temporal experience is changed. Distortions in the perception of time's passing, and also in the sense of "past," "present," "future," and how they interrelate, occur in certain other psychiatric conditions too, as well as in more mundane circumstances.[27] Consider, for example, the difference in how time is experienced when listening to a boring talk and when giving the talk.

That moods have such effects is something Heidegger readily acknowledges, and he suggests that the mood of boredom is characterized by alterations in the sense of time. Moods, he says, are modifications of time and can thus be understood in terms of time. Although one might feel tempted to maintain, in the case of profound boredom, that "one feels timeless, one feels removed from the flow of time," a temporal structure still remains (GA 29/30: 213). However, many first-person accounts of depression not only report that things appeared *no longer* appeared significant. They also describe an inability to conceive of things *ever having been* significant: "There was and could be no other life than the bleak shadowland I now inhabited."[28] The loss of practical significance from experience is something that applies equally to past, present, and future. Consider the following: "What time is it? A little after ten in the morning. I try to remember what ten in the morning means, how it feels. But I cannot. Time means nothing to me anymore."[29] Of course, clock time, which is what Brampton refers to here, is not original temporality. But the reason she finds clock time meaningless is that she has lost the presupposed sense of practical significance that makes timing and scheduling one's activities intelligible. Granted, practical significance itself has a temporal structure: one finds something significant insofar as one encounters its possibilities in the context of a situation that is already the case. But it is not clear that a mood in which practical significance is no longer intelligible depends upon time in such a way as to warrant the view that time is somehow more fundamental than mood. The loss of significance is not a way of experiencing time but something that determines the ways in which time can be experienced. Numerous authors describe depression as somehow atemporal:

When you are depressed, the past and future are absorbed entirely by the present moment, as in the world of a three-year-old. You cannot remember a time when you felt better, at least not clearly; and you certainly cannot imagine a future time when you will feel better. Being upset, even profoundly upset, is a temporal experience, while depression is atemporal.[30]

This is partly because practical meaning is altogether gone from experience. The sense that anything *is* significant, ever *was* significant, or ever *could be* significant is absent. The overall structure of temporal experience presupposes this absence of significance; the loss thus seems irrevocable, prior to time, outside of time. One possibility is that mood and time are inextricable but that neither is wholly analyzable in terms of the other. A stronger claim that might be made on behalf of mood is that it is more phenomenologically fundamental than time, that mood is presupposed not just by the ways in which temporal experience is organized but by the possibility of any kind of temporal experience.

NOTES

1   The German term "Stimmung" does not have quite the same connotations as "mood." In any case, Heidegger's analysis certainly does not encompass all of the phenomena associated with everyday uses of the term "mood," and so it is important not to place too much weight upon choice of this particular term.
2   Hubert Dreyfus, *Being-in-the-World: A Commentary on Heidegger's* Being and Time Division 1 (Cambridge, MA: MIT Press, 1991).
3   Martin Heidegger, *Being and Time*, trans. Joan Stambaugh (New York: State University of New York Press, 1996).
4   William Blattner, *Heidegger's* Being and Time (London: Continuum, 2006).
5   John Haugeland, "Truth and Finitude: Heidegger's Transcendental Existentialism," in *Heidegger, Authenticity, and Modernity: Essays in Honor of Hubert L. Dreyfus: Volume 1*, eds. Mark Wrathall and Jeff Malpas (Cambridge, MA: MIT Press, 2000), 43–77.
6   This choice is to some extent arbitrary and other terms, such as "disposedness," would serve equally well. However, no English term has quite the same connotations as *Befindlichkeit*.
7   See, e.g., Robert Campbell Roberts, *Emotions: An Essay in Aid of Moral Psychology* (Cambridge: Cambridge University Press, 2003), 115.

8 I am using the term "experience" in a broad and noncommittal way here, so as to encompass both how we encounter things in the world and the background sense of belonging to a world.

9 See Matthew Ratcliffe, *Feelings of Being: Phenomenology, Psychiatry and the Sense of Reality* (Oxford: Oxford University Press, 2008).

10 See Ratcliffe, *Feelings of Being*, and Matthew Ratcliffe and Matthew Broome, "Existential Phenomenology, Psychiatric Illness and the Death of Possibilities," in *The Cambridge Companion to Existentialism*, eds. Mark Wrathall and Jeff Malpas (Cambridge: Cambridge University Press, 2012).

11 Heidegger distinguishes between inauthentic and authentic modes of understanding (e.g., *Being and Time*, 186), but both depend upon kinds of possibility that are already laid out by a mood. If one could not find anything practically significant in any way, neither authentic nor inauthentic pursuit of projects would be possible.

12 However, in Division II, Heidegger makes clear that fear is also essentially past-involving. When we are afraid, we are "bewildered" by the possibilities that we are faced with. So we fall back on habitual 'and thus past' ways of dealing with things (341–2).

13 There is also a distinction to be drawn between having a mood in the context of which being afraid is a possibility and having a mood that one might call *living in fear*. In the latter case, the fear is the mood. One does not merely encounter certain entities within the world as threatening. Instead, all experience is structured by a background sense of threat.

14 See Ratcliffe (2010) for a more detailed account of emotional depth.

15 The German term *Langeweile* (literally translated "long while") better conveys the temporal aspect of boredom that is central to Heidegger's discussion.

16 Richard Garrett, "The Problem of Despair," in *Philosophical Psychopathology*, eds. George Graham and G. Lynn Stephens (Cambridge, MA: MIT Press, 1994), 73–89.

17 Anthony Steinbock, "The Phenomenology of Despair," *International Journal of Philosophical Studies* 15 (2007): 435–51, 446.

18 See Strasser (1977) for an account of "levels" of feeling, which treats pre-intentional mood (*Stimmung*) as fundamental and complements Heidegger's discussion in several respects.

19 See Ratcliffe *Feelings of Being*, chapter 8, for an account of how such changes might be incorporated into phenomenological method and into philosophical method more generally.

20 Tanja Staehler, "How is a Phenomenology of Fundamental Moods Possible?," *International Journal of Philosophical Studies* 15 (2007): 415–33.

21 See Ratcliffe, *Feelings of Being*, and Matthew Ratcliffe, "The Feeling of Being," *Journal of Consciousness Studies* 12 (2005): 43–60.

22 Heidegger, M. 2001. Zollikon Seminars: Protocols – Conservations – Letters ed. M. Boss, Trans. F. Mayr and R. Askay (Evanston: Northwestern University Press).

23 Gerrit Glas, "Anxiety – Animal Reactions and the Embodiment of Meaning," in *Nature and Narrative: An Introduction to the New Philosophy of*

Psychiatry, eds. Bill Fulford, Katherine Morris, John Sadler, and Giovanni Stanghellini (Oxford: Oxford University Press, 2003), 231–49.

24 William Blattner, "Temporality," in *A Companion to Heidegger*, eds. Hubert Dreyfus and Mark Wrathall (Oxford: Blackwell, 2005), 311–24, 315.

25 Matthew Ratcliffe, "Depression, Guilt and Emotional Depth," *Inquiry* 53 (2010): 602–26.

26 Sally Brampton, *Shoot the Damn Dog: A Memoir of Depression* (London: Bloomsbury, 2008), 26.

27 Karl Jaspers, *General Psychopathology* (Manchester: Manchester University Press, 1962), part I, chapter I, describes several kinds of alteration in temporal experience that can occur in conditions such as depression and schizophrenia. However, he claims that time is always experienced, even though it can be experienced in a range of different ways. This is Heidegger's view too.

28 Fiona Shaw, *Out of Me: The Story of a Postnatal Breakdown* (London: Penguin, 1997), 25.

29 Brampton, *Shoot the Damn Dog*, 29.

30 Andrew Solomon, *The Noonday Demon* (London: Chatto and Windus, 2001), 55.

8   Heidegger on Human Understanding

An essential feature of human being is its understanding. We understand a language, we understand how to use tools and make things, we understand social norms, we understand theories, and, centrally for Heidegger, we understand a world and we understand being, including what it is to be human. Indeed, it is definitive of a being like us that "in its very being it comports itself understandingly to that being" (53).

Heidegger's account of understanding is meant to illuminate all of these forms of understanding, and this is a potential source of confusion, for these seem like very different activities. An understanding of theories seems, on the face of it, very different from an understanding of tool use or of social norms. We understand theories by grasping the meaning of concepts, and accurately applying those concepts to entities in the world while systematically relating the concepts to each other. Our understanding of tool use, by contrast, consists in being able to do things properly with those tools, regardless of whether we possess concepts that allow us to describe accurately what we are doing. And our understanding of worlds, or of our own existence, seems significantly different than either an understanding of a theory or an understanding of how to use a tool. It seems to involve, among other things, a sense for what kinds of events and entities are possible or impossible, a sense of what makes sense or what would be nonsensical, and a grasp of how to navigate from one setting to another or how to transition from one activity to the next.

I am indebted to many people for helping me refine and clarify my thoughts as I was writing this paper over many years. Among those deserving special thanks are Hubert Dreyfus, Samantha Matherne, and Joseph Schear. I have also benefited from the questions posed and suggestions made by many who have heard previous versions of this paper, including participants in my graduate seminar at the University of California, Riverside, *The Post-Kantian European Philosophy Seminar*, at Oxford University, a workshop held at Capital Normal University, Beijing, China, and the 2010 meeting of *The American Society for Existential Phenomenology*.

One possible way to make sense of this plurality of types of understanding is to array them vertically, so to speak. Some forms of understanding are viewed as providing a foundation on the basis of which other acts of understanding can be performed. The pragmatist interpretation of Heidegger reads his account of understanding and interpretation in this way. The most "primordial" form of understanding, according to the pragmatist Heideggerians, is "know how," the ability to cope skillfully and fluidly with the environment. Deliberate and conceptually mediated types of action (including interpretation) are performed on the foundation of our skillful understanding of the world.

While I accept the pragmatist account of the vertical relationships between more and less deliberate acts, and between conceptually mediated and preconceptual acts,[1] a vertical and foundationalist story about the relationship between types of action fails to map onto Heidegger's account of understanding and interpretation. I think what Heidegger actually offers us is a horizontal account, where each type of understanding-comportment is a concretization of a common structure. It is horizontal in the sense that the different types of understanding need not be derived from each other – insofar as they are types of understanding, they are all on the same level with each other. What makes one type of understanding more "primordial" than another, on a horizontal view, is a matter of its centrality to the primary ontological function of world disclosure. Thus Heidegger's discussion of understanding is intended primarily to describe the formal structure of understanding in general, for the purpose of explaining what function understanding plays in world disclosure. The *function* of a thing is the operation it performs, the part or role it plays in achieving an overall end or purpose (ψ). The *structure* is the way constituent features of a whole are organized so as to perform the function. With most entities, however, the influence of function on structure is not a one-way street; the structure opens up and constrains the function that the entity can perform. This becomes particularly apparent as contexts change and entities move into new situations where different ends or purposes come to organize the current world, for the function the entity is suited to perform in the new context will be constrained by its structure.

A *"formal structure of φ"* is the relationship between elements in virtue of which any φ thing can perform its function as a φ with the purpose of ψ. Thus everything that is a φ is understood in terms of possessing those elements in that relationship. If, in a particular case, a φ-thing lacks those elements, or its elements don't stand in their proper relationship, then it is understood as a deficient case of φ (and hence is still understood in terms of possessing those elements in that relationship). For example, bicycles perform the function of human locomotion. To describe the formal structure of bicycle-ness, one would designate the basic parts that allow a bicycle to perform this function (two wheels, handlebars for steering, a seat, and pedals for propulsion), and would describe the relationship between the parts (the wheels are behind one another, the pedals are linked to a wheel, the handlebars turn a wheel, the seat is in the appropriate proximity to the handlebars and the pedals, and so on). The structure is "formal" if it describes the form – the proper state – of any and every bicycle. Similarly, Heidegger will succeed in describing the formal structure of understanding if his description captures the elements and relations that constitute each different type of understanding *as* a type of understanding. Once he has described the formal structures, he is in a position to offer an account of several "deformalized"[2] variations of the structure – for instance, an account of the different types of understanding in their determinacy, which arise when the formal structure is applied to the particularities of different domains of entities.

On Heidegger's account, then, "understanding" names a structure – projection onto possibilities – that performs a function – disclosing the world as a setting for meaningful action. Thus vertical accounts are mistaken in even treating understanding as a *type* of act at all. All human actions (as distinct from mere behaviors or merely spatio-temporal events) involve understanding – that is, seeing in terms of possibilities. All human comportments, for Heidegger, are understanding-comportments. Interpretation, by contrast, is an act – an act in which one appropriates the understanding and develops it through a commitment to particular significations disclosed in the understanding.

In the first section of this paper, I will sketch out in a formal way Heidegger's account of understanding, interpretation, and the relationship between the two of them. In the second section, I will help explain and motivate a horizontal account by reviewing the difficulties and anomalies that vertical accounts run into in making sense of Heidegger's text. In the third section of the paper, I will develop and illustrate the structural-functional reading of understanding and interpretation in a phenomenological fashion.

UNDERSTANDING AND INTERPRETATION IN *BEING AND TIME*

We can indicate the essential formal characteristics of Heidegger's account of understanding and interpretation in three theses.

First Thesis: Understanding Has Primacy Over Cognition

The first thesis posits *the primacy of understanding over cognition*. "Understanding," Heidegger says, "is not an acquaintance derived from knowledge, but a primordially existential kind of being, which, more than anything else, makes such knowledge and acquaintance possible" (123–4; translation modified). This thesis is meant to deprive cognition of its traditional role in defining human nature.[3] To understand is to *be* in a certain way, to embody a particular way of existing in the world, rather than to think or believe or know that such and such is the case. Of course, as we will see, this is not to deny that thinking and believing and knowing are forms of understanding. Rather, it is to insist that not all understanding consists in cognition, and thus to recognize cognition as a specific mode of understanding rather than definitive of what it is to understand: "'understanding' in the sense of one possible kind of cognizing among others (as distinguished, for instance, from 'explaining'), must, like explaining, be interpreted as an existential derivative of that primary understanding which is one of the constituents of the being of the 'there' in general" (143; translation modified).

Second Thesis: Interpretation Develops and Appropriates What Is Understood in the Understanding

Interpretation takes what is projected in the understanding, and acts on the basis of the possibilities it has in view. In doing this, it makes the understanding its own, enriches it, and potentially even alters it: "The projecting of the understanding has its own possibility – that of developing itself. This development of the understanding we call 'interpretation.' In it the understanding appropriates understandingly that which is understood by it" (148, translation modified).

Third Thesis: Interpretation Pervades Understanding-Comportment

Heidegger repeatedly affirms that interpretation is not an occasional supplement to understanding. Interpretation is not a kind of activity – say, the explication of texts – that we can sometimes engage in, and at other times set aside. Rather, "it belongs to [Dasein's] ownmost being to have an understanding of that being and always already to maintain itself in a certain interpretedness of its being" (15; translation modified). Indeed, it is in interpretation alone that we can see and use or otherwise engage with entities in the world:

Concernful being amidst what is available gives itself to understand which involvements *it can have in each case* with what is encountered, and it does this from out of the significance that is disclosed in understanding the world. Circumspection discovers – that means, the world that is already understood is interpreted. (148; translation modified, emphasis supplied)

In this crucial passage, to which we shall have to return, Heidegger reaffirms the pervasiveness of interpretation in circumspective engagement with the world three more times:

All prepredicative simple seeing of the available is in itself already understanding-interpreting (149; translation modified)

and

The seeing with this sight is always already understanding-interpreting (149; translation modified)

and

every perception of available equipment is understanding-interpreting, and lets us circumspectively encounter something as something. (149; translation modified)

And further along in §32, Heidegger affirms that "understanding and interpretation make up the existential constitution of the there" (150; translation modified).

Later, in his existential account of spatiality, Heidegger argues that an interpretive discovery of places is a necessary condition of our ability to encounter any available totality of equipment at all:

Something like a region must first be discovered if there is to be any possibility of allotting or coming across places for a totality of equipment that is circumspectively at one's disposal. The regional orientation of the multiplicity of places belonging to the available goes to make up the aroundness – the "round-about-us" [das Um-uns-herum] – of those entities which we encounter as closest environmentally. A three-dimensional multiplicity of possible positions which gets filled up with occurrent things is never proximally given. This dimensionality of space is still veiled in the spatiality of the available. The "above" is what is "on the ceiling"; the "below" is what is "on the floor"; the "behind" is what is "at the door"; *all "wheres" are discovered and circumspectively interpreted as we go our ways in everyday dealings*; they are not ascertained and catalogued by the observational measurement of space. (103; translation modified, emphasis supplied)

Because having a place or a "where" is a condition of the possibility of equipment being encounterable as usable in our circumspective comportment, and because the where of equipment is only discovered and made available to us as it is circumspectively interpreted, it follows that interpretation underlies all our comportment with the available.

HERMENEUTIC AND PRAGMATIST ACCOUNTS OF
HEIDEGGER'S THREE THESES

The three theses give us a formal and schematic account of what human understanding consists in. To understand is to be in the world in such a way that everything is projected upon, that is, makes sense in terms of, particular possibilities. Projecting is not necessarily a cognitive act but a stance or orientation to things around us (which may, of course, involve cognition). In order to inhabit this understanding, however, I must develop it and appropriate it by acting on the basis of it. Interpretation is the appropriation of the understanding, and it is a pervasive, ongoing activity.

Attempts to deformalize this account and give it some phenomenological content have, however, run into difficulty. According to my diagnosis, the difficulty stems from two fundamental errors. The first, as I outlined above, is the tendency to think of understanding as a discrete type of activity rather than as a structure present in all meaningful activities. This is to misconstrue the primacy of understanding over cognition as the priority of one type of activity over another type of activity, and thus to treat Heidegger's account of understanding and interpretation as a vertical account. The second error is to think of interpretation as an activity of making explicit the content of what is, and must be, inexplicit in skillful comportment. Interpretation, on this view, is an activity in which the content of understanding is converted into a form suitable for cognition. These two errors convert Heidegger's three theses into the following inconsistent triad:

1. The primacy of practice: coping (know-how) is more basic than cognition (knowing that).
2. Interpretation brings understanding to cognition.
3. Interpretation pervades understanding-comportment.

The triad is inconsistent because if interpretation is necessarily cognitive in nature, and interpretation pervades all our understanding engagements with the world, then we have no grounds for asserting the primacy of practice over cognition.

For me, the inconsistency of this triad is prima facie grounds for thinking that we need to deformalize Heidegger's account in a different way. But before offering such an account, it is instructive to see how the inconsistency has played itself out in scholarly appropriations of Heidegger's work.

The Hermeneuticist Reading

The perceived inconsistency in Heidegger's three theses has led many interpreters to abandon or at least qualify their commitment to one of Heidegger's claims. For instance, the hermeneutic school (largely indebted to Hans Georg Gadamer's influential interpretation) tends to abandon or qualify the first thesis. The hermeneuticists, in other words, give interpretation pride of place in their account of human existence. "Interpretation," Gadamer argues, is not an occasional, post facto supplement to understanding; rather understanding is always interpretation, and hence interpretation is the explicit form [*die explizite Form*] of understanding. In accordance with this insight, interpretive language and concepts were recognized as belonging to the inner structure of understanding. This moves the whole problem of language from its peripheral and incidental position into the center of philosophy.[4]

In passages like this, we can see clearly that Heidegger's second thesis has been construed as arguing that interpretation renders the understanding in conceptual terms. This is a salient point of agreement with the pragmatist interpretation. This passage also, however, indicates the point at which hermeneuticists part ways with the pragmatists – namely, in their insistence on the third thesis regarding the pervasiveness of interpretation.

Holding on to the third thesis, as we have already noted, drives the hermeneuticists to abandon or modify their commitment to the first thesis. Ricoeur, for instance, insists that the priority does not amount to positing a kind of understanding that could exist unmediated by language. Rather, the priority points to the need to "anchor[] the whole linguistic system, including books and texts, in something which is not primordially a phenomenon of articulation in discourse."[5] Thus "the first function of understanding is to orientate us in a situation."[6] The understanding is viewed on this model, not as lacking in conceptual articulation, but as the moment in which we "anticipate" or "project" a particular range of concepts.[7] Understanding is a nominally distinct activity from interpretation, in that the latter exploits one set of concepts to articulate another set while the former is simply the "projection of meaning in a situation."[8] But the understanding has already received a thorough-going conceptual-linguistic articulation that we inherit by being raised in an historical linguistic community that has been engaged in an ongoing process of interpretation. Our every encounter with the world is thus mediated by an interpretation that takes the form of either conversation or textual transmission of the historical tradition.[9] Thus hermeneutic interpreters of Heidegger tend to see *Being and Time* as having failed to come to terms with the important role of language in articulating our understanding of the world. They see the later Heidegger's alleged turn to language as evidence that Heidegger himself eventually recognized this failing, and corrected it by rejecting the first thesis himself.[10]

The Pragmatist Version of the Primacy of Practice

Pragmatist approaches to Heidegger, by contrast, have abandoned or qualified the third thesis. Interpretation, according to the pragmatists, interferes with the functioning of the most basic form of human understanding, and thus cannot be a necessary component of our understanding-comportment.

On Hubert Dreyfus' influential interpretation of Heidegger, understanding is divided into three types: coping, interpretation, and assertion.[11] Understanding as coping or know-how "consists of dispositions to respond to situations in appropriate ways,"[12] and as such "it is not a belief system but is embodied in our skills."[13] This most primordial form of understanding is "unreflective, everyday, projective activity such as hammering."[14] Interpretation, the explicit form of understanding, is derivative of understanding as coping: "understanding ... becomes explicit in the practical deliberation necessitated when a skill fails to suffice, and what thus becomes thematic can be expressed in speech acts ... That which is laid out as the unavailable, in what Heidegger calls 'interpretation' [Auslegung], can then be privatively (selectively) thematized as occurrent by means of assertions stating propositions assigning predicates to subjects."[15] Dreyfus divides the most basic form of understanding, coping, into three further levels – manipulation (or "current coping as pressing into possibilities"), coping with the local background, and coping with the world. The most basic of these is coping with the world, because it makes the other more specific forms of coping possible.[16] Dreyfus divides interpretation into two levels, including (surprisingly enough) "everyday coping with the available" at the more primordial level and "theory of the occurrent" at a more derivative level.[17] But I take it that this was a mistake – that for Dreyfus, everyday coping is not a form of interpretation, since interpretation for him involves cognition, having become deliberate and reflective because our skills are insufficient to cope fluidly with the situation. If we correct for this error,[18] Dreyfus's picture looks like this:

Dreyfus's Vertical Account of Understanding

Types of Understanding	Levels of Action
Assertion	Theoretical assertion – "attaching an isolated predicate to an isolated subject"
	Ordinary assertion – "Calling attention to aspects"
Intepretation = "laying out the as-structure"	Theory of the occurrent
	"Deliberate but still context-dependent" use
Primordial understanding = "unreflective, everyday, projective activity"	Manipulation – everyday coping with the available
	Coping with the local background
	Coping with the world

Others have closely followed Dreyfus in treating understanding as skillful practical activity. For Blattner, "to understand something is to be able to do or manage or master it" (Blattner 2006: 85). Taylor Carman likewise explains that "understanding means competence, skill, know-how" (*Heidegger's Analytic*, 19).

INTERPRETATION AS MAKING EXPLICIT. In the pragmatists' reading, as we've seen already, the thesis of the primacy of understanding is linked to a very specific account of what it means for interpretation to "appropriate and develop what is understood" in the understanding. In contrast to the basic practical form of understanding – "our engaged abilities, our skills and capacities"[19] – Blattner explains that "interpretation" is "an act of understanding in which we make what we understand explicit."[20] "Explicit" means, for Blatter, "suffused with conceptuality,"[21] and that means linguistically expressible: "the distinction between understanding and interpretation in *Being and Time*," Blattner explains, is "the line between those forms of intelligence that can be captured in propositions and those that cannot."[22]

The priority thesis is thus formulated in this way: "understanding that has propositional content (i.e., interpretation) is derivative of understanding that does not."[23] As Blattner explains at greater length:

So, the primacy of practice, the thesis that the intelligence and intelligibility of human life resides primarily in precognitive practice, and that cognition is derivative of such practice, takes form in *Being and Time* by way of the distinction between understanding and interpretation. Cognition is taking-as, grasping things under a conceptually articulated aspect, in such a way that the content of one's taking-as can be expressed in propositional form, asserted. Understanding is what Dreyfus calls "absorbed coping," an inexplicit mastery of one's world and oneself. Such mastery is inexplicit, however, not in the sense that it is un- or preconscious (though it may well mostly be), nor in the sense that it is not rule-governed (though it surely is not), but rather in the sense that it is preconceptual, prepropositional. Pre-cognitive understanding cannot "be expressed in a proposition," it cannot be "retained and kept as something asserted."[24]

Taylor Carman, too, argues that "interpretation is understanding made explicit."[25] But Carman has a different take on explicitness than Blattner or Dreyfus. For him, something is explicit when it demonstratively shows what we understand. Carman's reason for departing from the orthodox pragmatist interpretation in this respect is that he, unlike Dreyfus and Blattner, acknowledges thesis three – the *pervasiveness of interpretation*. For, as Carman observes, in Heideger's account, "we are never entirely without *some* explicit interpretation of ourselves and the world."[26]

THE PERVASIVENESS OF INTERPRETATION. It is perhaps no surprise that orthodox pragmatist Heideggerians tend to overlook the third thesis.

In his commentary, Dreyfus on a couple of occasions quotes passages asserting the pervasiveness of interpretation, but he treats them as passages about understanding and everyday coping. For instance, having quoted Heidegger as asserting that "in no case is a Dasein untouched and unseduced by this [the everyday way] in which things have been interpreted" (169), Dreyfus glosses the passage as being about the pervasiveness of our *understanding* of being:

our *understanding* of being is so pervasive in everything we think and do that we can never arrive at a clear presentation of it. Moreover, since it is not a belief system but is embodied in our skills, it is not the sort of thing we could ever get clear about.[27]

This gloss is perfectly correct provided that one sees that *a* particular, actual, operative understanding of being simply is an interpretation (as I will argue it is below). But that is not what Dreyfus has in mind, and it is telling that his way of thinking about interpretation forces him to read such passages as if they were talking about understanding rather than interpretation.

Blattner does something similar when he addresses Heidegger's claim that "all prepredicative simple seeing of something available is in itself already understanding and interpretation." Blattner glosses the phrase "pre-predicative simple seeing of the available" as "cognition" or "intending." Thus he restates this passage as saying: "all cognition, all intending, is a taking-in or taking-as. All cognition is interpretation."[28] But this gloss is a nonstarter if, like Blattner, one understands interpretation as the propositional articulation of intelligibility. For then Heidegger would be saying that all pre-predicative simple intending is propositionally articulated. But to be propositionally articulated is necessarily to have a predicative structure.

Carman, as we noted, recognizes the pervasiveness claim, but he tries to moderate it. Although there is always some explicit interpretation going on, according to Carman, he insists that "interpretation is not an element in all our comportment and all our dealings with things and with each other."[29] Carman's reason for this insistence is the phenomenologically plausible claim that "Dasein is ordinarily far from understanding itself or its being in explicit, perspicuous, or even fully coherent terms."[30] If the pervasiveness of interpretation entailed that Dasein always does understand itself or its being "in explicit, perspicuous, or even fully coherent terms," this would count as a compelling reason for rejecting it. The same reasoning is also behind Carman glossing the explicitness involved in interpretation, not in cognitive terms – not as either conscious awareness or as propositional articulation – but in demonstrative terms. To make explicit is to manifest, indicate, or show "the *how* that we know in understanding."[31] This manifesting can, but need not, exploit propositional or even conceptual ways of grasping things – bodily postures like shrugging my shoulders, or facial expressions like wrinkling my nose are for Carman instances of expressive and thus interpretive comportment. I'm not sure how to understand in these terms the claim that "we are never entirely without *some* explicit interpretation of ourselves and the world" – I don't see why we would always necessarily have to be making some sort of communicative gesture or facial expression. That is to say, even Carman's moderate reading of the pervasiveness claim is hard to defend on his account of interpretation.

Like the pragmatists, and against the hermeneuticists, I want to argue that a correct reading of Heidegger holds on to the core of the "pragmatist" interpretation, the primacy of practices. In order to do this, we have to rethink the way the thesis of the primacy of practice was formulated in 1', and this will lead us, in turn, to a different way of thinking about understanding. We will also need to to recognize that 2' misconstrues 2 – we have, in other words, to reject the claim that Heideggerian interpretation is necessarily cognitive in nature. But in rejecting 2', we will open the door to appreciating the true significance of Heidegger's endorsement of a hermeneutic approach to ontology, and thus recover an important kernel of truth in the hermeneuticist appropriation of Heidegger. To do that, we need to recover a sense of "interpretation" that Dreyfus himself employs in his commentary on Heidegger when, for example, he says that "our most pervasive interpretation of being masculine and feminine ... is in our bodies, our perceptions, our language, and generally in our skills for dealing with the same and the opposite sex."[32] When Dreyfus treats "existence as the self-interpreting way of being in our practices,"[33] he is much closer to thinking of interpretation in the same way Heidegger does than when he defines interpretation as deliberate, reflective, and conceptually mediated coping. With a clearer grasp of what Heidegger is actually committing himself to when he asserts the pervasiveness of interpretation in all understanding comportment, we will also get a more profound insight into all of the ways in which interpretation figures in *Being and Time* – for instance, the sense in which *das Man* interprets the world, action interprets the self, conscience interprets our thrownness, tool use and being-towards death interpret time, and so on.

THE STRUCTURAL-FUNCTIONAL ACCOUNT OF UNDERSTANDING AND INTERPRETATION

I should confess at this point that I understand myself not as rejecting but as clarifying and defending the pragmatist interpretation of

Heidegger. The pragmatist reading is built on giving pride of place to Heidegger's insight that human engagement with the world is distorted by treating all of it as involving cognition. This insight is something I want to hold on to. But abandoning thesis three – Heidegger's insistence on the pervasiveness of interpretation – is the wrong way to hold on to the priority of practice over cognition. And the pragmatist construal of Heidegger's first two theses misses key elements of his account of human understanding.

I want to advance, in particular, two claims to counter what I view as the two principal errors of orthodox pragmatist accounts. First, while I accept Dreyfus' vertical account of types of understanding-comportment, I don't believe that this captures what Heidegger meant when he argued for the primordiality of understanding. Understanding is not the most basic kind of human activity. It is the structure that makes all human activities *activities* as opposed to mere movements or events. Second, I suggest that *making explicit* is not the primary function of interpretation. It is true that *Ausdrücklichkeit* or *expressness* is the structure of interpretation. And expressness names a structure that includes explicitness in some of its modes. But we're after the general structure that Heidegger has in mind. Interpretation, for Heidegger, is action in which we "enact" the understanding – we commit ourselves to definite possibilities projected by the understanding. Interpretive enactment makes "express" certain meanings – it lifts them into salience, gives them definiteness, and so on. It can do this without involving deliberateness (Dreyfus), conceptually mediated activity (Blattner), the use of language (Gadamer and Ricoeur), or demonstrative action (Carman), although it certainly does involves those things in particular instances.

The Structural-Functional Account of Understanding

For Heidegger, "understanding" names an *existentiale*, an ontological constitutent of our being in the world. Thus every human action, practice, skill, mental or perceptual state, emotion, mood, or disposition will manifest understanding. As I noted in the introduction, the aim of Heidegger's existential analytic is to "expose a fundamental structure in Dasein" (41; translation modified). A structure is fundamental if it contributes to the primary function of the thing in question. In the analytic of Dasein, the primary function of understanding is world disclosure. "In the understanding," Heidegger explains, "the relations which are constitutive of the world as world ... are held in disclosedness *in advance*. It holds itself in them *with familiarity*; and in so doing, it holds them before itself as that within which its referring operates" (86–7, translation modified). Or, put slightly differently, "the disclosing in advance of that on the basis of which the freeing of that which is encountered within the world occurs – this is nothing other than the understanding of the world, to which the Dasein as an entity always already relates itself" (86; translation modified).

The function of understanding, then, is (a) to disclose "in advance" – that is, before we engage in any particular concrete activities – the relations that constitute entities as the entities that they are; and (b) to place us "within" contexts of relationships "with familiarity" – that is, to enable us to know our way around the world, to find it intelligible or understandable. The structure that allows understanding to perform this function, Heidegger claims, is "projecting onto possibilities":

Why does the understanding, in conformity with all essential dimensions of that which can be disclosed in it, always penetrate into possibilities? It is because the understanding has in itself the existential structure which we call "projection." It projects the being of Dasein on its "for-the-sake-of-which" just as primordially as it projects it upon significance as the worldliness of its particular world. The projection character of understanding constitutes being-in-the-world with regard to the disclosedness of its there as a there of an ability to be. Projection is the existential constitution of the being of the leeway [Spielraum] of the factical ability to be. And as thrown, Dasein is thrown into the mode of being of projecting. (145; translation modified)

"Projecting onto possibilities" amounts to seeing events and entities in the world (including ourselves) in the light of the different ways they can meaningfully interact. Understanding opens up sight, which means "letting entities which are accessible to it be encountered uncon-cealedly in themselves ... ['Sight' is] a universal term for characterizing any access to entities or to being, as access in general" (147; translation modified). By projecting onto possibilities, thus holding open the relations of signification that constitute entities as the entities they are, Dasein holds itself in a meaningful, that is, understandable world.

Understanding performs the ontological function of disclosing "the there as a there of an ability to be" (145). That is, through understanding, we find ourselves in a setting (our "there") within which we can be who we are. It constitutes the setting as "a leeway ('Spielraum') for the factical ability to be" (145; translation modified). The "leeway" or "room for maneuver" that understanding opens up needs to be under-stood in existential terms – that is, the understanding doesn't open up physical space, but it does provide us with a range of possibilities for pursuing a particular course of activity or a particular identity. All the different kinds of understanding we catalogued at the beginning of this paper – understanding a tool, a language, understanding ourselves – count as instances of understanding because they perform the function of showing us a certain leeway or range of ways to be – ways to use the tool, ways to perform speech acts, ways to be who we are.

The structure of understanding is what allows it to open up this leeway for a factical ability to be. The structure consists, as we saw, in projecting onto possibilities. But what does Heidegger mean by "projection"? "In its projective character, understanding makes up existentially what we call the sight of Dasein" (146; translation modified). As a kind of "sight," that is, a mode of access to entities, projection is to be understood in its differentiation from other forms of sight, in particular both introspection and what Heidegger sometimes calls "pure perception" or "pure apprehension." Pure apprehension is perception stripped of all evaluations or goals that are peculiar to the perceiver. It is a sight that terminates in the object, and discloses its objects "as in themselves already occurrent, as encountered of themselves on their own account" (GA 24: 167, translation modified). Understanding as projection "deprives pure intuition of its priority" (147; translation modified). "Projection," unlike pure perception, does not terminate on an object, but "unveils without making what is unveiled as such into an object of contemplation" (GA 24: 398). "What is *most proper* to this activity and occurrence," that is, to projection, "is what comes to expression linguistically in the prefix 'pro-', namely that in projecting, this occurrence of projection *carries* the projecting one *out and away from itself* in a certain way" (GA 29/30: 527).[34] And in going outward, projection carries us past the "object" of perception and *to* its interaction with other things. Think of a film projector. One sees a film projected, not by looking *at* the film, but precisely by looking away from it to the pattern it makes when it is illuminated and thrown onto something else.

Projecting in Heidegger's sense, then, is "apprehending x by looking at y." The "x" is the particular entity or event that we understand. The "y," Heidegger tells us, is a possibility. To be specific, the y-term of projection is the pattern of possibilities in terms of which the projector can incorporate the x into the world, thus making sense of it. For projection, the world shows up as a possibility space: "the world, qua world, is disclosed as possible significance ... The totality of affordances is revealed as the categorial whole of a possible interconnection of the ready to hand" (144, translation modified).

In projecting, we grasp a thing not in terms of its present, self-contained, occurrent properties but in terms of "what it becomes or respectively doesn't become" (145; translation modified). Heidegger also describes projection in terms of transparency – we understand things to the degree they are transparent, meaning we understand them better as we can see through to more and more of the possibilities that they afford (146).

Projection has a recursive structure, meaning that to understand the y-term, it must itself be projected onto something else. The "stratification" or "layers" (*Schichtung*) of projection, Heidegger argues, are interwoven (see GA 24: 398). For example, we understand a baseball bat by projecting it onto the rules of baseball, which govern the possibilities that determine what can and cannot be done with the bat during the game. But we only understand the rules of baseball by projecting them in turn onto (among other things) bats and balls and bases and pitches and swings. And ultimately, Heidegger argues, the possibilities must be projected onto time. The game of baseball affords a certain patterning of the temporal structure of life.

Of course, in each case, there is some particular, factical me who is projecting something onto its possibilities:

We shall now attempt to clarify the structure of the understanding that is constitutive of existence. To understand means, more precisely, to project oneself upon a possibility, in this projection to keep oneself at all times in a possibility. An ability to be, a possibility as possibility, is there only in projection, in projecting oneself upon that ability to be. (GA 24: 392; translation modified)

The possibilities that the thing affords depend on the disposedness (*Befindlichkeit*) of the one doing the projecting – his or her skills, tastes, preferences, dispositions, aims, goals, ideals, and so on. A baseball bat affords a very different set of possibilities for Albert Pujols, for instance, than it does for me. Thus Heidegger explains that "projection is essentially a thrown projection" (GA 9: 357/257):

In every case Dasein, as essentially disposed, has already got itself into definite possibilities ... But this means that Dasein is being-possible which has been delivered over to itself – thrown possibility through and through. (144; translation modified)

I understand my own thrown disposedness by projecting myself out into the world, thereby discovering what kind of pattern of possibilities shows up for such a being as me:

If the Dasein projects itself upon a possibility, it is projecting itself in the sense that it is unveiling itself as this ability to be, in this specific being. If the Dasein projects itself upon a possibility and understands itself in that possibility, this understanding, this becoming manifest of the self, is not a self-contemplation in the sense that the ego would become the object of some cognition or other; rather, the projection is the way in which I am the possibility; it is the way in which I exist freely ... Understanding as the Dasein's self-projection is the Dasein's fundamental mode of happening. As we may also say, it is the authentic meaning of action. (GA 24: 392–3; translation modified)

Dasein projects itself "both upon its 'for-the-sake-of-which' and upon significance, as the worldhood of its particular world" (145) – my possibilities open up simultaneously in terms of what the world affords me given both the facticity into which I am thrown, and who I have chosen to be.[35]

The possibilities into which I project – the patterns of affordances in terms of which I understand anything at all – afford me a leeway only because I am always projecting any particular thing (including myself) onto a *plurality* of different possibilities. Projection "lets the possibility stand as a possibility" (GA 20: 439), and "when one is diverted into [*Sichverlegen in*] one of these basic possibilities of understanding, the other is not laid aside [*legt ... nicht ab*]" (146). To be in a possibility is to be oriented to a possibility space that is broader than any particular commitment to a course of action. As we shall see below, interpretation (*Auslegung*) is a "diversion into" (*Sichverlegen in*) a possibility that develops and appropriates the possibility as one's own. But one reason understanding is not reducible to interpretation is that we continue to hold open, and see in terms of, possibilities we have not diverted ourselves into.

The possibilities are not held open, however, in and through an act of cognition: "Understanding is not a mode of cognition but the basic determination of existing" (GA 24: 392; translation modified). Projecting is not a mental state, but rather a way of being oriented to the significances in the world:

When I am completely engrossed in dealing with something and make use of some equipment in this activity, I am just not directed toward the equipment as such, say, toward the tool. And I am just as little directed toward the work itself. Instead, in my occupation I move in the affordance relations as such. In understanding them I dwell with the equipmental contexture that is handy. I stand neither with the one nor with the other but move in the in-order-to. (GA 24: 415; translation modified)

This is true even of cognitive acts of understanding. Even in developing a philosophical theory or designing a scientific experiment or describing an event or cashing out a metaphor, I am moving in an open field of relations. I project each word or concept onto a field of possibilities that I know my way around, that immediately offers me affordances for thought: "All ontical experience of entities – both circumspective calculation of the available, and positive scientific cognition of the occurrent – is based upon projections of the being of the corresponding entities – projections which in every case are more or less transparent" (324).

With this observation, we are now in a position to recognize the true significance of Heidegger's first thesis about the primacy of understanding over cognition. He is not claiming that one particular type of comportment – skillful action – is foundational for the rest. The claim is instead that all comportments, including the cognitive forms that philosophers tend to treat as foundational, are instances of projection onto possibilities. Heideggerian understanding is offered as "a sufficiently primordial concept of understanding from which alone not only all modes of cognition but every type of comportment that relates to beings by inspection and circumspection can be conceived in a fundamental way" (GA 24: 390; translation modified).

In exposing the structure of understanding, Heidegger often focuses on paradigmatic states or activities – these are states or activities that most perspicuously allow us to see the ontological structure and the performance of the function in question. But it would be a mistake to focus on the paradigm case to the exclusion of all others. We should not, for instance, ask, "which of all the kinds of understanding someone possesses is *true* Heideggerian understanding?" Rather, we ask, "how do all of the things we do depend on our having projected onto possibilities in such a way as to 'open up a leeway for a factical ability to be'?"

The Structural-Functional Account of Interpretation

Of course, there is more to inhabiting a world than merely possessing a complex of bodily, cognitive, or linguistic skills for seeing the possibilities each thing affords. We are only truly *in* the world when we commit to applying those skills. Interpretation, for Heidegger, is "enacting" the understanding: commiting to exercise and develop skills by acting on some particular set of possibilities projected in the understanding.

If I commit myself to pursue some definite set of possibilities that the world affords me – if I let myself be solicited by some possibility, that possibility will, for its part, demand of me that I develop myself to respond appropriately to it. The possibilities "exert a counter thrust" [*Rückschlag*] (148) – they rebound or push back at us. As we commit to a definite possibility, then, we develop and refine and execute and perfect our skills for seeing what possibilities are afforded to us. Heidegger calls this "laying out" or "interpreting" the possibility:

The projecting of the understanding has its own possibility – that of developing itself. This development [*Ausbildung*] of the understanding we call "interpretation" [*Auslegung*]. In it the understanding appropriates understandingly that which is understood by it. In interpretation, understanding does not become something different. It becomes itself. Such interpretation is grounded existentially in understanding; the latter does not arise from the former. Nor is interpretation the acquiring of information about what is understood; it is rather the working-out [*Ausarbeitung*] of possibilities projected in understanding. (148; translation modified)

Just to emphasize, then, there are three key moments to this formal, structural-functional definition of interpretation. The first is that interpretation "works out" the possibilities projected in the understanding. "Working out" (*Ausarbeitung*) is executing, accomplishing, bringing about what is afforded as a possibility by our understanding. The second moment of the interpretation is the *Ausbildung*, the development or cultivation or refinement of the understanding. As we encounter the concrete particularities of a situation opened up in a projection, we acquire a more precise, more closely tailored understanding of what possibilities the world affords us. In the third moment, the interpretive act lifts into salience some particular set of relationships within which entities and actions lie at any given moment. In interpretation, as Heidegger puts it, things "come *expressly* [*ausdrücklich*] into the sight which understands" (149). Thus

interpretation as such does not actually disclose, for that is what understanding or Dasein itself takes care of. Interpretation always only takes care of bringing out what is disclosed as a development of the possibilities inherent in an understanding. The most proximate everyday mode of interpretation has the functional form of appresentation, specifically the appresentation of meaningfulness in the sense of bringing out the referential correlations accessible at any given time. (GA 20: 359; translation modified)

Appresentation means to let one thing be seen through another. In committing ourselves to a particular possibility, we also make salient a particular relationship between something and what it affords.

It is no accident that Heidegger's account of interpretation makes use of so many words built around a common prefix: the *aus-* or out-. Interpretation "lays out" the world in a particular way. As it does so, it "works out" or develops possibilities in concreteness. It "develops out" or refines our ability to project. And it "presses out" or makes salient particular relationships. How are we to understand in general the contrast between the "in"-ness of the understanding and the "out"-ness of interpretation?[36] It is the distinction between what is merely contemplated versus what is executed (in English, we call this "carrying out"). It is the distinction between what is perceived in general and imprecisely versus what is discerned with sufficient detail and richness (in English, we call this "making out" – discerning in detail). Interpretation, we could say, is "exacting," invoking here the etymology to inform our sense. The English adjective "exact" comes from the past participle of the Latin verb "*ex-agere*" – literally to act out, to drive out, force out. What is "exact" in the traditional sense is what has been driven or pursued until it has achieved perfection or completion. A person or an action that is exact is one that is highly skilled or accomplished. It is within such a context of semantic values that one is to hear Heidegger's use of the word *Auslegung*.

Thus, in interpretation, the world gets "laid out" in a particular, more precise, more detailed way. Only with a commitment to a particular possibility, Heidegger notes, do things "genuinely come into the environment as present" (GA 20: 359; translation modified). Only then is something "first genuinely understood" because that is "when one has come into the involvement which one has with the environmental thing" (GA 20: 359; translation modified).

THE HORIZONTAL ACCOUNT OF INTERPRETATION. Interpretation, Heidegger tells us, is "the mode of enactment of understanding ... specifically as the cultivation, appropriation, and preservation of what is discovered in understanding" (GA 20: 366; translation modified). It should not surprise us that there are many different forms in which this cultivation, appropriation, and preservation can take place.

Gadamer has given us a useful typology of interpretations. He distinguishes between cognitive, normative, and reproductive forms of interpretation.[37] The cognitive type of interpretation is exemplified by literary or art criticism – it is an effort to restate or spell out or linguistically describe the meaningful content that is understood. The normative type of interpretation is exemplified by legal interpretation, and consists in bringing a particular case under the meaning that is understood. The law, for instance, is interpretively illuminated when we see in what way it applies (or fails to apply) to some particular case. The reproductive form of interpretation is exemplified by performances of a dramatic work or a musical work – the understanding of the piece is illuminated and developed as the performer makes it her or his own in reproducing it.

As a crosscutting category, we can distinguish, as Heidegger does, between thematic interpretation and circumspective interpretation (see 150). This distinction, roughly speaking, is the distinction between deliberately taking something as something versus using or being solicited to use something as something. There can be both thematic and circumspective forms of both normative and reproductive interpretation. When an umpire calls a pitch a strike, this is a thematic normative interpretive act. When a soccer player holds his run to stay onside, this is a circumspective normative interpretive act. An important category of circumspective reproductive interpretive acts consists in taking up a for-the-sake-of-which afforded by our culture. When Albert Pujols steps onto the field, he does it as the Los Angeles Angels' first baseman, and not as a pitcher, a manager, a trainer, football midfielder, and so on. In doing so, he is interpreting himself as a baseball player, but also interpreting the baseball player role in his own, reproductive way. Commitments to a particular course of action contribute to the function of world disclosure by involving us in the significations of the world in such a way that we own or appropriate them, develop them, and, in the process of developing them, enrich our skills for coping by giving us a more precise ability to anticipate and respond to the solicitations of our actual situation.

EXPRESSNESS. As I noted earlier, one of the principle errors of both the pragmatist and hermeneuticist readings of Heidegger is to understand interpretation as making explicit in the sense of bringing things to language or conceptual articulation. While making explicit is *one form* that interpretation can take, it is only one of many. Focusing on it leads one to misconstrue the essential structure of interpretation in general. The error is driven, I believe, by misconstruing Heidegger's use of the term *Ausdrücklich*, and thus it is worth addressing in some more detail the expressness that is a constitutive moment of interpretation.

Expressness is itself a functional term. It points, as we saw, to the moment of interpretation in which a particular relationship is lifted into salience. There are a number of different ways in which this can occur – through a linguistic act, through a thought, through deliberate action, but also through circumspective action in which we are solicited by and act upon a particular significance. Heidegger calls the thematic forms of expressness "explicit" (*explizit*) to distinguish them from more circumspective forms of expressness. But when a pitcher throws to first base to check the runner instead of, for instance, throwing a pitch, he is enacting one possibility and lifting one affordance into salience – he is expressing it, without making it explicit:

The circumspectively-interpretive coping with what is environmentally available, which "sees" this as a table, a door, a carriage, a bridge, does not necessarily need to lay apart in a determining assertion. All prepredicative simple seeing of the available is in itself already understanding-interpreting. (149; translation modified)

"The 'as,'" Heidegger explains, "makes up the structure of the expressness of what is understood; it constitutes the interpretation" (149; translation modified). Something is constituted when matters are so organized or arranged or set up that it can be the thing that it is. Thus the claim is that when a domain receives an "as-structure," then an interpretation can perform its function within that domain – the function of enacting the understanding in a way that develops it and lifts some particular significance into salience. The structure of expressness, which constitutes the interpretation as what it is, is the "as structure."

But what is the "as structure"? The "as structure" is the structure of affordances – the structure by which something is seen as affording something else. Something has an *as* when it draws us into acting with it in a particular way. At the circumspectively interpretive level, the desk simply shows up as affording writing (see GA 21, §12). At a thematic level, it shows up (perhaps) as affording description in such and such terms.

THE PERVASIVENESS OF INTERPRETATION. Now if I'm right that "interpretation" names whatever performs the function of developing and appropriating possibilities through a commitment to a particular course of action, then we can see that some form of interpretation will be pervasive in all particular instances of worldly action. Although pervasive, however, interpretation does not completely permeate the world, as there are possibilities projected in the understanding that are left standing while we divert ourselves into a particular interpretation. Moreover, there is a hermeneutic circle at work linking the understanding and interpretation. This is *not* the hermeneutic circle of the hermeneuticists – it is not a circle of explication. Rather, taking a particular stand on one's possibilities develops and refines those possibilities, thus altering and enriching our understanding of the world.

To be caught up in conventions, norms, and publically shared modes of behavior is one way to inhabit a particular interpretation. Our immediate, unthinking reaction to the world focuses on particular possibilities "in accordance with the way things have been interpreted by the 'one.' This interpretation has already restricted the possible options of choice to what lies within the range of the familiar, the attainable, the respectable – that which is fitting and proper" (129; translation modified). The "one," *das Man*, "sketches out in advance the most immediate interpretation of the world and being in the world. Dasein is for the sake of the 'one'-self in an everyday manner, and the 'one'-self articulates the referential context of significance" (129; translation modified). We always encounter the world, in other words, as soliciting us to pursue particular possibilities. When responding to these solicitations and doing what "one" does in our culture, we "maintain" ourselves "in an average interpretedness" (406).

CONCLUSION

We have seen that all our understanding-comportments are enabled by the structure of projecting onto possibilities. It is this structure that Heidegger names "understanding." Bodily skills are paradigmatic cases in which to recognize the structure of projection, and they present our most basic forms of insertion into a world.[38] But insofar as all forms of understanding comportment involve projection onto possibilities, they are all horizontally arrayed by Heidegger as instances of understanding. The world-disclosive function of the understanding is to insert us into a world, which shows up as a space within which we can pursue a variety of possibilities and take one of an indeterminate number of possible stands on our own existence.

Any action we perform involves a commitment to developing a particular way of projecting into possibilities, which amounts to an "interpretation" of ourselves and the world. Thus all actions are also horizontally arrayed as instances of interpretation. The world-disclosive function of interpretation is to involve us in developing, refining, and articulating the possibilities projected by the understanding. And it is at this point that we can acknowledge the truth in the hermeneuticist account. We always take over, in the first instance, an understanding to the world that has already been interpreted in a certain way by the community of which we are a part. Our background grasp of possibilities is always already illuminated for us by a particular interpretation.

One consequence of this structural-functional reading is that we need to draw a distinction between Heidegger's pragmatism and the foundationalism of most pragmatist Heideggerians. Nothing I have said here is inconsistent with the pragmatist version of the priority thesis – the primacy of practice over cognition. It might well be the case that practice has a priority in, for instance, fixing the content of cognitive states, or in illuminating how projection onto possibilities works. That is, skillful coping might well be both foundational to many acts of cognition, and it might be a paradigmatic case of projection. Heidegger, I would agree with the pragmatists, can be plausibly read as affirming both these forms of priority of practice over cognition. But when he asserts that *understanding* makes cognition possible, he means that the structure of projection is constitutive of cognition (as well as all other forms of understanding-comportment). Thus Heidegger himself is not committed to the view that *all* intelligence and intelligibility is derived from practical intelligibility – at least, he is not committed to this view by his account of understanding and interpretation. Rather, his pragmatism is more modest in scope: it claims only that intelligence and intelligibility do not reside *only* in cognition.

NOTES

1 See, for example, Hubert L. Dreyfus, "Overcoming the Myth of the Mental: How Philosophers Can Profit from the Phenomenology of Everyday Expertise," in *Proceedings and Addresses of the American Philosophical Association*, Vol. 79, Issue 2 (November 2005).

2 A formal account of the structure of φ is deformalized when we consider how the structure is instantiated in a particular type of φ in its determinacy.

3 Some form of cognition has historically been central to philosophical accounts of human being, from the *zōon logon echon* to the *res cogitans* to human beings as "autonomous rational beings." Heidegger's account does not deny that our ability to think, speak, and reason are important features of our existence. But they are not determinative of what it is to be human, on his account, since human understanding can also express itself in other, noncognitive ways.

4 *Truth and Method* (London: Continuum: 1982), 306; first paragraph of Part II; chapter 4, §2(A).

5 Paul Ricoeur, "The Task of Hermeneutics," in *Hermeneutics and the Human Sciences*, trans. John B. Thompson (Cambridge: Cambridge University Press, 1981), 56.

6 Ricoeur, "The Task of Hermeneutics," 56.

7 See "Phenomenology and Hermeneutics," in *Hermeneutics and the Human Sciences*, 106–7.

8 "Phenomenology and Hermeneutics," 107.

9 "Phenomenology and Hermeneutics," 107–8.

10 For my account of the significance of language in later Heidegger's work, see "Discourse, Language, Saying, Showing," in my *Heidegger and Unconcealment: Truth, Language and History* (Cambridge: Cambridge University Press, 2010), 118–55.

11 Hubert L. Dreyfus, *Being-in-the-World*, 195.

12 Ibid., 117.

13 Ibid., 32.

14 Ibid., 195.

15 Ibid., 195

16 Ibid., 186.

17 Ibid., 202.

18 Bert Dreyfus confirmed to me in conversation that this was an error.

19 William Blattner, *Heidegger's Being and Time: A Reader's Guide* (London: Continuum: 2006), 94.

20 Ibid., 92.

21 Ibid., 96.

22 "Ontology, the A Priori, and the Primacy of Practice," in *Transcendental Heidegger*, eds. Steven Crowell and Jeff Malpas (Stanford, CA: Stanford University Press: 2007), 14. See also "the line between understanding and interpretation is just this line between what can and cannot be expressed in assertion" (Blattner, *Heidegger's Being and Time*, 97).

23 Blattner, *Heidegger's Being and Time*, 85.

24 Blattner, "Ontology, the A Priori, and the Primacy of Practice," 17.

25 Taylor Carman, *Heidegger's Analytic* (Cambridge: Cambridge University Press, 2003), 20.

26 Ibid., 22.

27 Dreyfus, *Being-in-the-World*, 32. See also Dreyfus, *Being-in-the-World*, 197–8, where Dreyfus quotes Heidegger's assertion that "when we have to do with anything, the mere seeing of the things which are closest to us

bears in itself the structure of interpretation" (149). Dreyfus passes by in silence the interpretive structure of all our dealings with anything, while explaining that Heidegger is indeed talking about "everyday coping" in this passage.

28   Blattner, "Ontology, the A Priori, and the Primacy of Practice," 11.
29   *Heidegger's Analytic*, 21.
30   Ibid.
31   Ibid., 210.
32   Dreyfus, *Being-in-the-World*, 22.
33   Ibid.
34   The *pro-* in projection, like the *ent-* in *entwerfen*, has the sense of outward movement. See GA 29/30: 527.
35   See also: "The Dasein becomes what it is in and through this understanding; and it is always only that which it has chosen itself to be, that which it understands itself to be in the projection of its own most peculiar ability-to-be" (GA 24: 393; translation modified). Indeed, one way that Heidegger cashes out the distinction between authentic and inauthentic Dasein is in terms of whether one understands oneself primarily in terms of one's for the sake of which, or primarily "in terms of its world" (see 146).
36   "In" is in scare quotes to keep us alert to the fact that the "in"-ness of understanding is in no sense an internal state of the agent – no more than, for example, something implicit is "in" the mind before getting worked out.
37   See *Truth and Method*, 309.
38   That specifically *bodily* skills should be taken as paradigmatic is not a thesis for which I have argued in this chapter. The interested reader is encouraged to consult Merleau-Ponty's *The Phenomenology of Perception*, as well as the works by Dreyfus, Blattner, and Carman listed in the references section, for arguments to this effect.

9   Heidegger's Pragmatic-Existential Theory of Language and Assertion

Assertion has played a central role in philosophy of language, particularly in the twentieth century. It has been designated as the paradigmatic linguistic form, the most neutral propositional form or attitude, so much so that assertoric force has more often than not gone undetected. Heidegger, by contrast, claims that assertion is a derivative form of interpretation and that the entire tradition of analyzing language, or rather sentences, in terms of the attribution of predicates to subjects is wrongheaded because it conceives language as an *object*. Given that assertions continue to enjoy a privileged position in philosophy of language, even in the wake of Wittgenstein, Austin, et al., it is worthwhile to examine closely what exactly Heidegger means by these claims and what his alternative to the objectification of language is.

There are two conceptions of language that run through the relevant sections of *Being and Time*. One I shall call *instrumental*, the other *constitutive*. According to the former, language is a tool; according to the latter, it is an *Existenzial*, an essential attribute of Dasein. These two conceptions are reflected in the secondary literature on Heidegger's views on language in *Being and Time*, though scholars usually opt for attributing one or the other to him.[1] To acknowledge the presence of both and to explore the potential tension between them helps us to understand better Heidegger's analysis of assertion, as well as his account of discourse and language. I aim to show that, for Heidegger, the two conceptions are interrelated and that language moves between the two poles of fully absorbed coping and fully theoretical assertion.

I would like to thank audiences in the departments of philosophy at the University of Connecticut and the University of New Hampshire, where I presented earlier versions of this chapter. Thanks to John McCumber, Jonathan Maskit, and Bob Scharff for their comments and discussion. The leave during which this chapter was written was made possible by a Research Fellowship at the University of Connecticut Humanities Institute and an R. C. Good Fellowship from Denison University.

I first outline Heidegger's ontology of absorbed coping, with particular attention to his notion of reference and the role and nature of signs. Heidegger introduces meaningfulness and language against the background of this ontology. I then discuss the structure of assertion. Finally, I show that Heidegger's distinction between language (*Sprache*) and discourse (*Rede*) can be mapped onto the distinction between an instrumental and constitutive conception of language inasmuch as *Sprache* refers to (de facto) linguistic articulations and *Rede* to the activity of articulating an ontological ground of possibility of language. Yet rather than seeing this merely as a tension or contradiction between two competing views of language in Heidegger, I want to explore the thesis that this vacillation is in the nature of language and that Heidegger should be understood as defending a *pragmatic-existential* view of language on which the instrumentalist and constitutive views can be reconciled.

THE REFERENTIAL TOTALITY OF SIGNIFICANCE AND INSTRUMENTALISM

Heidegger's turn to language in *Being and Time* is preceded by a discussion of referentiality (*Verweisung*). Even though ontology is prior to language in *Being and Time*, questions of meaning and meaningfulness enter the picture long before explicit discussions of language, namely, in Heidegger's account of absorbed coping, of being-in-the-world, and of being-ready-to-hand (*Zuhandenheit*). This latter notion, of course, is contrasted with being-present-at-hand (*Vorhandenheit*), sometimes translated as what is "occurrent" or "extant." Presence-at-hand, as we shall see, plays an important role in Heidegger's account of assertion, while discourse is fundamental to his ontology of being.

Not only is the analysis of meaning (*Sinn*) and signification (*Bedeutung*) preceded by Heidegger's analysis of reference, Heidegger is in fact prompted to give an analysis of signs as a way of explaining what he means by reference, claiming that signs are essentially referential, for their very function, their reason for being, is to refer to something else. Even though the signs he uses as paradigms are not linguistic, the upshot of this argumentative structure is that Heidegger introduces language in an instrumental context: signs are tools; words, presumably, are a kind of sign; hence words are a kind of tool.

For Heidegger, our most fundamental (or, as he says, ontologically primary or primordial) way of encountering objects in the world is as "ready-to-hand" *pragmata*. That is, we encounter things in the practical context of engaging in our environment. It is surely no accident that Heidegger uses tools (*Werkzeuge*) to illustrate his point here, for he calls the things we thus encounter "equipment" or simply "stuff" (*Zeug*). Any one piece of stuff is what it is only relative to the totality of equipment. Thus a spatula is what it is relative to a bowl used for scraping batter in the service of baking a cake to bring to a fundraiser to support special school projects, and so forth. The pragmatic context of our engaged coping with the world is therefore holistically structured. Every piece in this structure stands in a relation to all the others. What Heidegger calls "reference" (*Verweisung*) plays a central role in that it is constitutive of this totality: 'The structure of being of what is at hand as useful things is determined by references" (74),[2] and ultimately, it derives its meaningfulness from Dasein's goals, purposes, and projects. Thus a certain duality of constitutiveness and instrumentality is already present in Heidegger's account of the referential totality of what is ready-to-hand.

Usually, Dasein is fully absorbed in this referential context. It doesn't notice it, but goes about its business functioning smoothly within it. An example of absorbed coping is driving home without knowing how one got there. Clearly, one turned the steering wheel, used the turn signals, stopped at lights, merged into lanes, and so on, yet without explicitly attending to doing any of these things. Similarly, when baking a cake, I may be paying attention to the recipe I am following, but I scoop flour, turn on the mixer, and so on automatically. In fact, noticing any of these things is indicative of something going wrong – or at least going not quite right, of there being some disturbance in my ordinary absorbed coping with the world. This can happen in a variety of ways. When my car's engine light comes on, for instance, I become aware not only of the instrument panel, which I now monitor consciously, but also of stepping on the gas, and so forth. I may also become more explicitly aware of what I am doing when I make a mistake in my absorbed coping, as when I accidentally run a stop sign and then pay particular attention to stopping at all remaining stop signs during the drive. Here, the breakdown does not have to do with the equipment but with my own performance. Such breakdowns are ways of becoming aware of the referential whole as such.

Insofar as the things we encounter in our absorbed coping are useful to us, they are characterized by their "serviceability," which Heidegger also says is a form of reference and an ontological condition of possibility of our encountering things as ready-to-hand:

Serviceability (reference) as constitutive of equipment, however, is not an appropriateness [*Geeignetheit*] of some entity; it is rather the condition (so far as Being is in question) which makes it possible for the character of such an entity to be defined by its appropriatenesses. (83, translation modified)

In other words, we encounter objects as appropriate or inappropriate tools with which to accomplish our goals.[3] Thus we notice their features insofar as they are apt to be of service, to be useful, to us or not. Features that are neither useful nor frustrating to us do not show up for us; they are not relevant to us. What makes it possible for something to be appropriate to a task is the fact that it is usable in the first place. Serviceability – or usability – is a form of reference because for something to be usable implies its being usable *for something*, which in turn implies reference to something else. The notion of "appropriateness" contains an ambiguity. On the one hand, it refers to how well something is suited for performing a given task in virtue of its own nature. Now whether or not something is an appropriate tool for a task depends on the thing used, the user, and the task. Therefore, appropriateness, too, is a relation. A whisk made of metal or bamboo will do; one made of clay or chocolate probably won't. If I am left-handed, the most perfect right-handed spatula will be frustrating to me; and while I can use a spatula to stir as well as scrape, I would have a hard time using a pizza peel to do so. This insight is important for blocking the idealist reading of Heidegger, for it shows that what we use to accomplish our tasks it not simply up to us but depends on how the world is. I shall have more to say about what we consider the "objective" properties of something below in the context of assertion and the present-at-hand. On the other hand, "appropriateness" carries a normative connotation, referring to how something is "supposed" to be used. This notion is grounded more in social sanctioning and cultural practices than the qualities of the objects themselves. One can, of course, argue that the two are closely connected and that objective appropriatenesses are the basis for social normative proprieties.[4] Furthermore, in both English and German, "appropriateness" is etymologically connected with "appropriation" in the sense of making something one's own. Dasein thus appropriates things by using them as appropriate equipment in the service of its projects.

Signs, Heidegger claims, are paradigm examples of how ordinary objects are referentially constituted, since their very function is to refer to something else. His famous example is the signaling arrow on a motor car to indicate turns. The sign itself is part of the referential totality "traffic." Without the context of cars, drivers, roads, and so forth, the arrow would have no purpose, no meaning; it would not refer to anything. As it stands, it refers to all of these things. As a sign, it also refers in a more privileged way, namely, it points in a given direction *and* represents the driver's intention to other drivers, thus serving as a *tool* of communication. The idea of signs as tools of communication provides the basis for attributing an *instrumentalist* understanding of language to Heidegger. It is analogous to Wittgenstein's account of language based on the builders' game, where words are an integral part of an interactive context.

Heidegger does not explicitly state that words are signs, and some of what he does say seems to suggest that he wishes to distinguish signs as forms of ready-to-hand equipment from linguistic expressions. Thus, for instance, he lists indicators, markers, and so on as examples of signs, and says that "these 'signs' are to be distinguished from trace, remainder, monument, document, symbol, expression, appearance, significance" (78, translation modified).[5] Nonetheless, it seems that we do often use words as signs. Consider, for example, the word "STOP" on stop signs or simply written on the street. Anaphora also functions in the language in order to refer or point back to other words. And, finally, the function of indexicals such as "this" is, precisely, to point. At minimum, then, at least sometimes words are signs much like the arrow on the motor car. By the same token, as we shall see, words – especially in the form of assertions – turn out to be tools unlike any others.

As we shall see, *pointing* also plays an important role in Heidegger's account of assertion.[6] There is a *deictic* theme running through the Division I of *Being and Time*, a theme that via the analysis of assertion can be connected to the book's *aletheic* theme. "Zeigen" means both "to point" and "to show," and hence already refers to a certain kind of disclosure and not a mere indicating of something.

Perhaps curiously, it is only after his analysis of signs and reference, but prior to any discussion of linguistic meaning as such, that Heidegger introduces *Bedeutung* or "signification." Inasmuch as signification is grounded in Heideggerian reference,[7] we might say that, for Heidegger, reference determines meaning. Because of our engagement in this referential totality, we have an (implicit) understanding of these relations, which we grasp as signifying (*be-deuten*) (87).

The relational totality of what Heidegger calls signifyings, namely, significance (*Bedeutsamkeit*), is what makes possible "significations" (*Bedeutungen*). *Bedeutungen* in turn make possible the being of "words and of language" (87). Interestingly, Heidegger talks more about "signifying" (the activity) and "significance" (the overall structure) than "signification(s)" themselves. Significations return again only in the section on assertion, where he talks about the relationship between words and *Bedeutungen* – a context in which it seems natural to talk about *meanings* or even, for that matter, reference or referents in the Fregean sense. This suggests that, in the earlier passages, Heidegger wants to say that the broad structural notion of significance is prior to the idea that there are individual, identifiable, and articulable meanings. These are what arise from the articulation of the referential totality of being-in-the-world. This in turn connects Heidegger's ontological holism with his linguistic holism. The former implies the latter. If significance is holistically structured and significations are the condition of possibility of words (and language), language, too, will be holistically structured. Throughout these passages, Heidegger aims to counter the tendency to think of meanings as entities and develops an essentially pragmatic account of meaning. In this effort, he prefigures the later Wittgenstein, Quine, and Davidson.

ASSERTION

The analysis of assertion in §33 (*"Assertion as a derivative mode of interpretation"*) follows immediately upon Heidegger's discussion of meaning (*Sinn*) in §32 (*"Understanding and Interpretation"*). Heidegger says that meaning is that wherein intelligibility (*Verständlichkeit*) lies, that which can be articulated in an understanding disclosure (*verstehenden Erschliessen*), as encompassing the formal framework of what necessarily belongs to that which interpretation articulates (151). Things make sense to Dasein, and only Dasein can therefore be meaningful or meaningless (*sinnvoll* vs. *sinnlos*).

When human beings encounter things in their environment, they always already encounter objects in their experience as something or other – as tables, doors, vehicles, bridges, and so on – never, in other words, as "bare" objects. This basic hermeneutic condition is what Heidegger calls the fundamental "as"-structure of human experience. Assertion (*Aussage*) is introduced negatively in this context. He describes hermeneutic understanding as a pre-predicative kind of seeing that need not be articulated in a determining assertion, but that is nonetheless a form of interpretive understanding:

> The articulation of what is understood in approaching an entity interpretively in terms of "something as something" is *prior* to the thematic assertion about it. The "as" does not appear only in the latter, but is merely uttered (*ausgesprochen*), which is only possible because it lies before us as something that can be uttered (*Aussprechbares*) ... The simple seeing of the things closest to us in our coping with them bears in itself the structure of interpretation in such a primordial fashion grasping something in a way that is *free of any as*, as it were, precisely requires somewhat of a reorientation. When we merely stare at something, our just-having-it-before-us lies before us as a form of *no-longer-understanding*. (149, translation modified)[8]

Interpretation thus precedes linguistic articulation; moreover, our involved (circumspect) coping with the world is always already interpretive. This is certainly borne out ontogenetically: children experience the world as meaningfully structured long before they can talk about their experience. To thematize – to make explicit – this absorbed hermeneutic understanding in the form of an assertion requires a "reorientation" and, at its most extreme, involves a *loss* of understanding. Here

Heidegger reveals his ambivalence toward assertion: he is quite critical of the philosophical tradition's privileging of assertions, yet also aims to provide an alternative analysis of the phenomenon.

Heidegger opens §33 by defining meaning as "that which is articulated as such in interpretation and what is sketched out in understanding as articulable" (153, translation modified). Meaningfulness and intelligibility are thus prior to linguistic meaning. The very next thing he says is that, insofar as assertion (judgment)[9] is grounded in understanding and represents a derivative mode of interpretation, it, *too*, has a meaning. Thus, assertions are meaningful, but they are not the paradigm of meaning, contrary to their treatment in much philosophy of language. Hence, although meaning and assertion are discussed together, assertion is not the primary locus of meaning. One might nonetheless retain the view that assertion is the primary locus of *linguistic* or semantic meaning.[10] However, this is a view that certainly the later Heidegger rejects, emphasizing instead the power of poetry to create new meanings (GA 12, also PLT), and one that unnecessarily narrows the account of linguistic meaning presented in *Being and Time*.

The idea that the meaning of assertions is derivative from another, more primary kind of meaning suggests what we might call a merely "articulatory" conception of language (or of assertion, at least) that is a variant of the instrumental conception. According to such a conception, language is a kind of *code*. Linguistic articulation simply puts into words already pre-existing meanings; it makes them explicit. This makes such meanings public and enables their dissemination – a point to which I'll return. The articulatory conception is compatible with an instrumental conception of language, since words are a tool for dealing with meanings, as it were, without altering them. After all, the idea of a code is to translate (encode, decode) from one medium to another while preserving sameness of meaning. This can be contrasted with a "transformative" conception, according to which articulating and making explicit what is implicit alters the playing field, the totality of significance. This kind of transformation is consistent with and indeed part of a constitutive view of language.

It is clear that at least a weak version of the transformative view must be correct for a Heideggerian account. It follows from the referentiality of absorbed coping that what is articulated is meaningful against a holistic background of referential relations that remain unarticulated. By extension, explicit linguistic meaning depends on an implicit background of linguistic and pragmatic referential relations. If language allows us to articulate and make explicit what is implicit, this eo ipso changes the background. Such an understanding of linguistic articulation also fits better than the merely articulatory view with a dynamic

and temporal conception of meaning, which I take Heidegger to espouse
(see below). Furthermore, it helps us to understand why Heidegger both-
ers with assertion at all.

There are two reasons. One is internal to Heidegger's positive
account; the other has to do with his critique of metaphysics in general. First, he says that assertion can be used to demonstrate how the
"as"-structure that is constitutive of understanding and interpretation
can be modified. What does he mean by this? The analysis of assertion
explicates what happens when we make aspects of our absorbed coping
linguistically explicit. Heidegger thus indicates his tendency toward a
transformative-constitutive view of language: assertoric articulation
changes something about how we understand and interpret the world.
There are two levels of modification: (i) that as what things appear can
change, as when we encounter a table as opposed to several joined pieces
of wood or a collection of molecules; (ii) the manner in which something
appears can change, as when we encounter something as ready-to-hand
as opposed to as present-at-hand. Assertion is capable of effecting both
kinds of modification. Second, Heidegger wants to provide an analysis of
assertion precisely because he recognizes its privileged place in the philosophical tradition as the "primary and authentic 'locus' of *truth*" (154,
Macquarrie and Robinson translation). Assertions are by definition paradigmatic truth-apt sentences. They form the basis for a correspondence
theory of truth, since sentences are taken to be true if they correspond to
reality. Because Heidegger ultimately wants to replace a correspondence
conception of truth with a conception of truth as disclosure (aletheia), it is
important to him to show that assertion, too, is grounded in disclosure.

The fact that Heidegger talks about assertions (*Aussagen*) rather than,
say, *propositions* (*Sätze*) is noteworthy and not merely an indication
of his remove from early analytic philosophy. *Aussage* can be translated as "proposition" (as well as "statement" or "testimony"), but it
would be a distortion of his positive view to do so. His choice of term
emphasizes his pragmatism and the idea that language is meaningful in
contexts of use. Frege, Russell, and the early Wittgenstein focus on the
logic and structure of propositions – sentences abstracted from use. But
for Heidegger, treating propositions in abstraction from such contexts
as the paragon of meaningfulness is illusory.

By the same token, Heidegger, too, elaborates on the structure of
assertion. He defines assertion as a "pointing-out which gives something a definite character and which communicates" (*mitteilend
bestimmended Aufzeigung*, 156, Macquarrie and Robinson translation).
What does he mean by this?

(1) An assertion is – primarily[11] – an *Aufzeigung*, a pointing-out or, one
might also say, showing. Both pointing out as well as showing (*zeigen*)

connote the disclosive nature of this aspect of assertion. The assertion draws something to our attention, but, in the sense of *Aufzeigung*, it also makes something manifest or evident. Interestingly, Heidegger – rather like Wittgenstein or, perhaps even more so, Davidson – says that in an assertion, such as "The hammer is too heavy," "what is discovered for sight is not a 'meaning' ('*Sinn*'), but an entity in the way that it is ready-to-hand" (154, Macquarrie and Robinson translation). The sentence does not refer to a semantic content or proposition. Rather, we encounter the entity directly, though we do so through our mode of experience. Heidegger is thus a kind of semantic externalist.

(2) Assertion "connotes" (*besagt*) *predication*. Here, Heidegger's analysis is pre-Fregean.[12] A "predicate," he writes, is "asserted" of a "subject," whereby the subject is *determined* by the predicate (154). Heidegger characterizes the subject, in accordance with the first signification, as what is asserted (*das Ausgesagte*) and the predicate as what does the asserting (*das Aussagende*). That determination by the predicate implies what he calls a "narrowing" of what is asserted:

What is asserted in the second signification of "assertion" (that which is determined as such) has undergone a narrowing of content as compared with what is asserted in the assertion in the first signification of this term. Every predication is what it is, only as a pointing out. (154–5, translation modified)

Predication is *also* a pointing out; it, too, *shows* something, but it does so by focusing the way in which what is shown or disclosed in the assertion appears to us by drawing our explicit attention to some particular feature of it, now articulated as a *property*. The hammer is asserted to be too heavy – rather than having a wooden handle or being red. Our perspective on the object under discussion is thus rendered more precise. In order to do this, Heidegger claims, we must take a step back from what is already evident to us, what we already understand in our coping with the world. Another way to put this is that we must abstract away from our practically engaged knowledge.

Determination first takes a step back from what is already manifest; the "positing of a subject" leaves beings in the shadows in order to cast light on "the hammer there," in order to make what is manifest visible in its determinable determinacy by means of carrying out this bringing into the light [*Entblendung*]. Positing a subject and positing a predicate are, along with their simultaneous conjunction [*Hinzusetzung*], thoroughly "apophantic" in the strict sense of the word. (155, translation modified)

In assertion, we posit a subject and a predicate and we *posit* their connection. In other words, we impose a propositional structure on our everyday activity. It is this move that makes possible explicit truth talk.

Assertion is a "derivative mode of interpretation," according to Heidegger. It is still a mode of interpretation because, like all interpretation, it presupposes what he calls a fore-having and fore-sight, and fore-conception. That is, a certain conceptual framework or perspective on and anticipation of what is disclosed must be presupposed. So, in that sense, assertions are never entirely decontextualized. What makes assertion a *derivative* mode of interpretation? As already indicated above, interpretation consists primordially not in a theoretical assertion but in absorbed coping. Thus the derivativeness of assertions has to do with Dasein distancing itself from this absorbed stance and narrowing its focus. Whence, Heidegger asks, does assertion arise from the interpretation of absorbed coping (157)?

When we make assertions about the things we initially encounter as ready-to-hand equipment and thus make them the "objects" of our assertions, Heidegger claims, there is a change in how we intuitively think of them (*Vor-habe*). He conceives of this as a transition from thinking of things as ready-to-hand to thinking of them as present-at-hand. We become interested in identifying the objective properties of something, of what it is really like independently of our interests and purposes, and so forth: "Fore-sight aims at something present-at-hand in the ready-to-hand" (158, translation modified). Indeed, Heidegger says that only with this change in perspective do we gain access to something like *properties*. What happens is a "leveling" of the originary "as" of circumspect interpretation in absorbed coping to the "as" of determining something as present-at-hand. Heidegger describes this as an advantage (*Vorzug*) of assertion: it makes possible detached contemplation (objectivity, if you will, or merely looking at, examining things as they are). Herein lies the distinction between what he calls the "hermeneutic" and the "apophantic" *as* (158). The hermeneutic *as* refers to circumspect interpretation; the apophantic *as* to propositional judgment and truth. Apophansis is an Aristotelian term for a categorical or declarative sentence; in other words, for a sentence with a truth value. An assertion is standardly understood as putting forward a proposition as true. Propositional truth is itself taken to be a property of the sentence or proposition asserted and is, presumably, to be cashed out in terms of a correspondence theory of truth.[13] This kind of truth is a narrower kind of truth than what Heidegger is ultimately interested in capturing, namely, *aletheia*: truth as disclosure rather than correspondence. According to Heidegger, the original meaning of apophansis is to let things themselves be seen. We might think that this means letting them be seen as they are *independently* of Dasein. So assertion in its pure form would be aimed at pure presence-at-hand in the sense of "grasping something in a way that is free of any *as*" that we saw earlier. Yet given the ontology of being, we can have no access to beings independently of our ways of grasping them. It is impossible for us to make assertions that capture the *pure presence-at-hand* of something, for any assertion we make will employ words of our language. As I argued above, that language is a holistic web that articulates (and transforms) the referential totality. As such, it cannot be severed from how things are meaningful to us, from our interests and purposes. Therefore, assertions cannot represent the world purely as present-at-hand. This is a now-familiar point, driven home by various critiques of objectivity in philosophy of science and in feminist epistemology. Indeed, in the same previously quoted passage, Heidegger claims that merely *staring* at things as purely present-at-hand is a form of *no-longer-understanding*. Understanding, as he tells us over and over again, is always to understand something as something.

Hence, the apophantic *as* exhibited in assertions is nonetheless a seeing of something as something, namely, seeing something as present-at-hand. Yet, as Brandom emphasizes, "the move from equipment ready-to-hand, fraught with socially instituted significances, to objective things present-at-hand, is one not of decontextualization, but of recontextualization."[14] Based on the above analysis, we can think of assertions as another kind of tool or equipment that makes possible new kinds of activities and projects. Assertions make possible a different way for us to engage with the world. Once we see something *as* having a property, that property can be discussed as one among many other properties it has. We have here the dual modification identified above: the manner in which something (the hammer) appears is modified and what it is that appears (properties) changes. Assertions make it possible to communicate our understandings of something as something, "of this as that," to talk about things not in our immediate presence, to spread knowledge.[15] Okrent has argued persuasively that assertions allow Heidegger to account for the fact that so much of our knowledge is propositional rather than practical.

I claimed at the outset that language moves between the poles of absorbed coping and theoretical assertion for Heidegger, and it is now time to make good on this claim. Let us return to the example Heidegger uses to elucidate assertion: "This hammer is too heavy." It is an instance of one's taking notice of something because it is not working as it is supposed to; that is, one notices its *lack of serviceability*. The example therefore illustrates how we become aware of the referential totality of significance in which we find ourselves. Still, in our everyday engagement with the world, we don't need to utter this explicit judgment in the form of an assertion. We might just as easily say, "Too heavy!"; or we might simply pick up a smaller hammer. To be sure, the utterance makes explicit what is implicit in this situation,[16] but it is the kind of *utterance* that is routinely produced in our absorbed coping with the world. In that sense, it is not a paradigmatic kind of assertion in the sense of a theoretical statement. It also shows that ordinary language is intimately intertwined with everyday activities. Heidegger himself writes that "circumspectly uttered (*ausgesprochene*) interpretation is not necessarily already an assertion in the sense defined" (157, translation modified). Why not?

Consider in what sense "This hammer is too heavy" can be seen to focus on something that is present-at-hand in the ready-to-hand. Heidegger claims that we become aware of the referential totality of equipment when *things break down* and, as a result, are suddenly no longer ready-to-hand but present-at-hand. So by saying that the hammer is too heavy, I make explicit the fact that it is no longer useful for what I am trying to do. But now imagine that I have been spending a lot of time by myself and I start talking to myself, a kind of running commentary on what I am doing, as part of which I might say, "The spatula cleans the sides of the bowl nicely." This seems to be a case of an assertion that is perfectly in tune with my absorbed coping and makes no reference to anything merely present-at-hand in the sense just identified. Why, in other words, could linguistic articulation – including in the form of assertions – not be part of absorbed coping? Indeed, Heidegger's own example remains, by its very content, tied to its pragmatic context. Contrast "This hammer is too heavy" with "This hammer weighs 567 g." The hammer is determined as too heavy only relative to the speaker (or hammerer) and her project (cf. 360–1): it is too heavy because I cannot hammer effectively, because it damages the surface I am hammering, and so forth. It is only the assertion of its mass in grams that is (relatively) indifferent to Dasein's purposes in this sense, that discloses the hammer "as it is in itself."[17] It is clear that what matters here is the *function* of the utterance, not its grammatical form. Most of the time, we use language absorbedly: we do not pay special attention to how or to the fact that we are using it, much as we take other aspects of our environment and context for granted. This everyday absorption is what is disturbed in the proverbial case of the monolingual speaker who, when confronted with someone who does not speak her language, responds by speaking more loudly.

Heidegger acknowledges that interpretation in fully absorbed coping and interpretation in explicit theoretical assertion are at opposite ends of a continuum and that there are many intermediary stages between them. Since we often do use language in our absorbed coping – especially when doing something with another – it follows that language moves between the poles of absorbed coping and fully theoretical assertion. Yet Heidegger clearly, on the one hand, treats the former as ontologically primary and does not give examples of the latter (at least not in this section) – lest of course we take all of *Being and Time* to be nothing but examples of theoretical assertions. On the other hand, Heidegger, too, can be seen as privileging the assertoric function of language. On Brandom's interpretation, language is viewed first and foremost as the tool that allows us to take an objective perspective on the world and to impose a propositional structure on it. Furthermore, when we look at Heidegger's account of language in his technical sense itself, it turns out that he tends to treat it as something ready-to-hand.

To a degree, the move of instrumentalizing language assimilates the apophantic to the hermeneutic as and implies that the dichotomy between them is a false one, since assertions are treated as another kind of tool for coping with the world. In Division II of *Being and Time*, Heidegger seems to corroborate this interpretation by arguing against any kind of sharp dichotomy between praxis and theory on the grounds that practical engagement with the world is as much guided by its own vision (theory) as theoretical research has its own praxis (357–8). Yet assertions qua tools differ from, say, screwdrivers, computers, the wheel, or other tools we have crafted to serve our purposes. As we will see in the next section, they differ not only in function but in kind. Therefore, it is a mistake to read Heidegger as endorsing an instrumentalist conception of language. What makes assertions special is not so much that they afford the opportunity to engage in truth talk but that they derive from language in the sense of logos as the *Existenzial* of Dasein. To try to understand what his alternative conception of logos is that underwrites this reading, we have to look at Heidegger's conceptions of language and discourse. Before doing so, however, we still need to discuss the third defining feature of assertion.

(3) Assertion, finally, signifies *communication* (*Mitteilung*) or, as Heidegger glosses it, a speaking-out: *Heraussage*. What is asserted or said (*das Ausgesagte*) is *shared* or, at minimum, is shareable among interlocutors. Here there is a significant shift in emphasis from traditional approaches to assertion to a deeply pragmatic view. The point of assertions is not to represent the world as it is, not to state the truth (at least not as correspondence), but to communicate one's way of seeing the world (i.e., the way the world is disclosed to me) to another. Heidegger says that part of this communication is *Ausgesprochenheit* (155), rendered by Macquarrie and Robinson as "the requirement to be expressed." What is at issue, however, is specifically *linguistic* expression, namely, utterance. Recall that interpretation or articulation need not be linguistic. Moreover, *Ausgesprochenheit* is a perfective term, that is, it indicates the fact that something *has been* said or uttered. In other words, it signifies "the fact of utterance." What Heidegger is getting at

is that assertion is an utterance, a speech act, laying the ground for the primacy of the social nature of linguistic communication and of *spoken* language. This will be important for our understanding of the distinction between language and discourse.

What is asserted can be shared without the hearer having had direct experience of what is being said,[18] and it can be transmitted further (*weiter-gesagt*). This is a distinct advantage of assertion, for it makes possible the expansion of community and makes possible the "social preservation of a common subject matter."[19] It means that we can talk about something absent and without actually using it.[20] By the same token, this very feature can easily become a disadvantage, since it also brings the possibility of obscuring that which has been pointed out. This can happen in two ways. First, as we have already noted, predication limits what is shown; it discloses and highlights one property of something at the expense of concealing others. Second, repeating assertions made by others (or oneself) absent the original context or without checking their validity leads to making unjustified assertions (Brandom) and to inauthentic speech (idle talk or chatter). That is, the very conditions of possibility of linguistic articulation and communication contain the possibility of inauthenticity, error, and miscommunication. Repeating the assertions of others might be like playing the telephone game.[21] More generally, this point bears on the question of semantic normativity. To say that utterances are norm-governed, that they have correctness conditions, means that it is possible to violate these norms or rules. Otherwise, the rules would reduce to laws.

LANGUAGE AND DISCOURSE: TOWARD AN EXISTENTIAL-PRAGMATIC ANALYSIS

This third characteristic of assertions, their communicative nature, leads Heidegger to the concept of saying and speaking (*Sagen und Sprechen*; 160). So it is only *after* his analysis of assertion that he explicitly takes up the question of *language* (*Sprache*). There is a close etymological link between *Sprache* and *sprechen* in German that is lost in English: language is what is spoken, and speaking is an activity. By contrast, Heidegger emphasizes that "the existential-ontological foundation of language is discourse [*Rede*]," which he regards as equiprimordial with attunement and understanding and which also emphasizes the practice of talking.[22] Discourse, then, is clearly not a tool for articulating meanings already present (or even for transforming them or passing them along to others), but is constitutive for Dasein as its way of being. Discourse is the articulation of intelligibility, Heidegger tells us (161). What is articulated is nothing less than the totality of significations

(*Bedeutungsganze*). The latter in turn can be broken up into significations, which in turn are always meaningful (*sinnhaft*; 161). In speech,
the totality of significations of intelligibility "is put into words." But
again, Heidegger denies that this is a matter of assigning significations
(*Bedeutungen*) to word-things: "The way in which discourse is uttered
or put into words (*Hinausgesprochenheit*) is language" (161, translation
modified).

Heidegger describes language as the *totality of words* that constitutes
the "worldly being" of discourse so that it can be encountered in the
world as something *ready-to-hand*. In terms of Heidegger' fundamental distinction between the ontological and the ontic, discourse is the
ontological condition of possibility of the ontic existence of language.
While this supports an instrumentalist understanding of language, it
is a somewhat puzzling claim. Heidegger does not mean by language
something like what Saussure, for instance, means by *langue*, which in
one variation or another has been the dominant conception of language.
He does not, in other words, conceive it as a system of rules subject
to objective inquiry, an abstraction from usage (*parole*) yet nonetheless logically or conceptually prior to it.[23] Characterizing such a system, according to Heidegger, requires that language can be "broken up
[*zerschlagen*] into word-things that are *present-at-hand*" (161, translation modified, italics added). A theoretical linguistic characterization
of language, in other words, turns it into something present-at-hand.
Thus, when we break our utterances into individual words for purposes
of analysis, we destroy language.[24] While such theoretical analysis can
still treat language holistically and semantic value as relational, it is
easy to see how it can lead to semantic atomism.

Heidegger asks what mode of being philosophers ultimately want to
attribute to language: that of innerworldly, ready-to-hand equipment, or
that of Dasein, or neither (166). I would like to suggest that it is neither
or, perhaps rather, both. As the totality of meaningful words, language
is ready-to-hand as another ensemble of equipment. As ready-to-hand
equipment, it can be seen as a toolbox of prior articulations we can draw
on in our linguistic dealings with the world and others. It is part of our
shared cultural background, our life world. Its function is the articulation of discourse; it is, as it were, uttered (or instantiated) discourse. If
language is the "worldly being" of discourse, this naturally raises the
question: what is discourse?

The answer is that it is an *Existenzial*, an "existential state of Dasein's
disclosedness." An *Existenzial* cannot be a mere tool of Dasein. Rather,
it specifies its way of being. That is, it is *constitutive* of the very existence of Dasein – not, in other words, a mere tool but the ontological
basis for that tool. Dasein, by its very essence, is the being that has

language (165). According to Heidegger, the interpretation of human beings as "logon echon" in the sense of being a *rational* animal developed subsequent to and obscures the originary meaning of logos as speech. In its originary sense, "The human being shows itself as the entity which talks (*redet*)" (165, translation modified). Talking, then, is not simply a type of activity we happen to engage in among others. Discourse is ontologically prior to rationality. Heidegger thinks that the philosophical tradition's focus on logos in terms of "assertion" has been mistaken because it has led to looking at language as something present-at-hand, treating words, word order and, eventually, judgments, for instance, as kinds of things. *Rede* is not to be conceived in terms of assertion. Human beings are essentially beings that *talk* – not, *pace* Brandom, beings that assert. This is not to say that assertion is not an essential part of talking; it is merely that "talking" does not privilege asserting over storytelling, linguistically establishing intersubjective relationships, or any number of other things we do in talking. In short, there are countless non-assertoric uses of language. The following passage illustrates the point:

Talking [*Reden*] is the "signifying" articulation ["*bedeutende*" *Gliedern*] of the intelligibility of being-in-the-world, of which being-with is a part and which is always in a particular mode of concernful being-together. The latter is discursive (*redend*) as assenting or refusing, demanding, warning, pronouncing, consulting or interceding on someone's behalf, or as "making assertions," and speaking in the form of giving a speech. Talk is talk about... (161–2, translation modified)

One might thus expect Heidegger to be sympathetic to ordinary language philosophy and particularly to speech act theory. It is difficult not to think of "talking" here in terms of speech acts (or at least types of speech acts). In German, "pronouncing," "consulting," and "interceding" are all modifications of "*Sprache*," and "assenting" and "refusing" modifications of "*Sagen*." Discursiveness, in other words, is manifested in linguistic utterances. Where Heidegger would part ways with ordinary language philosophy, presumably, is over the latter's emphasis on the ontic rather than the ontological. Semantics, for him, must be grounded in the ontology of being, in Dasein (166). Talking is not simply a matter of performing speech acts; it is a way of being. This is why both significance and meaning precede the analysis of language proper in *Being and Time*. It is also why Heidegger can say that talk is most primordially disclosed in silence.

Being-in-the-world-together is linguistic in the form of speech acts, whose primary function is action coordination among individuals. This is not to be understood instrumentally but in the sense that we are social animals and our social nature is expressed linguistically. Heidegger draws an immediate link between discourse and community. In fact, in discourse, our being-with becomes explicit as something shared (162). In other words, if discourse is constitutive of Dasein, Dasein is essentially social – and language is essentially shared.

Only a few paragraphs later he seems almost to repeat himself, but on closer examination, the juxtaposition of the two passages reveals, once more, the vacillation between the instrumental and the constitutive conceptions of language:

In discourse the intelligibility of Being-in-the-world (an intelligibility which goes with a state-of-mind) is articulated according to significations; and discourse is this articulation. The items constitutive for discourse are: what the discourse is about (what is talked about [das Beredete]); what is said-in-the-talk [das Geredete], as such; the communication; and the manifestation [Bekundung]. (162, translation modified)[25]

Whereas the first passage presents discourse as *signifying* articulation, that is, as engaged in the activity of creating significance, the second presents it as articulating *in accordance* with signification, which would logically precede discourse. How are we to make sense of the apparent contradiction between saying that discourse constitutes meaning (signification) and that it (merely) articulates it? Is Heidegger simply being careless or getting carried away by the poetry of his own writing? Do the two passages once more manifest the tension between the constitutive view, suggested by the former, and the instrumental, suggested by the latter? An alternative answer is that he is trying to get at discourse as a living, dynamic thing. When we articulate what has been implicit, we also generate a new meaning and thus change the existing holistic structure and the equipment available to us. I referred above to language as a toolbox. But of course, we do not simply repeat what others have said before, but constantly produce novel utterances, a point driven home by Chomsky. Hence, the contents of the toolbox, as it were, are constantly changing. Neither discourse nor language are static objects. This reading fits with what Heidegger says when he returns to discourse in Division II of *Being and Time*, this time emphasizing its temporality. He accords the "making present" (*Gegenwärtigen*) that occurs in the expression or utterance of discourse through language a "privileged constitutive function" and says that "discourse is inherently temporal, insofar as all talking about…, of…, and to … is grounded in the ecstatic unity of temporality" (349, translation modified).

In both passages, Heidegger maintains that discourse always has an intentional object: what is talked about. Dasein is always already involved with and directed toward the world. He further differentiates between the propositional content of discourse (what is said), the

communicative or intersubjective component, and the expressive element (*Bekundung*). These formal constitutive moments of discourse
are what make possible language, according to Heidegger. Moreover,
he writes that attempts to get at the essence of language have always
focused on some one of these (e.g., communication as "assertion") –
something he is trying to overcome.[26]

At the end of §34 (166), Heidegger proclaims that philosophy must
ask itself what kind of being language has: is it ready-to-hand equipment, or is it Dasein, or neither? Although Heidegger makes references
to languages dying and uses other organic metaphors, he does not provide a direct answer. Nor can he, if he endorses both the instrumental
and constitutive conceptions of language in the text. It is one thing to
establish that there is a tension between a constitutive and an instrumental conception of language in *Being and Time*. It is another to assess
the import of such a tension or to try to resolve it. The above analysis may suggest that we draw a neat distinction between language as
a kind of (instrumental) equipment and discourse as its (constitutive)
ontological foundation. Yet once we think of discourse as grounding
the possibility of a dynamic, temporal language that does justice to its
representational, communicative, and expressive moments, a different alternative emerges, namely that of a unified pragmatic-existential
account. Reconciling the two views requires modifying our understanding of the instrumental-pragmatic view. I noted earlier that assertions
are a different kind of tool than screwdrivers, computers, or wheels. This
is because, given our nature as linguistic beings, we cannot but have the
former, whereas whether we have the latter is quite contingent. We can
imagine worlds in which we never invented computers. Yet that we use
language is not thus contingent, for it is constitutive of who we are.
Language is not a tool I can pick up and put away again when I no longer
need it. It is not a type of ready-to-hand equipment among other types
because of its rootedness in discourse. At the same time, language itself
does not have the kind of being belonging to Dasein itself. Language is
not by itself conscious, for example, nor does it not have projects of its
own, and so forth. It is not Dasein. Insofar as we use language as a tool,
we do so not in the way we use these other tools but in the way we use
our body. We are linguistic beings just as we are embodied ones. That is,
we have not invented language to serve any purpose any more than we
invented the body, and without them, we would not be the kind of being
that we are. We cannot imagine not having a language any more than
we can imagine not having a body, pace Descartes. This is not to say
that we cannot adapt language to our purposes – as indeed we also adapt
our bodies, which quite literally have changed their shapes over the centuries as a result of what we do with them, how we eat, and so on.

Heidegger concludes §34 on language by saying that philosophy must forego "philosophy of language" and investigate "things themselves" in order to attain conceptual clarity about the problems that need to be addressed. By seeing language as grounded in discourse while also part of the referential totality of our pragmatic coping in the world, we do get a clearer picture of the conceptual ground of a Heideggerian philosophy of language. Comparing language to embodiment opens up a wide range of new ways of thinking of language: as something biological, something changing, something that is both individual and shared with other members of our species, something that involves rules and conventions as well as expressive creativity, and so forth. A pragmatic-existential philosophy of language will no longer consider itself to be autonomous of other branches of philosophy. It will make connections not only with philosophy of mind and epistemology, but also with philosophical accounts of social practices, aesthetics, and so on. And it will treat assertions as one linguistic form among others, albeit a form whose specific structure makes possible to speak of objects, properties, and truth.

NOTES

1   The interpretation of Heidegger championed by Hubert Dreyfus in *Being-in-the-World: A Commentary on Heidegger's* Being and Time, *Division I* (Cambridge, MA: MIT Press, 1991) attributes an instrumental conception to him. Similarly, Charles Taylor reads *Being and Time* as developing an instrumental conception and only the later Heidegger as having a constitutive conception of language in "Heidegger on Language," in *A Companion to Heidegger*, eds. Hubert L. Dreyfus and Mark A. Wrathall (Oxford: Blackwell, 2005), 433–55. Mark Okrent also offers a powerful pragmatist reading of Heidegger in *Heidegger's Pragmatism: Understanding, Being, and the Critique of Metaphysics* (Ithaca: Cornell University Press, 1988). In contrast, Cristina Lafont reads Heidegger as a linguistic idealist and to that extent can be read as attributing a constitutive conception to him in *Heidegger, Language, and World-Disclosure*, trans. G. Harman (Cambridge: Cambridge University Press, 2000). John McCumber, *Poetic Interaction: Language, Freedom, Reason* (Chicago: University of Chicago Press, 1989) also maintains that if Heidegger in *Being and Time* assigned any type of Being to language, it would be that of equipment. He locates what I am calling the constitutive view in "The Origin of the Work of Art" and subsequent works. However, McCumber recognizes a tension in *Being and Time* insofar as readiness-to-hand, which, as we shall see, is tantamount to instrumentality, does not allow Heidegger to formulate the concept of authenticity (*Poetic Interaction*, 122). Terminologically, my distinction parallels but is not identical to Charles B. Guignon, *Heidegger and the Problem of Knowledge* (Indianapolis: Hackett Publishing, 1983). Guignon's instrumentalist view regards language as a tool and takes our ability to use language to derive from a "prior grasp of the *nonsemantic significance* of the contexts in which we find ourselves" (*Problem of Knowledge*, 117),

whereas on the constitutive view, language structures our world and gener-
ates and makes possible our contexts of activity such that the distinction
between logos and language is dissolved (*Problem of Knowledge*, 119, 127).
Taylor Carman argues, I think rightly, that this is a mistake in *Heidegger's
Analytic: Interpretation, Discourse, and Authenticity in* Being and Time
(Cambridge: Cambridge University Press, 2003).

2   Unless otherwise indicated, I rely (with frequent modifications) on Joan
Stambaugh's translation of Martin Heidegger, *Being and Time* (Albany:
SUNY Press, 1996).

3   This is a point exploited by Robert Brandom in his inferentialist reading
of Heidegger as a normative pragmatist in "Heidegger's Categories," in *A
Companion to Heidegger*, 219ff. Brandom's interpretation will at times
serve as a foil to my own.

4   Ruth Millikan's work on functions and, more recently, conventions can be
seen as making such an argument. See *Varieties of Meaning: The 2002 Jean
Nicod Lectures* (Cambridge, MA: MIT Press, 2004). Also see "A Difference
of Some Consequence Between Conventions and Rules," *Topoi* 27 (2008):
87–99.

5   The scare quotes around "signs" here are puzzling, since the text suggests,
if anything, that it is the latter rather than the former phenomena that may
be taken to be but are not really signs. The passage that follows claims that
these latter phenomena are easily formalized because their relational nature
is formal. The idea here, I presume, is that signs, in their paradigmatic form,
are not formalizable because they are pragmata (see below).

6   *Being and Time* is, of course, rife with etymological connections and allu-
sions. Thus there is a semantic connection between *verweisen* and *zeigen*
and *(be-)deuten*, and between *zeigen* in the sense of showing and *aletheia*
and disclosure. These all form an intricate conceptual web. This very
feature of Heidegger's work illustrates an important fact about language:
words, qua signs, not only stand for things; they also point to other words,
to which they stand in relation. That is, language, as a linguistic system,
forms a holistic web.

7   "Understanding can itself be referred in and by [the relations constituting
the worldliness of the world]. We shall call the relational character of these
referential relations [*Bezüge des Verweisens*] signifying. In its familiarity with these relations, Dasein 'signifies' to itself. It primordially gives
itself to understand its being and potentiality-of-being with regard to its
being-in-the-world ... We shall call this relational totality of signification
significance. It is what constitutes the structure of the world, of that in
which Da-sein as such always already is" (87, Stambaugh translation).

8   Maquarrie and Robinson render "*aussprechbar*" as "expressible" as
opposed to "utterable." However, expression, unlike utterance, is possible
nonlinguistically.

9   This gloss is Heidegger's own, and we shall see below what he means by it.

10 This is Brandom's reading of Heidegger in "Heidegger's Categories."
Brandom's own view in *Making It Explicit: Reasoning, Representing, and
Discursive Commitment* (Cambridge, MA: Harvard University Press: 1994)
is that semantic or conceptual content is based on and makes explicit
normative (and already meaningful) social practices. The making explicit

happens in the form of the game of giving and asking for reasons, which take the form of assertions. Brandom's interpretation of Heidegger's conception of language is not strictly instrumentalist, since he emphasizes that we are by nature linguistic beings (see below), beings, as he puts it, that *thematize*. However, by claiming that "assertional language is an essential structure of the basic constitution of Dasein" (Robert Brandom, "Dasein, the Being That Thematizes" in *Tales of the Mighty Dead: Historical Essays in the Metaphysics of Intentionality*, Cambridge, MA: Harvard University Press: 2002, 331), Brandom reinscribes a new version of the historical privileging of assertions that Heidegger criticizes. In associating "making explicit" with linguistic articulation, Brandom privileges assertions.

11 Brandom claims that the "central" signification of assertion is communication (Brandom, "Heidegger's Categories," 225). As a result, he ends up downplaying the *disclosive* function of assertion.

12 Heidegger had not read Frege, according to John Haugeland, "Reading Brandom Reading Heidegger," *European Journal of Philosophy* 13 (2005): 427. For a discussion of Heidegger and Frege on reference, see my "Referentiality in Frege and Heidegger," *Philosophy and Social Criticism* 31 (2005): 37–52.

13 See Thomas Sheehan, "*Hermeneia* and *Apophansis*: The early Heidegger on Aristotle," in *Heidegger et l'idée de la phenomenology*, eds. Franco Volpi et al. (Dordrecht: Kluwer, 1988), 67–80.

14 Brandom, "Heidegger's Categories," 227.

15 Okrent, *Heidegger's Pragmatism*, 67. Also see Brandom's "Heidegger's Categories."

16 There is disagreement in the literature about what counts as implicit and explicit. For Brandom, for example, interpretation and articulation are conceptually divorced from explicitation, and making explicit is accomplished paradigmatically through assertion. In contrast, Taylor Carman takes *interpretation* to be *understanding made explicit* and hence what is explicit is not necessarily linguistic on his reading in *Heidegger's Analytic: Interpretation, Discourse, and Authenticity in* Being and Time (Cambridge: Cambridge University Press, 2003), 208.

17 Of course, even this assertion is not divorced from our interests. The purpose of the metric system is to allow us to measure things, usually not merely for the sake of measuring but for some other reason.

18 This is a corollary of the predicative nature of assertions.

19 Brandom, "Heidegger's Categories," 226.

20 Okrent, *Heidegger's Pragmatism*, 68.

21 Jacques Derrida bases his concept of différance on this phenomenon, arguing that no reiteration of a word carries exactly the same meaning as another.

22 "*Rede*" could be translated as speech, in the sense of giving a speech. The verb "*reden*" translates as "to talk" or "to speak."

23 Nor does Heidegger's language correspond to Saussure's *langage*, though that is a broader notion than *langue*.

24 Note that whereas in English, the etymology of "language" refers to "tongue," the German "*Sprache*" is cognate with "speaking" and "speech." The OED defines speech as "The act of speaking; the natural exercise of the vocal organs; the utterance of words or sentences; oral expression of

thought or feeling," "Speech," *The Oxford English Dictionary*, 2nd edition (Oxford: Clarendon Press, 1989). That means that there is a closer connection between *Sprache* and *Rede* than between "language" and "discourse" or "talk."

25 While "*bekunden*" literally means to manifest or to evince, it is usually used with subjective, often mental states (as in "*sein Beileid bekunden*," to express one's condolences).

26 Heidegger's account of what may be termed the formal conditions of discourse strikingly prefigures Habermas' analysis of communicative action and speech acts, as well as his critique of philosophy of language. See Jürgen Habermas, *The Theory of Communicative Action, Volume 1: Reason and the Rationalization of Society*, trans. Thomas McCarthy (Cambridge, MA: Beacon, 1984). Also see Habermas, "Toward a Critique of the Theory of Meaning," trans. William Mark Hohengarten in *Postmetaphysical Thinking: Philosophical Essays* (Cambridge, MA: MIT Press, 1992), 57–87.

10 The Empire of Signs

Heidegger's Critique of Idealism in *Being and Time*

The differentiation of standpoints lies at the very root of philosophical labor.
—A closing remark by Martin Heidegger from the debate
with Ernst Cassirer at Davos, Switzerland, 1929

INTRODUCTION

Throughout Division I of *Being and Time*, Heidegger returns with some frequency to the problem of idealism. A major burden of the existential analytic is to demonstrate that coping practices in particular and care in general are constitutive of Dasein's world. But if this is so, then it might seem to follow that the world depends for its very reality on Dasein's own manner of being. Heidegger seems to court precisely this idealistic interpretation at several points in the book. In §43, he explains that "only as long as Dasein *is* (that is, only as long as an understanding of being is ontically possible), 'is there' Being." This implies that "Being (not entities) *is dependent upon* the understanding of Being" (212). On this interpretation, Being itself is apparently dependent on Dasein. But Heidegger says even further: He observes that idealism has a clear "advantage" over realism if one understands idealism as the theory that "Being and Reality are only 'in the consciousness'" (207). This is a striking formula, especially since it resorts to the kind of cognitive language one might have expected Heidegger would avoid at all costs. It should be noted that he places the phrase "in the consciousness" in inverted commas as if to signal his discomfort with its idealistic implications. Yet many passages in the book's methodological overture would seem to reinforce the notion that Heidegger aims to interrogate the *understanding of Being (Seinsverständnis)* or the *meaning of Being (Sinn von Sein)*, formulae suggesting that the major purpose of the ontological inquiry is to get at a phenomenon that *inheres in human understanding* (1). Heidegger seems to dance even closer toward the edge of the idealistic abyss when he provides the following apparent endorsement of idealism:

If what the term "idealism" says, amounts to the understanding that Being can never be explained by entities but is already that which is "transcendental" for every entity, then idealism affords the only correct possibility for a philosophical problematic. If so, Aristotle was no less an idealist than Kant. (208)

This is a remarkable affirmation, and it should prompt us to ask just how Heidegger distinguishes his existential analytic from an idealistic doctrine that asserts that the world's intelligibility depends on our own cognitive faculties. More specifically, it raises the question as to whether Heidegger understood Being as a *transcendental condition* in the Kantian sense.

The resemblance, real or merely apparent, between Heidegger's argumentation in *Being and Time* to Kant's own doctrine of transcendental idealism remains a touchstone of considerable controversy in the secondary literature.[1] We should recall that this controversy began almost at the very moment of the book's original publication. In 1929, the neo-Kantian philosopher Ernst Cassirer, Heidegger's interlocutor in the famous debate in Davos, observed that "I must confess that I have found a neo-Kantian here in Heidegger" (GA 3: 274).[2] The passage cited above from *Being and Time* might seem to confirm this suspicion. But at several places in the book, Heidegger goes out of his way to ward off the misinterpretation of his doctrine as in any deep sense compatible with neo-Kantianism. Throughout *Being and Time* (and elsewhere), Heidegger is especially keen to emphasize his disagreements with Hermann Cohen and Ernst Cassirer. In what follows, I will shed further light on this polemical aspect of the book's engagement with the predominant philosophies of its time, so that we might come to a deeper understanding of just how Heidegger distinguished his doctrine from a certain kind of philosophical idealism. This endeavor is worthwhile not only because it helps us to appreciate the intellectual context in which *Being and Time* made its debut. It also helps us to discern some points of persistent irresolution in the core arguments of the book.

This chapter breaks down into four parts. First, I provide a brief historical and philosophical overview of Heidegger's complex relationship with his neo-Kantian contemporaries so as to prepare the reader for understanding some pivotal though unacknowledged references in the book. Second, I reconstruct the discussion of signs and reference in *Being and Time* in order to show how this discussion is addressed to a potentially idealistic reading of Heidegger's doctrine. Third, I explore Heidegger's remarkable and rarely discussed analysis of fetishism and magic within the horizon of so-called "primitive Dasein," phenomena that on Heidegger's view may help to explain the salience of ethnography for existential ontology. Finally, in the fourth section, I will briefly revisit the question as to whether Heidegger actually succeeds in defeating an idealistic interpretation of his philosophy.

Heidegger and Neo-Kantianism

The vigor of Heidegger's philosophical confrontation with his neo-Kantian contemporaries is well known. The confrontation owed its unusual intensity to the fact that Heidegger remained bound to the neo-Kantian movement in manifold ways. His earliest studies brought him into the neo-Kantian circle at Freiburg dominated by Heinrich Rickert, whose attempts at developing a transcendental groundwork for historical knowledge remained an important inspiration and foil as the young Heidegger labored to formulate his own doctrine of historical being.[3] In fact, he earned his doctorate in philosophy under Rickert's tutelage in 1913. Heidegger's relations with the neo-Kantian movement associated with the University of Marburg were rather more conflicted. In his own lecture series on Kant (given at Marburg during the winter term 1927–8, just following the publication of *Being and Time* and only one year preceding his inauguration as full professor at Freiburg), Heidegger introduces his account of the Transcendental Aesthetic with the following note:

With the phenomenological interpretation we oppose in principle the conception of Kant of the Marburg School ... But we want to stress that precisely this radical one-sidedness of the Marburg School has advanced Kant-interpretation more than all attempts at mediation which in the beginning to not bother with the central problematic. Here again we see that a radically mistaken course, when pursued with scientific rigor, is far more fruitful for research than a dozen so-called half-truths, in which each and everything (and that is to say nothing) comes into its own. (GA 25: 79)

The intensity of Heidegger's dislike for Marburg neo-Kantianism has aroused much speculation. There is even reason to suspect that Heidegger's animosity was nourished by extra-philosophical prejudice. Hermann Cohen, the founder of the Marburg School, was a German Jew and an outspoken supporter of democratic socialism. But Heidegger also disputed Marburg neo-Kantianism on genuinely philosophical grounds. Indeed, Heidegger believed that a variant of neo-Kantianism had misled even his teacher, Edmund Husserl. During the Davos encounter, Heidegger observed that "Husserl himself fell into the clutches of neo-Kantianism between 1900 and 1910." The key to this dispute lies in Heidegger's remark that neo-Kantianism was "one-sided" or "radical" – an idealistic doctrine that installed *logic* as the ground of reality. As we shall see, much of the argumentation in *Being and Time* that implies an apparent rapprochement with idealism will only make sense if we understand the deeper philosophical sources of Heidegger's objections.

Hermann Cohen left his mark on German academic philosophy as early as 1871 in his *Kant's Theory of Experience*, a strongly anti-metaphysical interpretation that enjoined readers to appreciate the importance of the modern sciences for Kant's project overall. But the true radicalism of Cohen's interpretation became fully apparent only in 1902 with the publication of the *Logic of Pure Knowledge*, in which Cohen fulfilled his ambition of abolishing the thing-in-itself as a residue of precritical metaphysics. On Cohen's view, Kant's first *Critique* still subscribed to an illicitly metaphysical and nonscientific picture of the world insofar as it posited the thing-in-itself as a mind-independent mystery that affects us through sensible intuition. Cohen followed the neo-Kantian injunction that all modern philosophy could only achieve true progress if it first returned "back to Kant." But in his *Logic*, Cohen rejected the metaphysical residue of sensible intuition as inconsistent with a truly logical groundwork for science, and he declared instead that the critical philosophy must begin with "pure thought" alone:

While we place ourselves again on the historical grounds of Critique, we must not permit logic to emerge from a theory of sensibility. *We begin with thought.* Thought must not have any origin outside of itself if its purity is to be uninhibited and untroubled. Pure thought, exclusive and in itself [*Das reine Denken in sich selbst und ausschließlich*], must be the exclusive source for the generation of pure knowledge.[4]

It was the trademark distinction of Cohen's neo-Kantianism to develop an *a priori* or transcendental foundation for natural scientific knowledge developed out of nothing else but pure thinking. Forms of intuition could have no place in this doctrine because, as Cohen had announced already in *Kant's Theory of Experience*, "the *a priori rests* in our mind."[5] Later in his career, Cohen would elaborate upon this idealistic insight by means of an instrument borrowed from calculus. In calculus, we conceive of an infinitely small magnitude (the "infinitesimal") as the originating point for the measurement of spatial areas. So, too, Cohen suggested that all of scientific discovery moves forward by positing a purely ideal limit-point as the unknown "x" that science aims to explain. Science therefore proceeds via the thought of a negation. It posits an infinitely small magnitude by negating finite being: "Via the route of the Nothing judgment presents us with the origin of something."[6] Without risk of exaggeration, we might regard this "principle of origins," or *Ursprungsprinzip*, as the trademark of Marburg neo-Kantian logicism. Its dramatic (and ultimately controversial) premise was the "reality" itself is generated in an act of thought.[7]

Ernst Cassirer was surely the most prominent and creative philosopher to emerge from the logicism of Marburg neo-Kantianism. Following Cohen's death in 1918, Cassirer moved beyond the constraining logicism of Marburg orthodoxy to develop a novel philosophy of culture, as presented in *The Philosophy of Symbolic Forms* (published in three volumes: *Language*, 1923; *Mythical Thought*, 1925; and *The Phenomenology of Knowledge*, 1929). But even before his celebrated movement into cultural philosophy, Cassirer had already earned a name for himself as one of the most consequential philosophers of the modern sciences. In his 1910 *Substance and Function*, Cassirer deployed principles borrowed from neo-Kantianism to develop a theory concerning the function of signs in scientific explanation. A sign, Cassirer observed, is a crucial instrument for natural-scientific reasoning insofar as it permits us to dispense with metaphysical commitments about reality so that we may forge pure and perfectly idealized *a priori* laws. The progress of science therefore exhibits a movement from substance to function – or, in other words, from substantialistic concepts about metaphysical reality to purely logical relations between signs:

The reduction of the concept of thing to a supreme ordering concept of experience disposes of a dangerous barrier to the progress of knowledge … No matter how complete our knowledge may be in itself, it never offers us the objects themselves, but only *signs* of them and their reciprocal relations.[8]

As Cassirer explained, scientific postulates guide our knowledge; they "signify not so much the known properties of things, but rather the logical instrument, by which we know."[9] Appealing to Helmholtz's theory signs, Cassirer observed that "The sign … does not require any actual similarity in the elements, but *only a functional correspondence* of the two structures."[10] Scientific explanation does not require that we should know "the real absolutely in its isolated, self-existent properties."[11] Rather, we know the logical relations between signs, or, in other words, "the rules under which this real stands and in accordance with which it changes."[12] Cassirer compressed this doctrine into a single aphorism: "The lawfulness of the real means ultimately nothing more and nothing else than the reality of the laws."[13]

Cassirer's theory of signs clearly built upon and extended Cohen's logicism, from which it borrowed the characteristic Marburg view of science as an orderly web spun out of "pure thought." The idealistic character of Cassirer's theory was unusually pronounced, as it suggested that, in the modern sciences, any robust kinds of ontological commitment must dwindle away. For as Cassirer explained, when natural science emerges from its metaphysical infancy, it gradually dispenses with all concepts of absolute "being" and supplants them with "mere expressions of being."[14] In summary, we can say that the neo-Kantians wished to supplant ontology with an idealistic relationism among signs whose logical dignity they sought to ground in pure *a priori* cognition. In *Being and Time*, this theory of signs was to serve Heidegger as an important foil, as we shall see below.

Heidegger on Signs

The remarks on signs and reference as presented in *Being and Time* (§§17 and 18) are surely among the most perplexing passages in Heidegger's entire book.[15] Much of the confusion is due to the author's failure to explain what argumentative purposes have prompted the discussion. Heidegger takes care to distinguish between a sign (*Zeichen*) and a reference (*Verweisung*). By this point in the book, we have already learned that Dasein's world is a holistic structure of *references*. The objects encountered in the mode of everydayness have the character of readiness-to-hand and they are understood as equipment. Dasein first comes across any item of equipment when it is already immersed in the flow of some activity that has been undertaken for some purpose. As Heidegger explains, equipment just is "something-in-order-to." Now because this purposeful structure implies that Dasein already takes any one item of equipment to *refer* to another item of equipment, it follows that Dasein understands the entire world of its everyday action as a *"referential context."* Heidegger therefore suggests that Dasein's world is constituted as a "totality of reference" or *Verweisungsganzheit* (76). Now this referential context is understood in the mode of purposeful activity rather than conceptual analysis. Just as one best understands the hammer through hammering rather than by stepping back to simply stare at it, so too the entire context of equipment is understood in a mode of *circumspection*. In other words, although the holistic context of reference is constitutive of everyday intelligibility, the phenomenon of referentiality *itself* remains submerged in the background of my experience. Heidegger's problem is that he wishes to understand the phenomenon of reference even though his analysis suggests that referentiality does not readily present itself for our philosophical inspection.

When Heidegger introduces the phenomenon of signs in §17, it might seem as if he does so precisely because signs appear as if they could provide us with a generic illustration as to the nature of reference as such. After all, a sign is itself a kind of equipment. We come across signs in the midst of purposive action. Heidegger offers several examples: signposts, boundary stones, the ball for the mariner's storm warning, signals, banners, signs of mourning, and so forth. In all these cases, the sign is a special sort of equipment that serves to "indicate" (*zeigen*) in an explicit manner. Moreover, these signs seem to have a "formal relational character" such that we may be led to believe they are serviceable models for the nature of reference as such. To take Heidegger's own example from 1920s technology, the arrow on a car is a sign that indicates what direction the driver will go. As Heidegger explains, "This sign is ready-to-hand within-the-world in the whole equipment-context of vehicles and traffic regulations. It is equipment for indicating, and as equipment, it is constituted by reference [*Verweisung*]" (78).

One might therefore be tempted to regard *all* reference as having a structure similar to that of a sign. But the ensuing discussion immediately defeats this expectation. For Heidegger hastens to inform us that although a sign "indicates" or points to some situation or event, this peculiarly indicative character is by no means due to its status as equipment. All equipment is referential, but not all equipment has the indicative character of a sign. A hammer, for example, is simply *understood* in and through the event of hammering. One does not need to have a *conceptual grasp* of the hammer *as indicating*, for example, one's intention of building a house. One simply goes about the activity in the appropriate way. Dasein's understanding and the referentiality that underwrites Dasein's world is simply *built into* its purposive activity. In other words, all equipment has a referential character insofar as it gains its intelligibility from an equipmental context, though not every item of equipment is a sign.[16] But if signs in particular do not serve to illustrate some crucial aspect of reference as such, then why does Heidegger take the time to discuss signs at all?

My suggestion is that Heidegger's discussion of signs in *Being and Time* fits into the book's broader argument against idealism. For the great risk of the sign is that it is easily construed as a phenomenon that depends primarily upon *thought*. After all, an arrow does not achieve its indicative role merely in virtue of its being a line with a triangular shape at one end. This shape in itself would accomplish nothing if it were not *taken as* indicating a direction. But it might seem to follow that the world *in itself* does not provide us with any reference whatsoever. And we might accordingly believe that the referential structure of the world is therefore something that *depends on human understanding*. Heidegger's account of how a sign achieves this indicative role is meant to ward off this idealistic conclusion. It aims to show that we can still understand the world's referential structure without succumbing to the idealistic distinction between *the (non-referential) world in itself* and *the world as a (thought-dependent) referential totality*.

To banish such an idealistic reading, Heidegger uses the example of signs to as a limit-case to drive home his global argument for the priority of ready-to-hand understanding. He therefore tries to show that *even* the referential status of a sign cannot be due to some sort of conceptual phenomenon called "indication" that has been superadded to the physical thing. It is "not a sort of bonus over and above what is already present-at-hand in itself" (80). We can see how ready-to-hand understanding retains its priority if we consider those special cases when we find it helpful to establish some given entity *as* a sign. A farmer, for example, might accept the south wind *as* a sign of imminent rain. But even in such a case, the wind is not first presented to us as a merely occurrent thing that only *afterwards* gets folded into the referential context of the farmer's concern for the weather. It is instead encountered "as equipment which has not been understood" (81). Heidegger also gives the rather quaint example of a person who ties a knot in a handkerchief. The knot can serve as a sign for various things, but it would make no sense to imagine that one could establish its referential status apart from a context of everyday concern. The referentiality that makes a sign an item of equipment is therefore dependent upon the wider context of involvements, and in this sense it is no different from the referentiality that belongs to other sorts of equipment. The analysis of signs thus does nothing to threaten Heidegger's broader argument as to the priority of ready-to-hand understanding.

Magic, Fetishes, and Primitive Dasein

It is at this point in the argument that Heidegger indulges in what may seem a peculiar digression concerning the character of fetishism and magic in "the primitive world."[17] The theme is certainly unusual, but it is important to note that Heidegger has already prepared the terrain for this digression in the book's first chapter, where he suggests that the study of "primitive Dasein" might offer certain advantages for a phenomenological inquiry into Dasein's everyday manner of being. He warns the reader that "everydayness does not coincide with primitiveness." But he goes on to suggest that anthropological study might nonetheless reveal certain facets of our everyday existence that have become obscured in our modern and highly conceptualized daily comportment: "To orient the analysis of Dasein towards the 'life of primitive peoples' can have positive significance as a method because 'primitive phenomena' are often less concealed and less complicated by extensive self-interpretation on the part of the Dasein in question" (51).

It is worth noting that this argument, which arguably conveys a certain nostalgic and Rousseauist admiration for the simplicity of savage life, was already a commonplace of anthropological research in the decades preceding Heidegger's *Being and Time*. Émile Durkheim appeals to a

similar premise to justify his study of Australian aboriginal ritual in his
1912 *The Elementary Forms of Religious Life*. And the early Heidegger's
own attempt at working out a phenomenology of religious experience
(in the 1920–1 seminars on *The Phenomenology of Religious Life*) takes
off from the premise that "the point of departure of the path to philosophy is *factical life experience*." In these lectures, Heidegger implies that
neo-Kantians have distorted philosophical work by beginning with *concepts* rather than the phenomena we understand via our involvement.
Their idealistic point of departure insures that "the object is merely
drawn from the object into the subject, whereas cognition qua cognition remains the same unclarified phenomenon" (GA 60: 11). Against
this idealistic tendency, Heidegger proposes to describe the "core phenomena" of religion by means of a description that resists conceptual
distortion. This same impulse to resist conceptual distortion animates
Heidegger's favorable remarks in *Being and Time* on the anthropological study of primitive life: "Primitive Dasein," he claims, "often speaks
to us more directly in terms of a primordial absorption in 'phenomena'
(taken in a pre-phenomenological sense). A way of conceiving things
which seems, perhaps, rather clumsy and crude from our standpoint,
can be positively helpful in bringing out the ontological structures of
phenomena in a genuine way" (51).

This preparatory excursus helps to explain what might otherwise
seem to be nothing more than an exotic digression from the rarefied
analysis of signs and referentiality. Once again, Heidegger wishes to
address the referential status of signs:

> One might be tempted to cite the abundant use of "signs" in primitive Dasein,
> as in fetishism and magic, to illustrate the remarkable role which they play in
> everyday concern when it comes to our understanding of the world. Certainly the
> establishment of signs which underlies this way of using them is not performed
> with any theoretical aim or in the course of theoretical speculation. This way
> of using them always remains completely within a Being-in-the-world which is
> "immediate."(81)

Heidegger opens the discussion by entertaining the possibility that the
primitive's understanding of signs may bear a superficial resemblance
to the sort of understanding that underwrites equipmental referentiality. It is therefore all the more intriguing to see how Heidegger *rejects*
examples drawn from primitive religion. On his view, the primitive
understanding of a sign does not exhibit the right sort of articulation
that is necessary for equipmental reference:

> But on closer inspection it becomes plain that to interpret fetishism and magic
> by taking our clue from the idea of signs in general, is not enough to enable us to
> grasp the kind of "Being-ready-to-hand" which belongs to entities encountered
> in the primitive world. (81–2)

Heidegger's objection runs as follows. For the sort of Dasein that we are (i.e., not primitives), understanding depends upon a referential totality of equipment. But this sort of referentiality has an *articulated* structure: one item of equipment refers to another without either of the items effacing the other. The knot may remind us of the bottle of milk we are intending to purchase on the way home, but we would never mistake the knot for the milk it indicates. When we consider the "primitive world," however, Heidegger suggests that this simple differentiation may be lacking. When one fashions a fetish and then makes it an object of worship, "the sign coincides with that which is indicated." But this means that the worshiper has failed to effect even the rudimentary articulation that is required for a referential totality: "Not only can the sign represent this in the sense of serving as a substitute for what it indicates, but it can do so in such a way that the sign itself always *is* what it indicates" (82).

Let us leave aside the question as to whether this is an accurate (or appealing) portrait of aboriginal fetishism. From the philosophical point of view, what is its purpose? We can appreciate Heidegger's aims only if we keep in mind that, on the one hand, he wants to reject a certain species of idealism, but, on the other hand, he wishes to avoid falling into the opposite picture of Dasein as immersed in a world of undifferentiated action. The idealist has an inflationary account of human understanding. He begins by breaking apart entities into discretely present-at-hand things. He thereby exaggerates the articulation amongst entities to such a degree that he can only picture them as linked together by concepts. By contrast, the fetish-worshiper has a deflationary account of human understanding. He has not yet understood the articulation of his world at all. Entities just "coincide" with one another:

This remarkable coinciding does not mean, however, that the sign-Thing has already undergone a certain "Objectification" – that it has been experienced as a mere Thing and misplaced into the same realm of Being of the present-at-hand as what it indicates. This "coinciding" is not an identification of things which have hitherto been isolated from each other: it consists rather in the fact that the sign has not as yet become free from that of which it is a sign. Such a use of signs is still absorbed completely in Being-towards what is indicated, so that a sign as such cannot detach itself at all. This coinciding is based not a prior Objectification but on the fact that such Objectification is completely lacking. (82)

Heidegger's conclusion is that the fetish-worshiper presents us with a rather inapt illustration for the ready-to-hand understanding. For primitive Dasein, "signs are not discovered as equipment at all." In other words, "ultimately what is 'ready-to-hand' within-the-world just does not have the kind of Being that belongs to equipment." We have therefore come up against the limits of comparative ethnography. As Heidegger observes, "Perhaps even readiness-to-hand and equipment have nothing to contribute as ontological clues for an interpretation of the primitive world" (82, translation modified). The problem is that such a being still exists in a kind of magical and undifferentiated communion with its surroundings. It has not developed the articulated mode of understanding that permits us to regard our world as a specifically *referential* whole. But the need to dissociate our own Dasein from primitive Dasein simply amplifies the urgency of combating an idealistic interpretation. For how are we to distinguish between our own more sophisticated understanding of the world as constituted by referential bonds of equipment from the idealistic portrait of the world as held together by nothing more than sheer thought?

Heidegger's Remarks on Neo-Kantian Idealism

I suggested above that we might think of the fetish-worshiper as a kind of uncomprehending idealist, that is, someone who fails to understand how the phenomenon he worships owes its being to his involvements. But then we might think of the modern idealist as a sophisticated fetish-worshiper, that is, someone who knowingly describes the world as a phenomenon that owes its reality to his mind. Heidegger's problem is that his own argument veers dangerously close to the idealistic premise common to both alternatives. For Heidegger has argued that Dasein's world is a "referential totality" constituted by Dasein's own involvements. But he has also suggested that "references" have to be in some sense *thought*. It might seem to follow that Dasein has not yet overcome the possibility that worldhood as such depends on Dasein's *thinking*. Heidegger expresses this idealistic worry in an explicit fashion toward the end of §18:

> If we have thus determined that the Being of the ready-to-hand (involvement) is definable as a context of assignments or references, and that even worldhood may be so defined, then has not the "substantial Being" of entities within-the-world been volatilized into a system of Relations? And inasmuch as Relations are always "something thought," has not the Being of entities within-the-world been dissolved into "pure thinking"?[18] (87–8)

Although no one is cited by name in this passage, it is surely significant that Heidegger places "pure thinking" in inverted commas. The unstated target in this passage is neo-Kantian idealism, specifically as represented by the doctrines in Cohen's *Logic of Pure Knowledge* that extol "pure thought" as the uninhibited source of knowledge. Now what is perhaps most striking is that Heidegger introduces the implied comparison because he seems to recognize the risk that one might interpret his own argument along similar lines.

Heidegger tries to ward off the comparison by explaining that existential ontology begins with entities as they are understood *through our purposive involvement*, whereas neo-Kantianism mistakenly begins with decontextualized or present-at-hand entities that it *only then* binds together with mathematical relations. The neo-Kantian point of departure is in error insofar as it misses the deeper relations that are *already* constitutive of Dasein's world as a context of involvement or "concernful circumspection."

The context of assignments or references, which, as significance, is constitutive for worldhood, can be taken formally in the sense of a system of Relations. But one must note that in such formalizations the phenomena get leveled off so much that their real phenomenal content may be lost, especially in the case of such "simple" relationships as those which lurk in significance. The phenomenal content of these "Relations" and "Relata" – the "in-order-to," the "for-the-sake-of," and the "with-which" of an involvement – is such that they resist any sort of mathematical functionalization; nor are they merely something thought, first posited in an "act of thinking." They are rather relationships in which concernful circumspection as such already dwells. (88)

On Heidegger's view, the error in neo-Kantian idealism is that it takes off from a view of the world as composed of decontextualized bits of knowledge that it then knits together as a "system of relations." But this is the wrong way to think about referentialty, since not all reference has the character of a conceptually constructed sign. References are instead simple "relations" that "lurk" in involvements:

This "system of Relations" as something constitutive for worldhood, is so far from volatilizing the Being of the ready-to-hand within-the-world, that the worldhood of the world provides the basis on which such entities can for the first time be discovered as they are "substantially" "in themselves." And only if entities within-the-world can be encountered at all, is it possible, in the field of such entities, to make accessible what is just present-at-hand and no more. (88)

This argument is supposed to reinforce the distinction between Heidegger and neo-Kantian idealism. Heidegger now offers the same rejoinder to Cassirer, whose *Substance and Function* is the implied target in the passage that immediately follows:

By reason of their Being-just-present-at-hand-and-no-more, these latter entities can have their "properties" defined mathematically in "functional concepts." Ontologically, such concepts are possible only in relation to entities whose

Being has the character of pure substantiality. Functional concepts are never possible except as formalized substantial concepts. (88)

Again, Heidegger is trying to show that the neo-Kantians have missed the primacy of Dasein's *involvement*. Instead, they take decontextualized present-at-hand entities as their point of departure. In *Substance and Function*, Cassirer explains that modern science gradually cast aside its "substantive" picture of reality and has embraced metaphysically neutral mode of explanation that relies upon merely mathematized relations. Heidegger's objection is that this story about scientific progress only convinces us because it has first presupposed decontextualized substances and only afterwards "formalized" them until, once their metaphysical substance is evacuated, we find ourselves left with purely "functional concepts." Neo-Kantianism neglects the readiness-to-hand character of entities as they are encountered through purposive action and it therefore conceives of the world as nothing more substantial than an empire of signs.

CONCLUSION

I have suggested that Heidegger's remarks on signs are best understood as part of his larger attempt to offer a refutation of idealism. It may strike the reader as somewhat ironic that Heidegger directs his remarks against neo-Kantian idealism in particular, since the implicit model for his refutation is Kant's own "Refutation of Idealism" from the *Critique of Pure Reason*, where time already figures as a crucial factor in the argument.[19] Be this as it may, the reader may be left with a lingering doubt as to whether Heidegger's own refutation has wholly succeeded in silencing the idealistic interpretation.

There are reasons to believe it has not. The problem is that although Heidegger's refutation stands in striking contrast to the radically logicist character of neo-Kantian idealism, the very terms of Heidegger's refutation seem once again to raise the specter of Immanuel Kant himself. According to Heidegger, neo-Kantianism fails to appreciate the crucial role of *involvement* in the constitution of Dasein's world, and it is therefore misled into the cul-de-sac of intellectualistic constructivism. But if Dasein's own involvements are constitutive of the world, then it might seem that the world seems to depend for its very worldhood upon our purposive action. Heidegger has defeated an idealism of the mind, but in its place it may seem he has left us to contend with an idealism of human practices.

It is by no means obvious that Heidegger would have resented this characterization. After all, the remarks quoted at the opening of this paper suggest that Heidegger welcomed the comparison between existential ontology and transcendental idealism. Just as Kant stubbornly refused to deny the metaphysical independence of things-in-themselves, so too Heidegger did not contest the notion that "entities" enjoy an independent status quite apart from Dasein's *Seinsverständnis*. As Heidegger writes in *Being and Time*, "Being (not entities) *is dependent upon* the understanding of Being" (212, emphasis added). Insofar as Dasein's understanding of Being accompanies Dasein's involvement, it follows that while entities are disclosed *through* involvements they are not dependent *upon* them.

Two years after the publication of *Being and Time*, Heidegger offered a further validation for this reading of the book as a species of transcendental idealism in his 1929 inaugural lecture at Freiburg, "What is Metaphysics?" In this lecture, he would argue that when we are in the grips of anxiety, we find ourselves cast into the mode of the *unheimlich* or the uncanny. This means that all of our daily involvements and concerns sink into indifference such that the worldhood of Dasein's world (which is understood as a referential totality) seems to come apart at the seams. What remains is "the nothing." Here, Heidegger offers an explicit rejoinder to what he sees as the extravagant logicism of Cohen's principle of origins:

The nothing is the origin of negation, not vice versa [*Das Nichts ist der Ursprung der Verneinung, nicht umgekehrt*]. If the power of the intellect in the field of inquiry into the nothing and into being is thus shattered, then the fate of the reign of "logic" in philosophy is thereby decided. The idea of "logic" itself disintegrates in the turbulence of a more original questioning. (GA 9: 117/92; translation modified)

Anxiety therefore seems to undo the possibility of logicist idealism. In this condition, "we can get no hold on things," and we witness "the slipping away of beings as a whole" (GA 9: 112/88). What is left of the world in such a condition? Just meaninglessness and a sense of ourselves as "hovering where there is nothing to hold on to." In Heidegger's phrase, "pure Da-sein [*reine Da-sein*] is all that is still there" (GA 9: 112/89). This seems to ratify a species of inverted idealism: Heidegger overcame what he considered the "radical" and "one-sided" species of neo-Kantian idealism celebrating "pure thought" only to endorse its mirror image: the proposition that sheer existence, when torn from its worldly context, is disclosed as the ground of Being. Whether this is a more satisfactory solution is by no means obvious.

NOTES

1 For a comprehensive argument, see William D. Blattner, *Heidegger's Temporal Idealism* (Cambridge: Cambridge University Press, 1999). Also

see Theodore R. Schatzki, "Early Heidegger on Being, the Clearing, and Realism," in *Heidegger: A Critical Reader*, eds. Hubert L. Dreyfus and Harrison Hall (Oxford: Basil Blackwell, 1992), 81–98.

2 For further discussion on Heidegger's relationship to Cassirer and neo-Kantianism, see Peter E. Gordon, *Continental Divide: Heidegger, Cassirer, Davos* (Cambridge, MA: Harvard University Press, 2010). Also see Michael Friedman, *A Parting of the Ways: Carnap, Cassirer, and Heidegger* (Chicago: Open Court, 2000).

3 Charles Bambach, *Heidegger, Dilthey, and the Crisis of Historicism* (Ithaca: Cornell University Press, 1995).

4 Hermann Cohen, *Logik der reinen Erkenntniss* (Berlin: Bruno Cassirer Verlag: 1922), 1213. The German original reads thus: "Indem wir uns wieder auf den geschichtlichen Boden der Kritik stellen, lehnen wir es ab, der Logik eine Lehre von der Sinnlichkeit voraufgehen zu lassen. *Wir fangen mit dem Denken an.* Das Denken darf keinen Ursprung haben außerhalb seiner selbst, wenn anders seine Reinheit uneingeschränkt und ungetrübt sein muß. Das reine Denken in sich selbst und ausschließlich muß aussschließlich die reinen Erkenntnisse zur Erzeugung bringen. Mithin muß die Lehre vom Denken die Lehre von der Erkenntnis werden. *Als solche Lehre vom Denken, welche an sich Lehre von der Erkenntnis ist, suchen wir hier die Logik aufzubauen*" (emphasis added).

5 See quotation in Claude Piché, "Heidegger and the Neo-Kantian Reading of Kant" in *Heiegger, German Idealism, and Neo-Kantianism*, ed. Tom Rockmore (Amherst: Humanity Books, 2000), 191 n. 32.

6 Cohen, *Logik*, 84.

7 For a lucid explanation of this principle, see Friedman, *A Parting of the Ways*, 31; also see Peter E. Gordon, "Science, Finitude, and Infinity: Neo-Kantianism and the Birth of Existentialism," *Jewish Social Studies* 6.1 (1999): 30–53. And Walter Kinkel, "Das Urteil des Ursprungs: Ein Kapitel aus einem Kommentar zu H. Cohens *Logik der reinen Erkenntnis*," *Kantstudien* 17 (1912): 274–82.

8 Ernst Cassirer, *Substance and Function*, trans. W. Swabey and M. Swabey (New York: Dover, 1953), 302–3.

9 Ibid., 304.

10 Ibid. (emphasis added).

11 Ibid.

12 Ibid.

13 Ibid., 305.

14 Ibid., 303.

15 Excellent introductory remarks can be found in Hubert L. Dreyfus, *Being-in-the-World: A Commentary on Heidegger's* Being and Time, *Division I* (Cambridge, MA: MIT Press, 1991), 100–2.

16 "Now it is certain that indicating differs in principle from reference as a constitutive state of equipment; it is just as incontestable that the sign in its turn is related in a peculiar and even distinctive way to the kind of Being which belongs to whatever equipmental totality may be ready-to-hand in the environment, and to its worldly character. In our concernful dealings, equipment for indicating gets used in a *very special* way." (79)

17 The passages in question can be found at 81–2.

18 The German reads: "Wenn wir so das Sein des Zuhandenen (Bewandtnis) und gar die Weltlichkeit selbst als einen Verweisungszusammenhang bestimmen, wird dann nich das 'substanzielle Sein' des innerweltlichen Seienden in ein Relationssystem verflüchtigt und, sofern Relationen immer 'Gedachtes' sind, das Sein des innerweltlich Seienden in das 'reine Denken' aufgelöst?"

19 See Immanuel Kant, *Critique of Pure Reason*, trans. and ed. Paul Guyer and Allen W. Wood (Cambridge: Cambridge University Press, 1998), B274–9.

11   Heidegger on Skepticism, Truth, and Falsehood

The climax of Division I of *Being and Time* are two sections on the themes of reality and truth, with the former largely devoted to the problem of skepticism. After the long and complex elaboration of the unique cluster of concepts that articulate the structure of Dasein, Heidegger here draws morals for familiar and fundamental philosophical issues. But these sections are dense and difficult, and these morals raise many questions of their own (only some of which I can consider here). For example, just what can the persuasive force of §43's dismissal of skepticism be, and, as Tugendhat asked, why would one think of the notion of truth that §44 spells out – and promotes as "deeper than," and "founding," the "traditional" correspondence notion of truth – as a notion of *truth* at all?[1] And why do these topics come to sit alongside one another in Heidegger's thought? As is well known, *Being and Time* was a work completed in some haste, but also one that emerged from years of reflection, some of which notes for, and transcripts of, Heidegger's lecture courses document. There one finds a case for a claim that this chapter will suggest sheds much light on the puzzles of §§43 and 44 of *Being and Time*: the claim that belief is a "founded mode" of being-in-the-world.

I. "THE SCANDAL OF PHILOSOPHY"

Heidegger sees skepticism about the external world as a "sham" problem (GA 20: 218), one that one comes to pose only by having embraced a

I'm grateful to Tom Sheehan and Adam Beck for access to their translations of the *Logik* and *Einleitung* lectures respectively. For useful comments on work out of which this paper emerged, I would like to thank Maria Alvarez, Adam Beck, John Divers, Sebastian Gardner, Joanna McManus, Adrian Moore, Stephen Mulhall, John Preston, Aaron Ridley, Graham Stevens, and, in particular, Daniel Whiting, as well as members of audiences at the Universities of Amsterdam, Bristol, Cambridge, Durham, Paris I, Reading, and Southampton. I would like to thank the University of Southampton and the Arts and Humanities Research Council for periods of research leave during which this work was carried out.

confused ontology. "Starting with the *construct* of the isolated subject," one does indeed come to wonder how this "fantastically conceived," "denatured" entity "comes out of its inner 'sphere' into one which is 'other and external'" (206, 60, GA 20: 223, emphasis added). To refute the skeptical worry that it can't would indeed "call ... for a theory and metaphysical hypotheses" (GA 20: 223). But *Being and Time* famously insists that we must not answer that call:

Kant calls it "a scandal of philosophy and of human reason in general" that there is no cogent proof of ["the existence of things outside us"] which will do away with any scepticism ... [But the] "scandal of philosophy" is not that this proof has yet to be given, but that *such proofs are expected and attempted again and again.* (203, 205)

Rather than attempting to offer such a proof (explaining how an "isolated subject" "comes into" an "other and external" "sphere"), Heidegger instead presents an ontology in which nothing corresponding to that "subject" and that "sphere" can be found. Heidegger acknowledges that "someone oriented to the traditional horizon of epistemological questions" will see his ontology as simply "nullify[ing] the problem of knowledge"; his response is to ask "what authority decides *whether* and *in what sense* there is supposed to be a problem of knowledge?" (GA 20: 217).

But it is not as if (what for simplicity's sake I will refer to here as) the Cartesian ontology is embraced without reason: rather we are driven to embrace it by seemingly innocent reflections on errors and dreams and by what many feel are intuitively compelling thought-experiments, such as those of the evil demon and the brain-in-a-vat. The "isolated subject" answers to the sense that there reflections seem to make vivid, that, as Tugendhat puts it, "our relation to beings is a specifically mediate one."[2] It is reflections such as these that seem to *prove* that there is "a problem of knowledge." So why think – with Heidegger – that there isn't?

Heidegger was clearly suspicious of the notion that one might compel the person of "traditional orientation" to change her view through argument.[3] Such an argument would presumably have to be offered in terms that that person accepts; but Heidegger believes that her confusion lies precisely in accepting those terms. Nevertheless, it seems much less plausible to think that Heidegger thought persuasion of any sort impossible, that a case or argument in some extended sense might not be made for his view. So what might that case be?

The charge he levels against the Cartesian is that her ontology is "indefinite," "indeterminate" (321). Only a kind of "neglect" – "the ontological indifference in which Descartes and his successors took" the thinking subject (GA 20: 305, 296) – allows one to believe that one can make sense of knowing on the basis that that subject provides. That one cannot is not news, of course, if all this means is that the ontology leads to skepticism; Heidegger's claim would instead seem to be that the ontology cannot make sense of the intentionality of belief, its power to represent states of affairs, or – to point to a topic that will be central here – to misrepresent them.

Crucially, Heidegger claims that "[k]nowing is a mode of Dasein founded upon being-in-the-world" (62). Our mode of being is one of *Sein-bei* the entities that the Cartesian would have us see as populating an "other and external sphere." *Bei* lacks any straightforward equivalent in English but corresponds roughly to the French *"chez"*; Heidegger's translators have offered for *Sein-bei* "being-alongside" (Macquarrie and Robinson in *Being and Time*), "being-involved-with" (GA 20), and "being-familiar-with" or "being-at-home-with" (GA 21), while Dreyfus has proposed "being-amidst."[4] As we will see, such differences matter.

On any of these construals, however, the Cartesian faces the collapse of an "inner"/"outer" distinction and, in its place, an intimacy of some sort to which she will naturally respond, "What of error? What of the various ways in which we can become disconnected from the world around us?" Heidegger's reply is that having false beliefs is also a "mode of Dasein founded upon being-in-the-world":

All delusion and all error, in which in a way no relationship of being to the entity is secured but is instead falsified, are once again only modes of *Sein-bei*. (GA 20: 221)[5]

If this is so, the skeptic's worry about the very existence of the world, based on the question of whether all of our ordinary beliefs might be false, represents "a misunderstanding of the very questioning": "For such a questioning makes sense only on the basis of a being whose constitution is being-in-the-world" (GA 20: 294).

My approach here will be to try to shed light on Heidegger's reflections on skepticism and truth by considering the rarely discussed[6] pre-*Being and Time* discussions where he explores the "founded" character of falsehood at some length. Heidegger identifies a set of "conditions of the possibility of falsehood," and I will argue that these point to a way of understanding, first, why Cartesian ontology might be thought "inadequate" because "indefinite," second, how this insight naturally leads to a notion of "truth" that might be seen as deeper than – by virtue of being presupposed by – the "traditional" correspondence conception of truth, and hence, third, why §§43 and 44 belong together; finally, it will also provide us with another way of thinking about the notions central to *Being and Time*'s "fundamental ontology," "being-in-the-world" and *Sein-bei*.

In the discussions to be explored, the figure Heidegger takes as his patron saint, as it were, is Aristotle. His thinking is free of "sham" concerns that bedevil ours:

Kant and Aristotle have this in common, that for both of them the external world exists. For Aristotle, knowledge of that world is not a problem. He treated knowledge quite differently, as a clarification of the surrounding world. He can be called a realist only inasmuch as he never questions the existence of the external world. (GA 61: 4–5)[7]

Heidegger claims that *De Anima* is "no psychology in the modern sense" but instead contains "[t]he central investigation of the human manner of being in the world" (GA 17: 6, 298), and he claims to find an anticipation of his view of truth in Book Theta of the *Metaphysics*, in the distinguishing of two forms of "truth," one that stands opposed to a form of falsehood or "covering-over," and one that does not.[8] In roughest outline, falsehood is possible when we describe "composite entities": in the "synthetic" work of articulating a proposition, "if one synthesises what is not together, there is covering-over," and if one synthesizes "what is together, there is uncoveredness" (GA 21: 177). The "synthetic" truth and falsehood of propositions is distinguished from our grasp of "non-synthetic entities," *asyntheta*, with which Heidegger compares our knowledge of "colour ... essence, movement, time, and the like" (GA 21: 185). Here, what stands in falsehood's place, so to speak, is a pure failure to grasp the *asyntheta*: here "there is no covered-overness at all, not even deception," but "only not-apprehending," a "lack of access," "an utter inability to apprehend at all" (GA 21: 177, 183). On the other hand, when the thinking subject does grasp the *asyntheta*, its "relation" to them is one of *thigein*, "touching": here there is "no distance" (GA 21: 180, 181). The discussion I summarize so briefly here is difficult and Dahlstrom claims that Heidegger's reading of Aristotle is characterized by "audaciousness ... violence and even rapaciousness" (2001: 218). But, as Heidegger himself seems to have done, we will find that some of its motifs have a resonance in the reflections to come.

2. "CONDITIONS OF THE POSSIBILITY OF FALSEHOOD"

The 1925–6 *Logik* lectures present Heidegger's most sustained examination of falsehood. Here, he identifies three related "structural conditions of falsehood" (GA 21: 187) and elaborates upon them through an example, that of his mistakenly declaring of a bush seen while he walks through a dark wood, "It's a deer." As in *Being and Time*'s well-known discussion of the understanding implicit in recognizing a hammer, Heidegger's "unearthing" of these "conditions" reveals a presupposed

understanding that a "traditional orientation" obscures: "a false statement ... too [is] grounded in a prior knowledge" (GA 21: 208).

The first condition is a "prior intending and having of the subject
matter" (GA 21: 187):

It is necessary that beforehand I already have something given to me, something
coming toward me. If something did not already encounter me from the outset,
there would be no occasion to regard it *as* ... (GA 21: 187, ellipsis in the
original)

Now the most natural interpretation of these remarks surely takes the
"something already given to me" to be the bush, the "it" – the "subject
matter" – of the mistaken judgment. But that construal is problematic
philosophically and textually. Philosophically, it limits the applicability of this condition to judgments where there *is* a subject matter, so to
speak. What would we say was the "something already given to me" in
a case where I mistakenly think I see something of a certain sort where
there is, in fact, nothing at all (as I do in the case that GA 20: 38 mentions,
that of being "beset by a hallucination such that I now perceive an auto-
mobile being driven through the room over [our] heads")? One response
would be to treat the judgment as, to use John McDowell's expression,
"object-dependent" and declare that when there is no relevant "object" –
no "It" – the sentence in question "fails to express a proposition," "fails
to express a thought" (Thornton 2004: 146). According to this view, one
has not merely failed to depict how things are in such a case; rather it
has become unclear whether anything *has* been said about how things
are: "About which things?" one might ask. This view has perhaps its
most natural application precisely to the kind of perceptual demonstrative thoughts that Heidegger's example illustrates:

The defining function of perceptual demonstrative thoughts is to convey
information about the perceptible world – and, hence, to be assessable as true or
false. So we have little reason, if any, to protest that there simply must be such a
thought when there is nothing for it to be true about – that is, when the question
of its truth or falsity cannot even arise. (De Gaynesford 2004: 136)

Heidegger's Aristotelian motifs could find an application here. If it
does indeed make sense to say that a claim, proposition, or thought
is absent in such cases, there is instead, one might say, "an utter
inability to apprehend at all," a "lack of access"; moreover, the object-
dependence of my thoughts makes for a connection between my
thought and its "subject matter" of such an intimacy that it merits
description as "touching." This "having-present the about-which"
would indeed be a "direct having, and in a certain sense a *thigein*"
(GA 21: 189).

But, as I mentioned, this interpretation sits uncomfortably with the text. Heidegger concludes the passage quoted above by saying, "Always already there is *a priori* disclosure of world" (GA 21: 187).

A similar slide away from a full-blown object-dependence to what one might call "context-" or "world-dependence" can be found at the point where, in the following gloss on the first "condition," Heidegger attempts to put his point "concretely":

In order for me to be able to be deceived, in order for something to misrepresent itself to me and to appear as something it is not, the thing that so appears has to have already encountered me. It has to appear, in some way or other, precisely "during" the misrepresentation. To put it concretely: I have to be moving in the forest, for example, or if not in the forest then someplace else, if I am to be able to be deceived about things in the world and in the knowledge of the world. (GA 21: 211–12)

What then must we already "touch" in making our judgment? In these passages, Heidegger seems to vacillate between identifying this with an entity judged and the setting, context, or "world" within which such an entity shows itself. The following is another example:

The that-about-which appears as something that encounters me within a persisting *thigein*, as something that is already uncovered from the outset, as something approaching in the woods. (GA 21: 189)

We will return to this vacillation; but a stress upon the need for a grasp of the already meaningful context within which an entity we might mistake might be found is echoed in Heidegger's elaboration of his second "condition of falsehood." My mistakenly taking the "it" I approach as something that it is not is only possible because I take the "it" in question as ... in the first place:

Only because I let whatever encounters me encounter me *on the basis of* the act of envisioning [*aus Hinblicknahme auf*] something (say, a deer), can that thing appear as a deer. (GA 21: 188)

Heidegger depicts that feat too as calling for a broader grasp of the situation in which the entity shows up:

As I approach the thing, I take it *as something* ... something that is already articulated *as something* and, as such, is expected and accepted in my way of dealing with the world. (GA 21: 187)

This "act of envisioning" harbors a further complexity, and a third condition must hold: taking something as ... assigns that which is so taken a particular place in what one might call "logical space," a place characterized by how it is distinguished from a determinate range of other possible places: "Envisioning a 'that as which' is possible only when there is a possible 'other'" (GA 21: 188).[9] It is a further feature of the already understood situation within which we find the object we (mis) judge that it restricts that "space" of possibilities. I am ready, one might say, to mistake a bush in a wood for a deer; more fancifully, I might imagine that the "it" approaching is the Shah of Iran since "the Shah is a being that *could* appear among the trees in a German forest at night"; but "there is not a chance that I would see anything like the cubed root of sixty-nine coming toward me" (GA 21: 188).

In sum, these conditions seem to require that, in order for one to hold a false belief of the sort Heidegger considers, one must have a grasp of the kind of entity that is the subject matter of that belief, of the kind of circumstances in which it can be found, and the range of alternative states of affairs that might be found within those circumstances. One's belief may be mistaken; there may indeed be nothing at all where one supposes the "deer" stands; but one must grasp the space or – to adapt an expression of Heidegger's – the "there" where the "deer" is thought to stand; one must grasp its place within its broader context and the kinds of entity that might come to stand "there."

3. SOME IMPLICATIONS: TRUTH AND BEING-IN-THE-WORLD

A schematic rationale emerges in the preceding reflections for regarding the "traditional conception of truth" as "superficial" (GA 19: 15). Heidegger identifies that "conception" as maintaining that the "'locus' of truth is assertion (judgment)" and that "the essence of truth lies in the 'agreement' of the judgment with its object" (214). He attacks this conception as "by no means ... primary" (33); it obscures the fact that "assertion is grounded in *Dasein*'s ... *disclosedness*" (226); quite how we ought to characterize "disclosedness" is a difficult issue, not least because Heidegger states that it "embraces the whole of that structure-of-being which has become explicit" in the course of Division I of *Being and Time* (221). But, by virtue of the fact that Heidegger identifies this "most primordial 'truth'" with "the ontological condition for the possibility that assertions can be either true or false" (226), the previous section's discussion promises to shed some light. What its three "conditions of the possibility of falsehood" identify is a kind of familiarity with the world that must be in place if we are to entertain propositions about how things are; in identifying a form of understanding of the world that our making true or false claims about the world presupposes, we identify a way in which that world is revealed to us that outstrips and is, in a recognizable sense, more fundamental than the revelation that arises when, through successful inquiry, we replace particular false beliefs with true beliefs. If so, such a deeper revelation would seem to merit identification with (or as playing some part in) the "most primordial 'truth.'"

While this clearly invites Tugendhat's earlier question – why ought one to think of this revelation as a kind of *truth*? – let us note here that, if we do, we also acquire a sense of why it must be the case that – as §44 gnomically puts it – "*Dasein is 'in the truth'*" (221). Heidegger depicts the "prior knowledge" in which even false statements are "grounded" as realized in "the prior act of letting something encounter us" and that act as "a comportment with which we constantly live" (GA 21: 209): "we live constantly in this state of letting-things-encounter-us" (GA 21: 209). There is one reasonably clear sense in which this might well be so. We cannot have acquired the "knowledge" in question by, as it were, reading it off the world itself; we cannot have acquired this "familiarity" by seeing that things are thus-and-so, because this "familiarity" grounds – and hence is presupposed by – our capacity to see that things are thus-and-so. "The constant letting-encounter/already-having of something," which "is existentially and *a priori* a *being-unto* [*Sein-zu*] and *Sein-bei* something," is not a condition into which "I first must bring myself" (GA 21: 209, 212).[10] Without it, I am incapable of entertaining true or false propositions, of possessing views on how things are, and only in it – if I am indeed an intentional agent – can I "live" (GA 21: 209). But – again – why think of this "condition," in which I must stand "insofar as I am at all" (GA 21: 212), as a form of *truth*?

And what of Heidegger's insistence that Dasein is being-in-the-world? The rhetoric of the passages that we considered in the last section (§2) is one of "having," "givenness," and "touch" (*thigein*); the three conditions require of us a certain understanding, but it is of something immediately present to us, one might say; this is no abstract knowledge: instead there is "something coming towards me," the thing judged "has already encountered me," "I have to be moving in the forest." Is this anti-Cartesian rhetoric justified by the reflections considered so far? Supposing there is a sense in which I have to "have" the "subject-matter" of my judgment and the world in which that "subject matter" is found, must I therefore be *in* that world? The notion of "being-in" at stake here is not, Heidegger insists, the familiar spatial sense; here "'in' primarily does not signify anything spatial at all but means primarily *being familiar with* [*vertraut sein mit*]" (GA 20: 213).[11] But why think of familiarity with something as a form of being *in* it in *any* sense? And to what extent does the anti-Cartesian force of these reflections depend on our continuing to hear this "in" in "spatial" terms and "*Sein-bei*" as "being-amidst" rather than "being-familiar-with"?

There remains a powerful intuition that understanding "lies within," such that there will always remain a question (the skeptical question, *in nuce*) of how it relates to that which lies "without."[12] We have, of course, already mentioned a view which challenges that intuition, namely, McDowell's postulation of object-dependent thoughts. Although I think it would be wrong to ascribe that view to Heidegger,[13] I think we may ascribe to him a view that shares with it certain features and which ascribes a not-unnatural sense both to his insistence that we live amidst the entities that we think about and to the rhetoric of "touch" witnessed in §2.

4. TWO HEIDEGGERIAN MODELS

The Cartesian who reads the *Logik* lectures' discussion of what one might call our "pre-propositional understanding" will find the charge that her own ontology is "indeterminate" galling, as the most obvious feature of that discussion is its abstraction. So just what kind of "understanding" does Heidegger have in mind when he tells us that "the statement is grounded in a prior understanding" (GA 21: 208)?

There are many ways through the complex works that Heidegger assembles in the 1920s, this being a characteristic of *Being and Time* just as of other more obviously exploratory texts: a variety of roads lead us to recurrent motifs and most of the core claims are surely overdetermined.[14] The notion that knowledge is a "founded mode" of being-in-the-world is embedded within discussions of Dasein's temporality, its capacity for authenticity and inauthenticity, and of what one might call its "'practical' and economic" (57) engagement with the world around it. That the latter might be key to understanding our "pre-propositional understanding" is interpretively highly plausible, not least because of the interspersing of the discussion of the conditions of judgment in §2 with one precisely examining how statements arise out of our "prescinding" from such forms of engagement (GA 21: 314). Heidegger there presents a picture of Dasein as a creature at work in the world, actually laying its hands upon and using the entities around it as it goes about its "practical and economic" business; awareness that takes a propositional form enters the scene only when that business is disrupted, when the tool we are using breaks and we are forced to step back, as it were, and examine that entity in relation to the purpose it has been serving.

Without wishing to suggest that this story is not an important part of Heidegger's thinking (or that it cannot be developed into a much more refined story than that which I have sketched here), I don't think that it embodies his best thoughts, for reasons at which I can only gesture here. Philosophically, I believe there are some significant difficulties in store when we claim, for example, that "[c]ognition and knowledge [are] derivative from ('founded upon') ... everyday practical understanding" (Rouse 2005: 125), in particular, when we try to demarcate what "everyday practical understanding" encompasses. Retrospective remark s certainly also suggest that Heidegger felt the significance of the analyses that inspire this kind of reading had been misjudged. His "*sole* intent," in taking his "departure from what lies to hand in the everyday realm, from those things that we use and pursue" was "to provide a preliminary characterization of the *phenomenon of world*" (GA 9: 155 n. 55/370 n. 59, GA 29/30: 262):

> It never occurred to me, however, to try and claim or prove with this interpretation that the essence of man consists in the fact that he knows how to handle knives and forks or uses the tram. (GA 29/30: 263)

But aside from those worries, there is another of more "strategic" importance given our present concerns. The Cartesian who reads the "practical and economic" proposal may well react as follows: "If holding beliefs about the world requires that I handle knives and forks or use the tram, then certainly skepticism is false. But does this Heideggerian story really tell me about what belief *is*? Isn't it just a 'genetic' story about how belief emerges in human life? A story about 'the order of discovery' rather than 'the order of justification'?"

In light of these worries, I will try to take a different tack and draw on a different model, one that I have used elsewhere to answer a number of questions about how Heidegger's fundamental ontology ought to be understood. It helps us escape the "genetic" charge just mentioned[15] and to keep clearly in focus our three "conditions of the possibility of falsehood." The textual basis for thinking that this model has some relevance to Heidegger's own thinking lies principally in another "strand" in his remarks on the nature of observation and of science, where he stresses the need for a mastery of certain kinds of "praxis" if we are to observe what one might think of as mere natural fact.[16]

Simple practices of measurement provide our model. In teaching a child the difference between talking, on the one hand, about large and small objects and, on the other, about objects being two meters long and ten meters long, we teach them the practice of measuring length. We show them standard rulers and how to lay them against the sides of objects; we teach them to check that the ruler is straight along those sides rather than held crisscross along them, and to check that the ruler doesn't bend or slip when the measurement is being made. We regard someone who fails to acquire these habits and concerns as having failed to understand what we mean by "measuring length," and only once this practice has been acquired do we think of them as capable of arriving at measurements of length and as having a grasp of propositions such as "This object is two meters long." They may see large objects and small objects; they may, as a matter of fact, see objects that happen to be two meters long; but they will not see them *as* two meters long.

The notion of thought as "embedded" in practices and in skills has always loomed large in interpretations of Heidegger. The above model merely lets us give that notion a new twist and a new application. But how then can this model help us here? The next section (§5) will consider how it sheds light on the "three conditions" discussed in §2, and on another important pre-*Being and Time* discussion of falsehood; the concluding sections of the paper (§§6 and 7) will then return to the particular issues that were raised by the schematic interpretation – which we derived from the three "conditions" – of Heidegger's remarks on skepticism, truth and being-in-the-world.

5. FALSEHOOD AND ERROR AS "FOUNDED MODES OF BEING-IN-THE-WORLD"

Crucially, the mastery that our model illustrates is presupposed if someone is to make *mistaken* measurements of length. Such a person is distracted at the crucial moment and doesn't notice that the ruler slipped or wasn't quite straight; without a general concern with such eventualities and a reasonable degree of success in preventing them coming about, what we have before us is not someone who makes mistaken measurements but someone who isn't measuring at all; rather, we'd say they were "playing at measuring" or just "messing about with a stick." So, corresponding to Heidegger's first "condition of the possibility of falsehood," one's capacity to arrive at mistaken measurements presupposes a certain facility with the relevant practice of measurement, which itself requires a certain familiarity with the "ways" of those entities that use of that practice allows us to describe: "In a certain sense, I must already have the subject matter if I am to make a mistake about it" (GA 21: 183).

Turning to the two other "conditions," in arriving at our (potentially mistaken) judgment, we assign the object judged an already "envisioned" place ("five meters") in the "world" of spatial location, one place within an already "envisioned" range. This is best illustrated, just as Heidegger does in his example, by considering the range of intelligible errors one might make. In arriving at a particular measurement – in seeing the object as five meters long – there are already in place a determinate set of possible "other" answers at which we could have arrived (seeing it as four meters long, six meters long, etc., etc.) and possible errors are restricted to measurements that correspond to these "others": while we may mistakenly conclude the object is six meters long, we won't end up reporting that its length is "a deer" or "the Shah of Iran."[17]

A further question, of course, is how do errors actually come about? One may well think that the ease with which the ontology of the "isolated subject" can answer this question is only apparent, because one might believe – with Heidegger – that it cannot actually make sense of falsehood, let alone error. But Heidegger's depiction of us as essentially always already amidst other entities and *in*-the-world that they populate may also seem unable to accommodate those intuitions that suggest that "our relation to beings is a specifically mediate one."[18] Our model suggests a simple answer: "our relation to beings" is "mediated" in that only successful performance of measurement tasks yields the truth about them.[19]

But how then does that answer square with Heidegger's own (few and difficult) remarks on how error comes about? In the 1923–4 lecture series, "Introduction to Phenomenological Research," Heidegger singles out for blame two features of the world:

The world is capable of deceiving, first, by virtue of its circumstantial character and the fact that the objects with which we deal are present for us concretely in a respective setting so that an assortment of possible ways of discussing them presents itself. The world is capable of deceiving, second, by virtue of its elusive character, obscured by fog, darkness and the like. Facts of the matter of this sort are inherent in the manner of being of the world itself. (GA 17: 39)

Though the surrounding discussion is tricky, I take the "the circumstantial character" of the world to correspond to the condition necessary for propositions to be capable of truth or falsehood that the entities those propositions concern are "given in more than one way," making possible "synthetic" claims that declare – truly or falsely – that one and the same thing is both, for example, a blackboard and in the room.[20] This is essentially Aristotle's requirement that propositions that can be true or false must concern "composite entities" and, on the face of it, tells us nothing about how errors actually come about. But I will return to this matter when I consider the connection that Heidegger sees between "elusiveness" and the "circumstantial": "the elusiveness of things comes to life by virtue of the fact that we encounter them circumstantially" (GA 17: 36–7).

Heidegger characterizes the world's "elusiveness" in the following way:

The facts are here in an utterly peculiar character of not being here. Th[is] elusiveness is something that lies in the being of the world itself, the phenomena of which include the daylight and darkness with which we have become acquainted. (GA 17: 36)

Our model suggests the following line of thought. Different descriptive practices, which reveal different bodies of fact, face different obstacles. Fading light makes judging colors difficult but not the judging of weights; one's own temperature affects one's estimates of temperature but not of distance, pitch, or style, and so on. These differences reflect, one might say, features "inherent in the manner of being of the world itself." Heidegger also states that "the possibility of deception ... lies in the manner in which the existing entity lives and encounters the world itself" (GA 17: 36).[21] But this also can be squared with our account: one only encounters particular possibilities of error because one engages in particular kinds of descriptive practice, though particular such practices are also necessary if one is to encounter particular bodies of fact.

Why then should "the elusiveness of things come ... to life by virtue of the fact that we encounter them circumstantially?" Heidegger elaborates on this by stating that "the more concretely I am in the world, the more genuine the existence of deception" (GA 17: 37). These are certainly puzzling remarks, suggesting as they do that I might exist in the world more or less concretely. But one reason why "the elusiveness" might be said to be "much more encompassing" (GA 17: 37) when we "live concretely" would be that, in "concrete life," we are subject to the competing demands that can arise on the basis of "the circumstantial character" of the world. The "*possibility of deception* is at hand" when demands that arise out of the other "dimensions" of our "concrete lives" dictate that we cannot execute our observational tasks with the necessary care. So we bodge that temperature measurement because our other expenses mean we cannot afford a decent thermometer; we hazard a guess at that judgment of length because our other commitments mean we cannot afford the time to measure it properly, and so on. Here, "we do not see the things as subject matters in the sense that they are an object of a scientific observation," as our "concrete lives" are pulled simultaneously in many directions: the "existence of things" that those lives encounter "is much richer and affords much more fluctuating possibilities" (GA 17: 37).

6. TRUTH AND BEING-IN-THE-WORLD REVISITED

I return now to the schematic implications set out in §3, beginning with the notion of a "truth" upon which the truth and falsity of propositions rests. Our model does seem to present a form of insight or understanding that "precedes" and makes possible the entertaining of certain kinds of belief, true or false. To grasp what it is for such beliefs to correspond to the relevant facts turns out to require mastery of "practical," "worldly" skill, a kind of insight quite unlike discovering that a proposition holds; and one cannot acquire that mastery by amassing knowledge of the relevant facts because one cannot take in those facts prior to acquiring that mastery.[22] But, to return to Tugendhat's worry, why think of this insight as embodying a form of *truth*? One reason – and we will soon encounter another – is that it seems apt to describe it as embodying a kind of insight into – or a "disclosure" of – the world. Failure to master these practices would mean that a whole dimension of reality, so to speak, would remain in darkness for us; an entire body of facts hidden. To revert to our earlier example, we would not know what it *is* for an object to have what one might call a quantitative length, and we would be incapable of making correct or *incorrect* determinations of facts of that form.

Our model also sheds some light on the notions of being-in-the-world and *Sein-bei*. With the model of understanding as skill before one's mind, the intuition that understanding "lies within," as I put it earlier, seems much less powerful. Most obviously, the skills in question are recognizably "worldly": they involve picking up and manipulating physical objects, both the tools we use to measure and the objects measured. This provides an obvious-enough sense for the notion that we live amidst the entities that we think about.

But perhaps more interestingly, mastery of skills has a feature that suggests a basis for the rhetoric of "having," "givenness," "touch," and "being-amidst," which is more in line with the (for want of a much better word) "cognitive" construal of our being-in-the-world that Heidegger explicitly favors over the "spatial," which the previous paragraph's gloss might instead suggest. The feature in question is one that this mastery shares with successful use of perceptual demonstratives as McDowell understands it.

The notion that someone might possess a skill but be incapable of applying it in any particular case seems incoherent; an incapacity to apply the skill in question are grounds for withholding ascription of the skill and the possession of this kind of understanding seems to require that generally one *actually* succeeds in grasping how the world around one is. We distinguish the maker of incorrect measurements from the person who messes about with a stick by reference to a background capacity to make successful measurement in the first case and its absence in the second. If a person were to lack this generally happy – if imperfect – acquaintance with the domain of facts in question, we would not see that person as holding beliefs true *or false* about those facts – just as, for McDowell, failure to identify an object with your perceptual demonstrative deprives you of the associated thought, true or false.

We also perhaps see some basis for the vacillation that we saw in Heidegger's specification of his first "condition" of falsehood: we cannot distinguish neatly here what one might call an understanding of "the domain" – or "context" – "in general" from a capacity actually to judge particular occupants of that domain or context correctly in the majority of cases. The urge to depict that which we "touch" as the particular objects judged may reflect the fact that understanding the "domain" or "context in general" requires that particular occupants of it must also generally yield to our thinking.[23]

These conclusions seem to me to provide some justification for talk of *being-in*-the-world; the world must very largely be unproblematic, not separated from us by any gulf of difficulty. If we are driven to think of ourselves as "outside" of the world by its being epistemically "distant," the above considerations suggest that fundamentally it must be the case that there is "no distance" after all; one might describe the relationship instead as one of "touch," *thigein*. Without the world being in this sense, at one's disposal, then one is not the intentional agent we might have supposed; faced with such a failure, no such agent withdraws back into its own "inner sphere"; whatever might so withdraw lacks intentional states, even false beliefs; its "mind" – though why we call it that is now puzzling – is dark. Or might even that metaphor mislead? Perhaps we should speak here of "an utter inability to apprehend at all" (GA 21: 177) – a "total absence of the faculty of thinking," as Ross translates Aristotle's phrase (1052a4) – or speak, as Heidegger in his *Habilitationschrift* did, of thought becoming still:

Everything that stands "over against" the ego in experience is in some way *comprehended*. The "over against" itself is already a definite *regard* (*respectus*) in which the ego deals with the object ... If there isn't this first moment of clearness, I would not even be in some sort of absolute darkness ... I have no object at all ... I cannot get myself mentally, intellectually in motion; thinking stands still.[24]

The need for a background facility *with* the world – a mastery of skills that necessarily involves the power to apply them successfully – also provides another reason to think of §44's "deeper," "pre-propositional," "disclosive" "truth" as a form of truth. The world must actually reveal itself to me "insofar as I am at all" (GA 21: 212, quoted above). Hence, Dasein must be "*in the truth*'"; as that section equally telegraphically states, "the presupposition of truth" "has been 'made' already with the Being of the 'we'" (221, 228). The intimacy of the relationship between the thinker and its world is such that if this "touch" is lost, then even if a sentence passes my lips, it "fails to express a proposition," "fails to express a thought" (Thornton, quoted above).

7. SKEPTICISM REVISITED

The vision of thought as "world-dependent" in the manner described here is clearly incompatible with skepticism. But how powerful a *criticism* of skepticism does it embody?

It would have power if we could tell of it an analogous story to that which Macarthur tells of McDowell's broader conception of thought, of which his notion of object-dependent thought is a part:

> The very possibility of empirical content depends on the fact that some or other of our experiences *must* be non-deceptive in the sense that the relevant objects figure in them ... Non-deceptive experience plays, as McDowell puts it, a "primary role" in the availability of empirically contentful thought quite generally, that is, in cases of *both* non-deceptive and deceptive experience. On this view, unless there are in fact *some* actual cases of veridical perception then we could not enjoy empirically contentful thought at all, so there can be no threat that we are *always* suffering from illusions, dreams, or hallucinations.[25]

According to the account developed in §6, contentful thought requires some – indeed the majority – of cases of perception to be actually veridical. So, if that account is correct, "there can be no threat that we are *always* suffering from illusions, dreams, or hallucinations." But is it correct? For what it's worth, it seems to me that the skeptic must accept some version of the "three conditions" discussed above (§2), fuzzily specified though they are. But the fit between those conditions and the account that I offered in §5 of those conditions – and indeed the "practical and economic" version I avoided – is plainly loose. Might it not then be possible to provide an account of those conditions that does not require the thinker to be "worldly" after all?

Take, for example, the first condition; there is at least one answer out there for the Cartesian to give to the question of how – as that condition states – I "have the subject matter" of my judgment even if it lies in the "outside world." That answer is: my inner states are intentionally related to the "outer" because they are mental states and such relatedness is an intrinsic property of the mental.

The most sensible response to this supposed answer for Heidegger to make is one which is very much in line with his own description of his response to skepticism. As §1 mentioned, Heidegger's characteristic complaint about the ontology upon which skepticism rests is that it is "indefinite," and the reflections we have considered here are perhaps best seen as Heidegger putting pressure on the skeptic to explain himself, to make definite what remains indefinite in his thinking. In articulating his three "conditions of the possibility of falsehood," he anticipates the kinds of question that Wittgenstein, Putnam, and McDowell have posed since. What the skeptic ought to worry about is "not ... that our contact with the external world seems too *shaky* to count as knowledgeable," but that it is "quite unclear that the fully Cartesian picture is entitled to characterize its inner facts in content-involving terms – in terms of it seeming to one that things are thus and so – at all": how can the inner states it envisages "be anything but dark," "blank or blind?"[26] The kind of story told here about the "founding" of knowledge and error in a necessary "having" of the world expressed through our actual mastery of practices – like Wittgenstein's discussions of "language-games," which "bring into prominence the fact that the speaking of language is part of an activity, or a form of life,"[27] and Putnam's reflections on the "division of linguistic labour"[28] – serves to build up the pressure on the kind of answer that the Cartesian gave in the preceding paragraph. Through such pressure, that answer comes to seem a "magical theory of reference,"[29] its invocation of the notion of "the mental" such that here "the word 'mental' indicat[es] that we mustn't expect to understand how these things work."[30]

   Can we not hope for more? Can we not be more aggressive here? Efforts to turn externalism into a refutation of skepticism seem to founder,[31] and some of its advocates distance themselves from any such attempt; so, for example, McDowell maintains that "the thing to do is not answer the skeptic's challenges, but to diagnose their seeming urgency";[32] and, according to Williamson,

If a refutation of scepticism is supposed to reason one out of the hole, then scepticism is irrefutable. The most to be hoped for is something which will prevent the sceptic (who may be oneself) from reasoning one into the hole in the first place. (Williamson 2000: 27)

Such responses still face the difficulty that the thought-experiments that motivate skepticism (dreaming, being a brain in a vat, etc.) have great intuitive power and the anti-skeptic has her work cut out if she is to make her own story as – let alone more – intuitive. One might think this is a mere matter of "presentation"; but I'm not sure that it is. One thing that is quite clear is that, if Heidegger's ideas do point to a way of "defusing" these thought-experiments, it is yet to be shown how.[33]

   But I will end with one tentative suggestion that may allow us to see the pro-skeptical thought-experiments, and their intuitive appeal, in a different light. In Heidegger's description in *Being and Time* of our everyday lives with "ready-to-hand" tools, he points to the manner in which they become "transparent"; as long as they and the practices within which they are embedded function as ordinarily required, then "that with which we concern ourselves primarily is the work – that which is to be produced at the time," "not the tools themselves," which "must, as it were, withdraw in order to be ready-to-hand authentically" (69). The account of "pre-propositional understanding" that I have given clearly gives pride of place to what one might think of as "cognitive tools" embedded within "cognitive practices." By analogy, one should expect such tools and such practices to become "transparent" – to "withdraw" – when functioning appropriately. There is indeed a sense in which we have to *remind* ourselves of the demands involved in mastering those practices – which become clearest when we think about bringing children to master them – and the demands that we make upon the tools involved – which become clearest when we think about possibilities such as the ruler bending or shrinking or (roughly speaking) my ruler turning out to be different from yours. But in the course of our ordinary and proficient dealings with these matters and the domains of fact that these practices reveal, all of these demands become "transparent," such that the dependency of our thought about these facts upon those practices and tools becomes "invisible." If this is indeed so, one would expect to be able to imagine that such thoughts would remain even if one were a brain in a vat or dreaming. The dependency of thought on these practices and tools is not part of what one might call the "phenomenal content" of our ordinary engagement with the facts that they allow us to uncover; indeed, that engagement requires that this be so. A master of these practices effortlessly looks to the facts, one might say, not at the structures that make such looking possible. If then the Heideggerian story told here were to be true, that the pro-skeptical thought-experiments have intuitive appeal is just what one would expect.

NOTES

1   Ernst Tugendhat, "Heidegger's Idea of Truth," in *Critical Heidegger*, trans. and ed. C. Macann (London: Routledge, 1996).
2   Tugendhat, "Heidegger's Idea of Truth," 234.
3   Heidegger declares that "the existential analytic ... does not do *any* proving *at all* by the rules of the 'logic of consistency'" (315) and comments on "the exaggerated rage for method which proves everything and in the end proves nothing" (GA 24: 59). Cf., for discussion, Richard Rorty, "Overcoming the Tradition: Heidegger and Dewey," *The Review of Metaphysics* 30 (1976): 280–305, and Hubert L. Dreyfus, *Being-in-the-World: A Commentary on Heidegger's* Being and Time, Division I (Cambridge, MA: MIT Press, 1991), 60, 120, and Denis McManus, "The Provocation to Look and see: Appropriation, Recollection and Formal Indication," in *Wittgenstein and*

Heidegger, eds. D. Egan, S. Reynolds, and A. Wendland (London: Routledge, forthcoming).

4 Dreyfus, *Being-in-the-World*, xi.

5 Cf. also GA 19: 602–3, GA 20: 40, GA 24: 294, and GA 27: 152–3.

6 One notable exception, from which I have profited, is Mark Wrathall, "On the 'Existential Positivity of Our Ability to Be Deceived,'" in *The Philosophy of Deception*, ed. Clancy Martin (Oxford: Oxford University Press, 2009), 67–81.

7 Of the host of issues that §§43–4 raise but which I leave untouched here, the most conspicuous is that of whether Heidegger ought to be characterized as a realist or an idealist. Denis McManus, "Heidegger, Measurement and the 'Intelligibility' of Science," *European Journal of Philosophy* 15 (2007): 82–105 sets out a case (based on the model of understanding summarized in §4 below) for thinking that there may be sense to Heidegger's claim to reject both alternatives; to do so would be to recapture something akin to the Greek perspective for which, he insists, "there is no such contrast" (GA 17: 9). (Here, Heidegger can be seen to have anticipated an insight into Greek philosophy for which the Anglophone philosophical world had to wait till the 1980s and the work of Bernard Williams and Miles Burnyeat. Cf. Bernard Williams, "The Legacy of Greek Philosophy," in *The Legacy of Greece*, ed. M. I. Finley (Oxford: Clarendon Press. 1981); and Miles F. Burnyeat, "Idealism and Greek Philosophy: What Descartes saw and Berkeley missed," *Philosophical Review* 91 (1982): 3–40.

8 For related discussions, cf., e.g., GA 17 §2 and GA 19 §26.

9 In the discussion of falsehood in GA 17, Heidegger makes a similar point: "A human being is the sort of entity that in its way has the world here by making things accessible to itself in setting them off from one another," and "in this process of setting something off from others, what is offset becomes accessible and can be grasped as here" (GA 17: 26).

10 A natural worry here is: is this "familiarity" learnable then, or must it instead be somehow *innate*? The model I will offer below suggests that acquiring such "familiarity" is a feat quite unlike establishing that a proposition holds.

11 Cf. also *Being and Time*, 54 and 132.

12 We see this intuition at work in what McDowell calls "the master thesis," "the thesis that whatever a person has in her mind, it is only by virtue of being interpreted in one of various possible ways that it can impose a sorting of extra-mental items into those that accord with it and those that do not" in John McDowell, *Mind, Value and Reality* (Cambridge, MA: Harvard University Press, 1998), 270. In §2.3 of "Rules, Regression and the 'Background': Dreyfus, Heidegger and McDowell," *European Journal of Philosophy* 16 (2008): 432–58, I argue that Heidegger anticipated the diagnostic use to which McDowell puts this notion.

13 The question of how Heidegger's ideas relate to established brands of externalism is explored in Taylor Carman, *Heidegger's Analytic* (Cambridge: Cambridge University Press, 2003); Cristina Lafont, *Heidegger, Language, and World-Disclosure*, trans. G. Harman (Cambridge: Cambridge University Press, 2000) and "Was Heidegger an Externalist?," *Inquiry* 48 (2005): 507–32; and Mark Wrathall, "Social Constraints on Conversational

Content: Heidegger on Rede and Gerede," *Philosophical Topics* 27 (1999):
    25–46.
14 My "Heidegger and the Measure of Truth" (Oxford: Oxford University Press,
    2012) presents other – though, I believe, compatible – ways of understanding
    Heidegger's route to the conclusion that the correspondence theory of truth
    is "superficial." Other valuable treatments of Heidegger's discussion of
    truth can be found in Taylor Carman, *Heidegger's Analytic* and "Heidegger
    on Correspondence and Correctness," *Graduate Faculty Philosophy Journal*
    28 (2007): 103–16; David R. Cerbone, "Realism and Truth" in *A Companion
    to Heidegger*, eds. Hubert L. Dreyfus and Mark A. Wrathall (Malden:
    Blackwell, 2005), 48–64; Daniel O. Dahlstrom, *Heidegger's Concept of
    Truth* (Cambridge: Cambridge University Press, 2001); Hubert L. Dreyfus,
    "How Heidegger Defends the Possibility of a Correspondence Theory of
    Truth With Respect to the Entities of Natural Science," in *The Practice
    Turn in Contemporary Theory*, eds. Theodore R. Schatzki, Karin Knorr
    Cetina, and Eike von Savigny (London: Routledge, 2001), 151–62; Lafont,
    Heidegger, Language, and World-Disclosure; William H. Smith, "Why
    Tugendhat's Critique of Heidegger's Concept of Truth remains a Critical
    Problem," *Inquiry* 50 (2007): 156–79; and Mark Wrathall "Heidegger and
    Truth as Correspondence," *International Journal of Philosophical Studies*
    7 (1999): 69–88 and "Unconcealment" in *A Companion to Heidegger*,
    337–57. Interesting discussions of Heidegger's response to skepticism
    include Stephen Mulhall, *Heidegger and* Being and Time, 2nd edition
    (London: Routledge, 2005); and Edward H. Minar, "Heidegger's Response to
    Skepticism in *Being and Time*," in *Future Pasts: The Analytic Tradition in
    Twentieth-Century Philosophy*, eds. J. Floyd and S. Shieh (Oxford: Oxford
    University Press, 2001), 193–214.
15 A version of that charge certainly could be raised against it, but I answer
    that charge, I believe, in McManus, "Intelligibility," 91–2.
16 My "Intelligibility" and "Measure of Truth" present that evidence and also
    consider many of the worries that this model naturally raises but which I
    will not attempt to address here.
17 A further interpretive benefit of my proposal that I will mention only
    briefly is that it naturally allows us to concur with the Greeks, for whom
    "*[p]seudos* is the *ostensive presenting of something as something*": "it is
    more than merely concealing something without presenting it as something
    other than it is" (GA 17: 32). Cartesianism invites one to think of falsehood
    as a kind of disconnection: there is nothing out there to which our proposi-
    tion corresponds. Heidegger instead praises the Greek conception of false-
    hood as a kind of "covering over," and the above proposal captures that
    intuition in that a failure in measuring yields not – as it were – nothing,
    but a measurement that presents the length as other than as it is: it covers
    over.
18 Tugendhat, "Heidegger's Idea of Truth," 234.
19 D. McManus, "Error, Hallucination and the Concept of 'Ontology' in the
    Early Work of Heidegger," *Philosophy* 71 (1996): 553–75 developed a version
    of this proposal, though with scant reference to the textual basis to be found
    for it in Heidegger's work. (I confess that I retain that earlier paper's negative

assessment of what Heidegger can tell us about how extreme hallucination comes about.)

20 Cf. also GA 17: 294.

21 As Wrathall notes in "On the 'Existential Positivity of Our Ability to Be Deceived,'" in *The Philosophy of Deception*, ed. Clancy Martin (Oxford: Oxford University Press, 2009), 75, Heidegger seems to want a much more "equitable division of labor" in attributing blame for deception to both ourselves and the world.

22 This talk of "priority" may give the misleading impression that learning such a practice is one feat and then, on the basis of that, one can go on to make measurements of length. But what one learns in learning the practice is – and is only – how to make measurements of length. The two feats come as a package and it might be more accurate to say not that the general practice *has* priority but that the particular measurements *don't*.

23 This provides a response to both the species of skepticism (specifically about knowledge claims *as opposed to* more primordial forms of "access") that Blattner distinguishes and the worry that our Being-in-the-world may require that there be *some* world in which we dwell but not that that world be anything like the world we believe we dwell in. See William D. Blattner, *Heidegger's* Being and Time (London: Continuum, 2006), 112.

24 GA 1: 223–4/*Duns Scotus' Theory of the Categories and of Meaning*, trans. H. Robbins, Ph.D dissertation, De Paul University, Chicago, Illinois, 1973, 39–40 (translation modified).

25 D. Macarthur, "McDowell, Scepticism, and the 'Veil of Perception,'" *Australasian Journal of Philosophy* 81 (2003): 179.

26 John McDowell, *Meaning, Knowledge, and Reality* (Cambridge, MA: Harvard University Press, 1998): 242–3, 249.

27 Section 23, Ludwig Wittgenstein, *Philosophical Investigations*, ed. G. E. M. Anscombe and R. Rhees, trans. G. E. M. Anscombe (Oxford: Blackwell, 1967) (italics removed).

28 Hilary Putnam, "Meaning and Reference," *The Journal of Philosophy* 70 (1973): 704.

29 Hilary Putnam, *Reason, Truth and History* (Cambridge: Cambridge University Press, 1981), 3.

30 Ludwig Wittgenstein, *The Blue and Brown Books* (Oxford: Blackwell, 1958), 39.

31 For a summary of related discussion, cf. Tony Brueckner, "Brains in a Vat," *The Stanford Encyclopedia of Philosophy*, ed. Edward N. Zalta (Winter 2011 Edition), URL http://plato.stanford.edu/archives/win2011/entries/brain-vat/.

32 McDowell, *Meaning, Knowledge, and Reality*, 410.

33 Dreyfus remarked in 1991 that "one can only guess what Heidegger would say about dreams" (*Being-in-the-World*, 251); subsequent publications mean we need no longer guess, but the remarks of which I'm aware (cf., e.g., GA 17: 38) don't suggest anything like a response to the dreaming argument.

12 Death and Demise in *Being and Time*

Mortals die their death in life.

Martin Heidegger[1]

INTRODUCTION: THE STATE OF THE DEBATE

This chapter seeks to answer the question of what Heidegger means by "death" (*Tod*) in *Being and Time*. I take up this weighty topic with some trepidation (if not quite fear and trembling), in part because to say that the meaning of "death" in *Being and Time* is controversial is to strain the limits of understatement. In addition to the emotionally freighted nature of the topic itself (to which we will return), I think four main factors contribute to and perpetuate this controversy: (1) Heidegger's confusing *terminology*; (2) the *centrality* of the issue to the text as a whole; (3) the *demanding* nature of what is required to adjudicate the matter; and (4) the radically *polarized* scholarly literature on the subject. One of my main goals here is to suggest a way to move beyond the controversy that currently divides the field. So let me begin by saying a bit about its four main contributing factors.

The first and most obvious cause of the controversy is that those passages in *Being and Time* where Heidegger describes phenomenologically what he means (and does not mean) by "death" are initially quite obscure. Heidegger deliberately employs a non-commonsensical terminology, for example, when he formally defines "the full existential-ontological concept of death" in the following important but initially mysterious terms: "*death, as the end of Dasein, is Dasein's ownmost, non-relational, certain and as such indefinite, and non-surpassable possibility*" (258–9), or, more famously, when he describes death "*as*

For helpful comments on and discussion of earlier versions of this paper, I would especially like to thank Bill Blattner, Taylor Carman, Steve Crowell, Bert Dreyfus, Charlie Guignon, John Haugeland, Kevin Hill, Piotr Hoffman, Michael Jennings, Stephan Käufer, Wayne Martin, Robert Pippin, John Richardson, and Mark Wrathall.

the possibility of the impossibility of existence in general" (262, trans-lation modified). Conversely, and even more confusingly (at least for unwary readers), he also misleadingly employs an only apparently commonsensical terminology, using ordinary words such as "death," "demise," "perishing," and "possibility" in ways that turn out to have decidedly non-commonsensical meanings. We will thus need to spend a fair amount of time clarifying Heidegger's terms of art in what follows.

The second source of the controversy is that a great deal turns on Heidegger's phenomenological analysis of death. John Haugeland rightly observes that "death, as Heidegger means it, is not merely relevant but in fact the fulcrum of Heidegger's entire ontology."[2] The reason death plays such an important part in the overarching ontological project of *Being and Time*, in a nutshell, is that the experience of the phenome-non Heidegger calls "death" discloses "futurity," which is itself the first horizon we encounter of originary temporality, that fundamental struc-ture of intelligibility that makes possible any understanding of being at all.[3] More to the point for us here, death is also crucial to the text's exis-tential ambitions because (as we will see) one must understand death in order to understand authenticity. The pivotal role played by Heidegger's phenomenology of death in *Being and Time* means that critical readers of the text cannot indefinitely postpone the difficult task of evaluating Heidegger's understanding of the phenomenon.

This brings us directly to the third reason for the controversy sur-rounding the meaning of death in *Being and Time*, which is that the phe-nomenological method we are supposed to use to adjudicate the matter is particularly difficult to employ in this crucial case. The problem, put simply, is that many readers seem to have trouble experiencing the phe-nomenon Heidegger describes as "death" for themselves. Without such a personal experience, however, readers can neither contest nor confirm *Being and Time*'s phenomenology of death. This is a general problem for critical readers of phenomenological works. Absent our own experi-ence of the phenomenon at issue, we can neither attest to (and so con-firm for ourselves) nor testify against (and so contest, refine, or seek to redescribe) the phenomenon at issue. This general phenomenological problem is greatly exacerbated in the case of death, however, because unlike phenomenological descriptions of more mundane phenomena (such as using a hammer, staring at a Gestalt figure or optical illusion, or even unsettling experiences such as being stared at by a stranger or feeling the pangs of a guilty conscience), the phenomenon by means of which we first encounter what Heidegger means by "death" – namely, the affective attunement of "'real' or 'authentic' anxiety" (*"eigentliche" Angst*), in which, as we will see, we experience ourselves as radically "not-at-home" in the world of our everyday projects – is both quite "rare" (190) and extremely difficult to endure.[4] The requirement that we must personally undergo an anguished experience of the utter desolation of the self in order to be able to testify for or against the adequacy of Heidegger's phenomenological analysis of death thus seems excessively demanding; Heidegger himself acknowledges that this demand "remains, from the existentiell point of view [that is, from the ordinary perspective of our everyday lives and concerns], a fantastically unreasonable demand [*eine phantastische Zumutung*]" (266). Nonetheless, without experiencing the phenomenon at issue for ourselves, we can at best approach Heidegger's phenomenological descriptions of death from the outside, and so find them, for example, suggestive, impressive, or deep sounding, or else fanciful, idiosyncratic, or even absurd.

It is revealing to contrast that kind of superficial evaluation – typical of but not limited to neophyte readings of *Being and Time* – with the critical interpretations advanced in the 1940s by Heidegger's first "existentialist" readers, especially Levinas but also, to a lesser degree, Sartre. Both sought to contest and revise Heidegger's phenomenology of death by drawing on their own experiences of the phenomenon at issue (or, in Sartre's case, his experience of an alternative phenomenon, namely, "the look of the other [person]," which is similarly supposed to result in "the death of my [existential] possibilities").[5] Perhaps the commendable quest for scholarly objectivity, which has yielded such important advances in clarity and argumentative rigor in the last sixty years, has also rendered us much more reluctant to inject ourselves into the discussion by testing Heidegger's descriptions for – or on – ourselves. Or perhaps Heidegger's own appalling misadventure with Nazism has led interpreters to distance themselves from the fact that, as he acknowledged in *Being and Time*, "a definite ontic interpretation of authentic existence, a factical ideal of Dasein, underlies our ontological interpretation" (310). Yet, should not Heidegger's admission that his phenomenological analyses derive ultimately from his own idealized personal experiences have precisely the opposite effect? That is, should not Heidegger's demonstration of his own susceptibility to the grossest of errors of judgment instead encourage us to subject his phenomenological analyses to the most careful scrutiny for ourselves, as his early existentialist readers undoubtedly sought to do, in part for this very reason? Because it is only by relying on such personal experience that one can advance either an internal confirmation or an immanent critique of Heidegger's phenomenology of death, the post-existentialist interpretations of Heidegger seem to me to have made a significant step backward in this critical regard.

Finally, the fourth reason for the persistent controversy about the meaning of "death" in *Being and Time* is that, owing to the combined effect of the aforementioned factors, the interpretive field is now radically polarized, with the secondary literature starkly divided into two diametrically opposed and seemingly incommensurable camps. In the first (and much larger) camp, most traditional scholars, critics, and readers of *Being and Time* adopt the straightforward view that, by "death," Heidegger must mean the same sort of things that we normally mean when we talk about "death," such as *demise* (Edwards), *decease* (Hoffman), or *mortality* (Mulhall). In the second (and significantly smaller) camp, a number of cutting-edge Heidegger scholars think that what *Being and Time* means by "death" has almost nothing to do with the ordinarily sense of the word (the two share a merely "metaphorical" connection, as Haugeland said). Instead, Heidegger means something like *the global collapse of significance* typified by a depressive episode (Blattner), *the collapse of an understanding of being* exemplified by a scientific paradigm shift (Haugeland), or *the end of an historical world*, which allows a new historical epoch to take shape (White).[6] Despite the hermeneutic liberties taken by Haugeland and White, I shall argue that the second camp is much closer to Heidegger's idiosyncratic understanding of death as an existential phenomenon that stands revealed when our everyday worlds collapse. Still, the interpretations of death in terms of existential world collapse advanced by this second camp leave it largely baffling why Heidegger should call the phenomenon he is interested in "death." Indeed, his doing so only seems to muddy the waters of *Being and Time*, encouraging the much more commonsensical misreadings of death as demise (or loss of life) that are typical of the first camp. To such a charge of misreading, moreover, those in the first camp will respond forcefully that (as Hoffman once objected to me): "One can stretch the meanings of words, but only so far: *Up* cannot mean *down*; *black* cannot mean *white*, and *death* cannot mean *something that you can live through!*"

The endeavor might initially seem rather unlikely, but in what follows I would like to suggest a way beyond the current deadlock over the meaning of "death" in *Being and Time*. What I shall show is that if we understand the phenomenological method *Being and Time* employs, then we can see exactly how Heidegger is able to move from our relation to the event we ordinarily call *death* (which he calls "demise") to that ontological phenomenon, revealed in world collapse, which he calls "death." To follow this path, we need to avoid conflating Heidegger's existential conception of death with that life-ending event he calls "demise," as the first camp tends to do, but we also cannot treat demise and death as radically heterogeneous phenomena, as those in the second camp tend to do. Instead, we need to understand how "death" is both distinguished from and related to "demise" if we want to transcend these longstanding hermeneutic controversies and begin to grasp the full existential-ontological significance of "death" in *Being and Time*. That will be the goal of this chapter.

PERISHING, DEMISING, AND DYING

In a crucial passage in *Being and Time* (which I shall refer to subsequently as P1), Heidegger distinguishes between three terms we might otherwise tend to use interchangeably, namely, "perishing" (*Verenden*), "demising" (*Ableben*), and "dying" (*Sterben*):

[P1] The ending of that which [merely] lives we have called *perishing* [*Verenden*]. Dasein too "has" its physiological death of the kind appropriate to anything that lives ... but ["has" it] as co-determined by its primordial way of being [namely, "existing" or "standing-out," *Ek-sistere*, into temporally structured intelligibility].[7] Dasein can also end without authentically dying [*eigentlich stirbt*], although in this latter case it does not, *qua* Dasein, simply perish. We designate this intermediate phenomenon as *demise* [*Ableben*]. Let the term *dying* [*Sterben*] designate the *way of being* in which Dasein *is toward* its death [*Tod*].[8] We must thus say: Dasein never perishes. Demising, however, is something Dasein can do only so long as it dies. (247)

What exactly is Heidegger saying here? The primary stumbling block to understanding Heidegger's phenomenology of "death" in *Being and Time* comes from the fact that the phenomenon Heidegger is referring to is not what we normally mean by *death*. For Heidegger, "death" means neither the ending of our biological lives, which he calls "perishing," nor even our experience of that end as a collapse of our intelligible worlds, which he calls "demise" – a terminal collapse that, by all appearances, accompanies perishing, the cessation of our biological functions.[9] When we reach the end of our lives, the physiological systems that kept us alive "perish" and (if we are awake and the event is not too sudden) we experience our intelligible worlds terminally collapse in "demise," but neither perishing nor demise is necessary for what Heidegger calls "death."

In other words, we experience the perishing of our physical bodies (insofar as we experience it) *as* demise, the apparently permanent collapse of our intelligible worlds, but what Heidegger calls "death" is functionally independent of both perishing and demise. How, then, does Heidegger distinguish death both from perishing and from demise? First, he distinguishes death from perishing. As P1 starkly puts it: "Dasein never perishes." (Dasein, of course, is Heidegger's name for our "being-here": we are the place where being takes place, that is, where intelligibility becomes an issue for itself, and *Dasein* designates this making-intelligible of the place in which we find ourselves.) *Pace*

Derrida, "Dasein never perishes" does not mean that "I do not end, I never end" (regardless of whether this alleged inability to experience our own end is recited as a calming mantra, with Epicurus, or as a heartbroken lament, with Kierkegaard and Blanchot).[10] Derrida misses the crucial point that, for Heidegger, Dasein *can* experience its end (indeed, as we will see, this experience is precisely what Heidegger calls "death"). "Dasein never perishes" does not mean that I am endless but, instead, that to describe the distinctive type of ending that is proper to Dasein as "perishing" is to make the category mistake of trying to conceive of the distinctive end of Dasein's existence, the end of our standing out into an intelligible world, in terms drawn from the occurrence of "worldless" objects. As I like to put it: *Pears perish, but Daseins demise and die.* Thus, even when the physical systems that support Dasein's life functions perish, Dasein, as Dasein, does not perish – it *demises*, if it is conscious and the event is not too sudden. But if a person is in a dreamless sleep when his body suddenly perishes (and he never wakes up), then his Dasein will cease to be without ever having experienced the terminal collapse of his world in demise.[11]

Heidegger thinks that the converse is also possible; one can experience one's own end without yet having demised. As this suggests, after distinguishing perishing from demise, Heidegger then goes on to distinguish demise (the "intermediate phenomenon") from death. Heidegger insists that we need not demise in order to die, in large part because of his aforementioned conviction that Dasein *can* experience its own end. Indeed, Heidegger thinks we can experience our intelligible world's having ended (and that we do so in what he calls "death"), even though, by all appearances, we cannot live through our own *demise* in order to experience *that* end from beyond it. With this latter point, Heidegger incorporates his understanding of Epicurus' famous paradox – that I never experience my own demise, since "When I am, death is not, and when death is, I am not" – into his discussion of "demise" (*Ableben*). As his German nicely suggests, "an 'experience' of [one's own] demise [*ein "Erleben" des Ablebens*]" literally (and paradoxically) means "a 'living-through of [one's own] ceasing to live" (251), an apparent absurdity.[12] For Heidegger, "demise" designates this ultimately paradoxical "experience" of the end of one's own life (an "experience" of the approaching end or absence of all experience), an event that we seem to be able to experience as it approaches but not when it has arrived, since once demise arrives our Dasein is no longer "here" to experience anything.[13]

This paradox means, Heidegger points out, that if death is understood only as demise, then Dasein (our being-here) can never comprehend itself as a whole. For it appears that, up until we demise, our intelligible worlds will always be constituted by worldly projects that stretch into an unknown future (such that our sense of self will never be fully transparent to itself), but then, once we demise, we will no longer be here at all (i.e., we will no longer be Dasein). *Being and Time*'s discussion of death begins (§§46-7) by setting up this problem at great length (indeed, this is the very problem that motivates Heidegger's phenomenological interpretations of death and demise in the first place): how can Dasein – an entity whose being is constituted by worldly projects that stretch into an unknown future – ever comprehend itself as a whole? What most readers seem to miss, however, is that Heidegger is able to solve this problem only by introducing his existential-ontological conception of death in distinction from demise. (The fact that Heidegger does not distinguish death from demise while setting up the problem has undoubtedly encouraged many readers to conflate the two.) Even though we cannot "experience" all experience having ended in demise, Heidegger remains convinced that there is an end proper to (or distinctive of) our being-here which we *can* experience, and that in this experience Dasein *can* grasp itself as a whole. As he puts it: "In such being-toward-its-end, Dasein exists in a way which is authentically whole, as that entity which it can be when 'thrown into death.' Dasein does not have an end at which it is simply stops, but instead [it has an end at which it] *exists finitely* [existiert endlich]." (329)[14]

Heidegger's solution to the Epicurean paradox, in other words, is that in the desolate experience he calls "death," the self – temporarily cut off from the world in terms of which it usually understands itself – finds itself radically alone with itself, and so can lucidly comprehend itself in its entirety for the first time, since there is no worldly, futural component of itself to elude its self-transparent grasp. When Dasein experiences itself as desperately unable to project into the worldly projects in terms of which it usually understands itself, then "the future itself is closed" for Dasein (even though objectively "time goes on"). Bereft of all its worldly projects, Dasein can fully grasp itself in its own "finitude" for the first time – and thereby come to understand itself as a "primordial existential projecting" (330), as we will see.[15]

Heidegger's phenomenologically grounded conviction that there is a kind of end that is distinctive of Dasein – that we can experience our intelligible world as having ended and so exist in a way that is radically "finite" (*endlich*) – is what leads him to distinguish this "existential conception of death [*die existenziale Begriff des Sterbens*]" from demise (251). As he clearly states (in the paragraph that follows P1), "when Dasein dies – and even when it dies authentically – it does not have to do so *with* an experience of its factical demising, or *in* such an experience" (247, my emphasis).[16] The main point behind this provocative assertion that *we can die without demising* is that neither "death" nor "dying" (nor even "authentically dying," to which we will return) requires us to suffer the *terminal* world collapse of demise. (This is fortunate, because if experiencing "death" in Heidegger's sense meant experiencing the permanent foreclosure of our intelligible worlds in demise, then we would have to write our phenomenologies of death from beyond the grave, by séance or Ouija board!)[17] Heidegger's distinctive contribution here – that we do not need to demise in order to die – is so contrary to our commonsensical notion of death that most traditional readers of *Being and Time* seem simply to repress and ignore it. For it suggests that what Heidegger calls "death" is in fact something we can live through! Indeed, despite the forceful protestations of Hoffman and the first camp, Heidegger himself is quite clear about this. Death does not require demise, our paradoxical experience of the "event" of the end of our lives (240). Instead, as *Being and Time* plainly states: "Death is a way to be, which Dasein takes over as soon as it is" (245).[18] For Heidegger, that is, "death" designates a fundamental modality of existence that is filled-in (and so covered over) by our everyday worldly experience.

To help accustom his audience to this strange use of the word "death," Heidegger immediately quotes a famous line from the Christian mystic, Jakob Böhme (1575–1624): "'As soon as a human being comes to life [*zum Leben kommt*], he is at once old enough to die'" (245). Stambaugh translates this important quotation as follows: "'As soon as a human being is born, he is old enough to die right away,'" but that is a bit misleading because Heidegger is not using Böhme to make the morbid suggestion that newborns can die in a way that late-term fetuses cannot.[19] Instead, Heidegger is suggesting that one is capable of experiencing the collapse of one's world as soon as one has an intelligible world to collapse, that is, as soon as one has come to embody an existential stand on oneself and thereby become a full-fledged Dasein (which is something a newborn infant has yet to do). As the reference to Böhme indicates, Heidegger has in mind the kind of "dying with Christ" or "dying to the world" familiar to Pauline Christianity, a spiritual passage through despair that Kierkegaard describes philosophically in *The Sickness Unto Death*. The basic point, *The Sickness Unto Death* explains, is that "in the Christian understanding, *death is itself a passing into life*."[20] To anyone familiar with Kierkegaard's brilliant text (as Heidegger was), it is clear that *Being and Time*'s phenomenology of existential death seeks to secularize the mystical Christian idea that, in order for one to be born truly into the life of the spirit, one must first die to the material world – so that one can be *reborn* to the world in a way that will unify the spiritual and material aspects of the self.[21]

The parallels between Kierkegaard's and Heidegger's thinking about death are profound and important. According to the view Kierkegaard (or, more precisely, his spiritually elevated pseudonym, "Anti-Climacus") presents in *The Sickness Unto Death*, when we acknowledge and confront our own despair, we are led to abandon our familiar, everyday self, "the fully clothed self of immediacy" that is constituted by all our worldly "projects." This seemingly disastrous loss of our "actual self" turns out to be our salvation, however, because when despair alienates us from the world of our ordinary projects, we discover that what survives this expulsion from the world is our true or "infinite" self. This infinite self, the "naked and abstract" self at our volitional core, is then able explicitly to repossess its "actual self," the world of its immediate projects, from the perspective it discovers in that very expulsion from the world.[22] There are significant differences between Kierkegaard's profoundly religious and Heidegger's thoroughly secularized versions of conversion. Grasped in their broad outlines, however, there can be no mistaking the momentous influence on *Being and Time* of Kierkegaard's view that confronting the despair intrinsic to the structure of the self can allow us to pass through a kind of salvific death and rebirth to the public world. It is thus not surprising that Heidegger's notoriously ambivalent acknowledgements of Kierkegaard in *Being and Time* should be so colored by the anxiety of influence, because Kierkegaard's religious view provides the obvious philosophical prototype for Heidegger's secularized conversion narrative. Kierkegaard paved the way for Heidegger's phenomenological account of the way that confronting our inescapable anxiety can allow us to turn away from the world, break its grip (in death) so that we can turn back to the world (in resoluteness), and thereby gain (or regain) our grip on the world – thereby making the transition from inauthenticity to authenticity (however temporarily).[23]

In other words, Kierkegaard's view of the necessity of confronting despair and so passing through such spiritual death in order to "become oneself" clearly had a formative impact on what I have elsewhere characterized as Heidegger's *perfectionist* account of "how we become what we are."[24] The crucial point for us here is that recognizing Kierkegaard's subterranean but unmistakable influence on Heidegger's thinking helps us to see that Heidegger too conceives of death as something we can live through.[25] So, with Böhme and Kierkegaard having primed the pump, let us delve more deeply into our main question: What exactly does Heidegger mean by "death" in *Being and Time*? Why does he say not only that "Death is a way to be, which Dasein takes over as soon as it is," but also that death is "the possibility of the impossibility of existence in general"?

THE POSSIBILITY OF IMPOSSIBILITY

As *Being and Time* famously maintains, "Higher than actuality stands *possibility*" (38). The sense of "possibility" celebrated here is not "logical possibility," mere alternatives arrayed in a conceptual space, but rather *existential possibility*, "being possible" (*Möglichsein*), which is for Heidegger "the most primordial and ultimately positive way in which Dasein is characterized ontologically" (143–4). Our existential possibilities are what we forge ahead into: the roles, identities, and commitments that shape and circumscribe our comportmental navigation of our lived environments. Dasein *exists* – that is, "stands out" (*ek-sistere*) into intelligibility in a meaningful way – through such a charting of "live options," choices that matter and that are made salient to us by these fundamental life projects, this sense of self embodied and reflected in our worlds.

To see what Heidegger means when he calls death "the possibility of the impossibility of existence in general," it helps to think, first, of someone whose fundamental life project was being a teacher (or a husband, son, communist, pet owner, or any other identity-defining self-understanding) but who then experiences the catastrophic collapse of this life project. What is crucial to recognize is that when such world collapse occurs, we do not instantly forfeit the skills, capacities, and inclinations that this identity previously organized. Instead, in such a situation, we tend to continue projecting ourselves upon an absent project (for a time at least – the time it takes to mourn that project or else replace it, redirecting or abandoning the forces it organized). After that world collapses, we tend to keep pressing blindly ahead (absentmindedly filling the food bowl of a recently deceased pet, for example), even though the project that previously organized this projection is no longer there for us to press ahead into (since, in this example, one no longer owns that pet). Thinking about such a paradoxical (but not uncommon) situation – in which we project ourselves toward a life project we can no longer project ourselves into – helps us grasp what Heidegger means when he calls death the possibility of an *impossibility*. For when not just one but all of our life projects break down in what Heidegger calls "anticipation" (*Vorlaufen*) or "running-out" toward death, we experience ourselves as a kind of bare existential projecting without *any* existentiell projects to project ourselves into (and so understand ourselves in terms of). We can thereby come to understand ourselves as, at bottom, a "primordial existential projecting" (330), a brute projecting that is more basic than and independent of any of the particular projects that usually give our lives content and meaning.

Heidegger distinguishes between our "being-possible" (*Möglichsein*) and our "ability-to-be" (*Seinkönnen*) in order to mark the difference between our life projects, on the one hand, and our projecting ourselves into those life projects, on the other. Usually we project ourselves into our life projects by skillfully navigating, rather than theoretically deliberating over, the live options these projects implicitly delimit and render salient for us – except in cases when something goes wrong or breaks down, and we become explicitly aware of what we were previously trying to do. Heidegger thinks it is possible, however, for all of our projects to break down simultaneously; indeed, this is precisely what he thinks will happen to anyone who endures a true confrontation with his or her existential *Angst*. Rather than acknowledging and confronting the underlying *Angst* that subtly accompanies the thought of death throughout our lives, Heidegger points out, we normally flee this "anxiety" (or "dread") by seeking to adopt *das Man*'s "indifferent tranquility as to the 'fact' that one dies" (telling ourselves, for instance, that "everyone dies, of course, some day," by which we really mean "but not me, not today"), a repression that transforms the existential anxiety that continually accompanies us "into fear in the face of an oncoming event" that remains somewhere off in the future (254). But if we can endure our existential anxiety instead of seeking to deny and tranquilize it (by adopting such common strategies as "hurrying" and "keeping busy"), then it becomes possible, *Being and Time* suggests, for us to trace this baseline anxiety back to its source in our basic "uncanniness" (or *Unheimlichkeit*), the fundamental existential *homelessness* that follows from the fact that there is no life project any of us can ever finally be at home in, because there is ultimately nothing about the ontological structure of the self that could tell us what specifically we should do with our lives.

When we confront our existential *Angst* (i.e., when we "pursue what such moods disclose and ... allow ourselves to confront what has been disclosed" through them [135]), we can come to recognize our essential *Unheimlichkeit*, that is, our not being at-home in-the-world, the fundamental lack of fit between our underlying existential projecting and the specific existentiell (or everyday) worldly projects in terms of which we each flesh out our existence and so give shape to our worlds. (Here, again, we can see the influence of *The Sickness Unto Death*, which insists on the radical heterogeneity of our "naked and abstract" self before God and our "fully clothed self of immediacy."[26] In fact, Heidegger's insistence on the "uncanniness" or "not-being-at-home" in the world seems to be his way of secularizing – and so preserving the core phenomenological insight contained in – the Christian idea that we are *in* but not *of* the world.) Heidegger's basic idea here is that there can be no seamless fit between Dasein's existing and the projects that allow us to make sense of our existing by giving content to our worlds, and thus no one right answer to the question of what we should do with our lives. Our sense of uncanniness or not-being-at-home in the world derives from and testifies to this anxiety-provoking lack of fit between Dasein and its world.[27] This means that, insofar as one lives in an unquestioned sense that one is simply doing what one should be doing with one's life, confronting one's *Angst* will expose one's fundamental lack of fit with the world and thereby catalyze the temporary collapse of the life projects one has been pursuing with a sense of naïve good conscience. Just such a scenario – in which I pursue my anxiety to the point where all my life projects, foundering on the reef of their own contingency, forfeit their unquestioned inertia and so temporarily break down or collapse, no longer allowing me to make sense of myself in their terms – is what Heidegger means by "anticipation" of (or "running-out" toward) death, and it forms the first component of *authenticity* understood in its two structural moments as *anticipatory resolution*.[28]

To grasp what Heidegger thinks the self ultimately boils down to (in this existential version of Husserl's phenomenological reduction), it is crucial to remember that when my projects all break down or collapse, leaving me without any life project to project myself into, projection itself does not cease.[29] When my being-possible becomes impossible, I still am; my ability-to-be becomes insubstantial, unable to connect to the world, but not inert. My projects collapse, and I no longer have a concrete self I can be, but I still *am* this inability-to-be. Heidegger calls this paradoxical condition revealed by anticipation "the possibility of an impossibility" or *death*. In his words:

Death, as possibility [i.e., as something we project ourselves into], gives Dasein nothing to be "actualized," nothing which Dasein could itself actually *be*. It is the possibility of the impossibility of every way of comporting oneself toward anything, of every way of existing. (262)

We thus see the phenomenon Heidegger has in mind when we generalize from the case in which one project breaks down to the catastrophic collapse of them all. A student can explicitly encounter his computer, a carpenter his hammer, and a commuter his car as a tool with a specific role to play in an equipmental nexus organized by his self-understanding, when this tool breaks down – when the hard drive crashes the night before a paper is due, the hammer breaks and cannot be fixed or replaced in the middle of a job, or the car breaks down on the way to an important meeting, leaving the commuter stranded by the side of the road. Just so, Dasein can explicitly encounter its structure as the embodiment of a self-understanding when its projects all break down in death. Dasein, stranded (as it were) by the global collapse of its projects, can come explicitly to recognize itself as, at bottom, not any particular self or project, but rather as a *projecting* into projects, that is, as a being who fundamentally takes a stand on its being and is defined by that stand.

Thus, qualifying his description of Dasein – radically individualized by its confrontation with anxiety – as a "self alone" (*solus ipse*), Heidegger distinguishes the existential reduction he is describing from the famous Cartesian reduction of the self to an isolated thing that is certain only of its own thinking:

> But this existential "solipsism" is so far from transposing an isolated subject thing ["subject thing" is a jab at Descartes' paradoxical conception of the self as a *res cogitans* or "thinking substance"] into the harmless emptiness of a worldless occurring, that what it does is precisely to bring Dasein in an extreme sense face to face with its world as world, and thus face to face with itself as being-in-the-world. (188)

That is, when our worlds collapse in death, we discover ourselves not as a worldless *cogito* but as a "world-hungry" Dasein (as Dreyfus nicely puts it), a "world hunger" we discover explicitly when we find ourselves utterly unable to eat anything – unable, that is, to project into any of the life projects that ordinarily constitute our worlds – despite our desperate desire to do so.[30] Hence, Heidegger's description of this radically individuated "self" of pure "mineness" as "a naked 'that-it-is-*and*-has-to-be'" (134, my emphasis).

By anxiously "running out" toward death and so embodying this possibility of an impossibility, "Dasein is taken back all the way to its naked uncanniness, and becomes fascinated by it. This fascination, however, not only *takes* Dasein back from its '*worldly*' possibilities, but at the same time *gives* Dasein the possibility of an *authentic* ability-to-be" (344). That anxiously running out toward death not only radically individuates Dasein, but also gives it an authentic ability-to-be brings us back to the point that, for Heidegger, death is something I can live through. (Remember that Heidegger himself stresses the paradox that Dasein lives through its death when he writes, "Death is a way to be, which Dasein takes over as soon as it is.") Heidegger's point is that the pure, world-hungry projecting we experience when we are unable to connect to our projects is what is most basic about us. This existential projecting is implicit in all of our ordinary *projecting* into projects, and it also inalienably survives the nonterminal loss of Dasein's any and every particular project (which is precisely why Heidegger frequently refers to death as Dasein's "ownmost ability-to-be"). How, then, can we "live through" death? The passage through death is what Heidegger calls "resoluteness," and it is the second structural moment in his phenomenological account of *authenticity*.

Resoluteness is at least as complex a phenomenon as anticipation, but at its core is Dasein's accomplishment of a reflexive reconnection to the world of projects lost in death, a recovery made possible by the lucid encounter of the self with itself in death. On the basis of the insight gained from this radical self-encounter, it becomes possible for us to recover ourselves and reconnect to the practical world we are usually connected to effortlessly and unreflexively. As I understand it, this reconnection turns on our giving up the unreflexive, paralyzing belief that there is a single correct choice to make, since recognizing that there is no such single correct choice (because there is no substantive self to determine such a choice) is what gives us the *freedom* to choose among the existential possibilities (the roles, goals, and life projects) we face (as well as the subsequent responsibility for having so chosen). As Heidegger puts it:

If Dasein, by anticipation, lets death become powerful in itself, then, as free for death, Dasein understands itself in its own *greater power*, the power of its finite freedom, so that in this freedom, which "is" only in its having chosen to make such a choice, it can take over the *powerlessness* of abandonment to its having done so, and can thus come to see clearly what in the situation is up to chance [and, correlatively, what is up to Dasein]. (384).

"Resoluteness" (*Entschlossenheit*) is Heidegger's name for such free decisions, by which we recognize that the self, as a (projectless) projecting, is more powerful than (that is, *survives*) death (the collapse of its projects), and so become capable of "choosing to choose," of making a lucid reconnection to the world of its existential projects. The freedom of such meta-decisions is "finite" because it is always constrained: by Dasein's own *facticity* and *thrownness* (the fundamental fact that each Dasein is, and has to be, as "thrown" into a world and so already possessing a variety of ontic talents, cares, and predispositions, which can often be altered piecemeal but not simply thrown off in some Sartrean "radical choice"); by the pre-existing concerns of our time and "generation" (to which we cannot but respond in one way or another); by the facts of the specific situation we confront (which of these facts can be altered, Heidegger stresses, we cannot fully appreciate until we act and so enter into this situation concretely); as well as by that which remains unpredictable about the future (including the responses of others). Nevertheless, it is by embracing this finitude – giving up our naïve desire for either absolute freedom or a single correct choice of life project and instead accepting that our finite freedom always operates against a background of constraint (in which there is usually more than one "right" answer, rather than none at all) – that we are able to overcome that paralysis of our projects experienced in death. It is thus important that Heidegger sometimes hyphenates "*Ent-schlossenheit*" (literally "un-closedness") in order to emphasize that the existential "resoluteness" whereby Dasein freely chooses the existential commitments that define it does not entail deciding on a particular course of action ahead of time and obstinately sticking to one's guns come what may, but, rather, requires an "openness" whereby one continues to be responsive to the emerging solicitations of, and unpredictable elements in, the particular existential "situation," the full reality of which only the actual decision itself discloses.

In resolve's decisive "moment of insight," Dasein is (like a gestalt switch) set free rather than paralyzed by the contingency and indeterminacy of its choice of projects, and so can project itself into its chosen project in a way that expresses its sense that, although this project is appropriated from a storehouse of publicly intelligible roles inherited from the tradition, it nevertheless matters that this particular role has been chosen by this particular Dasein and updated, *via* a "reciprocative rejoinder" (386), so as, ideally, to develop its particular ontic and factical aptitudes as these intersect with the pressing needs of its time and generation. Instead of simply taking over our projects from *das Man* (by going with the flow, following the path of least resistance, or simply doing "what one should do"), it thus becomes possible, through resolve, to take over a project reflexively (whether lucidly or explicitly), and thus to reappropriate oneself, to "become what we are" by breaking the previously unnoticed grip arbitrarily exerted upon us by *das Man*'s ubiquitous norms of social propriety, its pre- and proscriptions on *what one does*.[31]

In sum, then, authenticity, as anticipatory resoluteness, names a double movement in which the world lost in anticipating or running out into death is regained in resolve, a (literally) revolutionary movement by which we are involuntarily turned away from the world and then voluntarily turn back to it, in which the grip of the world upon us is broken in order that we may thereby gain (or regain) our grip on this world.

HEIDEGGER'S BRIDGE FROM DEMISE TO DEATH: FORMAL INDICATION

With this overview in mind, let us return to the specific question of how the phenomenon Heidegger calls death is related to – and distinguished from – our ordinary notion of "demise." By "death," we have seen, Heidegger means the experience of existential world collapse that occurs when we confront the ineliminable anxiety that stems from the basic lack of fit between Dasein and its world, an anxiety that emerges from the uncanny fact that there is nothing about the structure of the self that can tell us what specifically to do with our lives. By "dying," I have suggested, Heidegger means the mere *projecting, disclosing,* or *ek-sisting* ("standing-out") that we lucidly experience when our projects collapse in death. By "authentically dying," let me now suggest, he means the *explicit* experience of undergoing such world collapse and thereby coming to understand ourselves as, at bottom, a mere projecting, that is, a *projecting* into projects, a fundamental existential projecting that survives even the (nonterminal) global collapse of these worldly projects.[32]

If this is right, then (to come back to passage P1 for a final time) Heidegger's claim that "Dasein can demise only as long as it is dies" just means that only so long as one is dying, that is, simply projecting, existing, or disclosing at all, can one demise, that is, project into or disclose the terminal collapse of one's world. We are driven to such an initially strange view of what Heidegger means by "death" by the fact that Heidegger claims not only that we can "die" in his sense without having to demise but also, conversely, that most human beings reach their demise without ever undergoing his kind of "death." This functional independence of death from demise (the fact we can die without demising and demise without dying) justifies distinguishing the two phenomena in even a non-commonsensical way, as Blattner and Haugeland have long done well to argue against numerous critics who, like Hoffman, simply cannot accept that Heidegger would be so confusing as to use the word "death" to refer to something we can live through. This is precisely what Heidegger is doing, however, leading to the almost inevitable confusion experienced by the legion of readers who enter his hermeneutic circle already armed with the commonsensical conviction that "death" *must* mean demise, that when Heidegger writes about "death," he must surely be describing the phenomenon we colloquially (and euphemistically) call "kicking the bucket," "taking a dirt nap," "buying the farm" (as if finally making good on our *"mort-gage,"* our promise to die), or simply "passing away." (Again, he is not.) At the same time, however, rightly insisting on the difference between death and demise should not lead us to err in the opposite direction, as Haugeland and White clearly do, prying death and demise so far apart that they entirely overlook the crucial interconnections linking the two phenomena together.[33] For, I now want to show, demise and death remain intimately related, of methodological necessity, and these connections are what rightly generate the undeniable *existential pathos* that has led readers to expect to find a discourse about the ontic event of demise (or kicking the bucket) in Heidegger's ontological analysis of death as the type of end proper to and distinctive of Dasein.

I think we can begin to understand the crucial connection between death and demise if we notice that the six structural characteristics that "define" Heidegger's "full existential-ontological conception of death" – namely, that *"death, as* [1] *the end of Dasein, is* [2] *Dasein's ownmost,* [3] *non-relational,* [4] *certain and* [5] *as such indefinite, and* [6] *non-surpassable possibility"* (258–9) – are all drawn from a formal analysis of *demise*. This, I submit, is no accident but rather the deliberate result of Heidegger's phenomenological method. The fulcrum of Heidegger's broader method of *phenomenological attestation* is what he calls "formal indication"; formal indication is the pivot that allows Heidegger to move from the ontic to the ontological level of phenomenological analysis (as he does, for example, with ontic and ontological guilt, ontic and ontological conscience, demise and death, and time and temporality). In a formal indication, Heidegger explains, "The empty content, viewed with respect to the structure of its meaning [*das leer Gehaltliche in seiner Sinnstruktur*], is at the same time that which indicates the direction of its fulfilling enactment [*die Vollzugsrichtung*]."[34] In other words, "formal indication" enables Heidegger to extract from the ontic phenomenon under consideration only its formal *structures*, which he then fleshes out quite differently in his analysis of the corresponding ontological phenomenon. We then have to project ourselves into this ontological phenomenon in order to be able to understand (in the "fulfilling enactment") *how* it actually conditions the ontic phenomenon. By providing a bridge from the ontic to the ontological in this way, formal indication allows Heidegger to present an ontological interpretation that is not simply arbitrary or idiosyncratic. On the contrary, Heidegger's ontological interpretations may be judged compelling only insofar as we too can experience and so recognize and personally attest that the more basic but previously unnoticed ontological phenomenon Heidegger describes does indeed condition our own experience of the everyday ontic phenomenon with which we are all familiar and from which the formal features of the more fundamental ontological phenomenon are first drawn.[35]

Like Aristotle, who thought philosophy should begin by surveying the expert wisdom of the past that is preserved in common sense, Heidegger maintains that "All ontological investigations of such phenomena as guilt, conscience, and death must start with what the everyday interpretation of Dasein 'says' about them" (281). Heidegger's phenomenological attestation of *death* thus begins with an analysis of our everyday understanding of *demise*. After isolating and "formally indicating" the most significant structural characteristics of the ordinary ontic phenomenon of demise (in which, however, these formal characteristics have quite different meanings), Heidegger then seeks to flesh out these structural characteristics, collectively, in a way that will reveal the heretofore unnoticed ontological phenomenon of "death" that supposedly conditions the phenomenon of ordinary ontic demise. I try to summarize Heidegger's rather complex analysis in the following table:

Shared formal structures	Demise (ontic)	Death (ontological)
1. End	In demise, I experience the terminal collapse of my world. But this experience is ultimately paradoxical, since I do not live through demise to tell the tale.	Death is a global collapse of my world's mattering, in which, unable to project myself into the projects that normally give my world meaning, I experience myself as a mere *projecting*. I do live through death (constantly in my ordinary *projecting* into projects, repeatedly in authentic death – a periodic re-confrontation with the inauthentic one-self I continually accrue, by which I repossess myself).
2. Ownmost	No one can take demise away from me, in the sense that no one can demise in my place. (Even if someone sacrifices his or her own life for me, I myself will still have to demise in the end.)	My very being is at issue in death. When my worldly projects break down in death, I can experience myself (lucidly in death or explicitly in authentic death) as a being whose world is made meaningful by *projecting* into projects. In death, I discover this *projecting* (or *disclosing*) as the most basic aspect of my self (as "stronger than death"), for I recognize that this projecting can survive the collapse of any and all my particular projects.
3. Non-relational	No one else can experience my demise with me; I demise alone.[36]	In death, I encounter myself as having to project into projects, and thereby choose myself, of my own resources, experiencing the fact that no one can do this for me. In this moment (of collapse and reconnection), I am radically individuated.
4. Certain	Demise is empirically certain: We know no exceptions to the proposition that "all men are mortal." *Das Man* reduces this to the certainty that *one dies* (someday), or that *we all die* (but not me, not now).	Death is transcendentally or ontologically certain. The projecting it reveals as my ownmost self is the baseline horizon of all experience, and experiencing this projectless projecting supplies us with the very benchmark of certainty. (All worldly intelligibility requires projecting into projects, which in turn presupposes mere projection; so, phenomenologically, nothing could be more certain.)[37]

(and as such)	(and, experienced as the empirical certainty that *one dies* (someday), demise takes on the inevitability of)	(and, experienced as a pure *projecting* in death, the self rebounds back from the intentional horizon of a world which it cannot project into and so experiences itself as)
5. Indefinite[38]	An impending event ("indefinite as to its 'when'"). The *imminence* of demise (in its unpredictable and often sudden arrival) is obscured by the *indefiniteness* of "one dies."	The pure temporal horizon of futurity (i.e., the coming-toward itself of the self in existing). Here, the *indefiniteness* of demise becomes the *immanence* of death, the fact that this fundamental temporal horizon encountered in death underlies all experience.
6. Un-surpassable	Nothing comes after demise; it is the last moment of my life.	Death is not something I can get beyond; rather, I live through what it discloses – again, constantly in my ordinary *projecting* into projects, and repeatedly in authentic death.[39]

Obviously, this sketch remains incomplete, but I hope it sufficient to illustrate Heidegger's method and so show that he does not arbitrarily choose to rechristen some unrelated phenomenon "death" and analyze it outside of any relation to what the rest of us normally mean by *death*. This is important because it helps us see that, here as elsewhere, the ontic and the ontological are not *heterogeneous* domains (*pace* orthodox Heideggerians and influential critics like Habermas) but rather necessarily overlap and interpenetrate, and *must*, in order for the method Heidegger uses in *Being and Time* (which I have called phenomenological attestation) to work, that is, to be convincing.[40]

CONCLUSIONS: FEAR OF DEMISE AND ANGST ABOUT DEATH

I mentioned at the beginning that a significant obstacle to checking the phenomenological evidence for Heidegger's analysis of death comes from the fact that what he calls "death" – namely, the projectless *projecting* we experience in the wake of the global collapse of the inauthentic one-self each of us continually accrues – seems to be an extremely difficult experience for most people to endure. The magnitude of this difficulty is conveyed by Heidegger's aforementioned acknowledgement that requiring his readers to undergo what he means by death in order to be able to evaluate his account of the phenomenon seems, from the ordinary perspective, to be a "fantastically unreasonable demand" (266), as well as by *Being and Time*'s suggestion that the avoidance of a confrontation with our anxiety before death may be the real engine of Western history.[41]

By *anxiety before death*, however, it is once again crucial to recognize that Heidegger means anxiety about the core self revealed in the collapse of my world, not fear concerning my eventual demise. In fact, Heidegger considers such fear of demise – which "perverts anxiety into cowardly fear" (266) – to be one of the main ways we flee from our anxiety about death. He goes so far as to assert that even those who seem heroically to confront and overcome their fear of demise, in so doing, merely reveal their "own cowardliness in the face of anxiety" (ibid.). Heidegger's startling claim – that our fear of our eventual demise is really just a way of fleeing our anxiety about the core self laid bare by the global collapse of worldly projects in what he calls "death" – is so strange that, as far as I know, no interpreter has explicitly thematized and addressed it. Instead, it is most often miscognized: death is misunderstood as demise, and Heidegger's view is thereby reduced to that of Ernest Becker (a later sociologist who taught that we construct all systems of meaning in order to deny the demise we nevertheless cannot escape).[42] On grasping Heidegger's strange claim, moreover, many readers will suspect the opposite, namely, that Heidegger himself has just reinterpreted "death" so as to transform it into an experience that can be survived, thereby inadvertently exposing his own fear of demise. Further evidence that Heidegger is indeed making the strange claim I am attributing to him can thus be found in the fact that he anticipates that table-turning suspicion and goes out of his way to deny it as one of "the grossest perversions," asserting that: "Anticipatory resoluteness [i.e., authenticity understood as existential death and rebirth to the world] is not a way of escape, fabricated for the 'overcoming' of death" (310). Instead, we have seen, Heidegger believes that if we dare to endure a genuine confrontation with our existential *Angst*, rather than fleeing it back into *das Man*'s "indifferent tranquility as to the 'fact' that one dies" – a flight by which we displace "this anxiety into fear in the face of an oncoming event" (254) – then we will end up experiencing a global collapse of our identity-defining life projects in existential "death."

As I see it, then, what will ultimately be decisive in evaluating Heidegger's phenomenological attestation of death is that we be able to recognize the phenomenon he calls *death* as conditioning, and so explaining at a deep experiential level, the main features of our relationship to ordinary demise, including, perhaps most saliently, the widespread *fear* of demise from which, he recognizes, we habitually flee. Accordingly, I want to suggest that the strange provocations on the subject of the relation between death and demise just rehearsed are best understood as Heidegger's attempt to show that what he calls "death" is what we are really afraid of about demise, and thus that fleeing demise is really just a distorted way of repressing death. What, then, does this mean?

We might think that Heidegger is suggesting that what scares us about demise is the fact that, insofar as we experience demise, we will experience a world collapse without any subsequent reconnection to the world. In this case, we would fear and so flee demise because in it we will suffer an irreversible world collapse, undergoing an apparently permanent foreclosure of our worlds. If this were what Heidegger meant, then he would be suggesting that our fear of such demise is ultimately a cover for our deeper *Angst* about running out into death and then failing subsequently to reconnect to the world in resolve. In other words, Heidegger might seem to be suggesting that what drives our fear of demise is our underlying anxiety that, like the legendary shark that must keep swimming in order to stay alive, should we ever lose that unquestioned existential inertia driving us through our daily lives, should we ever stop and step back from our worlds in a radical way, we might lose our worlds never again to regain them.[43]

I do not want to deny that this is a real worry (perhaps even one to which Heidegger's own somewhat depressive nature might have inclined him), but I think it cannot be correct as an attempt to reconstruct Heidegger's analysis of the ultimate motivations behind our own fear of demise. For, if it were correct, then this would actually be an argument in favor of the interpretation Heidegger dismissed as "the grossest of perversions," namely, the view that Heidegger's call for us confront our *Angst* before death is really just his way of repressing his fear of demise. Because demise is *terminal* world collapse, the dread we might feel about *permanently* losing our unquestioned existential inertia seems to stem from our fear of demise, that is, our fear of our intelligible world coming to an *irreversible* end (think of Poe's haunting words, "Quoth the raven, 'Nevermore'"). That, however, is to derive *Angst* in the face of death from our fear of demise, which is exactly the reverse of what Heidegger seeks to do. For Heidegger to make his case that our fear of demise is ultimately motivated by our *Angst* about death, then, his view must be that what we are really afraid of about demise *is* what he calls death, namely, *losing our world and still being here to experience that loss*. In other words, Heidegger is suggesting that what we fear about demise is the same thing that suicidal people desperately hope to gain from it, namely, that in demise we will *be rid of ourselves*, as it were. Yet, as Epicurus pointed out long ago (and as Heidegger repeatedly stresses in *Being and Time*), we will not be rid of ourselves in demise because, once we demise, we will not *be* at all.[44]

If Heidegger is right, our fear of demise is really our fear of a paradoxical state in which we *are not* – or, more precisely, in which we are not
and yet somehow are in order to be aware that we are not. Our fear of
demise is thus a *misplaced* fear, but it is not (*pace* Nagel) an *unfounded*
one.[45] For there is an experience in which what we are afraid of about
demise – namely, not being, or, more precisely, being our not being –
can actually happen to us. As we have seen, this strange experience
of being in a way in which we are not able to be anything is precisely
what Heidegger calls *death*. When all our worldly projects collapse in
death, leaving a projectless projecting as the sole survivor of the ship-
wreck of the self, we do indeed experience the paradoxical "possibility
of an *im*possibility of existence – that is to say, the utter nothingness of
Dasein" (306), as Heidegger provocatively puts it.

In order to confirm Heidegger's phenomenological analysis for ourselves, then, we would need to be able to attest to the fact that death
conditions demise; that is, we would need to recognize that what we are
really afraid of about demise is not just losing our world but also being
here to experience that loss. So, is Heidegger right about this? I have
suggested that this is a *phenomenological* matter and, as such, one that
we must each decide for ourselves, but here are some leading questions
that I think help make Heidegger's case. In our fear of demise, do we not
torture ourselves precisely by paradoxically imagining, that is, trying to
project ourselves into, our own nonexistence (e.g., by imagining what
the world will be like after we are gone)? Is this paradoxical projection
into our own nonexistence, perhaps, also what is ultimately so unsettling about *the very idea* of a world in which we no longer exist? And,
finally, does not this paradoxical idea of projectless projecting also help
explain what is so frightening about various forms of dementia such as
Alzheimer's disease, which present us with the terrible possibility of
being here to experience the gradual disintegration of our being-here,
the slow-motion implosion of our worlds? If we answer "Yes" to these
questions, this suggests that the phenomenon Heidegger calls *death*
is not only related to but actually conditions our ordinary relation to
demise. Indeed, it suggests that projectless projecting, not terminal
world collapse, *is* what we are really afraid of about demise.

I think the best *confirmation* of Heidegger's phenomenology of
death, moreover, would come if this existential recognition that death
conditions demise can help us no longer to fear demise – which it
should do, because *in demise* we really will not be here not to be here.
Interestingly, I have repeatedly been told after presenting this chapter
that those wracked by fear on their deathbeds can often be helped by
hospice workers (or others) who guide them in visualizing their own
demise; when the terminally ill imaginatively project themselves into

such projectlessness, they reportedly experience a cathartic release of
their mortal fear. This is very strong evidence in favor of Heidegger's
initially strange but, I think, ultimately quite compelling view. What
Heidegger's phenomenology of death and demise in *Being and Time*
seeks to show us, in the end, is that if we want to shed the mortal
fear of demise that will otherwise pursue us throughout our lives, then
we need to muster the courage to confront our anxiety about death,
thereby learning calmly and simply to be here – instead of continuing
to rush blindly toward the very thing we fear in our desperate attempts
to evade it.

NOTES

1 *"Die Sterblichen sterben den Tod im Leben."* Martin Heidegger, "Hölderlin's
   Earth and Heaven [1959]," GA 4: 165/190.
2 See John Haugeland, "Truth and Finitude: Heidegger's Transcendental
   Existentialism," in *Heidegger, Authenticity, and Modernity: Essays in
   Honor of Hubert L. Dreyfus*, Volume 1, eds. Mark Wrathall and Jeff Malpas
   (Cambridge, MA: MIT, 2000), 44.
3 In anxiety, our being is, or becomes, becoming; we exist as a pure or empty
   existing, deprived of the world. See William Blattner, *Heidegger's Temporal
   Idealism* (Cambridge: Cambridge University Press, 1999).
4 As Heidegger puts it, "this primordial anxiety ... clears away everything
   covering over the fact that Dasein has been abandoned to itself. The 'nothing' with which anxiety brings us face to face unveils the nullity [or "emptiness," *Nichtigkeit*] by which Dasein, in its very *basis*, is defined; and this
   basis itself *is* as thrownness into death" (308). Hence, "Being-toward-death is
   essentially anxiety" (266; see also 251). Blattner nicely articulates this connection in terms of Heidegger's existentials: "Death is the self-understanding that belongs to this experience, anxiety is the mood, and conscience its
   discourse" (see William Blattner, *Heidegger's Being and Time: A Reader's
   Guide* [London: Continuum, 2006], 140). By "primordial" (*ursprüngliche*) or
   "real or authentic anxiety," Heidegger means anxiety that stems not from
   individual physiological peculiarities or unrelated neurochemical imbal-
   ances but, instead, from the ontological structure of the self, specifically,
   from what I shall explain as the "uncanny" lack of fit between the empty
   self at our volitional and intentional core, on the one hand, and the world of
   particular ontic choices by which we give this self concrete meaning, on the
   other. This lack of fit is common to everyone whether we realize it or not,
   Heidegger suggests, and so the source of an ineliminable existential anxiety
   in all our everyday lives (about which more later).
5 See Jean-Paul Sartre, *Being and Nothingness*, trans. H. E. Barnes (New York:
   Philosophical Library, 1956 [original 1943]), pp. 271, 288; and Emmanuel
   Levinas, *Time and the Other*, trans. R. A. Cohen (Pittsburgh: Duquesne
   University Press, 1987 [original 1947]). When a stranger stares at me, Sartre
   argues (using his famous example of being caught looking through a key-
   hole [pp. 259–61]), my subjectivity temporarily becomes objectified by this
   stranger's gaze; that is, I implicitly experience myself not as stretching out

into a world of practical projects that define me but instead as frozen by his stare like a bug on a pin, reduced by a subjectivity outside myself to this one moment and possibility. Levinas, for his part, still explicitly discusses "anguish" and "death" in terms very close to Heidegger's – much closer than is usually recognized, in fact. On this latter point, see my "Rethinking Levinas on Heidegger on Death," *The Harvard Review of Philosophy*, Vol. XVI (Fall 2009), 23–43.

6 See Paul Edwards, *Heidegger's Confusions* (New York: Prometheus, 2004; which reprints Edward's incredibly confused articles from 1975 and 1976); Piotr Hoffman, "Death, Time, History: Division II of *Being and Time*," in *The Cambridge Companion to Heidegger*, ed. Charles Guignon (Cambridge: Cambridge University Press, 1993); Stephen Mulhall, "Human Mortality: Heidegger on How to Portray the Impossible Possibility of Dasein," in *A Companion to Heidegger*, eds. Hubert L. Dreyfus and Mark A. Wrathall (Oxford: Blackwell, 2005); William Blattner, "The Concept of Death in *Being and Time*," *Man and World* 27 (1994), 49–70 (this is the seminal article for this way of reading Heidegger); John Haugeland, "Truth and Finitude: Heidegger's Transcendental Existentialism" (op. cit.); and Carol J. White, *Time and Death: Heidegger's Analysis of Finitude*, ed. Mark Ralkowski (Aldershot: Ashgate, 2005). With the exception of Edwards, these are all serious and informed scholars, and a detailed response to their views (which I am brutally simplifying here) would be a worthy but massive undertaking. For my detailed critique of White's interpretation, however, see "On the Advantages and Disadvantages of Reading Heidegger Backward: White's *Time and Death*," *Inquiry* 50:1 (2007): 103–20.

7 The scare quotes Heidegger puts around "has" here signal his awareness of the Epicurean paradox concerning our experience of demise. The paradox (to which we will return below), put simply, is how can we experience demise? If demise means the absence of all experience, then how can we experience the absence of all experience? Heidegger frequently uses scare quotes to signal such Epicurean worries (see also, e.g., 251).

8 "*Being*-toward" means *existing* in terms of, i.e., actually projecting oneself into; it does not mean simply thinking about or imagining some future event. So, as we will see, being-toward-death means existentially projecting oneself into the phenomenon Heidegger calls death; it does not mean imagining or adopting some attitude toward one's eventual *demise*.

9 Dasein "demises" insofar as the perishing of its physical body causes it to experience its own terminal world collapse. The relation between *perishing* and *demise* is suggestively illustrated by a scene in *The Matrix* when several minor characters are murdered by being "unplugged" while still in the Matrix world. Their Daseins, cut off from their actual physical bodies, suddenly "demise" in the world of the Matrix, and shortly thereafter their physical bodies "perish," having thus "given up the ghost." (That is perhaps an intentional pun in this scene, as one of the characters is named "Ghost." Yet, the fact that one's physical body would perish so quickly after being deprived of its Dasein suggests, in good Heideggerian fashion, that being Dasein in the Matrix world involves much more than what mind/body dualism imagines as the "mind," including all sorts of subconscious and even apparently "autonomic" processes without which the body cannot

maintain even its minimal life functions.) The same relation is then enacted in reverse later, when Neo demises in the Matrix but is then "resurrected" there, apparently jump-started (in some unexplained way) when Trinity kisses his physical body, still living outside the Matrix world from which he has been disconnected. (I thank Mark Wrathall for a conversation about this and related matters.)

10 See Jacques Derrida, *Aporias*, trans. T. Dutoit (Stanford: Stanford University Press, 1993), 40. Derrida gets this point from Blanchot; see my "Can I Die? Derrida on Heidegger on Death," *Philosophy Today*, 43:1 (1999): 29–42. Heidegger is quite right to distinguish Dasein's distinctive mode of being, *existence*, from the on-hand occurrence of objects and the hands-on availability of equipment, but these distinct realms obviously interpenetrate and act on one another in a wide variety of ways.

11 Our culture, testifying to its pervasive fear of demise, euphemistically calls this "passing peacefully" and often presents it as an ideal death. But from an existential perspective, such a demise looks more like the thief in the night who steals our whole life, stealing even our ability to notice the theft. The euphemism bears witness to the rather cowardly and dubious idea that it would be better never to experience such an irreversible foreclosure of our worlds. Absent such an experience of the terminal collapse of our intelligible worlds, however, we will not have *demised*; we will not have experienced our worlds' collapsing but, instead, will merely have ceased to be. (I shall suggest that this Epicurean paradox at the heart of the idea of an experience of demise motivates Heidegger's distinction between demise and existential death, which we can experience.)

12 See also note 7.

13 It is for this reason that Levinas criticizes Heidegger's phenomenology of death for deliberately remaining one-sidedly "this-worldly," alleging that Heidegger ignores the possibility that one might look back on one's life from some eternal beyond. But here Levinas seems to confuse death with demise, and, even if we restrict the question to the phenomenology of demise, is not clear how Heidegger – as a phenomenologist who must deliberately confine himself to what we are capable of experiencing concerning the phenomenon at issue – could avoid restricting himself to what Dasein can experience here, in *this* world. (Surely "near-death" experiences, e.g., could not settle the question of whether there is an other-worldly beyond.) For that very reason, in fact, Heidegger is careful to acknowledge that the phenomenological necessity of methodologically privileging what Dasein can experience (in our being-here) with respect to death and demise remains neutral on the religious question of whether or not there is any life after demise (see 247–8).

14 To understand "being toward," notice that Heidegger equates it here with "thrown into" (and see note 8).

15 Understanding this point allows us to answer another difficult question careful readers often pose, namely why does Heidegger think that the collapse of projects that we experience in what he calls "death" has to be *global*? It is necessary that *all* Dasein's projects break down because, as we have just seen, existential "death" is introduced in *Being and Time* in order to solve the puzzle of how we can have a *complete* existential analysis of

our Dasein (or "being-here"), given that there always seems to be something still outstanding about Dasein so long as it exists in the world, and
once Dasein demises, it is no longer here at all. A grasp of Dasein "as a
whole" is only possible, then, if Dasein undergoes an experience in which
all its existentiell possibilities have collapsed so that it finds itself retracted
from the world like a turtle into its shell. (A second reason is that, as we
will see at the end, fear of demise is fear of being not at all, not fear of being
diminished – although that can be a real fear too.) It is natural to worry that
the idea of total world collapse is problematic phenomenologically, and so
to suspect that Heidegger is either generalizing from his own depressive
nature or else letting the hermeneutic dictates of the existential analysis
trump phenomenology – which, I think, should instead have led him to recognize that *all* our projects do not need to collapse in order for us to come
to understand the existential structure of the self. Nonetheless, undergoing
such a global collapse is possible and seems to yield precisely the insight
Heidegger suggests, which is all he needs. I think he believes in such global
collapse not only because he himself experienced it repeatedly (on this point
see my forthcoming philosophical biography of Heidegger), but also because
he thinks that if Dasein experiences the collapse of its "ultimate for the
sake of which" – that is, the single project which ultimately organizes all
Dasein's other projects (i.e., the project we would give up last) – then its
whole world will collapse like a house of cards. (See also the analogy from
Gestalt psychology that Sartre uses to argue for Heidegger's same point in
Being and Nothingness, pp. 469–70.) As this suggests, Heidegger is committed to a robust neo-Kierkegaardian notion of a unified self, not a postmodern fractured self whose identity transforms from one context to the
next, and at least this much is right about this analysis: The collapse of our
defining projects can easily paralyze our peripheral projects, making it seem
as if our world has ended, whereas the collapse of peripheral projects only
completely paralyzes the most neurotic of individuals.

16 Here, "does not have to" clearly implies *but can*. Death can take place
without demise, but the two can at least partly coincide, and, by all appearances, they will if one is conscious when one demises and one's demise is
not too sudden. In such cases, it seems to me that demise and death will
at least temporarily coincide in the experience of terminal world collapse.
On this point, it has been suggested to me that the worlds of some Daseins
(some Buddhists, e.g., or perhaps a resolutely authentic person who has
become thoroughly at-home in their own existential homelessness) might
be structured in such a way that the conscious experience of demise would
not lead their world to collapse. But my own sense is that anyone who has
any contentful world at all will experience the collapse of that particular
world if they are conscious when they demise (and *if* demise does in fact
involve the arrival of a kind of permanent wordlessness, as seems to be the
case from the outside looking in), even if they greet the dissolution of this
world in demise as a blessed experience of union with the nothingness of
Nirvana or, on a more mundane level, as a joyful release from suffering,
etc. Such persons will still lose their worlds, whether they greet such world
collapse with ecstatic joy or with terrified despair. (Of course, my second
parenthetical conditional above oversteps the methodological boundary

Heidegger himself is careful to establish; as mentioned in note 13, we cannot as phenomenologists rigorously discuss what happens after the end of conscious experience.)

17 The basic distinction between death and demise, put another way, is that the first-person phenomenology of demise – of terminal world collapse – leaves no record. We might be able to *witness* the terminal collapse of our worlds (Epicurean paradoxes notwithstanding), but we Dasein (or being-here) cannot subsequently bear witness to it, since we will no longer *be here* to do so.

18 See also: "Dasein is dying, factically and indeed constantly, as long as it has not yet come to its demise" (259). Or, as Heidegger wrote in 1925, "I myself am my death precisely when I live." See Heidegger, "Wilhelm Dilthey's Research and the Current Struggle for a Historical Worldview," in *Becoming Heidegger: On the Trail of His Early Occasional Writings, 1910–1927*, eds. Theodore Kisiel and Thomas Sheehan (Evanston: Northwestern University Press, 2007), 263.

19 See Joan Stambaugh's translation of *Being and Time* (New York: SUNY Press, 1996), 228.

20 See Søren Kierkegaard, *The Sickness Unto Death*, trans. A. Hannay (London: Penguin Books, 2004), 47, my emphasis.

21 As others have observed, Heidegger's notion of "being toward death" (*Sein zum Todes*) seems deliberately to echo the title of *The Sickness Unto Death* in its German translation (*Krankheit zum Todes*); see White, *Time and Death*, 61. As White also rightly suggests (60), *The Sickness Unto Death* advances the view that "in 'Christian terminology,' the word 'death' means 'spiritual wretchedness,' not physical dying."

22 "This self, naked and abstract, in contrast to the fully clothed self of immediacy, is the first form of the infinite self and the progressive impulse in the entire process through which a self infinitely takes possession of its actual self along with its difficulties and advantages." See Kierkegaard, *The Sickness Unto Death*, 86.

23 Interestingly, Kierkegaard's version of conversion seems to leave the world just as it was (as if "rendering unto Caesar"), whereas Heidegger's core self (the *solus ipse*) can (but, *pace* White, need not) choose quite different projects, and so a different world, for itself. Sartre notoriously exaggerates this difference even further in his appropriations of Heidegger (which, like Heidegger's appropriations of Kierkegaard, are similarly creative and, when not explicitly critical, typically unacknowledged).

24 I elaborate this view in "Heidegger's Perfectionist Philosophy of Education in *Being and Time*," *Continental Philosophy Review* 37:4 (2004), 439–67, as well as in *Heidegger on Ontotheology: Technology and the Politics of Education* (Cambridge: Cambridge University Press, 2005), ch. 4.

25 Like Heidegger, moreover, Kierkegaard uses paradox in order to distinguish what he means by *death* from our ordinary use of the term; e.g., Anti-Climacus informs his readers that "to die death itself means to live to experience dying." See Kierkegaard, *The Sickness Unto Death*, 48.

26 Kierkegaard similarly suggests that confronting despair "begins that act of separation in which the self becomes aware of itself as essentially different from the environment and the external world and their effect on it." See Kierkegaard, *The Sickness Unto Death*, 85.

27 This means, I think, that if one could imagine a Dasein-like being (a kind of android, say) who fit perfectly into its world without leaving any remainder of self (a being for whom one and only one life project made perfect sense), then this being would not experience any anxiety. (Of course, if the world changed, or such a being changed (think, e.g., of *Wall-E*), then even such a being could find itself no longer entirely at home in the world.)

28 Heidegger's heroic image of "charging forward into death [*Vorlaufen in den Tod*]" seems to have been drawn from Jünger's grim yet romantic description of German soldiers charging blindly from the trenches through clouds of poisonous gas meant to cover and aid the *Blitzkrieg* – gas attacks which Heidegger's own "weather service" unit helped plan. See Ernst Jünger, *Storm of Steel*, trans. M. Hofmann (New York: Penguin, 2004), and chs. 3 and 4 of my *Heidegger on Ontotheology*.

29 See Steven Crowell, "Subjectivity: Locating the First-Person in *Being and Time*," *Inquiry* 44:4 (2001): 433–54.

30 See Hubert L. Dreyfus, "Foreword" to White's *Time and Death*.

31 I develop this line of thinking much further in *Heidegger, Art, and Postmodernity* (New York: Cambridge University Press, 2011). Heidegger's understanding of "finite freedom" is bolstered by Bernard Williams' suggestive speculation concerning the roots of the very idea of "liberty," viz., that "it is a plausible guess at a human universal that people resent being, as they see it, arbitrarily pushed around by others." See Williams, "Liberalism and Loss," in *The Legacy of Isaiah Berlin*, eds. Mark Lilla, Ronald Dworkin, and Robert B. Silvers (New York: New York Review of Books, 2001), 93.

32 See §61, where Heidegger rhetorically asks: "What if resoluteness ... should bring itself into its authenticity only when it projects itself ... upon the uttermost possibility which lies ahead of Dasein's every factical ability-to-be [i.e., death]?" (302). In authentic death (the first moment of authentic resolve), I explicitly *repeat* the experience I have previously undergone lucidly; i.e., I explicitly project myself into my own brute projecting and so come to exist my own existing or become my own becoming. (See also notes 3 and 39.)

33 Haugeland asserts that: "What is important about these ['demise and perishing'] is *only* that neither is to be identified with death, *existentially* conceived." See John Haugeland, "Truth and Finitude: Heidegger's Transcendental Existentialism," in *Heidegger, Authenticity, and Modernity: Essays in Honor of Hubert L. Dreyfus, Volume 1*, eds. Mark Wrathall and Jeff Malpas (Cambridge, MA: MIT Press, 2000), 66 (first emphasis mine). Although I think Haugeland is wrong on this important point, many of his other observations about death remain insightful and suggestive.

34 GA 61: 33 (these are lectures from 1921–2). As Karin de Boer writes, "Heidegger emphasizes that the formal indication, despite its formal character, must *intimate something* about the concrete possibilities that inhere in the concept." (See de Boer, *Thinking in the Light of Time: Heidegger's Encounter with Hegel*. Albany: SUNY Press, 2000, p. 88 [my emphasis], see also 91.) Theodore Kisiel contends that: "Formal indication, as hermeneutic phenomenology's guiding method ... would have become a main theme of the [unwritten] third division" of *Being and Time*. (See Kisiel, "The Demise of *Being and Time*," in *Heidegger's Being and Time: Critical Essays*, ed.

Richard Polt. Lanham: Rowman & Littlefield, 2005, 192.) Kisiel also points
to the connection between formal indication as a method and what I have
called Heidegger's *perfectionism*, quoting Heidegger's 1929–30 view that:
"The meaning content of these [formally indicating] concepts [Heidegger
mentions "death," *Tod*, as his first example] does not directly intend or
express what they refer to, but only gives an indication, a pointer to the
fact that anyone who seeks to understand is called upon by this conceptual
context to undertake a transformation of themselves in their Dasein." (See
GA 29/30: 428–30; quoted by Kisiel, ibid., p. 208.) Using formal indication
to pass from the ontic to the ontological level of analysis thus requires us to
practice existential phenomenology ourselves.

35 I shall suggest at the end that the force of such a recognition comes from the
way that it simultaneously illuminates and transforms our ordinary ontic
experience.

36 Amusingly, this is the reading of Heidegger advanced by Ethan Hawke's
character in the film *Reality Bites*, in response to which Ben Stiller's character suggests that this belief that we all die alone explains why Hawke's
character does not deserve to be in a romantic relationship with Winona
Ryder's character. This problem disappears, however, if one does not reduce
death to demise; see note 39.

37 For more on Heidegger's underexplored view of the paradigmatic certainty
of death, see my "Can I Die? Derrida on Heidegger on Death," *Philosophy
Today* 43:1 (1999), 29–42. It may also be that this recognition empowers
the self's meta-choice and is carried over into the "wholeheartedness"
of its commitments, as Taylor Carman suggests in *Heidegger's Analytic*
(Cambridge: Cambridge University Press, 2003).

38 By "indefinite" Heidegger specifies "'the *indefiniteness* of its 'when,'" i.e.,
"*that it is possible at any moment*" (258) or imminent.

39 Heidegger suggests that experiencing authentic death teaches me a kind of
existential humility by reminding me that my projects are vulnerable – not
only because a successful reconnection to the world through resolve is not
guaranteed, but also because my existence is finite and will predictably end
with a terminal world collapse that will separate me from my incomplete
projects for a final time. Recognizing this, Heidegger suggests, helps me to
acknowledge that others' projecting into projects will continue after mine
has ended, encouraging me to recognize the independence of others and treat
them as potential collaborators in or heirs to shared projects I cannot complete. (On this existential community, see the conclusion of my *Heidegger
on Ontotheology* and the opening acknowledgments of *Heidegger, Art, and
Postmodernity*.) Moreover, the fact that *what* resolve resolves is to repeat
itself suggests that the repeated reconnection to the ontological core of the self
(a kind of repeated removal of the barnacles of worldly habit) is part of what
makes it possible and important to try to disclose a sense of continuity and
coherence in my life as a whole (a requirement Heidegger also *inherits* from
Kierkegaard). How frequently, then, is existential death supposed to occur? If
we recall the reason that confronting one's *Angst* leads one's world to collapse
in the first place – namely, because the confrontation with *Angst* reveals the
uncanny lack of fit between the self and its world, revealing a contingency
that undermines one's naïve sense that one is doing the right thing with one's

life – then we can see that this kind of global collapse can only happen to one *again* insofar as one has settled back into this kind of naïve good conscience that one is doing the right thing with one's life. Yet, this is exactly what we do tend to do (living in the everyday public world of *das Man*), which helps explain why Heidegger specifies that *"authentic resoluteness ... resolves to keep repeating itself"* (308). This means that we must hold ourselves open to the occasional experience, typically in a moment of radical breakdown, of a certain distance with respect to our defining existential projects, a distance from which we can reevaluate or recommit to them. (This commitment to such reevaluation is not paralyzing, I think, both because it is only periodic, dictated by the accumulation of the conformist "one-self" that alienates us from *leading* our own lives, and also because it is only required for our ultimate for-the-sake of which, not for every project organized by that ultimate project.) In authentic death and resoluteness, we explicitly re-experience ourselves as a projectless projecting that makes sense of itself by projecting into projects, and we do thereby *explicitly* experience that disconnection from and reconnection to the world that we tend to experience only *lucidly* the first time we undergo it, a repetition Heidegger seems to think necessary in order to evaluate his phenomenology for ourselves. Nonetheless, this aspect of Heidegger's view seems phenomenologically problematic to me; I think we need only live through death at least once, lucidly (and that this world collapse can be partial; see note 15), in order to be able, in retrospect, to explicitly understand the experience thus lived through.

40 For a detailed explanation of the phenomenological argument that allows Heidegger to move from an ontic work of art (Van Gogh's painting of a pair of shoes) to the ontological truth of art in general, see my *Heidegger, Art, and Postmodernity*, ch. 3. There I also develop Heidegger's later view that art can teach us to embrace the nothing that death discloses (by helping us see this "noth-ing" as the source of meaningful possibilities for the future), instead of anxiously fearing it (as what reveals the limits of our subjectivistic fantasies of extending total control over our worlds).

41 See Haugeland, "Truth and Finitude," 74; Robert Pippin, *Idealism as Modernism* (Cambridge: Cambridge University Press, 1997), p. 383, n. 16. (I think the larger point Pippin makes here is right and insightful, but we need to emend the details so as not to equate "death" with "mortality," the latter having to do with "demise," because, as I shall now explain, Heidegger himself insists that our fear of demise is a way of fleeing from our anxiety before death.)

42 Heidegger believes something close to Becker, but thinks that this denial of demise is itself motivated by our flight before what Heidegger calls death. See below and cf. Ernest Becker, *The Denial of Death* (New York: Free Press, 1973).

43 This is close to Thomas Nagel's reason for thinking life absurd. As Nagel puts it: "What sustains us, in belief as in action, is not reason or justification, but something more basic than these ... If we tried to rely entirely on reason, and pressed it hard, our lives and beliefs would collapse – a form of madness that may actually occur if the inertial force of taking the world and life for granted is somehow lost." See Nagel, *Mortal Questions* (Cambridge: Cambridge University Press, 1979), 20.

44 In demise, we will not be here either to enjoy or to suffer not being here. Here, we come close to Kierkegaard's argument for the inevitable failure of suicide. In his view, the suicidal person does not want not to be, full stop; instead, the suicide really wants to *be* without those aspects of his experience that torture him. For Kierkegaard, moreover, we are all in a similar situation, even if unknowingly, because what ultimately tortures us are contradictions built into the nature of selfhood (the fact that the self is both determined and free, finite and infinite, temporal and eternal, etc.). Hence, his view that "despair is precisely the inability to die," where "to die means that it *is* all over." (See *The Sickness Unto Death*, p. 48.) In the end, Kierkegaard suggests that only faith in a God for whom "everything is possible" – even the resolution of such contradictions – can save us. Secularizing Kierkegaard, Heidegger suggests that only the radically individualized Dasein can *resolve* such existential contradictions for him- or herself. (Levinas falls in between Kierkegaard and Heidegger here; see my "Rethinking Levinas on Heidegger on Death.")

45 See Thomas Nagel, "Death," in *Mortal Questions*. Nagel, we might say, did not anticipate Heideggerian *anticipation* or "running out" into death, in which (as Heidegger already wrote in 1925) "the world withdraws, collapsing into nothingness." (See Heidegger, "Wilhelm Dilthey's Research and the Current Struggle for a Historical Worldview," *Becoming Heidegger*, 265.)

13 Freedom and the "Choice to Choose Oneself" in *Being and Time*

What Heidegger means by "freedom" in *Being and Time* is somewhat mysterious: while the notion crops up repeatedly in the book, there is no dedicated section or study, and the concept is repeatedly connected to a new and opaque idea – that of the "choice to choose oneself." Yet the specificity of *Being and Time*'s approach to freedom becomes apparent when the book is compared to other texts of the same period, in particular *The Metaphysical Foundations of Logic*, *The Fundamental Concepts of Metaphysics*, *The Essence of Grounds*, and *The Essence of Freedom*. Although there are some differences, the definition of freedom that can be found there identifies it with "existence" or "transcendence,"[1] Dasein's ek-static opening onto the world. Thus "being in the world must also be primordially bound up with or derived from the basic feature of Dasein's existence, *freedom* ... Dasein's transcendence and freedom are identical! Freedom provides itself with intrinsic possibility: a being is, as free, necessarily in itself transcending" (GA 26: 238; Heidegger's italics). Note the apodictic modality of the claim: it is not simply the case that Dasein, as transcending, is free. Anything that has the structure of being in the world *must* be free: freedom is co-extensive with Dasein. Yet Dasein is often pictured in *Being and Time* as anything but free: it "ensnares itself" (268), is "lost" (264), "alienated" (178), and needs to be "liberated" (264, 303). Thus comparison between *Being and Time* and other texts on freedom yields an important paradox: although by definition it transcends toward the world, the Dasein of Division I is deprived of freedom. It must be free, and yet phenomenological analysis shows that it is not free. To understand the specific meaning of freedom in *Being and Time*, one has to square this circle.

I am grateful to David Batho, Jeff Byrnes, Hubert Dreyfus, Fabian Freyenhagen, Jeff Haynes, Stephan Kaüfer, Wayne Martin, Stephen Mulhall, Edward Pile, Naomi Van Steenbergen, Dan Watts, and Mark Wrathall for their comments. I am especially indebted to Jeff Haynes for several discussions on the topic, and to Dan Watts for his help with the Kierkegaard material and for feedback on an earlier draft.

The most likely candidate for such resolution is to view the paradox in light of the ontological difference and to understand the apodictic claim as pertaining to Dasein's ontological structure, on the one hand, and the phenomenological observations as relevant to Dasein's ontic situation, on the other. This is suggested by Heidegger's own remark that "it is unimportant here [in *The Metaphysical Foundations of Logic*] to what extent something defined as free is, in fact, free, or to what extent it is aware of its freedom. Nothing is said regarding the extent to which it is free or only latently free, bound or enthralled by others ... Only a free being can be unfree" (GA 26: 247). So to understand *Being and Time*'s particular approach, we need to distinguish between two sorts of freedom: ontological freedom (transcendence), which is the condition of possibility of ontic, or existentiell freedom, itself the main concern of *Being and Time*. Heidegger states this relation of ontological dependency as follows: "in being ahead of oneself as being towards one's ownmost potentiality for being [ontological freedom as transcendence] lies the *existential ontological condition* for the possibility of *being free* for authentic existentiell possibilities" (193, first italics mine).[2] Since, by definition, Dasein cannot but be in the world, ontological freedom is inalienable: it consists in having a projective understanding of oneself and of the world focused by having oneself as one's for the sake of which: "it is Dasein's defining character that it is concerned with this being, in its being, in a specific way. Dasein exists for the sake of Dasein's being and its capacity for being ... This selfhood, however, is its freedom" (GA 26: 239, 241). Although I do not have the space to develop this here, for Heidegger, being ontologically free entails (a) that Dasein can comport itself, as opposed to animal behavior; (b) that in doing so, it opens up a normative space;[3] and (c) that it has alternative possibilities.[4] In short, it is the condition of possibility of *all* forms of Dasein's agency, including existentiell freedom. However, distinguishing between these two levels only solves the paradox formally: much remains to be asked, and said, about freedom.

Hubert Dreyfus, one of the few interpreters who noticed the need to make this distinction, briefly defines ontological freedom as "Dasein's ability to take part in the opening of a world" and adds that "the power of the particular Dasein to press into some possibilities rather than others is ontic freedom, or transcendence."[5] Yet, as such, this cannot be right. *The Metaphysical Foundations of Logic* and *The Essence of Reasons* state unambiguously that transcendence *is* ontological freedom. So while Dreyfus' first claim is correct, the assimilation of ontic freedom with transcendence is not. Furthermore, the proposed definition of ontic freedom is strongly reminiscent of the lowest degree of Cartesian freedom: in Heidegger's own words (which closely follow

Descartes' in the *Fourth Meditation*), "being able to do and not to do one and the same thing set before us" (GA 17: 149). Yet even the enthralled Dasein of Division I is able to press ahead into some possibilities rather than others: it can have its lunch at its desk, or at the cafeteria, or skip lunch altogether to write its paper. So there must be more to existentiell freedom than a modified interpretation of the Cartesian free arbiter – but what?

There is a further puzzle. Heidegger repeatedly links ontic freedom to the "choice to choose oneself." But why the doubled structure? Both Kierkegaard and Sartre talk about a "choice of the self." But Heidegger himself feels the need to distinguish between a first and a second choice. So what does each choice refer to, and how do they relate to each other? Furthermore, given his rejection of rationalist themes such as the primacy of consciousness and epistemic self-transparency, why use the vocabulary of choice, which is central to the tradition that runs from Descartes to German idealism, at all? Prima facie, the idea of a choice, both in its common use and within the rationalist strand, involves at least three aspects: I must know (a) *that* I choose, since otherwise I would simply be moved causally one way or another, for example by my drives or my desires; (b) *what* I choose, even if I am mistaken about it, as otherwise the choice would be void; and finally, (c) that *I* choose, as otherwise I could not be held responsible for my choice. All three aspects put a high premium on reflective awareness, both about the choice and myself. They also rest on a voluntaristic conception of choice as decision making. Yet much of *Being and Time* is intended to bypass the primacy of consciousness and to show that being in the world, in its everyday forms, does not require self-awareness (on the contrary, this would prevent us from responding appropriately to the affordances of the world). If the "choice to choose oneself" turned out to involve a rationalist model of choice, then the definition of existentiell freedom would bring back to the heart of *Being and Time* some of the very themes that the book was meant to criticize – a risk that is made even more salient by the consideration of Sartre's hyper-rationalistic reformulation as the radical choice of *Being and Nothingness*.

It is perhaps in implicit recognition of this danger that most interpreters do little more than mention the notion. Yet the vocabulary of choice crops up so often in *Being and Time* that it seems hermeneutically wrong to ignore it. Dreyfus and Rubin, to their credit, do acknowledge the importance of the theme, but raise three objections: (a) as a world-defining choice, it is contradictory because one cannot choose the criteria according to which the choice itself needs to be made; (b) since "inauthentic Dasein fails to make the choice, and authentic Dasein is produced by the choice," there is no one to make the choice except, most implausibly, "some sort of noumenal self";[6] and (c) it is unclear when the choice would take place, "again and again or ... in and for eternity."[7] These are important objections that will need careful consideration. But they are taken as decisive without discussion (except for the first), and, crucially, are addressed to the choice of the self, not the choice *to choose* the self. Dreyfus and Rubin reject the idea of a choice, and conclude that "as we might expect, the 'choice' of authenticity is not a *choice* at all ... Heidegger ... describes the 'choice' of authenticity as a 'way of letting the ownmost self take action in itself and of its own accord'"(295).[8] Yet the end of the same sentence takes us back to the idea of a self-defining choice: "in terms of that potentiality for being which it has *chosen*" (295, my italics). Clearly, more needs to be said about what such choosing amounts to. Thus I shall try in this paper to make sense of the choice of choosing the self in its relation to existentiell freedom while rescuing it from its rationalistic overtones.

ANXIETY AND THE CHOICE TO CHOOSE ONESELF

The section on anxiety plays a genetic part in the emancipation process by allowing Dasein to see for the first time that it is both ontologically free and ontically unfree. By breaking down its involvement with the world, anxiety enables Dasein to become pre-reflectively aware of its self-interpretative nature, and faces it with an ultimatum: Dasein has to choose to choose itself, or not. In the first case, it will become existentielly free; but either way, it will be irreversibly transformed.[9]

So "anxiety makes manifest in Dasein its *being towards* its ownmost potentiality for being – that is, its *being free for* the freedom of choosing itself and taking hold of itself. Anxiety brings Dasein face to face with its *being free for* (*propensio in* ...) the authenticity of its being" (188, Heidegger's italics). The doubling "being [ontologically] free for the [ontic] freedom" indicates the dependency of existentiell freedom on its ontological counterpart as the condition of possibility of all forms of Dasein's comportment. But the further characterization of ontological freedom as a "*propensio in*" authenticity is rather puzzling: why use Latin? Why talk of a "*propensio*" at all? This is, somewhat surprisingly, a reference to Descartes. In his study of Cartesian freedom in the *Introduction to Phenomenological Research*, Heidegger had made the following comment: "in order to be free, it is not required that I can move in both directions but rather: *quo magis in unam propendeo eo liberius* (the more I incline to the one, the freer I am). Here the Augustinian concept of freedom comes to the fore: the more primordially the *propensio* is for the *bonum*, the more authentic the freedom of acting ... I am genuinely free if I go towards what I understand" (GA 17: 151, italics in original). So freedom of indifference is only the bad textbook version of Cartesian freedom: the highest degree of freedom is achieved when the human will is fully enlightened by our understanding of the good. That my will should be "inclined," as opposed to "determined," makes this higher degree of freedom consistent with its lower form by allowing it to fit the model of free choice as having alternative possibilities central to *liberium arbitrium*: in theory, one could refuse to follow the inclination, although there is little reason to do so.[10]

This characterization of ontological freedom as a "propensio" toward authenticity is interesting in at least two respects. First, in Cartesian fashion, it suggests that freedom is structurally inclined toward authenticity. Seen on the background of the tripartite structure of care, that is, "facticity (thrownness), existence (projection), and falling" (284), such inclination could have the functional role of preventing ontic fallenness from being unavoidable by providing a counterweight to falling as an "ontologico-existential structure" (176). If falling is indeed the "downward plunge (*Absturz*) ... [which] constantly tears the understanding away from the projecting of authentic possibilities" (178), then the counter pull of ontological freedom as a *propensio toward* authenticity may be what enables Dasein to resist falling and to make the existentiell choice of ontic freedom. Second, the reference to Augustine suggests that authenticity is Dasein's good (since, for the early Augustine of the *De Libero Arbitrio* (c. 387 AD), at least the will is naturally inclined toward the good, although in its post-lapsarian state, the latter has become harder to see and to understand).[11] This confirms that, as pointed out by T. Carman,[12] Heidegger's views on authenticity are not neutral but evaluative. It may also help in answering the somewhat vexed question of why Dasein should be authentic, at least formally: there is no need for a specific motivation if Dasein is structurally inclined toward authenticity simply by virtue of its transcending toward the world and toward itself. Note, however, that this suggestion comes at the cost of the possible reintroduction of a form of essentialism. The claim that ontological freedom is a *propensio* to authenticity suggests that Dasein can derive *a priori* ethical guidance from its very constitution. But the idea that Dasein should have such a constitution is in tension with Heidegger's pronouncements about Dasein's essence residing in its existence (see, e.g., 12). Furthermore, Heidegger's account of authenticity goes beyond a transcendentally inclined reading, which would understand the concept of essence in a non-metaphysical way – that is, as a set of existential conditions that must apply on anything that is Dasein rather than as the core properties of a substance. The idea that Dasein is inclined toward authenticity by virtue of being ontologically free represents a further step in that it involves a moral, and not just transcendental,

form of normativity. It does not simply uncover the existential conditions on being Dasein, it also tells us what Dasein ought to be. Perhaps
Heidegger is right to make this claim, but he provides no argument
for it and does not say anything more about ontological freedom as a
propensio.

Regardless of the status of ontological freedom, anxiety also gives us
our first insight into existentiell freedom: it is "the freedom of choosing
[oneself] and taking hold of [oneself]" (188). Such choice is further specified by several passages as a "choice to choose oneself": thus Dasein
must "make up for not choosing ... [by] choosing to make this choice"
(268). Its "finite freedom ... 'is' only in having chosen to choose such
a choice" (285), and conversely one must "choose the choice which
makes one free" (385). This peculiar, doubled structure is echoed in *The
Metaphysical Foundations of Logic* (GA 26) by the oft mentioned idea
of "choosing oneself *expressly*" or of making an *"express* choice" (GA
26: 244, my italics). So why would it not be enough for existentiell freedom that Dasein should simply choose itself, as in Kierkegaard? A first
answer is that the doubled structure allows Heidegger to account for the
difference between authenticity, inauthenticity, and undifferentiatedness in a way a single choice could not. To see this, it is useful to look
at the double choice in the negative. Call the first and second choices
"C1" and "C2" respectively.[13] Anxiety makes manifest the possibility
of performing C1(C2), which §40 suggests (and we shall explore further)
is a necessary condition for authenticity. But Dasein could very well
choose *not* to choose itself [C1~(C2)]. Although this would not result
in the sought-after existentiell modification, it would still be a choice,
and it would still have transformative power. Indeed, once Dasein has
seen in anxiety that there is a choice to be made, it cannot return to its
pre-anxiety state. Yet explicit awareness of its having shied away from
the choice of the self C2 would be painful, for it would reveal to Dasein
that it is not up to embracing an authentic way of life. So if Dasein
chooses in C1 not to perform C2, presumably because it is too hard or
the cost is too high, the only way it can avoid facing its open disavowal
of existentiell freedom is to deceive itself into taking itself as a sort of
being who does not need to choose at all – an attitude that Sartre will
expound on as bad faith.[14] Thus the choice not to perform C2 can be seen
as involving the following steps (separated for clarity's sake): (1) Dasein
pre-reflectively understands the double choice disclosed by anxiety as
threatening and difficult; (2) this affect hints at something unpleasant
about Dasein, perhaps that it is not resolute enough to make such a
choice; (3) to prevent these negative affects and what they express from
coming to awareness, Dasein persuades itself that there is no choice to
be made (most likely by understanding itself as causally determined by

its idiosyncrasies and a situation it cannot change).[15] Consequently, it exonerates itself from all responsibility in the matter, but at the cost of an intentional misinterpretation its own ontological make-up and thus of inauthenticity.[16]

So anxious Dasein can choose to choose itself [$C_1(C_2)$] and become existentielly free, or choose not to choose itself [$C_1{\sim}(C_2)$] and become self-deceived. But the double choice opens up yet another, important option: it is equally possible and even common for Dasein not to perform C_2, but this time *without having chosen to do so* {${\sim}[C_1(C_2 \oplus {\sim}C_2)]$}, simply because the possibility of C_1 hasn't been disclosed to it.[17] Then Dasein is not self-deceived but, in Heidegger's words, "undifferentiated": it is absorbed in its world and in particular with "being with one another insofar as the latter is guided by idle talk, curiosity and ambiguity" (175). Not having been faced with explicit anxiety, it does not have enough self-awareness to realize, even at a pre-reflective level, that there is a choice to be made. Note that it doesn't follow from this that the "undifferentiated" mode is evaluatively neutral. In line with the deflationary account of self-deception presented by Mele, undifferentiatedness can be construed as a motivated failure of self-knowledge.[18] On such a picture, the undifferentiated mode is also inauthentic but to a lesser degree, the significant difference with fully fledged inauthenticity being that undifferentiatedness does not involve a violation of Dasein's epistemic standards, nor any deceptive intent: Dasein is motivated by its desire to maintain the more comfortable status quo of its immersion in the They into failing to see that it has a choice to make. But it is not aware of this failure to see and does not intend it. By contrast, $C_1({\sim}C_2)$ involves both the pre-reflective awareness of the double choice and an intentional attempt to repress both this awareness and Dasein's choice not to choose itself. Significantly, the watershed line between weaker and stronger forms of inauthenticity is the face to face with the double choice brought about by anxiety.

So the doubling of the choice is crucial in two respects. First, it allows Heidegger to distinguish between more passive cases of existentiell indifferentiation and more active cases of self-deception – in other words, between absorption as the ontic consequence of falling, on the one hand, and Dasein's "fleeing in the face of itself" (184), on the other. This helps explain Heidegger's well-known pronouncement according to which "this potentiality for being [existence], as one which is in each case mine, is [ontologically] free either for authenticity [$C_1(C_2)$] or for inauthenticity [$C_1{\sim}(C_2)$] or for a mode in which neither of these has been differentiated {${\sim}[C_1(C_2 \oplus {\sim}C_2)]$}" (232). Second, and importantly, the doubling shows that the ability to choose is a necessary but *non-sufficient* condition for existentiell freedom. If Dasein performs C_1

but not C2, it still chooses. Yet it is not existentielly free: it is enthralled more deeply than it was before, this time not by blind conformity to the They but by its own self-deception. Thus existentiell freedom requires one to make the *right* choice. To understand what this entails, I shall turn to Kierkegaard.

WHAT IS INVOLVED IN THE CHOICE? HEIDEGGER AND KIERKEGAARD

The Metaphysical Foundations of Logic mentions Kierkegard's "talk of choosing oneself and of the individual" and states that, although Kierkegaard's "purpose is not ours," this "doesn't prevent us from learning from him but obliges us to learn what he has to offer" (GA 26: 246). So what did Heidegger learn from Kierkegaard and his various pseudonyms about the choice of the self and its relation to freedom? I shall suggest that he reinterpreted four important ideas: (a) freedom consists in a specific choice which (b) is paradoxically transformative of the self and (c) works through the self-ascription of responsibility (d) in a "transparent" manner. I'll discuss each of these in turn, bearing in mind that my purpose is not to analyze Kierkegaard's views for their own sake but in relation to Heidegger's.

Throughout the second letter in *Either/Or*, Judge William repeatedly states that to choose oneself is to become free: "this choice is freedom"[19] and whoever makes it "possesses himself as posited by himself – i.e., as chosen, as free."[20] Freedom resides in a specific kind of self-relation, which is brought into existence by the choice. Yet this process is hard to understand because it said to both transform the individual and leave him unchanged: "the self that he chooses in this way is infinitely concrete, for it is he himself, and yet it is absolutely different from his former self, because he has chosen it absolutely. This self had not existed before, because it came into existence through the choice, and yet it has existed, for it was indeed 'himself.'"[21] One way to untangle the paradox is to borrow Paul Ricoeur's distinction between two kinds of identity: "identity-idem" and "identity-ipse."[22] The first is numerical, quantitative, and consists in the possession of a certain number of fixed features (such as being a certain size, a certain shape, etc.). It allows for the identification/recognition of a particular individual from the third-person point of view. By contrast, the second is qualitative and consists in this individual's reflexive self-relation. This self-relation is interpretative, fluid, largely unreflective, and first personal. So from the quantitative perspective of identity-idem, the choice indeed leaves everything as it is: the individual "remains himself, exactly the same as before, down to the most insignificant feature."[23] Yet from the qualitative standpoint of identity-ipse, the self-relation is radically modified: "and yet he becomes another, for the choice penetrates everything and changes it."[24] The reason for this is that by choosing himself, the individual acquires a "transparent" self-understanding and makes the leap of taking responsibility for what and who he is. Thus "the ethical individual is transparent to himself."[25] Yet the "sober reflecting about oneself" through which self-knowledge is acquired is performed with the quasi-biblical aim of "rendering an account of every careless word that is spoken."[26] As a result, "the individual, then, becomes conscious as this specific individual with these capacities, these inclinations, these drives, these passions, influenced by this specific social milieu, as this specific product of a specific environment. But *as he becomes aware of all this, he takes upon himself responsibility for it all* ... And this choice is freedom."[27]

So the main function of the choice of the self is the self-ascription of responsibility: "not until a person in his choice has taken himself upon himself, has put on himself, has totally interpenetrated himself so that *every movement he makes is accompanied by a consciousness of responsibility for himself* – not until then has a person chosen himself ethically."[28] There are of course many significant differences with *Being and Time*, several of which are linked to the predominance of religious and salvific concerns in Kierkegaard's thought – in particular, the Judge's version of the choice of the self is linked to repentance and to the search for the absolute – two aspects I have left out. Yet Heidegger takes up the crucial idea that existentiell freedom resides in a transformation of the self-relation through the self-ascription of responsibility. Before I explore the form taken by this in *Being and Time*, however, let me point out two important and problematic differences between Heidegger's double choice and even my largely secularized account of the single choice in *Either/Or*. The first one has to do with the proposed resolution of the paradox of the self being both presupposed and produced by the choice. As we have seen, Ricoeur's distinction between identity-idem and identity-ipse is helpful to understand William's view that the choosing individual can both be the same and another. Yet it is of little help to understand Heidegger's choice to choose oneself, quite simply because the ontic features picked out by identity-idem were never part of Dasein's ontological make-up in the first place. Like Ulrich in Musil's novel, Dasein has no "qualities," no present-at-hand properties it could legitimately identify with. So the paradox, and the associated issue of who makes the choice, will need re-examining – and what we have to take responsibility *for* is bound to be significantly different. Second, the Judge's notion of the "transparency" required for the choice is highly reflective: it is a "sober *reflecting* upon oneself," a "consciousness" or "awareness" of one's own features. Or yet, most explicitly, "the person who lives ethically has seen himself, knows himself, penetrates his whole concretion with his consciousness."[29] Judge William qualifies this by explaining that such self-knowledge "is not simply contemplation" but a "collecting of oneself which itself is an action" (ibid.). In other words, the reflecting is not performed from a detached perspective but is performative in that it transforms the individual's sense of identity ipse. Still, the predominance of the vocabulary of epistemic clarity seems too strong to ignore, and whatever Heidegger means by "transparency" in relation to the choice to choose oneself, it is very unlikely to share this high threshold of reflective awareness.

THE CHOICE TO CHOOSE AS THE TRANSPARENT SELF-ASCRIPTION OF RESPONSIBILITY

After having been introduced in the anxiety section, the theme of the double choice is developed in the sections on conscience and guilt. It is presented as the answer to the search for an existentiell "attestation" to the possibility of authenticity, itself analyzed formally in the sections about death. Whereas anxiety presents Dasein with the choice of freedom, the later sections explain how Dasein may actually come to make that choice, and what is involved in it. Importantly, they do not do so by explaining what the second choice, C_2, might be, independently from whether C_1 is made in the first place; it is not a matter of first clarifying a particular option for further deliberation. For Heidegger, hearing the call of conscience, which specifies the meaning of C_2, means performing C_1: "to the call of conscience there corresponds a possible hearing. Our understanding of the appeal unveils itself as our wanting to have a conscience. But *in this phenomenon* lies that existentiell choosing which we seek – the choosing to choose a kind of being one's self" (270, my italics). So anxious Dasein may perform C_1 and reject C_2 without understanding exactly the implications of the latter, but it cannot perform C_2 without performing C_1. This is another reason why the doubling is important: it points toward this peculiar aspect of C_1, namely the fact that genuinely understanding its object means choosing it. This may be seen as the practical consequence of ontological freedom as *propensio*: just as for Descartes, seeing the good is choosing it because our nature inclines us toward it, so for Heidegger understanding the call to C_2 is making the choice C_1 because we have an ontological inclination toward authenticity: "in understanding the call, Dasein is *in thrall* to its ownmost possibility of existence. *It has chosen itself*" (287, my italics). We knew from above that existentiell freedom lies in making the *right* choice. We now discover that such a choice is not a matter of deliberation, of weighing pros and cons, but of understanding oneself in the right way and being "in thrall" to such understanding, two aspects I'll come back to when discussing objections.

So what is the right choice? As suggested above, Heidegger takes from Kierkegaard the idea that freedom resides in the transparent self-ascription of responsibility: "understanding the call is choosing ... What is chosen is *having a* conscience as being free for one's ownmost being guilty" (288, Heidegger's italics). A few pages before, Heidegger had referred the "ordinary significations" of "being guilty" (*schuldig*), namely "having debts to someone" and "having responsibility for something" to "a kind of behaviour which we call '*making oneself responsible*'" (282, Heidegger's italics). Note the transition from the passive ("having responsibility") to the active ("making oneself responsible"): responsibility is not simply something that befalls Dasein but something it must take hold of. To understand this, it is helpful to distinguish between third-person accountability and first-person responsibility, and this in the light of the difference between ontological and ontic forms of freedom. Because it is ontologically free and thus has a specific, norm-responsive kind of agency, Dasein is accountable for what it does and can legitimately be praised or blamed for it. Thus "in the projection of the for the sake of as such, Dasein gives itself the primordial commitment [*Bindung*]. Freedom makes Dasein the ground of its essence, responsible [*verbindlich*] to itself, or more exactly, gives itself the possibility of commitment" (GA 26: 247). Ontological freedom is the ground of responsibility. But the end of the quote introduces an interesting amendment by stating that ontological freedom gives Dasein "the *possibility* of commitment" only. This needs to be actualized by the choice to choose itself so that Dasein becomes responsible *in its own eyes*: then "Dasein commits itself to a capability of being itself as able to be with others in the ability to be amongst extant things. *Selfhood is free responsibility for and toward itself*" (ibid., my italics). Note that the existentiell commitment lies primarily in the choice of a potentiality for being ("being itself") rather than the adoption of a particular course of action: it is the "choosing to choose a *kind of being one's self*" (270, my italics).[30] In other words, the choice to choose makes Dasein responsible not only for what it does but also for what it is in the pressing ahead into a particular possibility, and this is what we need to explore now.

As we saw, for Kierkegaard, too, the choice of the self involved the self-ascription of responsibility for what we are, not just what we do. But what we are was played out as a collection of features (e.g., psychological, physical, or social) that the individual had to take reflective stock of and own up to by acknowledging them as his. Yet, for Heidegger, Dasein *is* none of these features on the mode of presence at hand: it is the projection of its existentiell possibilities, or abilities-to-be, constrained by thrownness and falling. So when a particular possibility faces Dasein with the double choice, what it needs to take responsibility for is not a set of present-at-hand properties but the very way in which it deploys this possibility in relation to its understanding of itself and of its situation. Yet from the undifferentiated point of view of the pre-choice Dasein, the natural assumption is precisely to view itself as indeed endowed with objective features for which it is not responsible: in Blattner's terms, it tends to understand its ability-characteristics as state-characteristics.[31] Thus the choice of choosing oneself simultaneously involves two aspects. On the one hand, breaking away from undifferentiatedness by understanding pre-reflectively that I don't have any essence in the traditional sense of inalienable properties which, in conjunction with various empirical laws, would determine my comportment causally. "Dasein is, *in its existing*, the basis of its potentiality for being" (284, Heidegger's italics). What I "am" is what I understand myself to be in relation to the constraints of falling and thrownness (such as a constitutive tendency to avoid anxiety for the former and bodily characteristics, social environment, cultural milieu, etc., for the latter) focused by a particular possibility, and this not through conscious reflection, but through existentiell projection. On the other hand, choosing to choose oneself entails making the leap of realizing that, since I don't have any essence, I must take responsibility for my understanding of myself and of the possibility I am deploying, and this, without ever being caused to do so: "the self, which as such has to lay the basis for itself, can never get that basis into its [causal] power; and yet, as existing, it *must* take over being a basis" (ibid., my italics). Note that there is no relation of logical entailment between the two aspects: Dasein could very well understand pre-reflectively that it is not causally determined by anything and decide that its life is going to be a free for all, with no responsibility involved from anyone and especially not from itself. This is why Dasein needs to be "called," and why answering involves a leap.

Thus the self-ascription of responsibility is not a logical conclusion but a response to an ethical demand, a response that is *necessitated* by nothing but by which Dasein freely owns up to itself. But then where does the call derive its normative force from (Heidegger's "must")? As we saw, Heidegger himself links it to the idea that ontological freedom is a *propensio* toward authenticity, although this is not without its difficulties. Another answer, more relativistic but perhaps less metaphysically laden, could be that the demand for responsibility is predominant in our culture, and that in taking responsibility for itself, Dasein is responding to an important aspect of its normative environment. This, however, may call for a further question: if Dasein is simply responding to the environing normative pressure, how then is this a free choice? How different is that from just doing what One does? Yet there is a difference between responding to normative pressure without knowing that one is pressurized into doing so, and responding while being pre-reflectively aware that one's comportment is a *response* to one's normative environment. This difference is, again, what the doubled structure of the choice brings to the fore: the first attitude is that of ~[C1(C2 s ~C2)] or C1~(C2) Dasein (i.e., undifferentiated or inauthentic); the second, that of the C1(C2) Dasein. In the latter case, while the self-ascription of responsibility happens in C2, the performing of C1 indicates Dasein's pre-reflective awareness that, in taking responsibility for itself in the pressing ahead into a particular possibility, it is responding to its normative environment *as such*, rather than just going with the flow.

The choice of choosing oneself thus involves a degree of what Heidegger, following Kierkegaard, calls "transparency." Significantly, the theme is first introduced in relation to freedom: "there is also the possibility of a kind of solicitude which ... helps the Other to become transparent to himself *in* his care and to become *free for* it" (122, Heidegger's italics). The idea of a link between freedom and transparency is taken up by the next occurrence of the notion: "Dasein is the possibility of being free *for* its ownmost potentiality for being. Its being-possible is transparent to itself in different possible ways and degrees" (144). The combined quotes suggest that existentiell freedom requires a significant degree of transparency. So what does Heidegger mean by it? As we saw, for the Judge, transparency is the full epistemic clarity afforded to the individual by the reflective scrutiny of his character and deeds. But not so for Heidegger. In the section on understanding, he characterizes Dasein's projective openness to the world as a form of existential "sight": "Dasein *is* this sight equiprimordially in each of those basic ways of its being" (146, Heidegger's italics – he mentions as examples circumspection and solicitude). Sight is not thematic knowing: it is Dasein's practical grasp of a particular situation on the background of its pre-reflective comprehension of itself and its world. Transparency is a particular kind of sight: "the sight which is related primarily and on the whole to existence we call '*transparency*' [*Durchsichtigkeit*]" (ibid.). Thus the proper object of transparency is not ontic but ontological: it is the structure of existence itself – transparency is Dasein's pre-reflective grasp of its own ontological make-up. In Heidegger's words, "it is not a matter of perceptually tracking down and inspecting a point called 'the self' but rather one of seizing upon the full disclosedness of being-in-the-world *throughout all* the constitutive items which are essential to it, and doing so with understanding" (ibid., Heidegger's italics). No wonder then that the development of such transparency should intrinsically be linked to existentiell freedom: without it, Dasein would keep understanding itself in terms of natural or social features, which in turn would make the self-ascription of responsibility impossible.

Note, however, that the transparency required for existentiell freedom is not the highest possible degree. This would require an anticipatory understanding of my existence as a finite temporal whole, which can only be provided by being-toward-death: "the existential structure of such being [toward death] proves to be the ontologically constitutive state of Dasein's potentiality for being a whole" (234). There is much debate on what such "wholeness" might mean for Dasein, from Guignon's psychological account as a narrative that would allow authentic Dasein to "live each moment as an integral component of the overall story it is shaping in its actions,"[32] to Carman's reinterpretation as the "wholeheartedness" of Dasein's commitment to itself. In my view, Heidegger's emphasis on transparency as an *ontological* kind of sight significantly complicates psychological accounts (either of freedom or authenticity).[33] But either way, existentiell freedom per se is not enough to satisfy the requirement of total transparency: only "when one has an understanding of being-towards-death – towards death as one's *ownmost possibility* – one's potentiality for being becomes authentic and *wholly* transparent" (307, second italics mine). The choice to choose oneself allows Dasein to take responsibility for itself as it presses ahead into a particular possibility. But it does not disclose to Dasein that death impends at every moment of its life and that each and every of its possibilities, including the current one, may very well not come to be. By contrast, full ontological transparency reveals that, in S. Mulhall's words, it must "make its every projection upon an existentiell possibility in the light of an awareness of itself as mortal."[34] This is why existentiell freedom is a necessary but non-sufficient condition for authenticity: "making up for not choosing signifies *choosing to make this choice* – deciding for a potentiality for being and making this decision from one's own self. In choosing to make this choice, Dasein *makes possible*, first and foremost, its authentic potentiality for being" (268, Heidegger's italics). In existentiell freedom, the choice of choosing oneself is made wholeheartedly in the sense that Dasein takes without reservation as much responsibility for itself as is allowed by its finitude and the relative degree of ontological transparency achieved. Authenticity requires the further step of making the same self-commitment, but with a pre-reflective awareness of the radical fragility of each and every commitment.[35] Should this happen, then freedom is fully expressed and becomes an "*impassioned* freedom towards death – *a freedom which has been released from the*

*illusions of the 'they,' and which is factical, certain of itself and anx-
ious"* (266, Heidegger's italics). Such "passion" is needed because this
intensification of ontological transparency (the "release from the illusions of the They") makes the choice to choose oneself even harder: it
forces Dasein both to understand that it is temporally finite *and* not to
succumb to the nihilistic temptation of holding this finitude against the
very possibility of commitment. "Only being-free *for* death ... pushes
existence into its finitude" (384), and with the awareness of finitude
come the twin shadows of despair and resignation. Being free for death,
the highest form of freedom, is an implicit response to this risk, which
involves both the acknowledgement of the relative powerlessness
entailed by finitude and the – equally relative but intensely passionate –
overcoming of such powerlessness through the choice to choose a self
that can still own up to itself *even though* it has a pre-reflective awareness of its own limitations. Thus "if Dasein, by anticipation, lets death
become powerful in itself, as free for death, Dasein understands itself in
its own *superior power*, the power of its finite freedom, and that in this
freedom, which 'is' only in its having chosen to make such a choice, it
can take over the *powerlessness* of abandonment to its having done so"
(384, Heidegger's italics).

REPLIES TO OBJECTIONS

There are, however, three objections pending: (a) the idea of a
world-defining choice is contradictory, (b) the choosing self is both presupposed and produced by the choice, and (c) the temporality of the
choice is unclear. I shall consider these in turn.

As far as the first is concerned, the objection seems simply misplaced,
both for Kierkegaard and for Heidegger. A contrast with Sartre's radical
choice may help bring this out. For Sartre, choosing one's fundamental
project involves the creation of all of one's values. Such creation is a voluntaristic act by which "freedom makes [value] exist as value by the sole
fact of recognising it as such."[36] This generates a vicious circle because
the choosing individual is required to bring into existence *by* his choice
the very values which are required *for* such a choice: "it is this original
choice which originally creates all causes and all motives which can
guide us to partial actions; it is this which arranges the world with its
meaning, its instrumental complexes, and its coefficient of adversity."[37]
Yet if there is nothing in the pre-choice world to derive some normative
orientation from, then the very idea of a choice becomes contradictory:
no choice can be made without some commitment to preexisting (even
conflicting) values that will exert a draw on us and give us reasons for
choosing. So the Sartrian choice, instead of providing the radically new

and free values Sartre claims for it, becomes groundless.[38] Thus Dreyfus and Rubin's criticism, if it were addressed to *Sartre*, would be well taken. Yet there is nothing, either in the Judge's letter or in *Being and Time*, which points toward this criterion-less choice or to the creation of entirely new values by a sheer act of will. For the Judge, the choice of the self requires the individual to reflect on his idiosyncrasies and his relation to his social environment in order to take responsibility for it all. But this self-ascription of responsibility, while it radically trans-forms the individual's self-relation, leaves the normative framework intact: "he has his place in the world; in freedom he himself chooses his place – that is, he chooses *this* place."[39] In a similar way, for Heidegger, the choice to choose oneself does not involve a radical reconfiguration of the normative framework opened up by ontological freedom: it bears on the here and now, and requires Dasein to take responsibility for itself *as it is*: "in the express self-choice there is essentially the complete self-commitment, *not to where it might not yet be, but to where and how it already is, qua Dasein*" (GA 26: 245, my italics). Such "complete self-commitment" is only possible on the background of Dasein's cur-rent understanding of its world and its major normative orientations. Thus the demand that one should take responsibility for oneself has been central to our culture at least since the Enlightenment, arguably for much longer.[40] The choice to choose oneself may *modify* it to some extent, for example by requiring that Dasein should take responsibility not just for what it does but for what it "is" in the pressing ahead of a particular possibility. But this does not involve the *ex nihilo* creation of the new normative framework involved in radical choice. The point of existentiell freedom is not to bootstrap Dasein into a brave new world of private values but, as we saw, to foster its pre-reflective awareness, amongst other things, *that* it lives in a shared normative framework so that it can take responsibility for its understanding of it.

The second objection needs reformulating, as it was originally made in relation to the choice of the self. It faces us with a two-pronged dilemma: call S_1 the self who makes the choice to choose itself, and S_2 the self who is chosen. In some sense, S_1 and S_2 must be the same, for otherwise Dasein could not be said to choose to choose *itself*. Yet if the choice is to set Dasein free existentielly, then it must be genuinely transformative, and therefore S_1 and S_2 cannot be the same. So either I genuinely choose myself but then the choice is not transformative and thus pointless, or the choice is transformative but then I cannot choose myself. Can Heidegger get out of this impasse? He can, provided that one doesn't collapse the double structure into a single choice. Recall that we are talking about the conjunction of *two* choices, C_1 and C_2. S_1 is the self that makes the first choice C_1. Yet the proper object of that choice is *not* S2 but the second choice C2: thus in Heidegger's version, S1 was never *meant* to choose S2 directly, which prevents the dilemma from arising. But there is more to the story. As we have seen, the choice C1 is per se transformative of S1, whether C2 is performed or not: if Dasein chooses *not* to make the choice C2, then it becomes self-deceived (call that S1'). If it chooses C2, then it is transformed into S2 but by virtue of having made that first choice C1, not because it has chosen itself. So S2 takes responsibility for itself by making the choice C2, which thus can be spelled out as "S2 chooses S2." This may look tautological from a third-person point of view, but from the first personal perspective of the choosing Dasein, the doubled structure makes manifest the reflexive (but not necessarily reflective) character of the self-ascription of responsibility. Thus the form of Heidegger's choice of the self is not the problematic "S1 chooses S2" but "S1 performs C1 and by performing C1 transforms itself into S2 who takes responsibility for itself in C2." There is indeed a transformation of S1 into S2, which is the whole point of existentiell freedom, but crucially this is mediated by the choice C1.[41]

The third objection concerns the temporality of the double choice: when is it made? Is it made in time at all? Here again, it may help to compare it briefly with Sartre's choice of the fundamental project and Kant's choice of our *Gesinnung* [disposition] in *Religion Within the Limits of Reason Alone*. In Thomas Baldwin's pithy words, for Sartre "there is no time within a man's life when he makes this choice: rather, his whole life is the choice."[42] Although it is never fully visible in any of his actions, the choice is presupposed by everything a man does. Just like a three-dimensional object is only visible through two-dimensional surfaces, our fundamental project is disclosed through our deeds but not reducible to any of them. So although it is not made at any particular time, it is involved in everything we do and allows for a holistic account of the totality of a person's life. Similarly, Kant's choice of our moral disposition was developed in relation to subjective freedom[43] to provide an ultimate account for *Willkür*'s ability to opt consistently for some maxims rather than others. Thus all our maxims ultimately point toward the adoption of an original maxim whereby we choose our *Gesinnung*. Such choice is "the subjective ground of the exercise of man's freedom in general."[44] Although it is an "intelligible action, cognizable by means of pure reason alone, apart from every temporal condition,"[45] all our empirical choices are grounded in it. As noted by Schopenhauer in his reinterpretation of Kant's choice of our intelligible character, a thief may steal all kinds of objects in his life, but each theft will point toward the same choice of his moral disposition (dishonesty). So both for Sartre and for Kant, the choice is meant to allow for moral responsibility for

actions that otherwise could be viewed as causally determined by natural laws, a feature shared by Heidegger's understanding of existentiell
freedom. But Heidegger's double choice is different from either of its
two counterparts because it is not meant to account for the intelligibility of our lives as unified totalities. As we saw, Heidegger's own sense
of the "wholeness" of our existence is not provided by freedom, but
by being-toward-death. In other words, the choice to choose oneself is
not meant to build up to an incremental picture of the self over time
through which one would acquire a sense of a person's psychological
characteristics but which would preserve freedom, as in Sartre and
Kant. Thus it makes more sense to suggest that we choose to choose
ourselves in a discrete way when we answer the call and act responsibly
in the pressing ahead of a particular possibility: the choice is made each
time my comportment exhibits a pre-reflective awareness of my ontological make up and of my owning up to it, and this without guarantee
that I shall *always* behave responsibly.

THE CHOICE TO CHOOSE AS MEDIO-PASSIVE

If these replies are convincing, then there is nothing flawed in principle to Heidegger's idea that existentiell freedom resides in a choice
to choose oneself. Yet such choice remains paradoxical. It forces us to
depart from the rationalist model of decision making and to consider a
much less voluntaristic version that, although it involves some awareness of one's own ontological make up (transparency), does not require
reflective deliberation – as we saw, C_2 is not really an option open for
prudential calculus, since truly understanding it is to make the first
choice C_1. What are we to make of this?

Heidegger is very clear that his version of the choice is not a primordial act of willing, as for Kant or Sartre. For one thing, willing itself is not
primary but dependent on the structure of care (194). More importantly,
performing $C_1(C_2)$ is tantamount to hearing the call of conscience, and
whether we hear the call is not a matter of willing ourselves to do so.
Heidegger states that it cannot be "cultivated voluntarily": one must
be "ready to be appealed to" (288). Or again: for Dasein, "becoming
free for the call" means *"understandingly letting itself be called forth"*
(287, my italics). Thus rather than the deliberative making of a decision, the choice involves a special kind of readiness, halfway between
self-possession and abandonment ("letting oneself"). Just as the call
ambiguously comes both from outside and within me, the choice seems
made *in me* almost as much as *by me*. Thus the choice is neither fully
active nor fully passive: it involves a particular kind of agency, which,
following Greek grammarians, I shall call "medio-passive."[46] So how

are we to make sense of such a choice, since it is so far removed from the ordinary conception? It may help to note that medio-passivity is characteristic of *understanding* in general. Whether I understand something or not is not up to me (alas). Yet I have a measure of control over this in that I can lay the ground appropriately, for example by working very hard at familiarizing myself with the relevant material or bringing about the right kind of circumstances. Not doing so would significantly decrease the chances of the dawning of comprehension. So up to a point, I am responsible for what I understand, precisely because if I don't prepare myself for it, it is quite possible and even likely that understanding will not blossom. Even though it is not fully dependent on me, this understanding is an achievement that I can be praised for. And as with understanding, so with the choice to choose oneself – since the latter is largely a matter of self-understanding, it is hardly surprising that it should share this medio-passive feature. Ultimately, hearing the call is not up to me: yet I can take some responsibility for doing so in the sense that, unless I try to attune myself in the right way, it may never be heard at all.

Yet there is more: the choice of existentiell freedom is not just a choice I'm accountable for from a third-person standpoint. It is that by which, in Heidegger's terms, I "take hold" of myself in the first place. Yet given the medio-passive modality of the choice, such "holding" cannot be the active and explicit self-positing of freedom intended by both Sartre and Kant. Nor can the responsibility involved be absolute, since the choice itself is not fully within Dasein's control. Dasein is responsible *up to a point*, and this is as good as it gets. To demand more would be to exceed the limits of Dasein's finitude. Still, how do we understand such responsibility, limited as it is? It may help to do so *via* a reconsideration of mineness. In Division I, Heidegger states that Dasein is always mine: "that being which is an *issue* for this entity in its very being, is in each case mine.... Because Dasein has *in each case mineness* [*Jemeinigkeit*], one must always use a *personal* pronoun when one addresses it" (42). At the level of ontological freedom, this formal, quasi-grammatical sense of mineness does not require any awareness from Dasein's part that its possibilities are its own: it can and does press ahead into them unreflectively, responding selflessly to the various affordances of the world in the context of its activities. Yet each time Dasein is faced with the choice of existentiell freedom, this thin sense of mineness acquires a more substantive meaning. Having achieved a degree of ontological transparency, Dasein becomes pre-reflectively aware that it is nothing but the particular possibility it is pressing ahead into. Moreover, the way it "is" this possibility is not a matter of possessing present-at-hand qualities but of projective understanding, both of the world and of itself.

It is its thrown basis "only in that it projects itself upon possibilities into which it has been thrown" (284). Dasein is called to realize that although such projection is not fully under its control, it is not either something that simply happens to it. Thus answering the call means owning up to a particular possibility in a sense that is neither merely grammatical, as previously, nor even psychological. The possibility is not Dasein's own because it can recognize itself in it, for example by intuitively seeing it as expressive of a particular character trait or by connecting it with its past – such naïve, everyday identification is precisely what is prevented by ontological transparency.[47] By contrast, the more substantive sense of mineness gained in existentiell freedom is that of pre-reflective moral appropriation: even though it is aware that it does not have full control over its projection, Dasein is still prepared to *own up* to it. This means, inter alia, that it is prepared to take the negative consequences of its pressing ahead into the possibility (if any) as consequences rather than as accidents that befall it and about which it could complain. It is also means that Dasein stands ready to answer for its choice and to make reparations to other parties should they be affected adversely by these consequences. Such pre-reflective moral appropriation, in turn, transforms the meaning of Dasein's comportment: its very pressing ahead into the relevant possibility becomes the implicit endorsement of its responsibility for doing so.

How can we tell the difference, then, between cases in which the choice of choosing oneself has or has not been made? The pre-reflective awareness of responsibility is not directly available *as such* to Dasein in the first person, because the very process whereby it would become available would transform it from pre-reflective into reflective. So I would suggest that whether Dasein is pre-reflectively aware of its responsibility for itself or not is expressed through its comportment, and can thus be observed from the third-person standpoint. This, in turn, requires a non-psychological version of expressivism. According to C. Taylor,[48] our actions are neither the result of causal or psychological determinism nor narrowly intentional. They are the expression of our self-understanding rather than the result of our executive powers, and such self-understanding is not reducible to a narrow intentional content because its meaning cannot be isolated from our wider understanding of the world. To say that an action is expressive means that the expressed content can be seen directly from the action itself, without the need for any inference: I may infer from a flashing light on a car that it's about to turn left, but I can see from the smile on someone's face that they are in a good mood. Expression itself, and not the relation between signifier and signified, is the primitive. Naturally, all of Dasein's comportment may be seen as expressive of its understanding both of itself and the world, and makes the latter publicly available. But there are some forms of comportment that seem expressive of precisely the sort of pre-reflective appropriation of responsibility that is character-istic of existentiell freedom. Perhaps a particularly clear example could be found in T. E. Lawrence's narrative in *The Mint* of how, after hav-ing returned from the Middle East and resigned from his duties at the Foreign Office, he sought to enroll himself in the RAF as J. H. Ross. Yet, at the age of thirty-six, he was barely under the age limit for enrolment, at five feet five inches almost too short, and he had to start totally from scratch. Combined with his age, the wounds received during the Arab wars made it hard for him to satisfy the harsh requirements of the RAF training program. Given his accomplishments and his fame, he could certainly have obtained a much more comfortable and lucrative posi-tion. And yet he did enroll. And not just once. After having been recog-nized and kicked out of the RAF, he *re*-enrolled, this time as T. E. Shaw and in the Royal Tanks Corps. It does not seem unreasonable to see such resolute comportment as expressive of a degree of ontological transpar-ency and the self-ascription of responsibility involved in Heidegger's choice. Lawrence did not do any of the things that his physical abili-ties, sociocultural background (he was highly educated and spoke eight languages), or previous career could have been seen to predispose him to do. Had he understood himself as causally determined by his past, it seems highly unlikely that he could have chosen such a course. Yet he appropriated this unlikely possibility and took responsibility in pressing ahead into it. This may be, to use Heidegger's expression, an "extreme model" (188); yet, for most of us, there is no need (or capability for) such heroism. Think back on your life: there are hard-to-pin-down but cru-cial moments in our existence when we are pre-reflectively aware that, even though nothing prepared us for it and there is nothing necessary about it, a possibility has opened up that calls to us in such a way that we have to make the leap of appropriating it inasmuch as we can. Such a leap is the choice of existentiell freedom.

CONCLUSION

So the choice to choose oneself is a strange beast: while it involves a pre-reflective form of self-awareness that Heidegger (following Kierkegaard) dubs "transparency," it is not an exercise in deliberation. Although it admits of an alternative possibility (to choose not to choose oneself), existentielly speaking, if we hear the call, the alternative is not there, and the double choice is made. As Kierkegaard beautifully put it, "the content of freedom is decisive for freedom to such an extent that the very truth of freedom of choice is: there must be no choice, even though there is a choice."[49] Furthermore, while the double choice is in each case made *by* Dasein, it is not entirely *up to* Dasein. It is the self-ascription of responsibility and yet it is not, as in Sartre's willful reinterpretation, an absolute self-positing of freedom whereby man would "carry the weight of the whole world on his shoulders" and be "responsible for the world and for himself as a way of being."[50] Such could only culminate – as it does indeed for Sartre – in the desire for man to be God.[51] Even when it chooses to choose itself, Dasein's responsibility remains limited to the possibility into which it now transparently presses ahead. Its understanding remains constrained by its thrownness, and the possibility it was called to needs to be one that it finds available in its world, or at least one that would make sense within it. It is not invented out of nothing – thus for Lawrence, joining the RAF was a publicly available possibility, albeit not one that would have seemed relevant in his case from the third-person standpoint. Yet if I am right in seeing his comportment as expressive of existentiell freedom, then he appropriated this possibility and made it right *for himself* by taking as much responsibility for it as is humanly possible.

But then, why, one may ask, should the choice of choosing oneself count as a form of *freedom* at all? It does not free Dasein from its thrownness, nor from the normative pressure of its environment, nor from its facticity. It does not enable Dasein to give itself its own laws nor to have full control over itself and its life – it does not make it autonomous. On the contrary, it reveals the vacuity of the rationalist ideal of absolute mastery and the pernicious way it denies the constraints of finitude by blinding us to the medio-passive character of some of the most important aspects of our lives. It shows that Dasein needs to give up on freedom as total control to realize that, in Freud's words, it is not the master in its own house and needs the call of conscience that brings the choice home to it. Yet by developing its receptivity to the pull of possibilities that cannot be disclosed without a greater degree of ontological transparency, the double choice gives Dasein more *Spielraum*, more room for maneuver. It frees it from the alleged constraints of its "nature" and expands its range of existentiell possibilities, opening up the perspective of a richer and more "experimental" life, as Nietzsche would say. At the same time, by calling Dasein to take as much responsibility for itself as these constraints allow, it prevents the risk of such a life becoming meaningless. Thus Heidegger emphasizes the limits of spontaneity by drawing attention to the importance of receptivity and departs radically from the Kantian tradition: at the end of the day, existentiell freedom is mostly a matter of understanding in its medio-passivity, not will. By transforming its self-understanding, it frees Dasein both from the indifferentiation that enthralls it to the They, and from the self-deception by which it further ensnares itself if it refuses to make the double choice. Of course, none of this is permanent: Dasein is only existentielly free in the pressing ahead of a particular possibility, and the reason why it is free does not lie in a specific ontic content for that possibility (Heidegger does not propose any "ideal of existence with any 'special content'" (266),[52] but in the *form* taken by Dasein's self-relation in this particular case. The change in the self-relation brought about by the choice to choose can fade, and Dasein can lapse into self-deception. Such fragility is the hallmark of finitude; yet perhaps it is also a blessing, and the possibility of making the choice again and again can per se be seen as a reason for hope.

NOTES

1 Note that, etymologically, the two are very closely related: *ek-sistere* means to stand forth from a static or standing position (*stare*) and *trans-scandere* means "to climb over or beyond." In both cases, the prefix indicates a dehiscence from a fixed or enclosed position.
2 Lest one should put too much weight on the word "ownmost," the rest of the passage goes thus: "for the sake of its potentiality for being, any Dasein is as it factically is. But to the extent that this being towards its potentiality for being is itself characterised by [ontological] freedom, Dasein *can* comport itself towards its possibilities, even *unwillingly*" (193, Heidegger's italics).
3 See: "within the particular comportment and ability that can spring from freedom and with which we are now solely concerned ..., something like conforming to ... or being bound to ... is possible such that what this binding binds itself to, namely beings, are announced in their binding character. And this is possible only if there is an underlying freedom that is structurally articulated in this way, and for its part articulates" (GA 29/30: 492).
4 See, e.g., "in every case Dasein, as essentially having a state of mind, has already got itself into definite possibilities. As the potentiality-for-being which it *is*, it has let such possibilities pass by; it is constantly waiving the possibilities of its being, or else it seizes upon them and makes mistakes" (144); or "projection always pertains to the full disclosedness of being-in-the-world; as potentiality-for-being, understanding has itself possibilities which are sketched out beforehand within the range of what is essentially disclosable in it" (146).
5 Hubert Dreyfus, *Being-in-the-World: A Commentary on Heidegger's* Being and Time. Division I (Cambridge, MA: MIT Press, 1991), 302.
6 Dreyfus, *Being-in-the-World*, 317.
7 Ibid.
8 Ibid. Dreyfus and Rubin's italics.
9 By "pre-reflectively aware," I mean, first, that such awareness doesn't involve any thematizing form of intentionality: it is not representational (self-)knowledge; second, that although it is not at the time reflectively available to Dasein, this awareness it is not *structurally* inaccessible to it. Dasein may retrospectively become aware that it acted with a pre-reflective awareness of its having made the choice of the self, perhaps when challenged about the reasons for an action by someone else or through introspection.

Equally, such full awareness may never arise, or the reasons for its actions may never be fully articulated, and Dasein would still be existentielly free. Yet the possibility of such awareness arising explains why the choice cannot be said to be unconscious.

10 See, e.g., Letter to Father Mesland, February 9, 1645: "When a very obvious reason inclines us toward something, although from a moral point of view we can hardly go the other way, absolutely speaking we still could. Indeed, it is always possible for us to refrain from pursuing a clearly known good or to accept an obvious truth, provided that we think that it is a good thing that we should assert our freedom in this way" (my translation).

11 Note that by the time Augustine wrote the *De Civitate Dei* (427 AD), his views had changed significantly: the consequences of the Fall are now seen as so severe that the human will has been irremediably damaged and is only free to sin. Ignorance has become an unsurpassable obstacle and only grace can transfigure our will toward the good again. See, e.g., John Rist, "Augustine on Free Will and Predestination," in *Augustine: A Collection of Critical Essays*, ed. R. A. Markus (Garden City: Anchor Books, 1972), 223 ff.

12 Taylor Carman, *Heidegger's Analytic: Interpretation, Discourse, and Authenticity in* Being and Time (Cambridge: Cambridge University Press, 2003).

13 It may be tempting to conceive of the two choices in analogy to desires, in terms of a first- and second-order hierarchy (respectively, choosing oneself and choosing to choose oneself). However, there are reasons to think that such temptation should be resisted. In the case of preferences, desires, etc., the second order desire is most often formed *in response* to a first-order desire: thus I may desire to read a novel and form the second-order desire to work on this paper instead. But in the case of freedom, it would not be true to say that the "second-order" choice is formed in response to the making of the "first-order" choice; it is not the case that I need to choose myself first in order to have a choice about that. On the contrary, the "second-order" choice would *open up the possibility* of making the "first-order" one, hence the breakdown of the analogy.

14 Self-deception is a notoriously problematic topic in that it is equally hard to describe the phenomenon appropriately and to present a coherent account of the psychological factors that supposedly make it possible (on the so-called "static" and "dynamic" puzzles that challenge any account of self-deception, see, e.g., A. Mele, *Self-Deception Unmasked* (Princeton: Princeton University Press, 2001), 6 ff. Furthermore, the sort of description and explanation available varies considerably depending on how weak or strong the cases envisaged are: instances of weak self-deception are very close to wishful thinking in that they can be construed as requiring no self-deceptive intent and no violation of our normal epistemic standards. See, e.g., A. Mele, "Real Self-Deception," in *Behavioural and Brain Sciences* 20 (1997): 91 ff. By contrast, strong cases are often said to exhibit both an intention to deceive oneself (although it does not take the self-defeating form of a deliberative choice) and a failure of reflective self-knowledge. For an illuminating account of the structure of strong self-deception, see S. Gardner, *Irrationality and the Philosophy of Psychoanalysis* (Cambridge: Cambridge University Press 2006), 17–32. According to Gardner, strong

self-deception can be distinguished both from its weaker counterpart (i.e., motivated self-misrepresentation) and from neurosis by two key features: the first is that it requires an intention to deceive oneself ("a subject is self deceived when he believes one thing in order not to believe another ... Self-deception is a structure of motivated self-misrepresentation in which S and S' are beliefs and the process occurs through an intention of the subject" (Gardner, *Irrationality*, 19). The second is that strong self-deception involves two distinct beliefs: one that is false but useful to the subject, and another that is true but painful ("let's call the psychological states S and S' which are involved in strong self-deception the promoted and buried beliefs respectively," ibid., 21). For a discussion and defense of these two claims, see Gardner, *Irrationality*, 23–6. Note that in the case of C1(~C2), the intentional structure of the choice C1 suggests that the appropriate model is that of strong self-deception.

15 Note that the process differs from sublimation in that the negative affect is not displaced or discharged by being transformed into another emotion or attached to another object. Although it is not recognized as such, the negative affect remains (and keeps motivating the process of self-deception).

16 The whole process is made logically possible by the fact that none of these three steps is reflectively available to Dasein at the time. There are several possible types of explanation for such lack of availability. Subsystem theories such as Davidson's and Pears' suggest that in cases when the coming to awareness of a particular belief would cause significant anxiety to an individual, a subsystem is set up within the mind that, unbeknownst to the main system, manipulates the latter so as to insulate it from that belief. See D. Davidson, "Deception and Division," in *The Multiple Self*, ed. J. Elster (Cambridge: Cambridge University Press), 79–92; and D. Pears, *Motivated Irrationality* (Oxford: Oxford University Press, 1985). As pointed out by Poellner, another – in my view, preferable – account can be found in Sartre's distinction between thetic and non-thetic forms of awareness. See P. Poellner, "Self-Deception, Consciousness and Value," in *Hidden Resources*, ed. D. Zahavi, special issue of the *Journal for Consciousness Studies* 10–11 (2004): 44–65. While the former is fully reflective and thus cannot fail to be noticed by the subject, the second is pre-reflective and easily overlooked. The reason for such ease is that for Sartre self-deception (as a psychological form of ontological bad faith) also involves a pre-reflective commitment from the part of the subject not to submit certain aspects of herself or her life to reflective scrutiny (what Sartre calls the "original project" of bad faith, see J.-P. Sartre, *Being and Nothingness*, trans. H. Barnes (London: Methuen 1969), 67–8.

17 This is a significant difference with Sartre, for whom the (single-order) choice of the self is unavoidable: "the choice is absurd, not because it is without reason but because there never has been any possibility of not choosing oneself." Sartre, *Being and Nothingness*, 479.

18 See, e.g., Mele, "Real Self-Deception," 91 ff. A standard example is that of the anxious husband whose anxiety and desire to be reassured about his marriage motivate him to disregard potential evidence of deceitful behavior from his wife and to over-interpret elements in her conduct that may assuage his worries.

19 S. Kierkegaard, *Either/Or Vol. II*, eds. and trans. H. V. and E. H. Hong (Princeton: Princeton University Press, 1987), 251.

20 Ibid., 223.

21 Ibid., 215.

22 See P. Ricoeur, *Soi-même comme un autre* (Paris: Seuil, 1990).

23 Kierkegaard, *Either/Or*, 223.

24 Ibid.

25 Ibid., 258.

26 Ibid., 223.

27 Ibid., 251, my italics. Judge William draws a contrast with the mystic who "chooses himself abstractedly and therefore lacks transparency" (ibid., 248). Rather than acquiring concrete self-knowledge, the mystic identifies with humanity as a type and is thus unable to choose and take responsibility for himself as an individual.

28 Ibid., 248, my italics.

29 Ibid., 258.

30 See also "in understanding the call, Dasein lets its ownmost self take action in-itself *in terms of that potentiality for being which it has chosen*. Only so can it *be* answerable" (288, my italics).

31 W. Blattner, *Heidegger's Temporal Idealism* (Cambridge: Cambridge University Press, 1999), 34 ff.

32 C. Guignon, *On Being Authentic* (London: Routledge, 2004), 85.

33 Such accounts usually rely on an identification condition: Dasein must be able to recognize itself in its deeds, which conversely are viewed as expressive of who and what it is. Yet note that this condition can be satisfied by even the alienated Dasein of Division I: the They-self can perfectly well identify with what it does – such naïve identification is in fact one of the main ways in which the They-self can secure its grip on Dasein, by fostering conformism and the lack of critical awareness of Dasein's self-interpretative essence. By contrast, the sort of self-awareness characteristic of ontological transparency, while it would not make such identification impossible, would complicate it significantly because it would now involve the pre-reflective understanding that I am not naturally endowed any of the qualities that I recognize in my deeds, and that they themselves are a matter of interpretation and need to be freely owned up.

34 S. Mulhall, *Heidegger and* Being and Time (London: Routledge, 1996), 120.

35 See also "the existentiell way of taking over this guilt in resoluteness is therefore authentically accomplished only when that resoluteness, in its disclosure of Dasein, has become *so transparent that being-guilty is understood as something constant*. But this understanding is made possible only insofar as Dasein discloses to itself its potentiality for being, and discloses it right to its end ... As *being towards the end which understands* – that is to say, as anticipation of death – resoluteness becomes authentically what it can be" (305, first italics mine).

36 Sartre, *Being and Nothingness*, 38.

37 Ibid., 465. See also: "we choose the world ... in its meaning by choosing ourselves ... The value of things ... does nothing more than outline my image – that is, my choice" (ibid., 463).

38 A similar criticism can be found in the final chapter of Maurice Merleau-Ponty, *Phenomenology of Perception* (London: Routledge, 2002). A more analytic version features in Galen Strawson, "The Impossibility of Moral Responsibility," *Philosophical Studies* 75/1–2 (1994): 5–24.

39 Kierkegaard, *Either/Or*, 251 (my italics).

40 See, e.g., Aristotle, *Nichomachean Ethics*, III, 5. If one is to believe Nietzsche's account in the *Genealogy of Morals*, it is coextensive to the humanization process of proto-human forms of consciousness.

41 Note that the mediation is logical not chronological: in other words, it is not the case that Dasein first chooses C1 and only then, C2. As we saw, Dasein may opt out of the choice C1(C2) disclosed to it by anxiety: it then becomes S1' and is not in a position to choose S2 (and thus remains ensnared). But if it makes C1(C2), it does so simultaneously, by hearing the call of conscience. One can still distinguish between the two choices logically but not chronologically.

42 Thomas Baldwin, "Sartre, Kant and the Original Choice of Self," *Proceedings of the Aristotelian Society* 80 (1979–80): 33.

43 I.e., *Willkür* as free arbiter, by opposition to positive freedom as the self-determination of *Wille* through the moral law.

44 Immanuel Kant, *Religion within the Limits of Reason Alone* (New York: Harper & Brothers, 1960), 16.

45 Ibid., 26–7.

46 Although most Indo-European languages only allow for passive and active modes, ancient Greek had a third mode to refer to such cases where agency is ambiguous. The middle voice was meant to capture the modality of situations in which the agent participates in the action but without being fully in control of it. There is a large amount of secondary literature on the middle voice, and the one thing scholars seem to agree on is that it is a very elusive notion. See, e.g., P. K. Andersen, *Empirical Studies in Diathesis* (Münster: Nodus Publikationen, 2004), 10: "there are as many definitions of voice or diathesis as there are theoretical frameworks in the relevant literature"; S. Kemmer, *The Middle Voice: Typological Studies in Language* (Amsterdam: John Benjamins, 1993), 1: "there is no generally accepted definition of the middle voice"). One of the reasons for this is that the Greeks themselves did not elaborate on the matter. Andersen notes that the first grammar to use the three categories is a work attributed to Dionysios of Thrax. He focused on the opposition between active performance (*energeia*) and passive experience (*pathos*) and introduced *mesothes* as an intermediate category that applies to verbs that have a grammatical form that doesn't fit in either of the two previous ones (e.g., active verbs with a passive ending, such as deponents). Roman grammarians, in particular the Stoa (Zeno of Citium, the founder of the Stoic school) reappropriated this active/passive distinction by referring it to agency. Current grammar manuals of ancient Greek emphasize that the middle voice refers to actions that the subject performs on or for himself. See, e.g., H. W. Smyth, *Greek Grammar* (Cambridge: Harvard University Press, 1956), §1713: "the middle voice shows that the action is performed with special reference to the subject: *loumai* (I wash myself). Such actions often involve an ambiguous form of

agency, neither fully active nor fully passive, as one is both the agent and the recipient of the action." Benvéniste and Gonda picked up on this particular feature of the middle voice; see Benvéniste, *Problèmes de Linguistique Générale* (Paris: Gallimard, 1966), 172 ff.; and Gonda, "Reflections on the Indo-European Medium," *Lingua* IX/4 (1960), 30–67 and 175–93. According to the first, the middle voice does not so much indicate that the subject has an interest in the action as point toward the fact that s/he is the medium in which something takes place. It indicates that the subject is part of a process (expressed by the verb) to which s/he participates but which is not reducible to such participation. To emphasize this dimension, he introduced the notion of internal diathesis (as opposed to the external diathesis) of the active mode, in which the subject accomplishes an action that is under his control and carried out outside of him. Gonda underlines this peculiar active/passive mode of the middle voice in relation to a particular example in ancient Greek, that of marrying someone (Gonda, *Reflections*, 53 ff.). The active form (*gameô*) was standardly used by men and denotes an action in which the agent is fully in control, namely the taking of a wife. This is grammatically reflected by the fact that the complement is in the accusative. The middle voice form (*gameomai*) was normally used by women: it denotes activity (the woman takes a husband) but also passivity (she gives herself over to him, a fact that is grammatically expressed by the complement being indirect and in the dative). Furthermore, the middle voice has an eventive dimension: it indicates that "the process of marriage befalls the subject" (ibid., 59), in such a way that she participates in it without controlling it. Llewelyn follows his lead in his studies of Heidegger and Derrida and indicates that "we need a notion of power which does not merely pass through the subject, and a notion of subject which is neither merely a conduit or passage (the 'through' of pure passivity) nor the conductor entirely in charge of a performance (the 'by' of pure agency) but is performed as much as it performs the process"; J. Llewelyn, *The Middle Voice of Ecological Consciousness: A Chiasmic Reading of Responsibility in the Neighborhood of Levinas Heidegger and Others* (New York: St. Martin's Press, 1991), IX. For a useful account of the various conceptions of the middle voice, see P. Eberhard, *The Middle Voice in Gadamer's Hermeneutics* (Tübingen: Mohr Siebeck Verlag, 2004) in particular: "The Middle Voice from a Linguistic Perspective" and "Philosophical Perspectives on the Middle Voice" (7–31).

47 Note, however, that a more critical kind of psychological identification remains possible on the condition that Dasein does not view itself as naturally endowed with the psychological traits it assigns to itself, nor determined by them.

48 See in particular C. Taylor, "Action as Expression," in *Intention and Intentionality*, eds. C. Diamond and J. Teichman (New York: Cornell University Press, 1979); and C. Taylor, "Hegel's Philosophy of Mind," in *Human Agency and Language: Philosophical Papers 1* (Cambridge: Cambridge University Press, 1985).

49 Kierkegaard, *Either/Or*, 67.

50 Sartre, *Being and Nothingness*, 553.

51 Thus "human reality is the pure effort to become God ... Desire expresses this endeavour" (Sartre, *Being and Nothingness*, 576).

52 The full quote goes thus: "in our existential projection of anticipation, we have of course clung to those structures of Dasein which we have arrived at earlier, and we have, as it were, let Dasein itself project itself upon this possibility, without holding up to Dasein an ideal of existence with any special 'content' or forcing any such ideal upon it 'from the outside.'"

14 Authenticity and Resoluteness

Early in *Being and Time*,[1] Martin Heidegger gives notice that he will draw a distinction between authentic and inauthentic existence.[2] He writes:

And because Dasein is in each case essentially its own possibility, it *can*, in its very being, "choose" itself and win itself; it can also lose itself and never win itself; or only "seem" to do so. But only in so far as it is essentially something possibly authentic – that is, something of its own – can it have lost itself and not yet won itself. As modes of being, *authenticity* and *inauthenticity* (these expressions have been chosen terminologically in a strict sense) are both grounded in the fact that Dasein is in general determined by mineness. (42–3, translation modified)

Dasein is "in each case mine," which is to say that human existence and experience always belongs to or is owned by a person. *Who* that person is, according to Heidegger, is not obvious:

The word "I" is to be understood only in the sense of a non-committal *formal indicator*, indicating something which may perhaps reveal itself as its "opposite" in some particular phenomenal context. In that case, the "not-I" is by no means tantamount to an entity which essentially lacks "I-hood," but is rather a definite kind of being which the "I" itself possesses, such as having lost itself. (116)

Heidegger is willing to grant that the word "I" designates in each case the "owner" of existence, but he rejects the subjectivist or egoistic philosophical baggage that the term often carries. The self who I in each case am is not a sphere of subjectivity, a domain of inwardness, or a field of self-consciousness. Rather, the "I" is in each case simply that which can embrace or own existence, or lose or disown existence.[3] This contrast between owning and disowning or losing existence is the "terminologically strict" meaning of the terms "authentic" and "inauthentic."

The word "authentic" has been used in many ways in modern discussions of the self, uses that have been explored by Charles Taylor, Charles Guignon, and Lionel Trilling, among others.[4] Typically, it is used to indicate some form of being true to the self, which in turn contrasts with alienation or being unable to identify with the life one leads.

It is clear that Heidegger has no such expressivist notion of authenticity in mind, as Taylor Carman has persuasively argued.[5] So, what does he have in mind? In the extant secondary literature, there are a number of approaches to interpreting Heidegger's concept.

One approach (the "existentialist approach") understands authenticity as a form of life liberated from the illusions and distortions of everyday "idle talk" and conformism, in which Dasein faces up to the finitude of death and the demands of conscience. According to Charles Guignon, authenticity involves grasping the "ultimate contingency" of one's life and lucidly resolving upon an understanding of one's existence as a whole.[6] Hubert Dreyfus and Jane Rubin present almost the negative image of Guignon's reading. They interpret authenticity as "undertaking all my specific projects in a style of openness that manifests my understanding that no specific project can fulfill me or give my life meaning," which is motivated "by the revelation that all that [I] accepted as serious does not matter at all."[7] Existentialist approaches to authenticity emphasize the tension between finding a fulfilling purpose for one's life and realizing that neither an illusive human essence nor the world of the everyday can provide anything more than a contingent self.

A second strategy (the "Aristotelian approach") places authenticity in proximity to Aristotle's notion of *phronesis* and departs from Heidegger's explorations of Aristotle's practical philosophy in the early and mid-1920s.[8] *Phronesis*, which has traditionally been translated "practical wisdom," involves the capacity to see what a practical situation requires and to act on that insight. Theodore Kisiel has made much of this connection,[9] and Hubert Dreyfus has attempted to fuse the Aristotelian and existentialist approaches by interpreting authenticity as the ability virtuosically to innovate a new way of life in the face of having to surrender or give up on everything to which one has heretofore been committed.[10]

A third approach (the "Christian approach") focuses on the connections between the language of authenticity and Heidegger's interpretations of Christian experience in Paul and Luther, as well as Kierkegaard's existentialist appropriation thereof. John van Buren has explored this approach in greatest detail.[11] It strikes even the casual reader that Heidegger's term "falling" carries at least unintended religious connotations. Van Buren shows that a significant amount of Heidegger's vocabulary for inauthenticity is drawn from Paul, Luther, and Kierkegaard's descriptions of the state of sin and the ways in which the fallen hide their fear and suffering from themselves.[12] In the late 1910s and early 1920s, Heidegger explored the phenomenology of religious experience and the tensions, as he saw them, between original Christian experience and Greek philosophy. It is not clear, however, that Luther and

Kierkegaard's religious thought is a key to unraveling Heidegger's conception of authenticity. It is better to take Heidegger at his word[13] and to treat his ontology of Dasein, including his understanding of authenticity, as a foundation on which to build a clarified phenomenology of religious experience and a theology of sin and redemption. This is not to say, however, that Heidegger did not arrive at some of his insights and novel concepts through a fresh look at the New Testament, Luther, and Kierkegaard.[14]

A fourth approach (the "transcendental approach") views authenticity, or at least conscience, which "attests" the possibility of authenticity, as a condition of the possibility of agency. Heidegger characterizes resoluteness as "wanting-to-have-a-conscience," and conscience is a transcendental condition of the possibility of Dasein being responsible at all. It is Dasein's responsiveness to norms in general. In resoluteness, then, Dasein clear-sightedly experiences that it is not subject to norms in the way that physical events are subject to scientific laws of nature. Rather, Dasein is a participant in a sphere of normativity. This insight frees Dasein from unquestioning subservience to anonymous, public rules and constraints, freeing it to take responsibility for who it is and how it lives. This is a more recent line of approach to authenticity and has been developed by John Haugeland, Rebecca Kukla, and Steven Crowell.[15]

In what follows, I aim to weave the insights of the existentialist, Aristotelian, and transcendental approaches to Heidegger's conception of authenticity into a single synthetic position.

SOME PRELIMINARY EXEGETICAL OBSERVATIONS AND CHALLENGES

Authenticity is a mode of existence, according to Heidegger, that is, a manner in which Dasein can lead its life. By this phrasing, I do *not* mean to suggest that self-ownership is a way of life or life-style as these phrases are commonly used. Ways of life (e.g., the modern American way of life or the traditional Crow way of life) and lifestyles (the Southern California lifestyle or the lifestyle of the suburban Bible Belt) are particular factical configurations of culture. They come and go through history, are culturally localized and limited, and serve therefore as concrete possibilities for Dasein. Self-ownership is an intrinsic possibility for Dasein, however, not a factically contingent one. Thus authenticity and inauthenticity are formal modes of human existence because they are modes of living whatever other possibilities one might have.

Resoluteness is the mode of disclosedness that attends authenticity.[16] To own one's self requires disclosing one's life or being. Further, resoluteness bears a complex relation to *running-forth into death*

(M&R: "anticipation of death"). Running-forth is, Heidegger says, "the possibility of *authentic existence*" (263). He adds, "Thus only *as running-forth* does resoluteness become an originary being toward Dasein's ownmost ability-to-be" (306, translation modified), and for this reason, he fuses the two terms into "resoluteness that runs forth" (M&R: "anticipatory resoluteness").

The relationship between resoluteness and anxiety represents a further complexity in the text. In some passages, Heidegger states that the attunement (*Stimmung*, M&R: "mood") that belongs to resoluteness is anxiety:

The disclosedness of Dasein that lies in wanting to have a conscience, is thus constituted by the disposedness of anxiety, by understanding as a self-projection upon one's ownmost being-guilty, and by discourse as reticence. (296, translation modified)

However, in the very next passage, he writes that readiness for anxiety, not anxiety itself, is constitutive of resoluteness:

This distinctive and authentic disclosedness, which is attested in Dasein itself by its conscience – *this reticent self-projection upon one's ownmost being-guilty, in which one is ready for anxiety* – we call *resoluteness*. (296–7)

How one resolves this complexity necessarily interacts with what one thinks anxiety *is* in *Being and Time*. Is anxiety the sort of attunement or mood in which one can, to put it crudely, function, or is it rather disabling? Whatever else resoluteness is meant to be, it is a condition in which "Dasein is already *taking action*" (300). So, one can maintain that anxiety is constitutive of resoluteness only if one avoids interpreting anxiety as disabling.

Finally, the contraries of authenticity and resoluteness are inauthenticity and irresoluteness. It is not clear, however, whether the contrast between authenticity and inauthenticity is exhaustive, that is, whether there are any other modes of existence available to Dasein. Possible additional modes of existence are anxiety[17] and an "undifferentiated" mode in which Dasein is neither authentic nor inauthentic because the existential issues that force the choice have not yet arisen. Hubert Dreyfus, who was the first interpreter of whom I am aware to identify the undifferentiated mode as a third possibility, cites passages that clearly make reference to it,[18] but it is odd that the passages are so infrequent and that Heidegger sometimes treats the authentic/inauthentic distinction as exhaustive. In what follows, I will adopt both of these alternative modes of existence, thus assuming that Dasein can live in the undifferentiated mode, or in anxiety, or in authenticity or inauthenticity, the latter two primarily a response to anxiety.

RESOLUTENESS AS A RESPONSE TO AN EXISTENTIAL CRISIS

The existentialist approach to Heidegger's conception of authenticity treats it as a response to an existential crisis. The two crisis-like conditions to which Heidegger refers are *anxiety* and *death*. I have argued elsewhere, and due to limitations of space must assume here, that anxiety and death are in fact two facets of the same basic existential condition.[19] Heidegger writes, "In anxiety ... [t]he 'world' can offer nothing more, and neither can the Dasein-with of others" (187). Now, in I.3, we learned that Dasein's self-understanding is inextricably enmeshed in the practical world of equipment and tasks to be completed. To understand oneself is to project oneself or press ahead into some concrete possibility of living, which in turn is defined by the place it occupies within the matrix of equipmental roles and human purposes that constitutes the concrete social world in which we live. Further, this worldly matrix is defined by and shared with others; the world is a "with-world" (118). To understand oneself is to be tuned in to what matters and is at stake in a shared practical situation and to be able to forge ahead with some course of action that makes sense in terms of the way things matter. To exist, according to Heidegger's formal conception of existence (53), is to understand oneself, but in anxiety, Dasein cannot understand itself, hence is unable to exist. And that is exactly how Heidegger characterizes death: "Its death is the possibility of no longer being able to be-there" (250).[20]

So, the attunement of anxiety discloses Dasein in its death. "Death," in this unconventional way of writing, does not refer to "terminal world collapse" (as Iain Thomson aptly describes it), but rather to a condition in which Dasein can find itself: cut off from the practical world, isolated from others, existentially alienated. Let us call this "existential death." Death, so conceived, is a disabling condition, one in which one cannot press ahead with one's life because one finds everything insignificant or unimportant. Because significance and mattering are constitutive of Dasein's everyday familiarity with the world in which it lives, its being at home in the world, anxiety and death constitute a condition in which Dasein is not at home, in which it is uncanny (188). It thus also makes sense that Heidegger argues that death is disclosed most properly in anxiety (251). This is, then, the existential crisis Dasein can face: the inability to understand itself insofar as the world and the others with whom it shares that world "have nothing to offer."

How can Dasein respond to this crisis? One possibility is to hide from it, to bury it over, to "flee," in Heidegger's language. Heidegger describes flight as a form of "tranquilization" about death, in which the Anyone (*das Man*, M&R: "the 'They'") "does not permit the courage for anxiety in the face of death to arise" (254). Rather, "The Anyone concerns itself with transforming this anxiety into fear in the face of an oncoming event" (254), namely the ending of one's life, which Heidegger calls "demise" (*Ableben*). That is, the Anyone distracts Dasein from an anxious confrontation with death by substituting demise for death and then addressing itself to Dasein's rather natural fear of demise. Alternatively, Dasein can "run forth into," that is, embrace the existential crisis. In §53 on "The Existential Projection of an Authentic Being-towards-death," Heidegger distinguishes two things one might hear in "running-forth into death" (*Vorlaufen in den Tod*, M&R: "anticipation of death").[21] One might think that to run forth into death is to "live dangerously until the end," perhaps even to seek death, or at least to welcome it as it approaches. Such ways of living, which have been variously lauded in some existentialist literature and film,[22] are ways of relating to demise, not existential death (261). Running forth into existential death is, therefore, not closely related to any of these valorizations of "living dangerously."

What then is running-forth into death? Heidegger characterizes running-forth into death as letting "death reveal itself *as a possibility*," as "what first *makes* this possibility *possible*, and sets it free as a possibility" (262). Running-forth into death thus appears to be the act of holding on to death, not letting it be buried over and degraded into fear of demise. The paradox is that running-forth also "frees" one for one's death so that "one is liberated in such a way that for the first time one can authentically understand and choose among the factical possibilities lying ahead of" death (264). How could holding on to anxiety promote clear-sightedly choosing among the worldly possibilities currently available to one? This hardly seems possible if anxiety is the attunement in which the world slips into insignificance.

It is worth looking carefully at the critical paragraph on 264. Existential death is unsurpassable in that there is nothing one can do to put it behind one or insulate oneself from it.[23] It is constantly possible. In this crisis, one "gives oneself up" in that one surrenders or gives up on who one has been: one's commitments and self-understandings to date no longer matter. This is Heidegger's way of expressing what we might think of as the ineradicable vulnerability of life. We are vulnerable to "dying to the world," however, rather than dying in the sense of passing away, demise. Heidegger associates being lost in the Anyone with "stubbornness [*Versteifung*] about the existence one has achieved."[24] To be stubborn is to have a sort of tunnel vision or to be inflexible. There is a sense of freedom that contrasts rather plainly with such stubbornness: the flexibility to see beyond the narrow confines of one's rigid vision. The suggestion is, therefore, that by embracing existential death one expands one's vision, limbers up one's self-understanding. But how? By coming to understand, not just intellectually but more importantly practically, that one is not pinned down by the life one has achieved. How does one come to understand that? It is an aspect of vulnerability: one would not be vulnerable to "dying to the world" if one had a practical essence, an identity that defined one come what may.

How is this stubbornness realized in daily life? By "misinterpreting the existential possibilities of others" in such a way as to "force them upon its own possibilities" (264, translation modified). The idea seems to be that the encounter with existential death shatters the "obviousness" of the social expectations that one buys into as a participant in the communal life of the public. Recall that for Heidegger the Anyone is not "the others" in the sense of everyone else but me. Rather, we all belong to the Anyone and enhance its power (126). The "misinterpretation" to which Heidegger refers is taking the possibilities that the public insists upon as being somehow unchallengeable.

Heidegger concludes the critical paragraph by arguing that running-forth toward death allows Dasein to develop an understanding of the whole of its existence. Running-forth casts all of one's factical possibilities in a new light. That is, it discloses the whole of one's existence in a new light. So, embracing or running forth toward the existential crisis of death and anxiety shatters the rigidity of one's life, freeing one from the obviousness of the possibilities in terms of which one has come to understand oneself and the assumptions of one's social context. In doing this, it brings the whole of Dasein, that is, the full range of Dasein's existential possibilities, into view.

CONSCIENCE, GUILT, AND THE SELF

The existential crisis of death and/or anxiety is not a total collapse of self. Here a distinctively transcendental theme enters Heidegger's analysis: conscience. As a first approximation, we may characterize conscience as the disclosure of one's responsibility for one's choices, decisions, way of life. The word "conscience" evokes all sorts of moral connotations, which are not irrelevant to Heidegger's analysis but which are also not fundamental. In moral conscience, the disclosure of responsibility is focused on the moral dimensions of one's life. A "guilty conscience" attends moral transgressions; one may be led by one's conscience not to commit a crime or violate a moral norm. Conscience is, thus, an awareness of one's actual or possible guilt, or in the case of a "good conscience," innocence. Moral guilt presupposes a more basic form of responsibility: one is responsible for what one has done or might do and is subject to the implications of the norms one does or might violate. Conscience in this ordinary sense, therefore, presupposes one's being subject to or bound by norms. Further, to "feel guilty" – as opposed to merely noting intellectually that one has violated a norm – requires that one be responsive to the norms to which one is subject or bound, to feel the *pull* of the norms, to experience them as having a *claim* on one. One is "summoned" or "called" to a course of (in)action or way of being. Heidegger uses the term "conscience" to pick out this fundamental phenomenon of responsiveness to norms. We are responsive not just to moral norms but to epistemic, logical, social, and mathematical norms, among others.

In anxiety, the world in which one lives and the fellows amongst whom one leads one's life slip into insignificance. In death, one is unable to understand oneself. Why are anxiety and death unsettling, uncomfortable conditions of existence? Dasein is in its very being called upon to understand itself. To understand oneself is not just to have a cognitive grasp or interpretation of one's life. "Being is that which is *an issue* for every such entity" (42, emphasis altered). Dasein's being is a matter of concern to it; it is *called* to take a stand on who it is. In anxiety and death, however, Dasein cannot satisfy this demand. Another way Heidegger formulates this idea is that in conscience Dasein is called to its self: "The call reaches the Anyone-self of concernful being with others. And to what is one called? To one's *own self*" (272–3, translation modified).

One's "own self," as Heidegger describes it, is oddly empty: "The self to which the appeal is made remains indefinite and empty in its what" (274; see also 273 and 276). It is tempting to read in well-known existentialist ideas about the emptiness of life, of the vacuity of the self (as Sartre, Kafka, and Musil are often read). This would not be right, however. The empty own, ownmost, or authentic self to which Heidegger refers is not a concretely existing vacuous self. Nor is it a "true self," who one should really be. It is not a "deep self" hidden behind an everyday façade.[25] It is not the sort of thing one can find on a "journey of self-discovery."

The call does not appeal to a self *other than* the everyday self who one is, which Heidegger calls "the Anyone-self." Instead, "and because only the *self* of the Anyone-self gets appealed to and brought to hear, the *Anyone* collapses" (273). The Anyone-self is one's everyday self, who one is in going about one's business in an average everyday way. The Anyone-self is a *self* because it is responsive to norms, to the solicitations of the world and of one's self-understanding. I am a father because I respond to the solicitations of the for-the-sake-of-which, being a father, to which I am called by finding myself already enmeshed in the factical possibilities and attunements of family life. In existential crisis, I am stripped of these concrete for-the-sakes-of-which that make up my identity, and am left to confront my conscience pure and simple. Conscience discloses me as "my own self," as the target of norms, as the one who is called forth to understand who I am.[26] This "own self" is not something other than the everyday self. It is a transcendental aspect of the everyday self, a condition of the latter's possibility.[27] Thus the Anyone-self is an "existentiell modification of the authentic self" (317).

Heidegger also characterizes conscience as an awareness of one's own being guilty. Once again, however, he does not have the everyday moral sense of guilt in mind, nor the sense of being indebted that the German world *schuldig* also invokes. In the everyday sense, one is guilty if one is the cause or author of some evil or transgression of a moral norm. Heidegger formalizes this everyday meaning thus: "*Being-the-ground* for a lack of something in the existence of an other, and in such a manner that this very being-the-ground determines itself as 'lacking in some way' in terms of that for which it is the ground" (282). That is, if one wrongs someone, one is the ground or author of some lack or deprivation in the other's life, and one's being the author derives from some lack or failure of oneself. Heidegger further formalizes the notions of lack, failure, and deprivation as "nullities" – phenomena characterized by a "not." So, he finally arrives at the following streamlined formalization of guilt: being the null ground of a nullity.

Heidegger then argues that guilt in this formalized sense always and necessarily characterizes Dasein and serves as a condition of the possibility of everyday guilt. "[I]n being-able-to-be [Dasein] always stands in one possibility or another: it constantly is *not* other possibilities, and it has waived these in its existentiell projection" (285). Dasein is always someone in particular who is already enmeshed in concrete possibilities. Every such possibility excludes a range of alternative possibilities that are in principle available to one within one's culture. Being a father excludes the life of the single man free of family responsibilities. Being employed excludes a life devoted mostly to blogging. This is a nullity of Dasein – that it is always *not* possibilities it has forgone in being who it is. Heidegger refers to it as the nullity of Dasein's projection: "*as projection* it is itself essentially *null*" (285). Dasein is, further, the ground of this nullity.

"Being-the-ground" formalizes the notion of authorship used to explain everyday guilt. To be the author of something in the everyday sense is to have brought it about in such a way that one is, depending on the context, morally or legally responsible for its occurrence. Heidegger's ontology of Dasein is not focused on responsibility for individual actions and their consequences, but rather on the more basic phenomenon that he calls "projection" and that he describes as "press[ing] forward into possibilities" (145). One's entire way of being-in-the-world, how one conducts oneself in daily life, speaks and thinks about oneself, one's fellows, and one's world, all of these are a matter of projection. To project oneself is to cast oneself forward in life, press ahead into being who one is.[28] Projection is, further, always *thrown*, that is, situated in a concrete factical situation and oriented by the way things matter to Dasein. As he puts it in a oft-cited passage from I.5:

Possibility, as an *existentiale,* does not signify a free-floating ability-to-be in the sense of the "liberty of indifference" (*libertas indifferentiae*). In every case Dasein, as essentially disposed, has already got itself into definite possibilities.... But this means that Dasein is being-possible which has been delivered over to itself – *thrown possibility* through and through. (144, translation modified)

Thus Dasein is the ground for its projection in that it projects on the basis of or in the light of the way it is already disposed: how things already matter to it, to what it is already committed, where, when, and how it finds itself entangled in the world.

Such being disposed or thrown involves responding to the normative claims of the world in which one lives and of the person who one already is: I press forward into being a father because my children are dear to me; I press forward into being a teacher because education is exciting. These normative claims are not generally experienced as moral rules, duties, or obligations, though of course sometimes they are. Typically normative claims on my activity are disclosed affectively through the way things already matter to me, the ways in which they are important or significant, that is, the ways in which I am attuned to the world, my community and fellows, myself. "Although it has *not* laid that ground *itself*, it reposes in the weight of it, which is made manifest to it as a burden by Dasein's attunement" (284, translation modified). Dasein is thus the ground of itself in that it is responsible for, because responsive to, who it already is. *We* are the ones who are in each case *answerable for* or *accountable to* the normative claims that are disclosed to us in our "attuned self-finding," in our thrownness. This answerability or accountability is disclosed to us in conscience.

Finally, this answerability or being-the-ground is itself null, characterized by a "not," because Dasein is *not* able to get control over the ground that it is. "To this entity, it has been delivered over, and as such it can exist solely as the entity which it is; and *as this entity* to which it has been thus delivered over, it *is, in its existing*, the ground of its ability-to-be" (284, translation modified).

Dasein "reposes in the weight" of who it already is; it cannot choose how things matter to it. It is, thus, a null ground of a nullity, guilty in Heidegger's formal sense of the term. This guilt is not a matter of being responsible for evil; it is not any kind of feeling or emotion. It is rather the formal characteristic of Dasein that it is always responsible for, because responsive to, who it finds itself already to be, and this being already someone in particular limits and structures who it is able to be going forward.

AUTHENTICITY AS SELF-OWNERSHIP

Heidegger first characterizes resoluteness as "wanting to have a conscience":

Our understanding of the appeal [of conscience] unveils itself as our *wanting to have a conscience*. But in this phenomenon lies that existentiell choosing which we seek – the choosing to choose a kind of being-one's-self which, in accordance with its existential structure, we call *resoluteness*. (269–70)

Conscience discloses that Dasein is in each case responsive to norms that govern who it is called upon to be, that it is in each case account-able for who it is. So, wanting to have a conscience is to want, that is, to accept or embrace this accountability. To clarify this, let us contrast authenticity with "being lost in the Anyone."

"Losing itself in the publicness and idle talk of the Anyone, [Dasein] fails to hear its own self in listening to the Anyone-self" (271). One can listen to the Anyone-self *rather than* one's own self. What can this mean? As we have seen, "one's own self" is the transcendental dimen-sion of the self in virtue of which it is responsive to norms. Since one cannot be *un*responsive to norms, on pain of not being a self, Heidegger must mean that one's responsiveness to norms is diminished or com-promised while lost in the Anyone. To spell out this idea, he draws a distinction between "the situation" and "the general situation":

For the Anyone, however, the situation is essentially something that has been closed off. The Anyone knows only the *"general situation,"* loses itself in those *"opportunities"* which are closest to it, and pays Dasein's way by a reckoning up of "accidents" which it fails to recognize, deems its own achievement, and passes off as such. (300, translation modified)

The general situation is a generic situation, one that is experienced in terms of crude and prepackaged elements, rather than in terms of all its normative subtlety and nuance. Responding to the general situation, rather than the fully concrete actual situation in which one acts, is a form of diminished responsiveness.

To be lost in the general situation, rather than to listen to one's own self, must then mean that one loses touch with the normative claims

inherent in who one already is and responds, instead, to a generic understanding of how one should be. There are gripping literary and cine-
matic presentations of this. Consider two examples. Lester Burnham in
the film *American Beauty* leads a life of unreflective conformism, one
in which he holds down a boring job, phones in his relationships with
his wife and daughter, takes no real pleasure in his daily existence. A
similar pattern may be found in Sinclair Lewis's 1922 novel *Babbitt*, in
which George Babbitt finds that he is suffocating in his philistine and
bourgeois life. Both men have lost themselves and feel cut off from the
immediacy of life. They live as one is supposed to live, conforming to
the expectations of the communities in which they reside. They live
with little imagination or risk.

Publicness proximally controls every way in which the world and Dasein get
interpreted, and it is always right – not because there is some distinctive and
primary relationship of being in which it is related to "things," or because it
avails itself of some transparency on the part of Dasein which it has explicitly
appropriated, but because it is insensitive to every difference of level and of
genuineness and thus never gets to the "heart of the matter." By publicness
everything gets obscured, and what has thus been covered up gets passed off as
something familiar and accessible to everyone. (127)

Such unimaginative and conformist modes of living are responsive only
to the general situation, what the Anyone sketches out as an appropriate life.

Resoluteness, in contrast, is open to alternative possibilities obscured
in the general situation. One might be tempted to read in expressivist
ideas of a deep self that one betrays in succumbing to conformism. We
have seen, however, that the authentic self to whom one is called in
conscience is not a deep or true self behind the façade of the everyday.
We have also seen that who Dasein already is always grounds who it can
be, which entails that resoluteness also cannot require making a clean
break with one's past and setting out on some wild adventure (as Lester
Burnham and George Babbit do). At this point, we seem to have backed
ourselves into a corner. One must be open to alternative possibilities
not acknowledged by the public, yet these possibilities can be neither
expressive of one's true self nor a clean break with who one is. What is
left? Resoluteness returns Dasein to the everyday, to who it already is,
but with a clear-sighted understanding of the normative demands inherent in who it already is.

Resolution does not withdraw itself from "actuality," but discovers first what is
factically possible; and it does so by seizing upon it in whatever way is possible
for it as its ownmost ability-to-be in the Anyone. (299, translation modified; see
also 297–8)

Resoluteness is a mode of living in the Anyone, a modification of everydayness.

This is where the Aristotelian themes emphasized by some commentators enter the picture. It is important to note, however, that Heideggerian resoluteness cannot be equivalent to Aristotelian *phronesis*, for as Aristotle famously states, "we say this is above all the work of the man of *phronesis*, to deliberate well."[29] Deliberation is a decidedly secondary phenomenon for Heidegger, one he does not discuss until II.4 and which he presents as a response to breakdown, rather than a basic form of Dasein's activity. Instead, Heidegger appropriates Aristotle's notion of *phronesis* and adapts it to the context of his own thinking. In his *Sophist* lectures, he paraphrases Aristotle thus: "*Phronesis* is ... 'a disposition of human Dasein such that in it I have at my disposal my own transparency'" (GA 19: 52). He also writes, "*Phronesis* is nothing other than conscience set into motion, making an action transparent" (GA 19: 56).[30] For Heidegger, *phronesis* is the ability to see what a situation requires. It is a fluid mastery of the practical context that allows one to respond effectively and immediately to the normative demands of the situation. Resoluteness, likewise, "does not first take cognizance of a situation and put that situation before itself; it has put itself into that situation already. As resolute, Dasein is already *taking action*" (300). Thus resoluteness is responsive to the immediate, concrete, and factical situation, rather than to a generic understanding of the situation.

But what is the point of this notion of resoluteness, if all it does is bring Dasein into transparent contact with the current factical situation in which it lives? How does this combat or undermine conformism? How does it cause the Anyone to "collapse" (273)? If who one already is clashes with the expectations and demands of the public, then one does require extra fortitude in order to remain who one is, a sort of fortitude to which the word "resolute" might naturally apply. So, Heidegger's conception of resoluteness does have *some* overlap with the expressivist notion of authenticity, in which one stands up to social pressure to express who one really is. Heidegger's modification of the expressivist notion is to deny that this self to whom one returns, to whom one remains loyal, is a deep self. It is just one's ordinary, everyday self.

Heidegger's conception of resoluteness does not *require*, however, that one break ranks with the public and go one's own direction, find one's unique voice. In fact, since every way of being is sketched out and located by the Anyone,

Authentic being-one's-self does not rest upon an exceptional condition of the subject, a condition that has been detached from the Anyone; *it is rather an existentiell modification of the Anyone as an essential existentiale.* (130, translation modified)

Resolute Dasein is more flexible and attuned in how it navigates the world of the Anyone. This flexibility requires the ability to "take back" prior commitments and habitual modes of activity. As the situation changes and as one's attunements alter, one is called upon to adapt and change with the situation. If one falls out of love, if the community in which one lives disintegrates, or if the for-the-sakes-of-which to which one is committed are no longer possible, then one is called upon *by the situation* to change. That is, one must be open to the vulnerability of existence. This vulnerability is disclosed to Dasein in its anxious confrontation with existential death. Thus "resoluteness is authentically and wholly what it can be, only as *resoluteness that runs forth* [toward death]" (309, translation modified).

Such resoluteness that runs forth in turn demands of Dasein that it understand concretely and practically that who it has been up to the present time is not necessarily who it is now, who it is called upon to be. Thus in §64, Heidegger describes the self-constancy of the authentic self as "steadiness and steadfastness" (322). To be constant is not to be unchanging; it is, rather, to be *loyal*, loyal to who one now finds oneself to be, which is to say loyal to the situation. Resolute Dasein has a steady hand, or is surefooted, in its persistence or insistence upon being who it is. Thus what is distinctive of resolute Dasein is *not* the *content* of who it is but rather *how* it is who it is. Resolute Dasein is itself in a persistent and surefooted way, even if the conformism of the general situation seeks to make it back down from who it finds itself to be.[31]

Thus Heidegger's conception of authenticity borrows and remixes elements from the existentialist notion of embracing the threat of anxiety and "existential death," the Kantian transcendental concept of the self as a locus of normative responsiveness, and Aristotle's vision of *phronesis* or practical wisdom. Each of these elements is adapted to the novel ontology of Dasein that Heidegger offers. Anxiety and the indefinite certitude of existential death reveal that one is constantly vulnerable to the collapse of one's commitments and the dissipation of one's attunements. The normative responsiveness that defines the authenticity of the self is not responsiveness to norms that are themselves transcendental, that is, not to a categorical imperative or transcendent good, but rather to the everyday goods or for-the-sakes-of-which of practical life. Finally, the *phronesis* that constitutes resoluteness is not an excellence of deliberation, but rather a transparent attunement to what matters here and now in this concrete factical situation. Heidegger combines these elements so as to create a vision of a life liberated from the rigidity and stubbornness of everyday conformism, so that one may clearly see what the current situation in which one lives normatively demands of one. One is called upon to be true to one's self, but the self one must be true to is not one's true self, some deep self hiding behind the façade of the everyday. What authenticity requires is steady and steadfast loyalty to who one factically and currently is.

NOTES

1 I will generally rely on Macquarrie and Robinson's 1962 translation of Heidegger's *Sein und Zeit*, but will make alterations as I feel are necessary. To indicate a systematic divergence in technical terminology from Macquarrie and Robinson's translation, I will note their translation like this: "M&R: state of mind." I will also refer to chapters of *Being and Time* in the standard format: "I.3" to refer to Division I, chapter 3.

2 In this chapter, I will translate *eigentlich* with "authentic," both because the latter is a neutral translation and because it better mirrors Heidegger's grammar. I will often refer to the *concept* in question as "self-ownership."

3 Heidegger's formulation also leaves open which existence is mine. That is, on a traditional subjectivist understanding, I am the field of experience that is in principle accessible to my self-consciousness. Heidegger problematizes the "boundaries of the self," opening the door to potentially revolutionary reconfigurations of our understanding of the self. For more on this theme, see my *Heidegger's "Being and Time:" A Reader's Guide* (London: Continuum Books, 2006).

4 Charles Taylor, *The Ethics of Authenticity* (Cambridge, MA: Harvard University Press, 1992); Charles Guignon, *On Being Authentic* (New York: Routledge, 2004); and Lionel Trilling, *Sincerity and Authenticity* (Cambridge, MA: Harvard University Press, 1972). The term "expressivism" as used in this chapter derives from Charles Taylor's work.

5 Taylor Carman, "Authenticity," in *A Companion to Heidegger*, eds. H. L. Dreyfus and M. Wrathall (Oxford: Blackwell, 2005), 285–96.

6 Charles Guignon, "Becoming a Self: The Role of Authenticity in *Being and Time*," *The Existentialists: Critical Essays on Kierkegaard, Nietzsche, Heidegger, and Sartre*, ed. Charles Guignon (Lanham: Rowman & Littlefield, 2004), 130. Guignon develops similar ideas in his *Heidegger and the Problem of Knowledge* (Indianapolis: Hackett, 1983).

7 Hubert Dreyfus and Jane Rubin, "Kierkegaard, Division II, and Later Heidegger," *Being-in-the-World: A Commentary on Heidegger's "Being and Time,"* Division I (Cambridge, MA: MIT Press, 1991), 322–3, 315.

8 See especially *Phenomenological Interpretations of Aristotle: Initiation into Phenomenological Research* (GA 61), *Plato's Sophist* (GA 19), and *The Basic Concepts of Aristotelian Philosophy* (GA 18).

9 See Part II of Theodore Kisiel, *The Genesis of Heidegger's "Being and Time"* (Berkeley: University of California Press, 1993).

10 Hubert Dreyfus, "Could Anything Be More Intelligible Than Everyday Intelligibility? Reinterpreting Division I of *Being and Time* in the Light of Division II," in *Appropriating Heidegger*, eds. James E. Faulconer and Mark A. Wrathall (Cambridge: Cambridge University Press, 2000).

11 John van Buren, *The Young Heidegger: Rumor of the Hidden King* (Bloomington: Indiana University Press, 1994). See especially chapter 8. For Heidegger's phenomenology of Christian experience, esp. Paul and

Augustine, see Martin Heidegger, *The Phenomenology of Religious Life* (GA 60).

12 This is true also of Heidegger's word for the temporal present of authentic experience, "Augenblick," which is an ordinary German word for moment or instant, but also the word that Luther used to translate what the King James Bible renders as "the twinkling of an eye" (I *Corinthians* 15:52). Kierkegaard used the Danish cognate *Øjeblikket* for the title of his work translated into English as *The Instant*. In *Being and Time*, Heidegger cites Kierkegaard on 338n.

13 See 10 and 306n.

14 If one reads *Being and Time* through the lens of Christianity, then one also exposes oneself to the sorts of criticisms presented by Herman Philipse, *Heidegger's Philosophy of Being: A Critical Interpretation* (Princeton: Princeton University Press, 1998), which ascribes a "Pascalian Grand Strategy" (240) to *Being and Time*.

15 John Haugeland, "Truth and Finitude: Heidegger's Transcendental Existentialism," *Heidegger, Authenticity, and Modernity: Essays in Honor of Hubert L. Dreyfus*, vol. 1, eds. Mark Wrathall and Jeff Malpas (Cambridge, MA: MIT Press, 2000), 43–78; Steven Crowell, "Subjectivity: Locating the First-Person in Being and Time," *Inquiry* 44 (2001): 433–54; and *"Sorge* or *Selbstbewußtsein*? Heidegger and Korsgaard on the Sources of Normativity," *European Journal of Philosophy* 15 (2007): 315–33; Rebecca Kukla, "The Ontology and Temporality of Conscience," *Continental Philosophy Review* 35 (2002): 1–34.

16 Disclosedness consists of three (or maybe four) moments or structural elements, or what we might call "facets." These are understanding (*Verstehen*), disposedness (*Befindlichkeit*, M&R: "state-of-mind"), and discourse (*Rede*). Sometimes Heidegger substitutes falling (*Verfallen*) for discourse, and in other places, he lists all four facets.

17 I have argued for such a proposal in *Heidegger's "Being and Time": A Reader's Guide* (London: Continuum Books, 2006), and so has Piotr Hoffman, *Doubt, Time, Violence* (Chicago: University of Chicago Press, 1986).

18 "[The] undifferentiated character of Dasein's everydayness is *not nothing*, but a positive phenomenal characteristic of this entity. Out of this kind of being – and back into it again – is all existing, such as it is" (43). "But this *ability-to-be* ... is free either for authenticity or for inauthenticity or for a mode in which neither of these has been differentiated" (232, translation modified). See Hubert L. Dreyfus, *Being-in-the-World* (Cambridge, MA: MIT Press, 1991), 27.

19 See William Blattner, "The Concept of Death in *Being and Time*," *Man and World* 27 (1994): 49–70, and Blattner, *Heidegger's "Being and Time."* My treatment here will abstract from whether Heidegger's notion of anxiety is best captured by the contemporary psychiatric conception of agitated depression. For a related and more detailed discussion of death, see Iain Thomson, "Heidegger's Phenomenology of Death in *Being and Time*" (in this volume). In *Heidegger's "Being and Time,"* I interpreted conscience as the mode of discourse characteristic of the existential crisis. I now think that that is incorrect. *Reticence* is the mode of discourse in the existential crisis.

20 *"Nicht-mehr-dasein-könnens."* Here, Heidegger uses the verb "dasein," "to be there," rather than the gerund "Dasein."

21 Van Buren points out that Heidegger's phrase *"Vorlaufen in den Tod"* is a literal translation of Luther's phrase *"cursus ad mortem"* from his commentary on Genesis 3:15, to which Heidegger refers in his WS 1921–2 lectures. (*"Cursus ad mortem"* is also prominent in Augustine's *De Civitate Dei*, Book XIII.) Luther wrote, "Although we do not wish to call the life we live here a death, nevertheless it surely is nothing else than a continuous journey toward death [*perpetuus cursus ad mortem*] ... Right from our mother's womb we begin to die." (Martin Luther, *Lectures on Genesis, Chapters 1–5* (St. Louis, MO: Concordia Publishing House, 1958), 196). This is a characterization of original sin, the condition of fallenness. Heidegger's phrase *"Vorlaufen in den Tod"* may echo Luther's (and Augustine's) language, but its meaning is very different. It refers to the authentic embrace of death and the *route out* of fallenness. Thanks to Julia Lamm and Alan Mitchell of the Georgetown Theology Department for clarifying the Luther for me.

22 Perhaps most famously in Nietzsche's imperative to "live dangerously" in *The Gay Science*, Book IV, §283. Hubert Dreyfus, "Discussion of Film: Breathless" (UC Berkeley, 2008, Podcast: http://webcast.berkeley.edu/stream.php?type'download&webcastid'22733), makes a strong case for interpreting Michel in *Breathless* as a Nietzschean "living dangerously until the end."

23 This is an important idea that we cannot explore here. In "Existence and Self-Understanding in *Being and Time*," I argue that it follows from the more fundamental thesis that Dasein has no essence, hence no commitments, entanglements, attunements, or passions it is immune from losing.

24 M&R render *Versteifung* as "tenaciousness." To my ear, tenacity can well be an admirable trait, whereas Heidegger pretty clearly has something neutral or even negative in mind. *Versteifung* is also used to describe rigidity or stiffness, as when joints become stiff. Hence, there are overtones of inflexibility in Heidegger's phrasing.

25 This "deep self" is the sort of "expressivist" authentic self discussed by Taylor, *Authenticity*.

26 This is not far from Haugeland's conception of "units of accountability" in John Haugeland, "Heidegger on Being a Person," *Noûs* 16 (1982): 15–26.

27 It is critical to distinguish, using Kantian language, between a "transcendent" self and a "transcendental" self. A transcendent self would be a self other than and apart from the concrete person who I am, one that transcends the limitations of everyday life. A transcendental self is a formal and essential element of any concrete self.

28 This is not the same as, nor even analogous with, being "the author of oneself" in a literary or aesthetic sense. Heidegger does not use the word "author" outside of the context of responsibility in the ordinary sense. Heidegger's view is thus not close to those who use literary authorship as a model, such as Nietzsche or Ortega y Gasset.

29 Aristotle, *Nicomachean Ethics*, Book VI, 1141b8.

30 Some commentators construe Heidegger here as identifying *phronesis* with conscience, but this is not precise: conscience *set into motion* is conscience as it leads to action, i.e., resoluteness.

31 This way of unifying the Aristotelian and existentialist elements in Heidegger's notion of authenticity is related to Dreyfus's attempt in "Could Anything Be More Intelligible Than Everyday Intelligibility?" Dreyfus takes running-forth into death to liberate Dasein for a creative world-founding response to the current situation. There is not much evidence of this in *Being and Time*, however.

15 Temporality as the Ontological Sense of Care

INTRODUCTION

In §65, "Temporality as the Ontological Sense of Care," Heidegger argues that a basic temporal structure makes existence possible. It is one of the crucial sections of the overall argument of *Being and Time*. It wraps up Heidegger's existential phenomenology of death, guilt, and authenticity; it provides the conceptual grounding for the phenomenology of being-in-the-world in Division I; it sets up the analysis of the historicality of Dasein; it constitutes Heidegger's answer to his repeated questions about the wholeness of Dasein and the nature of the self; and it establishes the connection between being and time, although the notion of time here is unusual.

For all its importance, the argument of §65 is obscure, as Heidegger does not provide a lot of detail. The connections to the existentialist theme of authenticity are unclear. The transcendental argument that temporality makes care possible is so quick that it is easy to miss altogether. Heidegger claims that temporality somehow *unifies* the various aspects of care, but it is hard to see what justifies this claim. Even the terms in which the question is posed are confusing: what does "temporality" mean here, and what does it mean to ask about the "ontological sense" of care?

My interpretation of §65 in this chapter answers these questions. It rests on two fairly uncontroversial insights that I take to be fundamental for any successful reading of Division II. The first of these is that Heidegger's argument in *Being and Time* combines two different strategies: a phenomenological analysis and a transcendental argument. Division I consists almost entirely of phenomenology. At the beginning of Division II, Heidegger says that these analyses are incomplete or partial. He proposes to remedy this shortcoming through a phenomenological analysis of the limit conditions of existence, death, and thrownness. Throughout this existential phenomenology, Heidegger is laying the groundwork for a transcendental argument, whose point is to establish the *possibility* of the phenomena revealed in the existential analytic.

338

For Heidegger, this means to show that the various aspects of these phenomena belong together necessarily, that is, that they form a unity and that each aspect is only intelligible as an aspect of the underlying unity. Section 65 brings these two strategies together as Heidegger connects the phenomenology of human existence with a structural analysis of the possibility of existence.

The second basic insight is that Heidegger models his transcendental argument on his interpretations of Kant's *Critique of Pure Reason*, particularly his readings of the transcendental deduction and the schematism, which he gives for the first time in his 1925–6 *Logic* lectures and continues to develop over the next few years. I cannot here rehearse the many textual, historical, and philosophical reasons that motivate this basic insight. Division II of *Being and Time* is intimately intertwined with the work that culminates in Heidegger's 1929 book on Kant, and Heidegger's claims about originary temporality are central to both. This connection is especially clear in §65, and paying attention to it helps fill in the details of the transcendental argument Heidegger constructs here. Two points stand out. First, we can make some headway in understanding Heidegger's claim about the necessary unity of the three temporal ecstases by extrapolating from his interpretation of Kant's analysis of the threefold synthesis in the A-deduction. Second, Heidegger insists that Kant's text indicates a structural connection between time and apperception. Section 65 also asserts a basic connection between time and a notion of the self that lies hidden in care.

SENSE, PROJECTION, AND PRIMARY PROJECTION

The main claims of §65 are that temporality is the transcendental condition of existence, that it unifies the various aspects of existence, and that it constitutes the structure of the self. Heidegger frames these claims by stating that temporality is the "ontological sense of care."[1] We need to begin by clarifying how "sense" and the associated notion of "projection" set up the issue.

Heidegger first discusses sense in §32, "Understanding and Interpretation." To understand an entity is to disclose it in its being or, in Heidegger's terminology, to project it onto its being. For example, I understand a piece of chalk in terms of my ability to hold it and write with it in the course of lecturing. The chalk shows up *as* chalk in the context of a background of possibilities that I navigate skillfully. In using the chalk, I am "projecting" it onto this background, or the chalk *makes sense* in terms of this background. Strictly speaking, Heidegger says, I understand the chalk, not its sense, but "sense is that, in which the intelligibility [*Verständlichkeit*] of something

maintains itself" (151). The sense, in this example, consists of the practices of classrooms and blackboards that I have mastered and in terms
of which I understand the entities that show up within them. Hence,
Heidegger defines sense more generally as the "upon-which of projection, in terms of which something becomes intelligible as something"
and as the "formal existential scaffolding of disclosure that belongs to
understanding" (151). We do not understand sense, but we understand
entities in terms of their sense, by projecting them onto their sense.[2]

Heidegger begins §65 by reprising this definition of sense:

> Sense is that wherein the understandability [Verstehbarkeit] of something
> maintains itself, although it does not explicitly and thematically come into
> view. Sense means the upon-which of the primary projection, in terms of which
> something can be comprehended in its possibility as that which it is. (324)

This is virtually the same definition as the one he gave in §32, but
Heidegger here adds the word "primary." While sense is the intelligible background of all projection, when considering temporality as the
sense of care in §65 Heidegger focuses on what he calls the "primary"
projection.

The relation between projection and primary projection parallels the
relation between understanding and understanding of being. The primary projection is the projection of the understanding of being. I understand an *entity* insofar as I understand what it is, that is, understand it in
its *being*; so each instance of understanding an entity is also an instance
of understanding the being of that entity. I understand the chalk, that is,
I am familiar with classrooms, blackboards, and lecturing; this means
that I understand the being of the chalk, that is, that I skillfully disclose
it as an available piece of equipment to be used in determinate ways
within a holistic context of involvements.

> When we say: an entity "has sense," this means it has become accessible in
> its being, which first of all "has sense" properly. The entity only "has" sense
> because, already disclosed as being, it becomes intelligible in the projection of
> being, i.e. in terms of the 'upon-which' of that projection. (324)

Further, each instance of understanding the *being of an entity* requires
a more basic understanding of *being in general*.[3] Classrooms, blackboards, and lecturing can only make sense of the chalk insofar as they
make sense to me at all. And they make sense to me insofar as they
constitute possible ways for me to be. This general background understanding is my understanding of being. It consists of basic abilities that
disclose background practices as purposive, existential possibilities.[4]
These basic abilities make up the primary projection.

> The primary projection of the understanding of being [Verstehens von Sein]
> "gives" the sense. The question regarding the sense of the being of an entity has

as its topic the upon-which of the understanding of being [*Seinsverstehens*] that lies at the basis of all *being* of entities. (325)

In other words, the sense, the "upon-which" Heidegger wants to make explicit in §65 is not the sense of this or that type of entity, but the sense of the understanding of being in general.[5]

This basic understanding of being, which Heidegger says "nourishes" all understanding of particular entities, is bound up with the self-understanding of existing Dasein. My background understanding of classrooms and lectures makes sense of entities because it discloses possible ways for me to be, as an academic or a student. "Being-in-the-world, which is disclosed to itself, understands with the being of the entity that it itself is, also the being of the entities it discovers within the world" (324). On the one hand, understanding entities requires a set of basic abilities that enable us to disclose existential possibilities and, on the other hand, these very same abilities also constitute our own being. We are, as existing Dasein, an ability-to-be. So, Heidegger points out, the sense of the primary projection of the being of worldly entities is the same thing as the sense of the primary projection of the being of Dasein.

The disclosed being is the being of an entity, for whom this being is at stake. The sense of this being, i.e. of care, ... makes up the being of ability-to-be. The sense of the being of Dasein is not a free-floating something else and "outside" of itself, but rather the self-understanding Dasein itself. (325)

This is why the question about the "sense of care" is about Dasein's self-understanding. What basic structure explains that Dasein discloses possibilities and understands itself in terms of its ability to be those possibilities? To use our example: how can I disclose being an academic as a possible way to be? And how can I understand myself as an ability to be that possibility? Heidegger answers these questions by explicating the structure he calls temporality.

AUTHENTICITY

The question Heidegger poses in §65 is this: what basic structure explains how we disclose possibilities and understand ourselves as an ability to be those possibilities? It is not obvious what kind of "basic structure" Heidegger is looking for. What would count as an answer to this question?

Heidegger states his requirements for an answer in terms of the unity and wholeness of the various aspects of care.

With the question about the sense of care we ask: what makes possible the wholeness of the articulated structural whole of care in the unity of its unfolded articulation? (324)

This reprises the two main points of the methodological considerations that Heidegger uses to introduce Division II. In §45, he says that an "originary ontological interpretation" of an entity must explicitly thematize the *whole* of the entity and explain it with respect to the *unity* of its structural moments (232). So the explanation of care in terms of temporality in §65 is such an "originary ontological interpretation." This is why Heidegger calls the §65 notion "originary" temporality.

Regarding wholeness, in §45, Heidegger claims that the interpretation of Dasein in Division I cannot be originary because it does not thematize existence as a whole. He proposes to remedy this shortcoming with the analysis of authentic Dasein. The phenomenological description of authentic existence in the chapters on death and guilt is meant to provide this explicit thematization of existence as a whole. Scholars disagree about how exactly authentic existence is more "whole" or complete than inauthentic existence, and I can only sketch the answer here. In the section on "Dasein as Understanding" (§31) and again in "The Temporality of Understanding" (§68a), Heidegger says that inauthentic, un-owned existence understands itself in terms of the world, or the successes and failures of its dealings, while authentic, owned existence understands itself in terms of its own being, namely the ability to be purposively (337; cf. 146). For example, if I exist inauthentically, I might understand myself as a successful college professor, or a second-rate race-car driver. If I exist authentically, I might also press into those possibilities and understand the world in light of these possibilities; however, I understand myself as purely being-possible, as the ability to pursue possibilities. Inauthentic Dasein identifies itself with a role or profession (college professor), while authentic Dasein identifies itself *entirely* as being-possible. So authentic existence comprises a thoroughgoing self-identification with being-possible. This is why authentic existence, which Heidegger characterizes as ability-to-be-wholly (*Ganzseinkönnen*), is constituted by forerunning into death and ability-to-be-guilty: these are two ways of disclosing possibilities that also disclose that beyond them I am nothing. Heidegger's "extreme" phenomenology of death and guilt in Division II thus thematizes existence as a *whole* because it makes explicit this thoroughgoing self-identification with possibilities. The analyses of Division I cover all aspects of care, but they do not show that these are *all* there is to existence.

Wholeness implies unity. Entities or abilities only form a whole insofar as they belong together, that is, insofar as something explains their unity. Familiar examples of this are organisms or systems, where the overall function explains what each part of the system is; or texts and narratives, in which the meaning of each part is determined by its place in the whole. Similarly, the care structure, which consists of future-directed understanding, past-directed disposedness, and present absorption, forms a whole insofar as there is an underlying unity that makes sense of each aspect of care. As we just saw, the wholeness of existence consists of disclosing oneself as pure being-possible. Each aspect of care belongs to this whole insofar as care can be explained in terms of this self-disclosure. The basic structure Heidegger is looking for in §65, then, is the structure of self-disclosure implicit in existence that, first, makes sense of each aspect of care and, second, explains how each aspect of care necessarily involves every other aspect of care.

THE SELF

What unifies the aspects of care? The short answer to the question of §65 is simply "the self." Dasein is in each case mine, which means that each Dasein is a self and can have her possibilities as her own. In understanding, you disclose *your* possibilities; in being disposed, you disclose things as mattering to *you*; in being amidst entities, you encounter them in *your* concernful dealings.

This is indeed Heidegger's answer, but it takes some interpreting to make this clear. To begin with, it is not obvious that Heidegger is talking about the self in §65. He does not mention the self (*das Selbst*) or selfhood (*Selbstheit*) at all in this section.[6] In the preceding section, "Care and Selfhood," however, Heidegger makes it clear that the argument about originary temporality is his account of the self. This section, too, starts with the question about the "unity and wholeness of the articulated structural whole" of care and says that we can only understand Dasein's unity insofar as "in each case *I* am this entity. The 'I' seems to 'hold together' the wholeness of the structural whole" (317). The remainder of §64 consists of a sharp rejection of the conception of the self as a subject or a substance in the philosophical tradition and in Kant.[7] Nevertheless, Heidegger does not reject the notion of the self altogether. His point in §64 is that the self is not a substrate, but that selfhood is already implicit in the care-structure. To understand the self, we must interpret the care structure more carefully: "Fully understood, the care structure includes the phenomenon of selfhood within it. This is clarified in the interpretation of the sense of care" (323). This is both the conclusion of §64 and the introduction to §65 on originary temporality. The goal in this latter section is precisely to interpret the care structure in such a way as to make the "selfhood" that unifies it explicit. Accordingly, just *after* §65 Heidegger summarizes the upshot of this interpretation: "Now that selfhood has been *explicitly* brought back to the structure of care, and therefore of temporality" (332).

The bigger interpretative difficulty we will face below is to see how Heidegger's explanation of originary temporality and its ecstases amounts to an explanation of anything like a "self" or an "I" at all, and how it confers necessary unity onto all aspects of care. We just saw that in §64 Heidegger criticizes the traditional conception of the self, and it helps to recall the upshot of those criticisms. Heidegger faults traditional explanations for treating the self as an occurrent thing, rather than an existential structure. This is true both for views like pre-Kantian rational psychology that conceive of the self as a substance, and for Kant's own view of the self as subject.

> For the ontological concept of the subject does not characterize the selfhood of the I qua self, but rather the sameness and enduringness of something always already occurrent. To determine the I ontologically as subject means to always already treat it as something occurrent. The being of the I is understood as the reality of the res cogitans. (320)

Occurrence, however, is not the mode of being of Dasein. The self must be conceived in terms of existential phenomena, that is, in terms of abilities and possibilities. Here, too, the phenomenology of authentic Dasein is crucial, for it reveals that existence is nothing but being possible, while inauthentic existence covers up its own mode of being. Therefore, says Heidegger, "existentially selfhood can only be read off from the authentic ability-to-be-a-self, i.e. from the authenticity of the being of Dasein as care" (322).

OUTLINE OF TEMPORALITY IN SECTION 65

The main argument in §65 occupies four dense paragraphs on pages 325 and 326, one for each dimension of temporality, and one to tie them together. In each case, Heidegger first states the relevant aspect of care as it shows itself in authentic existence, then claims that this aspect is only possible on the basis of some further structure, and finally asserts that this further structure is part of originary temporality. In the case of the future, this goes as follows:

> Forerunning resoluteness is *being toward* your ownmost, distinctive ability-to-be. This is only possible insofar as you *can* come toward yourself in your ownmost possibility *at all* and maintain this possibility as a possibility in this letting-yourself-come-toward-yourself, i.e. exist. Maintaining the distinctive possibility and letting yourself come toward yourself in it, this is the originary phenomenon of the future. (325)

Similarly, existing authentically also means "taking over your thrownness, or being your Dasein authentically in the way it always already was." And this is "only possible" insofar as you "can *be* your 'been-ness'" (326). This phenomenon of being your beenness Heidegger calls the originary past. And, finally, resolute being-amidst entities is only possible in making present or "enpresenting" these entities. This enpresenting is the originary present. With coming-toward, having-been, and enpresenting, Heidegger thus points out three aspects of originary temporality. He calls these the temporal "ecstases" (329), in order to emphasize their character of "standing beyond." Together they form the "unitary phenomenon" of temporality.

These dense paragraphs leave many questions open. Most importantly, we need to explain what accounts for the unity of the temporal ecstases. Further, we need to make sense of Heidegger's claim that the ecstases are the condition of the possibility of care, that is, that authentic existence is "only possible" on the basis of temporality. As I indicated above, the answer to both of these questions involves Heidegger's conception of the self. The unity of temporality is the unity of the self; and, similarly, the condition of the possibility of existence as care is that in each case existence is mine, that is, owned by a self.

In the remainder of §65, Heidegger spells out two consequences of his conception of originary temporality: first, that the future has priority over the past and present; and second that originary temporality is finite. Both of these highlight a more basic claim, that originary temporality is not to be conceived in terms of ordinary notions of time as a flow or sequence of moments. In the ordinary conception, time is infinite, and the future does not have priority. Although Heidegger calls the originary ecstatic unity "temporality," he is quite explicit that he does not mean time in any straightforward sense. Time as we ordinarily think of it is not originary because it is derivative from, that is, arises out of, originary temporality.

HEIDEGGER'S KANT-INTERPRETATION

A good way to explain the unity of the three temporal ecstases is to compare Heidegger's argument in §65 to his various interpretations of Kant's threefold synthesis. Historically, we know that Heidegger develops much of his thinking about originary temporality in confrontation with Kant. Heidegger begins to focus on Kant in 1925 as he notices the temporal underpinnings of his phenomenology of everyday care. Reading Kant against the background of phenomenology, Heidegger says "the scales fell from my eyes" (GA 25: 431), and he goes on to develop detailed interpretations in the 1925/6 *Logic* lectures (GA 21) and the 1927/8 lectures on the *Critique of Pure Reason* (GA 25), culminating in the 1929 book *Kant and the Problem of Metaphysics* (GA 3).

Throughout, Heidegger focuses on the originary notion of time that, he argues, underlies and unifies the Kantian faculties, even though Kant himself does not make such a notion of time explicit. Heidegger claims that Kant is trapped in a traditional ontology that privileges concepts and the understanding, but that the phenomena of originary temporality nevertheless come to the fore in Kant's analyses of the threefold synthesis.

Kant discusses the threefold synthesis in the A-edition version of the transcendental deduction. He uses this analysis to explain how it is possible that cognition can be given a manifold of representations, such as sense impressions. Earlier empiricists take this possibility for granted. The thrust of Kant's analysis is to show that a given determinate manifold requires an active cognitive capacity to distinguish, identify, and organize indeterminate sensory inputs, and that the resources of this cognitive capacity suffice to establish the objective validity of the *a priori* structures that constitute them. For example, as I look at my desk, I see a number of books and papers on a gray surface. In order to see them as such, I must first be given the sense data of white rectangles, tiny black print, and so on. But, Kant argues, I am not simply given these sense data. My mind has to apprehend them as such. My given representation is not a bland, indeterminate blob because my mind actively distinguishes elements of the given from one another, sets them alongside one another, and organizes them into a determinate manifold. Each of the three syntheses presents one aspect of these capacities. The synthesis of apprehension in intuition is the action of "running through and taking together" the manifold of an intuition (A 99).[8] The synthesis of reproduction in imagining is the ability to distinguish an element in a series of representations from a preceding one, which requires that the preceding representation be reproduced. And the synthesis of recognition in the concept supplies a rule according to which the manifold is organized and unified into the cognition of a determinate object.

Four features of Kant's discussion of the threefold synthesis are especially relevant to Heidegger's conception of originary temporality. First, Kant argues all along that each synthesis requires the others. In apprehending, the mind runs through a series of representations, which it constitutes as a series by reproducing previous elements alongside each newly apprehended one. "The synthesis of apprehension is therefore inseparably combined with the synthesis of reproduction" (A 102). Further, the mind is only able to reproduce a representation insofar as it is able to identify the reproduction with the original. This self-sameness of the representation in reproduction requires "consciousness that that which we think is the very same as what we thought a moment before"

(A 103), which takes place in the synthesis of recognition in a concept. There are, then, not three separate syntheses but a single, unified synthesis with three aspects.

Second, empirical instances of the synthesis presuppose a pure or transcendental synthesis. It is clear to Kant that there must be an *a priori* version of the threefold synthesis. Our representations of space and time, for instance, are nonempirical representations of a manifold, and must therefore be apprehended, reproduced, and recognized nonempirically. More importantly, this pure synthesis is connected to the empirical synthesis insofar as it makes the latter possible. In running through an empirical manifold, I put it in an order and sequence; I apprehend distinct elements of the manifold by sequencing them in distinct moments. I can only do so insofar as I am able to represent such an order and sequence at all, prior to and independent of any empirical manifold, and this happens in my pure representations of space and time.

Third, the syntheses are immediately related to time. This is clear from the fact that they are "in" representations, that is, in intuitions, concepts, and imaginings. All representations, as modifications of the mind, are in Kant's words "subjected to the formal condition of inner sense, namely time, as that in which they must all be ordered, connected, and brought into relations" (A 99). The syntheses, as actions that constitute representations, are therefore also subject to time. The connection is stronger, though, for the syntheses are the very actions that order, connect, and bring representations into relations. They are therefore not "in" time in the same sense in which representations must be in time. Rather, they are the action that puts representations into a temporal order and thus constitutes them as representations in the first place.

Fourth, the syntheses presume an original unity of consciousness. In his discussion of the synthesis of recognition in the concept, Kant points out that a concept is a single consciousness of a manifold (A 103). In our experience, this unity often shows up late, as if it were an effect of cognition. First, I cognize the mess of papers and books on my desk, then I notice that all these objects are cognized by me. Nevertheless, Kant argues, the unity of consciousness is implicit in all concepts (A 104) and therefore, "however imperfect or obscure it may be," such a unity is inherent in all recognition, whether empirical or pure (A 106). Consequently, there must be, as he puts it, "a transcendental ground" that explains this necessary unity – and this is the transcendental apperception (A 106–7). This point is more familiar from the B-deduction, where Kant leads off with the famous statement that "the I think must be able to accompany all my representations" (B 131), and then goes on to establish this original apperception as the ground of the possibility of synthesis. The argument is ultimately the same in both versions of the deduction. Concepts can only do their work of unifying a manifold insofar as there is an original unity in which the manifold is brought together or synthesized. Since the threefold synthesis includes recognition in a concept, it too requires this original unity. We saw in the first point above that Kant already establishes the unity of the three-fold synthesis by showing how each synthesis requires the others. This fourth point establishes their unity at a deeper level. Besides mutually presupposing each other, the three syntheses are unified because they presuppose a more original unity, the transcendental apperception.

Heidegger thinks that Kant's analysis of the threefold synthesis comes close to articulating the notion of originary temporality.[9] To begin with, Heidegger finds that the syntheses correspond to the three dimensions of time. Apprehension enables representations of the present and reproduction enables representations of the past. As for recognition, it enables us to cognize a representation as the same again; we do so by identifying a representation as such-and-such and projecting the possibility of re-identifying it in the future. In his lecture course, Heidegger proposes to change Kant's term accordingly: "It would be appropriate to call this the synthesis of *pre*-cognition" (GA 25: 364). This relation to time, Heidegger claims, helps to explain the mutual presupposition of the three syntheses. "Insofar as the three modes of synthesis are related to time and these moments of time make up the unity of time itself, the three syntheses themselves obtain their own unified ground in the unity of time" (GA 25: 364). Time is a unity with three dimensions, each synthesis belongs to a dimension of time, and therefore the syntheses are unified. Apprehension requires reproduction just as the present requires the past.

Heidegger goes further. Consider Kant's third point above – that the syntheses are the actions that constitute representations as occurring in a temporal order in inner sense. In empirical cognition, the syntheses take up the given and form representations that appear in inner sense as ordered in a sequence of moments: *now* the white rectangle, *now* the black squiggle, *now* the other black squiggle, and so on as I apprehend the determinate manifold of sense data that I cognize as the papers and books on my desk. Heidegger argues that the same point holds for the pure, nonempirical representation of time. Not only are sense data given in a sequence of nows, but the very sequence of moments itself is constituted by the action of the threefold synthesis. The relation of the pure, transcendental syntheses to the dimensions of time is that the syntheses form or produce time. "The pure apprehending synthesis does not merely take place within the horizon of time, but it first forms such a thing as the now and the sequence of nows" (GA 3: 180).

Similarly, "the pure synthesis in the mode of reproduction forms the past [*Gewesenheit*] as such" and hence is "time-forming" (*zeitbildend*; GA 3: 182). On Heidegger's reading of Kant, the faculty that performs the threefold synthesis is the transcendental imagination.[10] So, Heidegger says, the sequence of nows that make up time as we usually understand it "is not time in its originary guise. The transcendental imagination lets time arise as a sequence of nows, and it is therefore the originary time" (GA 3: 175). Compare this to the parallel claim in §65 of *Being and Time*: "Since we demonstrate that the 'time' that is accessible to Dasein's understanding is *not* originary, but arises from authentic temporality, we can justify naming this temporality the originary time" (329).

The distinction between originary time and derivative time leads to a renewed question about the unity of the syntheses. The three syntheses relate to the past, present, and future. Since time is unified, so are the syntheses. However, time conceived as a sequence of past, present, and future moments is derivative. Hence, we cannot appeal to the unity of this derivative time to explain the unity of the syntheses from which it derives. Rather, there must be an originary unity of the syntheses that explains the unity of time. On Heidegger's view, Kant rightly claims that the transcendental apperception is this originary unity. However, Kant does not characterize the transcendental apperception in temporal terms. Heidegger thinks that, at precisely this point, Kant falls victim to the shortcomings of his ontological framework. "The inner rupture in the foundation of the Kantian problem becomes clear here: the lack of a connection between time and the transcendental apperception" (GA 25: 358). Heidegger therefore goes on to argue that the self has a temporal character, that is, that "time and the 'I think' do not incongruously oppose one another, but turn out to be one and the same" (GA 3: 191). Properly understood, they are both the originary unity of the threefold synthesis that first produces the pure representation of a temporal sequence within which the transcendental subject can encounter objects. Going beyond Kant, Heidegger here explicitly draws on his discussion of selfhood and originary temporality in *Being and Time*: "Only on the basis of this investigation was it possible for me to understand what Kant was seeking, or had to be seeking. Only against this background can the unity of time and the transcendental apperception be conceived as a problem" (GA 25: 394).

Let me rehearse the most important parallels and differences between Heidegger's Kant-interpretation and his argument in §65 of *Being and Time*. Kant distinguishes pure syntheses from empirical syntheses and claims that the former make the latter possible. Similarly, Heidegger argues that the originary temporal ecstases make Dasein's factical existence possible. Kant's three pure syntheses correspond directly to

Heidegger's three ecstases. "The pure syntheses are the basic forms according to which the subject must reach out" (GA 25: 388), and "in so reaching out the subject steps beyond itself. This reaching out and stepping beyond we call the ecstasis, the ecstatic basic character of the subject" (GA 25: 390). For our interpretation of the unity of the ecstases, this suggests that, like the three syntheses, the three ecstases of temporality show themselves to be unified by presupposing one another. However, Heidegger is concerned with showing a further ground for the unity of the ecstases, which, like Kant's transcendental apperception, is the temporally structured self. One indicator of this self qua originary temporality is that it constitutes the intelligibility of a sequence of moments as the horizon in which it can encounter objects. More centrally, though, it constitutes time in such a way that Dasein can in some sense own the objects and representations it encounters. In Heidegger's words, originary temporality "constitutes a dimension of possible belonging-to-me-ness [Mirzugehörigkeit] of all entities encounterable within this horizon" (GA 25: 388). This is Heidegger's gloss of Kant's famous claim that "the 'I think' must be able to accompany all my representations" (GA 25: 388).

Despite these parallels and despite Heidegger's efforts to interpret Kant as a proto-Heideggerian, there are deep differences between these two philosophical frameworks. Heidegger rarely uses the words "representation" or "synthesis" in his own work. These terms stem from Kant's cognitivism, the basic view that we relate to the objects of our experience is by cognizing them conceptually. Heidegger thinks of our relation to the world as disclosure, the skillful and attuned ability to press into possibilities. This is ultimately the reason for Heidegger's substantial disagreement with Kant on the nature of the self, for "with respect to the problems of self-identification, Kant takes the I as something that thinks and that can always find itself as this thinking thing" (GA 25: 396). Heidegger, however, argues that "the self must be able to identify itself *as existing*" and that means "extending into all dimensions of temporality" (GA 25: 395). There is more on this below.

TEMPORALITY MAKES CARE POSSIBLE

Returning to *Being and Time*, above, our brief survey of §65 raised three questions. First, in what sense does originary temporality make care possible, that is, in what sense is it the transcendental condition of care? Second, in what sense are the three ecstases a unity? And, third, what justifies Heidegger's claim that originary temporality is an analysis of the self? We are now in a position to develop the answers.

The transcendental claim, that temporality makes care possible, mirrors the relation between the pure and the empirical syntheses in Kant. The empirical syntheses arrange and organize an indeterminate mess of sensations into distinct empirical representations, of books, papers, white rectangles, and so forth. This is only possible because a pure synthesis constitutes the temporal order in which the empirical content can be organized in the first place. Similarly, factical existence is always pressing into some possibility or other on the basis of some concrete disposedness. Heidegger's chosen example of this in §65 is a resolute, authentic Dasein, who foreruns into death and takes over her guilt. As I pointed out above, Heidegger has methodological reasons for focusing on authentic existence. He wants to be sure that the care structure captures existence as a whole, that it does not leave out any possibilities of Dasein, and the extreme phenomenology of death and guilt reveal that beyond its ability-to-be Dasein is nothing. But there are countless other ways in which existence can factically press into particular possibilities.[11] The transcendental claim is that *any* comportment toward particular, factical possibilities (compare: empirical synthesis) presupposes the general ability (compare: pure synthesis) to disclose possibilities as possibilities and constitute them within a horizon of possible *Mirzugehörigkeit*, that is, disclose them as possibly mine. This general ability is originary temporality.

Imagine you are in a classroom in order to give a lecture, for the sake of being a professor. This is something you are able to do, that is, understand how to do, and it is tied up with your "for-the-sake-of-which" and hence your self-understanding. You position yourself within reach of the chalk and the blackboard; you project your voice to fill the large space; you let your gaze engage the students in front of you and occasionally glance at the clock behind you as you pace back and forth at the front of the room. The factical possibility toward which you are comporting yourself, in this example, is lecturing. You are taking up this possibility through your skillful comportment, movement, body position, tone of voice, head tilt, eye contact, pauses, and so forth. Heidegger's sketch of the originary future points out two basic features that first make it possible that you can comport yourself toward this possibility and exist for the sake of being a professor. First, you must be able to "maintain" or "hold out" this possibility as a possibility. By this, Heidegger means that you disclose the world through abilities and competences. Your ability to project and modulate your voice discloses the space as large; your ability to reach for and write with chalk discloses it as ready for you to use; your positioning and pacing discloses the front of the room as the optimal place to stand. You are not plunked down in a room indifferently; you are in a space that is already differentially disclosed by your abilities. Second, you must "let yourself come toward yourself" in this possibility. This means that you must be able to press into lecturing as *your* possibility, that is, that you do so for your own sake. Disclosing possibilities by itself is not enough. You must be able to disclose them as pertaining to you.

The case is similar for the originary past. All factical ways of being thrown and being disposed require the originary past. "The ecstasis of having-been first makes possible finding yourself by way of being disposed" (340). Using the same example, note how the situation is filled with ways in which entities already matter to you and solicit you. It matters that the clock is located behind you; it shows up as inconvenient; the space near the blackboard draws you near, it solicits you as the right space to stand and deliver the lecture; the space around the students shows itself as impenetrable. This disposedness, Heidegger says, is made possible by the originary past, that you *are* your beenness. What you *are*, as Dasein, is ability-to-be, and ability-to-be is always disposed, always finds itself already in a situation.

Here is a good way to characterize Heidegger's transcendental claim in analogy to Kant. For Kant, the empirical syntheses provide us with determinate representations. These are made possible by the pure temporal order in which representations can have their determinacy. For Heidegger, care discloses the world as meaningful, constituted by solicitations and purposes. These are made possible by the temporal ecstases that first constitute you as a discloser in such a way that the possibilities can be yours and the solicitations have a grip on you.[12]

THE UNITY OF THE ECSTASES AND HEIDEGGER'S EXISTENTIAL NOTION OF THE SELF

Originary temporality consists of three ecstases, which form a unified phenomenon and hence unify care. In what sense are the three ecstases a unity? As with Kant's threefold synthesis, there are two arguments for the unity of the ecstases. The first argument is that each of them presupposes the others; or, more precisely, that the originary future and past presuppose one another and the present presupposes both. Heidegger says that "only insofar Dasein is as 'I have-been' can it futurally come toward itself in such a way that it comes back" and "Dasein can only be its beenness insofar as it is futural" (326). And he says that the originary future and past "release" the present: "Beenness arises from the future, in such a way that the having-been future releases the present" (326).

The originary future consists of maintaining possibilities as possibilities and letting yourself come toward yourself. You can only come toward your *self* insofar as the originary future includes some kind of identification with the person, for whose sake you press into the possibility. This self-identification is given insofar as the Dasein that you are *coming toward* is the one that you *already are*. In other words, the possibility of letting yourself come toward yourself depends on the unity of the originary future and beenness. This is what Heidegger means by saying that Dasein can only come toward itself "in such a way that it comes back." In our example, this unity shows up readily. You lecture for the sake of "coming toward yourself" as a professor. At the same time, your lecturing already discloses the situation in a "professorish" way, and so you are coming toward yourself as you already find yourself. That the clock is inconveniently located, for example, is a matter of both your ability to lecture (for the sake of being a professor) and your disposedness (finding things mattering the way they matter to professors). This connection between the relevant ability and attunement is rooted in your ownership of the possibility: *you* competently position your body, face the students, and make eye contact, and *you* are affected by the solicitation of the clock behind you. Without this unity – if one person skillfully lectures while another is affected by the solicitations of the clock – the clock would not show up as inconvenient. In fact, without some combination of an ability and some kind of attunement, the clock would not show up at all. Hence, these two temporal ecstases "release" the present.

This first argument for the unity of the ecstases points to the second, more fundamental one. The three ecstases, and hence the various aspects of care, are unified because they are the fundamental determinations of the self. The analysis of temporality as the sense of care aims to uncover the selfhood that is "already included in the fully conceived structure of care" (323). So the ecstases and the aspects of care belong together because they are all *mine*. In Kant, the "I think" unifies all his representations, because the I that thinks is itself a unity. This does not require further argumentation. Similarly, Heidegger does not argue here that the self is unified; and from the fact that originary temporality makes care possible, it follows that it "accompanies," or better "pervades," all of Dasein's abilities and attunements. Rather, the question we face as interpreters of §65 is why Heidegger's description of ecstatic temporality should count as an analysis *of the self*.

For Heidegger, the self is not an act of self-reflection or a noumenal activity. It is not any one thing, locus, or activity. Care does not need, and cannot have, a "foundation in a self" as some separate thing behind the caring (323).

The sense of care, that which makes the constitution of care possible, makes up the being of ability-to-be in an originary way. What makes sense of Dasein's being is not some free floating other thing "outside" itself, but the self-understanding Dasein itself. (325)

Instead, Heidegger analyzes the self as an existential structure that is already implicit in care, that is, a self that consists of ability-to-be and disposedness.

What features of originary temporality should convince us that Heidegger here has articulated a genuine existential notion of the self? In Division II, Heidegger addresses three different criteria for selfhood. The first of these is familiar from historical and contemporary discussions of personal identity. The self holds existence together, or makes up the unity of events over time. Heidegger raises this issue with his question whether the existential analytic has thematized the Dasein as a whole (181, 233, 310, 317), which he later links explicitly to the "connectedness of life" (372, 387). Ecstatic temporality can reasonably count as the existential self if it explains the connectedness of life. In the historicality chapter, especially §75, Heidegger indeed argues this, albeit with a twist. The question, he argues there, arises from a misinterpretation of the nature of existence in inauthentic Dasein that appears to gather itself together from a disconnectedness of occurring events (390). This apparent disconnectedness, however, is grounded in an originary "extendedness." Existence is already connected because temporality is already extended (391).

The second criterion for selfhood is the possibility of owning one's experiences, what Heidegger called *Mirzugehörigkeit* in his Kant lectures. In Kant's cognitivist conception of experiences, this "belonging-to-me-ness" is given by the possibility that the "I think" can accompany all my representations. If ecstatic temporality explains how you can own experiences, then once again Heidegger is justified in claiming that temporality is the structure of selfhood. But this is clearly a central aspect of ecstatic temporality. The originary future, that is, letting yourself come toward yourself, and the originary past, that is, being your having-been, together determine the disclosure of possibilities that Dasein can be. They do not first disclose independent possibilities to which a Dasein then somehow needs to add its existence; rather, the most originary disclosure of possibilities is already permeated by self-relating existence. So by virtue of the structure of originary temporality, Dasein discloses possibilities as already accompanied by its own ability-to-be itself. This constitutes *Mirzugehörigkeit* in *Being and Time*.

The third criterion for selfhood is self-identification. Part of the concept of a self is that it stands in a relation to itself in which it identifies itself as itself. In Kant and in most of the philosophical tradition, this self-relation is cognitive. In fact, Kant claims there are two types of self-identification. On the one hand, "through inner sense we intuit ourselves only as we are internally affected by our selves, i.e. as far as inner intuition is concerned we cognize our own subject only as appearance but not in accordance with what it is in itself" (B 156). On the other hand, "in the synthetic unity of apperception, I am conscious of myself not as I appear to myself, nor as I am in myself, but only that I am. This is a thinking, not an intuiting" (B 157). So we know ourselves both as we appear to ourselves in intuition and as the subject of thinking that unifies experience. This doubling of self-consciousness is a special case of the transcendental idealism that underlies Kant's analysis of cognition in general.

In contrast to Kant and the tradition, Heidegger argues that self-identification is not a cognitive relation but an existential one.

The self must be able to identify itself *as existing*. It must be able to understand itself in every concrete instance as the self-same futural-having-been, uniting the resolve to a possibility and the commitment to the past. This displacing-yourself-into-yourself [*Sich-in-sich-versetzen*], extending into all dimensions of temporality, makes up the real concept, the existential concept of self-identification. (GA 25: 395)

Self-identification is Dasein's ability to "understand" itself. Understanding, as always in Heidegger, consists of competence or know-how. In *Being and Time*, Heidegger calls it the "ability-to-be-yourself" (*Selbstseinkönnen*) (322). Understanding yourself is the ability to *be* yourself. To be yourself, here, means to exist in terms of the being of your Dasein, that is, in terms of care. Heidegger shows that care is fundamentally temporal, and therefore self-identification is the ability to exist temporally. In this quote from the Kant lecture, Heidegger explains this ability as the unity of resolve and commitment (*Entschluß* and *Verpflichtung*). This unity is precisely the unity of the originary future and past. As we saw above, coming-toward your*self* as what you already are requires the effective identification of your abilities that disclose possibilities (your "resolve" to a possibility for the sake of which you exist) with your attunement to the way things matter (i.e., your "commitment" to how you already find yourself existing). This identification obtains insofar as both the abilities and the attunement are *yours*. Existence is in each case mine; this makes up the self-identification in Heidegger's existential conception of the self.

To summarize, Heidegger uses originary temporality to explain the coherence and connectedness of experiences, the possibility of owning one's experiences, and a type of self-relation that makes it possible to understand oneself as a self. For these reasons, he can claim that originary temporality makes up the existential concept of selfhood, which replaces the ontologically misguided notions of the self, or the "I," as a subject or substrate. This existential concept of selfhood explains why the ecstases are unified and therefore also explains the unity of care.

FINITUDE AND THE PRIORITY OF THE FUTURE

In light of this interpretation, we can now explain Heidegger's claims that originary temporality is finite and that the future has priority over the other two ecstases. It is clear that originary temporality is not time. Heidegger calls it "temporality" because he claims that time "as it is accessible to the intelligibility of Dasein" arises from it (329; Heidegger argues for this claim later in the book, in §81). The distinction between temporality and time corresponds to Heidegger's ontic-ontological difference. "Temporality 'is' not an entity at all" (328), so strictly speaking, we should not say temporality "is" but temporality "temporalizes" (zeitigt). Zeitigen can mean bringing forth, producing, or ripening, and what temporality produces in each case is an existing Dasein for whom entities and the ordinary conception of time are intelligible. "Temporality temporalizes possible ways of itself. These make possible the variety of modes of being of Dasein, most notably the basic possibilities of authentic and inauthentic existence" (328).

In explaining the unity of the ecstases, Heidegger says that "been-ness arises from the future, in such a way that the having-been future releases the present" (326), and that "the future, as futurally having-been first awakens the present" (329). So in addition to the unity of the three ecstases, there is a sense in which the originary future has priority or precedence. This priority, Heidegger says, has to do with "different modes of temporalizing. The difference lies in the fact that temporalizing can primarily determine itself in terms of the different ecstases" (329). So each ecstasis requires the others, and all three are constitutive of the basic unity, the existential notion of the self. However, as the self temporalizes itself, that is, as temporality brings forth concrete existing Dasein, it does so primarily in terms of the future. This means that in each concrete case, the self shows up first and foremost in the purposive comportment toward possibilities, and the past and present show up in terms of this purposiveness. To return to our example, the classroom situation has the features it has because, first and foremost, in lecturing you are comporting yourself toward your possibility as a professor. This, in turn, makes sense of the way you find the situation mattering to you and the way entities show up in the situation. Concrete existential phenomena must be explained primarily in terms of the "for-the-sake-of-which." This is the priority of the originary future in temporalizing concrete existence.

Finally, Heidegger claims that originary temporality is finite. This does not imply that time, as we normally think of it, is finite. The finitude of originary temporality is not about the end of time at all; rather, it explains a feature of existence, that it "exists finitely" (329). With this, Heidegger reminds us of his phenomenology of being-toward-death. Dasein, he says, "factically and constantly" (259) exists toward its end insofar as it always somehow comports itself toward death, understood as the limit or impossibility of its possibilities. This is a constant feature of existence because it is grounded in the finitude of originary temporality itself. The ecstasis of the originary future explains Dasein's being-toward death. "The ecstatic character of the originary future lies precisely in this, that it closes ability-to-be, i.e. is itself closed off, and as such makes possible the resolute existentiell understanding of nullity" (330). Pressing into a possibility, you let yourself come toward yourself. In so doing, you identify yourself in terms of the possibility you project. Possibilities, however, are vulnerable or contingent. You may understand yourself in terms of your ability to be a professor, but that possibility is not essentially or unavoidably yours. You might lose interest, or lose your abilities, or the entire academic profession might go out of business, in which case this possibility ceases to be relevant and you can no longer exist for the sake of it. The only possibility that is unavoidably yours is this paradoxical one – that you exist as being-possible, as projecting and pressing into possibilities, without being able to safely be any one of the possibilities you disclose. This is death, the "unsurpassable" and "ownmost" possibility. In disclosing possibilities, you also understand this "nullity" that you cannot safely be any of your possibilities. Originary temporality is finite because you come toward yourself against the background of the limit or impossibility of your existence. "The originary and authentic future is the toward-yourself, toward your *self*, existing as the unsurpassable possibility of nullity" (330).

NOTES

1 It is better to translate Heidegger's German *Sinn* as "sense" rather than "meaning." One reason for this is that "sense," like *Sinn*, connotes the direction of projecting-upon. All translations in this chapter are my own.

2 Hence, sense is not primarily semantic. Heidegger claims that sentences "also" have sense, but in a derivative way. "Insofar as the assertion (the 'judgment') grounds in understanding and is a derivative form of carrying out construal, is also 'has' a sense" (153). Indeed, *Being and Time* §33 says that sentences have sense because they articulate bits and pieces of the

world that already have sense on their own. Statements about chalk and blackboards have sense because they articulate the sense of the blackboard itself.

3   On this point, we can already note a broad resemblance between the structure of Heidegger's argument and Kant's analysis of the threefold synthesis in the A-deduction. Kant points out that each empirical synthesis requires a pure synthesis that provides the unity within which an entity can be apprehended, reproduced, and recognized. Similarly, Heidegger here points out that understanding an entity requires "pure" understanding of being.

4   In the first two chapters of Division II, Heidegger argues that these "basic abilities" include comportment toward death, guilt, and the self. Without such abilities, Dasein could not disclose possibilities or find itself affected by things mattering; i.e., it could not be Dasein at all.

5   *Seinsverständnis* is what makes the analytic of Dasein relevant to the question of being: Heidegger asks about Dasein in order to ask about being because Dasein understands being. This is the basic reason why, in Division II, Heidegger moves the inquiry toward an explanation of *Seinsverständnis*: "We are looking for an answer to the question about the sense of being in general ... Laying bare the horizon in which something like being becomes intelligible at all amounts to clarifying the possibility of the understanding of being belonging to the make-up of the entity we call Dasein. But understanding of being can only be clarified *radically* as an essential feature of the being of Dasein, if the entity to whose being it belongs is itself interpreted *in an originary way* with respect to its being" (231).

6   Except for the first sentence, which reprises §64.

7   Note the scare quotes around "I" and "hold together." Heidegger uses these to indicate a basic disagreement with traditional ways of conceiving of the type of unity the self or the "I" constitutes. In §75, he argues that the question about the "connectedness" of the self arises from a misunderstanding of the nature of existence.

8   Immanuel Kant, *Critique of Pure Reason*, trans. and ed. Paul Guyer and Allen W. Wood (Cambridge: Cambridge University Press, 1998). In-text citations refer to the Academy pagination.

9   Heidegger's Kant-interpretation is often regarded as not faithful to Kant's own thought. As if apologizing for this, Heidegger himself writes in a 1973 preface to his Kant book that he forced the issues of *Being and Time*, which are foreign to Kant's set of problems, onto Kant's text (GA 3: xiv/xvii). Certainly, this is no reason to dismiss Heidegger's interpretation. In fact, it was and continues to be influential. In any case, in the present paper, we are concerned precisely with the issues of *Being and Time*, so we need not worry about the accuracy of his reading of Kant.

10 This claim is supported by the text of the A edition, see esp. A 118. It is central to Heidegger's opposition to neo-Kantian readings that, basing themselves primarily on the B edition text, argue that the transcendental deduction shows the understanding to be more fundamental than intuition, and that Kant is therefore a logical idealist. Béatrice Longuenesse explains

how Kant's claims in the two versions are compatible in *Kant and the Capacity to Judge* (Princeton: Princeton University Press, 1998), 63.

11 "The phenomenon attained with regard to resoluteness represents only one modality of temporality, which makes possible care as such in general" (327). Cf. "Projecting and understanding yourself in an existentiell possibility is grounded in the future as coming-towards-yourself from the possibility as which you exist" (336). Any existential possibility presupposes the originary future.

12 This analogy also extends to the schemata. For Kant, the schemata are temporal patterns in which the categories show up in representations (permanence, absence, sequence, etc.), and these representations hence are objectively valid for the cognizer. Heidegger's horizonal schemata are ways in which solicitations and purposes show up as yours: for-the-sake-of-which, in-order-to, in-the-face-of-which (365), i.e., are significant for the existing Dasein.

16   Historical Finitude

The late chapter on temporality and historicality (*Geschichtlichkeit*) is one of the most obscure parts of *Being and Time*. Most commentators pass over it in silence, while several others dismiss it as confused, or worse. The challenge is to make sense of it at all. In this chapter, I claim that Heidegger's distinctive notion of the *existential situation*, understood as a modality of death, is the exegetical key. A general situation (*Lage*) is one situation among others within a historical form of life. An existential situation (*Situation*) is a situation in which the viability of a historical form of life as a whole is at stake – a situation, that is, in which the very possibility of a general situation hangs in the balance. This reading places the finitude of death within a historical frame, hence my title.

The paper falls into six sections. In §1, I introduce Heidegger's project in *Being and Time*. In §2, I sketch the central idea of ontological understanding. In §3, I discuss the sense in which this understanding is structured by the finitude of death, and proceed to elaborate this finitude by outlining Heidegger's appropriation of Kant's conception of the finite intellect. This all sets the stage for the contrast between general situations and existential situations (§§4 and 5), which I then apply to Heidegger's theorization of "the basic constitution of historicality" (§74 of *Being and Time*). I conclude by briefly suggesting how my interpretation addresses two natural questions about finitude that often arise for readers working through *Being and Time*.

The paper is dedicated to my late friend and teacher, John Haugeland (1945–2010). He did not have the time to work out an interpretation of the existential situation, a late Division II theme. The reading I offer is inspired by his path-breaking work. I am grateful to Bert Dreyfus, Mike Inwood, Wayne Martin, Adrian Moore, Stephen Mulhall, George Pattison, Robert Pippin, B. Scot Rousse, Kate Withy, Mark Wrathall, and Natasha Yarotskaya for helpful conversation and comments.

What is Heidegger's project in *Being and Time*? The project is to concretely work out of the question of the sense (*Sinn*) of being. Being is the
intelligibility of what is; there can be little doubt that this is the notion
of being that interests Heidegger:

And if we are inquiring about the sense of being, our investigation ... asks about
being itself insofar as being enters into the intelligibility of Dasein. (152)[1]

"Entity" (*Seiend*) is Heidegger's term of art for that which is "everything
we talk about, everything we have in view, everything towards which
we comport ourselves in any way" (6–7). "Being" (*Sein*) is thus "that
which determines entities as entities, that on the basis of which entities are already understood (*verstanden*)" (6). While the sense of being is
an ancient and venerable philosophical problem, the problem has fallen
dormant, *as a problem*, and thus needs reawakening. We are thus being
invited by Heidegger to consider with fresh eyes, as one commentator
has recently well put it, "the truly remarkable and singular fact that
sense is made of anything, and to try and make sense of that."[2]

The question, then, asks about what it takes to understand entities
as entities, that is, what it takes to make sense of them in terms of
their being. Heidegger's almost obsessive insistence that we approach
this task "concretely" is rich and many-sided. The demand, in the first
instance, is to focus squarely on the one for whom things *actually* make
sense, namely Dasein. Dasein's distinctive feature is to understand being
(*Seinsverständnis*), which is a capacity or an ability. This, however, is
not one ability among others that Dasein might happen peculiarly to
have. For unlike being able to tie one's shoes or being able to speak, say,
English, understanding being is an ability that is definitive of Dasein
as the kind of entity that it is: "Dasein is ontically distinctive in that
it *is* ontological" (12) – hence Heidegger's characterization of this fundamental ability not as an ability one "has" but as an "ability-to-*be*."
Understanding being – the ability to make sense of things as such – is
the mark of the distinctively human.[3]

Heidegger calls his account an "existential analytic of Dasein," an
exercise self-consciously offered after Kant's transcendental analytic in
the *Critique of Pure Reason*. "Dasein" is a successor term for what Kant
and the German idealists tended to call "the subject." Using "Dasein,"
Heidegger wagers, guards against various myths and *aporia* wrapped up
with some traditional uses of the term "subjectivity," and so is less
risky. One conspicuous piece of baggage is an interiorized conception
of the human being as a self-contained "cabinet of consciousness" cut
off from any worldly existence. Heidegger is himself happy, at least at

times, to characterize his orienting theme as "the ontology of the sub-jectivity of the subject." However, he usually adds the qualifier "in the well understood sense."[4]

ONTOLOGICAL UNDERSTANDING

If to be Dasein is to be "in the business" of making sense of entities, what precisely is this business? To make sense of an entity, in the rel-evant sense, is to understand its being. To understand the being of an entity (including oneself) is to understand the ways that entity can be – and, no less, cannot be. Heidegger accordingly characterizes the under-standing at issue as "the projection of entities onto their possibilities."[5] Lizards and babies inhabit their respective environments. An adult human being, by contrast, understands its world. What is the differ-ence that makes the difference? An adult's understanding of the world is a matter of appreciating what is possible and not possible with the actual entities toward which it comports. More precisely, the human adult comports toward entities *as* actual or real in virtue of understand-ing the possibilities in terms of which those entities are what and how they are.

We can approach Heidegger's conception of ontological understanding by reminding ourselves that we, unlike lizards and babies, hold things to standards. Consider the following three brief examples to illustrate the phenomenon. To be a hammer is to be able, when well wielded, to drive in nails (among other things). The field of possibilities for being a hammer has developed through history by human agents engaging in the practice of carpentry. If one picks up a hammer to discover that it is made of butter, one has been taken in. It is a gimmick, or maybe a work of art. The "hammer" is flouting the functional standards that make hammers what they are, and so *could not* be a real hammer. Those who understand carpentry, and so make sense of hammers *as* hammers, appreciate this fake hammer for what it is, and would insist on its unre-ality if challenged. To be a real or actual hammer, after all, is to accord with certain ontological, in this case, functional, standards.

To be a rook is to move and capture in the appropriate ways. Those ways are specified by the rules of the game of chess, which lay out the field of possibilities for being, among other pieces, a rook. For exam-ple, if a rook is moved diagonally, like a bishop, something is awry. The "rook" in this case, thanks to a wayward chess player, is flout-ing the standards that make a rook what it is, and so, at least at this moment, *could not* truly be a rook.[6] Those who understand chess, and so make sense of rooks *as* rooks, would rule this move out, and then no doubt proceed to try and coax the piece back into the field of play. To be a rook, after all, is to accord with ontological standards, in this case the rules of the game.

To be an ordinary perceptible thing is to behave in more or less stable and predictable ways. The "laws" of ordinary medium-sized things lay out the field of possibilities for being such things. For example, if one were to see an object, say a rock, that pops in and out of existence depending on whether one is looking at it, something would be awry, and would be recognized as such by any competent perceiver. The "rock" would be flouting the standards of substantial independence and persistence that hold for ordinary objects as such, and so *could not* be any such thing. Those who understand ordinary objects, and so make sense of them as such, would find themselves compelled in this situation to look again, and might very well worry that they have been drugged, for to be an ordinary perceptible thing is to accord with certain ontological standards.

Heidegger is suggesting, then, with great plausibility, that entities must "live up" to standards in order to count as being. Such standards are accordingly ontological standards – standards concerning what it is for entities *to be* as opposed *not* to be. Ontological standards are, one might say, the "ground rules" of the real. To comport toward actual entities oriented by the standards that frame their possibilities – an orientation without which, Heidegger claims, there would be no comportment toward entities *as* entities – is to understand being. To understand being is to be able to appreciate, and look after, the distinction between the being and non-being of the entities. The possession of such understanding constitutes the human ability-to-be.

The totality of what is does not make up a homogenous structure. The totality of what is, rather, divides into regions of being. Three ontological regions figure prominently in *Being and Time*: the being of equipment, the being of substance ("mere things"), and the being of Dasein. Heidegger also discusses the regionalization of being from a lower altitude, in terms of "subject-matters" (*Sachgebiete*). These regions or subject matters are constituted in terms of basic concepts or categories (*Grundbegriffe*) that articulate the forms of intelligibility at work in the respective areas of that which is. These concepts or categories are "basic" because they lay out the basic constitution (*Grundverfassung*) of an entity qua occupant of its respective region of being. In the terms used above, the categories articulate the ontological standards that structure and govern the ways in which entities are intelligible.

Heidegger inherits the idea of ontological categories that fund the intelligibility of entities, and therewith the project of making sense of them, from a long tradition of philosophical reflection. The inheritance, however, does not bow to tradition. Previous philosophers tended to inquire into the following kinds of questions: What are the categories of being? How precisely are the categories constitutive of the being of entities? Are there relations of priority, in some sense, among categories? How are regions of being individuated? Do regions of being stand in relations of hierarchy and inclusion? What principle unites the respective regions: what makes the regions of being all regions of *being*? Heidegger is seriously interested in these questions and puzzles, particularly the last question. But he takes as basic, as previous philosophers did not, the way in which ontology demands reflection on human life. Approaching the inquiry into human understanding concretely, he asks: What is it to *live by* ontological categories in engaging in our characteristic endeavor, namely making sense of things? With this question, ontology in effect takes a reflexive turn: what categories are proper to the entity whose charge is to make sense of entities? In short, what is the ontology of the distinctively human form of life?

Heidegger is suggesting that, amid the variation and diversity in forms of intelligibility across distinct regions of being, there lies a more formal notion of ontological understanding that is at work "across" the regions. Any regional understanding of being is a species of the more formal notion, the subject of which is the human "ability-to-be" as such. The subject of an existing (deformalized) regional understanding of being is what Heidegger calls a "factical ability-to-be." Typically, an individual person – a "Dasein" in its use as a count noun – participates in multiple factical abilities-to-be at any given time, at least in the modern world. So if Sam is a practicing chemist, he lives out what one might call the "chemistry ability-to-be." If Sam fixes cars too, he lives out the "auto mechanic ability-to-be." If Sam is a teacher, he lives out the "teacher ability-to-be." These are distinct factical abilities-to-be, which embody their own respective (regional) ontological understandings, and so are instances of the human ability-to-be. A factical ability-to-be is roughly what one might call a *form of life*. Heidegger does not enter a discussion, in any detail, of what makes one factical ability-to-be distinct from another. His inquiry is devoted to the structure they all share in virtue of being forms of human life that embody an understanding of being.[7]

The categories of Dasein are dubbed "existentialia," leaving the traditional term "category" for the ontology of entities, no matter the region, other than Dasein. The point of introducing the piece of jargon is to remind the reader that Dasein has its own distinctive ontology. The reason for this particular piece of jargon is to stress that any particular *existentiale* under scrutiny will amount to an unfolding of the sense of the initial title reserved to designate the being of Dasein, namely "existence" (42). And the guiding claim of the existential analytic as a whole is that existence – the way of being of human mindedness such that it is capable of understanding being – has a distinctive temporal form. The task is to elucidate the temporal form of human existence and thereby explain the ability to make sense of entities.

DEATH AS ONTOLOGICAL FRAGILITY

Death, in Heidegger's systematic ontology, is an *existentiale*. It marks a sense of radical futurity characteristic of existence. While Heidegger is not the first to draw a constitutive link between death and human understanding – Hegel is one notorious predecessor – no philosopher has given death a more fundamental place. By "death," Heidegger does not mean biological death or croaking ("perishing"). Nor does he mean the biographical death of the obituary ("demise"). Death is no impending storm, for it is not an event at all: "[Dasein] does not have an end at which it just stops, but it *exists finitely*" (329). Death for Dasein is "a *way of being* that one takes over as soon as it is" (245, emphasis added).

Death, that is, is no more and no less than "being towards death." To be toward death is to live in a manner that is oriented by the possibility of one's own impossibility, the possibility of "no-longer-being-able-to-be-there" (254). Being *able* to be there, in Heidegger's technical use of that phrase, is being able to render the entities *there*, in the world, intelligible in their being. This is to live out a determinate factical ability-to-be. To be, for Dasein, is to be a sense maker, and thereby possess ontological understanding. So the possibility of one's own impossibility – the possibility of being *unable* to be – is the possibility of the comprehensive breakdown of the understanding in terms of which entities make sense. This would coincide with a breakdown in one's self-understanding. For the shape of who one is, the sense of one's life as meaningful, is given by the possibilities of making sense that participation in a form of life makes available. Death is the essentially threatened character of human understanding. The threat is one of unintelligibility, of a wholesale failure or loss of sense. To be *toward* death, then, is to live in the acknowledgment of the *fragility* of one's form of life. Heidegger characterizes this fragility as the possibility of having to "take it back," to "give up" on one's ability-to-be, rather than sustain allegiance to it as a basis for pressing on (308, 391).

Before turning to discuss how this conception of death stands in the legacy of Kant's conception of finitude, it is worth noting that this limitedness applies across the traditional distinction between theory and practice. Heidegger repeatedly expresses suspicion about this distinction, partly because any form of life that embodies an understanding of being is inseparably both. Moreover, both acting and judging are, in Heidegger's sense, forms of comportment: both amount to something we *do* as ways of making sense of things. Thomas Kuhn gave us the classic philosophical-cum-historical account of the crises and revolutions characteristic of theory in its empirical scientific setting.[8] Heidegger was surrounded during his time by various crises in the sciences at the foundational level of their basic ontological concepts. This destabilizing, or "tottering," was the first concrete reason offered for his raising anew the question of the sense of being in the first introduction of *Being and Time*.[9] Jonathan Lear has recently offered us a transcendental anthropological account of the breakdown of the traditional Crow form of life in North America. As their nomadic hunting life of intertribal warfare came under threat by white settlers, the central concepts that structured traditional Crow life and made it intelligible came to be unlivable. The opportunities that essentially enabled the exercise of those concepts, and indeed some of the objects (e.g., the coup-stick) to which those central concepts applied, ceased to be.[10] Though more practically inflected than Kuhn's case studies, the breakdown of the field of possibilities for making sense in this case, as narrated by Lear, is no less fundamental. What unites empirical science and Native American warrior culture – what makes them both distinctively human enterprises – is that both are forms of life that embody an understanding of being. Death is the *riskiness* of any such understanding: any projection of a space of possibilities for making sense of things stands *exposed* to being disabled by the course of a recalcitrant reality, and hence brought down as a sustainable form of sensemaking practice.

Kant made the finitude of human understanding the cornerstone of his system. This was, for Heidegger, a decisive insight.[11] The Heideggerian finitude of death stands in the legacy of Kant's conception of finitude. While this legacy introduces a large set of thorny issues, it is worth briefly outlining it to shed light on the Heideggerian notion of death as ontological fragility.

Kant distinguished finite sensible intuition from infinite originary intuition.[12] Infinite intuition creates or produces its objects (God said, "Let there be light" and there was light). Finite intuition, by contrast, is given its objects from without, and thereby must be affected by objects to know them. So whereas an infinite intellect is wholly self-sufficient, a finite intellect is dependent on existing objects that are *already there*. Heidegger says, expounding Kant:

The finitude of human cognition does not lie in humans' cognizing quantitatively less than God. Rather, it consists in the fact that what is intuited must be given to intuition from somewhere else – what is intuited is not produced by intuition.

The finitude of human cognition consists in being thrown into and onto entities. (GA 25: 86; translation modified)

Heidegger proceeds to appropriate this Kantian distinction as a notional contrast. His interest is not at all in the question of whether a divine intellect possessed of infinite intuition actually exists. Nor is the interest in whether we are required to postulate a divine intellect by the demands of reason in either its theoretical or practical application (or both). And the interest is certainly not in measuring the power of a finite intellect according to a standard set by a divine intellect. Heidegger's primary interest in the Kantian contrast lies in its promise to offer an illuminating entrée into appreciating the basic metaphysical condition of human understanding. The condition of divine understanding is to produce or create its objects, and thereby be conditioned by nothing other than itself; its condition is to be unconditioned. The condition of human understanding, by contrast, is to be dependent on, and therewith conditioned by, objects that exist independently of it.[13]

Heidegger, moreover, *generalizes* the range of finite comportment toward entities beyond cognition. For Kant, human understanding is fundamentally the capacity to judge, the function of which is to acquire knowledge. For Heidegger, human understanding is the ability to make sense of things. This ability crucially includes the capacity to judge but is far from exhausted by it.[14] Sense making is at work in the simple act of picking up a hammer to scooting by someone in a crowded pub. Heidegger offers a list to indicate the multiplicity and diversity of sense making: "having to do with something, producing something, attending to something and looking after it, making use of something, giving something up and letting it go, undertaking, accomplishing, evincing, interrogating, considering, discussing, determining" (56). Ways of comporting oneself toward entities – these types, and many more – are so many modes of living out the rich and complicated enterprise of finite making sense.[15]

More importantly for this discussion, Heidegger *deepens* the sense of finitude characteristic of human understanding in addition to generalizing it. Kantian finitude has to do with objects in our relation to them. This sense of finitude does not dig deep enough: Heidegger wants to place Kantian finitude within a more comprehensive finitude, a finitude to do with being and our understanding of it. Kant is blind to this sense of ontological finitude.[16] For Kant, the basic framework of possibilities for making sense of the world is fixed and invulnerable. The contours of intelligibility delivered by critique are advertised as "complete" and "certain."[17] The finitude of death, the fragility of ontological understanding, is foreign to Kant's thought.

However, the finitude that Kant rests content with, the finitude of intuition, opens up the possibility of the finitude of death. This is so even though death, so construed, does not figure in Kant's thought. Kantian finitude is in effect the recognition of the distinction between the sensibility through which objects are intuitively given and the understanding that thinks those objects. An intellect for which there is no such distinction, a divine intellect, is an intellect for which the distinction between the possible and the actual does not apply. Such a modal distinction, as Kant says, "would not enter into the representation of such a being at all."[18] After all, for such an intellect, to think something possible just is for that something to be actual; the realm of the possible and the realm of the real coincide. Since anything that is thought possible is thereby *guaranteed* to be actual, there is no sense to the actual *thwarting* this intellect's sense of the space of possibilities. And since the divine intellect is not in a position to be thus threatened by unintelligibility, the burden of its possibility is not to be shouldered. Things are otherwise for the finite intellect, for whom the distinction between the recognizably possible and the actual, and the threat that distinction engenders, is the medium of its existence.

The finitude of death, on Heidegger's view, has its characteristic mood, namely anxiety: "being toward death is essentially anxiety" (266). Heidegger first introduces Dasein as being-in-the-world, in his "preliminary sketch," as an entity that is "at home" in the world.[19] Much has been made of the way in which this depiction of human existence stands opposed to the modern skeptical representation of our condition offered paradigmatically by Descartes in the first of his *Meditations on First Philosophy*. While there is clearly something right about this stress, it must also be said that as one proceeds further into *Being and Time* beyond the preliminary sketches, it becomes exceedingly clear (starting at §40) that Dasein's being-in-the-world is always and everywhere informed by the possibility of the "not-at-home" (189), or uncanniness, made available by the anxiety of finitude. Anxiety is "*always* latent" (189) in being-in-the-world. And only because Dasein is "anxious in the very depths of its being," (190) Heidegger claims, is it so much as possible to be in the world – hence death's status as Dasein's "ownmost [*eigenste*] possibility" (263).

These two features of death – anxiety and ownmost possibility – come together by appreciating that the anxiety of death is the anxiety of responsibility. Division II of *Being and Time*, following its opening chapter on death that sets the agenda for the rest of the book, is a somewhat tortuous account of the existential structures at work in taking responsibility for one's ontological understanding. These existential structures together constitute an overall stance that Heidegger titles *resoluteness*.

Resoluteness is a matter of facing death head-on. It is a kind of openness to its possibility, marked by the etymology of the German word *Ent-schlossenheit*. Irresoluteness, by contrast, is a way of acknowledging finitude by backing away from it, a way of being closed off to its possibility, and therewith a falling away from the resolute stance.

"Ownmost" means constitutive of being a possessor of ontological understanding. Ontological understanding is fragile because it can fail, as we have seen, to be what it promises to be, a viable form of making sense. The anxiety of death discloses the burden of responsibility this fragility incurs. Anxiety "fully assigns" Dasein to its "ownmost ability-to-be," then, because one does not merely "possess" one's understanding of being, one also *sustains* it. Or better, ontological understanding is possessed *by* being sustained. Finite intelligibility does not take care of itself and it does not come with a guarantee. One's ownmost ability-to-be is accordingly to be *a sustainer of intelligibility*. And we come into our own as anxious but "resolute" because this stance expresses the vigilance of a lucid and responsible self-understanding of one's condition: the sustainability of any finite intelligibility is *on me*. It is of course not on me alone, for any understanding of being is embodied in a collective form of life, but that makes it no less *my* concern.[20]

This brings us to the third relevant feature of death, namely its disclosing to Dasein the possibility of existing as a *"whole-ability-to-be"* (264). Much of Division II is taken up by this problematic of the "whole" (*Ganze*).[21] While there is much to say about the issue, understanding death as ontological fragility at least allows us to place the "whole" in the right setting. Many commentators construe the relevant whole as the *narrative* whole of a biographical life from birth to death. Heidegger *does* raise an issue about biographical unity in the opening of chapter 5 of Division II. However, he does not raise this issue in his own voice. He indulges *that* notion of the whole only to reject it as the wrong question to be asking.[22] The relevant whole made available by the anxiety of finitude is the whole of one's factical ability-to-be, that is, the form of life *as a whole* that embodies one's understanding of being – as one is in the midst of living that form of life.[23] The anxiety of finitude is the unsettledness that is constitutive of taking responsibility for the sustainability of one's form of life as a whole. This unsettledness comes to a head in what Heidegger calls an existential situation, to which I will turn after first sketching its contrast, namely the general situation.

GENERAL (EVERYDAY) SITUATIONS

Heidegger endorses Kant's rejection of the givenness of entities to human understanding as a brute impact.[24] However, Heidegger disagrees with

Kant about the best starting point for bringing the receptive dependent character of human understanding into view. The Heideggerian successor to the Kantian exposition of the structural forms of our sensibility is the description of the structure of our everyday being-in-the-world (which includes spatiality and a form of time). The latter, Heidegger submits, serve as the more faithful and fruitful point of entry for capturing the modes of givenness of entities, and thereby discerning the concrete shape of finite human understanding.

Entities are first and foremost given to us in everyday being-in-the-world by figuring in contexts of purposive engagement, or contexts of "significance." These contexts are generally articulated by a nexus of entities upon which we rely throughout the course of our activity. In the carpentry workshop, the chemistry lab, meeting a friend at a cafe, or cooking at home, we *find ourselves* amidst meaningfully configured entities. The entities so configured are internal to the temporally extended activity; without the anchoring of the entities, the activity could not carry on as it does. This dependence on entities is the most immediate manifestation of the Kantian finitude characteristic of our ability-to-be – hence Heidegger's characterization of our Kantian finitude, in the above passage (§3), as our being "*thrown* into and onto entities."

There is of course much to say about these entities and our relation to them. The crucial point for our purposes is that these everyday entities are given to us as *world-involving* – a point marked by Heidegger's very title for such entities, "intraworldly entities." Consider one of Heidegger's favored examples, an item of equipment, to bring out the point. A tool is what it is for. To be what it is requires having a place, or a part to play, within an interconnected web of tools. The hammer, for example, is essentially a part bound together with other parts (nails) "working together" in appropriate ways within a particular nexus of engagement. However – and here is the crucial point – the even wider whole that situates any local context is the everyday world. After all, hammers have their point and significance within a "wide" world of contexts structured by the pursuit of carpentry projects.[25]

Accordingly, to comport toward a hammer *as* a hammer in a concrete context of significance – that is, with understanding – is to appreciate the tool's potential situatedness in *other* contexts of significance in which the tool would find its appropriate place. In Heidegger's terms, our concerned *absorption* in a concrete context always already involves a sense of orientation beyond that context, toward other appropriate contexts, thanks to our "*familiarity*" with the world (86). The world so understood is the space of possibilities onto which these entities are projected in their being: "[This] familiarity, constitutive for Dasein, goes to make up Dasein's understanding of being" (86).

There is, accordingly, an inherent generality at work in our situational engagement with things: such engagement essentially positions us within a broader field that reaches beyond the here and now that absorbs one's immediate concern. The familiar world is the prior unity in terms of which any concrete context of significance finds its place. Heidegger aptly characterizes the world as a "categorial whole" in the following passage:

> Not only is the world, qua world, disclosed as possible significance, but when that which is intrawordly is itself freed, this entity is freed for its own possibilities. That which is ready-to-hand is discovered as such in its service*ability*, its us*ability*, and its detriment*ality*. The totality of involvements is revealed as the categorical whole of a *possible* interconnection of the ready-to-hand. (83, emphasis added)[26]

An analogous structure can be seen in Heidegger's analysis of our relations with one another. People are encountered first and foremost in concrete contexts of everyday significance. They are encountered in terms of they *do*, or what they are called upon to do, within such contexts. We might call this one's "social role." To comport toward another person *as* an other in a particular context of significance – that is, with understanding – is to appreciate what the other is doing as more or less the *kind* of thing she would do, given her role, in *other* contexts of significance in which her respective role finds purchase. Our engagement with others, our "being-with" them, always already involves an orientation beyond the context at hand, toward others' contexts, thanks to our comprehending participation in a wider social practice. Once again, we see the inherent generality at work in our situational engagement with entities in context. For who others are, including who oneself is, is first and foremost a matter of rendering concrete, by participating in, a social practice. A social practice – more or less what Heidegger characterizes as "the anyone" (*das Man*) – is the prior whole in terms of which others, including oneself, make sense.[27]

No matter the entity, and whatever the style of comportment, to engage with entities understandingly is to be oriented with a wider whole of possibilities in terms of which those entities make sense. Everyday situations are thus characterized as "general situations" (*allgemeine Lage*, 300) by Heidegger precisely to register the sense of generality at work in our absorbed engagement within them. A situation is general not because it is not particular or concrete. It is general because the concrete situation is essentially integrated with and opens out onto a wider setting of other concrete situations within a form of life. An everyday context *is* in such a way as to *lead* to more of them. The one situation (yet another faculty meeting) ushers in another (a seminar) in more or less familiar ways as one lives out a factical ability-to-be (being a teacher). So we should hear the modifier "general" in "general situation" along the lines of ordinary, humdrum, or, to use Heidegger's preferred term, *average*. Any such situation, to be sure, is a particular set of circumstances that affords its own unique and fine-grained nuance. But it is, more fundamentally, a recognizable *excerpt of* how things *generally* stand within an ongoing form of life *as a whole*, the basic terms of which are framed in advance by one's orientation in the space of intelligible possibilities.

Heidegger asks his readers not to lose sight of the spatial overtone of the term "situation" (299). Following that lead, consider as a rough analogy the parts of space within the whole of space that Kant describes. As Heidegger explains in his lectures on the first *Critique*, space as a *unitary* whole is not a result of adding together determinate regions of space, for regions of space are not independent components that could exist by themselves. Rather, any region of space is only possible as part of the prior whole of space. A region of space is thus a "delimitation," as Kant puts it, of the whole of space.[28] Compare the generality of an everyday situation. An everyday situation essentially finds its place *within* the whole of an ongoing form of life. And like the way a determinate region of space opens out onto more space, the average everyday situation opens out onto more everyday situations. An everyday situation, akin to a determinate region of space, is a part of a whole that cannot be understood or identified independently of that whole. One might therefore call an everyday situation a "delimitation" of a form of life.

Public practices, including of course language, serve as reservoirs of intelligibility funding engagement in general situations, no matter the region of being. As Heidegger says, "'the one' prescribes that way of interpreting the world and being-in-the-world which lies closest" (127). Our participation in normative public practices thus deserves the status of a *source of intelligibility*, as Hubert Dreyfus has long insisted.[29] Here we see that not only are we thrown into and onto entities, we are, as individuals, thrown into and onto the terms in which such entities are to be made sense of. This elaboration of Kantian finitude is one consequence of Heidegger's starting with everyday being-in-the-world as the point of departure for discerning the givenness of entities. The self that comports toward entities in the everyday mode is titled the "anyone-self" (*Man-selbst*) by Heidegger to register the point. The anyone-self engages in general situations, maintaining itself in the "public interpretedness" afforded by the public practice into which one has been inducted.

Two crucial features of this everyday sense-making practice in general situations are worth noting before turning to the contrasting existential situation. First, the anyone-self is *dispersed* into the objects of concern that articulate general situations. By this, Heidegger means that in everyday comportment toward entities, as we are "on our way," we are occupied by what needs taking care of and *not* by the whole space of possibilities in terms of which entities make sense. This is obviously a matter of course. After all, one's comportment toward entities as entities is *enabled* by the understanding of their possibilities. Public practice is a reservoir of this understanding: thanks to one's induction into public practice, one finds oneself going about one's business in the relatively fluid manner characteristic of day-to-day life (at least for the most part). There is nothing therefore more natural than *relying* on that understanding as we make our way about general situations. In its everyday functioning, then, ontological understanding operates in the background, making "dispersed" situational engagement possible in the self-effacing manner appropriate to its role. The categorial whole of ontological understanding is *drawn upon*, rather than *at stake*. There is, as Heidegger remarks, a kind of security and comfort in this (384).

Second, and consequently, we are, as individuals, *disburdened* by our dispersal into the everyday world. Heidegger characterizes this tendency as "depriving the particular Dasein of its answerability" (127). By this, he means that in the everyday mode of sense making, we take for granted the basic possibilities in terms of which entities, within general situations, present themselves (294). That is, we navigate these situations as though intelligibility is *taken care of* by the public practice into which we have been inducted, "supplied," independently of one's participation in that practice. As Heidegger puts it, Dasein, as the anyone-self, gets "lived by" public practice (299). Such is the "irresoluteness" of the anyone-self in its "submission" to general situations. The anyone-self, in another formulation, "lives along abandoning oneself to one's thrownness" (345).

EXISTENTIAL SITUATIONS

The existential situation, by contrast, is one in which we are called upon to *take over* one's thrownness, rather than be taken along by it. As such, the situation demands the resolute stance of the owned self in contrast to the irresolute "fallen" stance of the anyone-self immersed in general situations. Heidegger makes clear in multiple passages that the existential situation, which he also dubs the "limit-situation," has everything to do with the anxious anticipation of death.[30] An existential situation is one in which the fate of a *whole* form of life, the understanding of being it embodies, hangs in the balance – hence its status as a limit-situation, that is, one in which the limitedness of one's form of life has come to fore.

Consider the following two passages:

We have defined resoluteness ... as a projecting which is reticent and ready for anxiety. Resoluteness gains its authenticity as anticipatory resoluteness. In this, Dasein understands itself with regard to its ability-to-be, and it does so in such a manner that it will go right under the eyes of death in order thus to take over in its throwness that entity which it itself is, and to take it over *as a whole*. The resolute taking over of one's factical there, means, at the same time, that the existential situation is one which has been resolved upon. (282; translation modified, my emphasis)

The temporality of the existential situation is marked by the "moment" (*Augenblick*) in contrast to the "present" of the general situation:

[As] something which has been thrown into the world, Dasein loses itself in the "world" in its factical submission to that with which it is to concern itself. The present, which makes up the existential meaning of "getting taken along" ... gets brought back from its lostness by a resolution, so that the current situation and *thus* primordial "limit situation" of being-toward-death, will be disclosed as a moment which has been held onto. (348; translation modified; my emphasis)

What phenomenon is Heidegger identifying? Take the following example as an illustration. In Kuhn's discussion of what is known as the "chemical revolution," he describes the context of the discovery of oxygen announced in Lavoisier's 1777 papers. These papers were the beginning of an extended episode that eventually ushered in the oxygen theory of combustion in place of the now-obsolete phlogiston theory. Lavoisier had apparently expressed anxiety about the phlogiston theory as early as 1772, depositing a sealed note with the Secretary of the French Academy. But by 1777, partly due to Joseph Priestly's experiments, this sense that something was awry had grown into the recognition that, in Kuhn's terms, a major paradigm shift might very well be necessary – a recognition Priestly resisted to the end of his life. Where Lavoisier saw oxygen, Priestly saw dephlogisticated air. Given the fundamental role these purported items had in shaping the field of possibilities for chemical entities as such, Kuhn famously urged us to acknowledge that, after discovering oxygen, Lavoisier "worked in a different world."[31]

The situation facing Lavoisier was an existential situation. It does not matter that Lavoisier turned out to be right (as far as we know). And it does not matter that the situation was scientific.[32] What matters is the peculiar possibility of a concrete situation *within* a form of life that in a sense comes to contain the *whole* of that form of life. An everyday general situation, recall, is a "delimitation" of a form of life. It is one situation that leads onto others. An existential situation, while concrete, makes the whole of which it is a part an issue, *as a whole* – hence the "fullness" of the existential situation [die volle Situation; GA 29/30: 224]:

a whole, paradoxically, comes to be concentrated into one of its parts. An existential situation puts the whole at stake by pressing the question of whether the ontological understanding informing the form of life as a whole can be sustained. It is a situation in which the possibility of a general situation – whether *this* form of life can go *on* – is at stake. The existential situation stops one short, and calls upon one to interrogate whether the ability-to-be at issue is capable of pressing forward. As Heidegger puts it, the anxious anticipation at work in the moment of an existential situation "brings one face to face with the possibility of repetition [*Wiederholbarkeit*]" (344). The existential situation, in short, is the finitude of death *made concrete* in the midst of life.[33]

To face the "repeatability" question head-on is to own up to the finitude of one's ability-to-be. One does not have to be Lavoisier, or a Plenty Coups, to enter into an owned relation to one's ability-to-be. One does not have be a history maker to live ownedly or "authentically." The sense of responsibility Heidegger is trying to capture leaves entirely open what one does in an existential situation, and how what one does is received, if one does anything at all.[34] Indeed, the notion of responsibility leaves entirely open whether one ever *actually* finds oneself confronting an existential situation.

The sense of responsibility is rather a certain form of commitment, understood as a way or manner of inhabiting one's form of life. The resolute stance, in the first instance, is manifest in the ability to *identify* an existential situation for what it is, were it to present itself. It includes, moreover, not letting oneself, when potentially confronted by an existential situation, back away from it and remain "dispersed" in general situations, as if the very possibility of a general situation is not at issue. The stance therefore includes refusing to "disburden" oneself of one's own answerability for the intelligibility of a form of life. Resolute responsibility is a matter of living in a way in which, as Heidegger puts it, one "holds oneself open" to the possibility of an existential situation. This, it should be clear, is not to compromise one's allegiance or attachment to the viability of one's form of life. It is rather to take responsibility for it in light of its constitutive fragility. The responsibility involves a standing readiness, in the background of everyday comportment, to take on the radical prospect of "giving up" (391) a form of life if it cannot be made to work. This is what Heidegger calls being "free for death," that is, finite freedom (384).[35]

The public practices into which we are inducted when we grow up into an ontological understanding have a history. The possibilities for making sense have *come to be*, and in that sense were born or founded. Heidegger calls these possibilities embodied in public practice, situated within the current of their history, a *heritage* (*Erbe*). The resolute stance of responsibility includes the recognition of the historicality of one's heritage. This recognition is at once the acceptance of the authority of that heritage and a preparedness to identify the "repeatable possibilities of existence" that it makes available. So the acceptance of authority, insofar as the question of repeatability of internal to it, is not a blind deference. Heidegger calls any such inheritance a "recripocal rejoinder." Owned recognition of one's heritage "hands" those possibilities "down to oneself in *anticipation*." For Dasein to enter into this form of relation to its own possibilities is for Dasein to truly *happen*:

> Once one has grasped the finitude of one's existence, it snatches one back from the endless multiplicity which offer themselves as closest to one ... and brings into the simplicity of its fate [*Schicksal*]. This is how we designate Dasein's originary happening [*Geschehen*], which lies in owned resoluteness and in which Dasein hands itself down to itself, free for death, in a possibility which it has inherited and yet chosen. (384)

Dasein accordingly comes to recognize itself as historical *in its being*: its finitude is a historical finitude. And with this, we can see why Heidegger claims, in what is perhaps the guiding claim of Division II, chapter 5, that "Owned being-towards-death is concealed ground of the historicality of Dasein" (383).

CONCLUSION

Let me conclude by noting one payoff of the foregoing interpretation. By this, I mean answers to two questions that naturally arise for readers working through Division II of *Being and Time*. The first question is why is genuine resoluteness a matter of *anticipating* death, as if running forward into it, to tap into the etymology of the German *vorlaufen*? This is an especially puzzling question for traditional views of Heideggerian death that see it not as ontological fragility but rather as the terminal conclusion of an individual biographical life. The second question, no less pressing for the traditional view, is why in the world would anyone, save the suicidal, *want* to press forward into death? Why isn't being toward death, as Heidegger puts it, a "fantastical exaction" (266)?

Heidegger's answer to the first question, as we have seen, is that, by anticipating death, one takes responsibility for ontological fragility. Compare "running ahead" into the facts about which you hold beliefs, that is, vigilantly checking them, as a way of genuinely *holding* one's beliefs. To take such responsibility is "the loyalty of existence to its own self" (391) as a sustainer of finite intelligibility.

This leads to an answer to our second question. If one is participating in a genuinely dying form of life, and if one has the courage of anxiety to identify the situation for what it is, anticipating the death of that form of life is at once the anticipation of one's rebirth in the founding of a new form of life. The prospect, while no doubt terrifying, could also be felt as exhilarating – at least for a being bent on a sustainably intelligible form of life, and so uniquely capable of fundamental change.

NOTES

1 This passage may be taken to represent the link between being and intelligibility in terms of Heidegger's topic of inquiry, insinuating the possibility of some other notion of being, a different topic, not linked to intelligibility. Heidegger forecloses this possibility at *Being and Time*, 183.

2 A. W. Moore, *The Evolution of Modern Metaphysics: Making Sense of Things* (Cambridge: Cambridge University Press, 2012), 472.

3 Heidegger does not consider the empirical question of whether any non-human beings are possessed of an understanding of being. Nothing he says, if I understand him, precludes the possibility. If they are out there, they fall under Heidegger's account. So in the sense that interests Heidegger, such beings would belong within the scope of the extension, whatever it is, of the "we" in the sentence "we are ourselves the entities to be analyzed" (41). This sense of being "one of us" must be a more expansive and open-ended sense of *the distinctively human* than the taxonomical sense employed in empirical biology, as specimens of *Homo sapiens*. Does Heidegger therefore adopt an intensionalist procedure for specifying the meaning of "Dasein"? That would be compatible with there be no existing Dasein among the entities that there are, which is incompatible with the ontical priority of the question of being. See *Being and Time* (13) on the "roots of the existential analytic" in the personal self-reflection of an existing entity. Heidegger's inquiry does not fit well into either an intensionalist or an extensionalist approach to "Dasein." See Wayne Martin's searching discussion in his chapter of this volume, "The Semantics of 'Dasein' and the Modality of *Being and Time*."

4 For example, Heidegger (not Bultmann, it is thought) characterizes his project shortly after the publication of *Being and Time* as follows: "The basis of this problematic is developed by starting from the 'subject' properly understood as 'human Dasein,' such that, with the radicalizing of this approach, the true motives of German Idealism come into their own." See the entry "Heidegger, Martin; Lexicon article attributed to Bultmann" in *Becoming Heidegger: On the Trail of His Early Occasional Writings, 1910–1927*, eds. Theodore Kisiel and Thomas Sheehan (Evanston: Northwestern University Press, 2007), 329.

5 See esp. §§31 and 32 of *Being and Time*, especially the sentence, "In the projecting of the understanding, entities are disclosed in their possibility" (151).

6 If, by chance, the player is using a rook figurine to serve the bishop role, then the piece is a bishop, not a rook.

7   Of course, there will be overlap among the above-mentioned factical abil-
    ities-to-be and the regions of being with which they are correlated, espe-
    cially if Sam is a university chemistry teacher that makes use of automobile
    engine parts as illustrations of chemical principles.

8   Thomas S. Kuhn, *The Structure of Scientific Revolutions*, 2nd edition
    (Chicago: University of Chicago Press, 1972).

9   See §3. A key passage of the section: "The real movement of the sciences
    take place when their basic concepts undergo a more or less radical revi-
    sion which is transparent to itself. The level which a science has reached is
    determined by how far it is *capable* of a crisis in its basic concepts. In such
    immanent crises the very relationship between positively investigative
    inquiry and those things themselves that are under investigation comes to
    a point where it begins to totter" (9).

10 See Jonathan Lear, *Radical Hope: Ethics in the Face of Cultural Devastation*
    (Cambridge, MA: Harvard University Press, 2006), esp. 32–3 and 56–7. The
    philosophical program to which this book is a contribution is originally
    set out in Lear's influential 1986 essay "Transcendental Anthropology"
    reprinted in his *Open Minded: Working out the Logic of the Soul* (Cambridge,
    MA: Harvard University Press, 1998), 247–81. The coup-stick is a ready-
    to-hand entity par excellence. For it to lose its functional role is for it to
    cease to be.

11 See GA 3 and the associated lecture course, GA 25, esp. §5.

12 Immanuel Kant, *Critique of Pure Reason*, trans. and ed. Paul Guyer and
    Allen W. Wood (Cambridge: Cambridge University Press, 1998), B72.

13 Where Heidegger's position places him on the question of whether, in the
    end, a divine intellect is intelligible, or at least fully intelligible, is a dif-
    ficult question. Such an intellect must at least be minimally intelligible,
    at least at the outset, for it to serve as one side of a contrast. In his notes
    on Odebrecht's and Cassirer's critiques of his *Kantbuch*, which appear as
    appendix V in that volume, Heidegger writes: "What ought we to find, or
    do we want to find, from the comparison of our knowing with the absolute?
    Simply to explain what is meant by the finitude of *our* knowing, where its
    finitude can be seen. Absolute knowing is a merely constructed idea, that
    is, it comes from our knowing, in which the specifically finite has been
    separated and its essence has been freed. The actual knowledge of the actual
    being-at-hand of absolute knowledge – which is to say, the being of God
    himself – is not needed here" (GA 3: 208).

14 I discuss the place of judgment in Heidegger's phenomenology in my
    essay "Judgment and Ontology in Heidegger's Phenomenology," *The New
    Yearbook for Phenomenology and Phenomenological Philosophy* 7 (2007):
    127–58.

15 Compare Wittgenstein's formulation of Kantian finitude in terms of the
    will rather than the intellect: "The world is given to me, i.e. my will enters
    into the world completely from outside as into something that is already
    there." Ludwig Wittgenstein, *Notebooks 1914–1916*, eds. G. H. von Wright
    and G. E. M. Anscombe (Oxford: Basil Blackwell, 1961), 74.

16 See Robert B. Pippin's "Necessary Conditions for the Possibility of What
    Isn't: Heidegger on Failed Meaning," in his *The Persistence of Subjectivity:
    On the Kantian Aftermath* (Cambridge: Cambridge University Press, 2005),

64. According to Heidegger, this blindness is a consequence of (i) Kant's neglect of the problem of being, and, with this neglect, (ii) Kant's failure to offer an ontological analytic of the subjectivity of the subject (i.e., Dasein). See *Being and Time*, 24.

17 Kant, *Critique*, A13.

18 Immanuel Kant, *Critique of the Power of Judgment*, trans. Paul Guyer and Eric Matthews, ed. Paul Guyer (Cambridge: Cambridge University Press, 2001), 273.

19 See §12 of *Being and Time*.

20 The relation between what I am calling the anxiety of finitude and Stephen Mulhall's perfectionist proposal for understanding our being not-at-home raises a number of questions that a more comprehensive investigation of the theme of *Unheimlichkeit* would address. See Mulhall's 2005 preface to the second edition of his *Heidegger and Being and Time* (London: Routledge, 2005) for one programmatic expression of an interpretive orientation that now puts the not-at-home at the center of his reading.

21 The issue is raised in the opening of the division, it is inscribed in the very title of the opening chapter, "Dasein's possibility of being-a-whole, and being-towards-death," as well as the title for chapter 3, and it returns to open our chapter 5 on temporality and historicality.

22 As Steven Crowell aptly notes in his paper, "Authentic Historicality," in *Space, Time, and Culture*, eds. David Carr and Chan-Fai Cheung (Dordrecht: Kluwer, 2004), 57–71.

23 There is also the more formal whole of what I earlier called the human ability-to-be as such, i.e., the whole of Heidegger's topic, which raises difficult methodological issues.

24 See §12 of *Being and Time* for the introduction of the idea that entities "encounter" us. For Wilfred Sellars, the givenness of entities as a brute impact is an epistemological myth about the rational justification of judgments of experience. For Heidegger, following Husserl, the giveness of entities as a brute impact is a phenomenological myth about the way in which things show up to subjects who are *in-der-Welt*. I raise the question of the place of reason and rationality in *Being and Time* in my essay, "Are we essentially rational animals?" in *Mind, Reason, and Being-in-the-World: The McDowell-Dreyfus Debate*, ed. Joseph K. Schear (Abingdon: Routledge, 2013).

25 In Heidegger's terminology, any environment (*Umwelt*) is situated within a world (*Welt*) (66).

26 And as Heidegger goes on to immediately add, nature too is a unified whole of possibilities in terms of which natural entities are understood in everyday (say) experimental comportment.

27 For individual persons as "concretions of *das Man*," see *Being and Time*, 129.

28 Kant, *Critique*, A25/B39. For Heidegger's analysis, see GA 25: 81.

29 Hubert. L. Dreyfus, *Being-in-the-World: A Commentary on Heidegger's Being and Time, Division I* (Cambridge, MA: MIT Press, 1991).

30 "Limit situation" (*Grenzsituation*) is a term borrowed from Karl Jaspers.

31 Kuhn, *Structure*, 118. The description of discovery takes place in Kuhn's chapter VI on "Anomaly and the Emergence of Scientific Discoveries," esp. 53–7.

32 Compare Lear's question, "Was there a last coup?" (26–34 of *Radical Hope*) in his narrative of the breakdown of traditional life of the Crow. The question arises in light of an episode in 1887 in which, as Lear puts it, "things came to a head." The episode as interpreted by Lear was an existential situation. The fate of traditional Crow life was sealed, on Lear's interpretation of events, in the burial of the coups-stick in Washington in 1921, at which Plenty Coups marks the end of the traditional Crow form of life.

33 Dreyfus claims that Heidegger is confused about the existential situation. In his paper delivered at the Inaugural Meeting of the International Society for Phenomenological Studies, Asilomar, California (July 1999), "Could anything be more Intelligible than Everyday Intelligibility? Reinterpreting Division I in light of Division II," (available at: http://socrates.berkeley.edu/~hdreyfus), Dreyfus says that Heidegger fails "clearly to distinguish two experiences of the source, nature, and intelligibility of decisive action" (15). The first experience, according to Dreyfus, is "the primordial understanding of the current situation." Dreyfus reads this in terms of his phenomenology of skill acquisition. The expert coper is better than merely competent because she is attuned to the distinctive character of the particular situation in all of its particularity, seizing the occasion, rather than relying on general rules and banal maxims to guide her. The second experience, according to Dreyfus, is the radical transformation described by St. Paul, Luther, and Kierkegaard, the "Christian experience of being reborn," (14) that long interested Heidegger in the lead-up to *Being and Time*. The reading of the existential situation I have offered opens up an avenue of reply to Dreyfus' charge of confusion. Heidegger *is* interested in the peculiar concreteness of the existential situation. However, its intensified concreteness consists in its pressing the issue of radical transformation. So understood, the existential situation is one coherent idea, not a confused conflation of two distinct ideas. The mastery that interests Heidegger is not the fine-grained coping that interests Dreyfus, but rather what one might call mastery of the art of being finite.

34 "In existential analysis we cannot, in principle, discuss what Dasein factically resolves in any particular case" (383).

35 Compare the remark, "Freedom makes Dasein in the ground of its essence, responsible to itself, or more precisely, gives itself the possibility of commitment" (GA 26: 192).

17   What If Heidegger Were a Phenomenologist?

The wonder of all wonders:
that things make sense.[1]

PRELUDE: A QUESTION OF LANGUAGE

Paid-up Heideggerians – call them Heideggeroids – are addicted to speaking in the idiosyncratic code that Heidegger himself concocted, an often perplexing idiom that Karl Jaspers once called *Heideggergegacker*, "Heidegger cackling."[2] Not unlike the American Derridoids, who follow their own mystagogue ("Everyone say *oui, oui*"), Heideggeroids are deeply devoted to channeling the Master's voice from the Great Beyond, a practice that follows from the Doctrine of Heideggerian Exceptionalism.

According to his devotees, the Master was attuned to mysteries that had never before been seen or heard (cf. Paul's ἄρρητα ῥήματα, ineffable sayings: II Corinthians 12:4), and he bequeathed these secrets to a small conventicle of initiates in an esoteric language that they alone, using their secret decoder rings, are able to understand. (Philosophers of other persuasions are *so* totally jealous.) And only by speaking in that secret cipher can Heideggeroids avoid the pitfalls of "metaphysical language" and the disasters attendant upon it.

And yet … this insistence on expounding Heidegger only in Heideggerese raises suspicions that such efforts merely express what John Henry Newman called a "notional apprehension" as contrasted with a "real apprehension" of the issues. Real apprehension, Newman argued, is a direct, firsthand understanding – today, we would say a phenomenological understanding – of a concrete issue, whereas notional knowledge consists in merely manipulating terms and propositions constructed around the issue.[3]

Channeling the Master's voice is not unique to the present day. In ancient Corinth in the first century C.E., Paul of Tarsus encountered glossolaliacs who claimed to be communicating divine mysteries in strange tongues. Clearly annoyed, Paul gave them a piece of his mind, including advice that Heidegger code talkers might want to take to heart:

If your language is unintelligible, how can anyone make out what you're saying? You're blowing smoke! People will think you're out of your mind! So if you insist on speaking in tongues, hold it down to small groups – two or three people at the most – and make sure that at least *one* of you translates what you're saying. (I Corinthians 14:9, 23, 27)[4]

The sad fact is that Heideggerian thinking has become a prisoner of its own hermetic jargon and shows little concern for the kind of translation that Paul demanded. Heidegger himself even insisted that two of his key terms, *Dasein* and *Ereignis*, could not be translated from the German, and Heideggeroids have generally followed suit.[5] As a result, practitioners of Heidegger discourse end up warbling to each other like a flock of narcissists

Who think the same thoughts without need of speech
And babble the same speech without need of meaning.[6]

The discussion of Heidegger's philosophy runs the risk of becoming ever more cultic, ever less a real apprehension of the issues at stake, and ever more sealed off from a wider array of philosophical interlocutors. How to escape from that prison? The confinement is not just a matter of arcane rhetoric but above all of completely missing Heidegger's point. And it must be said that such misunderstandings are fast becoming the norm. Just check out recent interpretations of Heidegger's *Seinsgeschichte*, not to mention translations of that phrase.

I argue that only a radical rethinking of Heidegger's texts and terminology can save his important project from disastrous distortion and self-imposed isolation. In recent publications, I have laid some groundwork for rereading Heidegger. Continuing in that vein, the present text offers further suggestions on how to carry out the task.[7]

BEING AS MEANING

The first step is to realize that Heidegger's work was phenomenological from beginning to end.[8] This entails that his work was focused not on "the being of beings" (*Sein*) but on "the meaning of the meaningful" (*Sinn, Bedeutung*).

In 1966, after he had composed his major works, Heidegger announced that "being" is a term "I no longer like to use."[9] *Sein*, he said, had been only "the preliminary word" in his thought (GA: 7, 234.13f./ EGT 78.21). Even more pointedly, he affirmed that "being is no longer the proper object of thinking" (GA 14: 50.2f./OTB 41.4–5). For Heidegger,

Sein is the outcome of *Ereignis*: it "belongs in *Ereignis*," and should be "taken back into *Ereignis*."[10] As we shall see, by *Sein* Heidegger meant *Anwesen*, the meaningful presence of things in understanding. In keeping with that, this chapter will employ the phenomenological term "meaning" in place of the potentially misleading ontological word

1. *das Seiende* = *das Bedeutsame*	1. beings = the meaningful
2. *die Seiendheit* = *die Bedeutung von etwas*	2. beingness = meaningfulness of something
3. *das Sein selbst* = *die Welt* = *Bedeutsamkeit*	3. being-as-such = world = meaning itself.

"being":
Heidegger said as much in his first course after the Great War. What is it, he wondered, that we immediately encounter in our lived experience? Do we meet beings? No. What we first encounter and always live with is

the meaningful [*das Bedeutsame*] – that is what is first and immediately given to you without any mental detour through a conceptual grasp of the thing. When you live in the first-hand world [*die Umwelt*], everything comes at you loaded with meaning, all over the place and all the time. Everything appears within a meaningful context, and that context *gives those things their meaning.* (GA 56/57: 73.1–5/61.24–8)

By calling the immediate objects of experience "the meaningful" rather than employing the ontological term "beings," Heidegger implies that the *being* of things is their *meaning.* Moreover, what makes things meaningful is their relatedness to human being as the only locus (*Da*) of sense or intelligibility (*Sinn*).[11]

When things within-the-world are discovered along with human being – that is, when they have come to be understood – we say that they have *meaning.*[12]

Thus the discussion moves from things "being-out-there" (*Sein* as *existentia*) to things being-understood by human beings (*Bedeutung* as *Verständlichkeit*). Only when things are present to mind do they have meaning (or as Heideggerians say, "being"). Once that fact becomes clear, saying that something "is" is the same as saying it *makes sense.*[13]

Heidegger's project proceeds in two steps: (1) laying out the structure of human existence so as to show that meaning is the relatedness of things to human being; and (2) asking the fundamental question: why there is meaning at all? Roughly speaking, the first topic occupied the early Heidegger (1919–30), while the second was the focus of his work from the 1930s on. In this chapter, the next three sections will cover the first topic, while the final four sections will take up the second.

THE PHENOMENOLOGICAL REDUCTION

The *sine qua non* of phenomenological method is the phenomenological reduction, the second-order reflective move by which the practitioner shifts from a natural to a phenomenological attitude. A natural involvement with things consists in understanding them naïvely as "always-already-out-there-now-real"[14] without regard for their correlation with or constitution by human beings. The phenomenological reduction, on the other hand, refrains from taking a stance on the reality of things when they are viewed as independent of any human involvement with them. It focuses instead on the *relatedness* between things-out-there and human concerns.

The phenomenological reduction is the act of reflection in which the practitioner concentrates on the "constitution" of the object in human awareness, that is, the disclosure of its meaning in understanding and the human contribution to that. In what follows, I call such *a priori* disclosure and presence "the essence of meaning" or "meaning itself" (cf. *das Sein selbst*). This sheer givenness of meaning is the central topic (*die Sache selbst*) of Heidegger's thinking. It is what led the young Heidegger to the remarkable and consequential insight that what Husserl was investigating under the banner of constitution (things becoming manifest in consciousness) had already been thought out more originally in ancient Greek philosophy under the rubric of ἀλήθεια (GA 14: 99.1–9/ OTB 79.17–25).

The phenomenological reduction issues in the practitioner's first-person experiential engagement with *phenomena*, that is, with things only insofar as they are manifest and meaningful within understanding. But these phenomena are neither the experienced objects by themselves nor the experiencing subject by itself. Phenomena are always correlations: an object-as-experienced-by-a-subject, or equally a subject-as-experiencing-an-object. The relation between a phenomenologically reduced object and human understanding is what constitutes the meaning of the object. It is clear that Heidegger's work presumes (but does not stop at) *die Wende zum Subjekt*, the turn to the constituting subject in its finite existential subjectivity. Prior to early modernity's historic turn to the subject, ontology's focus was on *esse* or *existentia*, the being of things. But the phenomenological reduction reenacts modern philosophy's shift away from being and toward meaning and its constitution. Heidegger's effort throughout his career was to disclose the *a priori* foundations in human being that make possible all *a posteriori* acts of making sense of things.

Then why did Heidegger continue to use the pre-phenomenological language of "being" in his work? He did so to keep continuity with the Greek ontological tradition, in whose philosophy of λόγος he had found a pre-reflective proto-phenomenology. According to Aristotle, humans have access to things only κατὰ τὸν λόγον,[15] that is, only under the aegis of meaning. Thus, Heidegger argued, the ancient Greeks implicitly understood τὸ ὄν and οὐσία as παρ-όν and παρ-ουσία, with emphasis on the παρά, the relatedness to human being. Heidegger's point about Greek ontology was reflected in his increasing preference for the German terms *Anwesendes* and *Anwesen*, not "beings" and their "beingness" but the meaningful and its intelligible presence to human awareness, whether practical or theoretical. In short, even when Heidegger continues to use the traditional ontological lexicon of "being," he intends by that word the phenomenological correlation of man and meaning.

Heidegger makes this point frequently in *Being and Time*, and his point becomes clearer and more effective when we interpret "being" as "meaning." For example:

The disclosure of meaning to understanding happens only insofar as and as long as human being exists.[16]

There is meaning only in human understanding, the very structure of which entails an understanding of meaning.[17]

There is meaning only insofar as there is the disclosure of meaning to human understanding. And there is such disclosure only insofar as and as long as there is human being. Meaning and the disclosure of meaning to understanding are co-original.[18]

A "ground" [and "being" is a ground] becomes accessible *only as meaning*, even if it itself is the abyss of meaninglessness.[19]

Meaning is given only so long as there is human existence, which is the ontic possibility of understanding meaning.[20]

[*Being and Time*] asks about meaning itself insofar as it enters into the intelligibility that is human existence.[21]

(As regards that last sentence, Gadamer argues that being that has entered intelligibility is "language," that is, meaning.[22])

These texts show that there is no *Sein* without *Dasein*, and vice versa. Or to state that in an explicitly phenomenological formulation: there is no *Sinn* without *Da-sinn* and no *Da-sinn* without *Sinn*. No human existence = no meaning. No meaning = no human existence. And the sheer facticity of this reciprocity of man and meaning – their inexplicable mutual interdependence – is what the early Heidegger calls thrownness into meaning. In his later work, he calls it *Ereignis*, or "appropriation," the *a priori* fact of man's being posited in the meaning-process. In appropriation, man and meaning come into their own, that is, into sustaining each other within the meaning process.

It has been claimed that when *Being and Time* analyzes tool use in the world of practical living, the investigation remains embedded in the natural as opposed to the phenomenological attitude. That is quite wrong. Heidegger's analysis of tools is dedicated to showing how they get their meaning from their involvement in human concerns. In other words, the investigation is conducted under the rubric of "correlation research."[23] The chain of relations that connects tools with practical tasks, and ultimately with human being itself, is what Heidegger calls "world." But as we have seen, relatedness-to-man is what determines all significance: things have meaning only to the degree that they are associated with human being.[24] Thus Heidegger defines the world – the network of relations connecting things to human beings – as meaning-bestowing meaningfulness (*Bedeutsamkeit*).[25] Heidegger declares: "As existing, human being *is* its world."[26] The world is human being writ large so as to embrace meaningfully whatever we can encounter. But we find ourselves to be intrinsically hermeneutical: able, indeed required, to make sense of things, with no exit except death. Therefore, with human existence as the τέλος, the world "teleologically" confers meaning on whatever gets caught up in that concatenation of relations.

The point of this section is that the primacy in Heidegger's work lies with sense, intelligibility, and significance (*Sinn, Verständlichkeit, Bedeutung*) rather than with "being" (*Sein*) understood merely as mind-independent existence. In Heidegger scholarship, the continued use of the ontological language of "being" – with its implicit traditional-ontological connotation and without reference to *Da-sinn* as the locus of all meaning – risks doing great damage to Heidegger's project by overturning the finely balanced achievements of his phenomenological reduction. Given the risk of entirely missing the phenomenological point, Heideggerians should bury the language of "being," or at least leave its corpse to the metaphysical discourses to which it belongs.

MINDING THE MEANT

Heideggerians seem wary of saying very much about consciousness, perhaps because Heidegger strongly cautioned against confusing Husserlian consciousness with *Dasein* (GA 15, 383.19–21/FS 71.4–6).[27] Fair enough; Heidegger's work is focused on the structural *basis* for consciousness, namely, being-in-the-world. But by assuming this focus, Heidegger does not banish conscious, existentiel sensemaking from the scene. Rather, he allows it its place in the meaning-process while grounding it in the existential condition of its possibility.[28] Consciousness, after all, is intentional; and intentionality is always embodied and as such "outside" any supposed immanence.[29] Consciousness is not locked up inside one's head. It is one's natural, inescapable, and always situational relation to worldly things in their meaningfulness. In Aristotle, all enactments of λόγος, whether theoretical or practical, have as their goal ἀλήθεια, that is to say, the meaningful presence of something.[30] So too in Heidegger, all acts of intentional awareness (including tool-use) grasp things as meaningful, and thus at least implicitly understand that those things receive their meaning from their relatedness to human being.

An intentional act entails making sense of something by taking it in terms of something else: tools in terms of tasks, subjects in terms of predicates. Regardless of whether an intentional act takes the form of studying physics, looking after a friend, enjoying a painting, or building a bookcase, in each instance, we may speak of it as *minding the meant*. I use the word "minding" as equivalent to "taking care of," "being concerned about," or "attending to" (as in minding your little brother or minding your manners). To mind something is to keep it present to mind, to retain it as a matter of concern.

For Heidegger, the mind is always a body-mind, and minding is always bodily-minding. Understanding, that is, mind, is always an embodied understanding (*befindliches Verstehen*). There is no dualism here. Body and mind (or attunement and understanding) are simply two ways of saying the same thing. The body (i.e., oneself) is always mindful. And the mind (i.e., oneself) is always embodied. As a unity, the "two" are intrinsically hermeneutical, always required, and able, to make sense of things. The one term says *befindliches Verstehen* or *geworfener Entwurf*: an embodied understanding. The other says *verstehende Befindlichkeit* or *entwerfende Geworfenheit*: a body that always understands.

Mind or body-mind is not a container of impressions and ideas but rather is intentionality itself: the worldly activity of minding the meant. Mind is "where" things come into knowability, clarity, and intelligibility – "the realm of unhiddenness or clearing (intelligibility) wherein all understanding or projecting (bringing into the open) is possible."[31] Minding, understanding, and making-sense-of-things all say the same and are equally qualified by Heidegger as "thrown" (we cannot *not* be minding things) and as "tuned-in bodily" to the meaning-process. In turn, all such acts of intentional consciousness are made possible by the very structure of human existence, namely, being-in-the-world. But what exactly is being-in-the-world?

ENGAGEMENT WITH MEANING

Heidegger's move from consciousness to its underlying structure reflects the medieval Scholastic axiom *operari sequitur esse*: activities

are consonant with and derive from natures; or in the reverse: natures
determine activities.[32] In the present case, one's sensemaking activities
follow from one's structure as being-in-the-world. Man is:

1. *Faktizität*: ... always already thrown
2. *Existentialität*: ... "ahead of" or "beyond" actual things
   a. into their various possibilities of meaningfulness and
   b. into the source of those meaningful possibilities: thrown human
      being as the locus of all meaning (*Da* as *Welt/Lichtung*)...
3. *Sein bei*: ... and thereby able to make sense of the things one
   encounters.

That is to say:

1. *Thrownness*: The fact that we cannot, short of death, escape from
   making sense of things reveals that we are structurally delivered
   over to the meaning-process.
2. *Projecting*: Our condition of always being intentionally "ahead"
   of the subject of the sentence and always already involved with
   predicates as possible meanings of the subject, reveals our structural "aheadness-in-the-possible" – in the same way that, in the
   practical order, pre-envisioning the fulfillment of a task means
   living "ahead" of the tools that might accomplish the task. From
   that, we infer that we ourselves are structurally ahead in the possible, right up to the possibility of our own death.
3. *Presenting*: Finding ourselves always mindfully involved with
   meaningful things reveals that our nature is structurally hermeneutical: always already thrown into the ability and need to make
   things meaningfully present.

Being-in-the-world as the *a priori* structure of human being is easily
misunderstood on two points: "world" and "in." As regards the first:
the world is not the collection of spatiotemporal things out there. As
we know, "the world" is Heidegger's term of art for *relatedness to
human understanding* as the source of the meaning of everything we
can encounter. It is the network that semantically relates things to
us and us to things, thereby granting them their meaning. As regards
the second point: the preposition "in" and its "in-ness" do not refer
merely to being ontically "within" the spatiotemporal universe.
Rather, the later Heidegger defines in-ness as *Inständigkeit*, structurally standing into (being engaged with) the meaning-process.[33] One's
living-in-meaning is the fundamental *a priori* of human being, the very
way human being is. I argue, therefore, that given this reading in which
"world" denotes relatedness to human being and "in" refers to our *a*

priori involvement with the meaning-process, we should interpret and translate *In-der-Welt-sein* not as "being-in-the-world" but rather as our *a priori* "engagement-with-meaning."

But engagement-with-meaning is the same as the disclosure of meaning to understanding (*Erschlossenheit*), and that in turn is what the Greeks implicitly understood by ἀλήθεια. We must rescue this crucial Greek term from its general translation as "truth." As Heidegger understands it, ἀλήθεια refers not primarily to the correct correspondence of thoughts and things. It refers, rather, to *meaningfulness*, the disclosure and presence of meaning in human being on at least three analogous levels. Only on the third and most derivative level does it mean "truth" as the conformity between a mental or spoken proposition and a given state of affairs.

1. ἀλήθεια-1: The most basic meaning of ἀλήθεια is human being's thrown openness (or dis-closedness at all), our freedom and ability to make sense of whatever we encounter. It is the world or clearing as sustained by thrown human being. Here, ἀλήθεια is the structure of human existence as both disclosed and disclosive: *erschließend erschlossenes*.[34] It is the *a priori* fact that meaning is ever-operative in human being.[35]

2. ἀλήθεια-2: In a second and derived sense, ἀλήθεια refers to the disclosedness *of things* to understanding in one's everyday, pre-propositional involvement with them. We cannot encounter anything except under the rubric of meaningfulness. Even if we merely ask, "What does that mean?" we have already brought the thing into the realm of possible meaning.

3. ἀλήθεια-3: The third and most derivative sense of ἀλήθεια refers to the particular state of meaningfulness that we call "correctness," the agreement of a propositional thought or statement with the already disclosed state of affairs it refers to. Only at this third level do we have truth as *adaequatio intellectus et rei*, a position that goes back through Kant and Aquinas to Aristotle.[36]

Heidegger's interests lie primarily with the first two senses above, and ultimately with the first. For him, our *a priori* engagement with meaning is the same as the fact (or "givenness") of meaning-at-all.

The point of the last two sections of this chapter has been that the existentiel-intentional minding of things is grounded in and rendered possible by human being's *a priori* engagement with meaning. Again, interpreting "being" phenomenologically as "meaning" clarifies Heidegger's project and avoids the trap of understanding "being" as existence-out-there.

HEIDEGGER'S BASIC QUESTION

Up to this point, we have dealt with the first phase in Heidegger's program: investigating the structure of human being so as to show that
human being is *a priori* involved with meaning and that meaning is a
thing's relatedness to understanding. We now turn to the second phase
and to the one and only question that motivated all of Heidegger's work.
He called it the "basic" or "fundamental" question (*die Grundfrage*)
to which everything else in his thinking was prelude. Arriving at that
question entailed four steps on Heidegger's part.

First: In the days of his pre-phenomenological studies, Heidegger
learned that Aristotle remained focused on the being *of things* without raising the question about being *itself*. Later, under the tutorship of
Husserl, Heidegger came to see that the Greek understanding of being
was itself phenomenological *avant la lettre*. As we have already noted,
he argued that the usual terms for being and beings – namely οὐσία and
τὸ ὄν – refer implicitly to παρ-ουσία and τὸ παρ-όν (*Anwesen* and *das
Anwesende*), the presence-in-understanding of things in their meaningfulness. But even then, the *correlation* of οὐσία as παρουσία with the
structure of human being was at best implicit in both the pre-Socratics
and in classical Greek philosophy.

Second: In the 1920s, through his phenomenological interpretations
of texts like *On the Soul* and *Nicomachean Ethics*, Heidegger managed
to thematize the Greeks' proto-phenomenological correlation of meaning and human existence. If, for Aristotle, humans relate to things only
κατὰ τὸν λόγον, Heidegger sorted out the various functions of λόγος (the
ability to make-sense-of) in terms of how they make things meaningfully present, both in the practical order of production and prudential
judgment (τέχνη and φρόνησις – ἀληθές-2) and in the theoretical order of
explicit synthetic knowledge (ἐπιστήμη – ἀληθές-3).

Third: Having investigated human openness within the phenomenological correlation, Heidegger in the 1930s went on to investigate the
fact of meaning itself, its *a priori* operation in understanding, under a
number of ex aequo terms, among them:

- *Es gibt Sinn* (cf. *es gibt Sein*): the givenness of meaning in
  understanding;
- *Sinn selbst* (cf. *Sein selbst*): the presence of meaning in
  understanding;
- *Wesen des Sinnes*: the occurrence of meaning in understanding;
- *das Offenbarung*: the "revelation" of meaning in understanding;
- *Lichtung des Sinnes*: the openness of meaning in understanding;
- ἀλήθεια-1 or *Wahrheit*: the disclosure of meaning in understanding.[37]

"The fact of meaning-at-all" says that meaning is always already given in the form of the phenomenological correlation. It comes *a priori* with being human, just as human being is *a priori* given over to meaning. Hence, the disclosure or presence of meaning is not an occasional event but is always already operative in and manifest as our ability to make sense of whatever we encounter. This is so, even when someone makes the wrong sense of something. When I mistakenly take up a tool that will finally prove to be inadequate to perform a task, I nonetheless make sense of it as a tool, even if I later discover that it is not serviceable for the work.

Fourth and most important (and here, he stepped beyond both Aristotle and Husserl, indeed beyond the entire tradition of Western philosophy): Heidegger raised the basic question that goes to the "limit of the possible"[38] in human being: *How come ἀλήθεια-1 at all?* Why the very fact of meaning? Is it possible to find something that is the source of and responsible for the *a priori* operation of meaning in understanding?

In traditional philosophy, whether it be called metaphysics or onto-theo-logy, the question of the cause of the being (οὐσία, *esse*, *Sein*) of beings is answered by an ultimate thing or person or process that is constantly present and operative, regardless of whether it be Aristotle's self-thinking thought, or the God of various religions, or even the Eternal Return of the Same. ("Even Nietzsche's metaphysics is *as ontology ... at the same time* theology.")[39] But in Heidegger's view, such an ultimate entity or process does not show up phenomenologically because phenomenology is about meaning, and the furthest one can get in search of the "causes" of meaning is one's inexplicable thrownness into the meaning-process.

How, then, can we discuss the fact of meaning-at-all? To put the matter more succinctly than we have so far, in Heidegger's work, the basic object of interrogation is the togetherness of man and meaning. From one perspective, we may discuss this phenomenological correlation in terms of man's disclosive thrownness into meaning. From another, we may speak of the *a priori* givenness (*Geschick*) of meaning in human being. From either side, their unity bespeaks the fundamental and factical interlocking of man and meaning. The early Heidegger's name for the *inevitability* of that togetherness is "thrownness" (*Geworfenheit*); the later Heidegger's name for it is "appropriation" (*Ereignetsein*, *Ereignung*, *Ereignis*); and in both cases, that into which man is thrown or appropriated is the meaning-process.

In his *Contributions to Philosophy*, Heidegger frequently expresses the equivalence of thrownness and appropriation. For example:

- *das Da-sein ist geworfen, er-eignet*: man is thrown, appropriated (GA 65: 304.8/214.22).

- *die Er-eignung, das Geworfenwerden*: being appropriated, that is, being thrown (GA 65: 34.9/24.32).
- *geworfener... d.h. er-eignet*: thrown, i.e., appropriated (GA 65: 239.5/169.12).
- *Übernahme der Geworfenheit* = *Über-nahme der Er-eignung*: taking over one's thrownness is the same as taking over one's appropriation (325.37/373.14–15 with GA 65: 322.7–8/226.13–14).[40]
- *Geworfenheit und damit die Zugehörigkeit zum Seyn*: thrownness, and with that one's belonging to meaning as such (GA 65: 239.7–9/169.14).[41]

There is nothing arcane about Heidegger's basic topic. For him, every human act is an act of making sense. But the most he can say about such pan-hermeneutics is that the phenomenological correlation of man and meaning, which is its basis, is an irreducible given. To ask for the cause of sensemaking is itself a sensemaking act; and therefore the question about why there is meaning-at-all gets caught up in circular reasoning and cannot be answered. Whether practically or theoretically, we can in principle make sense of everything – except why we can make sense of anything.

THE HIDDENNESS AND FORGOTTENNESS OF MEANING ITSELF

Even though it is essential to every act of sensemaking, the *a priori* givenness of meaning in understanding easily goes unnoticed in our everyday minding of the meant. There are three moments in this phenomenon of forgottenness.

1. There is the fact that the very togetherness of meaning and man is *intrinsically hidden* from understanding. Inevitably, every attempt to discover what is responsible for the presence of meaning in human understanding already presupposes that fact and thus leads to a *petitio principii*. Our inability to grasp the reason for meaning-at-all is due to our radical finitude.
2. Precisely because the givenness of meaning is hidden, one tends to *overlook* or "forget" it.
3. When the overlooking itself gets overlooked, the result is the *virtual occlusion* of the fact of meaning at all, with the result that the *a priori* disclosure of meaning falls into *oblivion*.

This last state of affairs Heidegger sees as growing exponentially in today's world of techno-think (*Technik*), in which everything, including human being, is treated as an endlessly exploitable resource for engineering and profit. In this age of the "Construct" (*Gestell* – less happily, "enframing"),[42] human beings float free of their grounding, oblivious of the primal fact that constitutes them as human. This state of affairs as a whole we may call *die Vergessenheit des Sinnes*, the "forgottenness of meaning itself" – that is (in the reverse order from above): (3) the *oblivion* of (2) *one's overlooking* of (1) the intrinsic *hiddenness* of the fact of meaning-at-all.

In *Being and Time* (1927) and "What is Metaphysics?" (1929), Heidegger deals with this hiddenness in terms of dread (*Angst*).[43] Dread is the rare and fleeting awareness of the *limit* of our ability to make sense of things. It is an encounter with the groundlessness of hermeneutical existence. Heidegger calls this groundlessness "the abyss of meaninglessness" – that is, the nothing or absurdity – that underlies the presence of meaning in understanding.[44] To recognize that the only alternative to sensemaking is death is to experience what he calls the *Abweisung*, the push-back (or thrown-back-ness) into sensemaking. Nothingness is not a mysterious something that lies just beyond the limits of sensemaking. No, nothingness = nothing, which is a way of saying that, short of the grave, the only thing human beings can do is to keep on making sense of things.

For Heidegger, confronting the limit (πέρας) of our ability to make sense is the same as encountering the empowering ἀρχή of such sensemaking (GA 40: 64.18–32/63.4–18). Experiencing this ἀρχή-πέρας might *seem* to be an experience of the *reason why* meaning is given in understanding. However, the confrontation with the nothing (and thus with one's own mortality) is one with the condition of being always thrown back into meaning. Dread is the awareness of standing just this side of death or, what comes down to the same thing, living ever at the point of death. In dread, we feel ourselves pushed back from the brink of absurdity and repelled back into the only place we can live: meaning. Heidegger notes that the way nothingness "functions" (i.e., its "essence") consists in this push-back into sense. *Das Wesen des Nichts = die Nichtung = die Abweisung.*[45] The essence or function of absurdity or nothingness is to push us back into making sense. But we can never know "what" throws us back because no such "what" can be found. The throw-back into sensemaking is "*ohne Warum.*" It is an irreducible given for which there is no reason.[46]

To encounter the limit of sensemaking is also to experience one's ability to be thrown out of the meaning-process at any moment.[47] As Heidegger puts it, dread means confronting the "possibility of our impossibility." In that phrase, "impossibility" refers to being dead. But the *possibility* of such an impossibility is not death (*mors*) but mortality (*posse mori*), our ability to die at any moment. That is what Heidegger means by *Sein zum Tode* – not our being *toward* death ("we'll all die some day") but our being ever at the edge of death (mortality as the ability to die at every moment). To encounter the limit and origin of sensemaking is to experience our mortality, the thin line that separates us from being dead. The ability to die at any moment is, in fact, the correlate of our inability to know why there is meaning at all. Both are due to our radical finitude and thus to the impossibility (not to mention undesirability) of being completely self-present. At the very edge of our disclosedness, we are bound up with a unique form of hiddenness – our complete not-there-ness – which we know in the form of death as our ever impending final possibility. Death is the complete opposite of (and repels us back into) sensemaking. It is hidden from us, but as hidden, it belongs essentially to our ability to make sense and needs to be sustained as the basis of our engagement with meaning.[48]

The only answer one can give to the question, "What is the reason for our throwness/appropriation into the meaning-process?" is that the question goes beyond our ability to answer it. Any supposed "cause" of the phenomenological correlation is, from within our lived-experiential perspective, impossible to find. Heidegger's stand-in for an answer to the basic question is *"es gibt Sinn"*: meaning is *a priori* operative in understanding – period. Even if there were some divine revelation from a supernatural realm, it would have to occur within the limits of our finite ability to make sense of it. We have no natural ability to contact an ultimate thing or process that is ever-operative as the ground of phenomenological experience.[49]

Others, perhaps, might postulate something that goes beyond the limit of possible experience – perhaps a person or process that can somehow reveal itself to the human mind that could otherwise not know it; or a "saturated" phenomenon whose content exceeds any human act of intentionality and points beyond the phenomenological correlation.[50] For Heidegger, every attempt to postulate something noumenal steps outside the realm of natural phenomenological experience and, by the very laws of human being, is phenomenologically illegitimate. Heidegger the phenomenologist rightly stops where he must: at the incomprehensible empowerment (πέρας-ἀρχή) of all possible sensemaking. The ultimate phenomenon we *can* experience is our throwness into the unanswerable disclosure of meaning in finite human being. That disclosure is what the later Heidegger called "the last god," which is what he was referring to by his famous gnome, "Only a god can save us."[51]

In short, in the early Heidegger, there is no escape from the fact of the meaning-process, except death. Moreover, the intrinsic unavailability (hiddenness, invisibility) of why there is meaning-at-all, registered as it is in our facticity and mortality, is what accounts for our "fallenness," our remaining absorbed in meaningful things instead of attending to the intrinsically hidden fact of meaning itself.

THE HISTORY OF THE FORGOTTENNESS OF MEANING

The later Heidegger begins with the same phenomenological premise as did the earlier: human existence is unable to discern any reason for its thrownness into meaning. But it is the later Heidegger who goes further by projecting the "epochs" of the intrinsic hiddenness of and the overlooking of meaning itself throughout the history of Western philosophy.

Heidegger finds in the Greek word ἀλήθεια an implicit negative sense (λήθ-) that is related to the verbs λήθω and λανθάνω, "to be out of sight and out of mind," that is, to be unnoticed and unknown.[52] When the negative sense of "being unnoticed" is cancelled out by the addition of an alpha-privative (ἀ-), the word ἀλήθεια conveys to Heidegger a double negative sense: the condition of "no longer ... being unnoticed" or, to state it positively, the state of having become noticed by human being. In its most basic sense (see section "Engagement with Meaning"), ἀλήθεια-1 bespeaks the human engagement with meaning, thanks to which things become knowable in their everyday meaningfulness (ἀλήθεια-2).

On the other hand, the λήθη or lethic dimension of ἀλήθεια-1 points phenomenologically to our inability to know *why* there is meaning-at-all. Given the circular reasoning involved in presupposing ἀλήθεια-1 while looking for its source, the best we can do is to experience and accept its unknowability in an act of resolve and draw the consequences of that. As intrinsically unknowable, the why-and-wherefore of meaning itself is "held back" from human knowing. The Greek verb for "to hold back" is ἐπέχω, and Heidegger discusses this "holding back" under the rubric of the related noun ἐποχή (epoché), which he uses in a radically different sense from Husserl's.

In Heidegger's view, the Western tradition since Plato has overlooked the lethic dimension of the *a priori* givenness of meaning in understanding while instead generating various names for the meaningfulness of the meaningful (*die Seiendheit des Seienden*). This leads Heidegger to dub the whole of metaphysics an ἐποχή, a "holding-back" or "hiding" of ἀλήθεια-1. In turn, this general ἐποχή yields the specific "epochs" of Western metaphysics. Thus Plato overlooked the original sense of ἀλήθεια-1 (he mistook it for ἀλήθεια-3, the correct correspondence between mind and meaning) and named the mental accessibility of things εἶδος and ἰδέα.[53] Likewise, Aristotle overlooked the very givenness of meaning and employed ἐνέργεια as a name for the intelligible accessibility of things. Heidegger finds the same pattern of overlooking in the whole line-up of Western philosophers, each of whom remains inattentive to the unknowable givenness of meaning itself. Instead, he ferrets out the names for the meaningfulness of the meaningful – for example: *esse, actualitas,* monad, objectivity, Absolute Spirit, Will to Power, and so on. Each of these defines a specific "epoch" within the history of metaphysics, the West's general ἐποχή or overlooking of meaning itself.[54] Clearly, an "epoch" is not primarily a period of time but rather a way in which a given thinker, or generally speaking a culture, understands the meaningfulness of things, and overlooks its source.

This history of forgottenness issues in the utter oblivion that characterizes the age of the *Gestell* or Construct. What, then, would it take in the current and climactic epoch of metaphysics to shake us out of the slumber of such oblivion? The early Heidegger presented the experience of dread (or equally, the voice of conscience) as the wake-up call that makes possible a resolute choice of one's mortality and the finite sensemaking that follows from it. The later Heidegger speaks of a pervasive and stifling atmosphere rooted in an implicit sense of profound alienation from the core of one's existence. According to him, all that we can hope for in the present age is a personal epiphany, an existentiel lightning flash of insight (*Blitz, Blick*) – analogous to the "moment of insight" (*Augenblick*) in *Being and Time*. This alone will cut through the oblivion, confront us with our mortal finitude, and make it possible for us to accept resolutely our finite condition as thrown or appropriated into the meaning-process.[55]

CONCLUSION

What if Heidegger really were the phenomenologist he claimed to be? And what if his followers took that claim seriously? That would entail a paradigm shift in how one reads him – including (1) a shift of the field of Heidegger scholarship from "being" to "meaning"; and (2) as a specification of that field, a shift from the meaningfulness (*Seiendheit*) of the meaningful to the irreducible givenness of meaning-at-all in human understanding.

Such a paradigm shift would understand man's thrownness into the phenomenological correlation as equivalent to what Heidegger later called man's "appropriation" (*Er-eignung*) to the meaning-process. It would understand thrownness/appropriation as man's *a priori* engagement with meaning, and would see that this is what is meant by "care" (*Sorge*). It would reinterpret the phenomenon of time and temporality (*Zeit, Zeitlichkeit*) as simply Heidegger's first and inconclusive attempt to work through the problematic of ἀλήθεια-1.[56] And it would maintain the utter centrality of human being in the meaning-process – for where else can one find meaning except in *Da-sinn*? This paradigm shift would avoid all the hypostasizing of "being" and of the "truth" of being that Heideggerian discourse is mired in. It would never claim that *Sein* "reveals itself" to *Dasein*, "calls" *Dasein*, "throws" (itself?) to *Dasein*, or other such reifying phrases, as if *Sein* were a hyper-entity with agency which addresses itself to man from a higher plane of reality.

However, even if all of the above were to be instantiated, it would still be merely a matter of phenomenological theory, of intellectually thematizing the structure and possible activities of human being – as Heidegger himself did in *Being and Time*. Heidegger's real goal, however, lies beyond theory, in existentiel practice. It has to do with taking up and instantiating in one's own personal life what his phenomenological investigations merely talk about. Heidegger argues for "a transformation in how we *exist*."[57] Such a decision is the ultimate focus of his project: a personal grasp of one's own existential thrownness, such that one personally becomes the finite self that one already is.

Why else read *Being and Time*? Is it to find out what Heidegger – one philosopher among many – thought? That might be enlightening, but it is not what Heidegger had in mind. For him, being a phenomenologist means *living* differently. "The question of existence is clarified only by how one exists."[58]

NOTES

1 Cf.: *daß Seiendes ist* (GA 9: 307.23–4/234.18). Preliminary remarks: (1) I cite texts by page and line, separated by a period. The line count does not include headers or empty spaces but does count titles within the text. (2) I use the term "man" as gender neutral and as referring to human being as such. (3) I translate *Wahrheit* ("disclosure") as "disclosure of meaning to understanding" lest the phenomenological correlation be overlooked. (4) I translate both *Sinn* and *Bedeutung* as "sense" or "meaning" and often render *verstehen* as "to make sense of [something]." (5) All translations should be considered modified.
2 Karl Jaspers, *Notizen zu Martin Heidegger*, ed. Hans Saner (Munich: Piper, 1978), 207.35.
3 John Henry Newman, *An Essay in Aid of a Grammar of Assent* (Notre Dame: University of Notre Dame Press, 2001), 36–48.
4 A free but faithful translation of Paul's text. "Blowing smoke" (εἰς ἀέρα λαλοῦντες) is usually translated as "talking into the air." "People will think you're out of your mind" (οὐχ ἐροῦσιν ὅτι μαίνεσθε;) is usually translated, "Will they not say you are mad?"
5 *Dasein* as untranslatable: GA 65: 300.13/211.41 and GA 49: 62.1. *Ereignis* as untranslatable: GA 11: 45.17–19/ID 36.16–17.
6 T. S. Eliot, "A Dedication to my Wife," in *The Complete Poems and Plays of T. S. Eliot*, ed. Valerie Eliot (London: Faber and Faber, 1969), 206.
7 Background for this chapter includes my essays "Facticity and *Ereignis*," in *Interpreting Heidegger: New Essays*, ed. Daniel Dahlstrom (Cambridge: Cambridge University Press, 2011), 42–68; "The Turn," in *Heidegger: Key*

Concepts, ed. Bret W. Davis (Durham: Acumen, 2010), 82–101; and "Astonishing! Things Make Sense!," *Gatherings: The Heidegger Circle Annual* 1 (2011): 1–25. Cf. Anthony Kenny, "…[A]ny interpreter who wishes to make [*Being and Time*'s] ideas readily intelligible has to write in a style very different from Heidegger's own." *Philosophy in the Modern World, A New History of Western Philosophy*, 4 vols. (Oxford: Oxford University Press, 2007), vol. IV, 86.22–4.

8 GA 14: 147.15–21: "The Understanding of Time in Phenomenology and in the Thinking of the Being-Question," trans. Thomas Sheehan and Frederick Elliston, *The Southwestern Journal of Philosophy* 10 (1979): 201.1–5. Cf. William J. Richardson, *Heidegger: Through Phenomenology to Thought* (The Hague: Martinus Nijhoff, 1963), xvi.1–7; 44.1–2 with note 47; and 537.26–8: "It is singularly important to realize that Heidegger never abandons the phenomenological attitude that seeks only to let the phenomenon manifest itself."

9 "Obwohl ich dieses Wort nicht mehr gern gebrauche…" (GA 15: 20.8–9/HS 1966/67, 8.34–5).

10 GA 14: 49.30–1/OTB 41.1–2. Cf. GA 81: 209.8: "Die Er-eignung, die, was vormals Sein geheißen…"

11 "Sinn 'hat' nur das Dasein, sofern die Erschlossenheit des In-der-Welt-seins durch das in ihr entdeckbare Seiende 'erfüllbar' ist. *Nur Dasein kann daher sinnvoll oder sinnlos sein*" (151.36–9/193.13–16).

12 "Wenn innerweltliches Seiendes mit dem Sein des Daseins entdeckt, das heißt zu Verständnis gerkommen ist, sagen wir, es hat *Sinn*" (151.22–4/192.35–7).

13 See note 1.

14 See Aristotle's ἔξω [τῆς διανοίας] ("outside of thinking") at *Metaphysics*, trans. W. D. Ross, in *The Complete Works of Aristotle, Vol. II.*, ed. J. Barnes, VI 4, 1028a 2, and ἔξω ὂν καὶ χωριστόν ("a thing that is outside and separate [from thinking]"), ibid., XI 8, 1065a 24.

15 Aristotle, *Physics*, II 1, 193b 2–3.

16 "Wahrheit 'gibt es' nur, sofern und solange Dasein ist" (226.28/269.20–1; italicized in the original).

17 "Sein aber 'ist' nur im Verstehen des Seienden, zu dessen Sein so etwas wie Seinsverständnis gehört" (183.29–30/228.12–13).

18 "Sein – nicht Seiendes – 'gibt es' nur, sofern Wahrheit ist. Und sie *ist* nur, sofern und solange Dasein ist. Sein und Wahrheit 'sind' gleichursprünglich" (230.5–6/272.34–5).

19 "…weil 'Grund' nur als Sinn zugänglich wird, und sei er selbst der Abgrund der Sinnlosigkeit" (152.14–15/194.2–3; my italics).

20 "Allerdings nur solange Dasein *ist*, das heißt die ontische Möglichkeit von Seinsverständnis 'gibt es' Sein" (212.4–5/255.10–11).

21 "die Untersuchung … fragt nach ihm [= Sein] selbst, sofern es in die Verständlichkeit … hereinsteht" (152.11–12/193.31–2).

22 "Sein, das verstehen werden kann, ist Sprache" (italicized in the original), Hans-Georg Gadamer, *Wahrheit und Methode, Gesammelte Werke*, 4 vols. (Tübingen: J. C. B. Mohr, 1986), vol. I, 478.29–30. In English: *Truth and Method*, trans. Joel Weinsheimer and Donald G. Marshall (London: Continuum, 1989), 470.3–4.

23 Cf. Edmund Husserl, *The Crisis of European Sciences and Transcendental Philosophy*, trans. David Carr (Evanston: Northwestern University Press, 1970), §§46–8; also 166, note, on the "*a priori* of correlation."

24 See note 12.

25 "Den Bezugscharakter dieser Bezüge des Verweisens fassen wir als *be-deuten*" (87.8–9/120.13–14); and "...die *Bedeutsamkeit* ... ist ... die Struktur der Welt" (87.18–19/120.24–5). Also GA 18: 300.16/203.28: Bedeutsamkeit. Cf. "Sinn gibt," GA 21: 275.20/229.8.

26 "Dieses [= Dasein] *ist* existierend seine Welt" (64.34–5/416.8).

27 In GA 15, Heidegger feared that *Husserlian* consciousness remained imprisoned in immanence. In *Being and Time*, Heidegger promised that (the unpublished) Part One, Division III, to be entitled "Time and Being," would show how "the intentionality of 'consciousness' is *grounded* in the ecstatic temporality of human existence" (363, n. 1/498, note xxiii).

28 Note the equation of *Verhaltungen, Bewusstseinsvorgänge*, and *Erlebnisse* at GA 21: 210.30–1/177–8. The earlier Heidegger expressed the *a posteriori/a priori* relation of intentionality and transcendence in the dictum "Intentionality is the *ratio cognoscendi* of transcendence, while transcendence is the *ratio essendi* of intentionality" (GA 24: 91.20–3/65.15–16). That is, transcendence – the *a priori* sustaining of meaning – is the structural basis that transcendentally makes possible, in the realm of cognition, being intentionally aware of and understanding anything at all, just as understanding is the concrete form that transcendence takes in the realm of cognition.

29 See "Draußen-sein" at 62.16–17/89.18; and "draußen" and "Draußensein" at 162.26–7/205.31–2.

30 ἀμφοτέρων ... ἀλήθεια τὸ ἔργον. Nicomachean Ethics, VI 2, 1139b 12; also ibid., VI 1, 1139a 1–2; and VI 2, 1139a 21–31.

31 It is the realm of Sinn: "der Bereich der Unverborgenheit oder Lichtung (Verstehbarkeit), worin erst alles Verstehen, d.h. Entwerfen (ins Offene bringen) möglich ist" (GA 16: 424.20–2); cf. "Das Offene des Begreifens" (GA 9: 199.21/152.24).

32 See, e.g., cf. Thomas Aquinas, *Summa theologiae*, I, 75, 3, respondeo, ad finem: "similiter unumquodque habet esse et operationem." Or to reverse the direction, "qualis modus essendi talis modus operandi": a thing's way of being determines its way of acting.

33 For example, GA 9: 374.24/284.16; GA 66: 174.9/152.15); GA 49: 54.27. See also "Innestehen" and "Ausgesetzheit ins Offene" at GA 49: 53.15 and 54.10.

34 GA 27, 135.13. Cf. GA 49: 68.19 "ein geworfener."

35 See "die Weltoffenheit des Daseins" (GA 21: 164.13/137.29).

36 Immanuel Kant, *Critique of Pure Reason*, trans. and ed. Paul Guyer and Allen W. Wood (Cambridge: Cambridge University Press, 1998), A58/B82; St. Thomas Aquinas, *Quaestiones disputatae de veritate*, quaestio 1, articulum 1, respondeo; *Truth: Questions I–IX*, trans Robert W. Mulligan (Chicago: Henry Regnery Company, 1952), Question 1, Article 1, Response; Aristotle, *Metaphysics*, IV 7, 1011b, 26–8.

37 Cf. "Wahrheit selbst noch *als der Grundcharakter des Seins*": (GA 88: 36.27–8; Heidegger's italics). And "'Wahrheit': ... 'daß' Seyn west und wir

instándig in ihm": ibid., 161.8–10. On the sameness of Sinn, Wahrheit, Lichtung, and das Wesen der Zeit, see GA 12: 104.22–4/OWL 20.21–3, with GA12: 104.27–8/OWL 20.26–8). The phrase "'Sein' als 'Sein' hinsichtlich des ihm eigenen Sinnes, d.h. seiner Wahrheit (Lichtung)" (GA 12: 104.23–4) I translate as: "'being' as 'being' with regard to its own meaning, that is, its disclosure to and clarification in understanding."

38 Heidegger, "For Edmund Husserl on His Seventieth Birthday," in *Becoming Heidegger*, ed. and trans. Theodore Kisiel and Thomas Sheehan (Evanston: Northwest University Press, 2007), 420.2–3.

39 GA 6.2: 314.3–5/N4 210.5–6.

40 Cf. likewise "Übernahme der Zugehörigkeit in die Wahrheit des Seins" (GA 65: 320.16–17/225.5–6).

41 See also GA 9: 377, note d/286, note d.

42 See Sheehan, "The Turn," 95–6.

43 I prefer "dread" as the translation of *Angst*. "Anxiety" sounds too much like a psychological state that could be treated with medication.

44 I use "absurdity" not in a Sartrean sense but rather as a translation of Heidegger's "der Abgrund der Sinnlosigkeit" (152.14–15/194.2–3).

45 GA 9: 114.5–16/90.16–24 (where the passage is mistranslated: "parting gesture" etc.). Re: human being as always returning from the encounter with the absurd: ibid., 115.1–3/91.2–5 (where the passage is awkwardly translated). Cf. GA 49: 69.5–6: "das Wesen – verbal verstanden – ist ja nur die Weise, wie etwas ist."

46 On "Ohne Warum": GA 10: 53.10ff/35.1ff. See GA 14: 101.35/OTB 82.8, where the fact of meaning itself "bleibt ein Geheimnis."

47 "Der Tod ist eine Weise zu sein, die das Dasein übernimmt, sobald es ist. 'Sobald ein Mensch zum Leben kommt, sogleich ist er alt genug zu sterben'" (245.25–7/289.25–6).

48 See GA 65: 324.16–21, 28–32/227.39–228.1–2 and 9–13.

49 Hence, the Catholic doctrine of antecedent grace. Heinrich Denziger, *Enchiridio symbolorum*, 31st edn., ed. Karl Rahner (Freiburg: Herder, 1957), no. 797; or in the Wesleyan-Arminian tradition, "prevenient" grace.

50 This position is a postmodern replication of the disposition that Kant called *metaphysica naturalis* (Kant, *Critique of Pure Reason*, 21; cf. Aristotle, *Metaphysics*, I 1, 980a 1), which, here as there, is beset by "unavoidable contradictions" (B 22).

51 Re: "last god": Dasein "hat sein Wesen in der Bergung der Wahrheit des Seyns, d.h. des letzten Gottes..." (GA 65: 35.2/25.16–17), where the "d.h." refers to the phrase "der Wahrheit des Seins." Re: "only a god can save us": GA 16, 671.26/"Only a God Can Save Us," in *Heidegger: The Man and the Thinker*, trans. William J. Richardson and ed. Thomas Sheehan (Chicago: Precedent, 1981), 57.30. See also Heidegger's translation of Heraclitus, fragment 19: "Der Aufenthalt ist dem Menschen das Anwesen des Gottes": GA 81, 253.15–16. Clearly, this is not the God of supernatural revelation.

52 See Aristotle, *Nicomachean Ethics*, VIII 2, 1155b 34–5: For there to be mutual love, it is required that φιλίαν ... μὴ λανθάνουσαν.

53 Actually, Plato had a name for the source of εἶδος/meaningfulness, viz., ἡ τοῦ ἀγαθοῦ ἰδέα, the ultimate enabling power. But he took τὸ ἀγαθόν, the "good" or "empowering," as (1) comprehensible: the object of the mind's

gaze, and as (2) enabling "truth" as the correct relation between mind and forms. See Plato, *Republic*, in *Plato: The Collected Dialogues*, trans. Paul Shorey and eds. E. Hamilton and H. Cairns (Princeton: Princeton University Press, 1961), VII, 517–18.

54 See the list of names for *die Seiendheit des Seienden* at GA 6.2: 432.3–434.18/EP 68.24–70.27. Another list appears in "The Understanding of Time" (note 8), 201.1–5.

55 See Sheehan, "The Turn," 96.28–97.33.

56 See GA 9: 377.4/286.13. Also see GA 14: 36.11–12/OTB 28.20–1; GA 88: 52.17–20; and GA 49: 57.2–3.

57 "Verwandlung des Menschseins": GA 45: 214.18/181.7–8. Italicized in the original.

58 Cf. 12.30–1/33.8–9, with 268.10–12/312.29–30; and 312.23–4/360.14–15.

Bibliography

Allison, Henry, *Kant's Transcendental Idealism: An Interpretation and Defense* (New Haven, CT: Yale University Press, 1983).

"Transcendental Idealism: A Retrospective," in *Idealism and Freedom: Essays on Kant's Theoretical and Practical Philosophy* (Cambridge: Cambridge University Press, 1996), 3–26.

Andersen, Paul K., *Empirical Studies in Diathesis* (Münster: Nodus Publikationen, 2004).

Aquinas, St. Thomas, *Summa Theologiae* (Oxford: Blackfriars, 1970).

Truth: Questions I–IX, trans. Robert W. Mulligan (Chicago, IL: Henry Regnery Company, 1952).

Arendt, Hannah, "Martin Heidegger at Eighty," in *Heidegger and Modern Philosophy*, ed. Michael Murray (New Haven, CT: Yale University Press, 1978), 293–303.

Aristotle, *Metaphysics*, trans. W. D. Ross, in *The Complete Works of Aristotle, Vol. II*, ed. J. Barnes (Princeton, NJ: Princeton University Press, 1984).

Nicomachean Ethics, trans. W. D. Ross, in *The Complete Works of Aristotle, Vol. II*, ed. J. Barnes (Princeton, NJ: Princeton University Press, 1984).

Physics, trans. W. D. Ross, in *The Complete Works of Aristotle*, Vol. I, ed. J. Barnes (Princeton, NJ: Princeton University Press, 1984).

Baldwin, Thomas, "Sartre, Kant and the Original Choice of Self," *Proceedings of the Aristotelian Society* 80 (1979–80): 31–44.

Bambach, Charles, *Heidegger, Dilthey, and the Crisis of Historicism* (Ithaca, NY: Cornell University Press, 1995).

Becker, Ernest, *The Denial of Death* (New York, NY: Free Press, 1973).

Benvéniste, Émile, *Problèmes de Linguistique Générale* (Paris: Gallimard, 1966).

Blattner, William D., "The Concept of Death in *Being and Time*," *Man and World* 27 (1994): 49–70.

"Existence and Self-Understanding in *Being and Time*," *Philosophy and Phenomenological Research* 56 (1996): 97–110.

Heidegger's Being and Time (London: Continuum, 2006).

Heidegger's Temporal Idealism (Cambridge: Cambridge University Press, 1999).

"Ontology, the A Priori, and the Primacy of Practice," in *Transcendental Heidegger*, eds. Steven Crowell and Jeff Malpas (Stanford, CA: Stanford University Press: 2007).

"Review of Heidegger Language and World Disclosure," *Philosophy and Phenomenological Research* 66 (2003): 489–91.

"Temporality," in *A Companion to Heidegger*, eds. Hubert L. Dreyfus and Mark Wrathall (Oxford: Blackwell, 2005), 311–24.

403

Bourdieu, Pierre, *Outline of a Theory of Practice* (Cambridge: Cambridge University Press, 1977).

Brampton, Sally, *Shoot the Damn Dog: A Memoir of Depression* (New York, NY: W. W. Norton, 2008).

Brandom, Robert B., "Dasein, the Being That Thematizes," in *Tales of the Mighty Dead: Historical Essays in the Metaphysics of Intentionality* (Cambridge, MA: Harvard University Press: 2002), 324–47.

"Heidegger's Categories," in *A Companion to Heidegger*, eds. Hubert L. Dreyfus and Mark A. Wrathall (Oxford: Blackwell, 2005), 214–32.

Making It Explicit: Reasoning, Representing, and Discursive Commitment (Cambridge, MA: Harvard University Press, 1994).

Bremmers, Chris (ed.), "Schriftenverzeichnis (1909–2004)," in *Heidegger und die Anfänge seines Denkens, Heidegger-Jahrbuch*, vol. 1, eds. Alfred Denker, Hans-Helmuth Gander, and Holger Zaborowski (Freiburg: Verlag Karl Alber 1, 2004), 419–598.

Brueckner, Tony, "Brains in a Vat," *The Stanford Encyclopedia of Philosophy* (Winter 2011 Edition), ed. Edward N. Zalta, http://plato.stanford.edu/archives/win2011/entries/brain-vat/.

Burnyeat, Miles F., "Idealism and Greek Philosophy: What Descartes Saw and Berkeley Missed," *Philosophical Review* 91 (1982): 3–40.

Carman, Taylor, "Authenticity," in *A Companion to Heidegger*, eds. Hubert L. Dreyfus and Mark Wrathall (Oxford: Blackwell, 2005), 285–96.

Heidegger's Analytic: Interpretation, Discourse, and Authenticity in Being and Time (Cambridge: Cambridge University Press, 2003).

"Heidegger on Correspondence and Correctness," *Graduate Faculty Philosophy Journal* 28 (2007): 103–16.

"Phenomenology as Rigorous Science," in *The Oxford Handbook of Continental Philosophy*, eds. B. Leiter and M. Rosen (Oxford: Oxford University Press, 2007), 9–29.

"Was Heidegger a Linguistic Idealist?" *Inquiry* 45 (2002): 205–16.

Cassirer, Ernst, *Substance and Function*, trans. W. Swabey and M. Swabey (New York, NY: Dover, 1953).

Cerbone, David R., "Heidegger and Dasein's 'Bodily Nature': What is the Hidden Problematic?" *International Journal for Philosophical Studies* 8 (2000): 209–30.

"Realism and Truth," in *A Companion to Heidegger*, eds. Hubert L. Dreyfus and Mark A. Wrathall (Oxford: Blackwell, 2005), 248–64.

Cohen, Hermann, *Logik der reinen Erkenntnis* (Berlin: Bruno Cassirer Verlag, 1902).

Crowell, Steven, "Authentic Historicality," in *Space, Time, and Culture*, eds. David Carr and Chan-Fai Cheung (Dordrecht: Kluwer, 2004), 57–71.

"Sorge or Selbstbewußtsein? Heidegger and Korsgaard on the Sources of Normativity," *European Journal of Philosophy* 15 (2007): 315–33.

"Subjectivity: Locating the First-Person in *Being and Time*," *Inquiry* 44 (2001): 433–54.

Dahlstrom, Daniel O., *Heidegger's Concept of Truth* (Cambridge: Cambridge University Press, 2001).

Davidson, Donald, "Deception and Division," in *The Multiple Self*, ed. J. Elster (Cambridge: Cambridge University Press), 79–92.

de Boer, Karin, *Thinking in the Light of Time: Heidegger's Encounter with Hegel* (Albany: State University of New York Press, 2000).

De Gaynesford, Maximilian, *John McDowell* (Cambridge: Polity Press, 2004).

Denker, Alfred, "Heideggers Lebens- und Denkweg 1909–1919," in *Heidegger und die Anfänge seines Denkens, Heidegger-Jahrbuch,* vol. 1, eds. Alfred Denker, Hans-Helmuth Gander, and Holger Zaborowski (Freiburg: Verlag Karl Alber 1, 2004), 97–122.

Denker, Alfred, Gander, Hans-Helmuth, and Zaborowski, Holger (eds.), *Heidegger und die Anfänge seines Denkens, Heidegger-Jahrbuch* (Freiburg: Verlag Karl Alber 1, 2004), vol. 1.

Denziger, Heinrich, *Enchiridio symbolorum,* 31st edition, ed. Karl Rahner (Freiburg: Herder, 1957).

Derrida, Jacques, *Aprorias,* trans. T. Dutoit (Stanford, CA: Stanford University Press, 1993).

Descartes, René, *Meditations on First Philosophy,* 3rd edition, trans. D. Cress (Indianapolis, IN: Hackett, 1993).

Meditations, The Philosophical Writings of Descartes, Vol. II, trans. J. Cottingham (Cambridge: Cambridge University Press, 1984).

Principles of Philosophy, The Philosophical Writings of Descartes, Vol. I, trans. J. Cottingham (Cambridge: Cambridge University Press, 1985).

di Pellegrino, G., Fadiga, L., Fogassi, L., Gallese V., and Rizzolatti, G., "Understanding Motor Events: A Neurophysiological Study," *Experimental Brain Research* 91 (1992): 176–80.

Dilthey, Wilhelm, *Descriptive Psychology and Historical Understanding,* trans. R. Zaner (The Hague: Martinus Nijhoff, 1977).

Dilthey: Selected Writings, trans. and ed. H. P. Rickman (Cambridge: Cambridge University Press, 1979).

Selected Works, eds. R. Makreel and F. Rodi (Princeton, NJ: Princeton University Press, 1985).

Dreyfus, Hubert L., *Being-in-the-World: A Commentary on Heidegger's* Being and Time, Division I (Cambridge, MA: MIT Press, 1991).

"Could Anything Be More Intelligible Than Everyday Intelligibility? Reinterpreting Division I in Light of Division II," in *Appropriating Heidegger,* ed. James E. Faulconer and Mark A. Wrathall (Cambridge: Cambridge University Press, 2000).

"Discussion of Film: *Breathless,*" UC Berkeley (2008), Podcast: http://webcast.berkeley.edu/stream.php?type'download&webcastid'22733.

"Foreword," in Carol J. White, *Time and Death* (Burlington, VT: Ashgate Publishing, 2005), ix–xxxvi.

"Overcoming the Myth of the Mental: How Philosophers Can Profit from the Phenomenology of Everyday Expertise," *Proceedings and Addresses of the American Philosophical Association* 79 (2005): 47–65.

Dreyfus, Hubert L., and Rubin, Jane, "Kierkegaard, Division II, and Later Heidegger," in Hubert L. Dreyfus, *Being-in-the-World: A Commentary on Heidegger's* Being and Time, Division I (Cambridge, MA: MIT Press, 1991), 283–40.

Dreyfus, Hubert L., and Wrathall, Mark A. (eds.), *A Companion to Heidegger* (Oxford: Blackwell, 2005).

Eberhard, Philippe, *The Middle Voice in Gadamer's Hermeneutics* (Tübingen: Mohr Siebeck Verlag, 2004).

Edwards, Paul, *Heidegger's Confusions* (New York, NY: Prometheus, 2004).

Eliot, T. S., "A Dedication to my Wife," in *The Complete Poems and Plays of T. S. Eliot,* ed. Valerie Eliot (London: Faber and Faber, 1969).

Franck, Didier, "Being and the Living," in *Who Comes After the Subject?*, eds. E. Cadava, P. Connor, and J.-L. Nancy (London: Routledge, 1991), 135–47.

Friedman, Michael, *A Parting of the Ways: Carnap, Cassirer, and Heidegger* (Chicago, IL: Open Court, 2000).

Fultner, Barbara, "Referentiality in Frege and Heidegger," *Philosophy and Social Criticism* 31 (2005): 37–52.

Gadamer, Hans-Georg, *Neuere Philosophie I, Gesammelte Werke*, 4 vols. (Tübingen: J. C. B. Mohr, 1987), vol. III.

  Truth and Method, trans. Joel Weinsheimer and Donald G. Marshall (London: Continuum, 1989).

  Wahrheit und Methode, Gesammelte Werke, 4 vols. (Tübingen: J. C. B. Mohr, 1986), vol. I.

Gallese, Vittorio, "The 'Shared Manifold' Hypothesis: From Mirror Neurons to Empathy," *Journal of Consciousness Studies* 8 (2001): 33–50.

Gardner, Sebastian, *Irrationality and the Philosophy of Psychoanalysis* (Cambridge: Cambridge University Press, 2006).

Garrett, Richard, "The Problem of Despair," in *Philosophical Psychopathology*, eds. George Graham and G. Lynn Stephens (Cambridge, MA: MIT Press, 1994), 73–9.

Glas, Gerrit, "Anxiety – Animal Reactions and the Embodiment of Meaning," in *Nature and Narrative: An Introduction to the New Philosophy of Psychiatry*, eds. Bill Fulford, Katherine Morris, John Sadler, and Giovanni Stanghellini (Oxford: Oxford University Press, 2003), 231–49.

Gonda, Jan, "Reflections on the Indo-European Medium," *Lingua* IX/4 (1960): 30–67 and 175–93.

Gordon, Peter E., *Continental Divide: Heidegger, Cassirer, Davos* (Cambridge, MA: Harvard University Press, 2010).

  "Science, Finitude, and Infinity: Neo-Kantianism and the Birth of Existentialism," *Jewish Social Studies* 6:1 (1999): 30–53.

Guess, Raymond, *Outside Ethics* (Princeton, NJ: Princeton University Press, 2005).

Guignon, Charles B., "Becoming a Self: The Role of Authenticity in *Being and Time*," in *The Existentialists: Critical Essays on Kierkegaard, Nietzsche, Heidegger, and Sartre*, ed. Charles Guignon (Lanham, MD: Rowman & Littlefield, 2004), 119–32.

  Heidegger and the Problem of Knowledge (Indianapolis, IN: Hackett, 1983).

  On Being Authentic (London: Routledge, 2004).

  "The History of Being," in *A Companion to Heidegger*, eds. Hubert L. Dreyfus and Mark A. Wrathall (Oxford: Blackwell, 2005), 392–406.

Habermas, Jürgen, *The Theory of Communicative Action, Volume 1: Reason and the Rationalization of Society*, trans. Thomas McCarthy (Cambridge, MA: Beacon, 1984).

  "Toward a Critique of the Theory of Meaning," trans. William Mark Hohengarten, in *Postmetaphysical Thinking: Philosophical Essays* (Cambridge, MA: MIT Press, 1992), 57–87.

Haugeland, John, "Heidegger on Being a Person," *Nous* 25 (1982): 15–26.

  "Reading Brandom Reading Heidegger," *European Journal of Philosophy* 13 (2005): 421–28.

  "Truth and Finitude: Heidegger's Transcendental Empiricism," in *Heidegger, Authenticiy, and Modernity: Essays in Honor of Hubert L. Dreyfus*, vol. 1, eds. Mark Wrathall and Jeff Malpas (Cambridge, MA: MIT Press, 2000), 43–7.

Hegel, Georg Wilhelm Friedrich, *Science of Logic*, trans. A. V. Miller (London: Allen & Unwin, 1969).

Heidegger, Martin, "Brief Martin Heideggers an Elisabeth Husserl," ed. Guy van Kerckhoven, *Aut aut* 223–4 (1988): 6–14.

"Briefe Martin Heideggers and Engelbert Krebs (1914–1919)," in *Heidegger und die Anfänge seines Denkens, Heidegger-Jahrbuch*, vol. 1, eds. Alfred Denker, Hans-Helmuth Gander, and Holger Zaborowski (Freiburg: Verlag Karl Alber 1, 2004), 61–8.

"For Edmund Husserl on His Seventieth Birthday," in *Becoming Heidegger*, trans. and eds. Theodore Kisiel and Thomas Sheehan (Evanston, IL: Northwest University Press, 2007), 415–20.

"Letter to Kark Löwith (1921)," in *Zur philosophischen Aktualität Heideggers*, vol. 2: *Im Gespräch der Zeit*, eds. Dietrich Papenfuss and Otto Pöggeler (Frankfurt: Klosterman, 1990), vol. II, 27–32.

"Only a God Can Save Us: The *Spiegel* Interview (1966)," trans. William J. Richardson in *Heidegger: The Man and the Thinker*, ed. Thomas Sheehan (Chicago, IL: Precedent, 1981), 45–72.

"The Understanding of Time in Phenomenology and in the Thinking of the Being-Question," trans. Thomas Sheehan and Frederick Elliston, *The Southwestern Journal of Philosophy* 10 (1979): 199–201.

Heidegger, Martin, and Blochmann, Elisabeth, *Briefwechsel 1918–1969*, ed. Joachim W. Storck (Marbach am Neckar: Deutschen Literaturarchiv, 1989).

Heidegger, Martin, and Rickert, Heinrich, *Briefe 1912 bis 1933 und andere Dokumente*, ed. Alfred Denker (Frankfurt am Main: Vittorio Klostermann, 2002).

Hoffman, Piotr, *Doubt, Time, Violence* (Chicago, IL: University of Chicago Press, 1986).

Homer, *Odyssey*, trans. Robert Fitzgerald (New York, NY: Macmillan, 1998).

Husserl, Edmund, *Die Konstitution der geistigen Welt* (Hamburg: Felix Meiner, 1984).

Ideen zu einer reinen Phänomenologie und phänomenologischen Philosophie, Erstes Buch, 2nd edition (Tübingen: Niemeyer, 1922). Translated as *Ideas Pertaining to a Pure Phenomenology and to a Phenomenological Philosophy, Bk. I*, trans. F. Kersten (Norwell, MA: Klewer Academic, 1998).

Logical Investigations, Vol. II, trans. J. N. Findlay and ed. D. Moran (New York, NY: Routledge, 2001).

The Crisis of European Sciences and Transcendental Philosophy, trans. David Carr (Evanston, IL: Northwestern University Press, 1970).

Jaspers, Karl, *General Psychopathology*, trans. Julius Hoenig and Maria W. Hamilton (Manchester: Manchester University Press, 1962).

Notizen zu Martin Heidegger, ed. Hans Saner (Munich: Piper, 1978).

Philosophische Autobiographie (Munich: Piper, 1977).

Jünger, Ernst, *Storm of Steel*, trans. M. Hofmann (New York, NY: Penguin, 2004).

Kant, Immanuel, *Critique of Pure Reason*, trans. and ed. Paul Guyer and Allen W. Wood (Cambridge: Cambridge University Press, 1998).

Critique of the Power of Judgment, trans. Paul Guyer and Eric Matthews, and ed. Paul Guyer (Cambridge: Cambridge University Press, 2001).

Religion within the Limits of Reason Alone (New York, NY: Harper & Brothers, 1960).

Theoretical Philosophy: 1755–1770, trans. and ed. D. Walford and R. Meerbote (Cambridge: Cambridge University Press, 1992).

Kaysen, Susanna, "One Cheer for Melancholy," in *Unholy Ghost: Writers on Depression*, ed. Nell Casey (New York, NY: William Morrow, 2001), 38–43.

Keller, Pierre, *Husserl and Heidegger on Human Understanding* (Cambridge: Cambridge University Press, 1999).

Kemmer, Suzanne, *The Middle Voice: Typological Studies in Language* (Amsterdam: John Benjamins, 1993).

Kenny, Anthony, *Philosophy in the Modern World*, *A New History of Western Philosophy*, 4 vols. (Oxford: Oxford University Press, 2007), vol. IV.

Kierkegaard, Søren, *Either/Or*, Vol. II, eds. and trans. H. V. & E. H. Hong (Princeton, NJ: Princeton University Press, 1987).

The Sickness Unto Death, trans. A Hannay (London: Penguin, 2004).

Kinkel, Walter, "Das Urteil des Ursprungs: Ein Kapitel aus einem Kommentar zu H. Cohens Logik der reinen Erkenntnis," *Kant-studien* 17 (1912): 274–82.

Kisiel, Theodore, "Das Kriegsnotsemester 1919: Heideggers Durchbruch in die Hermeneutische Phänomenologie," *Philosophisches Jahrbuch* 99 (1992): 105–12.

"The Demise of *Being and Time*," in *Heidegger's* Being and Time: *Critical Essays*, ed. Richard Polt (Lanham, MD: Rowman & Littlefield, 2005), 189–214.

The Genesis of Heidegger's Being and Time (Berkeley: University of California Press, 1993).

Kisiel, Theodore, and Sheehan Thomas (eds.), *Becoming Heidegger: On the Trail of His Early Occasional Writings, 1910–1927* (Evanston, IL: Northwestern University Press, 2007).

Kripke, Saul, *Naming and Necessity* (Cambridge, MA: Harvard University Press, 1980).

Kuhn, Thomas S., *The Structure of Scientific Revolutions*, 2nd edition (Chicago, IL: University of Chicago Press, 1972).

Lafont, Christina, *Heidegger, Language, and World-Disclosure*, trans. G. Harman (Cambridge: Cambridge University Press, 2000).

"Heidegger on Meaning and Reference," *Philosophy and Social Criticism* 31 (2005): 9–20.

"Was Heidegger an Externalist?" *Inquiry* 48 (2005): 507–32.

Lear, Jonathan, *Radical Hope: Ethics in the Face of Cultural Devastation* (Cambridge, MA: Harvard University Press, 2006).

"Transcendental Anthropology" reprinted in his *Open Minded: Working out the Logic of the Soul* (Cambridge, MA: Harvard University Press, 1998), 247–81.

Levinas, Emmanuel, *Time and the Other*, trans. R. A. Cohen (Pittsburgh, PA: Duquesne University Press, 1987).

Lewis, Sinclair, *Babbitt* (New York, NY: Grosset & Dunlap, 1924).

Llewelyn, John, *The Middle Voice of Ecological Consciousness: A Chiasmic Reading of Responsibility in the Neighborhood of Levinas Heidegger and Others* (New York, NY: St. Martin's Press, 1991).

Longuenesse, Béatrice, *Kant and the Capacity to Judge* (Princeton, NJ: Princeton University Press, 1998).

Luther, Martin, *Luther's Works* Vol. 1: *Lectures on Genesis, Chapters 1–5* (Saint Louis, MO: Concordia Publishing House, 1958).

Macarthur, D., "McDowell, Scepticism, and the 'Veil of Perception'," *Australasian Journal of Philosophy* 81 (2003): 175–90.

MacAvoy, Leslie, "Meaning, Categories, and Subjectivity in the Early Heidegger," *Philosophy and Social Criticism* 31 (2005): 21–35.

Malpas, Jeff, *Heidegger's Topology: Being, Place, World* (Cambridge, MA: MIT Press, 2006).

Matthews, Gareth, "Senses and Kinds," *Journal of Philosophy* 69 (1972): 149–57.

McCumber, John, *Poetic Interaction: Language, Freedom, Reason* (Chicago, IL: University of Chicago Press, 1989).

McDaniel, Kris, "Ways of Being," in *Metametaphysics*, eds. D. Chalmers, D. Manley, and R. Wasserman (Oxford: Oxford University Press, 2009).

McDowell, John, *Meaning, Knowledge, and Reality* (Cambridge, MA: Harvard University Press, 1998), 242–3, 249.

  Mind, Value and Reality (Cambridge, MA: Harvard University Press, 1998).

McManus, Denis, "Error, Hallucination and the Concept of 'Ontology' in the Early Work of Heidegger," *Philosophy* 71 (1996): 553–75.

  "Heidegger, Measurement and the 'Intelligibility' of Science," *European Journal of Philosophy* 15 (2007): 82–105.

  "Rules, Regression and the 'Background': Dreyfus, Heidegger and McDowell," *European Journal of Philosophy* 16 (2008): 432–58.

  "Heidegger and the Measure of Truth," unpublished manuscript.

Mele, Albert, "Real Self-Deception," *Behavioural and Brain Sciences* 20 (1997): 91–102.

  Self-Deception Unmasked (Princeton, NJ: Princeton University Press, 2001).

Mendes, Sam (dir.), *American Beauty* (Dreamworks SKG, 1999).

Merleau-Ponty, Maurice, *Phenomenology of Perception*, trans. Colin Smith (London: Routledge, 1962).

  Phenomenology of Perception, trans. Colin Smith (London: Routledge & Kegan Paul, 1981).

Millikan, Ruth Garrett, "A Difference of Some Consequence Between Conventions and Rules," *Topoi* 27 (2008): 87–99.

  Varieties of Meaning: The 2002 Jean Nicod Lectures (Cambridge, MA: MIT Press, 2004).

Minar, Edward H., "Heidegger's Response to Skepticism in *Being and Time*," in *Future Pasts: The Analytic Tradition in Twentieth-Century Philosophy*, eds. J. Floyd and S. Shieh (Oxford: Oxford University Press, 2001).

Moore, Adrian, *The Evolution of Modern Metaphysics: Making Sense of Things* (Cambridge: Cambridge University Press, 2012).

Moran, Dermot, *Introduction to Phenomenology* (London: Routledge, 2000).

Mulhall, Stephen, *Heidegger and* Being and Time, 2nd edition (London: Routledge, 2005).

  "Human Mortality: Heidegger on How to Portray the Impossible Possibility of Dasein," in *A Companion to Heidegger*, eds. Hubert L. Dreyfus and Mark Wrathall (Oxford: Blackwell, 2005), 297–310.

Nagel, Thomas, *Mortal Questions* (Cambridge: Cambridge University Press, 1979).

Newman, John Henry, *An Essay in Aid of a Grammar of Assent* (Notre Dame, IN: University of Notre Dame Press, 2001).

Nietzsche, Friedrich, *The Gay Science*, trans. Walter Kaufmann (New York, NY: Random House, 1974).

Ochwadt, Curd, and Tecklenborg, Erwin (eds.), *Das Mass des Verborgenen: Heinrich Ochsner zum Gedächtnis* (Hannover: Charis-Verlag, 1981).

Okrent, Mark, "Equipment, World, and Language," *Inquiry* 45 (2002): 195–204.
   Heidegger's Pragmatism: Understanding, Being, and the Critique of Metaphysics (Ithaca, NY: Cornell University Press, 1988).
Olafson, Frederick, *Heidegger and the Philosophy of Mind* (New Haven, CT: Yale University Press, 1987).
Ott, Hugo, *Martin Heidegger: Unterwegs zu seiner Biographie* (Frankfurt: Campus Verlag, 1988).
Pears, David, *Motivated Irrationality* (Oxford: Oxford University Press, 1985).
Philipse, Herman, *Heidegger's Philosophy of Being: A Critical Interpretation* (Princeton, NJ: Princeton University Press, 1998).
Piché, Claude, "Heidegger and the Neo-Kantian Reading of Kant," in *Heidegger, German Idealism, and Neo-Kantianism*, ed. Tom Rockmore (Amherst, MA: Humanity Books, 2000), 179–207.
Pippin, Robert B., *Idealism as Modernism* (Cambridge: Cambridge University Press, 1997).
   "Necessary Conditions for the Possibility of What Isn't: Heidegger on Failed Meaning," in *The Persistence of Subjectivity: On the Kantian Aftermath* (Cambridge: Cambridge University Press, 2005), 57–78.
Pius X, *Acta apostolicae sedis* 40 (1907).
Plato, *Sophist*, trans. F. M. Cornford, in *Plato: The Collected Dialogues*, eds. E. Hamilton and H. Cairns (Princeton, NJ: Princeton University Press, 1961).
   Parmenides, trans. F. M. Cornford, in *Plato: The Collected Dialogues*, eds. E. Hamilton and H. Cairns (Princeton, NJ: Princeton University Press, 1961).
   Republic, trans. Paul Shorey, in *Plato: The Collected Dialogues*, eds. E. Hamilton and H. Cairns (Princeton, NJ: Princeton University Press, 1961).
Poellner, Peter, "Self-Deception, Consciousness and Value," in *Journal for Consciousness Studies* 10–1 (2004): 44–5.
Putnam, Hilary, "Meaning and Reference," *The Journal of Philosophy* 70 (1973): 699–711.
   Reason, Truth and History (Cambridge: Cambridge University Press, 1981).
Ramachandran, Vilayanur S., "MIRROR NEURONS and imitation learning as the driving force behind "the great leap forward" in human evolution," http://www.edge.org/3rd_culture/ramachandran/ramachandran_index.html
   The Tell-Tale Brain: A Neuroscientist's Quest for What Makes Us Human (New York, NY: W. W. Norton, 2012).
Ratcliffe, Matthew, *Feelings of Being: Phenomenology, Psychiatry, and the Sense of Reality* (Oxford: Oxford University Press, 2008).
   "The Feeling of Being," *Journal of Consciousness Studies* 12 (2005): 43–60.
   "Understanding Existential Changes in Psychiatric Illness: The Indispensability of Phenomenology," in *Psychiatry as Cognitive Neuroscience*, eds. Matthew Broome and Lisa Bortolotti (Oxford: Oxford University Press, 2009), 223–44.
Ratcliffe, Matthew, and Broome, Matthew, "Existential Phenomenology, Psychiatric Illness and the Death of Possibilities," in *The Cambridge Companion to Existentialism*, ed. Steven Crowell (Cambridge: Cambridge University Press, 2012), 361–82.
Richardson, William J., *Heidegger: Through Phenomenology to Thought* (The Hague: Martinus Nijhoff, 1963).
Ricoeur, Paul, *Hermeneutics and the Human Sciences*, trans. John B. Thompson (Cambridge: Cambridge University Press, 1981).

Soi-même comme un autre (Paris: Seuil, 1990).

Rist, John, "Augustine on Free Will and Predestination," in *Augustine: A Collection of Critical Essays*, ed. R. A. Markus (Garden City, NY: Anchor Books, 1972), 218–52.

Roberts, Robert Campbell, *Emotions: An Essay in Aid of Moral Psychology* (Cambridge: Cambridge University Press, 2003).

Rorty, Richard, "Overcoming the Tradition: Heidegger and Dewey," *The Review of Metaphysics* 30 (1976): 280–305.

Rouse, J., "Heidegger on Science and Naturalism," in *Continental Philosophy of Science*, ed. G. Gutting (Oxford: Blackwell, 2005).

Sartre, Jean-Paul, *Being and Nothingness*, trans. Hazel E. Barnes (London: Routledge, 1989).

Schaber, Johannes, "Martin Heideggers 'Herkunft' im Spiegel der Theologie- und Kirchengeschichte des 19. und beginnenden 20. Jahrhunderts," in *Heidegger und die Anfänge seines Denkens, Heidegger-Jahrbuch*, vol. 1, eds. Alfred Denker, Hans-Helmuth Gander, and Holger Zaborowski (Freiburg: Verlag Karl Alber 1, 2004), 159–84.

Schatzki, Theodore R., "Early Heidegger on Being, the Clearing, and Realism," in *Heidegger: A Critical Reader*, eds. Hubert L. Dreyfus and Harrison Hall (Oxford: Basil Blackwell, 1992), 81–98.

Schear, Joseph K., "Are we essentially rational animals?" in *Mind, Reason, and Being-in-the-World: The McDowell–Dreyfus Debate*, ed. Joseph K. Schear (Abingdon: Routledge, 2013).

"Judgment and Ontology in Heidegger's Phenomenology," *The New Yearbook for Phenomenology and Phenomenological Philosophy* 7 (2007): 127–58.

Sheehan, Thomas, "Astonishing! Things Make Sense!" *Gatherings: The Heidegger Circle Annual* 1 (2011): 1–25.

"Facticity and *Ereignis*," in *Interpreting Heidegger: New Essays*, ed. Daniel Dahlstrom (Cambridge: Cambridge University Press, 2011), 42–68.

"Heidegger's *Lehrjahre*," in *The Collegium Phaenomenologicum: The First Ten Years, Phaenomenologica*, eds. John C. Sallis, Giuseppina Moneta, and Jacques Taminiaux (Dordrecht: Kluwer Academic, 1988), vol. 105, 77–137.

"*Hermeneia* and *Apophansis*: The early Heidegger on Aristotle," in *Heidegger et l'idée de la phénoménologie*, ed. Franco Volpi (Dordrecht: Kluwer, 1988), 67–80.

"The Turn," in *Heidegger: Key Concepts*, ed. Bret W. Davis (Durham: Acumen, 2010), 82–101.

Smith, William. H., "Why Tugendhat's Critique of Heidegger's *Concept of Truth* Remains a Critical Problem," *Inquiry* 50 (2007): 156–79.

Smyth, Herbert W., *Greek Grammar* (Cambridge: Harvard University Press, 1956).

"Speech," *The Oxford English Dictionary*, 2nd edition (Oxford: Clarendon Press, 1989).

Solomon, Andrew, *The Noonday Demon* (London: Chatto and Windus, 2001).

Spinoza, Baruch, *Ethics*, Bk. I, Def 3, trans. S. Shirley, *Baruch Spinoza: The Ethics and Selected Letters* (Indianapolis, IN: Hackett, 1982).

Staehler, Tania, "How is a Phenomenology of Fundamental Moods Possible?" *International Journal of Philosophical Studies* 15 (2007): 415–33.

Steinbock, Anthony, "The Phenomenology of Despair," *International Journal of Philosophical Studies* 15 (2007): 435–51.

Steiner, George, *Martin Heidegger* (Chicago, IL: University of Chicago Press, 1978).

Stiller, Ben (dir.), *Reality Bites* (Universal Studios, 1994).

Strasser, Stephan, *Phenomenology of Feeling: An Essay on the Phenomena of the Heart* (Pittsburgh, PA: Duquesne University Press, 1977).

Taylor, Charles, "Action as Expression," in *Intention and Intentionality*, eds. C. Diamond and J. Teichman (New York, NY: Cornell University Press, 1979).

  Ethics of Authenticity (Cambridge, MA: Harvard University Press, 1992).

  "Hegel's Philosophy of Mind," in *Human Agency and Language: Philosophical Papers 1* (Cambridge: Cambridge University Press, 1985), 77–96.

  "Heidegger on Language," in *A Companion to Heidegger*, eds. Hubert L. Dreyfus and Mark A. Wrathall (Oxford: Blackwell, 2005), 433–55.

Thomson, Iain, "Can I Die? Derrida on Heidegger on Death," *Philosophy Today* 43:1 (1999): 29–42.

  Heidegger, Art, and Postmodernity (New York, NY: Cambridge University Press, 2011).

  Heidegger on Ontotheology: Technology and the Politics of Education (Cambridge: Cambridge University Press, 2005).

  "Heidegger's Perfectionist Philosophy of Education in *Being and Time*," *Continental Philosophy Review* 37:4 (2004): 439–67.

  "Heidegger's Phenomenology of Death in *Being and Time*," in *The Cambridge Companion to Heidegger's* Being and Time, ed. Mark Wrathall (Cambridge: Cambridge University Press, this volume).

  "On the Advantages and Disadvantages of Reading Heidegger Backward: White's Time and Death," *Inquiry* 50:1 (2007): 103–20.

  "Rethinking Levinas on Heidegger on Death," *The Harvard Review of Philosophy*, XVI (2009): 23–43.

  "The End of Ontotheology: Understanding Heidegger's Turn, Method, and Politics," UCSD Ph.D. dissertation, 1999, ch. 5.

Thornton, Tim, *John McDowell* (Durham: Acumen, 2004).

Trilling, Lionel, *Sincerity and Authenticity* (Cambridge, MA: Harvard University Press, 1972).

Tugendhat, Ernst, "Heidegger's Idea of Truth," trans. C. Macann, in *Critical Heidegger*, ed. C. Macann (London: Routledge, 1996).

  Self-Consciousness and Self-Determination, trans. P. Stern (Cambridge, MA: MIT Press, 1986).

Van Buren, John (ed.), *Supplements: From the Earliest Essays to* Being and Time *and Beyond* (Albany: State University of New York Press, 2002).

  The Young Heidegger: Rumor of the Hidden King (Bloomington: Indiana University Press, 1994).

Wachowski, Andy, and Wachowski, Larry (dirs.), *The Matrix* (Warner Bros Pictures: 1999).

Weber, Max, *Wissenschaft als Beruf/Politik als Beruf* (Tübingen: J. C. B. Mohr, 1994).

White, Carol J., *Time and Death: Heidegger's Transcendental Existentialism*, ed. Mark Ralkowski (Aldershot: Ashgate, 2005).

Williams, Bernard, "The Legacy of Greek Philosophy," in *The Legacy of Greece*, M. I. Finley (Oxford: Clarendon Press. 1981).

  "Liberalism and Loss," *The Legacy of Isaiah Berlin*, eds. Mark Lilla, Ronald Dworkin, and Robert. B. Silvers (New York, NY: New York Review of Books, 2001), 91–104.

Williamson, Timothy, *Knowledge and its Limits* (Oxford: Oxford University Press, 2000).

Wittgenstein, Ludwig, *Notebooks 1914–1916*, eds. G. H. von Wright and G. E. M. Anscombe (Oxford: Basil Blackwell, 1961).

Philosophical Investigations, ed. G. E. M. Anscombe and R. Rhees, trans. G. E. M. Anscombe (Oxford: Blackwell, 1967).

The Blue and Brown Books (Oxford: Blackwell, 1958).

Wrathall, Mark A., "Heidegger and Truth as Correspondence," *International Journal of Philosophical Studies* 7 (1999): 69–88.

Heidegger and Unconcealment: Truth, Language and History (Cambridge: Cambridge University Press, 2010).

"Heidegger, Truth, and Reference,"*Inquiry* 45 (2002): 217–18.

"On the 'Existential Positivity of Our Ability to Be Deceived'", in *The Philosophy of Deception*, ed. Clancy Martin (Oxford: Oxford University Press, 2009).

"Social constraints on conversational content: Heidegger on Rede and Gerede," *Philosophical Topics* 27 (1999): 25–6.

"Unconcealment," in *A Companion to Heidegger*, eds. Hubert L. Dreyfus and Mark A. Wrathall (Oxford: Blackwell, 2005), 337–57.

Wrathall, Mark A., and Malpas, Jeff (eds.), *Heidegger, Authenticity, and Modernity: Essays in Honor of Hubert L. Dreyfus*, Volume 1 (Cambridge, MA: MIT Press, 2000).

Index